Lecture Notes
in Business Information Processing 29

W0230236

Terry Halpin   John Krogstie
Selmin Nurcan   Erik Proper
Rainer Schmidt   Pnina Soffer
Roland Ukor (Eds.)

Enterprise, Business-Process and Information Systems Modeling

10th International Workshop, BPMDS 2009
and 14th International Conference, EMMSAD 2009
held at CAiSE 2009
Amsterdam, The Netherlands, June 8-9, 2009
Proceedings

 Springer

Volume Editors

Terry Halpin
LogicBlox, Atlanta, GA, USA
E-mail: terry.halpin@logicblox.com

John Krogstie
Norwegian University of Science and Technology, NTNU, Trondheim, Norway
E-mail: john.krogstie@idi.ntnu.no

Selmin Nurcan
University of Paris 1 Pantheon Sorbonne, Paris, France
E-mail: selmin.nurcan@univ-paris.fr

Erik Proper
Capgemini and Radboud University Nijmegen, Nijmegen, The Netherlands
E-mail: erikproper@gmail.com

Rainer Schmidt
University of Applied Sciences, Aalen, Germany
E-mail: rainer.schmidt@htw-aalen.de

Pnina Soffer
University of Haifa, Carmel Mountain, Haifa, Israel
E-mail: spnina@is.haifa.ac.il

Roland Ukor
University of Manchester, Manchester, UK
E-mail: roland.ukor@cs.man.ac.uk

Library of Congress Control Number: Applied for

ACM Computing Classification (1998): J.1, D.2, H.4, H.3.5

ISSN   1865-1348
ISBN-10   3-642-01861-0 Springer Berlin Heidelberg New York
ISBN-13   978-3-642-01861-9 Springer Berlin Heidelberg New York

springer.com

© Springer-Verlag Berlin Heidelberg 2009
Printed in Germany

Typesetting: Camera-ready by author, data conversion by Scientific Publishing Services, Chennai, India
Printed on acid-free paper   SPIN: 12681877   06/3180   5 4 3 2 1 0

Preface

This book contain the proceedings of two long-running workshops held in connection to the CAiSE conferences relating to the areas of enterprise, business-process, and information systems modeling

- The 10th International Workshop on Business Process Modeling, Development and Support (BPMDS 2009)
- The 14th International Conference on Exploring Modeling Methods for Systems Analysis and Design (EMMSAD 2009)

BPMDS 2009

BPMDS 2009 was the tenth in a series of workshops that have successfully served as a forum for raising and discussing new ideas in the area of business process development and support.

The topics addressed by the BPMDS workshops are focused on IT support for business processes. This is one of the keystones of information systems theory. We strongly believe that any major conference in the area of information systems needs to address such topics independently of the current fashion. The continued interest in these topics on behalf of the IS community is reflected by the success of the last BPMDS workshops and the recent emergence of new conferences devoted to the theme.

During the previous BPMDS workshops, various issues were discussed that could be related to different but isolated phases in the life cycle of a business process. In the previous edition we arrived to a focus on the interactions between several phases of the business process life cycle.

In BPMDS 2009 the focus was on the drivers that motivate and initiate business process design and evolution. We distinguished three groups of drivers, which can exist separately or in any combination in real-life situations. These include (a) business-related drivers, where processes are changed to meet business objectives and goals, (b) technological drivers, where change is motivated or enabled by the availability, the performance or the perceived quality of IT solutions, and (c) drivers that stem from compliance requirements, facing standards and interoperability challenges.

The workshop discussions mainly dealt with the following related questions:

- What are the drivers or factors that initiate/demand change in business processes?
- How to cope with/introduce changes required by different drivers
- How to discover that it is time for a change
- How to discover that change has already happened (uncontrollable changes), and there is a need to explicitly change process definitions/operational instructions

The 17 papers accepted for BPMDS 2009 were selected from among 32 papers submitted from 14 countries (Australia, Brazil, France, Germany, Israel, Italy, Japan, Latvia, The Netherlands, South Africa, Spain, Switzerland, Tunisia, United Kingdom). They cover a wide spectrum of issues related to the drivers of business process change and how these affect the change process and are reflected in it. They are organized under the following section headings:

- Business and goal-related drivers
- Model-driven process change
- Technological drivers and IT services
- Technological drivers and process mining
- Compliance and awareness

We wish to thank all the people who submitted papers to the workshop for having shared their work with us, as well as the members of the BPMDS 2009 Program Committee and the workshop organizers of CAiSE 2009 for their help with the organization of the workshop. The conference was supported by IFIP WG 8.1

March 2009   Selmin Nurcan
                                                                Rainer Schmidt
                                                                   Pnina Soffer
                                                                  Roland Ukor

EMMSAD 2009

The field of information systems analysis and design includes numerous information modeling methods and notations (e.g., ER, ORM, UML, DFDs, BPMN), that are typically evolving. Even with some attempts to standardize (e.g., UML for object-oriented design), new modeling methods are constantly being introduced, many of which differ only marginally from existing approaches. These ongoing changes significantly impact the way information systems are being analyzed and designed in practice. EMMSAD focuses on exploring, evaluating, and enhancing current information modeling methods and methodologies. Although the need for such studies is well recognized, there is a paucity of such research in the literature.

The objective of EMMSAD 2009 was to provide a forum for researchers and practitioners interested in modeling methods in systems analysis and design to meet and exchange research ideas and results. It also provided the participants with an opportunity to present their research papers and experience reports and to take part in open discussions.

EMMSAD 2009 was the 14th in a very successful series of events, previously held in Heraklion, Barcelona, Pisa, Heidelberg, Stockholm, Interlaken, Toronto, Velden, Riga, Porto, Luxembourg, Trondheim, and Montpellier. This year we had 36 papers submitted from 18 countries (Argentina, Austria, Brazil, Canada, China, France, Germany, Israel, Italy, Latvia, Luxembourg, The Netherlands, Norway, South Africa, Spain, Sweden, Switzerland, United Kingdom). After an extensive review process by a distinguished international Program Committee, with each paper receiving at least three reviews, we accepted the 16 papers that appear in these proceedings. Congratulations to the successful authors!

Apart from the contribution of the authors, the quality of EMMSAD 2009 depends in no small way on the generous contribution of time and effort by the Program Committee and the additional reviewers. Their work is greatly appreciated. We also express our sincere thanks to the CAiSE Organizing Committee, especially the CAiSE Workshop and Tutorial chairs Paul Johannesson (KTH, Stockholm, Sweden) and Eric Dubois (CRP Henri Tudor, Luxembourg).

Continuing with our very successful collaboration with IFIP WG 8.1 (http://home.dei.polimi.it/pernici/ifip81/) that started in 1997, this year's event was again a joint activity of CAiSE and WG 8.1. The European INTEROP Network of Excellence (http://www.interop-vlab.eu/) has also sponsored this workshop since 2005, as has AIS-SIGSAND (http://nfp.cba.utulsa.edu/bajaja/SIGSAND/).

For more information on EMMSAD, see our website www.emmsad.org

March 2009
John Krogstie
Erik Proper
Terry Halpin

Organization

BPMDS 2009 Industrial Advisory Board

Ilia Bider	IbisSoft, Sweden
Ian Alexander	Scenario Plus, UK
Lars Taxén	Linköping University, Sweden
Gil Regev	EPFL and Itecor, Switzerland

BPMDS 2009 Organizing Committee

Selmin Nurcan	University Paris 1 Pantheon Sorbonne, France
Rainer Schmidt	University of Applied Sciences, Aalen, Germany
Pnina Soffer	University of Haifa, Israel
Roland Ukor	University of Manchester, UK

BPMDS 2009 Program Committee

Wil van der Aalst	Eindhoven University of Technology, The Netherlands
Sebastian Adam	Fraunhofer IESE, Kaiserslautern, Germany
Antonia Albani	Delft University of Technology, The Netherlands
Ian Alexander	Scenario Plus, UK
Ilia Bider	IbisSoft, Stockholm, Sweden
Stewart Green	University of the West of England, UK
Paul Johannesson	Royal University of Technology, Stockholm, Sweden
Marite Kirikova	Riga Technical University, Latvia
Peri Loucopoulos	Loughborough University, UK
Renata Mendes de Araujo	Federal University of the State of Rio de Janeiro, Brazil
Jan Mendling	Humboldt University of Berlin, Germany
Murali Mohan Narasipuram	City University of Hong Kong
Selmin Nurcan	University Paris 1 Pantheon Sorbonne, France
Louis-Francois Pau	Erasmus University, The Netherlands
Jan Recker	Queensland University of Technology, Brisbane, Australia
Gil Regev	Ecole Polytechnique Fédérale, Lausanne (EPFL), Itecor, Switzerland

Manfred Reichert	University of Ulm, Germany
Michael Rosemann	Queensland University of Technology, Brisbane, Australia
Rainer Schmidt	University of Applied Sciences, Aalen, Germany
Pnina Soffer	University of Haifa, Israel
Markus Strohmaier	University of Toronto, Canada
Lars Taxén	Linköping University, Sweden
Roland Ukor	University of Manchester, UK
Barbara Weber	University of Insbruk, Austria
Jelena Zdravkovic	Royal University of Technology, Stockholm, Sweden

BPMDS 2009 Additional Reviewers

Martin Henkel
Joy Garfield

EMMSAD Steering Committee

Keng Siau	University of Nebraska - Lincoln, USA
Terry Halpin	LogicBlox, USA
John Krogstie	NTNU, Norway

EMMSAD 2009 Organizing Committee

John Krogstie	NTNU, Norway
Terry Halpin	LogicBlox, USA
Erik Proper	Radboud University Nijmegen and Capgemini, The Netherlands

EMMSAD 2009 Program Committee

Wil van der Aalst	Eindhoven University of Technology, The Netherlands
Antonia Albani	Delft University of Technology, The Netherlands
Annie Becker	Florida Institute of Technology, USA
Egon Berghout	University of Groningen, The Netherlands
Giuseppe Berio	University of Turin, Italy
Nacer Boudjlida	Loria, France
Sjaak Brinkkemper	Utrecht University, The Netherlands
Andy Carver	Neumont University, USA
Olga De Troyer	Vrije Universiteit Brussel, Belgium
Mathias Ekstad	KTH, Sweden
John Erickson	University of Nebraska-Omaha, USA

EMMSAD 2009 Additional Reviewers

Namyoun Choi   Heiko Kattenstroth   Chun Ouyang
Jens Gulden   Ki Jung Lee   Pascal Ravesteyn
Martin Henkel   Dominique Mery   Ornsiri Thonggoom

Table of Contents

Technological Drivers and Process Mining

Compliance and Awareness

EMMSAD 2009

Use of Ontologies

UML and MDA

New Approaches

ORM and Rule-Oriented Modeling

Goal-Oriented Modeling

Alignment and Understandability

Enterprise Modeling

Patterns and Anti-patterns in Enterprise Modeling

Towards a BPM Success Model: An Analysis in South African Financial Services Organisations

Gavin Thompson, Lisa F. Seymour, and Brian O'Donovan

Information Systems Department, University of Cape Town, South Africa
Lisa.Seymour@uct.ac.za

Abstract. The improvement of business processes has recently emerged as one of the top business priorities for IT, and Business Process Management (BPM) is currently being seen as the best way to deliver process improvements. This research explores the enablers of BPM success, expanding on the Rosemann, de Bruin and Power theoretical BPM success model [1]. Qualitative research was conducted in four South African Financial Services Organisations with developing BPM capability. The research identified multiple success enablers categorised around Strategy, Culture, People / Resources, Governance, Methods and IT. Correlation between these factors was proposed and BPM, process and business success defined. Poor understanding of BPM within the participating organisations was found as well as insufficient supporting IT resources. It was found that the benefits of BPM investment had not yet been realised, which, increased the threat of funding being withdrawn.

Keywords: Business Process Improvement, BPM, Innovation Driver / Enabler / factors / process, IT Business Alignment / Value.

1 Introduction

For many organisations, success is based on how well they can model and optimise their processes in order to better manage the external value that the processes provide [2]. In a number of industries, organisations need to be able to create or modify business processes quickly to launch new product in a timely manner [3]. In the financial services industry, an increase in business competition and the amount of legislation being imposed by regulatory bodies has made it more difficult for companies to meet customer's service demands. This has resulted in process optimisation becoming a key strategic focus [4] and BPM (Business Process Management) being adopted.

BPM is the most recent stage in the advancement of process-oriented management theory with the overall goal of improving operational performance and increasing an organisation's agility in responding to dynamic market forces [5]. Although BPM is sometimes viewed as an IT focused extension of business process automation [6], we use the Melenovsky [7] definition of BPM as a management approach supported by technology components. By de-coupling the process from the underlying business application, BPM technology enables the business to design, deploy, change and optimise its business processes. As BPM is a fairly new discipline, there is limited research into the factors that contribute positively to BPM success. However recent

T. Halpin et al. (Eds.): BPMDS 2009 and EMMSAD 2009, LNBIP 29, pp. 1–13, 2009.

research by Rosemann, de Bruin & Power [1] has identified a theoretical BPM success model. This research will expand on their model by exploring the understanding of success and what enables BPM success.

The remainder of the paper is organised as follows. In the next section we briefly outline our research approach and methodology. This is followed by details about the collection of data and its analysis. Next, we present the results of the data analysis in an explanatory framework, from which we derive enablers of BPM success as well as their inter-relation and an expanded and modified BPM success model.

2   Research Questions and Method

The primary research question that this study set out to answer is "What are the enablers of BPM success?" Secondly the research wanted to answer "how success is defined". The Rosemann, de Bruin & Power [1] BPM success model, which is used as a meta-theory for this research, contains six independent categories that affect BPM success and these relationships are impacted by context. BPM success is seen to directly influence process success which in turn directly influences business success. Many of these categories are of a human interaction nature which would be difficult to measure without human interpretation. It was therefore fitting to adopt an interpretive philosophy for this research [8]. Given the limited research literature on BPM success, the research was conducted using the General Inductive Approach [9], in which the research is guided by the research objectives derived from a study of the current research literature. The inductive element allows additional research findings to emerge from the significant themes that are inherent in the research data [9].

Table 1. Data Sources with references (Ref.) used

Ref	Org.	Description	Ref	Org.	Description
Int1	Org1	BPM Program Manager	Int8	Org3	BPM Domain Owner
Int2	Org1	Business Leader	Int9	Org4	BPM Program Manager
Int3	Org2	Business Consultant	Int10	Org4	Business Analyst
Int4	Org2	Process Owner	Art01	Org1	Process Improvement Roadmap
Int5	Org2	Process Owner	Art02	Org2	Way Forward with Lean Six Sigma
Int6	Org2	Business Leader	Sem01		Lean Deployment. Executive
Int7	Org2	IT Architect			Breakfast July 2008.

Table 1 describes the sources of information used in this research. Organisations were selected that had made an investment in a BPM suite and are known to have, or be developing, BPM strategies and were willing and available to participate. The four participating organisations provide a good representation of South African Financial Services Organisations, with two (Org1 and Org2) being large, multi-national organisations and the other two (Org3 and Org4) being medium size organisations. Each organisation provided access to participants that could give good insight into both the business and IT view of BPM. The interview questions were open-ended and based on the BPM Success Model. Additionally, non-structured questions were asked depending on the information that emerged. Participants gave consent for interviews to be recorded and these were transcribed. Apart from semi-structured interviews, two artefacts were collected and one researcher attended a seminar (Sem01) on the application of Lean in South African Financial Services Organisations that had attendees from Org1 and Org2.

Data analysis was performed in accordance with the guidelines for the General Inductive Approach [9]. The researchers familiarised themselves with the transcriptions and documents through close reading; Key themes were identified and tagged; A data coding spreadsheet was populated with quotes, theme descriptors, low level and high-level categories; Categories were reviewed and consolidated; Common patterns between organisations as well as contradictory quotes within organisations were identified. Finally, a model was derived with key categories and linkages.

2.1 Context

The South African economic conditions had been very favourable up until the end of 2007 but had shifted in 2008 when this research was performed. This was attributed to an increase in interest rates and oil prices, and concerns around South Africa's political stability. In 2008, Org1 and Org2 had to reduce their operating costs in order to remain competitive. These conditions have a bearing on some of the attitudes to the enablers of BPM success, such as cutting costs and reducing head count. Further contextual elements include the age and maturity of the organisations involved in the research as well as the degree of previous process improvements undertaken. Both Org1 and Org2 had a history of Business Process Re-engineering (BPR). *"BPR has been on the agenda every now and again for the 10 – 12 years"* (Int6). In contrast, Org3 and Org4 were starting their process improvement journey with the purchase and implementation of a BPM suite. Considering the context that had a bearing on the research analysis, the following sections discuss the analysis of BPM enablers under the categories proposed by Rosemann, de Bruin and Power [1].

3 Strategic Enablers

Strategic alignment requires two approaches. Firstly there needs to be a clear link between the corporate strategy and the company's core processes [10] and secondly whenever the corporate strategy is altered, the required process changes need to be reviewed [11]. Three of the four participating organisations were confident that their processes were well linked to the strategy. However only in one instance this was performed consciously and there was acknowledgement that this linkage was difficult to achieve. *"...if you had to ask if we went through a process of saying "this is the strategy so this is what our processes should look like" then I can't point to a formal process that we went through to do that. I think intuitively in business planning we try and link it to strategy and make sure it is aligned"* (Int6).

Given the need for strategic intention to conduct BPM, Rosemann and de Bruin [12] believe that a BPM initiative needs to be driven from the top to ensure that it gets sufficient attention. There was general agreement on this. *"Due to the vastness of what it entails, it is not something you can drive from within the business; you need to do it from a higher level towards various businesses in the company"* (Int4).

While communication of the strategic intent to implement BPM was not mentioned in the literature, the analysis identified the need to have a conscious strategic intent to embrace BPM. Nevertheless, most organisations interviewed lacked a comprehensive BPM strategy. They either had a strategy that addressed the technology implementation of BPM or, alternately, the implementation of a process improvement methodology with only Org1 having a clear strategy addressing both the principles and the technology: *"There is an expressed intent that it be done overall. ..we believe that the BPM operational excellence approach is to raise standards"* (Int2).

In order for the organisation to link process to strategy, there first needs to be an awareness of the dimension of process in the organization [11]. In no cases did the participants agree that the dimension of process was well understood.

A number of BPM initiatives fail to launch due to an inability to build credible business cases and hence obtain funding [13]. Most interviewees agreed that BPM needed to be funded centrally. Two organisations started funding BPM as a project, subsequently shifting it to 'Business as Usual' while Org2 was still in project mode. *"It is starting off in the program space but is being seen as an operational budget as we realise the length of the journey if you want to get anything delivered"* (Int2).

Both Org1 and Org2 displayed concern over the need to fund BPM over the medium term before results could be visible and the impact of the current economic conditions on this perspective: *"External factors such as the economic pressure that the organisation might experience could result in the organisation going for short term gains rather than long term gains and to get BPM right completely you need to take a longer term view and take it slow and get things established"* (Int3). This supports the view of Bradley [14] that BPM offers good returns over the medium term but companies may choose initiatives that have quicker returns.

In summary the strategic enablers of BPM requires that corporate strategy be consciously linked to the core processes and that a clear strategy exists to implement both the technology and principles of BPM. There was some doubt about the need to recognise 'process' as an organisational dimension. Finally, BPM initiatives need to be driven from the top, with sufficient initial and ongoing central funding.

4 Cultural Enablers

The cultural enablers of BPM cover the organisational values and beliefs that support initiatives to improve organisational performance. BPM differentiates itself from BPR in that the changes are incremental and continuous as opposed to once-off [15]. Continuous improvement requires that the organisation cultivates a culture of support and encouragement for the process [10]. Org2 appeared to have a strong continuous improvement culture which was supported by channels that staff could use to make improvement suggestions. *"We promote it with our people that if they notice that a process is not working as expected or it can be improved that they send that through a channel that has been made available"* (Int4). Org2 also believed that their employees were aware of the consequences of not embracing continuous improvement if they were to avoid large process improvement initiatives that could have a disruptive impact on the organisation. *"Given that the organisation has been through a number of cost reduction initiatives, this has made people conscious that if we do not continuously improve, you are going to get these large (process improvement) interventions"* (Int6). Int2 stated that linking process improvement to cost savings, rather than improvements such as productivity, quality, and client experience was a concern and would discourage adoption. This echoes Lees [16] who cautions against making headcount savings the key objective for BPM initiatives.

All four of the organisations reported that they had a good culture of change. This appeared to be as a result of employees becoming accustomed to the organizational changes. *"I believe that they are equipped (to deal with change) as we have changed a lot in this organisation over the last two to three years"* (Int9). Int1 pointed out that if BPM is about continuous improvement then the change should be smaller and hence easier to absorb than change brought on by big process improvement projects.

Another cultural element that can contribute to the success of a BPM initiative is that of cross-functional team work [12]. The two large organisations reported that while their organisations were structured around the value chain, cross functional-team work was difficult and that it was difficult to find an optimal structure to manage processes. *"I do not think you will ever find an ideal structure as at some stage you will have to go across boundaries and you will need to make sure that your MIS and culture is such that you can manage that"* (Int6). An organisational culture of respect for another's opinion, collaboration and consensus building enables BPM [11]. Int2 suggested that the culture created by the remuneration system at Org1 actually inhibited cross-functional team work as employees were rewarded in how they worked in their own work areas. This response supports the concern raised by Lee and Dale [10] that some managers may create a competitive environment in which employees are incentivised to compete with colleagues and other departments rather than collaborate with them.

The relationship between business and IT is another area that impacts on BPM success. In general the co-operation between IT and business on BPM appeared to be good with good effect. *"IT sees ourself as part of business, so it is not us and them. Everything is working together with IT people and business people to come to a workable solution which will improve the process"* (Int9).

Staff need to be empowered and incentivised to improve process [16]. Three of the organisations did not feel that employees were sufficiently empowered to make changes. This is a result of productivity pressures and the tight legislation control in force on the financial services industry. *"If you look at our front office like the client contact centre, it is kind of a factory where you do not really want people to do things differently"* (Int6). Only Org1 reported an incentive scheme to improve process but suggested that it needed more work. Org2 and Org4 had Key Performance Indicators (KPI's) in place to measure employees' contribution to process improvement.

It was evident that the establishment of a continuous improvement culture could not be done in isolation of a clearly communicated BPM strategy. This is especially important as it was emphasised that the communicated strategic intention should alleviate any fears that BPM will result in headcount reductions. It was therefore considered appropriate to update the BPM success model to show a relationship between Strategy and Culture.

In summary, cultural enablers require that organisations instil a culture of continuous improvement and focus on process improvements that do not concentrate merely on cost savings. BPM is enhanced by a culture of cross cultural team work between business functions and between business and organisations. Part of the culture to enable BPM is empowerment and incentivising of employees to improve the process. Finally, it was evident that strategy has an impact on the culture.

5   People / Resource Enablers

The first theme under this heading that was identified in the literature was the need for all staff to have an understanding of process [10]. All participating organisations reported that process understanding was generally poor. It would, however, appear that, in each organisation, there are pockets of employees, mainly at a more senior level, that have a good understanding of process. *"There is an elite group that knows it inside out and they are quite knowledgeable about that".* (Int4). *"...people still tend to view things functionally and not necessary in a process dimension"* (Int8).

The literature reviewed did not separate the understanding of process from that of BPM. Yet these are not the same. The understanding of process is more aligned to the basic concepts of what a process is, as well as the principles that govern process behaviour. BPM understanding is more aligned to knowledge of all the factors of a BPM implementation including those factors presented in the BPM success model. There appeared to be a poor understanding of the more holistic view of BPM with many interviewees seeing it only in terms of the technology or the process improvement methodology. *"There is no specific understanding as to what is BPM versus what is process modelling versus what is BPR or how to position methodologies or tools in the bigger picture"* (Int3).

However, it may not be necessary for the majority of employees to know about BPM as long as they have an understanding of process and continuous improvement. Interviewees in both Org1 and Org2 raised concerns about BPM being viewed as another management fad. This is a good reason to be selective about how much 'holistic' BPM knowledge is imparted to employees as well as the pressing need for BPM to prove its value in. *"The communication of BPM into the organisation is low key, specifically because we are trying to move away from this being the next fad. It is more something that we build into the fibre of the organisation rather than a big bang, ho-ha, ra-ra type approach of implementation"* (Int2).

Employees involved in process improvement need to be skilled in process modelling, analysis and simulation [11]. In Org2, the training that had been provided to the business analysts was perceived to be ad-hoc with not real strategy or context behind it. Int2, referring to training they had received in Lean based process improvement methodology, reported that the first line managers at Org1 felt, for the first time, that they were being trained properly as operational managers.

A theme that emerged was the capacity to implement process improvements. Three organisations appeared to have IT capacity issues which hampered process improvements. *"It was run as a project but I do not think it was that successful as the improvements that they identified needed some IT support and in our business we struggle for IT resources"* (Int10). Int7 and Int9 specifically mentioned that their organisations had to try and find improvements that did not have an IT impact due to the IT resource constraints. This issue was also documented (Art02). There appears to be a real danger that organisations can become efficient at identifying improvement opportunities but not efficient enough at implementing the changes. While BPM technology can make the implementation of changes easier, there need to be sufficient IT resources available to implement improvements in a timely manner.

It was made clear that many of the People/resource enablers will be best addressed when there is a clearly communicated BPM strategy in place. This is especially true for the structured training as well as the creation of IT capacity to implement process improvements. As the provision of IT capacity has a monetary impact, it is believed that the average IT department will be unwilling to incur this extra cost unless it is in response to a stated corporate strategy. It is therefore appropriate to update the BPM success model to show this relationship between Strategy and People.

The people/resource enablers focus on the development of a process understanding amongst all employees, but caution over the need for the promotion of overall BPM process understanding. Important to the success of BPM was a well defined BPM training programme and sufficient IT resources.

6 Governance Enablers

The Governance enablers of BPM cover the establishment of relevant and transparent accountability, decision making and reward processes to guide individual's actions. The starting point of good process governance is clear process ownership [11]. This was considered necessary by the respondents and the majority of participating organisations had clear owners of departmental processes. However, this was not always the case for processes spanning multiple departments. *"If you look at it from a process point of view that crosses boundaries or business units, then someone needs to overlook the total process. Currently we are not set up like that so it is more silo driven for a specific piece of the process"* (Int5).

The establishment of a cross-functional facility that has responsibility for the management and improvement of processes is recommended [16]. Governance of process change can include formal and non-formal channels such as the linking to performance agreements, informal networks and internal audits [12]. All participating organisations referred to having adequate process management governance. The majority indicated that their process governance mechanisms were cross-functional. *"...they have a group that they call the Process Owner Team with representatives from Distribution Support and New Business and they talk through process issues across the boundaries"* (Int3).

Another dimension of process governance is the governance of process improvement initiatives [12]. This dimension also includes the methodology used to identify process improvement opportunity. The larger organisations had both adopted a formal process improvement methodology (based on Lean or Lean Six Sigma).

In summary, governance enablers clearly define the process owners and provide a cross-functional facility that has responsibility for the management and improvement of processes and the adoption of a formal process improvement methodology.

7   IT Enablers

While there is a wealth of literature on the IT required for BPM, not much is written about IT as an enabler. All participating organisations had made some investment in Business Process Management Systems (BPMS). BPMS selection criteria included successful implementation at other organisations; whether the cost was within budget and good vendor support. Despite this, three organisations reported that they were dissatisfied with vendor support levels as well as their level of technology knowledge.

Underlying BPM technology is the processes modelling language such as Business Process Execution Language (BPEL) that can be generated and executed on a process server. Another BPMS component is the Business Rules Engine which extracts business rules from the underlying legacy applications and stores and manages them in a separate database where rules can be changed and re-used by multiple process steps [4]. Once a process has been deployed into production, Business Activity Management (BAM) allows the business to capture real-time process event data and present it in a more intuitive graphical format [17]. All of the suites used had the basic capability to model and execute processes and had some BAM capability. However, it appeared that not all were using BAM and that the BPMS at Org1 was not BPEL compliant. Two organisations reported that their BPMS rules engine capability was not very powerful. Int1 highlighted the problem that a lot of rules were built into source applications and that they need to ensure that they only extract sufficient rules into the rules engine to allow the process to function.

Web services such as Service Oriented Architecture (SOA) are also required to integrate with fragmented legacy applications [18]. Int3 made specific mention of the dependence of BPM on SOA. Two organisations reported that integration was relatively easy. One of these organisations selected its BPMS based on compliance with its current technology stack and strategic technology plans. Both Org3 and Org4 reported integration issues. *"The integration into existing systems was not as easy as we had thought and it took a lot more effort than we had originally thought"* (Int9).

In summary, IT enablers include the need for an appropriately priced BPEL compliant BPMS, with good vendor support and proven implementation history. This technology needs to have a good BAM and process rules capability and needs to fit the IT architecture with good legacy system integration.

8   Methodological Enablers

The methodological enablers of BPM cover the approaches used to support and enable consistent process actions. Process mapping is an important part of BPM methodology and should be done in a hierarchical, consistent manner across the organisation [19], and stored on a central accessible repository, providing a central view [10]. The reviewed organisations had not reached that goal yet; Org2 had multiple process mapping standards which had evolved out of different process improvement initiatives and Org1 did not yet have high-level, end-to-end process maps. *"...because of the Lean initiative, people are doing process designs at a staff level but not all the way through yet"* (Int2). None of the organisations had managed to create a central process repository although there was good awareness that this was a weakness that needed to be addressed. *"We don't have a central process repository as such which is a weakness that we are working on but it is quite tough to come up with an answer that everyone is going to buy into"* (Int2).

In addition, none of the participating organisations had yet been able to generate BPEL code from their process maps. For example, in two organisations the Business Analysts performed their process mapping in Microsoft Visio, IT developers then re-did these in the BPMS interface prior to generating executable BPEL code. One organisation had attempted to generate BPEL from process diagrams on a previous project but had not been successful and had subsequently hand coded the BPEL.

Another important methodology discipline is the on-going measurement of process performance [10]. Success in this area appeared to be directly related to the extent to which the organisations had implemented processes on their BPM platforms. Org2 was not able to measure processes very easily and was also the least mature in terms of running their processes on their BPMS. *"We need a more formal strategy to measure process performance and simulations"* (Int5). The other organisations were all measuring their processes moderately well. However, only Org3 reported that they were able to measure process quality to an acceptable standard. *"All our current processes are reported on in terms of cost and SLA. With BPM, we will add to that a greater element of customer experience and customer value management"* (Int1).

Some BPMS provide optimisation capabilities which allow for the process to be emulated with numerous variables in order to find the optimum solution. Three of the organisations were using metrics to monitor and adjust process performance and make business decisions. This ranged from tracking season process variation to making organisational adjustments to optimise workflow. *" Decisions about team sizes can be made quite scientifically"* (Int8).

As BPM does not have an inherent process improvement methodology, organisations should incorporate a methodology which should then evolve over time [16]. These internal methodologies can be based on readily available methodologies such as Lean, Six Sigma [20], as-is and to-be mapping, and plan-do-check-act cycles [12] and Value Chain Analysis [11]. Two of the organisations were in the process of adopting Lean and embedding it as part of the organisational culture. One of these organisations had piloted Six Sigma but found that i had insufficient process metrics available. Consequently their use of Six Sigma tools had to be reduced until better metrics were available from implementing processes on the BPM platform (Art02). There was a feeling that employees in financial services organisations were put off by Lean's manufacturing background and terminology such as 'waste' (Sem01). Both Org1 and Org2 are developing their own internal process improvement methodology, based on Lean principles, but with an identity which fits with their own culture (Art01, Art02). In addition to Lean and Six Sigma, both large organisations were doing work around Client Experience and were starting to incorporate some of these techniques into their own process improvement methodology. *"We are now, through the whole client experience initiative, starting to do more work on making sure we know what the customer wants and what they need"* (Int6). Neither Org3 nor Org4 had done any work around the creation of a process improvement methodology and appeared to be more focused on the implementation of processes on their BPM platform then the improvement of processes. *"It is all quite a reactive manner of identifying opportunities and we do not yet look proactively for improvements"* (Int8).

Despite the talk of continuous improvement, BPM still needs to be implemented through projects [16]. Three organisations adopted a mixed approach where there was an element of 'Business-as-Usual' process improvement as well as specific improvement projects on a time to time basis. In contrast, all improvements to date at Org3 had been the first part of a bigger initiative.

Another aspect of implementation is the use of business cases. Two organisations drew up business cases for process improvements and then requested funding through the normal project approval mechanisms. Business cases were also used at Org4 but, these did not quantify the value of the benefits and only covered the IT costs to implement the changes.

There was a noticeable difference between the BPM implementation approaches at the large and the medium organisations. Org1 and Org2 had started with a process improvement methodology and was following that with a technology implementation. *"We did a lot of departmental level Lean improvements but realised that we could not get any further improvement until we started linking our value chain together and supporting that by BPM"* (Int1). In contrast, both Org3 and Org4 had gone the technology route first and still needed to develop their improvement methodologies. *"We have to bed the system down and then look at how we can improve the process"* (Int8). Although this research does not attempt to make any predictions on the success of the different implementation approaches, the technology-first approach may help to alleviate some of the IT resource constraints, making it easier to change processes that are executing on BPM technology. In addition, as Org2 reported that they had not been too successful with Six Sigma due to the lack of process metrics, adopting a technology-first approach would provide rich process metric to support Six Sigma's statistical data analysis requirements.

An additional theme that emerged from the interviews with Org2 was the need to start small and quantify the value of BPM through a pilot project. Mooney [13], recommends running smaller initiatives that demonstrate value quickly, building BPM credibility. Processes should be selected that are causing immediate pain and have a good chance of success and those that are politically charged, complex, highly distributed or require a high degree of buy-in from external parties need to be avoided [13]. *"We need to demonstrate value in smaller, more digestible chunks and we must be willing to let go of some of the control that we intuitively want to put in place if we want to tackle something like this"* (Int3). *"I think we first want to see what will come of this (pilot project) before it is driven as a company-wide initiative"* (Int4).

As mentioned, the process improvement methodology needs to be customised to the organisation's culture. This includes creating a process language that employees can identify with. The use of methodology is also dependent on the amount of technology implemented, specifically BAM. Hence we updated the BPM success model including a relationship from both Culture and IT to Methods.

The first methodological enabler is to ensure that there are standardised process mapping and storage practices. There is also a requirement for standardised process measurement; simulation and monitoring practices. Organisations also reported the need for the development of a flexible process improvement methodology that fits with the organisation's culture and maturity. There was evidence that it was useful to quantify the value of BPM through smaller projects. Finally, relationships were identified between culture and technology, and methods.

9   The BPM Success Model

From the themes that emerged around BPM, process and business Success, the BPM success model was expanded and modified (Fig. 1). We argue that process success does not necessarily result in business success and that BPM Success should only be achieved when BPM initiative leads to measurable degrees of business success. We therefore excluded the BPM success variable from the expanded model.

In terms of process success, three dimensions were highlighted, quality, efficiency and agility. Quality comments were consistent with the view that BPM can reduce processing errors as well as improve process consistency [22]. *"It definitely reduces error rates. ... The error rates were previously about 5 – 8% and are now down to 0.something %"* (Int8). Secondly, two respondents made specific mention of gains in process efficiency. Int2 attributed this to the application of their Lean process improvement methodology whilst Int9 attributed this to the automation of the processes on their technology platform. *"The automation saves time. We are definitely doing a lot more now with the same number of people than what we did two years ago"* (Int9). Process agility comments were consistent with Bradley's [14] statement that BPM architecture allows processes to be changed more easily than with hard-coded applications. Int3 reported that his organisation had to wait about six months to get process changes implemented on its legacy systems, with BPM technology, they would benefit from better process agility and flexibility. This was echoed by Int10 who stated that one of the key measurements of BPM success was the speed at which the business could implement process changes.

In relation to the contribution of Process Success to Business Success, multiple themes emerged from the analysis. Several interviewees mentioned that there was a real cost benefit from BPM attributable to improved process efficiency and a reduction in rework as a result of improved process quality (Int2). *"The value is that it makes you a lot cheaper in servicing a specific product"* (Int4). Client experience was

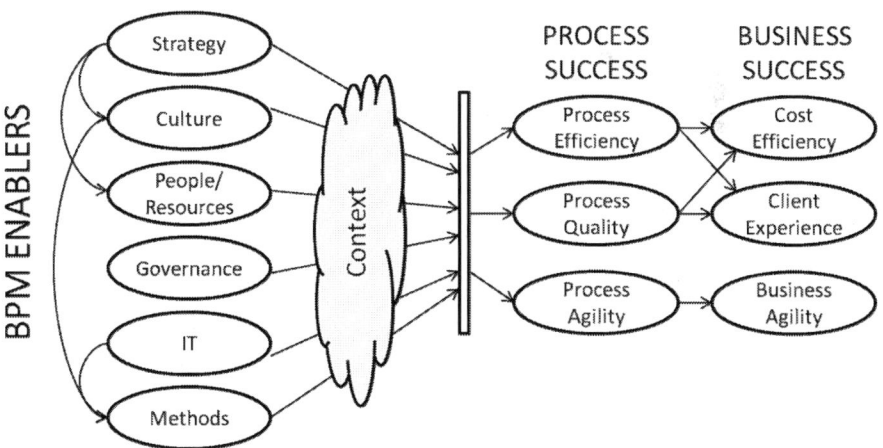

Fig. 1. The expanded BPM success model

another business success theme that emerged several times. *"The focus has always been around the client experience rather than the actual Rand value to the organisation with the thinking being that if the investor is happy and you are making him lots of money, we will be fine"* (Int8). Specific mention was made of the client experience benefit. *"BPM is a key enabler to improve your client service and your client experience"* (Int6). The final business success theme that emerged was the ability to implement change quickly when the process agility is improved (Int10). In financial services, there is a strong relationship between the product and the supporting process and to implement a new product one needs to design and implement the supporting processes quickly.

10 Conclusion

This research expanded on the Rosemann, de Bruin and Power [1] BPM success model through an analysis of BPM in South African financial services organisations. The research has found that there are more enablers within the Strategy factor than just the alignment of process to organisational goals. Organisations wishing to implement BPM must also develop a culture of change, continuous improvement and cross-functional team work. It was found that there may be a conflict between incentivising staff through building a competitive working environment (such as in Sales) and developing the culture of collaboration needed to improve process. While key people need to understand BPM, the majority need to have a general awareness of process. There was also evidence that insufficient IT resources and a lack of clearly defined process owners impacts BPM success. Yet these are all dependent on a well communicated BPM strategy. The degree of process measurement that an organisation was able to perform was related to the degree that the processes were implemented on the BPM technology. Therefore IT or the lack of it impacts on methodology. It was found that employees were resistant to methodologies like Lean and Six Sigma due to their manufacturing background and terminology. Organisations need to be aware of the impact of culture on methodology and might need to sanitise methodologies to fit their own culture. The research suggests that Process Success is achieved when processes are efficient, agile and produce good quality output. Process Success should lead to Business Success which can be measured through improved operational cost efficiency, improved client experience, and business agility. BPM Success is ultimately determined by business success through process success. It is hoped that this model will be able to assist organisations in making a success of BPM and that future research could validate this model in other industries.

References

1. Rosemann, M., de Bruin, T., Power, B.: A model to measure Business Process Management Maturity and improve performance. In: Jeston, J., Nelis, J. (eds.) Business Process Management, Butterworth-Heinemann, London, ch. 27 (2006)
2. Neubauer, T., Stummer, C.: Extending Business Process Management to Determine Efficient IT Investments. In: Proceedings of the 2007 ACM Symposium on Applied Computing, pp. 1250–1256. ACM Press, Korea (2007)

3. Leymann, F., Roller, D., Schmidt, M.: Web services and business process management (2002),
   https://www.research.ibm.com/journal/sj/412/leymann.html
4. Kung, P., Hagen, C.: The Fruits of Business Process Management: An Experience Report From a Swiss Bank. Business Process Management Journal 13(4), 477–487 (2007)
5. Hill, J.: Business Process Improvement Role Overview. Gartner, Stamford (2006)
6. Harmon, P.: Business Process Change: A Manager's Guide to Improving, Reengineering and Automating Processes. Morgan Kaufmann, San Francisco (2003)
7. Melenovsky, M.: Business Process Management as a Discipline. Gartner, Stamford (2006)
8. Klein, H.K., Myers, M.D.: A Set of Principles for Conducting and Evaluating Interpretive Field Studies in Information Systems. MIS Quarterly 23(1), 67–93 (1999)
9. Thomas, D.R.: A General Inductive Approach for Qualitative Data Analysis (2003),
   http://www.health.auckland.ac.nz/hrmas/resources/
   Inductive2003.pdf
10. Lee, R.G., Dale, B.G.: Business Process Management: A Review and Evaluation. Business Process Management Journal 4(3), 214–225 (1998)
11. Melenovsky, M.J., Sinur, J.: BPM Maturity Model Identifies Six Phases for Successful BPM Adoption. Gartner, Stamford (2006)
12. Rosemann, M., de Bruin, T.: Application of a Holistic Model for Determining BPM Maturity. In: Proceedings of the AIM Pre-ICIS Workshop on Process Management and Information Systems, Washington, DC, December, pp. 46–60 (2004)
13. Mooney, L.: Building a Business Case for BPM - A Fast Path to Real Results (2008),
   http://www.metastorm.com/ec/sf/
   WP_Building_a_Business_Case.asp
14. Bradley, R.: Fertile Ground for ROI in BPM: Three Unlikely Areas (2008),
   http://www.ebizq.net/hot_topics/bpm/features/9958.html?&pp=1
15. Valentine, R., Knights, D.: TQM and BPR - Can You Spot the Difference? Personnel Review 27(1), 78–85 (1998)
16. Lees, M.: BPM Done Right: 15 Ways to Succeed Where Others Have Failed (2008),
   http://whitepapers.silicon.com/0,39024759,60447963p,00.htm
17. Hill, J., Melenovsky, M.: Achieving Agility: BPM Delivers Business Agility through New Management Practices. Gartner, Stamford (2006)
18. Rosen, M.: BPM and SOA Where Does One End and the Other Begin (2006),
   http://www.omg.org/news/news_public-2006.htm
19. Engiles, M., Weyland, J.: Towards Simulation-Based Business Process Management. In: Proceedings of the 35th Conference on Winter Simulation: Driving New Orleans Innovation, pp. 225–227 (2003)
20. Henschen, D.: Six Sigma and Lean Meet BPM: Q&A With Software AG's Bruce Williams (2007),
   http://www.intelligententerprise.com/
   showArticle.jhtml?articleID=201802552&pgno=1
21. Rosemann, M., de Bruin, T.: Towards a Business Process Management Maturity Model. In: Proceedings of the 13th European Conference on Information Systems. DBLP, Regensburg (2005)
22. Silver, B.: BPMS Watch: BPM's Evolving Value Proposition (2006),
   https://www.bpminstitute.org/no_cache/articles/
   all-articles/news-browse/18.html

A Conceptual Framework for
Business Process Redesign

George Koliadis and Aditya Ghose

Decision Systems Laboratory,
School of Computer Science and Software Engineering,
University of Wollongong, NSW 2522 Australia,
{gk56, aditya}@uow.edu.au

Abstract. This paper addresses the problem of managing business process change at the level of design-time artifacts, such as BPMN process models. Our approach relies on a sophisticated scheme for annotating BPMN models with functional effects as well as non-functional properties. This permits us to assess the extent of change being made, as well as the performance characteristics of the resulting processes.

Keywords: business process redesign, conceptual modeling, conceptual framework, change management.

1 Introduction

Given the accelerating nature of change to business processes, decision support that permits reactive and deliberate control of business process designs is required. The decision support interface must: expose itself in a language analysts are fluent with (such as BPMN [1]); work with parsimonious descriptions of functionality that may be incomplete; provide change recommendations and elicit feedback from analysts; and, make complete use of available process, and other, knowledge.

In [2], process configuration is described, utilizing *explicit* configuration options, and [3] describe a detailed classification and correctness criteria associated with dynamic business process model changes (that include rule and goal based approaches). In [4], inter-task data and control dependencies are used in the design of an algorithm for generating process variants, [5] describe systems for managing process variants, and [6] provide techniques for conducting change impact scope analyses. In [7], formal tools are deployed for analysing the throughput time of processes. In [8] a formal model and method for context aware business process design is introduced. In [9], a scheme for annotating and propagating a restricted form of axiomatic task descriptions is introduced for a restricted class of process models (as is ours). In [10], process annotation is applied in order to check compliance against a deontic and temporal representation of obligations.

In comparison, our aim is to explore how functional and non-functional process annotations can be leveraged during design. We present a precise formulation of the how typical process change scenarios influence the greater context of a

T. Halpin et al. (Eds.): BPMDS 2009 and EMMSAD 2009, LNBIP 29, pp. 14–26, 2009.
© Springer-Verlag Berlin Heidelberg 2009

process in terms of resources involved, goals achieved, compliance rules satisfied, and objectives optimized. The general planning literature [11] does not usually construct plans by considering many factors we address here. The general verification literature [12] relies on complete axiomatizations, and implementations, of processes to be effective - we do not reject their applicability in this context, but choose to focus on parsimonious specifications of effect and how these may be leveraged in the tradition of "lightweight" approaches [13]. The theory in this paper is implemented in the ISORROPIA Service Mapping Software Toolkit available for download at: http://www.isorropia.org/.

Our focus in this paper is on change management at the level of design-time artefacts. In other words, we aim to better understand process re-design, driven by a variety of factors. We make progress to our work in [14] by: exploring the general dynamics of process change; extending our effect accumulation theory (with non-functional effects); reformulating SPNets algebraically for change.

2   Example

Consider Figure 1: a simple "Screen Package" process owned by a Courier Organization. Changes to this process may be required for a variety of reasons. For example: (1) resources (e.g. a Sort Officer) may no longer exist (due to a resourcing changes) or have the capacity to perform certain actions (e.g. Assess Package); (2) activities or their coordination may need to change (e.g. Route Package must be performed after Handle Package); (3) new compliance obligations may be introduced (e.g. requiring adequate package screening); (4) new process goals, or outcomes, may be required (e.g. requiring a Regulatory Authority to know whether a package has been routed); and/or (5) a process improvement initiative may be initiated (e.g. leading to an improved cycle time).

The scenario we will be considering (and describing) in the following sections will involve Figure 1 and the rule: C_1: *"Packages Known to be Held by a Regulatory Authority must not be Routed by a Sort Officer until the Package is Known to be Cleared by the Regulatory Authority"*; encoded in Linear Temporal Logic (LTL) [12] as: C_1: $\mathbf{G}(Knows(RA, Package, Status, Held) \Rightarrow (\neg Performs(SO, Route, Package)\mathbf{W}Knows(RA, Package, Status, Clear)))$.

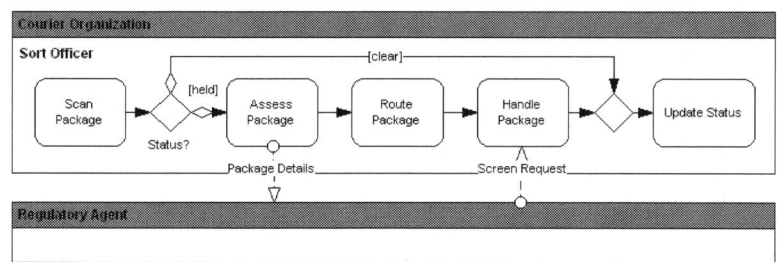

Fig. 1. Resolved Package Screening Process (O)

Finally, the set of non-functional objectives will include: *reliability* (O_R), measured as the number of successful completions per set of requests; *security* (O_S), measured as the length of the encryption scheme; and *cycle time* (O_{CT}) measured as the average number of seconds to completion.

3   Drivers for Process Change

Business process models, resource models, constraints (or rules), goals, and objectives are five key elements that play a role in business process change management, which we will formalize. The key intuition in our formalization is that processes/resources/constraints/goals/objectives influence each other. Changes occurring to processes, rules, and goals can lead to alternative contexts. Changes occurring to objectives can influence choice among alternative contexts. In most of our discussion, as well as in the relevant literature, the requirement of minimal change can be preferred over efficient but disruptive change. We consider both types of change in our formulation below.

Definition 1. *A process context is given by a tuple $\langle P, R, C, G, O \rangle$ where P is a process model, R is a resource model (or description), C is a set of constraints or business rules (e.g. compliance requirements or functional dependencies), G is a set of goals (or, without loss of generality, a single conjunctive goal assertion) and O is a set of objectives (or, objective functions), such that P, R, C, G are mutually consistent.*

We do not formally define the notion of consistency between a process model, a resource model, a goal assertion and a set of rules here, but the underlying intuition is clear. A process P achieves a goal G if the goal conditions are made true as a result of executing P, P satisfies C iff all of the business rules in C are satisfied by P, while P satisfies R iff P utilizes resources and resource attributes available in R. We can similarly talk about the consistency of G and C, given that some goal assertions could potentially violate business rules. We could also talk about the consistency of G and R, or R and C with respect to resource availability and attributes. O on the other hand, particularly in relation to P, determines a degree of satisfaction that allows alternative contexts to be compared on a multi-valued (rather than boolean) scale.

We shall use $P'' \leq_O P'$ (defined relative to a set of objectives O) to denote the weak dominance of P' over P'' with respect to all the possible execution scenarios of P' pairwise compared with the scenarios produced by P''. We shall also assume the existence of a process proximity relation $\preceq_P$ (defined relative to a background process model P) such that $P' \preceq_P P''$ denotes that P' is "closer", under this proximity relation, to P than P''. We shall also use the strict version of the relations $\prec_P$ and $<_O$ in the usual manner. We shall present several alternative means of defining such relations later in the paper.

3.1 Reacting to Change Requests

In the following, we assume O to be static and describe a strategy for reacting to requests to change P, R, C, or G. A change request is presented as a *process constraint, resource constraint, compliance (or rule) constraint* or *goal constraint*, depending on whether the change driver is operational, resource-related, rule-related or strategic. A process constraint is represented as a process model which must (or must not) be included in the revised process model. Below, $P \models P'$ denotes P *satisfies* a process constraint P' (using an inclusion relation or otherwise). A process constraint can thus represent a change involving the removal, addition or modification of elements in an existing process model. Goal, compliance, and resource constraints similarly represent sets of goal assertions, compliance rules, or resource descriptions, that must (or must not) be included in the changed process context.

We are interested in minimizing the extent of change, given a need to protect investments in existing process infrastructures. We are also interested in improving the profile of the process with respect to its objective. We are therefore interested in process contexts that implement a given change request, and are minimally different to the original process context. Among this set, we are interested in process models that are optimal with respect to a set of objectives.

We say a process context $\langle P, R, C, G, O \rangle$ *implements* a change request iff: for operational changes, $P \models P'$, given a process constraint P'; for resource changes, $R \models R'$. If R and R' is viewed as a sets of resource assertions (or descriptions), then $R' \subseteq R$; for rule changes, $C \models C'$, given a compliance constraint C'. If C and C' are viewed as sets of compliance rules, then $C' \subseteq C$; and, for strategic changes, $G \models G'$, given a goal constraint G'. If G and G' are viewed as sets of goal assertions, then $G' \subseteq G$.

Given a process context $\langle P, R, C, G, O \rangle$, a revised context $\langle P', R', C', G', O \rangle$ is a *minimal implementation* of a change request iff:

- $\langle P', R', C', G', O \rangle$ implements the change request in question;
- there exists no P'' such that: $P'' \prec_P P'$ (*minimal*); $P'' \preceq_P P'$ and $P' <_O P''$ (*optimal*); and $\langle P'', R', C', G', O \rangle$ is a process context implementing the change request;
- there exists no R'' such that $R' \subset R'' \subseteq R$ and $\langle P', R'', C', G', O \rangle$ is a process context implementing the change request;
- there exists no C'' such that $C' \subset C'' \subseteq C$ and $\langle P', R', C'', G', O \rangle$ is a process context implementing the change request;
- there exists no G'' such that $G' \subset G'' \subseteq G$ and $\langle P', R', C', G'', O \rangle$ is a process context implementing the change request.

3.2 Reacting to Improvement Requests

An improvement request is presented as a *proximity threshold* $\lceil P \rceil$. Given an initial process context $\langle P, R, C, G, O \rangle$, an improved process context $\langle P', R', C, G, O \rangle$ implements an improvement request $\lceil P \rceil$ iff:

- $P' \preceq_P \lceil P \rceil$ and there exists no P'' such that: $P'' \preceq_P \lceil P \rceil$; $P' <_O P''$; and $\langle P'', R', C, G, O \rangle$ is a process context implementing the improvement request;
- there exists no R'' such that $R' \subset R'' \subseteq R$ and $\langle P', R'', C, G, O \rangle$ is a process context implementing the improvement request.

4   Conceptual Framework for Process Redesign

A challenge analysts face is dealing with the relative paucity of process semantics available in BPMN models (which focus mainly on representing the coordination of process flows). One way of dealing with this is to leverage the formal semantics of BPMN, but this poses three problems. First, BPMN models alone do not convey sufficient semantic information to support change management in any signficant way (the only types of requests that we would be able to evaluate would be structural). Second, there is a lack of consensus as to what the best approach to defining semantics for BPMN might be [15]. Lastly, there are the usual problems associated with obtaining industry acceptance of formal techniques in domains that are not necessarily safety- or mission-critical.

Our approach, is to develop a framework (and an associated toolkit) that enables analysts to annotate BPMN models with effects in a *lightweight* fashion. Since change management clearly requires more information than is available in a pure BPMN process model, we propose a analyst-mediated approach to semantic annotation of BPMN models, in particular, the annotation of activities with functional effects. We also require an analyst to annotate each activity in a BPMN model with local QoS measures. This would be represented as a vector $\langle m_1, m_2, \ldots, m_k \rangle$ where m_i is the local measure for the i-th QoS factor (e.g., processing time for that specific activity), such that each measure is an element of the set of preference values in a c-semiring associated with the i-th QoS factor.

Quality of Service (QoS) properties have been difficult to describe in the past as: there are no obvious, or commonly agreed upon, ways of quantifying several key non-functional factors such as quality, usability, security; and, these factors are often assessed on multiple heterogeneous scales, requiring separate machinery to be defined for each distinct factor. We address these issues by deploying an algebraic framework that permits integrated multi-dimensional assessments of QoS factors by generalizing a wide range of heterogeneous assessment scales that can be both qualitative and quantitative. In the algebraic *c-semiring* framework [16] QoS scales can be represented via mappings to an abstract set of preference values. Recent work aims to model negative (as in the case of a c-semiring) and positive preferences under the same unified (bi-polar) scheme.

Definition 2. *A constraint semiring [16] is a 5-tuple $\langle A, \oplus, \otimes, \mathbf{0}, \mathbf{1} \rangle$ such that: A is a set of preference values; $\oplus$ and $\otimes$ are two commutative and associative operators closed in A; $\oplus$ compares preference values, $\mathbf{1}$ is its absorbing element, $\mathbf{0}$ is its unit element, and it is idempotent; $\otimes$ combines preference values, $\mathbf{0}$ is its absorbing element, $\mathbf{1}$ is its unit element, it usually decreases (i.e. $\alpha \otimes \beta \leq_s \alpha, \beta$), and distributes over comparison; $\mathbf{0}$ is the least preferred value; and, $\mathbf{1}$ is the*

Table 1. Non-Functional Annotation of Package Screening Process in Figure 1

Activity	O_R	O_S	O_{CT}
Scan Package	0.98	128	20
Assess Package	0.96	128	30
Route Package	0.94	64	600
Handle Package	0.88	128	50
Update Status	0.98	128	10

most preferred value. In addition, we include a parallel combination operator $\ddot{\otimes}$ (inserted after $\otimes$ in our examples) to deal with the merging of concurrent model sections. $\ddot{\otimes}$ satisfies the properties of $\otimes$.

For example, in our example process context described in Section 2, we can define our objectives for *reliability, security,* and *cycle time* in the following way: $O_R = \langle [0,1], max, \cdot, \cdot, 0, 1 \rangle$, (assuming independence); $O_S = \langle \mathbb{N}^+, max, min, min, 0, +\infty \rangle$; $O_{CT} = \langle \mathbb{R}^+, min, +, max, +\infty, 0 \rangle$; with annotations for Figure 1 outlined in Table 1.

Effect annotations can be *formal* (possibly augmented with temporal operators), or informal (such as simple English). Many of the examples we use in this paper rely on formal effect annotations, but most of our observations hold even if these annotations were in natural language. Controlled natural language involves offering an analyst a limited repertoire of sentence formats in which effects may be described in natural language. Each sentence format, once instantiated, can be automatically translated into an underlying formal assertion (the formats are determined by the choice of the underlying language). Formal annotations (i.e. provided, or derived from CNL) permit us to use automated reasoners, while informal annotations oblige analysts to check for consistency between effects.

Semantic Process Nets (SPNets) [14] are a structural encoding of extended BPMN models for use during change management operations.

Definition 3. *A Semantic Process Network (SPNet) is a graph $\langle V, E, s, t, l_V, l_E \rangle$ such that: V is a set of nodes; E a set of edges; $s, t : E \rightarrow V$ are source and target node mappings; $l_V : V \rightarrow \Omega_V$ maps nodes to node labels; and, $l_E : V \rightarrow \Omega_E$ maps edges to edge labels. Each label in Ω_V and Ω_E is of the form $\langle id, type, value \rangle$.*

We note that a unique SPNet exists for each model in BPMN. This can be determined objectively through transformation. Each event, activity or gateway in a BPMN model maps to a node, with the *type* element of the label indicating whether the node was obtained from an event, activity or gateway in the BPMN model. Actors also map as nodes, with the value label referring to the name of the role associated with the pool and lane of the actor. The *type* element of an edge label can be either *control, message, assignment, immediate effect, cumulative effect* depending on whether the edge represents a control flow, message flow, task assignment, immediate effect, cumulative effect or goal obligation descriptor. The *value* element of edge labels are: guard conditions (for control edges); message descriptors (for message edges); actor names (for assignment edges); post conditions (for immediate effect edges); or, context descriptors (for cumulative effect or goal obligation edges). Note, $s(e) = t(e)$ for an immediate effect, or cumulative effect edge $e \in E$.

The *value* elements for immediate effect, cumulative effect and goal obligation edges are triples of the form $\langle id, function, quality \rangle$. The *id* element of an immediate effect edge corresponds to the source node *id* label element. The *id* element of a cumulative effect or edge is a scenario identifier (a vector) where each element is either: a node identifier; or, a set whose elements are (recursively) scenario identifiers. A scenario identifier describes the precise path that would have to be taken through the process model to achieve the cumulative effect in question. The *function* element of an immediate effect or cumulative effect edge label is a set of assertions, whereas the *quality* element is a vector of QoS evaluations. The *function* and *quality* elements of an immediate effect annotation edge label can be viewed as a context-independent specification of its functional and non-functional effects. These must be accumulated over an entire process to be able to specify, at the end of each activity, the contextual *function* and *quality* elements of cumulative effect annotation labels. These labels indicate the functional and non-functional effects that a process would have achieved had it executed upto that point. The process of obtaining cumulative effect annotations from a BPMN model annotated with immediate effects can be automated in the instance of formal or controlled natural language annotations. We note that this approach to obtaining functional effects comes with no guarantee of completeness. In other words, the quality of the descriptions that we obtain is a function of the quality of immediate effects specified by analysts. Our experience suggests that the approach is nonetheless useful in providing an approximately adequate basis for change management.

4.1   Functional Effect Accumulation

We define a process for *pair-wise effect accumulation*, which, given an ordered pair of tasks with effect annotations, determines the cumulative effect after both tasks have been executed in contiguous sequence. The procedure serves as a methodology for analysts to follow if only informal annotations are available. We assume effect annotations have been represented in Conjunctive Normal Form (CNF) where each clause is also a *prime implicate*, thus providing a non-redundant canonical form. Cumulative effect annotation involves a left-to-right pass through a participant lane. Activities which are not connected to any preceding activity via a control flow link are annotated with the cumulative effect $\{e\}$ where e is the immediate effect of the task in question.

Let $\langle t_i, t_j \rangle$ be an ordered pair of tasks connected via a sequence flow such that t_i precedes t_j, let e_i be an effect scenario associated with t_i and e_j be the immediate effect annotation associated with t_j. Let $e_i = \{c_{i1}, c_{i2}, \ldots, c_{im}\}$ and

$e_j = \{c_{j1}, c_{j2}, \ldots, c_{jn}\}$ (we can view CNF sentences as sets of clauses, without loss of generality). If $e_i \cup e_j$ is consistent (where consistency can be established in a variety of ways - e.g. by an analyst or by including an appropriate type of domain theory), then the resulting cumulative effect, denoted by $acc(e_i, e_j)$, is $\{e_i \cup e_j\}$. Else, $acc(e_i, e_j) = \{e_i' \cup e_j | e_i'$ is a maximal subset of e_i consistent with $e_j\}$ (i.e. maximally incorporates as much of the prior cumulative effect as can be incorporated). We note that $acc(e_i, e_j)$ may result in multiple alternative effect scenarios in the case where there are multiple maximally consistent subsets of e_i. The process continues without modification over splits. Joins require special consideration. In the following, we describe the procedure to be followed in the case of 2-joins only, for brevity. The procedure generalizes to n-way joins.

In the following, let t_1 and t_2 be the two tasks immediately preceding a join. Let their cumulative effect annotations be $E_1 = \{es_{11}, es_{12}, \ldots, es_{1m}\}$ and $E_2 = \{es_{21}, es_{22}, \ldots, es_{2n}\}$ respectively (where es_{ts} denotes an effect scenario, subscript s within the cumulative effect of some task, subscript t). Let e be the immediate effect annotation, and E the cumulative effect annotation of a task t immediately following the join.

For an AND-join, we define $E = \{a_i \cup a_j | a_i \in acc(es_{1i}, e)$ and $a_j \in acc(es_{2j}, e)$ and $es_{1i} \in E_1$ and $es_{2j} \in E_2$ and $\{es_{1i}, es_{2j}\}$ are compatible$\}$. A pair of effect scenarios are compatible if and only if their identifiers (representing the path and decisions taken during construction of the scenario) are consistent (the outcomes of their decisions match). Note that we do not consider the possibility of a pair of effect scenarios es_{1i} and es_{2j} being inconsistent, since this would only happen in the case of intrinsically and obviously erroneously constructed process models. The result of effect accumulation in the setting described here is denoted by $ANDacc(E_1, E_2, e)$. For an XOR-join (denoted by $XORacc(E_1, E_2, e)$), we define $E = \{a_i | a_i \in acc(es_i, e)$ and $(es_i \in E_1$ or $es_i \in E_2)\}$. For an OR-join, the result of effect accumulation is denoted by $ORacc(E_1, E_2, e) = ANDacc(E_1, E_2, e) \cup XORacc(E_1, E_2, e)$. The role of guard conditions within effect annotations is also important. Consider the first activity t on an outgoing sequence flow from an OR- or XOR-split. Let E be the set of effect scenarios annotating the activity immediately preceding the XOR-split and let $E' \subseteq E$ such that each effect scenario is E' is consistent with the guard condition c associated with that outgoing flow. Then the set of effect scenarios of t is given by $\{a \mid a \in acc(e \wedge c, e_t)$ and $e \in E'\}$, where e_t is the immediate effect annotation of t and $e \wedge c$ is assumed without loss of generality to be represented as a set of prima implicates.

For example, consider Figure 1 with the following annotations:

- Assess Package: $Knows(RegulatoryAgent, Package, Status, Held)$;
- Route Package: $Performs(SortOfficer, Route, Package)$.

During accumulation we determine that the "Route Package" node will be labeled with an effect scenario es_1 where $Knows(RegulatoryAgent, Package, Status, Held) \wedge Performs(SortOfficer, Route, Package)$ is satisfied. It is also easy to see that the compliance rule C_1, described in Section 2 is violated.

We note that the procedure described above does not satisfactorily deal with loops, but we can perform approximate checking by partial loop unraveling. We also note that some of the effect scenarios generated might be infeasible. Our objective is to devise decision-support functionality in the change management space, with human analysts vetting key changes before they are deployed.

4.2   Non-functional Effect Accumulation

We use scenario identifiers to compute cumulative QoS measures. This leads to a cumulative measure per effect scenario. Recall that a scenario identifier is a sequence composed of activity identifiers or sets consisting (recursively) or scenario identifiers. We use the sets in the label to describe parallel branches. We therefore need to use our algebraic *parallel accumulation operator* ($\ddot{\otimes}$), one for each QoS factor, to specify how cumulative QoS measures, propagated along parallel branches, get combined together at a join gateway.

4.3   Identifying Candidate Prerequisites

The execution of task in a process must be qualified by the conditions achieved up-to the point preceding the tasks' execution. These conditions may be carried forward from a preceding task or the initial context. These prerequisites can be utilized in our framework in much the same way as is the norm in the [12] and [11] literature. Although these conditions may be provided by analysts, dealing with the sheer number of conditions that must be anticipated has been widely acknowledged as a significant problem [17]. In order to reduce the impact of this additional burden, the cumulative effect (as established by accumulation procedure) preceding a task can be queried to establish a set of candidate prerequisites that can be either: used as a strong approximation of the context required by a task; or, as a basis for further refinement by an analyst.

4.4   Business Process Metrics

Business Process Proximity. Business process proximity is used to establish a minimality criterion when selecting candidate SPNet revisions. Previously, in [14], we presented minimality in the context of compliance resolution.

Definition 4. *Associated with each SPNet is a* proximity relation $\leq_{spn}$ *such that* $spn_i \leq_{spn} spn_j$ *denotes that* spn_i *is closer to spn than* spn_j. $\leq_{spn}$, *in turn, is defined by a triple* $\langle \leq_{spn}^V, \leq_{spn}^E, \leq_{spn}^{EFF} \rangle$ *for evaluating node (V), edge (E), and cumulative effect (EFF) proximity respectively. Thus,* $spn_i \leq_{spn} spn_j$ *iff each of* $spn_i \leq_{spn}^V spn_j$, $spn_i \leq_{spn}^E spn_j$ *and* $spn_i \leq_{spn}^{EFF} spn_j$ *holds. We write* $spn_i <_{spn} spn_j$ *iff* $spn_i \leq_{spn} spn_j$ *and at least one of* $spn_i <_{spn}^V spn_j$, $spn_i <_{spn}^E spn_j$ *or* $spn_i <_{spn}^{EFF} spn_j$ *holds.*

These relations can be defined in different ways to reflect alternative intuitions. For instance, the following, set inclusion-oriented definition might be of interest: $spn_i \leq_{spn}^V spn_j$ iff $(V_{spn} \Delta V_{spn_i}) \subseteq (V_{spn} \Delta V_{spn_j})$, where $A \Delta B$ denotes the symmetric difference of sets A and B. An alternative, set cardinality-oriented definition is as follows: $spn_i \leq_{spn}^V spn_j$ iff $|V_{spn} \Delta V_{spn_i}| \leq |V_{spn} \Delta V_{spn_j}|$ (here $|A|$

denotes the cardinality of set A). Similar alternatives exist for the $\leq_{spn}^{E}$ relation. Both $\leq_{spn}^{V}$ and $\leq_{spn}^{E}$ define the structural proximity of one SPNet to another.

Defining the proximity relation $\leq_{spn}^{EFF}$ is somewhat more complicated, since it explores semantic proximity. One approach is to look at the terminating or leaf nodes in an SPNet (i.e. nodes with no outgoing edges). Each such node might be associated with multiple effect scenarios. The set of all effect scenarios associated with every terminating node in an SPNet thus represents a (coarse-grained) description of all possible end-states that might be reached via the execution of some instance of the corresponding process model. For an SPNet spn, let this set be represented by $T_{spn} = \{es_1, \ldots, es_n\}$ where each es_i represents an effect scenario. Let $Diff(spn, spn_i) = \{d_1, \ldots, d_m\}$ where d_i is the smallest cardinality element of the set of symmetric differences between $es_i \in T_{spn_i}$ and each $es \in T_{spn}$. In other words, let $S(es_i, T_{spn}) = \{es_i \Delta e \mid e \in T_{spn}\}$. Then d_i is any (non-deterministically chosen) cardinality-minimal element of $S(es_i, T_{spn})$. Then we write $spn_i \leq_{spn}^{EFF} spn_j$ iff for each $e \in Diff(spn, spn_i)$, there exists an $e' \in Diff(spn, spn_j)$ such that $e \subseteq e'$. The definition of $\leq_{spn}^{EFF}$ above exploited set inclusion. An alternative, cardinality-oriented definition is as follows: $spn_i \leq_{spn}^{EFF} spn_j$ iff $\sum |d_i| \leq \sum |d_j|$ for each $d_i \in Diff(spn, spn_i)$ and $d_j \in Diff(spn, spn_j)$.

The evaluation of the three relations we have discussed so far may be weighted with measures of investment (a key process change criterion). When applied in combination with performance measures, key metrics such as Return on Investment (ROI) can be calculated. As investment can be measured with respect to a variety of factors (e.g. time, cost, risk, return) and at varying levels of precision (e.g. using quantitative or qualitative scales), a scheme similar to the general c-semiring scheme we used for performance evaluation is also applicable here. As with any process, there may be many different ways of implementing a change request, leading to various investment profiles. For example, choosing between an off-the-shelf or in-house implementation, or even whether to implement changes in sequence or concurrently.

The two approaches to defining $\leq_{spn}^{EFF}$ presented above focus on the cumulative end-effects of processes, thus ensuring that modifications to processes deviate minimally in their final effects. In some situations, it is also interesting to consider minimal deviations of the internal workflows that achieve the end-effects. In part this is evaluated by the $\leq_{spn}^{V}$ and $\leq_{spn}^{E}$ proximity relations, but not entirely. Analysis similar to what we have described above with end-effect scenarios, but extended to include intermediate effect scenarios, can be used to achieve this.

Business Process Performance. Process performance, or QoS, metrics are a traditional criterion used alone, or in combination with proximity relations, for guiding selection during process change. In practice, there must be consensus and commitment among analysts when selecting the c-semiring QoS instances (values and their ordering) applied to a specific process (even if multiple scales are being used for similar QoS factors).

Definition 5. *Associated with each SPNet is a dominance relation $\leq_O$ such that $spn_j \leq_O spn_i$ denotes that spn_i performs as good, or better, for a set of QoS factors or objectives (O) than another spn_j. We say that spn_i weakly dominates spn_j if $spn_j \leq_O spn_i$ and $spn_i \not\leq_O spn_j$. We use $<_O$ to denote strict dominance. We say that spn_i and spn_j are intransitive iff $spn_j \leq_O spn_i$ and $spn_i \leq_O spn_j$.*

The set of cumulative QoS measures computed for each terminal effect scenario, denoted $O(spn)$ for a process spn, provide a basis for comparing performance. Associated with each aggregate QoS measure (an n-tuple of QoS specific measures) is a partial order $\leq_s$ produced by the aggregated c-semiring comparison operator. Therefore, we say that: $spn_j \leq_O spn_i$ iff $\forall o_i \in O(spn_i) \forall o_j \in O(spn_j)$ $o_j \leq_s o_i$. In reality, dominance can be difficult to establish as: aggregate QoS measures may be incomparable due to the multitude of factors used during analysis (e.g. one improves cost while the other improves quality); and/or, each process may have optimal cumulative QoS measures for certain criteria. To help deal with variability within the set of cumulative QoS measures for a single process, a summarization operator may be applied to the set of cumulative QoS measures. This operator would result in a single approximate cumulative QoS measure for the entire process. This operator can be based on existing operators (e.g. the comparison $\oplus$ operator for a best-case approximation), and may even be weighted (e.g. the approximate rate of each effect scenario).

4.5   Example

Consider the violation we identified in Section 4.1 between the effect scenario of the "Route Package" task: $es_1 \models Knows(RegulatoryAgent, Package, Status, H\text{-}eld) \land Performs(SortOfficer, Route, Package)$; and the rule: C_1: *"Packages Known to be Held by a Regulatory Authority must not be Routed by a Sort Officer until the Package is Known to be Cleared by the Regulatory Authority"* (described in FOL in Section 2). Considering the constraint that C_1 must hold in our example process context, we can consider changes to the process model in Figure 1 that are minimal with respect to the criteria outlined in Section 3 and implemented in Section 4.4.

The two models in Figures 2 and 3 are two candidates for resolution, which we will evaluate w.r.t. our proposed criteria. Figure 2 resolves the inconsistency

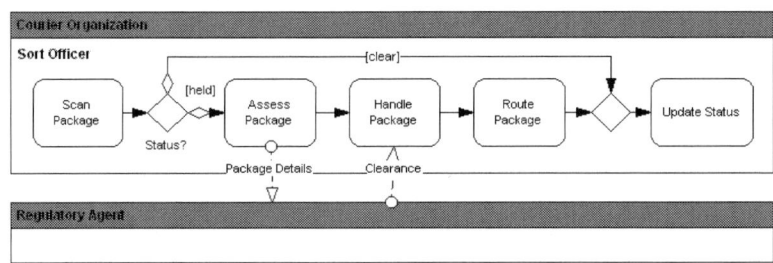

Fig. 2. Resolved Package Screening Process (R_1)

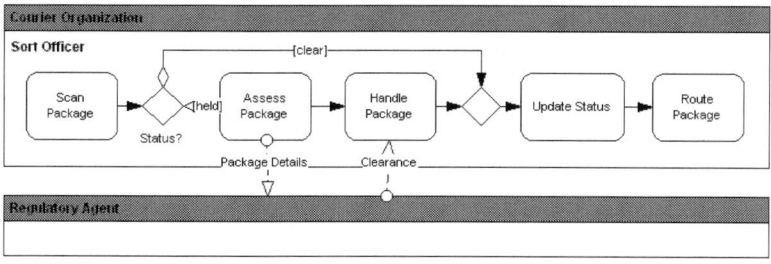

Fig. 3. Resolved Package Screening Process (R_2)

introduced by the request to satisfy C_1 by placing the "Route Package" task
after the "Handle Package" task. Figure 3 on the other hand appends the "Route
Package" task to the end of the process.

We apply the proximity metric and relation. Upon inspection Figures 2 and
3 share all their nodes with Figure 1. Therefore, no comparison can be made
across this structural dimension. We determine a significant edge difference
between Figures 2 and Figure 1, six edges in total, including the "Handle Package' $\rightarrow$ 'Route Package' edge. Figure 3 also differs with Figure 1 across four
edges in total including "Update Status" $\rightarrow$ "Route Package". In addition, the
final cumulative effect of both Figure 2 and Figure 3 result in two effect scenarios
such that Figure 2 actually remains identical to Figure 1. Figure 3 on the other
hand receives the additional effect of $Performs(SortOfficer, Route, Package)$
on the effect scenario now generated by placing the "Route Package" activity
in line with both process trajectories. With respect to structural inclusion, we
cannot differentiate Figure 2 and Figure 3, however when the cardinality based
evaluation is applied, Figure 3 is more proximally efficient. On the other hand
Figure 2 is more proximal semantically.

As discussed, we determine the cumulative quality of service for an effect
scenario by working through the path history for that scenario. Let the path
histories for our examples be: Figure 2: $1 : \langle SP, AP, HP, RP, US \rangle$, $2 : \langle SP, US \rangle$;
Figure 3: $1 : \langle SP, AP, HP, US, RP \rangle$, $2 : \langle SP, US, RP \rangle$.

We accumulate the measures in using the combination operator of each scale,
leading us to the following cumulative evaluations for our examples: Figure 2:
$1 : O_R = 0.76, O_S = 64, O_{CT} = 710$, $2 : O_R = 0.96, O_S = 128, O_{CT} = 30$;
Figure 3: $1 : O_R = 0.76, O_S = 64, O_{CT} = 710$, $2 : O_R = 0.90, O_S = 64, O_{CT} = 630$. Therefore, Figure 2 performs the same or better than Figure 3.

5   Conclusion

We have presented a conceptualization of extended business process models,
which permit improved decision support functionality for analysis and change
management. We have described how this conceptualization deals with change
in the context of requests to change a process or the artefacts that influence its
design. Finally, have presented a toolkit for managing change.

References

1. White, S.: Business process modeling notation (bpmn), Technical report, OMG Final Adopted Specification 1.0 (February 2006), http://www.bpmn.org
2. van der Aalst, W., Dreiling, A., Rosemann, M., Jansen-Vullers, M.H.: Configurable process models as a basis for reference modelling. In: Proceedings of the Workshop on Business Process Reference Models (BPRM 2005) (2005)
3. Rinderle, S., Reichert, M., Dadam, P.: Correctness criteria for dynamic changes in workflow systems - a survey. Data and Knowledge Engineering 50, 9–34 (2004)
4. Ponnalagu, K., Narendra, N.C.: Deriving service variants from business process specifications. In: Proceedings of the 1st Bangalore annual Compute conference (COMPUTE 2008), pp. 1–9. ACM, New York (2008)
5. Lu, R., Sadiq, S.: Managing process variants as and information resource. In: Dustdar, S., Fiadeiro, J.L., Sheth, A.P. (eds.) BPM 2006. LNCS, vol. 4102, pp. 426–431. Springer, Heidelberg (2006)
6. Soffer, P.: Scope analysis: identifying the impact of changes in business process models. Software Process: Improvement and Practice 10(4), 393–402 (2005)
7. van Hee, K.M., Reijers, H.A.: Using Formal Analysis Techniques in Business Process Redesign. In: van der Aalst, W.M.P., Desel, J., Oberweis, A. (eds.) Business Process Management. LNCS, vol. 1806, pp. 51–71. Springer, Heidelberg (2000)
8. Modafferi, S., Benatallah, B., Casati, F., Pernici, B.: A Methodology for Designing and Managing Context-Aware Workflows. In: Mobile IS II, pp. 91–106 (2005)
9. Weber, I., Hoffman, J., Mendling, J.: Semantic business process validation. In: Proceedings of the 3rd International Workshop on Semantic Business Process Management (2008)
10. Governatori, G., Hoffmann, J., Sadiq, S., Weber, I.: Detecting regulatory compliance of business process models through semantic annotations. In: Proceedings of the 4th International Workshop on Business Process Design (2008)
11. Hendler, J., Tate, A., Drummond, M.: Ai planning: Systems and techniques. AI Magazine 11(2), 61–77 (1990)
12. Huth, M., Ryan, M.: Logic in Computer Science: Modelling and Reasoning about Systems. Cambridge University Press, Cambridge (2004)
13. Jackson, D., Wing, J.: Lightweight formal methods. IEEE Computer, 21–22 (1996)
14. Ghose, A.K., Koliadis, G.: Auditing business process compliance. In: Krämer, B.J., Lin, K.-J., Narasimhan, P. (eds.) ICSOC 2007. LNCS, vol. 4749, pp. 169–180. Springer, Heidelberg (2007)
15. Puhlmann, F., Weske, M.: Using the pi-calculus for formalizing workflow patterns. In: van der Aalst, W.M.P., Benatallah, B., Casati, F., Curbera, F. (eds.) BPM 2005. LNCS, vol. 3649, pp. 153–168. Springer, Heidelberg (2005)
16. Bistarelli, S.: Soft Constraint Solving and Programming: a General Framework. PhD thesis, Computer Science Department, University of Pisa (2001)
17. Shanahan, M.: Solving the Frame Problem - A Mathematical Investigation of the Common Sense Law of Inertia. MIT Press, Cambridge (1997)

Supporting Change in Business Process Models Using Pattern-Based Constraints

Jens Müller

SAP Research CEC Karlsruhe,
Vincenz-Prießnitz-Str. 1, 76131 Karlsruhe, Germany
jens.mueller@sap.com

Abstract. When business processes are affected by changes in legal or organisational requirements, the corresponding process models have to be adapted accordingly. These requirements implicate constraints that influence how certain parts of business processes have to be modelled. If these constraints are not explicitly known to the modelling tool, the chance that a modeller accidentally violates them increases with the number of constraints. Therefore, we propose to explicitly model constraints and automatically verify them in order to support change. In this paper, we explain how to incorporate semantics into business process models and constraints in order to facilitate the verification process. In addition, we present ideas on how to model and verify these constraints.

1 Introduction

Business process models are dynamic and therefore change over time. For example, changes to process models could be necessary due to revised legal or organisational requirements. Such high-level requirements implicate technical constraints that influence the structure and semantics of business process models, as they specify how modellers have to model certain parts of business processes in a specific domain. Before changing process models according to the current constraints, modellers must ensure that process models do not contain parts that satisfy previous constraints but are incompatible with current ones.

The execution of business process models (by humans or machines) that violate constraints may lead to undesired results or, in the worst case, critical situations. If constraints are not explicitly known to the modelling tool, the chance that a modeller accidentally violates constraints during the modification of process models increases with the number of constraints. Therefore, we propose to explicitly model constraints and automatically verify them. The next section describes how change in process models can be supported.

1.1 Scenario from the Aviation Industry

Changes in organisational requirements can be found in maintenance, repair, and overhaul (MRO) processes of the aviation industry, which is threatened by the problem of suspected unapproved parts (SUP). An SUP is an aircraft part

T. Halpin et al. (Eds.): BPMDS 2009 and EMMSAD 2009, LNBIP 29, pp. 27–32, 2009.

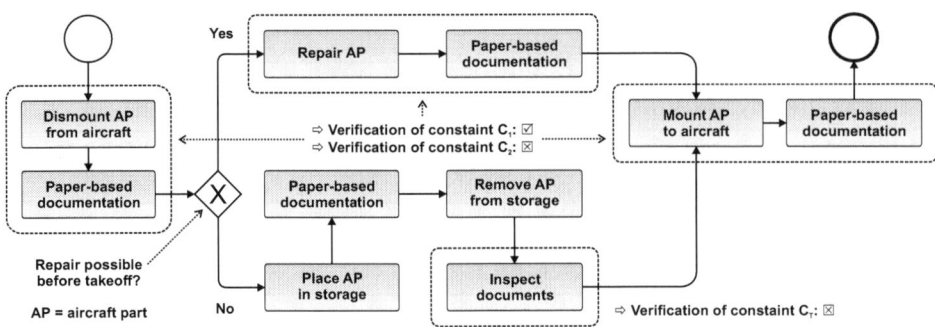

Fig. 1. Simplified model of a maintenance process from the aviation industry

that is not guaranteed to meet the requirements of an approved aircraft part (e.g., counterfeits, which do not conform to the strict quality constraints of the aviation industry). Thus, SUPs seriously violate the security standards of an aircraft. Apart from time-consuming material analyses, verifying the authenticity of aircraft parts can be performed by inspecting the accompanying documents, which can be easily forged. The aviation industry intends to solve this problem by introducing electronic pedigrees for certain categories of aircraft parts, which document their origin and safety-critical events during their lifecycle (e.g., modifications). The industry plans to store pedigrees on radio frequency identification (RFID) tags, which are meant to be securely attached to aircraft parts.

Figure 1 shows a simplified model of a maintenance process from the aviation industry. An example for a constraint on maintenance processes is that all activities that represent a safety-critical event have to be followed by an activity that represents the paper-based documentation of this event (constraint C_1). As depicted, the process model satisfies this constraint.

However, when implementing the maintenance process with RFID support, C_1 must be replaced by a new constraint (C_2), which assures that the model reflects the resulting changes. In addition, temporary constraints may be used to find parts within business process models that satisfy previous constraints but are incompatible with current ones:

- *No* activity that represents a paper-based inspection process *may exist* within a business process model (temporary constraint C_T).
- *All* structures of model elements within a business process model that represent the mounting, dismounting, or repair of an aircraft part *have to be followed* by an activity that represents a storage process of this safety-critical event on an RFID tag, which is attached to the aircraft part (constraint C_2).

As illustrated, the process model does not comply with C_T and C_2, since the planned introduction of RFID requires its modification. An automatic detection of such constraint violations would assist modellers in finding objectionable parts within process models during the implementation of revised requirements.

2   Enriching Business Process Models with Additional Semantics

The graphical representation of business process models is mostly based on an internal model with a more formal representation. Models themselves are typically based on a meta-model that defines modelling constructs and how they can be associated with each other. A standardised language for specifying technology neutral meta-models is defined by the Meta Object Facility (MOF) specification [1]. The inherent semantics of modelling constructs is usually described in a specification in an informal way. The Business Process Modeling Notation (BPMN) specification [2], for example, describes an activity as a generic term for work that a company performs. In order to assign meaning to activities, a modeller can either label the activity using natural language or specify a web service endpoint, in the case of an automated activity. When modelling constraints, it should be possible to refer to these labels or web service endpoints. However, despite its semantic complexity, natural language is not machine-readable. Even for a human, it is hard to decide if two activities with similar labels have the same meaning. It is easier to identify activities with a certain meaning if they are linked to web service endpoints. In this case, it is more likely that modellers use the same web service endpoint for a given operation, although other web services could offer the same functionality.

One solution to uniquely identify the meaning of model elements is to semantically enrich them via the assignment of classes from domain ontologies. Such ontologies could, for example, comprise descriptions of MRO activities. Although semantic enrichment poses additional overhead for modellers, business process analysis benefits from machine-readable semantics in the long term. To speed up the process of semantic enrichment, techniques like natural language processing of activity labels could be used to assist modellers. In contrast to other authors who proposed the combination of business process models with ontologies in the ontological technological space [3], we propose semantic enrichment in the meta-modelling technological space [4]. This implies representing ontologies as models (e.g., based on the Ontology Definition Metamodel [5]) and associating activities and ontology classes within the business process meta-model. Semantic enrichment using MOF associations leads to the tight coupling of activities and ontology classes. One advantage of this tight coupling over other approaches is that MOF-based repositories would delete the association between a model element and an ontology class automatically, in case the ontology class is deleted.

3   Modelling Constraints

When addressing the issue of modelling constraints on business process models that exhibit machine-readable semantics in order to support change, the question that arises is how to make these constraints explicit. Constraints refer to the structure and semantics of business process models. More precisely, constraints can be seen as conditions on sets of model elements with a certain meaning,

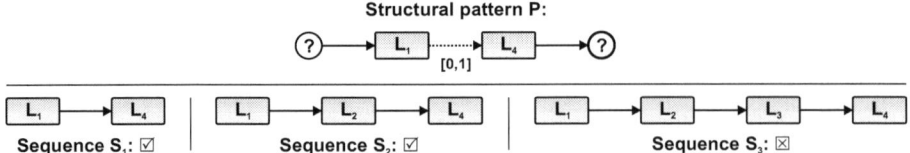

Fig. 2. Matching a structural pattern that includes a flexible sequence flow

which exist within the structure of business process models. These sets of model elements are referred to as structural patterns in the following.

To model constraints it is inevitable to introduce techniques for modelling structural patterns and corresponding conditions. We propose using a graphical notation for structural patterns in order to make the modelling as intuitive as the modelling of business processes. There have been several attempts to specify quality constraints and query patterns visually. In [6], the authors refer to constraints as conditions on single activities. These conditions, for instance, allow modellers to specify that all activities labelled L_1 must be preceded or followed by an activity labelled L_2. However, this approach does not consider conditions on structural patterns and does not support machine-readable semantics. In [7,8], the authors propose a graphical notation to specify queries on business process models using a pattern-based approach. Nevertheless, they do not address the specification of constraints on business process models. Furthermore, the above mentioned approaches do not provide enough flexibility when modelling sequence flows between model elements within structural patterns. For example, figure 2 depicts a structural pattern P. The modeller of this pattern is interested in a sequence of activities labelled L_1 and L_4. Moreover, occurrences of these activities within business process models with at most one additional activity in between, should match the structural pattern as well. As depicted, the sequences S_1 and S_2 within a business process model match the pattern, whereas the sequence S_3 does not. No existing approach offers a modelling construct to express this kind of limitation. For these reasons, we suggest the development of a new modelling language for structural patterns that tackles these issues.

The availability of a modelling language for structural patterns allows the introduction of constraints that support change in business process models, such as the following conditions on the structural patterns P_1 and P_2:

- At least n instances of P_1 must exist within business process models
- At most n instances of P_1 may exist within business process models
- Every instance of P_1 must be preceded/followed by an instance of P_2
- No instance of P_1 may be preceded/followed by an instance of P_2

It is important to note that the last condition should only be used for temporary constraints (cf. constraint C_T), as it is not possible to specify all combinations of patterns that must not exist within process models. In order to specify such conditions, additional modelling constructs are necessary. A modeller should also be able to correlate constraints, e.g., to express that a business process model should either comply with one constraint or another, which requires suitable modelling constructs as well. With this approach, business processes and constraints can be both expressed as models.

4   Verifying Constraints

Constraints on business process models alone are not sufficient if they are not enforced. To this end, a technique is required that verifies constraints with respect to a process model. One of the most important steps of the verification process is to find occurrences of structural patterns with a certain meaning within business process models. None of the existing approaches to verify constraints on (business process) models fulfils our needs. Certain types of constraints on MOF models can be specified by means of expressions based on the Object Constraint Language (OCL) [9]. Unfortunately, OCL is not expressive enough to refer to sets of model elements. In [10], quality requirements are translated into temporal logic formulas, which are then verified by a model checker. However, this approach only allows the verification of conditions on single activities.

To solve the problem of finding structural patterns, an appropriate algorithm is needed. We propose to apply the concepts of existing tools, which we use as search mechanisms. Two types of tools satisfy our requirements: model query processors, which evaluate requests written in languages comparable to SQL, and rule engines. To use these types of tools, structural patterns have to be transformed into queries or rules. An important feature of queries and rules is that they are declarative, i.e. they describe what to do instead of specifying how to do it, which facilitates the transformation process. In addition, most tools can access business process models directly and allow the generation of queries or rules during run-time. Furthermore, there are tools that support the usage of user-defined functions within queries or rules. A user-defined function is needed, for instance, in order to measure the distance between two activities that are indirectly connected via sequence flows. Using existing techniques, the verification process of a constraint can be divided into three fundamental phases:

1. Transformation of structural patterns that are associated with the constraint into a representation that can be used as input for an existing technique, which we use as a search mechanism
2. Execution of the respective technique
3. Evaluation of the condition of the constraint

While the first phase necessitates the development of a transformation algorithm, the second phase relies on existing tools. Once a constraint violation has been detected in phase three, there are several possibilities on how to react. One possibility is to notify the modeller and mark objectionable parts within the business process diagram. Another approach is to replace these parts automatically. While this is sometimes not possible, automatic replacement might frustrate the modeller who is not aware of what is happening behind the scenes.

5 Conclusions

In this paper we discussed the importance of specifying constraints on business process models explicitly. We explained the benefits of the semantic enrichment of activities within business process models and the advantages of using the meta-modelling technological space for this purpose. We proposed the development of a modelling language to specify constraints on business process models that overcomes the shortcomings of existing approaches. Finally, we outlined techniques on verifying constraints automatically.

We are currently implementing the presented ideas on top of a tool for modelling business processes with BPMN, which is based on a MOF-compliant infrastructure. The extension consists of a modelling tool for specifying constraints as well as a rule-based verification component. The tool will be evaluated in collaboration with an aircraft maintenance company that wants to implement maintenance processes with RFID support.

References

1. OMG: Meta Object Facility (MOF) Specification Version 1.4 (2002)
2. OMG: Business Process Modeling Notation: Version 1.2 (2009)
3. Thomas, O., Fellmann, M.: Semantic EPC: Enhancing Process Modeling Using Ontology Languages. In: 2007 Workshop on Semantic Business Process and Product Lifecycle Management, pp. 64–75 (2007)
4. Kurtev, I., Bézivin, J., Aksit, M.: Technological Spaces: an Initial Appraisal. In: OTM 2002 Federated Conferences, Industry Program (2002)
5. OMG: Ontology Definition Metamodel (Beta 3) (2008)
6. Förster, A., Engels, G., Schattkowsky, T., Straeten, R.V.D.: A Pattern-driven Development Process for Quality Standard-conforming Business Process Models. In: 2006 IEEE Symposium on Visual Languages and Human-Centric Computing, pp. 135–142. IEEE Computer Society Press, Los Alamitos (2006)
7. Awad, A.: BPMN-Q: A Language to Query Business Processes. In: 2nd International Workshop on Enterprise Modelling and Information Systems Architectures, pp. 115–128. Köllen Druck + Verlag, Bonn (2007)
8. Francescomarino, C.D., Tonella, P.: Crosscutting Concern Documentation by Visual Query of Business Processes. In: 4th International Workshop on Business Process Design (2008)
9. OMG: Object Constraint Language: Version 2.0 (2006)
10. Förster, A., Engels, G., Schattkowsky, T., Straeten, R.V.D.: Verification of Business Process Quality Constraints Based on Visual Process Patterns. In: 1st Joint IEEE/IFIP Symposium on Theoretical Aspects of Software Engineering, pp. 197–208. IEEE Computer Society Press, Los Alamitos (2007)

Eliciting Goals for Business Process Models with Non-Functional Requirements Catalogues

Evellin C.S. Cardoso, João Paulo A. Almeida, Giancarlo Guizzardi,
and Renata S.S. Guizzardi

Ontologies and Conceptual Modelling Research Group (NEMO)
Computer Science Department, Federal University of Espírito Santo (UFES),
Av. Fernando Ferrari, s/n, Vitória, ES, Brazil
ecardoso@inf.ufes.br, jpalmeida@ieee.org, gguizzardi@acm.org,
rguizzardi@inf.ufes.br

Abstract. While traditional approaches in business process modelling tend to focus on "how" the business processes are performed (adopting a behavioural description in which business processes are described in terms of procedural aspects), in *goal-oriented business process modelling* [23][24][6], the proposals strive to extend traditional business process methodologies by providing a dimension of intentionality to the business processes. One of the difficulties in enabling *goal-oriented business process modelling* is the identification of goals. This paper reports on a study conducted in an organization in which we have obtained several goal models which were represented in Tropos methodology, each one corresponding to a business process also modelled in the scope of the study. A preliminary goal elicitation activity has been carried out for collecting an initial version of the goal models. After that, we have obtained a second version of the goal models by using the NFR catalogues as a tool in goal elicitation. We have found the NFR catalogues to be useful in goal elicitation, uncovering goals that did not arise during previous interviews.

Keywords: business processes, goal models, non-functional requirements.

1 Introduction

The increasing competitiveness drives organizations to promote change in an attempt to improve the quality of the services and products they offer. In recent years, many of the efforts related to managing change in organizations have been conducted in the scope of Business Process Reengineering (BPR) activities [1][2]. BPR is based on the assumption that change in business processes should generate radical improvements in critical performance measures (such as cost, quality, service and speed) [1]. Moreover, it is believed that implementing radical changes in business processes is the way to achieve dramatic and satisfactory results [1][2].

However, predicting how a given enterprise environment should respond to changes by simply adopting a business-process centered view is unfeasible since there is a large number of issues to be considered, such as infrastructure, power and

T. Halpin et al. (Eds.): BPMDS 2009 and EMMSAD 2009, LNBIP 29, pp. 33–45, 2009.
© Springer-Verlag Berlin Heidelberg 2009

politics, organizational culture, etc [3]. Given this multitude of issues, understanding an organizational setting often requires a number of perspectives [3].

While traditional approaches in business process modelling tend to focus on "how" the business processes are performed (adopting a behavioural description in which business processes are described in terms of procedural aspects), in *goal-oriented business process modelling* [23][24][6], the proposals strive to extend traditional business process methodologies by providing a dimension of intentionality to the business processes [4].

In recent years, goal-oriented approaches have been largely addressed in the literature of requirements engineering (RE) which focuses on how these approaches support requirements elicitation and modelling for system development [4]. In this context, goals express, in multiple levels of abstraction, the objectives the system under consideration should undertake [8]. Although this field is mainly concerned with system development, a goal-driven nature of software engineering requires RE to pay attention to the organizational context [4]. The Zachman framework [22] also highlights the importance of motivation as a driver for enterprise management and system development. Therefore, in the context of business process modelling, goal modelling is extended not only to capture concerns and motivations of the stakeholders in the achievement of business processes, but to incorporate issues related with the strategy of the enterprise as a whole.

Although goal modelling provides a more strategic view for business processes, little attention is devoted to explicitly modelling goals as well as using the concept of goal to increase the value of the process modelling techniques [12]. To articulate an organization's business processes in terms of the enterprise's strategic goals, the first problem to be addressed is how to elicite goals from the organization context since goal identification is not an easy task [8]. Problems related with goal elicitation are firstly addressed by the requirements engineering (RE) literature, but essentially the same problems arise in the area of business process modelling. Some problems arising in the scope of business process modelling are: goals are difficult to formulate (often these formulations become vague and highly abstract) [7], the involved parties are unable to explicitly state their views [14] and even when they are capable the goals can be conflicting [15] (even when goals are drawn from the same individual), the analysts have limited knowledge about the environment [14], among others.

The purpose of this paper is to report a field work in which we addressed the problem of identifying goals. This field work took place in the Rheumatology Department of a hospital in Brazil. Our main purpose is to contribute in the area of goal elicitation with a systematic way to identify goals in a given organizational setting in the business process modelling activity prior to the identification of potential business process change. We suggest using Non-Functional Requirements (NFRs) [9][10] catalogues in order to tackle the difficulty in identifying business goals. The next section shows our motivation in adopting this approach.

This paper is structured as follows: section 2 describes the NFR framework (used as a starting point to derive (soft)goals), section 3 provides a description of our field work: the preliminary goal elicitation method (section 3.1), the results of this preliminary phase (section 3.2), the goal elicitation with catalogues (section 3.3), a discussion about these results (section 3.4). Section 4 points to related work and finally, section 5 concludes with some considerations as well as future research work.

2 The NFR Framework

Many important goals for an organization may be characterized as "softgoals", i.e., goals with no clear-cut criteria to determine their satisfaction [5]. Eliciting softgoals is particularly challenging, given their subjective, interactive and relative nature [16]. One of the solutions proposed to address the problem of identifying non-functional requirements in RE is the NFR framework. Basically, the NFR framework is an approach for specifying and analyzing non-functional requirements (NFRs). Although this framework has been primarily conceived for helping one to elicit NFRs in the system development life-cycle, we have used them to tackle the problem of systematic identifying business goals, helping one to reflect about the dimensions which a softgoal can assume in an organizational environment.

Although the concepts of NFRs and softgoals are commonly treated as the same in the literature, we must stress out that the differences between NFRs and softgoals cannot be ignored. On one hand, as explained in [25], NFRs refer to quality attributes that some system is expect to meet while executing a particular service. These services which the system must provide amounts to its set of functional requirements (FRs). NFRs are the opposite of functional requirements (FRs). On the other hand, hardgoals are defined as goals whose satisfaction can be determined by applying formal verification techniques [8][25]. Softgoals are the opposite of hardgoals, since they are "subject to interpretation" [3], "imprecise, subjective, context-specific, and ideal" [25]. This common association between NFRs and softgoals arises because there is a tendency in specifying quality attributes in an imprecise manner.

Since we have addressed the motivation behind using the NFR framework and the difference between NFRs and softgoals, we describe the NFR framework in the sequel.

The NFR Framework [9][10][16] comprises a proposal for addressing NFRs using catalogues that accumulates knowledge about specifying NFRs. The catalogues' specification ranges from representing to operationalizing NFRs, offering guidelines for prioritization and decomposition during the design process.

The Softgoal Interdependency Graphs (SIGs) represent particular kinds of NFRs, their decomposition structures and possible design alternatives to embody the requirement in the future system. Further, the interdependencies between the NFRs and their operationalizations are represented.

There are three kinds of catalogs used: the first kind (called *NFR type catalog*) contains particular types of NFRs, such as security or performance, and their associated terminology. The second type (called *methods catalogs*) represents development techniques for the system to meet a particular requirement and finally, the third type (*correlation catalogs*) shows the correlation and tradeoffs among softgoals.

Fig. 1 depicts a catalogue of some NFR types, where a NFR can be "performance", "security", "cost" and "user-friendliness" [9].

An application within a real example is also demonstrated in [9]. In this example, security is the NFR considered for developing a credit card system. Fig. 2 shows that to incorporate security in a given account, three subtypes of NFRs are necessary: integrity, confidentiality and availability. In turn, to incorporate integrity on credit card accounts, two additional NFRs are needed: completeness and accuracy. This

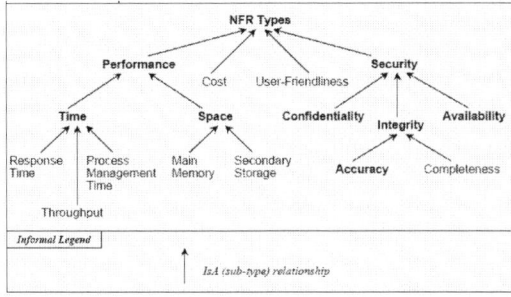

Fig. 1. A catalogue of some NFR types [9]

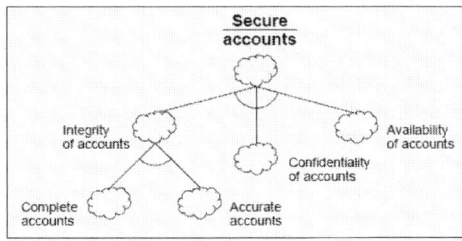

Fig. 2. Further decomposition of a security softgoal (adapted from [9])

example depicts that the process of decomposing some NFR is guided (and thus facilitated) by adopting these catalogues since they are helpful in reasoning about what qualities the system to-be is expected to meet.

3   Case Study: Goal Elicitation in a Healthcare Institution

This section describes the case study conducted in the Rheumatology Department of the Cassiano de Moraes University Hospital, which is part of the Federal University of Espírito Santo in Vitória, Brazil.

In the context of the hospital, the department has the following functions: provide educational training to form specialists in rheumatology, provide outpatient medical care and developing research to investigate the incidence de rheumatologic conditions in population. It has six specialists in rheumatology, two nurses and two physiotherapists, among other professionals for hosting patients. The department performs 15 business processes, such as outpatient care, drugs infusion, among others and performs an average rate of 5700 outpatient medical care by year.

In the scope of this study, we have produced 9 goal models which were represented using the Tropos Modelling Language and methodology [17]. Each of these models correspond to a business process also modelled in the scope of the study. A preliminary goal elicitation activity has been carried out for collecting an initial version of the goal models. After that, we have obtained a second version of the goal models by using the NFR catalogues as a tool in goal elicitation. Due to space restrictions, we focus on the goal models of the diagnosis process.

3.1 Preliminary Goal Elicitation Method

This preliminary goal elicitation and modelling effort was divided in four stages according to the source of information and technique used to interact with the process stakeholders. In the first and second stages, we have captured only hardgoals. From the second stage on, our goal models were composed by hardgoals and softgoals.

In a *first stage*, the available documentation about the organizational process has been assessed. This revealed some organizational characteristics such as: organizational structure and human resources, routines, business processes (with a brief textual explanation in natural language about these processes) and physical space. From the organization structure, we could infer internal actors and the business process they carry out. This documentation also provided goals previously achieved by the department (along with their impacts) and goals which were yet to be achieved by the department, giving us some insight about the nature of the business processes under consideration and about some relevant goals (stated in natural language). Further, a first interview was undertaken with a physician (who does not belong to the organization) for understanding general concepts about the medical domain. Additionally, concepts related with rheumatology (diseases, medicines and other technical terms) have been briefly surveyed in online information sources.

In a *second stage*, we have obtained a preliminary goal model along with a preliminary business process model. The approach used here consisted in observing the process performers during business process execution, i.e., we observed the daily routine of the organization. While this approach allowed us to understand how actors interact and how actor dependency relationships are established in practice, the actors' focus on getting the work done prevents one from revealing most of the intention and motivation behind their practices.

A *third stage* focused on interviewing the organizational actors during business process execution to reveal the goals of specific activities as well as goals related with a process as a whole. Thus, the model generated in previous stage could be incremented through *refinement/abstraction techniques* [3][8][18]. With the *refinement technique* one can find out subgoals of the parent goal by asking "HOW questions" about the goals already identified [8]. This is helpful in capturing the different ways of goal achievement. With the *abstraction technique*, more abstract goals can be identified by asking "WHY questions" about the goals previously modelled [8]. This enabled us to capture the rationale (more general goals) behind more specific goals. Although the interviews during the process execution provided a more strategic dimension (in the sense that they have captured details related with the organization's strategy in a lower level of abstraction), the goal models obtained were strongly related to the business process models, not capturing knowledge about the enterprise setting as a whole. This deficiency was addressed in *fourth stage*.

In a *fourth stage*, we concentrated in dedicated interviews not only with the business process actors but also with the department manager. (By "dedicated interviews" we mean that the interviewees devoted all attention to the elicitation process as opposed to being fully involved with activity execution). The elicitation interviews in this stage focused on raising internal problems of the organization, as well as problems associated with the relationship between the department and external organizations, highlighting all kinds of conflicting interests. The problems and deficiencies that the stakeholders believed to exist in the organization provided not just additional goals to enrich the models, but also some obstacles for goal realization, reasons for non-achievement of goals and possible solutions for these obstacles.

3.2   Results of the Preliminary Goal Elicitation Activities

Fig. 3 exhibits a Tropos diagram which shows the goals of a physician who conducts the diagnosis business process.

In Tropos diagrams, actors are represented as circles, goals as oval shapes and soft-goals as cloud shapes. (Soft)goals can be related with three kinds of relationships: *means-end analysis, contribution analysis* and *AND/OR decomposition.*[1]

The physician provides medical care to a patient (Provide medical care to patient goal) through a medical consultation (Provide medical care through medical consultation goal). During consultation, the physician diagnoses the patient's health state (Diagnose health state goal) and prescribes the treatment (Prescribe patient's treatment goal which uses, in turn, a Drugs prescription).

The main goal of the physician is to Diagnose patient's health state. During the process of diagnosis, the physician can find either rheumatologic or non-rheumatologic conditions (Diagnose rheumatologic conditions goal and Diagnose non-rheumatologic conditions goal). After diagnosing the patient's heath state, the physician is able to select the most suitable treatment for the disease (Select the most suitable treatment for patient softgoal). For this reason, Diagnose patient's health state is a mean for Select the most suitable treatment for patient.

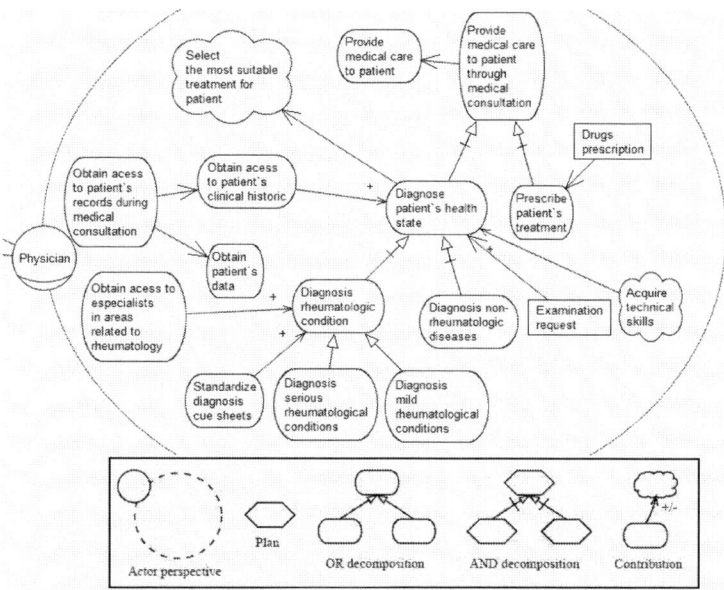

Fig. 3. Goal model resulted from the preliminary goal elicitation activities

---

[1] The AND/OR decomposition can be made by using the "HOW questions" previously mentioned.

The physician must have accurate knowledge for being able to discover the presence/absence of diseases (Acquire technical skills softgoal). He/she must also access the patient's data (Obtain patient's data goal) for being able to determine how the patient health condition is evolving along the time (Obtain access to patient's clinical historic goal). One of the means for accessing the patient's data and thus to know its clinical history is to obtaining access to patient's records (Obtain access to patient's records during medical consultation goal). Finally, the rheumatologist must confirm the diagnosis with other specialists in order to interpret the evidences in the whole clinical context (Obtain access to specialists in areas related to rheumatology goal).

3.3 Goal Elicitation with Catalogues

During the four stages we have reported here, we had the opportunity to understand the organization's context, its problems, deficiencies and so forth. By following the execution of the business process, interviewing the stakeholders and observing the organizational setting, we could keep direct contact with implicit factors that underlie the organizational context. These previous stages were crucial to provide *insights* about new concerns that could be added. These *insights* guided us to suggest which NFR types could be extracted from NFR catalogues [9][10][19][20] and subsequently adapted to the organizational context. According the NFR types catalogues, we have formulated additional goals for the business process, initially without participation of the stakeholders. The translation from NFR types in the catalogues to goals was highly related to the knowledge acquired in previous stages, i.e., to adequately refine the NFRs we had to consider the meaning of the NFRs' refinement in the context of the domain under consideration. After incorporating these additional goals into the model, we have applied the same techniques of abstraction/refinement previously applied for identifying additional goals without the participation of the stakeholders. Due to space constraints, we concentrate here on some relevant portions of the resulting goal models.

3.4 Results of the Goal Elicitation with Catalogues

Before discussing the outcomes related with the utilization of the catalogues with the stakeholders, we have translated the NFR types to goals in the context of the domain under consideration. The NFR types originated the following goals:

Accessibility [19]. Access patient's data records;
Confidentiality [19]. Maintain healthcare information private;
Completeness [19]. Obtain complete information about patient's treatment;
Accuracy [19]. Obtain accurate information about patient's treatment;
Traceability (Process and Data) [19][10]. Obtain traceability for information in patient's treatment refined into Obtain traceability in investigation of patient's condition, Obtain traceability in relation to treatment administered to patient and Obtain traceability in relation to physicians who prescribed patient's treatment.
Integrability [19]. Integrate service with other hospital departments, Integrate service with municipal and state health services (to obtain what is called "integrated treatment" exploring the benefits of information integration).

Trust and Confidence to the Provider (Assurance) [20]. Trust physician (not shown in the figures since this goal belongs to the patient's perspective.)
Empathy (Level of Caring and Personalized Attention Provided to the Requestor) [20]. Show empathy to patient.

The translation of NFR types from the catalogues to goals revealed that although catalogues address non-functional requirements, some goals elicited in this effort are not softgoals, but hardgoals instead. For instance, the requirement of Accessibility has led to the identification of the hardgoal Access patient's records. Besides, the translation seems to be highly domain-dependent. For example, traceability refers to the capacity of tracing patient's data along treatment. Another particularity concerned with the translation is that different NFR types are mapped to the same goal in the organization. Distributivity (capacity of reaching all decision-makers [19]) and integrability (capacity of adequately and efficiently integrating operational information [19]) mean the same in this context (in the sense that both mean the information must be integrated so as to reach all decision-makers caring about that information). Privacy and confidentiality are also mapped to the same goal.

With respect to the goals added, we were able to identify goals which had remained implicit in the preliminary study (Fig. 4). Most of these goals were either associated with quality aspects of the previously modelled goals (Obtain complete information about patient's treatment softgoal and Obtain accurate information about patient's treatment softgoal) or with quality aspects for the service as a whole (Integrate service with all stakeholders softgoal and the softgoals originated from its refinements). We also have noticed that some of some of the elicited (soft)goals address exceptional situations, for example, the softgoal Integrate services with specialists in areas related to rheumatology is relevant only in the case the rheumatologist needs to clarify further details about the diagnosis with other specialists (for example, a dermatologist or ophthalmologist) in the hospital.

Another interesting aspect in elicitation with catalogues was the fact that we could notice that some of the goals spontaneously mentioned are actually goals for

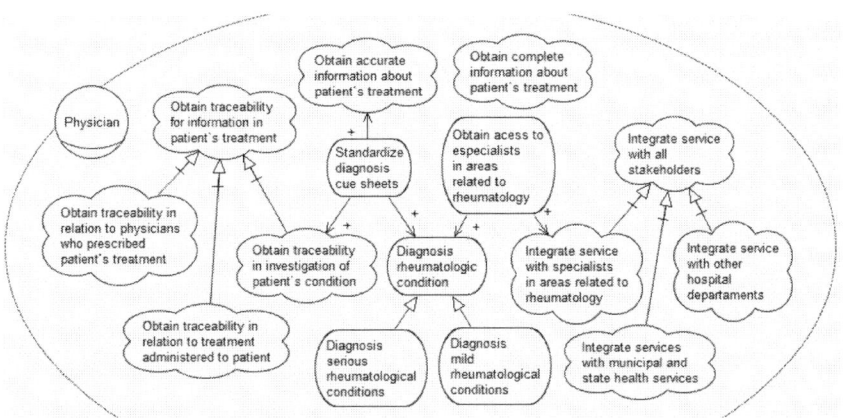

Fig. 4. Portion of the goal model obtained in goal elicitation activities with catalogues (1)

implementing mechanisms for the attainment of more abstract goals, which remained implicit when applying the abstraction technique, but that could be revealed through the use of the catalogues. For instance, in Fig. 4, from traceability we have suggested three types of traceability: Obtain traceability in relation to treatment administered to patient softgoal (obtain information about the drugs prescribed along the treatment), Obtain traceability in relation to physicians who prescribed patient's treatment softgoal (obtain information about the physicians who had already prescribed treatment to the patient) and Obtain traceability in investigation of patient's condition softgoal (obtain information about the conditions which had already been investigated previously by the physician). Actually, this last goal was the motivation for the standardization of diagnosis cue sheets (previously modelled). The standardization of diagnosis cue sheets was one of many means towards achieving traceability in the investigation of diseases.

Finally, all goals suggested through the use of catalogues were validated by the stakeholders in a validation interview. They acknowledged the need of these goals and were also able to spontaneously mention other goals (for example the refinements of the goal Provide medical care to patient goal, shown in Fig. 5). The goal Provide medical care to patient can be achieved in three forms: by achieving a consultation appointment (in this consultation the physician examines the patient and prescribes the treatment); by providing attendance for assessment of high cost drug (the physician examines the patient and in the case of the need of a high cost drug, he/she issues an certificate) and by an informal meeting. In these informal meetings, the physician can examine a patient who reports the presence of symptoms, or the physician just issues some document required by the patient (a prescription of drugs, a medical certificate or a medical report).

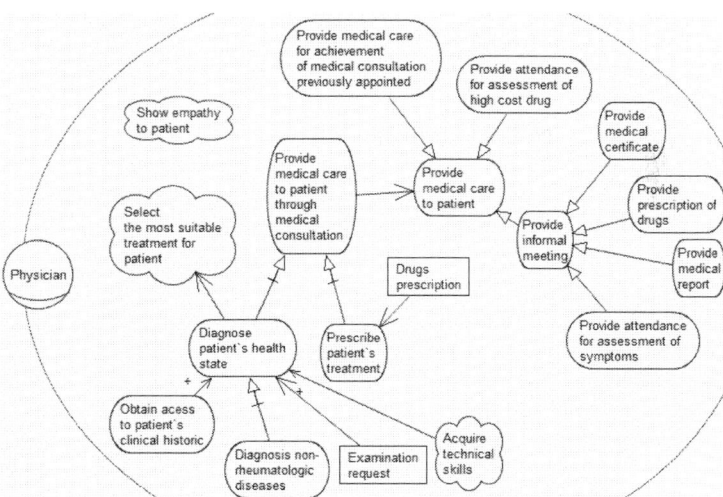

Fig. 5. Portion of goal model obtained in goal elicitation activities with catalogues (2)

4 Related Work

The NFR framework [9] [10] has been the first approach to propose softgoals and softgoal satisficing in the context of RE to cope with NFRs and their appropriate representation [11]. The main proposal of this framework is to provide means of specifying NFRs, decomposing them and recording the reasoning process of operationalizing and prioritizing NFRs in graphs. Although the catalogues proposed in that work serve as useful tools in identifying softgoals, they are only concerned with addressing these issues in the context of systems development, not considering them within the organizational scope.

In [12], Soffer and Wand propose a conceptual framework to enable the formal integration of goals and softgoals into process modelling (formal in the sense that the approach uses the BWW ontology [13] for the integration). The application of this framework drives the mechanism of systematically reasoning about the incorporation of the softgoals in process design. Although the initiative focuses on defining the existing dependencies between process and their respective softgoals, the method starts in the point where softgoals are already identified (it assumes that the goal elicitation phase has already been undertook) and thus, does not provide guidelines for systematic addressing goal elicitation from the organizational context.

Pavlovski and Zou [21] assume that business process modelling is concerned about capturing functional behaviour of business process but fail to cover non-functional requirements. To tackle this deficiency, the authors propose two new artifacts to capture these constraints denominated *operating condition* (to represent the business process constraints) and *control case* (to denote criteria to manage the risk associated with a given operational condition), to be applied in business process models. For that, it extends the Business Process Modelling Notation (BPMN) with these constructs. Although these artifacts have improved the communication about NFRs among the stakeholders, thus facilitated their acquisition, the proposal adopts a system-oriented view for non-functional requirements. It assumes that softgoals will later manifest themselves as non-functional requirements of an intended system, excluding those softgoals which are intrinsically related to the business process' dynamics and, as consequence, which should not be translated into system requirements.

Extending the notion of goals in business process modelling, Yu [3] has proposed the i* framework. The Tropos methodology has been derived from the i* framework, addressing the need of a methodology for software development based on the agent-oriented paradigm. The following explanation about the i* framework can also be applied to the Tropos methodology.

The i* framework is articulated in terms of two kinds of models: the Strategic Dependency model (SD) and Strategic Rationale model (SR). The SD model acknowledges actors as intentional agents within an organizational setting and represents them as a network of strategic dependencies. The SR assumes that the dependencies expressed in SD models are justified by actors' internal rationales. As explained in Yu's PhD thesis [3], the framework can be used to capture (soft)goals in business process modelling in order to provide a more strategic view of those processes. However, despite the usefulness of the i* approach to address intentions, motivations and vague aspects of business modelling, their work do not provide methodological guidelines for eliciting goals.

This paper proposes the use of NFR catalogues for goal elicitation within *goal-oriented business process modelling* in goal models based on Tropos modelling language. This combination the NFR framework and the Tropos modelling language has the following direct benefits. On one hand, it extends the use of NFR framework (initially conceived for addressing NFRs in system development) to support the identification of business goals within organizational scopes. On the other hand, it provides methodological guidelines for the identification of business goals in Tropos. In this manner, the SR and SD Tropos diagrams can be enriched by the additional goals identified through the use of NFR catalogues.

5 Conclusions

We have found the preliminary goal elicitation activities useful in addressing our need to understand the organizational setting. This has enabled us not only to capture details about the enterprise and its business processes, but also to provide us with proper understanding about the domain under consideration. However, we have found the preliminary stages to be deficient in the identification of strategic concerns related to the organization's goals. This difficulty was partly addressed through stakeholder interviews. Although these interviews addressed many organizational issues, much knowledge still remained implicit. With respect to that, the catalogues provided by the NFR framework have shown to be useful as a complementary tool to elicit goals.

Before discussing the nature of the additional goals identified with the support of catalogues, we must highlight some particularities about translating NFR types to goals. We have observed that the translation is highly domain-dependent, i.e., one must take into account how a NFR must be mapped to some goal in the organization domain such that this goal makes sense regarding the organizational context, as we have illustrated in section 3.4. Further, one must define whether a NFR type should be represented as a soft or hard goal. As observed in [11], there is a tendency in treating NFRs as softgoals, however, as demonstrated in the case study, some NFRs could be objectively specified in the context of the domain.

In relation to the goals uncovered with the help of catalogues, we believe that goals have enabled us to reason about the organization from a more strategic point of view. This can be confirmed by the fact that some additional goals referred to quality attributes; either for specifying qualitatively a hardgoal or for specifying quality metrics for the business process as a whole. We have observed in this case study that stakeholders have difficulties in explicitly stating quality attributes for business processes (the same difficulty is often reported to arise requirements in system development [16]). In that respect, the catalogues employed in this case study provided guidelines for identifying these attributes in a systematic way.

We have observed that, in certain cases, stakeholders formulate goals which are highly dependent on the current operationalization of the organization's objectives, i.e., much emphasis is given to the goal of applying successfully a particular solution for a problem. Catalogues partially helped to overcome this issue, revealing higher level goals not easily identified by the abstraction technique. Further, some of the goals uncovered through catalogues had initially been deemed an inherent organizational characteristic by stakeholders, and thus had not been spontaneously mentioned.

At first sight, the technique we have employed seems highly dependent on the experience of analysts in conducting the elicitation effort (experience in the sense that analysts must have broad knowledge about the domain). We believe this is the case partly because of the need to translate NFRs into goals which are specific to the organization's domain. Further investigation in NFR type catalogues for business process in a particular business domain may prove to be fruitful to reduce the dependency on analyst experience and improve goal elicitation in general. In this sense, NFR type catalogues can be seen as design patterns in goal modelling. The compilation of these catalogues in a format of design patterns allows one to reuse the knowledge by making available methodological connections which are tacit in an experienced modeller's mind and which are not typically available to the novice.

Further work will be necessary to associate particular goals with guidelines for business process (re-)design. Additionally, in our future work, we intend to investigate suitable representation and semantics to relate goal models and business process models (especially in the presence of softgoals). Moreover, we aim at investigating the impact which this approach of eliciting additional goals through the use of NFR catalogues shall have in business process structures as well in the systematic redesign of business processes.

Acknowledgments. This work was partially supported by FAPES in the scope of the INFRA-MODELA project and in the scope of grant DCR number 37274554/2007. We thank to all physicians, interns, residents and patients at the Cassiano de Moraes University Hospital for their cooperation in this research. In particular, we are grateful to Professor Dr. Valéria Valim and Érica Serrano, MD for providing invaluable assistance in the execution of this research in the Hospital.

References

1. Hammer, M., Champy, J.: Reengineering the Corporation: A Manifesto for Business Revolution. HarperBusiness (1993)
2. Hammer, M.: Reengineering Work: Don't Automate, Obliterate. Harvard Business Review (1990)
3. Yu, E.: Modelling Strategic Relationships for Process Reengineering, PhD Thesis, University of Toronto (1995)
4. Kavakli, E., Loucopoulos, P.: Goal Driven Requirements Engineering: Evaluation of Current Methods. In: Proceedings of the 8th CAiSE/IFIP8.1 Workshop on Evaluation of Modeling Methods in Systems Analysis and Design, EMMSAD (2003)
5. Mylopoulos, J., Chung, L., Yu, E., Nixon, B.: Representing and Using Non-functional Requirements: A Process-Oriented Approach. IEEE Trans. on Software Eng. 18(6), 483–497 (1992)
6. Neiger, D., Churilov, L.: Goal-Oriented Business Process Modeling with EPCs and Value-Focused Thinking. In: Desel, J., Pernici, B., Weske, M. (eds.) BPM 2004. LNCS, vol. 3080, pp. 98–115. Springer, Heidelberg (2004)
7. Halleux, P., Mathieu, L., Andersson, B.: A Method to Support the Alignment of Business Models and Goal Models. In: Proc. 3rd Workshop on Business/IT-Alignment and Interoperability (BUSITAL 2008) CEUR Workshop Proceedings (2008)

8. Lamsweerde, A.: Goal-Oriented Requirements Engineering: A Guided Tour. In: 5th International Symposium on Requirements Engineering. IEEE Computer Society Press, Los Alamitos (2001)
9. Chung, L., Nixon, B.A., Yu, E., Mylopoulos, J.: Non-functional Requirements in Software Engineering. Kluwer Academic Publishing, Dordrecht (2000)
10. Catalogues, http://math.yorku.ca/~cysneiro/nfrs/nfrs.htm (accessed in 19/02/2008)
11. Daneva, M., Kassab, M., Ponisio, M.L., Wieringa, R.J., Ormandjieva, O.: Exploiting a Goal Decomposition Technique to Prioritize Non-functional Requirements. In: Proceedings of the 10th International Workshop on Requirements Engineering (WER 2007) (2007)
12. Soffer, P., Wand, Y.: On the notion of soft-goals in business process modeling. BPM Journal, 663–679 (2005)
13. Wand, Y., Weber, R.: An ontological model of an information system. IEEE Transactions on Software Engineering 16(11), 1282–1292 (1990)
14. Dardenne, A., Lamsweerde, A., Fickas, S.: Goal-Directed Requirements Acquisition. Science of Computer Programming 20 (1993)
15. Alexander, I.: Modelling the Interplay of Conflicting Goals with Use and Misuse Cases. In: Proceedings of the HCI 2002 Workshop on Goal-Oriented Business-Process Modeling (GBPM 2002) (2002)
16. Cysneiros, L.M.: Evaluating the Effectiveness of using Catalogues to Elicit Non-Functional Requirements. In: Proc. of 10th Workshop in Requirements Engineering, pp. 107–115 (2007)
17. Bresciani, P., Perini, A., Giorgini, P., Giunchiglia, F., Mylopoulos, J.: Tropos: An Agent-Oriented Software Development Methodology. Autonomous Agents and Multi-Agent Systems (2004)
18. Regev, G., Wegmann, A.: Where do Goals Come from: the Underlying Principles of Goal-Oriented Requirements Engineering. In: Proceedings of 13th IEEE International Requirements Engineering Conference (2005)
19. Castro, J.F.B., Paim, F.R.: Enhancing Data Warehouse Quality with the NFR Framework. In: Proceedings of the V Workshop on Requirements Engineering. Universidad Politecnica de Valencia, Valencia (2002)
20. O'Sullivan, J., Edmond, D., Hofstede, A.T.: What's In a Service? Towards Accurate Description of Non-Functional Service Properties. In: Distributed and Parallel Databases, pp. 117–133. Kluwer Academic Publishers, Dordrecht (2002)
21. Pavlovski, C.J., Zou, J.: Non-functional requirements in business process modeling. In: Proceedings of the Fifth on Asia-Pacific Conference on Conceptual Modelling, vol. 79 (2008)
22. Zachman, J.A.: A framework for information systems architecture. IBM Systems Journal 26(3), 276–292 (1987)
23. Yamamoto, S., Kaiya, H., Cox, K., Bleistein, S.: Goal Oriented Requirements Engineering: Trends and Issues. IEICE - Trans. Information Systems E89-D, 11 (2006)
24. Bider, I., Johannesson, P. (eds.): Proceedings of the HCI 2002 Workshop on Goal-Oriented Business Process Modeling GBMP 2002, London, September 2 (2002)
25. Jureta, I.J., Faulkner, S., Schobbens, P.Y.: A More Expressive Softgoal Conceptualization for Quality Requirements Analysis. In: Embley, D.W., Olivé, A., Ram, S. (eds.) ER 2006. LNCS, vol. 4215, pp. 281–295. Springer, Heidelberg (2006)

A Business Process-IT Alignment Method for Business Intelligence

Jun Sekine, Takashi Suenaga, Junko Yano, Kei-ichiro Nakagawa,
and Shu-ichiro Yamamoto

Research and Development Headquarters, NTT Data Corporation
3-9, Toyosu 3-chome, Koto-ku, Tokyo, Japan
{sekinej, suenagatk, yanojn, nakagawaki,
yamamotosui}@nttdata.co.jp

Abstract. Business intelligence (BI) is becoming a key means of providing information necessary for achieving business goals such as improving profits or solving business process issues. This paper proposes a business process-IT alignment method for BI. The proposed method has two phases of business processes: the first phase extracts and checks the validity of hypotheses for achieving business goals and the second phase clarifies the actions needed to implement the hypotheses. Then, business information used in each business process is defined. Four levels of BI systems are proposed in accordance with the maturity of the enterprises they support, and each level is mapped to a subset of the business processes. Finally, three types of models used to clarify and organize the hypotheses and the actions are proposed. Case studies have shown that the method explains a variety of business processes for BI and BI systems.

1 Introduction

The concept of business intelligence (BI) that provides information for achieving business goals such as improving profits or solving business process issues is becoming important. The BI systems supporting the concept require business process-IT alignment in the sense that they should provide functionality useful for achieving the business goals. However, BI systems in reality vary from system to system depending on the maturity of the target enterprises and the quality of data available. For example, in some cases, users require such functionality as visualization of key performance indicators (KPIs) and related data using online analytical processing (OLAP) tools [3], while in other cases they require validation of hypotheses for achieving business goals using data mining methods, or support of actions implementing the hypotheses. Thus, we need a business process-IT alignment method for BI covering all these variations. In addition, it is essential for people engaged in BI, whom we call BI analysts, to convince enterprise management that their proposed hypotheses and the actions necessary to implement them are comprehensive and rational, which means that a kind of framework used to clarify and organize the hypotheses and the actions is required.

The Balanced Scorecard [4-8, 10-12] is a method of organizing business goals as a set of KPIs. It promotes management of KPIs corresponding to causes as well as KPIs

T. Halpin et al. (Eds.): BPMDS 2009 and EMMSAD 2009, LNBIP 29, pp. 46–57, 2009.

corresponding to effects. By managing both types of KPIs and related data with a BI system, it is possible for the system to support management of business goals. However, it is the responsibility of practitioners to extract KPIs corresponding to causes and to ensure that the KPIs are controllable by taking actions. The Fact Based Collaboration Modeling (FBCM) [9] is a method of evaluating the completeness of business goals and KPIs through end user observations, and it tells how to use business processes to align IT functions with business goals. It is applicable to business process-IT alignment for BI, however, it does not give sufficient consideration to business information, which is especially important in BI systems. The business data analysis framework [13] categorizes data analysis scenarios by the type of actions taken after data analysis is completed. It is useful for reusing data analysis scenarios, and the types of actions proposed are useful when considering future actions. However, its primary focus is on data mining and it does not cover all aspects of BI. It is only considered appropriate for use by skilled BI analysts. We, therefore, need a business process-IT alignment method that covers different levels of BI systems, enables identification of business information used in the BI systems, and gives frameworks for clarifying and organizing the hypotheses and the actions.

In this paper, we propose a business process-IT alignment method consisting of a two-phase business processes for BI, where the first phase extracts and checks the validity of hypotheses for achieving business goals and the second phase clarifies the actions necessary to implement the hypotheses. The method defines business information that should be managed by the BI systems, ensuring business process-IT alignment for BI. We also propose four different levels of BI systems covering different subsets of the business processes. An important part of the business processes is a modeling process. The model created in the process is used to clarify the hypotheses and the actions to be considered, and to help enterprise management understand their target domains, such as customers, products, or business processes.

Note that we did not consider a type of BI systems that enables ad-hoc queries and reporting of information, since the requirements for business information are not clearly specified at the time of system development, but rather they are specified at the time of defining queries or reports.

Section 2 proposes business processes for BI and the business information used in each business process. Then, Section 3 proposes four levels of BI systems, and shows that each of them can be mapped to a subset of the business processes. Section 4 categorizes models for BI, and Section 5 shows case studies of BI systems and the models used in them. Finally, Section 6 concludes and presents further issues to be solved.

2   Business Processes of Business Intelligence

This section proposes business processes for BI and the information used in them. The information is presumed to be managed by the BI systems supporting the processes.

We designed the business processes in two phases. The first phase extracts and checks the validity of hypotheses for achieving business goals. It includes the business processes for clarifying the causes and effects of goal achievement and produces minimal information for enterprise management to understand the situation surrounding business goals. Then the second phase clarifies the actions needed to implement the hypotheses for achieving goals. It includes the business processes ensuring that the actions are planned and achieved. Since the value of BI resides in achieving business goals, the second phase is essential for enterprises. The business processes of the two phases are explained here in more detail.

First Phase: Extraction and Validation of Hypotheses
Since BI is used to achieve business goals of enterprises or departments, the business processes for BI start by defining business goals and the KPIs that represent the measures of them. This is done using such methods as Balanced Scorecard [5] or FBCM [9]. Then hypotheses that contribute to achieving the goals should be extracted and organized. A hypothesis is a written idea that might improves KPIs and should comprise at least one causal factor affecting the KPIs. For example, "outsourcing of parts of work improves profits" is a hypothesis for improving the KPI "profits" and comprises the causal factor "outsourcing." By controlling the degree of "outsourcing," increase in "profits" might be achieved. Note that it is still an idea not proven at this stage.

The extraction of the hypotheses can be done in two ways. One way is to extract hypotheses through interviews with enterprise management. Since the hypotheses extracted through the interviews might be incomplete, we need a framework for mapping the hypotheses and checking their completeness. We call this framework a model. The model is manually developed by BI analysts. For example, the simplest types of models can be viewpoints of classifying profits, such as the locations of branches or the categories of products, usually called "dimensions" in OLAP tools. On the other hand, to decrease complaints from shops for an electric appliance company, the types of complaints related to the processes of selling products constitute a model. The models vary according to the business goals and the business environments surrounding the goals. Several examples are shown in Section 5. To summarize, hypotheses are created first, then a model is created, and the hypotheses are checked and reinforced using the model. The other way to extract hypotheses is to create a model first and then create hypotheses based on the model. Sometimes, models are created automatically using data mining methods. For example, the model might be the result of clustering customers based on their purchase history.

The hypotheses extracted in the processes explained above are still insufficient, since they are not proven. Therefore, the next process is to check whether controlling causal factors stated in hypotheses actually improves KPIs. The checking is usually done using statistical methods. For example, to improve profits of projects, the hypothesis "outsourcing of parts of work improves profits" might eventually be proven wrong, while the hypothesis "there is a relationship between the degree of employee satisfaction and the profits" might be proven true. Through these processes, we get a set of valid hypotheses for achieving business goals and a model organizing the hypotheses at the end of the first phase.

Second Phase: Clarification and Execution of Actions
The second phase starts by checking whether the hypotheses are achievable. There are cases where they are valid but not achievable because of circumstances surrounding the enterprises. For example, even if the hypothesis "the profits of their franchise shops can

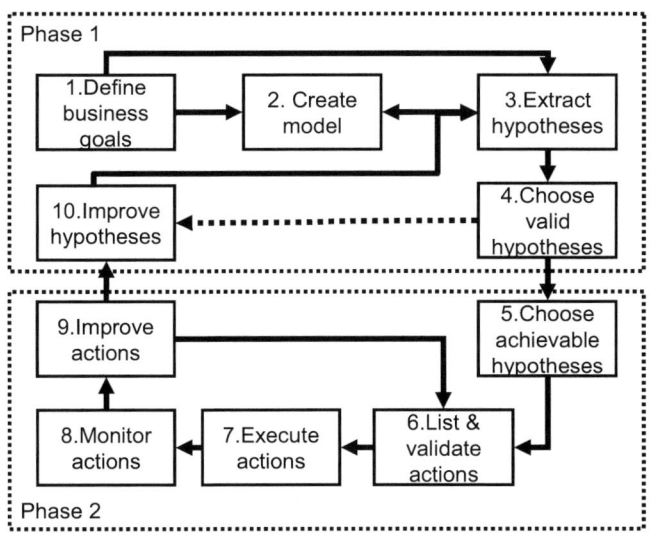

Fig. 1. Business processes of BI

be increased by locating them near stations" is extracted using data mining methods, it would be impossible to move the shops. The hypothesis can be used to choose the location of a new shop, but it is useless for increasing the profits of current shops. Once we get achievable hypotheses, the next process is to list and validate actions for achieving them. Each action might require a period of time to complete. We, therefore, need to manage the extent to which the actions are carried out. We call the extent a "monitoring index." For example, the hypothesis "at least 5% of the employees on each project need project management skill" needs to be monitored by a monitoring index "percentage of project management skill," which may not be achievable in a short time. After the actions are authorized by enterprise management, they are executed, monitored, and checked to see if they really contributed to achieving the business goals. If not, the actions or the hypotheses should be improved. All of the business processes form a plan-do-check-act (PDCA) cycle. The complete business processes are depicted in Fig. 1.

The business information is now shown for each business process and it should be managed by the BI systems covering the process. First, KPIs are extracted from business goals using Balanced Scorecard. There is a relationship between business goals and KPIs. Second, the data used to create a model and the model itself are extracted in the modeling process. The model is mapped to a set of metadata used to categorize the data and to describe the relationships among categories, and it would eventually be mapped to data models or dimensions in OLAP tools. Third, quantitative measures of causal factors are extracted from hypotheses. For example, if the business goal is to increase profits in a sales department, the KPI is the profits, and the quantitative measure of causal factor might be the average number of contact times with each customer per sales person a month. The relationship between KPIs and causal factors might be extracted through such method as multivariate regression. Finally, monitoring indices are extracted from actions.

If BI systems are used to implement actions themselves, some specific information might be used in addition to the information listed here. For example, a recommendation system for customers can be considered to be a BI system implementing an action "increase profits by promoting products that fit customers" and uses purchase history to derive groups of customers who are likely to buy similar products. Further examples are shown in Section 5.

3   Maturity Levels of Business Intelligence Systems

Although we analyzed data for more than one hundred cases as shown in Fig.2, it was not always possible to carry out the whole set of business processes proposed in Section 2. There were several reasons for this. First, enterprise management was not confident in the results of BI. Second, data that could be used to validate hypotheses were not available or the quality of the data was not sufficient. Finally, neither the customers nor the BI analysts could think of any feasible actions.

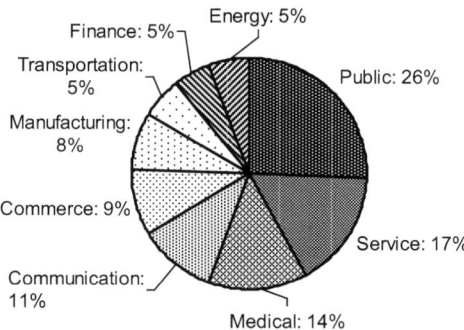

Fig. 2. Distribution of data analysis cases over business domains (number of cases is 111)

Because of this, we began to understand that there should be levels of BI systems depending on the maturity of the business environments, and classified the systems into four levels based on two viewpoints. One viewpoint is the scope of the BI systems, that is, if they cover management of KPIs or management of actions. The two alternatives correspond to the two phases proposed in Section 2. The other viewpoint is the functionality, that is, if the functionality provided by the BI systems covers just management of information loaded from other IT systems and then integrated, or management and creation of information useful for making decisions. The information is created using such technologies as data mining, simulation, or optimization. With two alternatives for each viewpoint, we have four levels of BI systems as shown in Fig. 3. In this section, each level is briefly described and is mapped to a subset of the business processes it covers.

Level 1: Visualization
The goal of this level of BI systems is to visualize KPIs, the model related to the KPIs, and causal factors of valid hypotheses, for reporting them to enterprise management. Validation of the hypotheses is also part of the goal. However, this level does not ensure that the business goals are achieved. Therefore, the return on investment of this level is often questioned by enterprise management in the long run.

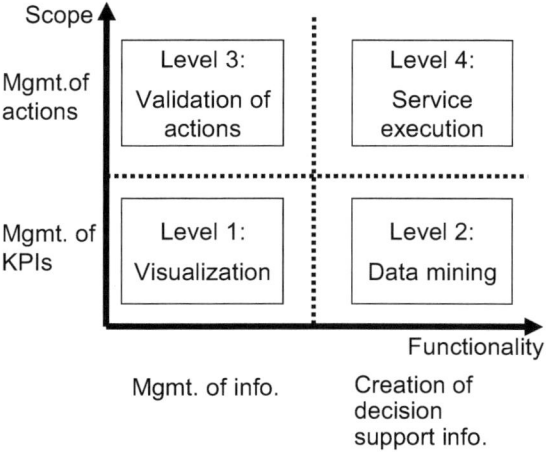

Fig. 3. Four levels of BI systems

Level 2: Data Mining

The goal of this level of BI systems is the same as that of level 1, however, the models or the valid hypotheses are created using such data mining methods [2] as multivariate regression, clustering analysis, or correlation analysis. The information used in this level is the same as in level 1.

Level 3: Validation of Actions

The goal of this level of BI systems is to validate the effectiveness of the proposed actions, and manage the causes and effects of the actions taken. There are two ways to do this. One way is to validate the actions after they are executed. The other way is to validate the actions before they are executed. In both cases, the validation process is done by human.

Level 4: Service Execution

The goal of this level of BI systems is to create new services for employees within enterprises or for customers outside enterprises, using such technologies as statistical analysis or mathematical programming. The important point of this level is to provide information that completely changes service levels by the technologies. Well known examples are Amazon's system of recommending books based on customer purchase history [1,14], and Capital One's system of recommending new services to customers when they contact a call center [14]. In addition to the information used in level 3, some specific information useful for validation and execution of services is generated in this level.

In some cases, technology such as simulation is used to estimate the effects of new services before they are actually provided. This avoids the risks of executing actions, has no negative effects, and does not confuse employees by changing their business processes. For example, the business goal of a call center was to decrease the response time for customer complaints. To this end, changes to business tasks were planned and simulated before they were actually put into action.

Table 1. Alignment of each level of BI systems to business processes of BI

Levels Business processes	Visualization	Data min-ing	Validation of actions	Service execution
1.Define business goals	H	H	-	-
2. Create model	H	S	-	-
3.Extract hypotheses	H	S	-	-
4.Choose valid hypotheses	H	S	-	-
5.Choose achievable hypo-theses	-	-	H	H
6.List & validate actions	-	-	H	S
7.Execute actions	-	-	H	S
8.Monitor actions	-	-	H	H
9.Improve actions	-	-	H	H
10.Improve hypotheses	H	S	-	-

H: The business process is executed by human, and the information related to the process is managed by BI systems of the level.

S: The business process is executed by human, and the information related to the process is generated and managed by BI systems of the level.

Table 1 shows how each level of BI systems covers the business processes proposed in Section 2. It is possible that a BI system could cover more than one level shown in this section.

4   Modeling

This section proposes the models, which are the frameworks for categorizing and organizing hypotheses and actions, and provide accountability for enterprise management. Although the models vary depending on the hypotheses or the actions, they can be categorized in 3 types.

Type 1: Categorization of Business Objects
This type of models describes the business objects that are the target of improvement, and categorizes the business objects into categories significant for enterprise management. For example, if the business goal is to increase the sales of shops, then the business objects are shops, and the model categorizes the shops into categories, such as shops in the suburbs, or shops in downtown, etc. Since the model should be used for mapping hypotheses and actions, it is expected that the hypotheses and the actions vary depending on the categories of the shops. In some cases, the relationships among categories are also described. An example of the relationships is shown in Section 5.

Type 2: Description of Relationships among Business Objects
This type describes business goals, business objects consisting of business environments, and the relationships among them. For example, if the business goal is to

increase the profit of each sales person, then the model consists of business objects "customers" and "sales person" and the relationships between them such as "sell" and "contact." Causal relationships among business goals and other business objects are special cases of the relationships.

Type 3: Description of Business Tasks
The last type describes business tasks which enterprise management would like to improve. In some cases, only the names of the business tasks are important for categorization, while in other cases the way business tasks are performed is more important. The latter are the cases often seen in level 3 or 4 since ways to improve business tasks or provide new services are the focus of BI systems of these levels.

Using the models, hypotheses and actions are mapped to the elements of the models, and through these mappings the comprehensiveness of the hypotheses and the actions is understood by enterprise management. Further examples of each type are shown in the next section.

5   Case Studies

This section shows several cases that we have encountered in the past.

Example 1: Increasing Profits in Project Management
The business goal of an enterprise was to increase the profit of each project, and the KPI was the profit per sale. To achieve this goal, hypotheses such as "high degree of employee satisfaction leads to large profits", "a certain number of skilled managers is necessary", and "proper outsourcing of part of the work is necessary" were extracted. The first hypothesis was validated by correlation analysis, however other hypotheses were not validated due to the lack of data. A simple model of Type 2 was developed as shown in Fig. 4 to map various hypotheses. The BI system covered the business processes 1 through 4, and its level was 1. The information used was profits, costs, number of employees per project, and the skills and the satisfaction degree of each employee.

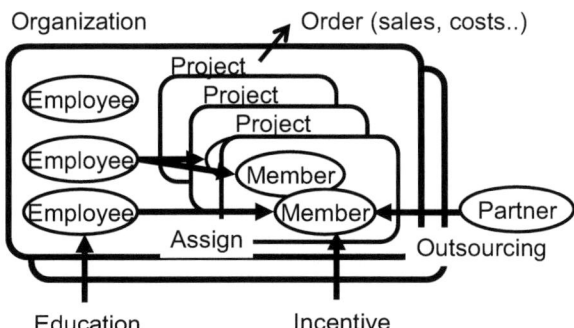

Fig. 4. A model of business environment surrounding projects

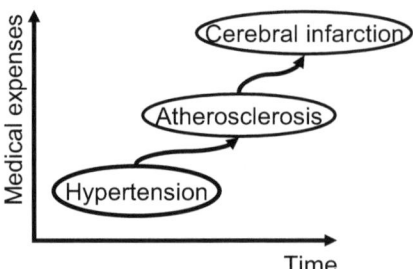

Fig. 5. State transition diagram of diseases

Example 2: Cost Reduction of Medical Expenses
The business goal of a health insurance organization was to decrease medical expenses, and the KPI was medical expenses per member. To achieve this goal, a model showing the transition processes between diseases was created from data as shown in Fig. 5. Each node of Fig. 5 denotes a disease and each arrow denotes that there is a possibility of transition from one disease to another with a given probability. This is a model of Type 1, with additional information, transition between diseases. By checking the model, the hypothesis "a cost effective reduction of medical expenses can be achieved by focusing on members whose diseases are likely to migrate to serious ones" was extracted. The BI system covered the business processes 1 through 4, and the level of it was 2. The information used was the history of medical expenses per member, and the model extracted from the patient histories.

Example 3: Decreasing Stock of Products
The business goal of an enterprise was to decrease the stock of products, and the KPI was the total amount of the stock. The key action to be taken was to estimate future demand of each product, but the estimation of the demand was usually done by a human and not always precise. To achieve the goal, a new estimation algorithm was created and validated by simulation using real sales data. The algorithm was able to decrease the stock by 10 percent. The BI system covered the business processes 5 through 9, and the level of this BI system was 4, since it used simulation to estimate the effects of new business tasks using the algorithm and the algorithm was actually adopted by the enterprise after the validation. In this case, the model was not explicitly described, however, business tasks for managing stock, with details of how and when products were ordered, were used for simulation, and this information actually constituted a model of Type 3. The information used in the BI system was sales and stock of each product.

Example 4: Decreasing the Number of Complaints at a Call Center
The business goal of a call center was to decrease the number of complaints it receives from service agents, and the KPI was the number of complaints. To achieve this goal, a model of business tasks used by the agents in selling services was developed as shown in Fig. 6. This model was Type 3. Using the model, the complaints were categorized by the business tasks, and a few business tasks that were related to most of the complaints

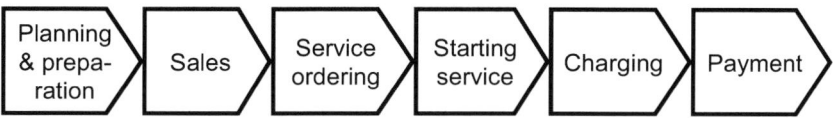

Fig. 6. Business tasks of service agents

were identified. Based on the finding, the reasons for the complaints were further investigated, and finally it was found that the guidance for the services was incomplete. The hypothesis in this case was "decrease the numbers of complaints of the business tasks that are responsible for most of the complaints." This BI system covered the business processes 1 through 9, and the levels of it was 1 and 3. The information used in this example was the complaints themselves and the model used to classify the complaints. Since the complaints were written in text, a text-processing functionality was used for the investigation.

Example 5: Increasing Sales in Membership Services
The business goal of an enterprise providing online membership services was to increase sales of new services, and the KPI was the sales of the services. To achieve this goal, the recency, frequency, and monetary value (RFM) analysis was conducted to categorize their customers. The categories derived constituted a model of Type 1. The results showed that the repetitive use of the services was insufficient. Therefore the hypothesis "increase the frequency of service usage for each member" became a valid hypothesis. The level of the BI system was 2, since it covered only the business processes 1 thorough 4 and was too early to find out any action. The information used was the purchase history of each member and the model extracted by the RFM analysis.

Note that the RFM analysis is often used to classify customers based on the last time they used services, the frequency of the usage, and the average sales of the services per customer. Another way of classifying customers is clustering analysis.

Example 6: Decreasing Cost of Delivery Service
The business goal of a delivery service enterprise was to deliver services in a cost effective way, and the KPI was the total time for delivery. An analysis of delivery persons' work records formed a basis for a model of how they delivered services from house to house. This was a model of Type3. Then, the hypothesis "a decrease in the variation of delivery time of delivery persons would decrease the total time for delivery" was formed. In fact, some delivery persons could finish their works in a short time because the distance between houses was short down town, while other delivery persons could not because distances were far in the suburbs. Then, an action was proposed that optimize the workload of each delivery agent to minimize variations among them. The BI system covered the business processes 1 thorough 9, and the levels of it were 1 for the investigation of hypotheses and 4 for optimization using mathematical programming. The information used in the BI system was the total time for delivery, the work records of delivery agents, and the results of optimization.

As shown in the examples, the levels of BI systems vary and the actual BI systems sometimes cover more than one level, as shown in Table 2. It is also shown that the types of models used also vary. Although only one type of models is used for each example, there would be cases where more than one type of models is used.

Table 2. BI system levels and model types for each example

Example #		1	2	3	4	5	6
BI system level	1)Visualization	Yes	-	-	Yes	-	Yes
	2)Data mining	-	Yes	-	-	Yes	-
	3)Validation of actions	-	-	-	Yes	-	-
	4)Service execution	-	-	Yes	-	-	Yes
Model type	1)Categorization of business objects	-	Yes	-	-	Yes	-
	2)Description of relationships among business objects	Yes	-	-	-	-	-
	3)Description of business tasks	-	-	Yes	Yes	-	Yes

6 Concluding Remarks

In this paper, we proposed a two-phase business processes for BI: the first phase extracts and checks the validity of hypotheses for achieving business goals and the second phase clarifies the actions needed to implement the hypotheses. Four different levels of BI systems are also proposed. These are mapped onto subsets of the business processes and the business information used in the processes. This mapping is used to align the business goals of BI with BI systems. Studies of real cases have shown the validity of the business processes and their mapping to BI systems. As shown in the examples, it is not easy to reach level 3 or 4. We understand that we should start from level 1 or 2, and if we are able to get enough support from enterprise management and if the data supporting BI systems are available, we may be able to proceed to the next levels.

We also proposed three types of models used to clarify the hypotheses or the actions to be considered. We believe that it is important to make enterprise management understand the whole picture of the hypotheses and the actions. The types of models that are useful for different situations are yet to be investigated. We would like to build a catalog of modeling methods with rationales and criteria for their use. As we are continuously analyzing data for our customers, we would like to feedback our experiences for improving the method, including the modeling process.

References

1. Recommendations. Amazon.com,
   http://www.amazon.com/gp/help/customer/
   display.html?nodeId=13316081
2. Berry, M.J.A., Linoff, G.S.: Data Mining Techniques: For Marketing, Sales, and Customer Relationship Management, 2nd edn. Wiley, Chichester (2004)
3. Golfarelli, M., Rizzi, S., Cella, I.: Beyond data warehousing: what's next in business intelligence? In: 7th International Workshop on Data Warehousing and OLAP (DOLAP 2004), Washington, DC (2004)
4. Kaplan, R.S.: Integrating Shareholder Value and Activity Based Costing with the Balanced Scorecard. Balanced Scorecard Report 3(1) (2001)

5. Kaplan, R.S., Norton, D.P.: The Balanced Scorecard Translating Strategy into Action. Harvard Business School Press (1996)
6. Kaplan, R.S., Norton, D.P.: Having trouble with your strategy? Then map it. Harvard Business Review 78(5), 167–176 (2000)
7. Kaplan, R.S., Norton, D.P.: The Strategy-Focused Organization: How Balanced Scorecard Companies Thrive in the New Business Environment. Harvard Business School Press (2001)
8. Kaplan, R.S., Norton, D.P.: Strategy Maps: Converting Intangible Assets into Tangible Outcomes. Harvard Business School Press (2004)
9. Kokune, A., Mizuno, M., Kadoya, K., Yamamoto, S.: FBCM: Strategy Modeling Method for the Validation of Software Requirements. Journal of Systems and Software 80(3), 314–327 (2007)
10. Norton, D.P.: The Unbalanced Scorecard. Balanced Scorecard Report 2(2) (2000)
11. Norton, D.P.: Building Strategy Maps: Testing the Hypothesis. Balanced Scorecard Report 3(1) (2001)
12. Norton, D.P.: The First Balanced Scorecard. Balanced Scorecard Report 4(2) (2002)
13. Suenaga, T., Takahashi, S., Saji, M., Yano, J., Nakagawa, K., Sekine, J.: A Framework for Business Data Analysis. In: Workshop on Business Intelligence Methodologies and Applications (BIMA 2008), pp. 703–708 (2008)
14. Davenport, T.H., Harris, J.G.: Competing on Analytics: The New Science of Winning. Harvard Business School Press (2007)

Analysis and Validation of Control-Flow Complexity Measures with BPMN Process Models

Elvira Rolón[1], Jorge Cardoso[2], Félix García[3], Francisco Ruiz[3], and Mario Piattini[3]

[1] Autonomous University of Tamaulipas – FIANS
University Center Tampico-Madero S/N, Tamaulipas, México
erolon@uat.edu.mx
[2] SAP Research, Germany and University of Coimbra, Portugal
jorge.cardoso@sap.com
[3] Alarcos Research Group, University of Castilla La Mancha
Paseo de la Universidad No. 4, 13071 Ciudad Real, Spain
{felix.garcia, francisco.ruizg, mario.piattini}@uclm.es

Abstract. Evaluating the complexity of business processes during the early stages of their development, primarily during the process modelling phase, provides organizations and stakeholders with process models which are easier to understand and easier to maintain. This presents advantages when carrying out evolution tasks in process models – key activities, given the current competitive market. In this work, we present the use and validation of the CFC metric to evaluate the complexity of business processes modelled with BPMN. The complexity of processes is evaluated from a control-flow perspective. An empirical evaluation has been carried out in order to demonstrate that the CFC metric can be useful when applied to BPMN models, providing information about their ease of maintenance.

Keywords: Business process models, BPMN, measurement, validation.

1 Introduction

Business process modeling is the first step towards the achievement of organizational goals, because its importance resides not only in the description of the process, but in that it also usually represents a preparatory phase for activities such as business process improvement, business process reengineering, technology transfer and process standardization [1].

But in all these activities the business process models are managed by different stakeholders (business process analysts, domain experts, technical analysts, software developers, among others). Therefore, one of their main purposes is support communication between stakeholders, and to fulfil this purpose business process models should be easy to understand and easy to maintain. High complexity in a process has several undesirable drawbacks: it may result in bad understandability, errors, defects, and exceptions, thus leading to the need for more time to develop, test and maintain the processes. Therefore, the first step towards reducing the complexity of processes is to first recognise its existence, and, then, measure it.

T. Halpin et al. (Eds.): BPMDS 2009 and EMMSAD 2009, LNBIP 29, pp. 58–70, 2009.

In this context, Cardoso [2] has defined process complexity as *the degree to which processes are difficult to analyze, understand or explain.* Along with this definition Control-Flow Complexity (CFC) metric for analyzing the degree of complexity of business processes has been presented. The metric is independent of the language used to model business processes. On the other hand, another stream of research [3, 4, 5] has concentrated efforts to develop a set of measures for the evaluation of models developed with BPMN (Business Process Modeling Notation) [6] which have been empirically validated. They are based on the measurement of the structural properties of process models. As a result of this empirical validation, several measures were correlated with the usability and maintainability of processes. However, we believe that since the measures proposed in both research streams are based on the analysis of the complexity of business processes models, it is important to analyze the influence of the CFC metric on the complexity of BPMN models from a control-flow perspective.

This paper therefore presents the analysis and empirical validation of the influence of the CFC metric on the usability and maintainability of BPMN process models. This is done by using the data obtained from two families of experiments which had previously been carried out to validate measures of the structural complexity of BPMN models [5].

This paper is organized as follows. Section 2 provides an overview of the related work in this area of research and Section 3 introduces the CFC metric, presenting an example of computation in a business process modelled with BPMN. Section 4 provides an overview of the two families of experiments carried out to empirically validate measures for BPMN process models. Section 5 presents the analysis of results in the validation of the CFC metric, using the data obtained from the experiments with the BPMN models. Finally, conclusions are outlined in Section 6.

2   Related Work

The complexity and other characteristics and aspects of business processes models (BPMs) such as size, density, cohesion, and coupling have been analyzed and measured by researchers who agree that, as with software processes, business processes should minimize their complexity in order to provide adequate support to the various stakeholders. The vast majority of the measures proposed for analyzing the complexity of BPMs have their origin in, or are adaptations of, measures previously defined for the evaluation of software. For instance, in [7, 8, 9, 10], this topic is analyzed and software complexity metrics (or other characteristics of software) are analyzed and compared with corresponding metrics for BPMs.

However, it is important to highlight the different perspectives from which the complexity of a business process has been evaluated. For instance, Gruhn and Laue [11] have adopted complexity measures based on cognitive weights, assuming that this is a good manner in which to measure the difficulty of understanding the BPM elements. In [12], Mendling investigates how the complexity of models influences errors observed in a wide range of existing BPMs by developing a set of metrics to measure the probability of error and testing 28 business process metrics as error predictors on a set of over 2000 process models from different samples [13, 14]. In [7], some ideas from McCabe's cyclomatic complexity are used and the CFC metric is defined, which can be used to analyze the complexity of business processes from a work-flow perspective (see Section 3).

Nonetheless, while a number of metrics have been proposed the work published about empirical validation of the measures is almost inexistent. In a recent study, the use of BPMN elements in practice and their implications were analyzed [15]. In this context, we use the CFC metric defined by Cardoso [2] to evaluate the control-flow complexity of several BPMs developed with BPMN standard notation [6]. The work presented in [2, 3] coincide in the study of the metrics defined for evaluating software processes complexity and their extension and adaptation to business processes. In addition, both share the idea that when information regarding process model complexity is obtained, the model is easier to understand and modify in order to perform maintenance tasks, and process quality improvement is more likely to occur.

3 Control-Flow Complexity Measure

An important aspect to consider in the quest to achieve an effective process management is the complexity analysis of processes. This is the aim of the CFC metric, whose definition is based on the hypothesis that the complexity of a process can be derived from its control-flow behaviour and it is affected by constructs such as splits and joins. As a result, the formula developed captures the complexity of XOR-split, OR-split and AND-split constructs as follows:

XOR-split Control-flow Complexity. Determined by the number of mental states that are introduced with this type of split. The function $CFC_{XOR-split}(a)$, where a is an activity, computes the control-flow complexity of the XOR-split a. For XOR-splits, the control-flow complexity is simply the fan-out of the split.

$$CFC_{XOR-split}(a)= \text{fan-out}(a) \tag{1}$$

OR-split Control-flow Complexity. Determined by the number of mental states that are introduced with the split. For OR-splits, the control-flow complexity is 2^(n-1), where n is the fan-out of the split.

$$CFC_{OR-split}(a)= 2^{\text{fan-out}(a)-1} \tag{2}$$

AND-split Control-flow Complexity. For an AND-split, the complexity is simply 1. The process designer needs only to consider and analyze one state that may arise from the execution of an AND-split construct, since it is assumed that all the outgoing transitions are selected and followed.

$$CFC_{AND-split}(a)= 1 \tag{3}$$

Mathematically, the Control-Flow Complexity metric is additive. This is done by simply adding the CFC of all the split constructs and is calculated as follows:

$$CFC = \sum CFC_{XOR-split}(a) + \sum CFC_{OR-split}(a) + \sum CFC_{AND-split}(a) \tag{4}$$

The greater the value of the CFC, the greater the overall structural complexity of a process will be. CFC analysis seeks to evaluate complexity without the direct execution of processes.

3.1 Example of CFC Calculation

Figure 1 shows a business process for an online ticket purchase modelled with BPMN. This process states that a customer has to choose between different outgoing paths once the process is initiated. Basically, it consists of selecting the type of tickets that is being sought on the Web, and for each option there are diverse outgoing paths. The process finishes when the purchase is carried out satisfactorily or when the customer cancels the purchase process. As example, the results of the Control-Flow Complexity calculation carried out in the process of Figure 1 are shown in Table 1.

The calculation of the overall CFC value basically consists of adding the individual CFC of each split. The value obtained gives an indication of the complexity of the ticket purchase process. With this example, it has been possible to verify that CFC metrics can be used to measure the complexity of BPMN models, thus fulfilling their objective of analyzing the control-flow complexity of business processes.

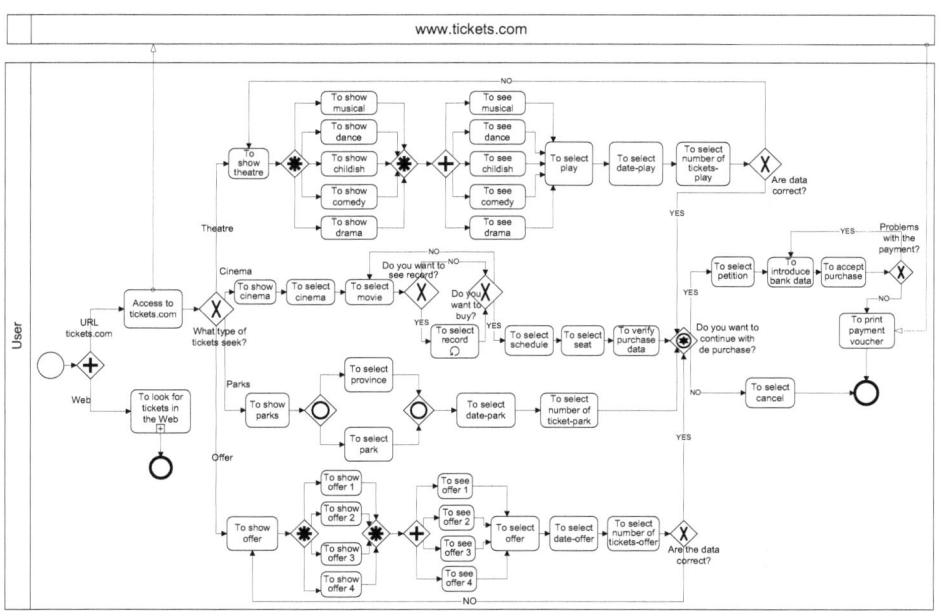

Fig. 1. Online ticket purchase process

Table 1. Values of CFC metrics for the process from Fig. 1

CFC Metric	Value	CFC Metric	Value
$CFC_{XOR\text{-}split}$(tickets type?)	4	$CFC_{XOR\text{-}split}$(shows offer type?)	4
$CFC_{XOR\text{-}split}$(to select theatre type)	5	$CFC_{XOR\text{-}split}$(offer data correct?)	2
$CFC_{XOR\text{-}split}$(theatre data correct?)	2	$CFC_{OR\text{-}split}$(to select province/park)	2^2-1
$CFC_{XOR\text{-}split}$(wants to see record?)	2	$CFC_{AND\text{-}split}$(to access the web)	1
$CFC_{XOR\text{-}split}$(wants to buy?)	2	$CFC_{AND\text{-}split}$(to select theatre type)	1
$CFC_{XOR\text{-}split}$(wants continue the purchase?)	2	$CFC_{AND\text{-}split}$(to select offer type)	1
$CFC_{XOR\text{-}split}$(payment' problems?)	2	**CFC (Online ticket purchase)**	**31**

4 Measures for BPMN Models

Our work consists of analyzing and empirically validating the CFC metric on the basis of previous work carried out to evaluate models developed with BPMN. Hence, in this section a summary of our previous works is included in order to place the results presented in this paper in context.

With the aim to evaluate the complexity of business processes by starting from the model which is a conceptual representation, we have previously defined a set of measures grouped into two categories: Base Measures and Derived Measures. Table 2 shows an example of some derived measures (the complete list of measures can be found in [3]).

Table 2. Derived measures for BPMN models

Measure	Definition	Formula
TNE	Total Number of Events of the Model	TNE = NTSE + NTIE + TNEE
TNG	Total Number of Gateways of the Model	TNG=NEDDB+NEDEB+NID+NCD+NPF
TNDO	Total Number of Data Objects	TNDO = NDOIn + NDOOut
CLA	Connectivity Level between Activities	$CLA = \dfrac{TNT}{NSF}$
PDOPOut	Proportion of Data Object as Outgoing Product and the total of Data Objects	$PDOPOut = \dfrac{NDOOut}{TNDO}$
PDOTOut	Proportion of Data Object as Outgoing Product of Activities of the Model	$PDOTOut = \dfrac{NDOOut}{TNT}$

The following subsections present the research context and an overview of the two families of experiments which were conducted to empirically validate the relationship between the proposed measures and the usability and maintainability of BPMN models.

4.1 Research Context

The objective of carrying out families of experiments to empirically validate the measures presented in [3] was to discover which of the measures defined could provide useful and objective information about the external quality of business process models. They focused mainly on two characteristics of the ISO 9126 external quality: usability (understandability) and maintainability (modifiability). The results obtained in the empirical validation of the first family are presented in [5].

Initially, the measures were theoretically validated according to the Briand *et al.* theoretical framework [16]. As a result, it was possible to group them in relation to the different properties of structural complexity (size, coupling and complexity) they evaluate (Fig. 2). So, the next step consisted of carrying out the empirical validation.

A set of experiments was planned and designed for the empirical validation of the measures defined. The GQM template (Goal Question Metric) [17], was used to define the research objectives as *analyse* measures of the structural complexity of BPMs *with the purpose of* evaluating them *as regards* their capability of being used as indicators of the understandability and modifiability of BPMs, *in the context of* PhD students, research assistants and others.

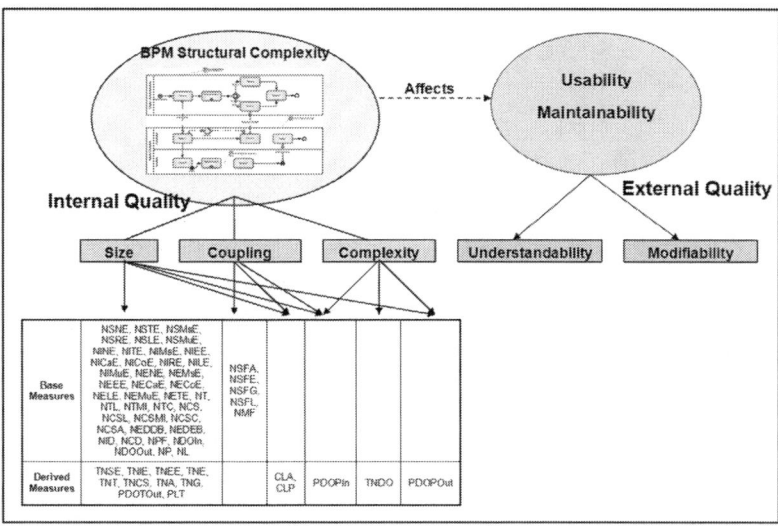

Fig. 2. Relationship between structural complexity and quality attributes

The hypothesis proposed with regard to the research objective was to ascertain whether there is a significant correlation between the measurements of structural complexity and the understandability and modifiability subcharacteristics. The independent variables were the measures defined for BPMN models and the dependent variables were those relating to the understandability and modifiability of BPMs. Later these were measured according to answer times, number of correct answers, subjective evaluation and the efficiency in the accomplishment of the tasks.

4.2   First Family

The first family of experiments was composed of five experiments. The experimental design used was the same for all five experiments. Thus, they were carried out in similar circumstances and in the same context, that is to say, by applying the same research objective, hypotheses and variables. In the experimental design a within-subjects design was carried out in which all the subjects had to do all the tests.

Material composed of ten randomly ordered BPMN models was given to each subject. These BPMN models had different structural characteristics; that is to say, different degrees of complexity; they included two questionnaires formulated for each process model. The first one was related to the understandability, and the second to the modifiability. A subjective question about the complexity of the model was also included. A more detailed description of the material can be found in [4].

The subjects (Table 3) were chosen since all of them had sufficient knowledge of modelling to carry out the experimental tasks. To leverage their knowledge about process modelling, a training lesson was carried out before the experiments run. This session consisted of an introduction to business processes and training about the BPMN standard notation.

Table 3. Groups of participants in the first family of experiments

Exp	Group	N° Sub.	Profiles
1	UCLM (Spain)	27	PhD students, research assistants and lecturers in Computer Engineering.
2	UAT (Mexico)	31	Master's students in Information Systems.
3	University of Sannio (Italy)	37	Master's Students in: • Software Technology • Software Management and Technology • Computer Science Technology for Organizational Management and Knowledge.
4	HGCR (Spain)	6	Health professionals.
5	UCLM (Spain)	8	PhD students

4.3 Second Family

The second family of experiments included the development of five experiments. In the experiments of the second family, understandability and modifiability aspects were also analyzed, the difference being that in this instance separate experiments were designed to analyze each aspect. From the five experiments included in the second family, the first three were carried out to analyze the understandability of the models, and the modifiability was evaluated in the last two experiments.

The experimental material used to analyze the understandability consisted of fifteen BPMN models with different structural characteristics and degrees of complexity. For each model, a questionnaire with three questions related to the understandability of the process model was elaborated. In order to analyze the modifiability, the experimental material consisted of twelve BPMN models and a questionnaire with two modification requirements for each model. Moreover, in all cases the subjects answered a subjective question regarding the complexity of the process model [5].

As with the first family of experiments, the participant subjects in the second family (Table 4) received a training session about BPMN.

Having described the families of experiments the following step in this paper is to present the descriptive and statistical analysis that was carried out to validate the CFC metric. This was done by taking the data obtained concerning the dependent variables to determine the feasibility of using the CFC metric to measure the structural complexity of business process models developed with BPMN.

Table 4. Groups of participants in the second family of experiments

Exp.	Group	N° Sub.	Profiles
1 (U)	UCLM (Spain)	22	PhD students and students in Computer Engineering.
2 (U)	UCLM (Spain)	40	Students of 4th year in Computer Engineering.
3 (U)	UCLM (Spain)	9	PhD students and students in Computer Engineering.
4 (M)	University of Bari (Italy)	29	Students in Computer Engineering
5 (M)	UAT – (Mexico)	15	Master's students in Information Systems.

As both the CFC metric and the measures proposed in [3] evaluate the structural complexity of BPMs, the same experimental design, hypothesis and variables in the two families of experiments can be stated. Consequently, the data obtained in the two former empirical studies can be used to analyze whether a correlation between the CFC metric and the maintainability of the BPMN models exists. The results of the CFC validation are shown in the next section.

5   Analysis and Validation of the CFC Metric

The CFC metric, presented in section 3, has been previously validated, by analyzing its values in different process models represented with the METEOR workflow management system and with regard to the subjective evaluation of such models by process designers [18]. As a result, the authors concluded that the CFC metric is highly correlated with the complexity of processes and, therefore can be used by business process analysts and designers to analyze the complexity of processes and to develop simpler processes when possible.

In this paper our aim is to corroborate whether the CFC metric can be used to analyze the complexity of business processes developed with a standard notation such as BPMN. Our goal is also to provide some insight, based on objective data, into the metric's influence on the ease of understanding and modifying BPMN models. With this objective in mind the stated research hypotheses are:

- Null hypothesis, H_{0u}: There is no significant correlation between the CFC metric and understandability.
- Alternative hypothesis, H_{1u}: There is a significant correlation between the CFC metric and understandability.
- Null hypothesis, H_{0m}: There is no significant correlation between the CFC metric and modifiability.
- Alternative hypothesis, H_{1m}: There is a significant correlation between the CFC metric and modifiability.

5.1   Descriptive Analysis

The first step, in order to carry out the descriptive analysis, was to obtain the values of the CFC metric of the models used in all the experiments (Table 5). The values of the CFC metrics reflect the degree of complexity of control-flows between process models. For example, process models 7 and 10 of the first family have the highest values of CFC. It is therefore possible to state that they have a greater structural complexity than process model number 1. In the second family, the highest CFC values were obtained with the first five models, as these models contained more gateways.

In both families of experiments, the dependent variables were measured based on: 1) the times that the subjects needed to carry out the required tasks, 2) the percentage of correct answers, 3) the subjective evaluation with regard to the complexity of the models, and 4) the efficiency of the answers (calculated as the ratio between the number of correct answers and the time needed to respond).

Table 5. Values of the CFC metric in experimental material

Process Model	1st Family			2nd Family	
	Exp. 1, 2 and 5	Exp. 3	Exp. 4	Exp. 1, 2 and 3	Exp. 4 and 5
1	2	2	2	25	25
2	2	2	2	25	25
3	6	6	6	33	33
4	8	8	8	31	--
5	7	7	7	2	2
6	6	6	6	7	--
7	11	11	8	9	9
8	2	2	3	5	5
9	2	2	8	8	8
10	14	15	15	0	0
11				2	--
12				4	4
13				8	8
14				4	4
15				0	0

Table 6 shows a summary of the results obtained from the experiments carried out, with regard to the time (in minutes) that the subjects needed to respond to the tasks related to understandability and modifiability.

By analyzing the time taken by the subjects to carry out the required tasks, it is possible to identify the process models in which more time was needed. For instance, for the understandability tasks in the first family, the subjects took more time to analyse process models 5, 7 and 10, whilst they took more time to carry out the modifications requested with process models 3, 4 and 7. On the other hand, the time taken by the subjects in the second family of experiments to carry out the tasks relating to the model's understandability is greater for process models 1, 2, 3, 4 and 13. For the modifiability tasks, the models 1, 2 and 13 had more spend time.

The results in both families reflect, in the first instance, the relationship of the understandability times - degree of model complexity, when comparing tables 5 and 6, since process models 7 and 10 in the first family and process models 1 to 4 in the second family coincide as being those of greater complexity. The descriptive analysis relating to correct answers, subjective evaluation and efficiency was carried out in a similar manner. Once the descriptive analysis of the data had been completed, the statistical correlation analysis was carried out and it is presented in the next section.

Table 6. Values of answer times (first family)

Process Model	First Family										Process Model	Second Family				
	Understandability Times					Modifiability Times						Underst. - Times			Mod. - Times	
	Exp. 1	Exp. 2	Exp. 3	Exp. 4	Exp. 5	Exp. 1	Exp. 2	Exp. 3	Exp. 4	Exp. 5		Exp. 1	Exp.2	Exp. 3	Exp. 4	Exp. 5
1	121	181	230	178	132	327	323	325	316	247	1	135	137	178	308	137
2	166	159	218	134	148	401	454	450	305	581	2	137	124	137	331	124
3	185	182	228	174	189	291	384	418	348	773	3	238	245	331	253	245
4	149	175	214	164	362	306	2546	1509	420	272	4	135	137	205	~	~
5	280	248	295	337	293	375	438	384	519	407	5	52	53	63	181	53
6	279	220	270	142	205	345	409	383	196	540	6	120	122	163	~	~
7	221	230	307	145	284	416	473	419	453	405	7	102	114	142	242	114
8	211	193	225	143	218	305	392	416	284	379	8	101	96	108	180	96
9	187	240	225	101	241	392	362	343	306	527	9	92	97	159	294	97
10	238	247	277	243	187	319	454	461	319	364	10	56	53	57	171	53
											11	123	126	178	~	~
											12	94	97	122	144	97
											13	174	161	262	312	161
											14	111	112	192	184	112
											15	49	53	116	162	53

5.2 Correlation Analysis

The first step of the correlation analysis was to ascertain whether the distribution of the data was Normal. Therefore the Kolmogorov-Smirnov test was applied. Since the data distribution was not Normal, we decided to use a non-parametrical statistical test. We have used Spearman correlation coefficient with a level of significance of $\alpha = 0.05$, which indicates the probability of rejecting the null hypothesis when it is certain (type I error). That is to say, a confidence level of 95% exists. The Spearman correlation coefficient was used to separately correlate each of the measures with the dependant variables as regards each of the aspects evaluated in the descriptive analysis (answer times, correct answers, subjective evaluation and efficiency). The following subsections show the results obtained in the two families of experiments.

5.2.1 Results of the First Family

Table 7 shows the results of the correlation of the CFC metrics with regard to the measures of the dependent variables. With regard to understandability, only the $CFC_{AND-split}$ metric was validated in the fourth experiment in correlation with the answer times and subjective evaluation. In this case, we can conclude that the number of AND-split construct affects the understandability of the model, which is reflected in the answer time.

With regard to modifiability, the correlation analysis shows that the $CFC_{XOR-split}$ and CFC metrics were validated in experiments 2 and 3 in relation to the answer times, subjective evaluation and efficiency. On the other hand, only the $CFC_{AND-split}$ was validated in the third experiment in relation to the subjective evaluation.

From the results of the correlations analysis obtained in the first family of experiments, we can observe that the relationship of CFC metrics to process complexity is greater with regard to the modifiability aspect in particular. Specifically, these results show that the XOR-split construct affects above all the modifiability of the model. In addition, the validation of the CFC metric (which adds all the split constructors) gives us an indication that the structural complexity of a process, from the point of view of control flows, affects modifiability.

5.2.2 Results of the Second Family

In the second family of experiments, understandability and modifiability aspects were also evaluated, but in separate experiments designed to analyse each aspect. By following the same procedure as the one carried out in the first experimental family, once we had obtained the summary of data for each of the dependent variables measures (answer times, correct answers, subjective evaluation and efficiency) we carried out the analysis of correlations.

Table 7. Correlations of the CFC metrics and understandability (first family)

Measure	Understandability		Modifiability				
	Times	Sub. Eval.	Times	Subj. Eval.		Efficiency	
	Exp-4	Exp-4	Exp-2	Exp-2	Exp-3	Exp-2	Exp-3
CFC (XOR)			X	X	X	X	X
CFC (OR)							
CFC (AND)	X	X			X		
CFC			X	X	X	X	

Table 8. Correlations of the CFC metrics and Understandability (second family)

Measure	UNDERSTANDABILITY												MODIFIABILITY							
	Times			C. Answer			Sub. Eval.			Efficiency			Times		C. Answer		Sub. Eval.		Efficiency	
	E-1	E-2	E-3	E-1	E-2	E-3	E-1	E-2	E-3	E-1	E-2	E-3	E-4	E-5	E-4	E-5	E-4	E-5	E-4	E-5
CFC (XOR)	X	X	X		X		X	X	X	X	X	X	X	X			X	X	X	
CFC (OR)	X	X	X		X		X	X	X	X	X	X	X	X			X		X	
CFC (AND)	X	X	X		X		X	X	X	X	X	X	X				X		X	
CFC	X	X	X		X		X	X	X	X	X	X	X	X			X	X	X	

Table 8 shows that the CFC metrics were, on the whole, validated in relation to the variables analyzed. With regard to the understandability the correlations with the answer time the CFC metrics were validated in all experiments. This same correlation exists with regard to the variables of subjective evaluation and efficiency. The correct answers were only validated in the second experiment.

The correlation analysis results with regard to the modifiability also indicate that all the CFC metrics are highly correlated with the modifiability of the process models. The influence of the control-flow complexity on the modifiability of the BPMN models is reflected essentially both in the answer time in the required tasks and in the subjective evaluation and efficiency in the accomplishment of the tasks.

There are significant differences between the results obtained from the correlation analysis in the experiments of the second family as compared to the first one. These differences were also observed when the validation of measures for BPMN models was carried out. One reason for this was that the experimental material used in the second family of experiments was an improved version of that used in the first one (which, according to the feedback obtained, did not have much variability in its structural complexity). The accomplishment of the second family was therefore based on two main characteristics: a) the selection of a subset of structural complexity measures which included only the most significant measures (29 from the 60 initially defined) according to empirical results and an analysis of principal components, and b) an increase in the variability of the structural complexity of the models. We can thus consider the results obtained in the second family to be more conclusive.

The results obtained indicate that XOR-split, OR-split, and AND-split constructors affect the understandability and modifiability of the model. Therefore, based on the results and as regards the hypothesis proposed, it is possible to reject the null hypotheses and to conclude that there is a significant correlation between the CFC metric and the understandability and modifiability of BPMN models.

Finally, as a result of this empirical study, we consider that the CFC metric is a suitable complement in measuring the structural complexity of business processes models with BPMN alongside the measures proposed in [3]. With the use and validation of the CFC metrics it is possible to obtain additional information with regard to the structural complexity of BPMs, in this case from a control-flow perspective. This allows designers building process models (given more than one possible and equivalent modelling alternative) to determine which of those models is more usable and maintainable.

6 Conclusions

In this work we have presented the evaluation and empirical validation of the CFC metric for measuring BPMN business process complexity from the point of view of control-flows. The empirical validation relied on the results obtained from two families of experiments which included the carrying out of a total of ten experiments. Initially, these experiments were carried out with the aim of evaluating the structural complexity of BPMs, as a means to obtain useful information concerning their understandability and modifiability.

The CFC is a design-time measure. It can be used to evaluate the difficulty of producing a BPMN process design before implementation. When control-flow complexity analysis becomes part of the process development cycle, it has a considerable influence on the design phase, leading to further optimized processes. It is a well-known fact in software engineering that it is cost-effective to fix a defect earlier in the design lifecycle rather than later. To enable this to be done we introduce the first steps with which to carry out process complexity analysis.

As a result of applying the CFC metric, we were able to obtain additional information regarding the structural complexity of business processes. It was also possible to validate the CFC metric and to establish that it is highly correlated with the control-flow complexity of a business process and, therefore with its understandability and modifiability. These results, along with the results on the validation of BPMN measures previously obtained, provide valuable information when carrying out improvements or maintenance tasks in process models. A better understanding of the process facilitates its later modelling and evolution.

We believe that the evaluation and measurement of business process complexity in early phases of development (such as design and modeling phases) can help to identify problems in a process model and, therefore, assist designers to create or choose process models that are easy to understand for all stakeholders. Understandable models also facilitate maintenance tasks, thus reducing implicit costs. Models that are easy to understand and maintain can provide support to development tasks, such as process reengineering, the redesign of business processes on a large-scale and refactoring.

Acknowledgments. This work has been partially financed by the INGENIO Project (Junta de Comunidades de Castilla-La Mancha, Consejería de Educación y Ciencia, PAC 08-0154-9262) and ESFINGE Project (Ministerio de Educación y Ciencia, Dirección General de Investigación/Fondos Europeos de Desarrollo Regional (FEDER), TIN2006-15175-C05-05.

References

1. Succi, G., Predonzani, P., Vernazza, T.: Business Process Modeling with Objects, Costs and Human Resources. In: Bustard, D., Kawalek, P., Norris, M. (eds.) Systems Modeling for Business Process Improvement, pp. 47–60. Artech House (2000)
2. Cardoso, J.: How to Measure the Control-flow Complexity of Web Processes and Workflows. In: WfMC (ed.) Workflow Handbook, pp. 199–212. Lighthouse Point, FL (2005)

3. Rolón, E., Ruiz, F., Garcia, F., Piattini, M.: Applying Software Metrics to evaluate Business Process Models. CLEI-Electronic Journal 9(1) (paper 5) (2006)
4. Rolón, E., Garcia, F., Ruiz, F., Piattini, M.: An Exploratory Experiment to Validate Measures for Business Process Models. In: First IEEE International Conference on Research Challenges in Information Science (RCIS 2007). IEEE, Ouarzazate (2007)
5. Rolón, E., Garcia, F., Ruiz, F., Piattini, M., et al.: Evaluation of BPMN Models Quality: a Family of Experiments. In: 3rd International Conference on Evaluation of Novel Approaches to Software Engineering (ENASE 2008), Funchal, Madeira (2008)
6. OMG, Business Process Modeling Notation (BPMN) Specification (2006)
7. Cardoso, J., Mendling, J., Neumann, G., Reijers, H.A.: A Discourse on Complexity of Process Models. In: Eder, J., Dustdar, S. (eds.) BPM Workshops 2006. LNCS, vol. 4103, pp. 117–128. Springer, Heidelberg (2006)
8. Ghani, A.A.A., Wei, K.T., Muketha, G.M., Wen, W.P.: Complexity Metrics for Measuring the Understandability and Maintainability of Business Process Models using Goal-Question-Metric (GQM). International Journal of Computer Science and Network Security (IJCSNS) 8(5), 219–225 (2008)
9. Gruhn, V., Laue, R.: Complexity Metrics for Business Process Models. In: 9th Int. Conference on Business Information Systems (BIS 2006), Klagenfurt, Austria (2006)
10. Cardoso, J.: Control-flow Complexity Measurement of Processes and Weyuker's Properties. In: 6th International Enformatika Conference. Transactions on Enformatika, Systems Sciences and Engineering, Budapest, Hungary (2005)
11. Gruhn, V., Laue, R.: Adopting the Cognitive Complexity Measure for Business Process Models. In: 5th IEEE International Conference on Cognitive Informatics (ICCI 2006), Beijing, China (2006)
12. Mendling, J., Neumann, G.: Error Metrics for Business Process Models. In: 19th International Conference on Advanced Information Systems Engineering (CAISE 2007), Trondheim, Norway (2007)
13. Mendling, J.: Detection and Prediction of Errors in EPC Business Process Models. Vienna University of Economics and Business Administration, Vienna, Austria (2007)
14. Mendling, J., Neumann, G., van der Aalst, W.M.P.: Understanding the Occurrence of Errors in Process Models based on Metrics. In: Meersman, R., Tari, Z. (eds.) OTM 2007, Part I. LNCS, vol. 4803, pp. 113–130. Springer, Heidelberg (2007)
15. Muehlen, M.z., Recker, J.: How Much Language is Enough? Theoretical and Practivcal Use of the Business Process Modeling Notation. In: Bellahsène, Z., Léonard, M. (eds.) CAiSE 2008. LNCS, vol. 5074, pp. 465–479. Springer, Heidelberg (2008)
16. Briand, L., Morasca, S., Basili, V.: Property-Based Software Engineering Measurement. IEEE Transactions on Software Engineering 22(1), 68–86 (1996)
17. Basili, V., Rombach, H.: The TAME Project: Towards Improvement-Oriented Software Environments. IEEE Transactions on Software Engineering 14(6), 728–738 (1988)
18. Cardoso, J.: Process control-flow complexity metric: An empirical validation. In: IEEE International Conference on Service Computing (SCC 2006), Chicago, USA (2006)

Vertical Alignment of Process Models – How Can We Get There?

Matthias Weidlich[1], Alistair Barros[2], Jan Mendling[3], and Mathias Weske[1]

[1] Hasso Plattner Institute, Potsdam, Germany
{matthias.weidlich, weske}@hpi.uni-potsdam.de
[2] SAP Research, CEC Brisbane, Australia
alistair.barros@sap.com
[3] Humboldt-Universität zu Berlin, Germany
jan.mendling@wiwi.hu-berlin.de

Abstract. There is a wide variety of drivers for business process modelling initiatives, reaching from business evolution and process optimisation over compliance checking and process certification to process enactment. That, in turn, results in models that differ in content due to serving different purposes. In particular, processes are modelled on different abstraction levels and assume different perspectives. Vertical alignment of process models aims at handling these deviations. While the advantages of such an alignment for inter-model analysis and change propagation are out of question, a number of challenges has still to be addressed. In this paper, we discuss three main challenges for vertical alignment in detail. Against this background, the potential application of techniques from the field of process integration is critically assessed. Based thereon, we identify specific research questions that guide the design of a framework for model alignment.

Keywords: process model alignment, business-IT gap, model consistency, model correspondences.

1 Introduction

The broad field of application of Business Process Management (BPM), from process analysis to process enactment, results in a variety of requirements for BPM methods and techniques. In particular, there is a huge difference in the appropriate level of abstraction of processes, as well as the assumed perspective. Both, abstraction level and perspective, depend on the purpose of the model and the involved stakeholders.

Evidently, real-world scenarios require multiple process models, each of them created for a specific objective. Such a model has to be *appropriate* in the sense that it incorporates a reasonable level of detail, focus on certain properties, and neglects unrelated aspects. As diverging modelling purposes cannot be organized in a strict top-down fashion, it is unrealistic that the corresponding models can always be derived through hierarchical refinement. Consequently, and most likely,

T. Halpin et al. (Eds.): BPMDS 2009 and EMMSAD 2009, LNBIP 29, pp. 71–84, 2009.

there will be a variety of differences between models. Arguably, these *mismatches* are in the nature of process models that serve different purposes. Thus, avoidance of mismatches might not only be impossible in certain scenarios, it might also be unnatural and counter-productive. That is to say that a resolution of these mismatches might impact the adequacy of a process model in a negative manner.

A widely known example for the problem of aligning high-level and low-level models is the missing fit between business process models and workflow models. For more than a decade, this notorious 'Business-IT Gap' has motivated various researchers to investigate a better alignment of such models [1,2,3,4,5]. The prominence of this mismatch has somewhat hindered the discussion of the problem in a more general setting. Due to a similar difference in purpose, we observe that process models that are created to reflect control objectives for Sarbanes-Oxley compliance can hardly be used for process reengineering. In the same vein, SIPOC process diagrams are hardly informative to workflow implementation projects. While process modelling builds on a certain core in terms of task description, the diverging application scenarios for these models (see [6]) result in models that cover accounting operations, web service invocations, control activities, or strategic to-dos.

This paper argues that various aspects of an alignment of process models have not yet been investigated in a sufficient manner. Results from various research fields, for instance process integration and behaviour inheritance, might be adapted for alignment purposes. However, the scope of model alignment goes beyond the requirements that have typically to be satisfied in these research fields. Therefore, this paper elaborates on the challenges for vertical model alignment in detail and outlines the steps to be taken in order to achieve a mature solution. Albeit complicated by the usage of different modelling approaches (with potentially varying expressiveness), the problem of vertical model alignment is independent of any language. For illustration purposes, we use the Business Process Modeling Notation (BPMN) [7] throughout this paper. In order to clarify our point, we explicitly exclude mismatches from the discussion that stem from a mismatch between different modelling languages (such as BPMN and BPEL).

Against this background, our contribution is twofold. First, we motivate the need for vertical alignment and elaborate on three major challenges in detail. Second, we discuss why existing techniques are not sufficient in order to address these challenges and identify open research questions. The remainder of this paper is structured accordingly. The next section introduces a motivating example along with the major use cases for an alignment. Subsequently, Section 3 reviews related work. In Section 4 we elaborate on the major challenges for an alignment of process models. Based thereon, a set of research questions that need to be tackled is presented in Section 5. Finally, Section 6 concludes the paper.

2   Motivating Example and Use Cases

In order to illustrate the need for vertical alignment of process models, Figure 1 depicts two process models describing a lead management process, which we

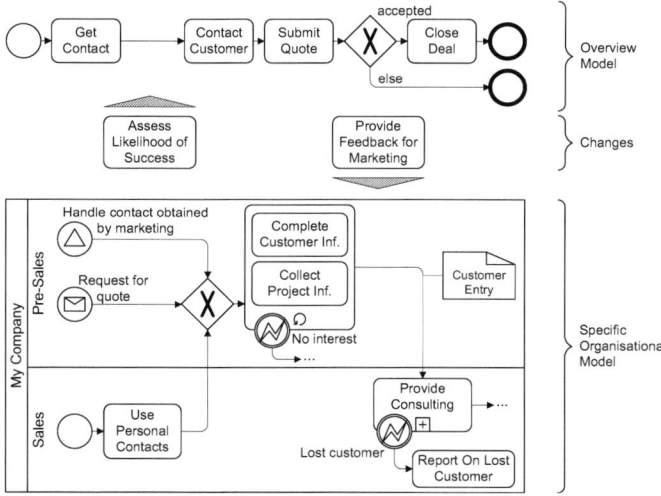

Fig. 1. A lead management scenario, described by two models that need to be aligned

encountered in the course of an industry corporation. The upper model shows solely the major activities, from getting a customer's contact details to arranging a deal with them. Here, an intuitive overview of the major processing steps, independent of any concrete organisational or technical environment, is in the centre of interest.

At the other end of the line, processes are specified in a fine-grained manner. They might aim at capturing technical aspects, such as the treatment of exceptional cases or data mediation. Furthermore, low-level models often also focus on the relation between the process and its execution environment. Organisational units that are mandated to execute the tasks and information systems that support their execution are assigned to certain parts of the process. The lower process in Figure 1 is an example for such a low-level model. It provides not only a more fine-grained view, but also relates activities to organisational roles.

Granted that there are multiple process models as described before, vertical alignment of process models is mainly driven by three use cases.

Validation. In various situations as, for instance, related to the 'Business-IT Gap' one process model is utilized as a specification against which a second, often more fine-grained model is validated. However, validation is not restricted to technical models. The upper model in Figure 1 might also be interpreted as a specification for the implementation of the process in a certain organisational environment, that is, the lower model.

Inter-Model Analysis. Process optimisation often requires an analysis across multiple process models. With respect to the exemplary processes in Figure 1, one might want to identify all roles that are involved when a customer is contacted. Starting from the activity *Contact Customer* of the high-level model, this information depends on one or more low-level models.

Change Propagation. Once potential improvements have been identified, all related models have to be updated accordingly. This can imply that changes in one model have to be propagated to the other models, and vice versa. While automatic change propagation appears to be unrealistic, the identification of affected processes or process regions, respectively, would already be a major benefit. Changes in process models can origin from all abstraction levels. Strategic management decisions will typically be reflected as changes in high-level models, whereas the replacement of a technical system enforces an adaptation of a low-level model. Consequently, change propagation has to happen top-down as well as bottom-up. Figure 1 illustrates both cases.

Addressing these use cases, any alignment has to embrace means for correlating elements of different models. These correspondences, in turn, have to respect certain consistency criteria in order to be exploited for model validation, analysis, or change propagation.

3   Related Work

Our work relates to the various research areas, namely *integrated system design, process integration, measures for process similarity,* and *behaviour inheritance.*

Integrated system design relates to various approaches that have been proposed to derive technical realisations from business requirements. In this case, consistency is achieved by deriving *information system models* directly from *business models.* In [1], the author raises the awareness for interdependencies between such models and introduces the notion of *vertical integration,* which comprises refinements for data objects and their relationships, as well as activities and their life-cycles. Considering also transactions, *realisation types* [4] that transform a business model into a technical model are another approach to derive technical models from business requirements. Bergholtz et al. [8] advocate the usage of communication patterns that guide the creation of process models from business requirements. This work has later been extended towards a framework, in which process models are derived from business models via activity dependency models as an intermediate step [9]. Due to the focus on the system development from-scratch, the aforementioned approaches are limited to rather strict refinements and do not deal with detection or resolution of inconsistencies. Taking existing informations systems into account, business-driven development (BDD) [5] aims at seamless transition from business-centred *analysis models* to technology-centred *design models.* Here, the authors describe transformation steps concerning the control flow, data representation, and service landscape in order to realise this transition. Other authors introduced a *process support layer* [10] realising common mismatch patterns to bridge the gap between process models and existing service landscapes. These patterns focus on differences related to service granularity, ordering, and interaction behaviour. Still, these approaches assume comprehensive derivation of technical models from business models, which implies a rather tight-coupling of these models.

Process integration assumes that process models originate from different sources and, therefore, are different yet similar. Common integration approaches for process models aim at unification of multiple views on a process, process harmonisation after an organisational merger, or the evolution of existing processes using reference models. Various publications define a merge operation for behavioural models based on model correspondences [11,12,13]. Nevertheless, this operation typically considers solely the control flow dependencies. A systematic classification of differences between similar processes has recently be published by Dijkman [14]. This work describes mismatches related to the control flow, resource assignments, and activity correspondences between two models that should be integrated. For control flow mismatches, a detection technique has also been presented [15]. Although process integration methods show how certain mismatches can be detected and resolved, they typically focus on *very similar* processes on the same level of abstraction. Thus, these models differ only slightly. The same delimitation holds for existing approaches to integrate different behavioural views, for instance [16], in which enterprise and computational views are aligned under the assumption of hierarchical refinement.

Measures for process similarity are related to our work, as vertical alignment assumes models to be similar to a certain extent. The authors of [17] present such a measure based on the enforced execution constraints. Moreover, a similarity measure might also be grounded on change operations [18]. Aiming at querying of models that are similar regarding their structure but reside on different levels of abstraction, Soffer introduced *structural equivalence* [19]. Still, focus is on hierarchical refinements between these models.

Behaviour inheritance aims at applying the idea of inheritance known from static structures to behavioural descriptions. In [20], Basten et al. introduced different basic notions of behaviour inheritance, namely *protocol inheritance* and *projection inheritance* based on labelled transition systems and branching bisimulation. A model either inherits the behaviour of a parent model, if it shows the same external behaviour when all actions that are not part of the parent model are *blocked* (protocol inheritance) or *hidden* (projection inheritance). Similar ideas have been presented in [21], in which the authors distinguish *invocation consistency* and *observation consistency*. These notions correspond to the notions of Basten et al. mentioned above [20]. Focussing on object life cycles, Schrefl and Stumptner built upon this work and argued that there is no exclusive choice between invocation consistency and observation consistency [22]. They also further distinguished *weak invocation consistency* and *strong invocation consistency*. The former implies inheritance of the interface, while the latter also enforces that added activities do not interfere with the inherited interface.

4   Challenges for Vertical Alignment

In this section, we discuss what we see as the major challenges for vertical alignment of process models. Section 4.1 first identifies the spectrum of differences

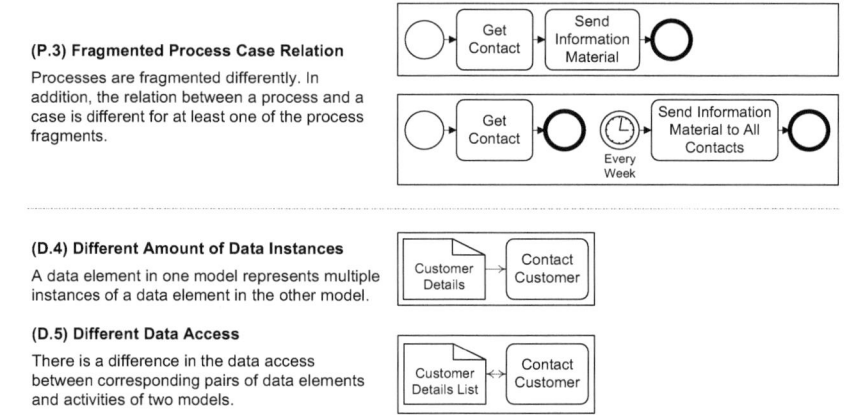

(P.3) Fragmented Process Case Relation

Processes are fragmented differently. In addition, the relation between a process and a case is different for at least one of the process fragments.

(D.4) Different Amount of Data Instances

A data element in one model represents multiple instances of a data element in the other model.

(D.5) Different Data Access

There is a difference in the data access between corresponding pairs of data elements and activities of two models.

Fig. 2. Examples for differences in process slicing, data access, and instance correlation

before Section 4.2 discusses challenges of defining model correspondences. Finally, Section 4.3 describes requirements for measuring a degree of consistency.

4.1   A Variety of Differences

Process models describing a scenario on different abstraction levels and from different perspectives, naturally show various kinds of differences. As mentioned above, there is related work on differences between quite similar processes. Nevertheless, existing classifications focus on resource assignments, activities, or the control flow, and neglect the process, and data perspective.

For instance, the upper part of Figure 2 illustrates differences related to the process perspective. Here, the slicing of processes is different as a process in one model is split up into two processes in the other model. In addition, we encounter differences with respect to instance correlation. In contrast to the most upper process, sending of information material is not an atomic activity in the process below. Here, sending is done via batch processing. As these mismatches cannot be traced back to elements of the process model, but refer to sets of process models, they are said to relate to the process perspective. The same kind of instance correlation issue can also arise with activities or data objects, illustrated in the lower part of Figure 2. Moreover, this example shows differing data access. While the first activity has only read-access, its counterpart might modify the respective data object. Due to space limitations, we have to restrict the discussion to these exemplary differences in this paper and refer to a technical report for an informal description of more differences relevant for vertical alignment [23]. An assessment of existing classifications of differences against our set of differences is shown in Table 1. This reveals only partial support for the differences that we identified and, therefore, motivates further investigation. The reason for the limited support is a predominant focus on comparison of rather similar processes. As these processes typically reside on the same level of abstraction, some of our differences are of minor importance for the purpose of process integration.

Table 1. Differences of process models (informal descriptions can be found in [23]) and how they are considered in existing classifications

	ID	Mismatch	Henkel [4]	Decker [10]	Dijkman [14]
Proc.	P.1	Process Fragmentation	–	–	–
	P.2	Process Case Relation	–	–	–
	P.3	Fragmented Process Case Relation	–	–	–
Activity	A.1	Activity Fragmentation	+	+	+
	A.2	Partial Activity Equivalence	–	–	+
	A.3	Non-Covered Activity	–	–	+
	A.4	Activity Iteration	–	–	+
	A.5	Activity-Case Relation	–	+	–
Flow	C.1	Different Causal Dependencies	+	+	+
	C.2	Rerouting	+	–	+
	C.3	Alternative Merge	–	–	+
	C.4	Decision Distribution	–	–	–
Data	D.1	Data Element Fragmentation	+	–	–
	D.2	Partial Data Element Equivalence	–	–	–
	D.3	Non-Covered Data Elements	+	–	–
	D.4	Different Amount of Data Instances	–	–	–
	D.5	Different Data Access	–	–	–
Resource	R.1	Resources Fragmentation	+	–	+
	R.2	Partial Resources Equivalence	–	–	+
	R.3	Non-Covered Resources	–	–	–
	R.4	Contradicting Resource Assignments	–	–	+
	R.5	Additional Resource Assignments	–	–	+

The variety of differences illustrated in table 1 raises the question of how they can be classified and formalized in a systematic manner. The most extensive collection of differences, published by Dijkman [14], is based on the notion of *black-box equivalence* and *white-box equivalence*. The first requires the effects of two related units of work to be the same, whereas the second criterion also requires the way these effects are achieved to be the same. Although it is mentioned that equivalence is defined between sets of activities, phenomena that result from different abstraction levels are not further investigated. However, in our context, we have to consider these effects. Therefore, we advocate to extend the classification of differences from two dimensions, i.e. *what* is specified and *how* it is achieved, with a third one, which takes the level of detail into account. Thus, differences can be clustered according to one of the following aspects, *model coverage*, *behavioural contradictions*, and *information density*.

Model coverage relates to the question, whether there is a difference in what is described in two models. That is, the process models are examined regarding the coverage of functionality and descriptions of data and resources. In other words, to which extent is the scenario described in one model reflected in the other model? An example is given in Figure 3. Compared to process (A), the process (B) contains an additional activity, i.e. *Notify Candidate*. Differences in model coverage can be coarse-grained (whole process parts of one model are without counterpart in the other model), as well as fine-grained (activities or data elements without counterpart).

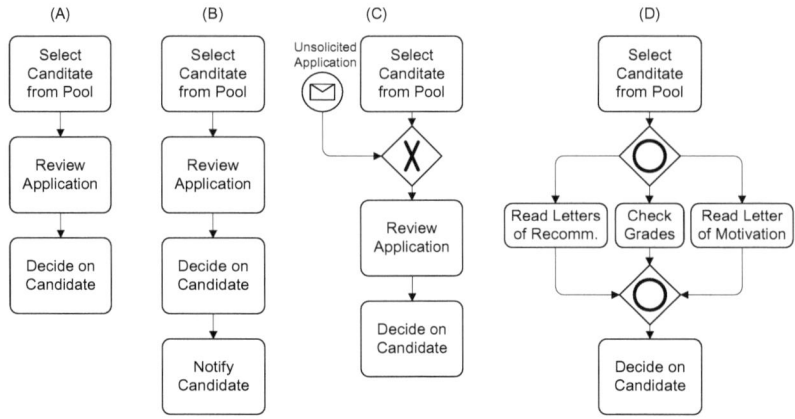

Fig. 3. A base process (A) and three process variants that differ with respect to model coverage (B), behavioural contradictions (C), and information density (D)

Behavioural contradictions relates to the question of how certain behaviour is achieved. Even in case the same functional part of a business scenario is captured by two models (no difference in model coverage), the realisation of this part might be different. For instance, there are differences in the execution order of corresponding activities, there is differing data access between corresponding activities, or a resource assignment in one model contradicts the one in another model. Again, Figure 3 illustrates such a difference with process (C) that specifies another entry point compared to process (A).

Information density relates to the question of how detailed the process is described. Two process parts realising the same scenario (no difference in model coverage) in the same way (no difference with respect to behavioural contradictions) might be specified in a different level of detail. Here, a typical example would be the refinement of an activity, as illustrated with process (D) in Figure 3, again compared to process (A). Different non-conflicting resource assignments of corresponding activities are another example for such a difference.

We summarize that vertical alignment has to deal with a broader variety of model differences compared to the existing work regarding process integration. Here, it is interesting to notice, that certain differences between processes that have been observed in practise, for instance in terms of enterprise integration patterns [24], have not yet been considered in the detection of differences to the best of our knowledge. Thus, the challenge is a comprehensive classification and formalisation of model differences. Such a formalisation might be inspired by the notions of *refinement* and *extension* as introduced for object life cycles [22].

4.2 Model Correspondences

A substantial requirement for vertical alignment of process models are means to correlate model elements. These *correspondence links* associate one or more

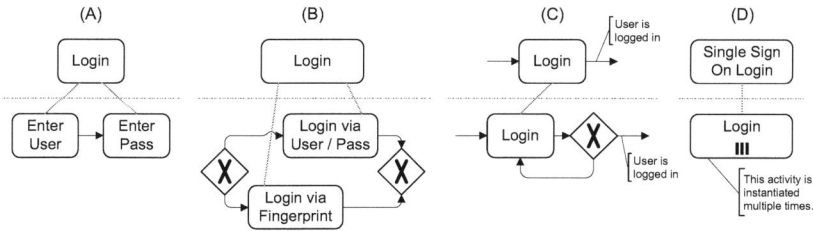

Fig. 4. Examples for model correspondences with different semantics

elements of one model, with its corresponding elements of a second model. Any validation and inter-model analysis, as well as change propagation depends on these connections. Concerning model correspondences, we can identify two major challenges. First, the question how correspondences are established has to be addressed. Second, semantics of correspondences have to be defined.

The question of the origin of model correspondences is crucial for the applicability of vertical model alignment. For real world scenarios, correspondences cannot be defined manually, owing to the pure number of models and model elements. Therefore, techniques that allow for automatic or at least semi-automatic definition of correspondences need to be exploited. Linguistic analysis of element naming, domain specific ontologies, or analysis of data dependencies are just a few examples of techniques that might be applied. It might also be necessary to select a set of related models from a repository prior to determining correspondences between them. That, in turn, results in additional efforts.

Besides their implications on techniques for finding correspondences, the aforementioned differences raise the question of semantics of correspondences. In other words, what is the meaning, if two (sets of) model elements *correspond* to each other. Figure 4 illustrates this challenge by four exemplary process pairs. We see that a 1-to-n correspondence might be interpreted such that the conjunction of n model elements corresponds to the single model element (A). On the other hand, it might be interpreted in way that the correspondences are mutually exclusive (B). Theoretically, it might even be the case that m-out-of-n model elements together correspond to an element in the other model. Thus, the latter element corresponds to more than one (i.e. different to case (B)), but not all (i.e. different to case (A)) of the model elements connected via correspondences. Sure enough, the same questions regarding correspondence semantics arise for fragment-to-fragment correspondence. It might be the case that for two elements of one model, the sets of corresponding elements of the other model are overlapping. Moreover, semantics of a correspondence might be that one activity instance in one model corresponds to all instances of the respective activity in the other model (C). While this scenario assumes sequential iteration of a corresponding activity, a correspondence might have also been defined between activities with a different notion of a case (D). Here, one activity is instantiated for a set of logins, whereas the other is instantiated multiple times, for each login. Thus, semantics of the correspondence are that one activity corresponds to multiple concurrent instantiations of the other activity.

Semantics for correspondences were proposed in the context of process integration. However, the semantic relationships observed during process integration, for instance counterpart-related processes [25], do typically not appear between processes that should be aligned. Correspondences, as whose by Dijkman that we discussed above [15], might be seen as a starting point, but are still not able to capture the examples of Figure 4. Please note that although this figure illustrates the ambiguity of link semantics only for activities, similar problems arise for other kind of process elements, e.g. data objects or resources.

4.3   The Notion of Consistency

Meaningful analysis across multiple process models has to be related to a certain degree of consistency between these models. However, there is no commonly agreed on definition of consistency for models on different abstraction levels that also assume different perspectives. Above, we discussed that differences between process models can be clustered according to the aspect they relate to, i.e. model coverage, behavioural contradictions, and information density. It seems reasonable to assume that differences in information density do not affect consistency. In other words, consistency is independent of the level of detail in which a process is specified. Consequently, we assume models to be consistent, if they cover exactly the same part of a scenario and there are no behavioural contradictions between them. Starting with this informal definition, formalisation of the coverage criterion seems to be straight-forward. In contrast, a formalisation of the second criterion, the absence of behavioural contradictions, i.e. behavioural consistency, appears challenging.

In Section 3, we discussed related work from the field of behaviour inheritance. Inheritance notions typically focus on the so called *visible* behaviour, while internal behaviour is neglected. Thus, we have to clarify the notion of visible behaviour for the purpose of vertical model alignment. Considering only the interactions with partners of a process might not be sufficient, as an interchanged order of corresponding internal activities of two processes might not be detected. Nevertheless, such a contradiction affects consistency in a negative manner, as it hampers change propagation. Depending on the purpose of the alignment, there might be no invisible behaviour.

Despite that, behaviour inheritance notions are too restrictive and support only a limited variety of mismatches. The authors of the most liberal notion, namely *life-cycle inheritance*, list a set of *inheritance preserving transformation rules* [20]. The insertion of activities between existing ones or the addition of loops containing new actions are examples for these rules. Everything that goes beyond these rules, for instance differences in the process instantiation mechanism, does not preserve inheritance and is inconsistent. Thus, these notions assume that behaviour is *added* in a *structural way* (e.g. iteration, choice, sequential or parallel composition) in the course of refinement of process models.

An assumption that does not hold for vertical alignment. Moreover, behavioural contradictions that relate to the data or resource perspective, for example differing data access and conflicting assignment of activities to resources, must be taken into account.

Even in case existing inheritance notions would be weakened to some extent, most of the real world alignment scenarios would probably be still inconsistent. Thus, a single Boolean answer to the question of consistency is not sufficient. Instead, consistency should either be assessed based on a set of distinguished criteria (similar to the different soundness criteria for the verification of control flow) or measured in a metric way. The former would be similar to the different soundness criteria for the verification of control flow or the *realisability levels* [26] that have been proposed for the alignment of business and technical models. Obviously, a pure metric (i.e. non-stepwise) consistency measure would have to be relative with respect to certain properties, e.g. size of models or the abstraction level. We consider the latter to be intuitive, as a big difference in the level of detail of two models might legitimate a certain degree of differences regarding model coverage or behavioural contradictions. Such a notion would ease change propagation, as the less invasive out of a set of change operations can be identified.

5   Empirical Research Questions

In the previous section, we outlined the major challenges for vertical model alignment. In order to address these challenges, this section identifies research questions that need to be answered through empirical research.

Specific Analysis Questions. In Section 2, we introduced three major use cases for model alignment. In case of change propagation, requirements for a model alignment framework are easy to derive. In contrast, the use case of inter-model analysis needs to be further refined. The *usefulness* of specific analysis questions has to be evaluated empirically. These analysis questions could be clustered according to the process perspective (e.g, activity or data perspective) or the difference categories (e.g., model coverage).

Synthesis of Model Correspondences. We mentioned before that it does not seem to be realistic to assume manual syntheses of model correspondences for real world scenarios. On the other hand, it also seems to be naive to assume that automatic techniques for deriving correspondences can approach the quality achieved by human-beings with specific domain knowledge. Therefore, the effort process modellers would be willing to invest needs to be analysed. In terms of the technology acceptance model [27], the potential *ease-of-use* of a framework for vertical model alignment needs to be investigated. There might be a trade-off between these results and the refined analysis use case; certain analysis questions might require a certain degree of manual alignment efforts.

Perception of Consistency. In order to shape a requirements framework for consistency notions applicable in the context of vertical model alignment, we need to know, which differences between processes affect consistency in a negative manner. First, our hypothesis on differences related to information density—we consider these differences to have no impact on consistency—has to be corroborated. In addition, the impact of the remaining differences on the *perceived consistency* of process models has to be further investigated. It seems reasonable to assume that certain differences are more likely to be tolerated than others. In contrast to an interchanged order of activities, a sequentialisation of concurrent activities might not be seen as a behavioural contradiction. Empirical evidence on the perception of consistency is therefore needed to define gradual or even metric consistency notions.

6   Conclusion

The need for an alignment of business-centred and IT-centred process models has been identified over a decade ago. In this paper, we argued that this alignment problem has to be generalised to more than two abstraction levels and two perspectives. That results from different drivers for process modelling, which requires an alignment of models serving a variety of purposes. Based on three use cases, we elaborated on three major challenges for model alignment, that is the characteristics of mismatches, the semantic ambiguity of model correspondences, and the definition of a consistency notion. Our main contribution is the assessment of existing techniques from the field of process integration in order to address these challenges. It becomes evident that these techniques cannot be applied in a straight-forward manner. Instead, they have to be extended and adapted in order to cope with the requirements for vertical model alignment.

On the one hand, some of the identified white-spots can directly be addressed in future work. For instance, mismatches that are not covered by existing work have to be formalised and classified. Subsequently, techniques for identifying differing semantics of correspondences have to be investigated. On the other hand, for other open issues, it is uncertain how existing techniques should be extended or adapted. In this paper, we pointed out three research questions that have to be answered as a prerequisite for the definition of an alignment framework. Currently, we are addressing these questions empirically. As a result, we hope to clarify the requirements framework for reasonable vertical model alignment.

References

1. Ramackers, G.J.: Integrated Object Modelling. PhD thesis, Leiden University, Thesis Publishers, Amsterdam (1994)
2. Grover, V., Fiedler, K., Teng, J.: Exploring the Success of Information Technology Enabled Businessprocess Reengineering. IEEE Transactions on Engineering Management 41(3), 276–284 (1994)

3. Rolland, C., Prakash, N.: Bridging the Gap Between Organisational Needs and ERP Functionality. Requirements Engineering 5(3), 180–193 (2000)
4. Henkel, M., Zdravkovic, J., Johannesson, P.: Service-based processes: Design for business and technology. In: Aiello, M., Aoyama, M., Curbera, F., Papazoglou, M.P. (eds.) ICSOC, pp. 21–29. ACM, New York (2004)
5. Koehler, J., Hauser, R., Küster, J.M., Ryndina, K., Vanhatalo, J., Wahler, M.: The Role of Visual Modeling and Model Transformations in Business-driven Development. Electr. Notes Theor. Comput. Sci. 211, 5–15 (2008)
6. Rosemann, M.: Preparation of Process Modeling. In: Process Management: A Guide for the Design of Business Processes, pp. 41–78. Springer, Heidelberg (2003)
7. OMG: Business Process Modeling Notation (BPMN) 1.1(January 2008)
8. Bergholtz, M., Jayaweera, P., Johannesson, P., Wohed, P.: A Pattern and Dependency Based Approach to the Design of Process Models. In: Atzeni, P., Chu, W., Lu, H., Zhou, S., Ling, T.-W. (eds.) ER 2004. LNCS, vol. 3288, pp. 724–739. Springer, Heidelberg (2004)
9. Andersson, B., Bergholtz, M., Edirisuriya, A., Ilayperuma, T., Johannesson, P.: A Declarative Foundation of Process Models. In: Pastor, Ó., Falcão e Cunha, J. (eds.) CAiSE 2005. LNCS, vol. 3520, pp. 233–247. Springer, Heidelberg (2005)
10. Decker, G.: Bridging the Gap between Business Processes and existing IT Functionality. In: Proceedings of the 1st International Workshop on Design of Service-Oriented Applications (WDSOA), Amsterdam, The Netherlands, pp. 17–24 (2005)
11. Frank, H., Eder, J.: Towards an Automatic Integration of Statecharts. In: Akoka, J., Bouzeghoub, M., Comyn-Wattiau, I., Métais, E. (eds.) ER 1999. LNCS, vol. 1728, pp. 430–444. Springer, Heidelberg (1999)
12. Mendling, J., Simon, C.: Business Process Design by View Integration. In: [28], pp. 55–64
13. Küster, J.M., Koehler, J., Ryndina, K.: Improving Business Process Models with Reference Models in Business-Driven Development. In: [28], pp. 35–44
14. Dijkman, R.M.: A Classification of Differences between Similar Business Processes. In: EDOC, pp. 37–50. IEEE Computer Society, Los Alamitos (2007)
15. Dijkman, R.M.: Diagnosing differences between business process models. In: Dumas, M., Reichert, M., Shan, M.-C. (eds.) BPM 2008. LNCS, vol. 5240, pp. 261–277. Springer, Heidelberg (2008)
16. Dijkman, R.M., Quartel, D.A.C., Pires, L.F., van Sinderen, M.: A Rigorous Approach to Relate Enterprise and Computational Viewpoints. In: EDOC, pp. 187–200. IEEE Computer Society, Los Alamitos (2004)
17. van Dongen, B.F., Dijkman, R.M., Mendling, J.: Measuring Similarity between Business Process Models. In: Bellahsene, Z., Léonard, M. (eds.) CAiSE 2008. LNCS, vol. 5074, pp. 450–464. Springer, Heidelberg (2008)
18. Li, C., Reichert, M., Wombacher, A.: On Measuring Process Model Similarity based on High-level Change Operations. In: Li, Q., Spaccapietra, S., Yu, E., Olivé, A. (eds.) ER 2008. LNCS, vol. 5231, pp. 248–264. Springer, Heidelberg (2008)
19. Soffer, P.: Refinement equivalence in model-based reuse: Overcoming differences in abstraction level. J. Database Manag. 16(3), 21–39 (2005)
20. Basten, T., van der Aalst, W.M.P.: Inheritance of Behavior. Journal of Logic and Algebraic Programming (JLAP) 47(2), 47–145 (2001)
21. Ebert, J., Engels, G.: Observable or Invocable Behaviour - You Have to Choose. Technical Report 94-38, Department of Computer Science, Leiden University (December 1994)
22. Schrefl, M., Stumptner, M.: Behavior-consistent specialization of object life cycles. ACM Trans. Softw. Eng. Methodol. 11(1), 92–148 (2002)

23. Weidlich, M., Decker, G., Weske, M., Barros, A.: Towards Vertical Alignment of Process Models - A Collection of Mismatches. Technical report, Hasso Plattner Institute (2008),
    http://bpt.hpi.uni-potsdam.de/pub/Public/BptPublications/
    collection_of_mismatches.pdf
24. Hohpe, G., Woolf, B.: Enterprise Integration Patterns: Designing, Building, and Deploying Messaging Solutions. Addison-Wesley, Reading (2003)
25. Grossmann, G., Schrefl, M., Stumptner, M.: Classification of business process correspondences and associated integration operators. In: Wang, S., Tanaka, K., Zhou, S., Ling, T.-W., Guan, J., Yang, D.-q., Grandi, F., Mangina, E.E., Song, I.-Y., Mayr, H.C. (eds.) ER Workshops 2004. LNCS, vol. 3289, pp. 653–666. Springer, Heidelberg (2004)
26. Henkel, M., Zdravkovic, J.: Supporting development and evolution of service-based processes. In: ICEBE, pp. 647–656. IEEE CS, Los Alamitos (2005)
27. Davis, F.D.: Perceived usefulness, perceived ease of use, and user acceptance of information technology. MIS Quarterly, 319–339 (September 1989)
28. Eder, J., Dustdar, S. (eds.): BPM Workshops 2006. LNCS, vol. 4103. Springer, Heidelberg (2006)

Ontology-Based Description and Discovery of Business Processes

Khalid Belhajjame[1] and Marco Brambilla[2]

[1] School of Computer Science, University of Manchester,
Oxford Road, M13 9PL - United Kingdom
[2] Politecnico di Milano, Dipartimento di Elettronica e Informazione
P.za L. Da Vinci, 32. I-20133 Milano - Italy
`Khalid.Belhajjame@manchester.ac.uk, Marco.Brambilla@polimi.it`

Abstract. Just like web services, business processes can be stored in public repositories to be shared and used by third parties, e.g., as building blocks for constructing new business processes. The success of such a paradigm depends partly on the availability of effective search tools to locate business processes that are relevant to the user purposes. A handful of researchers have investigated the problem of business process discovery using as input syntactical and structural information that describes business processes. In this work, we explore an additional source of information encoded in the form of annotations that semantically describe business processes. Specifically, we show how business processes can be semantically described using the so called *abstract business processes*. These are designated by concepts from an ontology which additionally captures their relationships. We show how this ontology can be built in an automatic fashion from a collection of (concrete) business processes, and we illustrate how it can be refined by domain experts and used in the discovery of business processes, with the purpose of reuse and increase in design productivity.

1 Introduction

The last two decades showed that *business process modeling (BPM)* is the solution of choice of multiple companies and government institutions for describing and enacting their internal and external work procedures. Generally speaking, a business process is modelled as a series of activities connected together using data and control dependencies. Once modelled, business processes can be made available either publicly or accessible to a specific community to share the know-how between institutions and promote the reuse of existing business processes, e.g., as building blocks for constructing new business processes. The success of such a paradigm depends partly on the availability of a means by which users can locate business processes that are relevant for their purposes.

A handful of researchers have investigated the problem of business process reuse based on similarity and repository management. Eyal *et al.* proposed a visual query language for discovering business processes modelled using BPEL [3].

T. Halpin et al. (Eds.): BPMDS 2009 and EMMSAD 2009, LNBIP 29, pp. 85–98, 2009.
© Springer-Verlag Berlin Heidelberg 2009

Goderis *et al.* developed a framework for discovering workflows using similarity metrics that consider the activities composing the workflows and their relationships [6]. Corrales *et al.* developed a tool for comparing the controlflow of business processes [5].

The above solutions to business process discovery use as input the workflows that model the activities that constitute the business processes and their dependencies in term of controlflow. Yet, a workflow is not a complete description of the business processes. In this paper, we argue that a more effective discovery of business processes can be achieved if they are semantically described. Specifically, we show how such information can be encoded within an ontology that can be used for:

– *Abstracting discovery queries:* The user is able to formulate his/her queries in terms of the tasks (semantics) fulfilled by the desired business processes.
– *Exploiting relationships between business processes:* Business processes are inter-dependent. These dependencies can be explicitly described in the ontology in the form of binary relationships that can be used, amongst other things, for increasing the recall of discovery queries.

The paper is structured as follows. We introduce business processes and formally define the concept of abstract business process in Section 2. We present the ontology used for describing business processes in Section 3, and then show how it can be created and populated automatically in Section 4, starting from a set of concrete business process models. We show how the business process ontology can be used for discovering business processes in Section 5, and present a simple case study in order to exemplify and assess the effectiveness of our solution in Section 6. We compare our solution with existing related works in Section 7, and close the paper in Section 8.

2   Preliminaries

2.1   Business Process

A business process is a collection of interrelated tasks, which aim at solving a particular issue. It can be decomposed into several sub-processes, which have their own peculiarities, but also contribute to achieving the goal of the super-process. Execution of tasks is typically constrained by dependency rules among tasks, that consist of sequence constraints, branching and merging rules, pre- and post- conditions, event management points, and so on.

A business process can be specified by means of a workflow model, i.e., a visual representation of the correct sequence of tasks that leads to the achievement of the goal. The notations for workflow modelling provide the proper primitives for defining processes, tasks, actors, control flow and data flow between tasks. In our work, we will adopt a particular business process notation, namely BPMN (Business Process Management Notation) [4] and the terminology defined by the Workflow Management Coalition and the Business Process Management

Initiative and the concepts specified by BPDM (Business Process Definition Metamodel) [11], a platform- and notation- independent metamodel for defining business processes. However, we propose a general purpose approach, which is valid regardless of the adopted notation. The workflow model is based on the concepts of Process, Case (a process instance), Activity (the unit of work composing a process), Activity instance (an instantiation of an activity within a case), Actor (a user role intervening in the process), and Constraint (logical precedence and enabling rules for activities). Processes can be structured using a variety of control constructs: sequence, gateways implementing AND-splits (a single thread of control splits into two or more independent threads), AND-joins (blocking convergence point of two or more parallel activities), OR-splits (point in which one among multiple alternative branches is taken), OR-joins (non-blocking convergence point), iterations, pre- and post-conditions, events (happenings categorized by type). The flow of the process is described by means of arrows, that can represent either the control flow, the exchanged messages flow, or the data flow between the tasks. Activities are grouped into pools based on the participating organization that is in charge of the activity. Pool lanes are usually used to distinguish different user types within the organizations.

Figure 1 exemplifies a BPMN workflow diagram of online purchase, payment, and delivery of goods. The customer can choose the products to purchase, then submits his payment information. Then, two parallel tasks are executed by the seller employees: the warehouse manager registers the shipping of the order, and a secretary prepares the bill.

For the purpose of this paper, we define a business process bp by the tuple: $\langle nameBP, A, CF \rangle$, where:

- $nameBP$ is the name identifying the business process.
- A is the set of activities composing bp. An activity $a \in A$ is defined as $\langle nameA, roleA \rangle$, where $nameA$ is the activity identifier, and $roleA$ is a string determining its role within the business process.

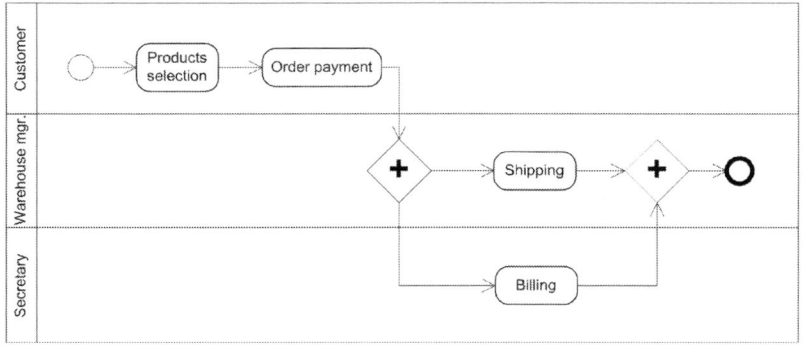

Fig. 1. Example of business process model expressed in BPMN

- $CF \subseteq (A \times OP) \cup (OP \times A)$ is the controlflow. OP is the set of operators used for defining controlflow dependencies between the activities in A. Specifically: $OP = \{Sequence, ANDssplit, ANDjoin, ORsplit, ORjoin\}$.

We say that a business process $bp1$ is a sub-process of a business process of $bp2$ if the activities of $bp1$ are activities of $bp2$, i.e., $bp1.A \subseteq bp2.A$, the control dependencies of $bp1$ are also controlflow dependencies of $bp2$, i.e., $bp1.CF \subseteq bp2.CF$, and the controlflow of $bp1$ forms a connected directed graph.

2.2   Abstract Business Process

An *abstract business process (ABP)* is a representative of a class of *equivalent* business processes, sharing the same set of activities and flow structure. In ABPs the activities are generic task descriptions, associated with semantic labels that provide information about the capabilities of the processing units able to perform the activities and descriptions of the data to be consumed and produced. An ABP can be implemented by several concrete business processes, which define the exact behaviour of the tasks and the names of the actors of the process and the association of the activities with the actors in charge of their execution. ABP descriptions are encoded in the form of annotations that map to concepts from ontologies that specify the semantics of these elements in the real world.

An ontology is commonly defined as an explicit specification of a conceptualisation [7]. Formally, an ontology θ can be defined as a set of concepts, $\theta = \{c1,\ldots,cn\}$. The concepts are related to each other using the sub-concept relationship, which links general concepts to more specific ones. For example, *CreditCardPayment* is a sub-concept of *OrderPayment*, for which we write *CreditCardPayment $\sqsubseteq$ OrderPayment*. The concepts can also be connected by other kinds of binary relationships.

To semantically annotate the activities of a business process, we use the task ontology, θ_{task}. This ontology captures information about the action carried out by the activities within a domain of interest. In bioinformatics, for instance, an activity can be annotated using a term that describes the *in silico* analysis it performs. Example of bioinformatics analyses include *sequence alignment* and *protein identification*. Another example of a task ontology can be defined in the electronic commerce context. In this case, activities are annotated in terms of business transactions they implement. For instance, business transactions may include *quotation request*, *order confirmation*, and *credit card payment*.

To retrieve the task annotation of service operations we consider the function *task()* defined as *task: $ACTIVITY \rightarrow \theta_{task}$*, where $ACTIVITY$ denotes the domain of business process activities. We can now formally define an ABP.

Abstract business process. An abstract business process *abp* is defined as the pair: $\langle T, CF \rangle$, where

- T is the set of tasks that constitute abp: $T \subseteq \theta_{task}$.
- $CF \subseteq (T \times OP) \cup (OP \times T)$ is the control flow relating the tasks in T.

To map the tasks of two abstract business processes, we consider two classes of functions the domain of which are denoted by *MapEquiv* and *MapSpec*. The functions that belong to *MapEquiv* are used to map the tasks of a given abstract business process to the tasks of another abstract business process that perform *the same or equivalent tasks*. Let $abp1$ and $abp2$ be two abstract business processes and let f_{map}: $abp1.T \rightarrow abp2.T$ a function that maps the tasks of $abp1$ to those of $abp2$. $f_{map} \in MapEquiv$ iff:

$$\forall\ t\ \in abp1.T,\ task(f_{map}(t))\ \equiv\ task(t)$$

The functions in *MapSpec* are used to map the tasks of a given abstract business process to the tasks of another abstract business process that perform equivalent or more specific tasks. Let $abp1$ and $abp2$ be two abstract business processes and let f_{map}: $abp1.T \rightarrow abp2.T$ a function that maps the tasks of $abp1$ to those of $abp2$. $f_{map} \in MapSpec$ iff:

$$\forall\ t\ \in abp1.T,\ task(f_{map}(t))\ \sqsubseteq\ task(t)$$

To construct the abstract business process abp corresponding to a (concrete) business process bp, we use the function *abstractBP()* with the following signature: *abstractBP*: $BP \rightarrow ABP$, where BP denotes the domain of business processes and ABP the domain of abstract business processes.

3   Ontology for Business Processes and Their Relationships

To describe business processes, we define the *business process ontology*, θ_{BP}. The concepts of this ontology designate abstract business processes. Given a concept c from business process ontology θ_{BP}, we use the function *getABP(abp)*: $\theta_{BP} \rightarrow ABP$ to retrieve the abstract business process designated by c. The concepts in the ontology θ_{BP} are related using binary properties that encode relationships between abstract business processes. Specifically, we identify four binary properties to encode process relationships, namely, *equivalence*, *specialisation*, *overlap*, and *partOf*.

Process equivalence. Two abstract processes are equivalent iff their respective constituent tasks are equivalent tasks and are connected using the same controlflow. Formally, let $c1$ and $c2$ two concepts from the business process ontology θ_{BP} that designate the abstract business processes $abp1$ and $abp2$, respectively. That is $abp1 = getABP(c1)$ and $abp2 = getABP(c2)$. The two concepts $c1$ and $c2$ are equivalent, for which we write $c1 \equiv c2$, iff there exists a mapping function f_{equiv}: $abp1.T \rightarrow abp2.T$ in *MapEquiv* such that:

$$abp2.CF = \{(f_{equiv}(t), op),(t, op) \in abp1.CF\} \cup \{(op, f_{equiv}(t)),(op, t) \in abp1.CF\}$$

Process Specialisation. Let $c1$ and $c2$ be two concepts from the business process ontology θ_{BP} that designate the abstract business processes $abp1$ and $abp2$, respectively. $c1$ specialises $c2$ iff the tasks of $abp1$ are equivalent to or more specific than the tasks of $abp2$, and that they have the same controlflow. Formally, $c1$ specialises $c2$, for which we write $c1 \sqsubseteq c2$, iff there exists a mapping function f_{spec}: $abp1.T \rightarrow abp2.T$ in *MapSpec* such that:

$$abp2.CF = \{(f_{spec}(t), op),(t, op) \in abp1.CF\} \cup \{(op, f_{spec}(t)),(op, t) \in abp1.CF\}$$

Part-of relationship. Let $c1$ and $c2$ be two concepts from the business process ontology θ_{BP} that designate the abstract business processes $abp1$ and $abp2$, respectively. We say that $c1$ is *part-of* $c2$ iff there exists a concept $c3$ that is equivalent to $c1$ and that designates abstract business process $abp3 = getABP(c3)$ that is sub-process of $abp2$.

Process overlap. Two concepts $c1$ and $c2$ overlap iff their respective ABPs have one or more tasks in common. Let $abp1$ and $abp2$ the abstract business processes designated by $c1$ and $c2$, respectively. $c1$ and $c2$ overlap iff: $abp1.T \cap abp2.T \neq \emptyset$.

As mentioned earlier, the concepts in the business process ontology designate abstract business processes. Given a concept c from the business process ontology, the function $getAbstractBP(c)$: $\theta_{BP} \rightarrow ABP$ returns the abstract business process designated by c.

To manipulate the business process ontology, we assume the existence of the following operations:

defineConcept: $ABP \rightarrow \theta_{BP}$
defineProperty: $PROPERTY \times \theta_{BP} \times \theta_{BP} \rightarrow Boolean$
addInstance: $BP \times \theta_{BP} \rightarrow Boolean$

To define a new concept c that represents an abstract business process abp in the business process ontology, we use the operation *defineConcept(abp)*. The operation returns the concept defined. The operation *defineProperty(p,c1,c2)* defines a property $p \in Property$ between the concepts $c1$ and $c2$. *Property* denotes the domain of binary properties, i.e., *Property= {equivalence, specialisation, part-of, overlap}*.

Business processes are defined as instances of the concepts in the business process ontology. Specifically, a business processes bp can be defined as an instance of a concept c iff c designate the abstract business process abp corresponding to bp: i.e., $abp = abstractBP(bp)$. To define bp as an instance of the concept c, we use the operation *addInstance(bp,c)*. The operation returns true if it is executed successfully and false, otherwise.

4   Creating and Populating the Ontology

The business process ontology is created and populated in an automatic fashion. Figure 2 illustrates the generation process: given a set of business processes together with semantic annotations describing the tasks of their constituent

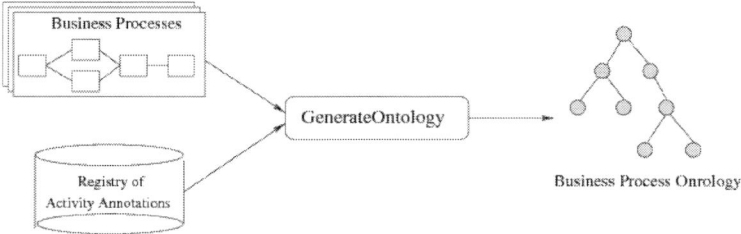

Fig. 2. Generation of the business process ontology

activities, the concepts of the business process ontology are defined. The binary properties that relate the concepts in the business process ontology, as seen in the previous section, are also automatically inferred. Furthermore, (concrete) business processes are defined as instances of the ontology concepts, thereby allowing the business process ontology to be used for business process discovery. The business process ontology is created according to the following algorithm:

```
Algorithm GenerateOntology
input BP
output θ_BP
begin
1       for each bp ∈ BP do
2           abp = abstract(bp)
3           if (∃ c ∈ θ_BP, abp = getAbstractBP(c))
4           then
5               addInstance(bp,c)
6           else
7               c := defineConcept(abp)
8               addInstance(bp,c)
9               deriveAndAssertProperties(c)
end
```

For each business process *bp*, the corresponding abstract process *abp* is built *(line 2)*. If the business process ontology contains a concept *c* that designates the abstract business process *abp* *(line 3)*, then *bp* is defined as an instance of *c* *(line 5)*. If not, then a new concept is defined within the business process ontology to represent the abstract business process *abp* *(line 7)*, and *bp* is defined as an instance of the concept defined *(line 8)*. Furthermore, the binary properties that relate the newly defined concept *c* to other concepts in the business process ontology are derived and asserted using the *deriveAndAssertProperties(c)* subroutine *(line 9)*, operating as follows. The ABP designated by the concept *c* is compared to the ABPs designated by other concepts in the business process ontology. If the two abstract processes are found to be equivalent (see Section 3) then an *equivalence* property is defined for the respective concepts in the business process ontology. The *specialisation*, *part-of*, and *overlap* are defined in a similar fashion.

5   Discovering Business Processes

Most of existing proposals to business process discovery adopt the following paradigm. The user first formulates a query specifying the business process of interests by describing the activities that compose the business processes (e.g., specifying the actors in charge) and the controlflow that connects them. Then, a matching operation extracts the business processes that match the user query.

We adopt a different approach that exploits information about business processes and their relationships encoded within the business process ontology. A discovery query takes the form of an abstract business process abp_{user} designed by the user by selecting concepts from the task ontology and connecting them using a controlflow graph. As a running example, consider that the user specifies the abstract business process illustrated in Figure 3. This is a simple process taken from the domain of bioinformatics and is composed of four tasks. First, the *RetrieveBiologicalSequence* fetches a biological sequence from accessible biosources. Then, the gene annotations associated with the sequence retrieved are fetched using the *FindBiologicalFunction* task, and its homologous sequences are fetched using the *FindSimilarSequences* task: these two tasks are concurrently performed. Finally, the phylogenetic tree of the sequence retrieved and its homologues is constructed using the *ConstructPhylogeneticTree* task. We distinguish the following cases for discovering the business processes that implement the abstract business process specified by the user.

- There exists in the business process ontology a concept *abp* that is equivalent to the abstract business process specified by the user, i.e., $abp_{user} = abp$. The result of the user query, in this case, is the set of business processes that are instances of *abp*: *instances(abp)*.
- Suppose now that there does not exist any concept in the business process ontology that is equivalent to abp_{user}. In this case, the concepts *ABP* in the business process ontology that are subconcepts of *abp* are retrieved: $ABP = \{abp \in \theta_{BP} \ s.t. \ abp \sqsubseteq abp_{user}\}$.

    As an example, the abstract business process illustrated in Figure 4 is subsumed by the abstract business process illustrated in Figure 3. Indeed, the task *RetrieveProteinSequence* is a subconcept of *RetrieveBiologicalSequence*, *FindSimilarBiologicalSequences* is a subconcept of *FindSimilarProteinSequences*, and the remaining two tasks, *FindBiologicalFunction* and *ConstructPhylogeneticTree* are subconcepts of themselves.

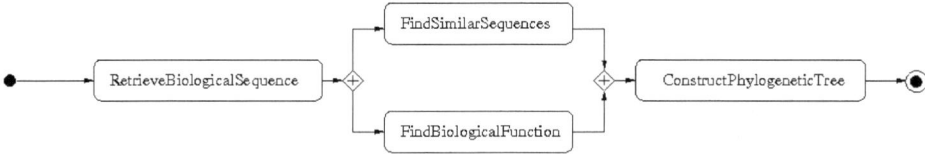

Fig. 3. Example of abstract business process specified by the user

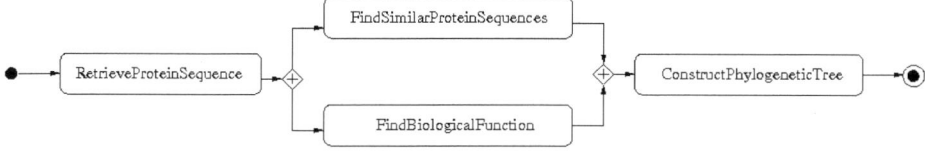

Fig. 4. Example of ABP that is subconcept of that illustrated in Figure 3

The query result in this case is the set of business processes that are instances of at least one abstract process in *ABP*. That is:

$$\bigcup_{abp_i \,\in\, ABP} instancesOf(abp_i)$$

- The business process ontology may not contain any concept that is equivalent or subconcept of the abstract business process specified by the user, abp_{user}. Instead of returning a null result to the user request, we attempt to create business processes that match the user request by aggregating other business processes.

The algorithm for building new aggregated business processes as further responses to the user queries is the following:

1. The set *ABP* of concepts in the business process ontology designating abstract business processes that are part of abp_{user} are retrieved. That is: $ABP = \{abp_i \in \theta_{BP} \ s.t. \ abp_i \ partOf \ abp_{user}\}$
2. Of the set *ABP* we extract a subset *ABP'* of abstract business processes, of which the union of tasks is a set that contains all the tasks required for building abp_{user}. Specifically:

$$\bigcup\nolimits_{abp_i \,\in\, ABP'} abp_i.T \ = \ abp_{user}.T$$

For example, the abstract business processes illustrated in Figure 5 are parts of the abstract business process illustrated in in Figure 3. Moreover, the union of the tasks that compose the abstract business processes in Figure 5 covers all the tasks that compose the abstract business process illustrated in Figure 3.
3. For each abstract process abp_i in *ABP'*, we retrieve its business process instances, i.e., $instancesOf(abp_i)$
4. The result of the user query are business processes that are obtained by substituting the abstract business processes abp_i that are part of abp_{user}, with business processes that are instances of abp_i. As an example, consider that abp_{user} is composed of two abstract business processes abp and abp' that are connected using a sequence operator. And suppose that:
   - $instancesOf(abp) = \{bp_1, bp_2\}$, i.e., there are two business processes bp_1 and bp_2 that are instances of abp.

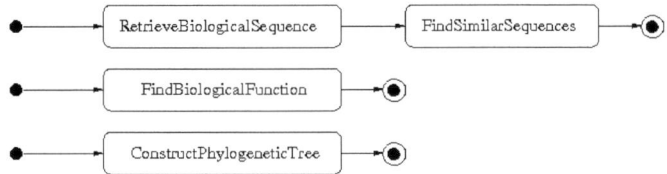

Fig. 5. Example of ABP that are parts of that illustrated in Figure 3

- *instancesOf(abp′)* $= \{bp'_1, bp'_2\}$, i.e., there are two business processes bp'_1 and bp'_2 that are instances of *abp′*.

The business processes returned to the user are those obtained by substituting *abp* and *abp′* with thier instances. The business processes obtained using any possible combination of the instances of the business processes of *abp* and *abp'* are returned: in total the following combinations are used to build the business processes that are instances of abp_{user}: abp_1 and abp'_1; abp_1 and abp'_2; abp_2 and abp'_1; abp_2 and abp'_2.

In addition to the query paradigm just described , we developed an additional method in which business processes are *discovered by example*. In this case, instead of specifying an abstract business process, the user specifies an actual business process bp_{user} that is composed of activities (instead of tasks). The processing of this kind of queries is implemented in two phases:

- In the first phase, we construct an abstract business process abp_{user} that corresponds to the business process specified by the user bp_{user}.
- Then, we use the method for discovering business process presented above using as input abp_{user}.

This paradigm for querying business processes is suitable for users who are not familiar with the task ontology and, therefore, may not be able to specify an abstract business process that reflects their true needs. Also, it can be useful for designers who already have specified a business process and are interested in finding similar business processes developed by other designers.

6   Case Study

To exemplify and give a flavour of the effectiveness of our method, we describe a simple case study aiming at: (1) showing that the business process ontology can be created automatically; and (2) showing that the recall of business process discovery queries increases when using the ontology.

Let's consider 10 business processes bp_i, $1 \leq i \leq 10$, covering all possible controlflow dependency types and with activities randomly annotated using a task ontology that we created for the sake of our evaluation. Using the algorithm presented in section 4, we automatically generated the business process ontology illustrated in Figure 6. Notice that the number of concepts in this ontology is 7

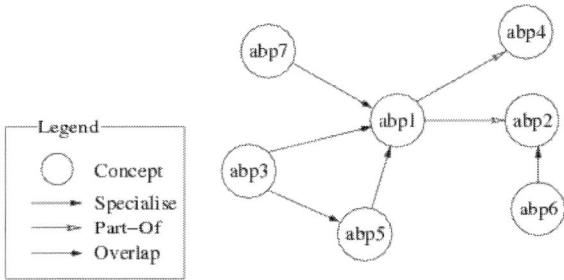

Fig. 6. The business process ontology automatically created using example BPs

instead of 10, because some of the business processes were instances of the same ABP (e.g., both bp_1 and bp_4 were instances of the abstract business process denoted by the concept abp_1).

The business processes $\{bp_1, \ldots, bp_{10}\}$ are pair-wise different. That is:

$$\forall\, i, j \,\in\, \{1, \ldots, 10\},\; i \neq j \,\rightarrow\, bp_i \neq bp_j$$

Therefore, discovery queries that rely solely on the structural properties of business processes always return as a result *1* business process at most. To see whether the use of the ontology for answering business process discovery queries increase the recall, we posed the following queries over the ontology illustrated in Figure 6.

Q1 : returns the business processes instances of the concept *abp1*.
Q2 : returns the business processes instances of *abp1* and its subconcepts.
Q3 : returns the business processes instances of the concept *abp1*, its subconcepts, and the concepts *abp1* is part-of.
Q4 : returns the business processes instances of the concept *abp1*, its subconcepts, and the concepts that are part-of *abp1*.
Q5 : returns the business processes instances of the concept *abp1* and the concepts that overlap with *abp1*.

Table 1. Number of results obtained using the business process ontology

	Q1	Q2	Q3	Q4	Q5
Number of returned business processes	2	3	6	3	10

Table 1 illustrates the number of business processes returned for each of the above queries. It shows an increase in recall compared to the case where the queries are evaluated relying only on structural information of business processes. For example, it shows that the number of business processes that are equivalent to or specialises the abstract business process abp_1 is *3*. Also, relaxing the discovery query conditions implies an increase in the recall. For example, by considering the abstract business processes of which abp_1 is part-of, the number of business processes returned is 6. In summary, this shows that:

- The ontology used for capturing semantic information about business processes and their relationships can be created in an automatic fashion.
- The use of the ontology for evaluating business process discovery queries increases the recall with respect to the structural information only.
- Discovery queries can be relaxed to increase the recall by considering relationships such as *part-of* and *overlap*.

7   Related Work

Recently, many proposals have attempted to facilitate the discovery of business processes. Most of the approaches only apply graph-based comparison or XML-based querying on the business process specifications, disregarding ontology-based similarity discovery. In early works, Van der Aalst *et al.* [12] posed the basis of the concepts of inheritance between business processes, that we exploit in the relationships described in our ontology. Other works [13], defined the formal foundations and the semantics of business processes and similarity, on which we base our definitions.

Eyal *et al.* [3] proposed BP-QL, a visual query language for querying and discovering business processes modelled using BPEL. Lu and Sadiq [9] proposes a way for comparing and retrieving business process variants. Corrales *et al.* [5] developed a tool for comparing the controlflow of business processes in the scenario of service matchmaking, by reducing the problem of behavioral matching to a graph matching problem (i.e., receiving as input two BPEL models and evaluating the graph-based distance between them). These proposal offer a query mechanism on the process structure and topology only.

Goderis *et al.* [6] developed a framework for discovering workflows using similarity metrics that consider the activities composing the workflows and their relationships, implementing a ranking algorithm.

[10] proposed a framework for flexible queries on BP models, for providing better results when too few processes are extracted. [1] proposes the BPMN-Q query language for visual semantic queries over BPMN models. Kiefer *et al.* [8] proposed the use of semantic business processes to enable the integration and inter-operability of business processes across organizational boundaries. They offer an imprecise query engine based on iSPARQL to perform the process retrieval task and to find inter-organizational matching at the boundaries between partners. The work of Zhuge *et al.* [14] is instead closer to our approach, presenting an inexact matching approach based on SQL-like queries on ontology repositories. The focus is on flexible workflow process reuse, based on a multi-valued process specialization relationship. The matching degree between two workflow processes is determined by the matching degrees of their corresponding sub-processes or activities. Differently from us, the ontology cannot be automatically built from the workflow models and does not include explicit relationships between business processes, but only exploits ontological distances.

Beco *el al.* [2] specified the language OWL-WS (OWL for workflow and services) for describing ontologies of workflows and services aiming at providing grid architectures with dynamic behaviour on workflow specification and service invocation. The resulting workflow ontology did not focus on relationships between business processes and was not exploited for querying workflow similarity. Instead, the language was mainly used for specifying adaptive business processes.

8 Conclusions

In this paper we presented an approach for describing, storing, and discovering Business Processes. We extended the concept of similarity between process models by exploiting ontology definitions and the concept of abstract business process (ABP). Queries based on ABPs allow reuse and matching of business process models, thus saving time and reducing cost of implementation of enterprise workflows. Thanks to ontology-based comparison, we can evaluate the similarity between processes in a more flexible way with respect to traditional approaches, and therefore identify more potential similarities, for instance based on activity descriptions that are semantically close.

Ongoing and future works include the development of a large-scale repository of real business processes in the banking field, where some real applications are being developed for a major European bank.

References

1. Awad, A., Polyvyanyy, A., Weske, M.: Semantic querying of business process models. In: Enterprise Distributed Object Computing Conference (EDOC), pp. 85–94 (2008)
2. Beco, S., Cantalupo, B., Giammarino, L., Matskanis, N., Surridge, M.: Owl-ws: A workflow ontology for dynamic grid service composition. In: e-Science, pp. 148–155 (2005)
3. Beeri, C., Eyal, A., Kamenkovich, S., Milo, T.: Querying business processes. In: Dayal, U., Whang, K.-Y., Lomet, D.B., Alonso, G., Lohman, G.M., Kersten, M.L., Cha, S.K., Kim, Y.-K. (eds.) VLDB, pp. 343–354. ACM, New York (2006)
4. BPMI and OMG. Business Process Management Notation (BPMN) 1.2 (2009), http://www.bpmn.org/
5. Corrales, J.C., Grigori, D., Bouzeghoub, M.: Bpel processes matchmaking for service discovery. In: Meersman, R., Tari, Z. (eds.) OTM 2006. LNCS, vol. 4275, pp. 237–254. Springer, Heidelberg (2006)
6. Goderis, A., Li, P., Goble, C.A.: Workflow discovery: the problem, a case study from e-science and a graph-based solution. In: ICWS, pp. 312–319. IEEE Computer Society, Los Alamitos (2006)
7. Gruber, T.: A translation approach to portable ontology specifications. Knowledge Acquisition 5(2) (1993)
8. Kiefer, C., Bernstein, A., Lee, H.J., Klein, M., Stocker, M.: Semantic process retrieval with iSPARQL. In: Franconi, E., Kifer, M., May, W. (eds.) ESWC 2007. LNCS, vol. 4519, pp. 609–623. Springer, Heidelberg (2007)
9. Lu, R., Sadiq, S.: Managing process variants as an information resource. In: Dustdar, S., Fiadeiro, J.L., Sheth, A.P. (eds.) BPM 2006. LNCS, vol. 4102, pp. 426–431. Springer, Heidelberg (2006)
10. Markovic, I., Pereira, A.C., Stojanovic, N.: A framework for querying in business process modelling. In: Multikonferenz Wirtschaftsinformatik (February 2008)

11. OMG. Business Process Definition Metamodel (2006),
    http://www.omg.org/cgi-bin/doc?bei/03-01-06
12. van der Aalst, W.M.P.: Inheritance of Interorganizational Workflows to Enable
    B-to-B ECommerce. Electronic Commerce Research 2(3), 195–231 (2002)
13. van Glabbeek, R.: The linear time - branching time spectrum i; the semantics of
    concrete, sequential processes. In: Bergstra, J.A., Ponse, A., Smolka, S.A. (eds.)
    Handbook of Process Algebra, pp. 3–99 (2001)
14. Zhuge, H.: A process matching approach for flexible workflow process reuse. Infor-
    mation & Software Technology 44(8), 445–450 (2002)

A Method for Service Identification from Business Process Models in a SOA Approach

Leonardo Guerreiro Azevedo[1,2], Flávia Santoro[1,2], Fernanda Baião[1,2], Jairo Souza[1],
Kate Revoredo[1], Vinícios Pereira[1], and Isolda Herlain[3]

[1] NP2Tec – Research and Practice Group in Information Technology
[2] Departament of Applied Informatics, Federal University of the State of Rio de Janeiro
[3] Petrobras – Petróleo Brasileiro S/A
{azevedo, flavia.santoro, fernanda.baiao}@uniriotec.br,
{jairofsouza, katerevoredo,viniciospereira}@gmail.com,
iherlain.POLITEC@petrobras.com.br

Abstract. Various approaches for services development in SOA propose business processes as a starting point. However, there is a lack of systematic methods for services identification during business analysis. We believe that there has to exist a integrated view of organizational business processes to promote an effective SOA approach, which will improve IS requirements understanding. In this context, we propose a method, and a detailed set of activities, for guiding the service designer in identifying the most appropriate set of services to support organization business activities. The method was applied in a real scenario of a Brazilian Petroleum organization.

Keywords: Service Identification, Business Process Model, Service Life-cycle.

1 Introduction

The deployment of SOA (Service-Oriented Architecture) in an organization presents a series of challenges. As new architectural roles and development tasks were introduced by the service-oriented approach, the life-cycle model of traditional software engineering may not be directly applied.

The need for an approach for service development is recognized by several authors, who also agree that services should be defined according to organizational business processes and their corresponding models [1][2][3][4][6][7][8]. These works, however, do not present detailed methods for business analysis towards services identification and, very commonly, propose principles or guidelines that are very difficult to follow in practice due to the lack of systematic process. Moreover, they do not explicitly consider the role of the system designer, which in practice is responsible for aligning the service development demands to the actual organization scenario (strategic objectives and goals, current demands, amount of available resources), thus turning the service identification activity into a complex decision-making process. Yet, related works are typically proposed in domains where business processes are

T. Halpin et al. (Eds.): BPMDS 2009 and EMMSAD 2009, LNBIP 29, pp. 99–112, 2009.

automated and services may be directly derived from them. In real scenarios, how-ever, automated activities are mixed with manual or system-supported ones, all in the same process. Also, the same activity may appear in several processes in the organiza-tion, being implemented or supported by several information systems, in different departments of the organization. We believe that there has to be an integrated view of the organizational business processes, where each process is derived from the organ-izational key-value chain. This integrated view means the relationship among proc-esses (and consequently their models) are explicit, since they are part of a common process repository, they are linked to each other through interface elements and they share global artifacts such as clusters of data, business rules and business require-ments. This infrastructure makes possible a SOA analysis on business process to know about commonalities (common element definitions) and interfaces (execution and derivation relationships) among processes. This view must be considered to choose which processes should not/be automated, and is determinant for an effective service identification approach. In the process repository, it is possible to create an explicit link between business processes' constructs and candidate services and physi-cal (implemented) services descriptions. So, it makes easier to identify which services must be updated when business process changes, and vice-versa. So, evolution of the services themselves can trigger evolution of the supporting business processes, and following the link it is possible to track changes.

This paper proposes a top-down method for systematic service identification from business process models. Our main contribution relies on a set of heuristics that were validated in a real scenario. The results of a case study are presented.

2   Service Life-Cycle

Services life-cycle models present some additional challenges when compared to tradi-tional software engineering, for example: it is even more important to align business requirements with service-based IT solutions; typical distributed service development scenarios requires more complex security constraints; and handling service versioning to accommodate business changes is an essential issue. Thus, a pre-defined life-cycle model for organizational services is vital for the smooth operation of SOA [12].

Gu and Lago [4] claim that there is no consensus for a service life-cycle model in the literature. They evaluated a number of proposals and pointed to a well-defined sequence of steps divided into three phases: *design time*, *run time* and *change time*. Services identification is not handled explicitly, even though it is essential for service modeling. On the other hand, the service modeling step must be presented along with a set of step-by-step instructions [6]. Arsanjani [1] proposes the use of business proc-ess modeling in SOMA methodology. However, it is not proposed a systematic ap-proach for service identification from business process. The same lack of systematic approach appears in [3] [7] [8][9] [10] and [11]. Klose *et al* [7] and Papazoglou and Heuvel [11] presented some principles that should be observed during services identi-fication (e.g, low coupling, high cohesion and high level of granularity), while Marks and Bell [9] emphasized use/reuse of services. Mcbride [10] proposes scanning a repository of business requirements and look for: services that meet this requirement; services that could be adapted to meet it; or a new service that should be implemented. The approach of Jamshidi *et al.* [5] considers both an enterprise business process model and an enterprise entity model and proposes an approach for identifying and specifying enterprise software services. The approach assumes that the business process model is highly detailed (up to the level of elementary business process, or EBP) and that the granularity of each business entity is the same of the EBP which creates it. Process models in such a level of abstraction are not easy to accomplish. Besides, this proposal does not consider process model elements (business rules, business requirements, process flows). So, finding the service which meets a specific business requirement is totally dependent on the SOA analyst expertise and memory, and there is a lack of systematic methods for services identification during business analysis.

3 A Service Identification Method from Business Process Models

This section presents a method for identifying candidate services from a set of business processes models considered as input. Erl [2] defines a candidate service as an abstract (not implemented) service which, during the design phase of a service life-cycle model, could be chosen to be implemented as a service or as an application function. We further define 2 types of candidate services, namely: candidate data service, which is a service that performs CRUD (Create, Retrieve, Update and Delete) operations on databases; and candidate business service, which is a service that performs business rules which are not so related to CRUD operations. The method includes the phases presented in Figure 1.

Service identification starts when a demand for software development is received. The demand is represented as a set of requirements to be implemented (either as services or application functions). Other entries for the method are: "to-be process" models (designed processes in which the new requirements are already represented), and a set of business requirements already implemented in existing applications. The to-be process models are used for identification and classification of candidate services, while the business requirements of existing systems and the business requirements of the demand are used for consolidation of candidate services. The method returns a set of elements (tables, charts, services dependency graph) that should assist the service designer in making decisions about the most suitable implementation for an identified candidate service. In other words, the output of our proposal is a set of candidate services that is input for the next steps in a service life-cycle model (for example, service analysis and design). In these steps, the designer will decide if a candidate service is implemented as a physical service or if it must be considered as part of another service or if it must be discarded for implementation.

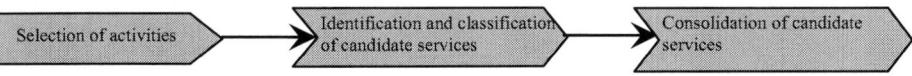

Fig. 1. Method for Service Identification

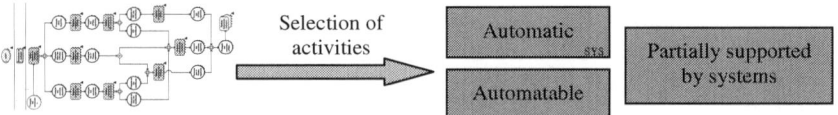

Fig. 2. Selection of Activities Phase

3.1   Phase 1: Selection of Activities

In the first phase (Figure 2), a set of activities are selected from to-be business process models. A process activity is selected if it is either automatic (performed entirely by a system with no manual interference), partially supported by systems or automatable (manually executed, but expected to be supported by a system). Manual activities (i.e., the ones that are not being considered for automation) are not selected, since it makes no sense to develop services for them.

3.2   Phase 2: Identification and Classification of Candidate Services

In the second phase (Figure 3), candidate services are identified by applying a set of proposed heuristics to the set of activities selected in phase 1. The proposed heuristics were defined in order to address both syntactical and semantic analysis of the process model.

Syntactical (structural) analysis of process models is carried out by considering the process model structure. Thus, we propose heuristics for service identification from each workflow pattern proposed in [13] [17]. A workflow pattern is the abstraction of a concrete form that remains repeatedly in specific contexts. The set of workflow patterns from [13] and [17] is often used as a benchmark for workflow management systems functionality. When relying on the workflow patterns specification for service identification, we assure covering all possible flow of activities that may be represented by a process model.

The semantic analysis of a process model towards service identification should consider all indications for process (total or partial) automation. Among all possible elements in a process model [15], it seemed obvious to address both "business requirement" and "business rule" elements in special, since their semantic indicates functionalities that should be implemented by a process-supporting service. Thus, we propose heuristics for service identification from each of these two elements, when it is associated to some of the activities selected from phase 1.

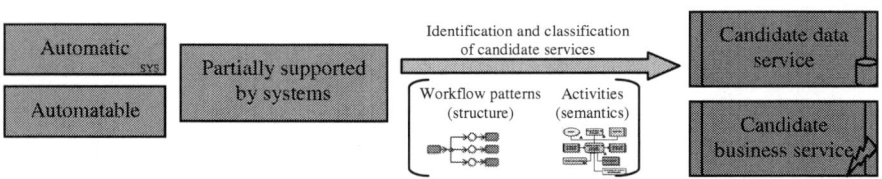

Fig. 3. Identification and Classification Phase

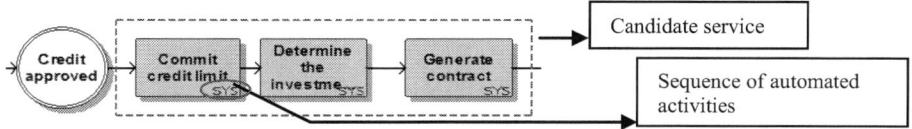

Fig. 4. Example of candidate service from a series of sequential activities

After being identified, each candidate service is classified (data, business or utility) according to its characteristics, i.e, if the service performs CRUD operations on databases or if it is a service that performs business rules; and utility service, which is a generalized service whose operations can be used in different context adjusting some of its parameters.

The following heuristics handle semantic analysis:

Heuristic 1 (Business Rule): A candidate service must be identified from a business rule.

Example: From the business rule "Select product supplier", described as "The selected supplier should be the one with the lowest price for the requested amount of product"; the candidate service *Select product supplier* must be identified. The candidate service has the same description than the rule from which it was identified.

Heuristic 2 (Business Requirement): A candidate service must be identified from a business requirement.

For example, from the business requirement "Retrieve quotes from suppliers", described as "The system ABC should retrieve prices of all suppliers who supply a certain product"; the candidate service "*Retrieve quotes from suppliers*" is identified. The candidate service description is the same of the requirement from which it was identified.

The following heuristics handle syntactical analysis:

Heuristic 3 (Sequence of Activities): A candidate service must be identified from a series of sequential activities.

For example, from the sequence of automated activities "Commit credit limit", "Determine the investment rate charged" and "Generate contract" (Figure 4), a candidate service must be identified.

Heuristic 4 (AND): A service candidate must be identified from an AND-pattern.

AND-pattern is a structure started in a point in the workflow where a single flow is divided into multiple streams, which can run in parallel, and finalized at a point in the workflow where multiple parallel streams converge into a single flow, synchronizing them, or where branches end in final event [17]. For example, a service candidate must be identified from the AND-pattern presented in Figure 5, for activities "Get customer's history", "Get financial information" and "Get information from stealing and robbery".

Heuristic 5 (XOR): A service candidate must be identified from a XOR-pattern.

XOR-pattern is a structure started in a point in the workflow where, based on a decision, one and only one of several branches of the flow is chosen, and finalized at a

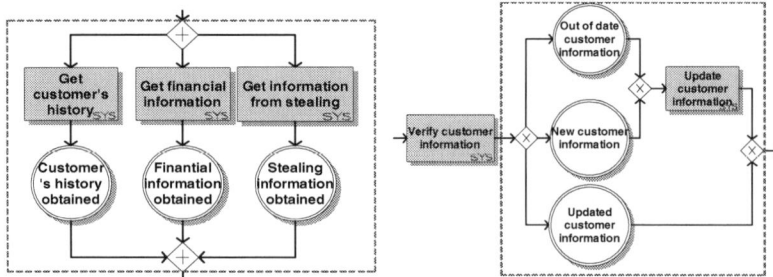

Fig. 5. Example of AND   **Fig. 6.** Example of XOR

point in the workflow where the ramifications of the flow come together without synchronization or when one or more of the ramifications ends in final event [17]. For example, a service candidate must be identified from the XOR-pattern of Figure 6.

Heuristic 6 (OR): A candidate service must be identified from an OR-pattern.

OR-pattern is a structure started in a point in the workflow where, based on a decision, one or more branches of the flow is chosen and ended at a point in the workflow where the various branches of the flow are joint. If more than one of the source streams was implemented, then it is necessary to synchronize them. Ramifications may also end in a final event [17].

Heuristic 7 (Loop): A candidate service must be identified from a Loop-pattern.

Loop-pattern is a structure of workflow where one or more activities can be performed repeatedly.

Heuristic 8 (Process Interface): Candidate services must be identified from the interaction between two processes: one candidate service to pass the information to the other process, and another service to receive the message.

Process interface is the representation of the mechanism that one process passes the flow to another process [15]. For example, in Figure 7, when the process "Treat store limit" (Figure 7a) identifies that the threshold of a commodity store was reached, it sends a request for goods to the process "Provide goods" (Figure 7b). In this case, a candidate service must be identified (in process "Verify stock level", Figure 7a) to pass the requirement for stock replenishment to the process "Process product order". On the other hand, another candidate service must be identified (in the process "Process product order", Figure 7b) to receive the request for stock replenishment and start to process product order.

Heuristic 9 (Multi-Instance Activity): Candidate services must be identified from a multi-instance activity: one candidate service to send the information to each instance of the multi-instance activity; one candidate service to represent each instance of the multi-instance activity; and, one candidate service to consolidate the outputs of the instances and to pass the result to the next step.

A multiple-instance task is a task that may have multiple distinct execution instances running concurrently within the same workflow case. Each of these instances executes independently. Only when a nominated number of these instances have completed, the task following the multiple instance task is initiated [13].

(a)   (b)

Fig. 7. Example of process interface service

Heuristic 9 is in accordance with patterns proposed in [13]. We propose: a sender service which is known as a broker and it is responsible for distributing the messages to each instance; a candidate service responsible for operating the rules and requirements described on the multi-instance activity; and, a candidate service to consolidate the outputs of each instance and pass the result to the next step.

3.3   Phase 3: Consolidation of Candidate Services

In the third phase, information about candidate services is consolidated. Service consolidation aims at gathering several characteristics about each candidate service so as to support the service designer in deciding upon its implementation. Services not selected to be implemented are removed, resulting in a refined candidate services list.

The proposed heuristics for service consolidation were based on the principles for high-quality service implementation mentioned in [1][2][5][6][7][8][9][11], thus reflecting the most important technical issues that should be observed by designers. Moreover, information regarding the candidate service usage (by process activities or other candidate services) and existing implementations are also considered.

However, we did not try to automatically select the candidate services to be implemented, since this is a very complex and subjective decision, influenced by not only technical but also political and cultural organizational objectives. We argue that with the information produced in this phase, the designer has more knowledge for deciding upon service implementation. The following heuristics are proposed:

Heuristic 10 (Service Reuse Degree): The degree of reuse of a candidate service is calculated by the sum of times the service is used by each process activity.

Service reuse corresponds to the number of occurrences of the activities from which the service was identified. The degree of reuse cannot be automatically calculated when a candidate service was identified from a multi-instance activity, in which the iteration granularity is not quantitatively represented (e.g., an activity that should be executed "for all company units").

Heuristic 11 (Link Candidate Service and System): A candidate service identified from a business requirement that is already implemented should be associated to the systems which implement it.

This should help in the design phase to identify which requirements are already implemented and could be exposed as services.

Heuristic 12 (Link Candidate Service and Demand Requirements): A candidate service identified from a business requirement of the demand must be associated to it.

A candidate service identified from the demand should be associated with its corresponding requirement. That information will allow the designer to identify the minimum set of services required to meet initial demand, or for prioritization.

Heuristic 13 (Link Candidate Service and Activities): A candidate service must be associated to the activities from which it was identified.

This enables the service designer to know all the services used by a process activity, or all the activities supported by (impacted by) a service. This information may be used in the future for choosing a unique service implementation that encapsulates all the identified functionalities indentified in the activity(ies).

Heuristic 14 (Identify Candidate Services Dependencies): A candidate service must be associated to other service candidates that use it.

This information is obtained from the association between business rule × business rule and business rule × business requirement, when they are explicit in modeling. The relationships allow the identification of the granularity of candidate services as well as the dependency between them. The candidate services that do not use any other candidate services are considered fine-grained, and are independent from other services, i.e., they are self-contained. The services that use other services are coarser-grained services. They depend on services they use. The more dependencies a service has, the higher is the susceptibility to failures.

Heuristic 15 (Utility Candidate Service Identification): A utility candidate service shall be identified from the observation of recurrent patterns.

Our previous experience in service development led us to pay a special attention to some recurrent flows of activities which are very typical in different processes of the same organization, or even in different organizations. Some of those domain-independent recurrent patterns were pointed by [16]. Thus, we also propose heuristics for service identification from recurrent patterns. The rationale for using recurrent patterns for service identification is that, once a pattern is detected in a process model instance, its corresponding service will probably be highly reused. Hence it is related to one of the main principles of service, which is "reuse". A service that is indentified from a recurrent flow is marked as a "Utility Candidate Service".

The method final product is the list of candidate services (with descriptions) as well as a table containing a series of information useful for service designers. Besides a dependency graph also assists the designer to make decisions about the implementing services. Next section describes a case study in a real scenario.

4   Applying the Proposed Method for Service Identification in a Real Scenario for Oil Production Diagnosis

The method proposed in Section 3 was experimented in a case study conducted at PETROBRAS, the largest Oil Company from Brazil. PETROBRAS is responsible for the majority of Oil and Gas derivatives exploration and production in this country. The

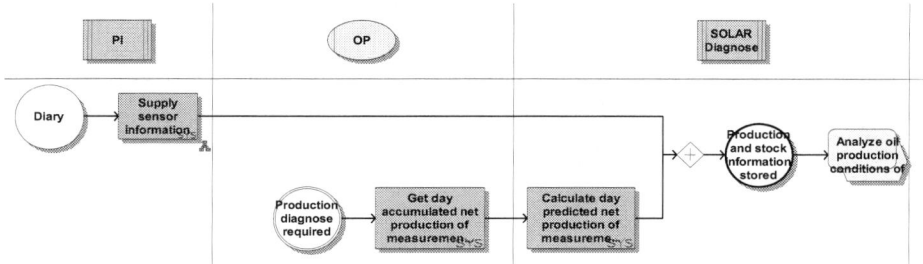

Fig. 8. EPC of "Send physical sensor information" process

case study was done in the "Diagnose daily oil production" business process model. Production Control is an important process within the Exploration and Production (E&P) area of PETROBRAS.

The "Diagnose daily oil production" is a to-be process model. The process was designed in detail, so that business users and application developers' needs were met. The designed model comprises 19 activities, control flows, 90 business rules and 37 business requirements. The process aims at maximizing company results. This is achieved using real time physical sensor information to fast and accurately identify the production variation related to previous oil production information (production of previous days or previous month). This process has two subprocesses: "Send physical sensor information" and "Analyze oil production conditions of measurement node".

Each process was detailed using EPC (Event-Driven Process Chain) diagrams and each process activity was detailed using an FAD (Function Allocation Diagram) [14]. Figure 8 illustrates the EPC of "Send physical sensor information" process. Figure 9 presents the FAD of the "Supply sensor information" activity, where business rules (i.e., "Stocks of non-automatic tanks") and business requirements (i.e., "Supply tank stock information") are also presented.

The service identification method takes as its inputs: (a) a set of to-be process models: for this experiment, it corresponds to "Diagnose daily oil production"; (b) a set of system requirements already implemented in applications: in this case, it is represented by an empty set, since it is a new business process, and there is no application supporting it; (c) a demand, i.e., a set of business requirements to be implemented: in this experiment, all business requirements were considered demand.

Phase 1 (Activity selection): all automatic, subject to automation, and partially supported by computers activities were selected, such as: Supply sensor information; Get accumulated measurement node net production from previous days; Calculate measurement node predicted net production for the day; Analyze characteristics of measurement node production; Query measurement node previous productions; etc.

Phase 2 (Candidate service identification and classification): candidate services were identified and grouped accordingly the proposed heuristics. Each service was

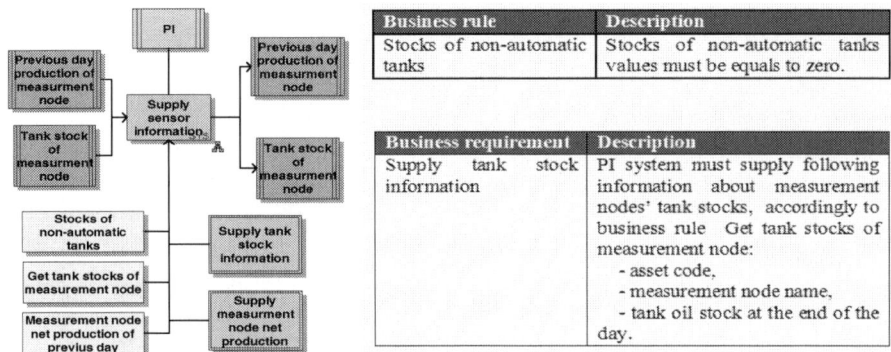

Business rule	Description
Stocks of non-automatic tanks	Stocks of non-automatic tanks values must be equals to zero.

Business requirement	Description
Supply tank stock information	PI system must supply following information about measurement nodes' tank stocks, accordingly to business rule Get tank stocks of measurement node: - asset code, - measurement node name, - tank oil stock at the end of the day.

Fig. 9. "Supply sensor information" activity's FAD

described with the following attributes: service name; service type (candidate business or candidate data service); input and output information; which element originates the service (business rule, business requirement, activity flow); activities where it was discovered from; service description. Table 1 and Table 2 present examples of candidate services. The experiments did not identify candidate services using heuristics 7 and 9 since there is no loop or multi-instance activity in the model.

Phase 3 (Candidate services consolidation): The results of this phase are presented in Table 3 and Table 4. Table 3 presents information related to Heuristic 10 (Service Reuse Degree), Heuristic 11 (Link Candidate Service and System) and Heuristic 12 (Link Candidate Service and Demand Requirements). It was identified 72% of candidate business services and 28% candidate data services. No candidate utility services were identified.

Table 1. Examples of service candidate information

Attributes	Service 1	Service 2	Service 3
Heuristic	Heuristic 1	Heuristic 2	Heuristic 3
Name	Calculate measurement node production of type appropriation of Estreito	Query measurement node tank information	Calculate predicted net production
Type	Business service	Data service	Business service
Input	Measurement node	Measurement node	Measurement node
Output	Measurement node oil production	Asset code, measurement node name, oil stock volume in the tank in the end of the day	Production variation of measurement node
Source	Business rule: "Production calculus of appropriation measurement node of Estreito to be analyzed"	Business requirement: "Supply information about tank oil stock"	Workflow pattern
Activities	Send sensor information	Supply sensor information	Get accumulated measurement node net production; Calculate daily predicted net production of measurement node
Description	Production of Estreito measurement node to be analyzed = Production of measurement node of Estreito B – Production of fiscal measurement node of Angico – Production of fiscal measurement node A – Production of fiscal measurement node B.	Asset code, measurement node name, stock volume of oil in the tank in the end of the day from Plant Information System	Get accumulated measurement node net production, and then calculate daily predicted net production of measurement node

Table 2. Examples of service candidate information

Attributes	Service 4	Service 5	Service 6
Heuristic	Heuristic 4	Heuristic 5	Heuristic 6
Name	Analyze production of measurement node	View production ATP diagnose summary	View production diagnose summary
Type	Business service	Business service	Business service
Input	Measurement node	Measurement node	Measurement node
Output	Loss of measurement node production		
Source	Workflow pattern	Workflow pattern	Workflow pattern
Activities	Analyze loss of production; Analyze production potential variation of measurement node; identify measurement node oil well that start to produce; Analyze tank oil stock information	View production diagnose summary; View diagnose summary	View production diagnose summary; Analyze loss of measurement node production; Analyze production potential variation of measurement node; analyze measurement node oil well that start to produce; Analyze tank oil stock information
Description	Analyze measurement node production calculating loss of production, potential variation of production, identify measurement node oil well that start to produce; Analyze tank oil stock	View production diagnose summary measurement node	View production diagnose summary of measurement node

Table 3. Table presents reuse, systems those implement candidate service functionality and association between candidate services and demand

Candidate service	Type	Reuse	Implem. Req.	Demand's requirements
Calculate measurement node production of type appropriation of Estreito	Business	1	-	
Calculate daily predicted net production of measurement node	Business	1	-	Calculate daily predicted net production of measurement nodes
Query measurement nodes for production diagnose	Data	1	-	Supply measurement node net production information

Table 4 presents the association between candidate services and activities, according to Heuristic 13 (Link Candidate Service and Activities). This information can be used to identify all services those were discovered from the same activity, which can originate one logical service that encapsulates all those functionalities.

Table 4. Candidate services and activities association

Candidate service	Activities					
	1	2	3	4	5	6
Calculate difference between daily predicted net production related to previous month						X
Calculate difference between daily predicted net production related to previous days						X

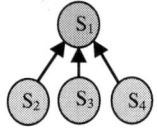

Fig. 10. Dependency graph of some candidate services

From Heuristic 14, dependency graphs can be built to represent dependencies between candidate services. Figure 10 presents an example of dependency graph. According to this example, the designer may choose to implement only one service merging functionalities of services S_2, S_3 and S_4 in service S_1, or develop S1 invoking (orchestrating) the others three services. This graph can be built for each service.

Heuristic 15 is related to identify candidate services that represent activity patterns based on recurrent functions or activity patterns based on organizational structural aspects. In spite of the literature demonstrate that these patterns may occur in business process, in our experiments they were not present.

The "Diagnose daily oil production" process has only 19 activities. This could mean that there were only some candidate services. However, the heuristics identified 147 candidate services. Business rule and business requirement heuristics produced 57% and 30%, respectively. It is because that this business process has a lot of business rules and business requirements, and it is strongly based on system.

The important aspect of our approach is that both fine-grained and coarse-grained candidate services were identified. We observed that Heuristic 1 (Business Rule), in general, produce fine-grained services, while Heuristic 2 (Business Requirement) and workflow pattern heuristic (Heuristic 3 to 9) produce medium- to coarse-grained ones.

After the application of the method, the services identified were validated by the specialists, i.e., System Analysts who developed physical services to support the automation of "Diagnose daily oil production" business process. All services they implemented were identified by our proposal; and the specialists agree that the consolidated information helped them in service implementation. One difference that must be highlighted is that candidate services and implemented services have different granularities. For instance, the functionalities of five candidate services were merged and implemented in only one physical service. Those five services correspond to methods that manipulate the same entity. The specialists pointed that the identification of those candidate services by the proposed method helped them to know which functionalities should be implemented as well as they would have more reuse if published in the same service. On the other hand, some candidate services where implemented and orchestrated in a higher level service. In this case, the specialists observed that the functionalities would have more use and reuse if published separated. Besides, they observed that it also would be useful if the functionalities were published as an orchestrated service according to a specific flow.

Hence the specialists confirmed that a method for service identification from business process models must identify candidate services and produce information that can assist the service design phase. Hence the experiment demonstrated good results, and pointed to the possibility of new heuristic for the design phase.

5   Conclusions and Future Work

The deployment of SOA in an organization presents a series of challenges, especially service modeling, design, monitoring and management. Proposals for service life-cycle models are typically abstract and lack from considering the integrated view of business processes in an organization. A service life-cycle not only facilitates the management of service-oriented systems but can also improve its governance.

Among the activities of a service life-cycle model, we emphasize the services identification step. We propose a top-down approach for services identification from business process models, applying heuristics to define services from the semantic analysis of process elements such as business rules and business requirements, and from a syntactic analysis of process models according to its corresponding structural patterns.

As a result, a set of candidate services is identified and scored according to a set of criteria (degree of reuse, existing implementations, presence in the input development demand, usage by process activities, relationship between services, and service granularity). This information helps service designer to better design and plan service implementation, while also considering subjective issues such as security, political decisions, and so on. Besides, an explicit link can be made between business process constructs and services descriptions. Business process evolutions can target changes in the services which support the process, and vice-versa. The association of services and process models helps in tracking changes within the models that directly impact IT, as well as changes in IT that should be reflected in the process models. Furthermore, changes in processes can trigger calls or automatic changes in the implementation of services.

The proposed method was assessed on a case study in a real organization. In this case study, a process model for oil production diagnosis was used as input. The method was manually applied, and resulted in 147 candidate services identified. We are currently working on a supporting tool for the method.

As future work we are studying the next steps (analysis, design, implementation, deployment and maintenance) and the changes on business process models resulting from service life-cycle steps. Another important future work is related to service reuse principle. A service can be reused in a variety of contexts. In other words, it can support different business process. So, a change in a business process can induce service maintenance, and consequently impact another business process. The management of these changes and business process impacts are important issues.

Acknowledgment

The authors thank Petrobras (TIC/TIC-E&P/GDIEP) for supporting this project.

References

1. Arsanjani, A.: Service-oriented modeling and architecture (2004),
   http://www.ibm.com/developerworks/webservices/library/
   ws-soa-design1/
2. Erl, T.: Service-Oriented Architecture: Concepts, Technology, and Design. Prentice Hall, Englewood Cliffs (2005)
3. Fareghzadeh, N.: Service Identification Approach to SOA Development. In: Proceedings of World Academy of Science, Engineering and Technology, vol. 35, pp. 258–266 (2008)
4. Gu, Q., Lago, P.: A Stakeholder-Driven Service Life Cycle Model for SOA. In: 2nd International Workshop on Service Oriented Software Engineering: in Conjunction with the 6th ESEC/FSE Joint Meeting, pp. 1–7 (2007)
5. Jamshidi, P., Sharif, M., Mansour, S.: To Establish Enterprise Service Model from Enterprise Business Model. In: 2008 IEEE International Conference on Services Computing, vol. 1, pp. 93–100 (2008)
6. Josuttis, N.M.: SOA in Practice: The Art of Distributed System Design. O'Reilly, Sebastopol (2007)

7. Klose, K., Knackstedt, R., Beverungen, D.: Identification of Services - A Stakeholder-based Approach to SOA Development and its Application in the Area of Production Planning. In: ECIS 2007, pp. 1802–1814 (2007)
8. Klückmann, J.: 10 Steps to Business-Driven SOA, ARIS Expert Paper (2007),
   `http://www.ids-scheer.com/set/6473/`
   `ARIS_Expert_Paper-SOA-10_Steps_to_SOA_Klueckmann_2007-03_en.pdf`
9. Marks, E.A., Bell, M.: Service-Oriented Architecture: A Planning and Implementation Guide for Business and Techonology. John Wiley & Sons Inc., Chichester (2006)
10. McBride, G.: The Role of SOA Quality Management in SOA Service Lifecycle Management. DeveloperWorks (2007),
    `ftp://ftp.software.ibm.com/software/rational/web/articles/`
    `soa_quality.pdf`
11. Papazoglou, M.P., Heuvel, W.-J.v.d.: Service-Oriented Design and Development Methodology. Int. Journal of Web Eng. and Tech. (IJWET) 2(4), 412–442 (2006)
12. Pulier, E., Taylor, H.: Understanding Enterprise SOA. Manning (2006)
13. Russell, N., ter Hofstede, A.H.M., Edmond, D., van der Aalst, W.M.P.: Workflow Data Patterns. QUT Technical report, FIT-TR-2004-01, Queensland University of Technology, Brisbane (2004)
14. Scheer, A.-W.: ARIS - Business Process Modelling. Springer, Berlin (2000)
15. Sharp, A., McDemortt, P.: Workflow Modeling: Tools for Process Improvement and Application Development. Artech House computing library (2001)
16. Thom, L., Iochpe, C., Reichert, M.: Workflow Patterns for Business Process Modeling. In: 8th Int. Workshop on Business Process Modeling, Development, and Support (BPMDS), pp. 349–358 (2007)
17. Van der Aalst, W.M.P., Ter Hofstede, A.H.M., Kiepuszewski, B., Barros, A.P.: Workflow patterns. Distributed and Parallel Databases 14, 5–51 (2003)

IT Capability-Based Business Process Design through Service-Oriented Requirements Engineering

Sebastian Adam, Özgür Ünalan, Norman Riegel, and Daniel Kerkow

Fraunhofer IESE, Fraunhofer Platz 1, 67663 Kaiserslautern
{sebastian.adam, oezguer.uenalan, norman.riegel,
daniel.kerkow}@iese.fraunhofer.de

Abstract. Besides goals and regulations, IT is also considered as a driver for business process development or evolution. However, as reuse becomes increasingly important in many organizations due to return of investment considerations, the available IT is not only an enabler but also a constraint for business process design. In this paper, we present a systematic approach that explicitly takes into account the capabilities of a (service-oriented) reuse infrastructure and that guides the business process design accordingly. An important element in our approach is the notion of conceptual services, which we have experienced as appropriate candidates for communicating the capabilities of a reuse infrastructure to business people[1].

Keywords: requirements engineering, business process, business process design, service orientation.

1 Introduction

Business goals, regulations, and technological capabilities can all trigger the evolution of business processes. However, each change is risky and expensive. The costs and times required to realize a change therefore play an important role due to return on investment considerations, and pose many constraints for the incorporation of changes, mainly with regard to information systems (IS). The aim of reusing as many established implementations as possible is therefore a widely observable trend in many organizations, both in organizations using IS and in those developing IS.

Even if the paradigm of Service Oriented Architecture (SOA) [4] is considered a powerful means for adopting the reuse idea to the business process context, a fit between available services and business requirements is hard to achieve as long as no systematic approaches are used to reconcile both views [5, 6]. As a consequence, the degree of reuse is often less than expected and many parts of the IT / IS still have to be renewed, leading to the situation that the desired benefits of reuse cannot be exploited.

Business stakeholders are often not aware of these problems, respectively the costs and the feasibility of their requirements. Requirements must therefore also *"depend*

---

[1] The research results described in this paper were obtained in the SoKNOS project (founded by the German Federal Ministry of Education and Research, No. 01ISO7009).

T. Halpin et al. (Eds.): BPMDS 2009 and EMMSAD 2009, LNBIP 29, pp. 113–125, 2009.
© Springer-Verlag Berlin Heidelberg 2009

on existing system capabilities and not just on what stakeholders believe they need" [7]. Several references such as [5, 11, 12] have therefore stressed that the capabilities of a reuse infrastructure must be taken into consideration already during the early requirements phase, as otherwise a high degree of reuse will not occur. In addition, [13] stress that it is inevitable to develop business processes and supporting IS in a coordinated manner in order to cope with their mutual dependency.

The major challenge to be managed by (good) requirements engineers and business analysts is therefore neither just to write down wishes nor to instantiate a predefined reference solution, but to satisfy and reconcile actual needs with a given reuse infrastructure. Hence, customer expectations must be negotiated against the capabilities and constraints of an underlying infrastructure [9, 10], and proactively refined into business processes and IS requirements that are actually realizable within the estimated time and budget.

However, as far as we can tell, negotiation and reconciliation are often done late, requiring significant and time-consuming rework on the requirements, or the renouncement of a high degree of reuse, and thus of cost- and time-savings in subsequent development phases.

In this paper, we therefore present a novel approach for IT capability-based business process design based on service-oriented requirements engineering principles that allow developing business processes and supporting IS with the early consideration of an existing service infrastructure in a cooperative manner. The aim of this method is to assure a high degree of reuse in a constructive rather than analytical way right from the beginning of each IS development project.

The remainder of this paper is structured as follows: In the next section, we give a brief overview of service-oriented requirements engineering to bring the method of this paper into context. In section 3, we then introduce conceptual services as the basis of our method for IT capability-based business process design, while the corresponding process is described in section 4. This process is the main contribution of this paper and presents concrete guidance on how to elicit and design business processes with the early consideration of existing services. Our preliminary experience with this approach made in the "SoKNOS" project is presented in section 5, and we show related work and open issues in sections 6 and 7.

2   A Short Overview of SORE

Service-oriented Requirements Engineering (SORE) is a still evolving [16] discipline dealing with the identification of services for reuse, as well as with the reconciliation of existing service capabilities and application requirements during reuse [6]. In order to emphasize the role we see for SORE in the strongly business-influenced SOA context, we have developed an approach integrating some concepts of business process management, SOA, and product line engineering (see Fig. 1 and [6] for more information).

According to this model, the role of SORE consists of mediating between the more business-oriented application engineering and the more technical-oriented service

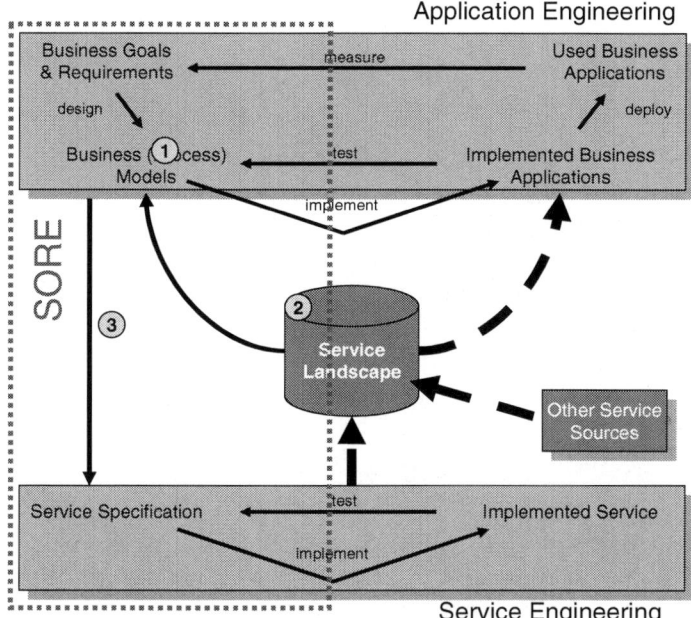

Fig. 1. SORE in SOA engineering

engineering in order to achieve a good fit between business needs and available services. Thus, SORE should provide support for

(1) **the process of reconciliation** of business needs with available services in order to support the achievement of both business goals and high reuse
(2) **the appropriate representation** of actual service capabilities to business people in order to make these capabilities explicitly visible already during an early phase
(3) **the process of defining services**, i.e., the determination and clustering of (innovative) features a service should provide in order to also be beneficial in future contexts.

3 Communicating IT Capabilities with Conceptual Services

The method for IT capability-based business process design described in this paper mainly aims at operationalizing task (1) of SORE as mentioned above. The purpose of our approach is the assurance that business processes do not pose many hard requirements that are not realizable with the existing IS, respectively service infrastructure, within the estimated time and budget. Hence, a high degree of reuse should be assured constructively right from the beginning of each IS project, i.e., already during business process design.

Especially to avoid late and thus costly negotiations and reconciliations, our approach aims at proactively guiding the business process design with the consideration of existing services. This, of course, requires an abstraction of service capabilities in business terms [6, 15], as these capabilities could otherwise not be sufficiently considered by business people (see also SORE task (2)).

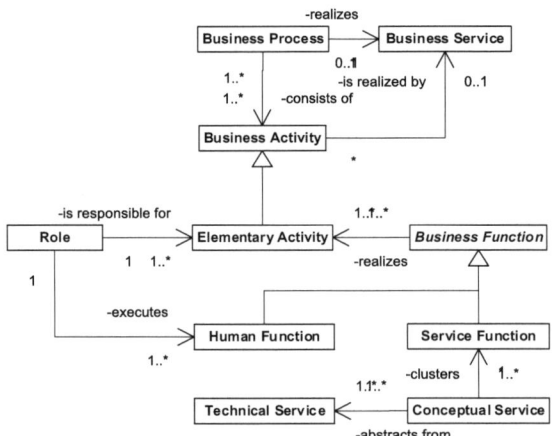

Fig. 2. Levels of abstraction

Based on our previous work concerning the identification of services [14], we propose representing service capabilities, i.e., their functionality, on the level of business functions within elementary business activities (see Fig. 2)[2]. This level has the advantages of being well understandable and beneficial for business people on the one hand, while remaining generic enough and thus, highly reusable, on the other hand. Especially the high reusability is caused by the fact that functionality on such a level of abstraction can be reused as-is and context-independent of its process integration.

However, as the amount of service functions provided on this level may exceed a manageable size in industrial settings, it is hard to communicate on this basis with business people even if they are able to understand the meaning of the functions. In order to provide these capabilities on an appropriate level of granularity, we therefore recommend clustering the service functions into so-called conceptual services [14], which, in our experience, have found out to be perfect candidates for communicating IT capabilities to business people due to their logical capsulation. This abstraction from the real technical services and the focus on understandability for humans rather than on interpretability for machines is especially an advantage with regard to requirements negotiation [1]. In particular, business people can better understand what is easily feasible with the existing IS, while developers can assess much faster how well their reuse infrastructure already covers the mentioned needs.

However, for facilitating actual service reuse during IS development, knowing the real technical services (e.g., backend components, legacy system interfaces, etc.) that implement the conceptual ones is also important, of course. Hence, both should be explicitly linked, i.e., the selection of a conceptual service function should automatically guide the developers in identifying and orchestrating the required technical services accordingly. However, we will not deal with this traceability issue in this paper.

---

[2] An elementary business activity is performed by exactly one role with an IS and fulfills exactly one goal (e.g., "change customer data"), while a service function within this activity is a recognizable IS reaction triggered by the involved human (e.g., "search customer").

4   Method Description

As [16] highlights the need for a domain-specific, framework-oriented analysis in SORE, we also propose a similar approach for IT capability-based business process design. Using a framework-driven approach when designing new business processes is hence the key concept of our method described in this paper. However, while traditional framework-oriented analysis approaches such as [3] use the real technical framework components, our approach makes use of the more abstract conceptual services belonging to a certain application domain (e.g., "incident management" in our later case study). The reason is, as already mentioned, that business requirements can only be reconciled with service capabilities in the early phase of business process design when both are described on a level of abstraction that is understandable and comparable for business people.

The basic steps of our method are depicted in Fig. 3. According to this method, the identification of relevant stakeholders in the business organization (respectively the organizational unit) of interest and their involvement in the elicitation process is the first step (1)[3]. The most important stakeholder groups are the actual end-users (business process participants) and people who are responsible for the regulations and policies (those with regard to IT as well as those with regard to business issues). Getting access to all "right" stakeholders is a crucial issue, and usually requires, for succeeding, the support of the (top) management. With the former group, the current business processes in the organization are systematically analyzed and modeled in joint workshops in order to get a common picture (2). In order to quickly obtain this comprehensive overview of the current business processes, a systematic, algorithmic-like elicitation checklist is used. This checklist (see Fig. 4) assures that a process model can be sketched already during the workshops, enabling the participants to directly make comments and corrections. Thus, misunderstandings, incorrectness, or incompleteness can be avoided right from the start. Furthermore, the business processes can be systematically elicited on a common level of abstraction; in our case, the level of elementary business activities.

Based on the elicited business processes, unsatisfied goals and problems that currently hamper more efficient and satisfactory work are therefore systematically analyzed in a next step (4). In particular, this step helps to understand which problems can be improved by IT (technical solution) and which problems rather require organizational improvements. Only if these problems are clearly understood and classified can an IS supplier provide solutions that really satisfy the organization.

The problem analysis is performed by iterating over each business activity and each activity sequence within the business processes modeled before. During this iteration, a detailed checklist with questions in three different categories is used: questions regarding problems (e.g., "Is the result of this activity reached satisfactorily?"), quality requirements (e.g., "Are there any quality constraints / requirements for this activity?"), and improvement possibilities (e.g., "Can this activity be left out?").

By posing such questions, typical problems in business processes such as media disruption, an insufficient degree of automation, or of parallelization can be identified systematically. Furthermore, based on this problem analysis, the IS supplier can preselect first conceptual services from his service framework as possible solution candidates.

---

[3] Our assumption in this paper is that the IS supplier is from an external organization.

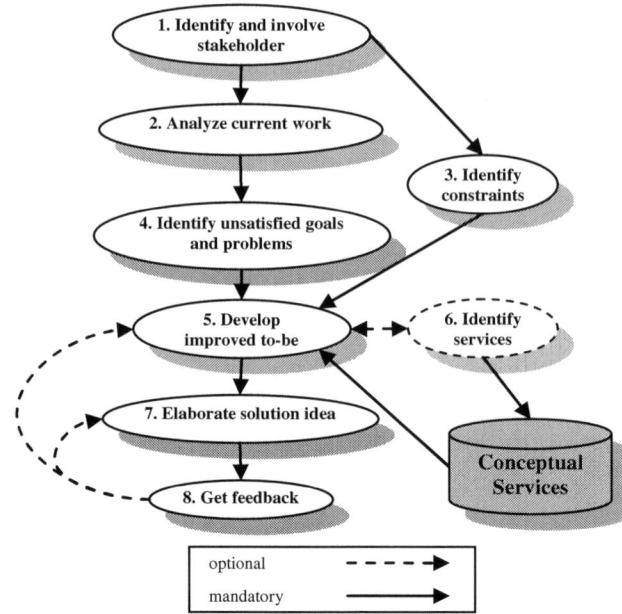

Fig. 3. Method Overview

In order to assure that all relevant information with regard to given constraints is also taken into consideration, the constraints posed by regulation and policies are systematically elicited from the responsible persons using a similar question- and checklist-driven approach (3). However, all elicited constraints should be classified into hard and soft constraints (i.e., if they absolutely have to be complied with or if it would be good to comply with them) in order to assess their impact on the solution space.

The constraints, the current business processes, and the identified problems and unsatisfied goals are then taken as input for cooperatively developing ideas for improvement, respectively improved to-be business processes (5). Hence, the IS supplier directly collaborates with the involved stakeholders in joint workshops in order to find a suitable solution that solves the organization's problems.

First, the improvement possibilities that have been identified in the previous step are used to improve the business processes from an organizational perspective with the consideration of the given constraints, e.g., through parallelizing or removing activities in order to increase the general process performance.

After that, the IS supplier's conceptual services framework comes into play. Based on the application domain, respectively the considered business process areas, specific sub-frameworks are chosen (see Fig. 5 for an example) and visualized for the involved stakeholders. Every conceptual service is presented by giving a short summary of its general purpose and functionality. Furthermore, based on the problem identification and the service preselection, the IS supplier can also motivate the specific benefit of a certain service for the organization, both for specific business processes and for cross-cutting issues.

- •   ...
- •   Which tasks / activities are performed in order to fulfill the responsibilities?
- •   For each task / activity:
    - o   Which material / devices / systems / etc. are uses to perform this task?
    - o   Which preconditions must be fulfilled that the task can be started?
    - o   ...
    - o   Which information / input is needed for this task?
    - o   For each input:
        - ▪   Who/ what delivers the input?
    - o   Which information / output is produced in this task?
    - o   ...
    - o   How often is this task performed?
    - o   ...

Fig. 4. Excerpt from an elicitation checklist

Then, together with the stakeholders, the conceptual services are annotated to corresponding activities in the processes (see Fig. 5 (left) for an example). In doing so, the stakeholders easily get an understanding of which activities can basically be supported by available services. Furthermore, they can discuss how this conceptual service, respectively which conceptual service functions, would concretely be used within each business activity. Hence, they can check the applicability of each service and make remarks on whether adaptations or extensions are needed.

As the IS supplier is interested in achieving as much reuse of existing services as possible, the following resolution strategy is applied when no conceptual service can be annotated to a business activity or when a conceptual service function is missing that would be needed to perform an activity. First, the IS supplier checks whether the required functionality is provided by another conceptual service, maybe even in a service framework belonging to another domain. If no appropriate functionality is found, IS supplier and stakeholder cooperatively discuss whether the activity (or even the entire process) could be changed in a way that existing services can be used but the goal of the activity / process is fulfilled nevertheless. Only if this is not possible, must new services be defined or existing services modified (6). In this way, missing functionality that cannot be solved by the existing services can be revealed early and can be prepared for future usage (SORE task (3)) [14].

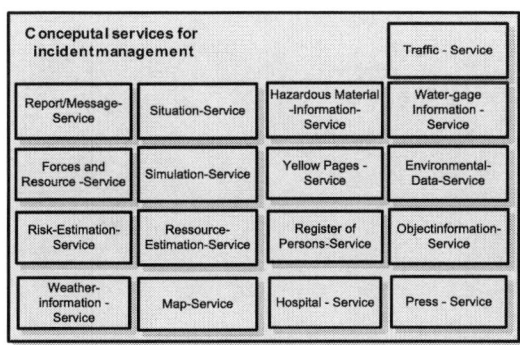

Fig. 5. Framework of identified conceptual services in SoKNOS

After these cooperative steps, the IS supplier elaborates the solution idea (7) by resolving the conceptual services, i.e., they develop a prototype. Then, a coherent IS concept is presented to the customer to get feedback (8) and make final adaptations, if necessary. This feedback from stakeholders who are affected by the discussed changes is very important. By getting feedback, the IS supplier can get an impression of whether his ideas are on the right track and are considered helpful for the organization's intended purpose. Depending on the feedback result, step 5 or step 7 of the method has to be repeated.

5   Preliminary Experience

The first experience with SORE in general, and the method described in this paper in particular, was made in the German research project "SoKNOS". The main goal of "SoKNOS" is to optimize the workflows within but also between public safety organizations in case of major incidents such as natural disasters by means of service-oriented technology.

During the first phase of the project, we elicited representative processes with scenarios, and, using our method for service derivation (SORE task (3)) described in [14], we derived a set of conceptual services that were used as input for developing the real technical services ("development for reuse"). Despite the fact that we were looking at a very large and fuzzy-bounded application domain, we were able to derive a manageable number of conceptual services in this way (see Fig. 5).

Then, during the second phase of the project, the aim was to evaluate the appropriateness of the developed service landscape for the purpose of "development with reuse", i.e., to check whether the developed services were sufficient for addressing the needs of as many organizations as possible. In order to perform this evaluation, we applied the method described in this paper several times with stakeholders from representative public safety organizations such as fire departments, and police organizations, which had not yet been involved in the first project phase.

After identifying a scenario about handling a large amount of injured people that was assessed as a very challenging scenario by the involved stakeholders, we started with the analysis of the currently foreseen reaction (business processes) to this

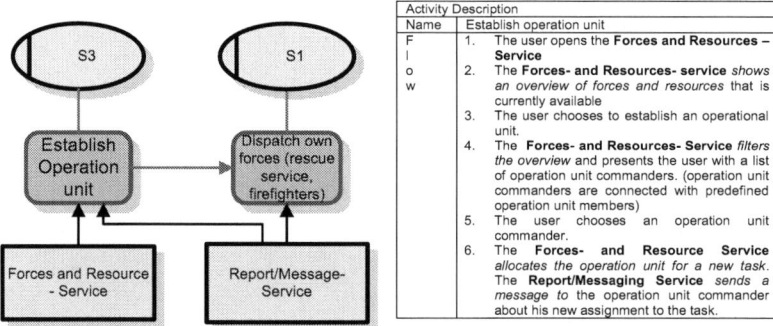

Fig. 6. Part of business process with annotated conceptual services and activity description

scenario. By using our method, we quickly came up with a corresponding business process model and could easily analyze unsatisfied goals, constraints, and possible problems to get a first impression of which conceptual services might provide significant support. After that, we presented the "incident management"-specific service framework (just like in Fig. 5) to the stakeholders, and we briefly explained each conceptual service one by one. We went through the whole scenario and annotated cooperatively the business processes with our conceptual services (see Fig. 6 (left) for an example using our own extension of EPC [23]).

After this annotation, we discussed each activity of the process with the stakeholders and how the functions of the conceptual services are actually used (see Fig. 6 (right) for an example) in order to perform the activity. When a certain function was still missing, we looked at another service to see whether the required functionality was included there, or we discussed whether the process could be modified in such a way that the existing services fit. Of course, as we were still in an early phase of a research project, a couple of functions were still missing and could thus not be taken from the reuse infrastructure. With regard to the evaluation of our method, however, we experienced the method as beneficial and learned the following lessons:

(1) We were able to communicate with the stakeholders in a predefined scope (conceptual services), which helped us to guide the business process design as far as possible towards reusable functionality. Thus, functionality that had already existed could actually be reused. Our hypothesis for future evaluations is therefore that this method leads to a higher degree of reuse in subsequent development phases, respectively to less effort when achieving a similar degree of reuse, compared to other approaches that propose to first refine a business process and then annotate services.

(2) The stakeholders appreciated the expression of service functionality in their domain terms using the conceptual services. Therefore, the stakeholders were enabled to abstract from detailed requirements such as user interface issues, etc. and could focus on their essential business needs. Thus, the complex phase of requirements analysis could be simplified (just business process design), which streamlined the entire requirements process. Furthermore, the abstraction from detailed requirements prevented the stakeholders from posing requirements that were too restrictive.

(3) We were able to easily identify whether the required functionality within the stakeholder's processes was already available in the service infrastructure, or whether new functionality had to be added. Therefore, we could use the method for systematically identifying deltas in the reuse infrastructure. Of course, a complete and systematic elicitation of reusable functionality cannot be performed this way and rather requires the approach described in [14].

(4) We were able to adhere to the real business processes and did not need to introduce reference business processes in order to achieve reuse. We think that this is a significant advantage over other reuse approaches, especially in domains that require support for rather ad-hoc processes than predictable production processes. This is also the case in the incident management domain.

(5) We experienced that the degree of technical innovation is very limited when the aim is to develop in a reuse-based manner. However, innovation and creativity are also quite important in "development with reuse" because solving unforeseen problems with a given reuse infrastructure is challenging. So far, we do not have systematic support for this aim.

6 Related Work

Reuse in the information systems domain can basically take place at any level of abstraction. In IS-COTS products such as ERP systems, reuse is typically achieved on the level of entire business processes through the configuration of predefined reference models [22]. Approaches aiming to apply product line engineering to the business process context also choose a similar approach, e.g., [8]. These approaches extend variant-rich reference processes with decision models and thereby allow an automatic instantiation of business processes and their implementations. However, due to the enormous process variety in today's organizations and the attempt to keep individuality in the way of work, the proactive prediction of all process variants to be supported is nearly impossible [5] and also not manageable through scoping [24], except for specific domains.

The level of business activities is therefore another level on which reuse can be applied and has basically already been part of the ARIS framework [18], for instance. Indeed, reuse at this level allows defining flexible business processes, as the order of activities is not predefined. However, this approach also has some shortcomings. First, how an activity is performed is already predefined (probably with certain variants, e.g., use case variants [25]). Second, we experienced in trials with such a reuse approach that it is more time-consuming and challenging for business people to click their way to a process while scrolling through an activity repository than frankly modeling a process using their own terminology and mapping this process to existing components afterwards.

The third level is the level of business functions (e.g., service functions) and is also the level basically addressed by SOA [4]. This level provides the highest flexibility in building business process applications but generally requires the most effort for refining requirements into an executable solution. However, as far as we can tell, most approaches in this area, including those proposed by leading BPM/SOA solution vendors (see, for instance, [17]), share two main shortcomings. First, they require specifying the business processes on a very low level of abstraction, as otherwise an annotation of the real service functions is not possible. This, of course, leads to an enormous complexity of process models and the service infrastructure, as no appropriate means for abstraction exist. Second, most SOA approaches are based on the assumption that an organization's IT infrastructure has been decomposed completely in a service-oriented way and that thus all required services are either actually available or very easy to (re)develop. As a consequence, most approaches still propose a pure top-down approach, i.e., a specification of business processes without reconciliation between the resulting requirements and service capabilities. While this might work in an in-house scenario, it is hard to apply in settings where IS supplier and IS users are two independent organizations with different strategies.

To cope with this reconciliation problem, only some initial work exists. [19] for instance, propose intentional services based on the MAP formalism to match high-level business requirements with service functionality. However, even though this approach provides a clear algorithm on how to match both views, we consider the required specification effort and the notations used not justified for a lightweight communication of IT capabilities.

Approaches from COTS-based requirements engineering (see [20] for a comprehensive overview) aim at matching high-level requirements in terms of goals with product features to find the "best matching" product. Our approach shares the idea that the requirements should remain on a high level of abstraction in order to prevent restrictions that are too severe. However, we are convinced that goals alone are not sufficient and that the detailed way of work must also be known. [21] is probably the first reference that introduces the notion of domain services as an encapsulating means to mediate between business requirements and the capabilities of real technical services without the need to predefine the process flows in which the services are used. Even though this idea is quite similar to our notion of conceptual services, [21] gives no guidance on how the domain services are to be used for the actual reconciliation process between business needs and service capabilities. In this regard, our proposed method is strongly influenced by the key concepts of [2], who also aim at using a framework of abstract components and a collaborative method for improving and defining new processes. The differences between this approach and the approach presented in this paper are the context (requirements engineering process improvement vs. business process evolution) and the fact that [2] consciously avoid explicit modeling of processes.

7 Conclusion and Outlook

Available IT is not only an enabler but also a constraint for business process design. In this paper, we presented an approach for IT capability-based business process design. The novelty of our approach lies in the fact that we embed reuse capabilities in terms of conceptual services into a systematic process for business process design and thereby allow achieving a high degree of reuse in an early phase already. Even though we have not been able yet to evaluate our approach in a controlled experiment, the case study experience confirms that we are on the right track with our approach.

Our hypothesis to be checked in a next step is that this approach leads to a higher degree of reuse when developing IS, respectively to less effort for a similar degree of reuse, compared to other approaches that propose to first refine business processes and to annotate services afterwards. Of course, the success of our proposed method also depends on the quality and completeness of the underlying service framework, and the involvement of the right stakeholders. Furthermore, our method is still limited to mid-term or long-term business process evolution and not applicable for short-time or even run-time adaptations. Besides the need to discuss the business processes with a group of people, also the degree of automated transition between conceptual services and real implementations influences the addressable time scope. So far, there is only a conceptual link requiring developers still to manually map the conceptual services within a business process model to an executable description.

Besides this weakness, we have to elaborate the method into a complete requirements engineering approach that goes beyond the activity of business process design. As we have shown in [6], non-process requirements, such as interoperability with already existing systems, must not be forgotten. In another project, we are therefore trying to integrate our approach with an engineering approach for a system of systems. In this project, the conceptual service functions incorporated into the business process models are used to customize each single system with the overall system. Thus, we plan to combine a rather workflow-oriented system development approach with a highly automated product derivation approach. Furthermore, we plan to investigate how development for reuse can also benefit from creativity techniques.

References

1. Maiden, N.: Servicing Your Requirements. IEEE Software (September / October 2006)
2. Doerr, J., Adam, S., Eisenbarth, M., Ehresmann, M.: Implementing Requirements Engineering Processes: Using Cooperative Self-Assessment and Improvement. IEEE Software (May/June 2008)
3. Zhu, F., Tsai, W.: Framework-Oriented Analysis. In: Proceedings of the 22nd International Computer Software and Applications Conference. IEEE, Los Alamitos (1998)
4. Erl, T.: Service-oriented Architecture. Concepts, Technology, and Design. Prentice Hall, Upper Saddle River (2005)
5. Adam, S., Doerr, J.: How to better align BPM & SOA – Ideas on improving the transition between process design and deployment. In: Proceedings of 9th Workshop on Business Process Modeling, Development and Support, Montpellier (2008)
6. Adam, S., Doerr, J.: The Role of Service Abstraction and Service Variability and its Impact on Requirements Engineering for Service-oriented Systems. In: Proceedings of the 32nd IEEE International Computer Software and Applications Conference. IEEE, Los Alamitos (2008)
7. Sommerville, I.: Integrated Requirements Engineering: A Tutorial. IEEE Software (January / February 2005)
8. Bayer, J., Kose, M., Ocampo, A.: Improving the Development of e-Business Systems by Introducing Process-Based Software Product Lines. In: Münch, J., Vierimaa, M. (eds.) PROFES 2006. LNCS, vol. 4034, pp. 348–361. Springer, Heidelberg (2006)
9. Boehm, B., Abi-Antoun, M., Port, D., Kwan, J., Lynch, A.: Requirements Engineering, Expectations Management, and the Two Cultures. In: Proceedings of the 4th IEEE International Symposium on Requirements Engineering. IEEE, Los Alamitos (1999)
10. Strong, D., Volkoff, O.: A Roadmap for Enterprise System Implementation. IEEE Computer (June 2004)
11. Lam, W., Jones, S., Britton, C.: Technology Transfer for Reuse: A Management Model and Process Improvement Framework. In: Proceedings of the IEEE International Requirements Engineering Conference. IEEE, Los Alamitos (1998)
12. Baum, L., Becker, M., Geyer, L., Molter, G.: Mapping Requirements to Reusable Components using Design Spaces. In: Proceedings of International Requirements Engineering Conference. IEEE, Los Alamitos (2000)
13. Regev, G., Soffer, P., Bider, I.: Coordinated development of business processes and their support systems. Requirements Engineering 10 (2005)
14. Adam, S., Riegel, N., Doerr, J.: Deriving Software Services from Business Processes of Representative Customer Organizations. In: Proceedings of Service Oriented Computing – Challenges for Engineering Requirements (SOCCER 2008), Barcelona (2008)
15. Rolland, C., Kaabi, R.: An Intentional Perspective to Service Modeling and Discovery. In: Proceedings of 31st International Computer Software and Applications Conference. IEEE, Los Alamitos (2007)

16. Tsai, W., Jin, Z., Wang, P., Wu, B.: Requirement Engineering in Service-Oriented System Engineering. In: Proceedings of International Conference on e-Business Engineering. IEEE, Los Alamitos (2007)
17. Klückmann, J.: In 10 Schritten zur Business-driven SOA. IDS Scheer AG (2007)
18. Scheer, A.-W.: ARIS – Modellierungsmethoden, Metamodelle, Anwendungen. Springer, Heidelberg (2001)
19. Rolland, C., Kaabi, R.: An Intentional Perspective to Service Modeling and Discovery. In: Proceedings of the 31st Annual International Computer Software and Application Conference. IEEE, Los Alamitos (2007)
20. Alves, C.: COTS-Based Requirements Engineering. In: Cechich, A., Piattini, M., Vallecillo, A. (eds.) Component-Based Software Quality. LNCS, vol. 2693, pp. 21–39. Springer, Heidelberg (2003)
21. Wang, J., Yu, J., Falcarin, P., Han, Y.: An Approach to Domain-Specific Reuse in Service-Oriented Environments. In: Mei, H. (ed.) ICSR 2008. LNCS, vol. 5030, pp. 221–232. Springer, Heidelberg (2008)
22. Recker, J., Mendling, J., Aalst, W., Rosemann, M.: Model-driven Enterprise Systems Configuration. In: Dubois, E., Pohl, K. (eds.) CAiSE 2006. LNCS, vol. 4001, pp. 369–383. Springer, Heidelberg (2006)
23. Keller, G., Nüttgens, M., Scheer, A.-W.: Semantische Prozeßmodellierung auf der Grundlage Ereignisgesteuerter Prozeßketten (EPK), Universität des Saarlandes (1992)
24. Schmid, K.: Planning Software Reuse – A Disciplined Scoping Approach for Software Product Lines. PhD Theses in Experimental Software Engineering. Fraunhofer IRB Verlag, Stuttgart (2003)
25. Fantechi, A., Gnesi, S., John, I., Lami, G., Doerr, J.: Elicitation of Use Cases for Product Lines. In: van der Linden, F.J. (ed.) PFE 2003. LNCS, vol. 3014, pp. 152–167. Springer, Heidelberg (2004)

Minimising Lifecycle Transitions in Service-Oriented Business Processes

Roland Ukor and Andy Carpenter

School of Computer Science, University of Manchester,
Oxford Road, Manchester M13 9PL, United Kingdom
{roland.ukor,andy}@cs.man.ac.uk

Abstract. Service selection involves the use of well-defined criteria such as Quality of Service (QoS) metrics to optimally select services for business processes. However in some cases, the service capabilities being accessed require non-trivial protocols for accessing them. When the protocol of a selected service is incompatible with the process, a lifecycle transition is triggered from operation and evaluation phase to the design phase of the process lifecycle. Such transitions can be expensive in terms of the technical and organisational resources required. In this paper, we introduce a conceptual framework for minimising such transitions in the process lifecycle by considering the relative protocol compatitbility between candidate services.

Keywords: business process, soa, web services, qos, process lifecycle.

1 Introduction

The web services paradigm enables an organisation to implement business processes by orchestrating existing services, some of which may be provided by external organisations. In order for a process to access a capability provided by a web service, the process needs to be aware of the existence of the web service. This is typically achieved by executing queries on service registries or by using other means of web service discovery. Here, we consider a capability to represent a set of functions that an organisation is able to realise by deploying some technical and/or organisational resources.

A registry holds two types of descriptions for web services - abstract and concrete service descriptions. The abstract service description (ASD) is called the interface and it contains information about the capabilities that are provided by any implementation of the service, whereas a concrete service description (CSD) describes an implementation of a web service by a concrete agent – that is a software or hardware that actually sends and receives messages. A concrete agent is owned by a service provider [1].

To implement a business process that accesses externally provided capabilities through web services, the following activities are usually carried out:

Initiation and Analysis. The process is analysed to determine which of the required capabilities should be outsourced to external agents. In a loan

T. Halpin et al. (Eds.): BPMDS 2009 and EMMSAD 2009, LNBIP 29, pp. 126–135, 2009.

process example, a simple choice could be to outsource credit rating checks to a third party credit management agency.

Discovery. For each outsourced capability, the user performs searches in one or more service registries (possibly through a *broker*), and obtains a list of provider agents for the required capability. This is referred to as *functional matchmaking*, since the results returned by the search are expected to include only those service provider agents claiming to provide an implementation of the required capability.

Selection. A set of non-functional properties is then used to rank the identified provider agents with the objective of selecting one for each required capability. Quality of Service (QoS) metrics are the most common type of non-functional properties used for service selection.

Monitoring. Where possible, metrics are collected during the execution of each process instance, for the non-functional properties that were used during the selection process. These actual metrics can be compared with expectations, and the results of such comparisons can potentially provide feedback to future selection processes.

Figure 1 shows the traditional business process lifecycle. The lifecycle phases in which the above activities are carried out are shown in Table 1. The initiation and analysis activity is obviously carried out during the design phase of the lifecycle, while discovery and selection can take place at any point in the process lifecycle, although at least one discovery activity must precede service selection. Furthermore, it is possible that after the first discovery activity for all the services in a process, subsequent discovery activities can occur independently of analysis and/or selection activities e.g. to routinely find new services that provide better QoS than the ones being used for currently running process instances. Any service selection activity after the initial one could potentially use the collection of services that have been discovered as at the last discovery activity.

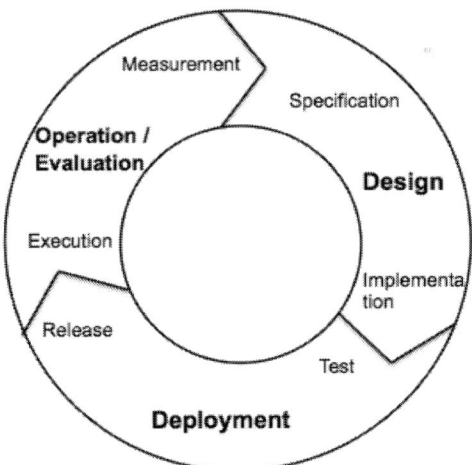

Fig. 1. Traditional business process lifecycle[2]

Table 1. Service Selection Activities in the Process Lifecycle

Activity/Phase	Design	Deployment	Operation and Evaluation
Initiation and Analysis	+		
Discovery	+	+	+
Selection	+	+	+
Monitoring			+

During the operation/evaluation phase of the process lifecycle, different instances of the process are instantiated, executed and then terminated. Each instance of the process can be associated with a particular context, which defines the criteria for determining the most appropriate set of service implementations that can be used by the process instance. For example, an instance of a loan process that is currently processing an application from a customer in the UK, will require a credit rating service that can provide rating for UK-based customers. This means that for a given process, several selection activities may be required for different contexts during the operation / evaluation phase. When a new service selection activity is carried out, two types of changes can occur:

1. A new CSD is selected from the list of available CSDs (which represent concrete service implementations) that are based on the same ASD.
2. A new CSD is selected from the list of available CSDs that are based on different but functionally equivalent ASDs

The first type of change does not require any transition in the process lifecycle. In fact, the idea of dynamic service binding makes it easy to bind a new service implementation to a new instance of a business process [3]. However in the second type, this is not always the case. If the differences in the ASDs are data structure related, then it may be possible to apply semantic techniques to reconcile and perform automatic data transformations [4]. On the other hand, if the differences are behavioural (i.e. incompatible protocols), then a lifecycle transition is often necessary to resolve the differences. This is because business process models are structurally constrained by the behavioural protocols with which they are expected to interact with other services (or systems).

For example, consider a procurement process that requires the capability to electronically order books for a school. The following lists the protocols associated with a set of three different capability definitions in a registry. Here the construct $b\text{-}s(m)$ is read as *buyer* sends message of type m to *seller*; a comma is used for sequencing and | implies concurrency.

- **def 1:** $b - s(order), s - b(invoice), b - s(payment, shipAddr), s - b(delivery)$
- **def 2:** $b\text{-}s(order), s\text{-}b(invoice), b\text{-}s(commitment, shipAddr), [s\text{-}b(delivery)|b\text{-}s(payment)]$
- **def 3:** $b\text{-}s(order, shipAddr), s\text{-}b(invoice), b\text{-}s(commitment), [s\text{-}b(delivery), b\text{-}s(deliveryConfirmation)|b - s(payment), s - b(paymentConfirmation)]$

Let us assume that process is designed to interact with service implementations based on *def 1*. Dynamic service selection can potentially identify candidates that implement the other two protocols. It is fairly easy to observe that if any of such is selected, the process will likely encounter an error after the message exchange $s - b(invoice)$ takes place except the process is modified to accommodate the behavioural differences.

In this paper, we examine how dynamic web service selection can act as a driver of business process development. Specifically, we examine how it affects the transition between the operation/evaluation phase to the design phase of the process lifecycle. We then discuss how the notion of a relative compatibility metric can be applied during service selection in addition to traditional QoS metrics (e.g. cost and availability). to reduce the number of induced lifecycle transitions.

The rest of this paper is structured as follows: In Section 2, we briefly introduce the service selection problem and discuss related work. Section 3 discusses the different types of change that may occur within the context of service selection, and how they affect the transitions in the process lifecycle. Section 4 outlines our approach to service selection based on the concept of relative protocol compatibility. In Section 5, we describe the limitations of the work presented, and summarise the contributions of the paper in Section 6.

2   Related Work

During the discovery phase, a set of service agents with descriptions that match the required functional criteria are identified by web service discovery engines [4]. However, it is possible for the list of agents matched solely on the basis of functional compatibility to grow very large over time. As a result, it is often useful to be able to filter and rank these agents based on non-functional properties as well (e.g. QoS metrics).

A number of service selection approaches have been proposed in the literature. In [5], the authors describe an approach to service selection by modelling the problem as a constraint satisfaction optimisation problem. They define a notion of conformance that indicates whether the requirements of a requester expressed as constraints on QoS metrics is satisfied by a provider based on the constraints on the QoS metrics supplied by the provider. The notion of confomance was refined in [6] to accommodate cases where the worst solution offered by a provider for a particular QoS metric exceeds the upper bound of the request for the same metric. In [7,8], the authors present heuristic algorithms for service selection. In particular, a set of aggregation methods for different categories of QoS metrics which can be used to determine the utility of a set of service selections was introduced in [7].

The research above and most of the others in the literature[9,10] describe approaches to service selection optimisation with support for end-to-end constraints on QoS metrics. However, they do not consider the situation where the invocation of a single service requires more than a single RPC-style service invocation. The work in [11] began to address that concern by introducing an

approach to selection optimisation that abstracted from the activities of the
process. It considered service capabilities as the unit of selection that may be
accessed within the process by non-contiguous process activities according to a
pre-defined protocol. However, it made a simplifying assumption that all candidates for a particular service capability implemented the same protocol. As
explained in Section 3, this assumption may not always hold in an open and
distributed environment such as the Internet.

There have also been various approaches in the literature for matchmaking
web services based on the bevavioural properties of web services where the protocols may not exactly be the same [12,13]. However, they have mainly focused
on verification and compatibility checking and do not address the issues that
arise with regard to the lifecycle transitions that may take place as a result of
matching and selecting such services. Furthermore, the relationship between QoS
metrics used for traditional service selection and the differences in behavioural
protocols have not been studied.

3   Service Selection and Lifecycle Transitions

A business process invokes a web service implementation using an interaction
protocol, which may be trivial or complex. The protocol defines the legal set of
message exchange sequences that may take place between the process and the
service provider. Considering the open nature of the Internet, it is reasonable to
expect that not all the candidate service implementations discovered for a service
capability will implement the same message exchange protocol (i.e. reference
the same abstract service description). In fact, a look at some public service
registries[1] indicate that most service providers supply their own ASDs along
with their CSDs.

In view of the above, we identify the following drivers, which may easily induce
transitions between the operation/evaluation and the design phases of a business
process implementation.

Performance. In the monitoring activity, which takes place after service selec-
    tion, metrics are collected and aggregated in various ways to evaluate key
    performance indicators for the selected services. If the actual QoS perfor-
    mance of a selected service does not measure up to expectation, then its
    chances of being selected in subsequent selection activities may be lower. As
    a result, there is a chance that a new service, which uses a different protocol
    may be selected. In such a case, the process may need structural adjustments
    in order to be able to *safely* interact with the new service implementation.
Context Senstive Selection. As mentioned earlier, one or more process in-
    stances can be associated with a context, which defines the actual set of
    candidate services that may be selected for each required service capability.
    Consequently, different services may be selected for the same service capabil-
    ity for different instances of the same process. Under such circumstances, it

---

[1] E.g. http://www.seekda.com, http://www.xmethods.com

is possible for the protocol associated with a selected service for one process instance to be different from the protocol associated with the selection for another instance.

New Protocols. The availability of new access protocols for service capabilities already being used in a process may cause a transition from the operation/evaluation phase to the design phase. For example, if the protocol for accessing a particular service capability is defined by an industry consortium (e.g. RosettaNet Partner Information Processes [14]), then an upgrade to the protocol might trigger updates by existing service providers to their service implementations. In subsequent discovery and selection activities, selecting such providers may require a transition to the design phase in order to support the new message exchange protocol.

One way of avoiding these transitions is to initially filter candidate services based on strict behavioural compatibility [15], and only make QoS-based selections from that pool. This means that only candidates that implement the exact protocol for which the process was designed to interact can be selected. However, this can result in very small set of candidates per service capability from which to choose. Furthermore, candidates with much better QoS may not even be shortlisted.

To take advantage of a larger pool of functionally compatible service candidates, any issues in behavioural compatibility has to be resolved. This often involves modifying the process structure to accommodate necessary changes or even creating multiple variants of the process structure to deal with the different services. The transitions induced by these drivers can cause significant overhead in terms of the technical and organisational resources needed to achieve them. As a result, methods are required to minimise the number of lifecycle transitions that take place due to service selection activities.

4   Relative Protocol Compatibility Based Selection

The approach outlined in this section is based on the concept of mediators[16] (also called adapters in [17,18]). A *mediator* enables a process, which is designed to use access a service using a certain protocol to access other functionally equivalent services using a different protocol. Although the use of a mediator can prevent the need to modify the definition of the original processs, the construction of a mediator is not always automatic. Often, human intervention is required to support the generation of a semantically correct mediator. Furthermore, recall that multiple instances of a process may be active at the same time, and dynamic service selection makes it possible to select different candidate services with different protocols for different instances. Consequently, it is of utmost interest to minimise the number of mediators that are created during the operational phase of the process lifecycle. To achieve this goal, we propose the design of mediators based on two principles:

- A candidate service that requires a mediator is only selected if its QoS is substantially better than the QoS of another candidate service, for which a

mediator is not required or already exists. This helps to ensure that mediators are not constructed for candidate services that provide only marginal QoS improvements.
- The relationships between the behavioural properties of candidate services are taken into consideration when creating mediators. This helps to ensure that when possible, a single mediator can be constructed such that it supports multiple instead of just one of the protocols used by candidate services.

Let a business process BP be required to realise n capabilities $C = \{c_1, \cdots, c_n\}$ by accessing a set of web services. For each service capability c_i, we identify three sets of candidate services: 1) the set of candidates that do not require mediation, 2) candidates that require mediation but a mediator already exists in a repository (e.g. based on previous selection), and 3) candidates for which mediators are not yet constructed. We denote the first two groups of candidates as K_i^0, and the third group as K_i^1. The set of all candidates for c_i is the union $K_i = K_i^0 \cup K_i^1$.

Traditional QoS-based service selection results in the selection of a candidate $k \in K_i$ for each selection context. If $k \in K_i^0$, then an existing mediator is used to interact with the service. However, if k is in K_i^1, then a mediator needs to be constructed. Sometimes, the difference in QoS between the selected candidate and another candidate in K_i^0 can be too small to justify the "notional cost" of creating and maintaining a mediator for the candidate service. In order to adhere to the first principle above, we introduce an additional weighted metric for service selection, which is termed *relative compatibility metric* and is based on the notion of behavioural compatibility. The weight assigned to this metric will enable the user to indicate how much the degree to which the notional cost of constructing and maintaining a mediator for a candidate service impacts on its suitability relative to the other candidates.

Given a process and the protocol used by a candidate service, the notional cost of creating and maintaining a mediator can be determined by considering a variety of factors e.g.:

- The structural complexity of the expected mediator, which may have some effects on the organisational maintainance cost.
- The syntatic / structural gap, which can be expressed in terms of the number of change operations needed to enable the process interact with a service that implements the protocol (e.g. graph edit distance [19,13]).
- The semantic gap (i.e. unresolvable differences between the message types used in the process and the protocol).
- The concessions required policy-wise. e.g. using a protocol that requires payment before delivery, when the policy of the business requires delivery before payment.

Admittedly, automatically determining a quantification for some of the factors above may not be trivial. However, a good start would be to use those that can be automatically determined such as the syntatic and semantic gaps.

The result of using this metric is that depending on the weight (or priority) assigned to the metric, a user can ensure that a candidate service that requires mediation is selected only if it provide substantially significant QoS for the particular selection context. This ultimately leads to a reduction in the number of intermittent lifecycle transitions that arise as a result of dynamic web service selection.

Assuming that a candidate service k_m, which requires mediation is selected, we can construct a mediator that exploits the relationships between the protocol associated with the candidate and protocols of other candidates in K_i^1. The idea is to construct the least costly mediator that enables the process interact with the largest number of other protocols. Where possible, this leads to the situation where candidate services implementing these protocols will all be part of K_i^0 in subsequent service selection activities. Let P_i represent the set of protocols for all $k_j \in K_i^1$, where $P_{ij} \in P_i$ refers to the protocol associated with candidate k_j.

Definition 1 (Protocol Refinement). *A protocol P_{ik} is considered a refinement of another protocol P_{ij} for the same capability c_i, if a process that can access c_i using P_{ik} can also access c_i using P_{ij} up to name substitution.*

Definition 2 (Horizontal Protocol Compatibility). *For a service capability c_i, two protocols P_{ij} and P_{ik} are horizontally compatible with respect to a process if a mediator M can be designed such that through M, the process can interact safely with two different services that implement protocols P_{ij} and P_{ik} respectively. M can be considered to be a trivial mediator if either P_{ik} or P_{ij} is a refinement of the other.*

Note that horizontal protocol compatibility is defined within the context of the behavioural interface of the process. For any protocol $P_{ij} \in P_i$, let $H_{ij} \subseteq P_i$ be the set of the protocols to which P_{ij} is horizontally compatible. This means that we can construct a mediator M_p for any set of protocols $p \in 2^{H_{ij}}$. Each M_p is associated with a 'notional cost' as described earlier and the number of protocols in p, denoted $|p|$. We can then associate this two parameters with weights and make a selection using the same standard techniques for service selection optimisation based on weighted metrics[11]. The result is the selection of an optimal mediator to be constructed. The parts of the mediator that can be auto-generated are then generated, after which a user can complete the specification. The mediator is then stored in a mediator repository. In subsequent service selection activities, candidates implementing the protocols in p will then be classified under K_i^0. As a result the subseqent selection of any candidate that implements a protocol in p will not trigger any lifecycle transition.

5 Limitations and Future Work

The approach described in this paper is currently a work-in-progress and a prototype is being developed to enable a comprehensive evaluation of the approach. Furthermore, there are a number of issues that are still yet to be addressed. For example in some cases, the use of a protocol to access a particular service capability within a process might have an impact on the use of another protocol for accessing another service capability within the same process (e.g. in the case of direct or indirect data dependencies between the message exchange protocols). Under such circumstances, a change to the protocol for accessing the first capability through mediation may require some changes in how the process interacts with the second service. Here, it is important to ensure that any such changes does not require the process to violate the protocol for accessing the second service. We term this notion of compatibility between the protocol for the first service and that of the second service as vertical compatibility.

If changes have to be made to the aspects of the process that deals with other services as a result of selecting a candidate service for a capability, then a quantification of those changes (whether automatic or semi-automatic) may be used as a factor that contributes to the relative compatibility metric that was introduced earlier. Also, we are interested in how the concept of worklets as introduced in [20] can be used to represent configurable mediators that support more than one protocol.

6   Conclusion

In this paper, we have outlined an approach to service selection that minimises intermittent lifecycle transitions for a business process, which uses web services that require arbitrarily complex interaction protocols. The approach introduces a new selection metric known as the relative compatibility metric, which is based on the behavioural properties of candidate services. It also introduces the concept of horizontal compatibility between candidate services, which is used to minimise the number of mediators that are constructed, while maximising their mediating capabilities. By assigning an adequate priority for the metric as a selection criterion, a user can potentially reduce the number of explicit lifecycle transitions that arise as a result of dynamic web service selections thus reducing the operational and maintainance cost of agile business processes.

References

1. Booth, D., Haas, H., McCabe, F., Newcomer, E., Champion, M., Ferris, C., Orchard, D.: Web services architecture. Technical report, W3C (2004), http://www.w3.org/TR/ws-arch/
2. Adam, S., Doerr, J.: How to better align bpm and soa – ideas on improving the transition between process design and deployment. In: 9th Workshop on Business Process Modeling, Development and Support, vol. 335, CEUR-WS (2008)
3. Weske, M.: Business Process Management: Concepts, Languages, Architectures, 1st edn. Springer, Heidelberg (2007)
4. Keller, U., Lausen, H.: Functional description of web services. Technical report, WSML Working Draft (2006)
5. Ruiz-Cortes, A., Martin-Diaz, O., Duran, A., Toro, M.: Improving the automatic procurement of web services using constraint programming. International Journal of Cooperative Information Systems 14, 439–467 (2005)
6. Kyriakos, K., Dimitris, P.: Semantic qos metric matching. In: ECOWS 2006: Proceedings of the European Conference on Web Services, Washington, DC, USA, pp. 265–274. IEEE Computer Society, Los Alamitos (2006)

7. Jaeger, C., Michael: Optimising Quality-of-Service for the Composition of Electronic Services. PhD thesis, Technische Universität, Berlin (2007)
8. Yu, T., Zhang, Y., Lin, K.J.: Efficient algorithms for web services selection with end-to-end qos constraints. ACM Trans. Web 1, 6 (2007)
9. Aggarwal, R., Verma, K., Miller, J., Milnor, W.: Constraint driven web service composition in meteor-s. Scc, 23–30 (2004)
10. Zhang, W., Yang, Y., Tang, S., Fang, L.: Qos-driven service selection optimization model and algorithms for composite web services. In: 31st Annual International on Computer Software and Applications Conference, COMPSAC 2007, vol. 2, pp. 425–431 (2007)
11. Ukor, R., Carpenter, A.: Optimising service selection for message oriented web services. In: IWSC 2009 (submitted, 2009)
12. Wombacher, A., Fankhauser, P., Mahleko, B., Neuhold, E.: Matchmaking for business processes based on choreographies. In: EEE 2004: Proceedings of the 2004 IEEE International Conference on e-Technology, e-Commerce and e-Service (EEE 2004), Washington, DC, USA, pp. 359–368. IEEE Computer Society, Los Alamitos (2004)
13. Grigori, D., Corrales, J.C., Bouzeghoub, M.: Behavioral matchmaking for service retrieval: Application to conversation protocols. Inf. Syst. 33, 681–698 (2008)
14. RosettaNet: Rosettanet partner information processes. Internet (2009)
15. Decker, G., Weske, M.: Behavioral consistency for B2B process integration. In: Krogstie, J., Opdahl, A.L., Sindre, G. (eds.) CAiSE 2007 and WES 2007. LNCS, vol. 4495, pp. 81–95. Springer, Heidelberg (2007)
16. Tan, W., Fan, Y., Zhou, M.: A petri net-based method for compatibility analysis and composition of web services in business process execution language. IEEE Transactions on Automation Science and Engineering 6, 94–106 (2009)
17. Dumas, M., Benatallah, B., Nezhad, H.R.M.: Web service protocols: Compatibility and adaptation. IEEE Data Eng. Bull. 31, 40–44 (2008)
18. Gierds, C., Mooij, A.J., Wolf, K.: Specifying and generating behavioral service adapter based on transformation rules. Preprint CS-02-08, Universität Rostock, Rostock, Germany (2008)
19. Lohmann, N.: Correcting deadlocking service choreographies using a simulation-based graph edit distance. In: Dumas, M., Reichert, M., Shan, M.-C. (eds.) BPM 2008. LNCS, vol. 5240, pp. 132–147. Springer, Heidelberg (2008)
20. Adams, M., Ter, Edmond, D., van der Aalst, W.: Worklets: A service-oriented implementation of dynamic flexibility in workflows, pp. 291–308 (2006)

Discovering Business Rules through Process Mining

Raphael Crerie, Fernanda Araujo Baião, and Flávia Maria Santoro

NP2Tec – Research and Practice Group in Information Technology
Department of Applied Informatics,
Federal University of the State of Rio de Janeiro (UNIRIO), Brazil
{raphael.silva, fernanda.baiao, flavia.santoro}@uniriotec.br

Abstract. Business rules guide the operation of an organization, thus its documentation provides an important source of information both for developing technological solutions (information systems, databases)and for evaluating information systems implementations. Despite its importance, manual creation and maintenance of business rule documentation is very costly, and practically infeasible in complex organizations. This paper describes a method for discovering business rules from the information systems event logs, through the use of process mining and data mining techniques. We exemplify the method execution to discover two selected sub-types of business rules, namely condition action assertions and authorization action assertions.

Keywords: Business Rules, Process Mining, Data Mining, Classification.

1 Introduction

Business rules play a key role in organizing daily activities, both in business and in scientific environments [13], because they determine how the activities should be executed to maintain the organization structure, thus influencing the organization as a whole [14]. Business rules also comprise essential information to the business models [6]. Under the focus of computing, the business rules are important input for conceptual modeling during the requirements elicitation phase for information systems development, where it is necessary to study the domain, i.e., understand and represent the automation context. Business rules are responsible for defining the concepts of domain, how these concepts can be related to each other, and regulate how various systems of an organization should handle the data sources they use.

According to Ross [18] [19], there must be a single, unified conceptual representation of current business rules. Despite its importance, many organizations do not have their business rules documented due to several factors, such as difficulty in formalizing them, high cost of documentation maintenance, and the existence of legacy systems implementing a large number of rules which are difficult to be extracted [6][18]. It is therefore important to develop automated mechanisms for discovering those business rules, extracting the rules actually implemented in information systems ("as-is" rules) and representing them in business rules models which are easy to understand and analyze.

T. Halpin et al. (Eds.): BPMDS 2009 and EMMSAD 2009, LNBIP 29, pp. 136–148, 2009.

The automatic constructed business rules models provide business analysts with a very insightful representation of actual rules implemented in the organization systems, and allow the assessment of those systems according to the functionalities they support, enabling the identification of gaps between intended business rules and those effectively implemented by IT supporting systems.

This paper presents a method for business rules discovery [28] from information systems event logs. Two selected sub-types of rules are examined: condition action assertion and authorization action assertion [7], which serve, respectively, to control the execution of an action in accordance with business restrictions and to limit the execution of some activity in accordance with who can run it.

Section 2 discusses the business rules concepts and exposes the adopted taxonomy in this study. Section 3 explains concepts related to process and data mining. Section 4 describes the method for discovering business rules and present two techniques for business rules discovery. Finally, Section 5 concludes the paper and describes future work.

2   Business Rules

The documentation of the procedures and concepts related to an organization is recently gaining more importance and attention. In this context, Business Rules are essential. In general, business rules should be specified by domain experts to define the structure, control or influence business conduction [7], thus assuring that information structures are adequate and facilitating decision making processes [22].

Following Ross's definition [18], a Business Rule is a guideline to influence or guide the conduct of business, a sentence that defines or qualifies any aspect of business, representing the knowledge of experts [7] [18]. Thus, they accumulate all the knowledge of the business built during time and by persons highly involved with it, making the rules a major structural and intellectual asset for organizations and creating the need for formal documentation to effectively make them a source of organizational knowledge dissemination and strengthen standard and efficient business processing by professionals [13].

Business Rules, from the IT perspective, can be seen as priority requirements for the development of applications to support the business; they tend to ensure that the objectives of the organization are aligned to the systems [13]. However, business rules must be generated without the involvement of IT professionals [5] and shall be represented in natural language so that they can be understood by everyone within the business scope. Current research is being conducted in order to formalize business rules so that the stored knowledge can be used for implementing automated processes and inferences [29] [36].

2.1   Business Rules Taxonomy

There are several initiatives to organize and classify business rules, but there is no universal standard. The classification used in our research is proposed by the Business Rule Group [7]. They present a taxonomy that classifies a business rule in one of 3 types: Structural Assertion, Action Assertion and Derivation (Figure 1).

Fig. 1. Classification of business rules (Business Rule Group [7])

An action Assertion is a restriction or condition that limits or controls the activities in the organization, that is, the dynamics of the business. Action assertions may be classified as Integrity Constraint, Authorization and Condition. The two last are the focus of this paper.

An authorization action assertion restricts who is allowed to perform a certain action. Examples of authorization action assertions are:

> *Only teacher can approve student.*
> *Only registered students can perform test.*

A condition action assertion serves to restrict the existence of certain business rules according to the application of others, or according to pre-existing conditions. Examples of a condition action assertion is:

> *Student registration is accomplished if:*
> I.   *Student has documents; and*
> II.   *Student had paid the registration;*

2.2 Business Rules Representation Languages

Recently, the OMG (Object Management Group) [37] adopted Semantics of Business Vocabulary and Business Rules (SBVR) as the standard language for representing business rules [29]. The SBVR meta-model allows business professionals to describe the organizational policies and rules in a clear, unambiguous and easily convertible to other representations. The SBVR is a MOF (Metadata Object Facility) [31]-compliant meta-model for the specification of business rules by business people with vocabulary based on XMI [32]. It enables interoperability of rules and vocabularies among software tools that handle business rules. An example of rule in SBVR can be seen below (words in bold are SBVR keywords):

> **It is obligatory that** Payment_order **has** customer.

3   Data Mining

Data mining (DM) is at the heart of all knowledge discovery approaches in large volumes of data, being an essential step in the knowledge discovery in databases (KDD) process [8]. Diverse types of patterns can be found through the application of different types of DM analysis, such as association analysis, cluster analysis and classification [38]. In the present work, we focus on the task of classification.

3.1 Classification

Classification is the process of searching for a set of models (functions) that describe and distinguish classes or concepts in terms of known object characteristics. The resulted model is used to predict the class of objects that have not yet been classified [38]. The model is constructed based on prior analysis of a sample dataset (training data) containing objects with known classifications, and evaluated against a test dataset with distinct objects from the training dataset. For example, suppose a scenario where a sales manager is interested in discovering if a customer is a "good buyer" or "bad buyer", that is, which customers may be classified in *status* = *"good buyer"* and *status* = *"bad buyer"*. The *status* attribute is called the class label attribute [38], which essentially represents the information to be discovered. A possible output from the classification task is a model including the following rule: "Customers with an income less than US$ 2,000 and aged between 50 and 60 are bad buyers".

The classification process is divided into two stages:

- *Creating the classification model*: uses a dataset called a "training database" which is a subset of the database to be evaluated, to create a model according to the available information;
- *Verifying the model*: uses another dataset, which is a subset of the database to be evaluated with no intersection 1 with the training database, which is called the "test database", where the model found is tested to assess its quality.

3.2 Process Mining

Traditionally, KDD techniques have been used to identify new, valid, potentially useful and understandable patterns in data [8]. And, more recently, the approach of processes mining has been exploited in many studies for extracting information from event logs to capture the business process throughout its implementation [1] [2] [3] [11], trying to identify how the processes are actually implemented and run analysis on their data. The flow of mining processes can be seen in Figure 2.

Process mining techniques assumes the existence of structured logs from information systems to store relevant events for the business. This is the case of organizations that adopt BPMS or ERP (Enterprise Resource Planning) systems, that record all transactions [1] [2] [9]. These events are a good source of information and make it possible to discover business processes from log data.

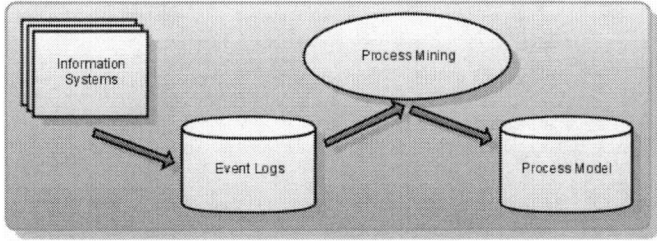

Fig. 2. Simplified flow of process mining

Developed by the Process Mining Group, the ProM (Process Mining Framework) [15] is an extensible framework that supports a wide variety of techniques for mining processes, implemented as plug-ins. This is an open source software and is used by several process mining approaches in the literature [2] [3] [11]. Our proposal is implemented on top of the ProM infrastructure. Event logs in the ProM framework are represented using the Mxml (Mining XML) common format [39] [40].

4 A Process Mining Approach for Business Rules Discovery

The proposed method for discovering business rules through process mining [28] consists of selecting and applying process mining techniques, and is implemented on top of the ProM framework infrastructure [15]. The method comprises the identification of implemented business rules and their representation in SBVR. Each type of business rule requires a different subset of information to be present in the event log.

The architecture shown in Figure 3 represents the proposal of this research. The information systems logs are captured and converted into Mxml. A technique of process or data mining is then applied on the logs, obtaining a set of rules that are then translated to SBVR [29].

4.1 Authorization Action Assertion Discovery

Two business rules sub-types were selected to test and validate the proposed method; the first method application used the sub-type Authorization Action Assertion (cited in session 2.1). As a first step the information requirements in the event log for the extraction of this type of rule of business have been identified:

- Name of the activity;
- Identification of the activity performer;
- Category of the performer (group access);

This log should be converted to the format with the aid of the tool Mxml ProM Import [27], or to be developed plug-in for the specific format of the log. The discovery of

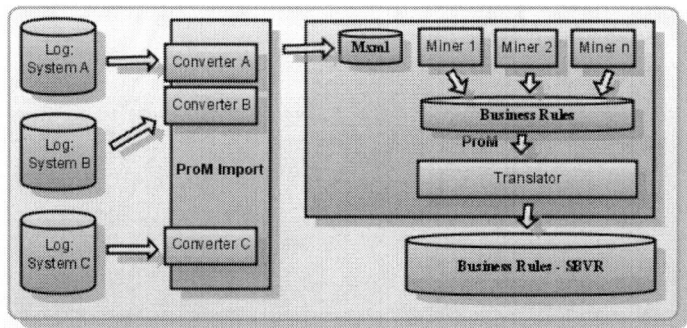

Fig. 3. Architecture of the business rules model generation through log mining

such a rule was made through an analysis of which groups have held that activities [28], making it possible to find rules like:

> Only "Manager" and "Seller" can perform the activity "Register claim".
> Only "Cashier" can perform the activity "Record of payment."
> Only "Manager" can perform the activity "Archive complaint."

For execution of this discovery, a plug-in for the ProM Framework was built. This plug-in loads the data and analyze the existing information in each execution. It identifies, for each existing activity in log, which categories of users (represented for the attribute group access) had executed instances of this activity.

4.2 Condition Action Assertion Discovery

The other business rules sub-type was selected to test and validate the proposed method, is the Condition Action Assertion (also cited in session 2.1). Condition action assertions, as explained in Section 2.1, restrict the existence of certain business rules according to the application of other ones, in other words, a particular rule will be valid for the business when other rules are applied. In order to find such a rule it is necessary to record as much information as possible at the time each an event is executed in the business. This information is known as "attributes of context", and among them, there should be an attribute that indicates how the event was completed (status of the event). Figure 4 shows an example of context information to the activity "Approve credit" with emphasis in the attribute "CREDIT SITUATION" that indicates the status of the event.

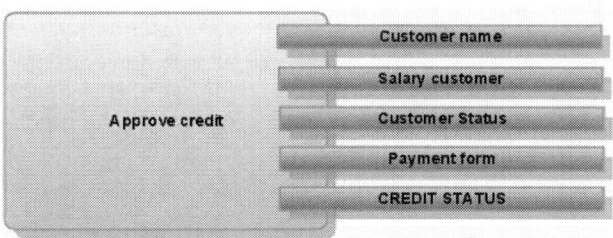

Fig. 4. Example of activity context attributes

Through the analysis of the each attribute values contained in a set of executions of the event, it is possible to discover new information about the context attributes: a set of possible values (Figure 5).

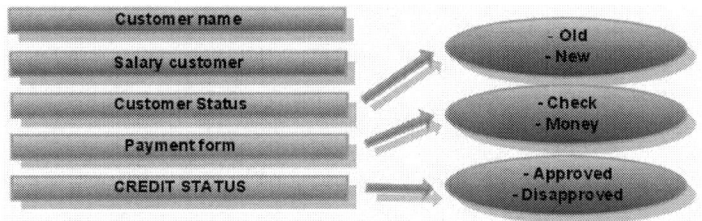

Fig. 5. Set of possible values for context attribute

Each set "context attribute" + "attribute value" represents a possible business rule that may have restricted its existence in accordance with the other attributes related to their context, when an analysis is made based on multiple instances of the activity. Through the analysis of this information, the following conclusion can be reached:

"CREDIT SITUATION" is approved when:
- "Form of Payment is Cash" or;
- "Form of Payment is Check" and "Status of Client is Old Client."

In this example we notice that the statements "Form of Payment is Cash," "Form of Payment is Check" and "Status of Client is Old Client" are conditions under which the statement "CREDIT SITUATION is approved" is true, i.e., there is a limitation for the context of the existence of this business rule. Analyzing the activity executions attributes makes possible to find this kind of business rules.

4.2.1 Classification Problem Characterization

As explained in Section 3.1, classification is the process of searching for a set of models (functions) that describe and distinguish classes or concepts. This definition fits to our necessity to find models that describe the existence of limitations by certain business rules. Furthermore, the classification process two sets of data (training and testing) can be represented as subsets of each activity instances execution to be analyzed, and besides, the classification attributes can be the context attributes.

4.2.2 Step by Step of the Condition Action Assertion Discovery

According to the method for business rules discovery using process mining [28], it is being developed a plug-in for ProM framework that searches for the data stored in an Mxml to perform the classification. The context attributes of each activity performed are grouped together and serve as a basis for the implementation of data mining (classification) for each activity. The following steps are implemented by plug-in:

- **Division of the Event Logs by Activity:** The Mxml, input file format of the PROM, have a structure guided to workflow, bringing the sequence of distinct activities executed. The first executed step is to group the information by activity so that can be made a mining based on all the executions of one determined activity;
- **Analysis of the Context Attributes:** In each activity, are identified the existing context attributes and the set of possible values for each attribute (for example, for the attribute sex, exist the values "Masculine" and "Feminine"). That is executed because was used the Weka library[41] of data mining for execution of classification algorithm, and the input file format for the execution of mining in this library (Arff [42]) demands that the information is organized in such a way;
- **Creation of Arff Files:** On the basis in the division of the events for activity and in the result of the analysis of the context attributes, is created Arff files [42], one for each different activity. One arff file contains: listing of the attributes with your specific domain and the set of values of the attributes for each execution;

- **Mining Execution:** Each context attribute is used as class label attribute [38] for execution of the data mining (classification). Numerical attributes are discarded because only text attributes are accepted as class label attribute for the algorithm;
- **Obtaining of the Rules Set:** The rules are gotten through of the analysis of the decision trees returned by the classification algorithm;

Rozinat and Aalst [20] identify Decision Points in process models through process mining. Decision points can be considered condition action assertions business rules, because they exhibit activities that are restricted by rules. However, this analysis is made only on the activities that have more than one successor activity, and analysis is always on the flow of activities. In our proposal, the assessment is made on the context attributes of each activity isolated, regardless its relationship with others of the flow.

4.2.3 Evaluation of the Method Application

To perform an evaluation of our proposal it was used the concept of automatic log generation through the tool CPNTools [25], that is a base model in the area of process mining [33] (Figure 6). This model was extended to add context information relevant to activities and guarantee the existence of such business rules in the workflow and thus, in a controlled environment, evaluate whether the rules that actually exist can be discovered through the application of this proposal.

The activities "SendBill" and "CloseCase" from the workflow used as base had been changed to add the following context attributes to be recorded (Figure 7):

- Role: indicates whether the profile of the activity executor is "role0", "role1" or "role2" (the activity "SendBill" should always de held by people with the profile "role0");
- Client_type: indicates whether the client is "Old_Client" or "New_Client";
- Payment_Type: records the type of payment used ("credit" or "money");
- Amount: records the total amount of the transaction. The possible values are: "130", "210", "200", "145", "1000", "1250", "515", "3100", "350", "45", "10000", " 125 "," 3000 "," 180 "," 1450 "," 5050 "," 900 "," 1430 "," 1700 "," 2000 "or" 5000 ";
- Credit_Status (only for activity "SendBill"): records whether the status of the operation was "Approved" or "Disapproved."
- Payment Status (only for activity "CloseCase"): records the status of the payment operation ("OK", "Denied" or " Failure");

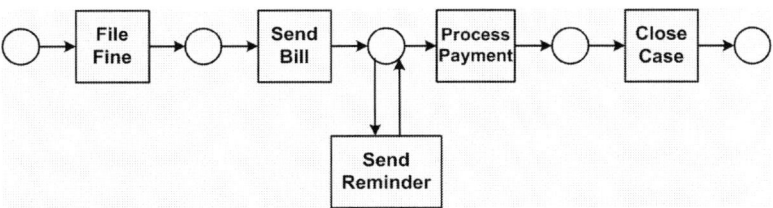

Fig. 6. Extract of the base process used as example [25]

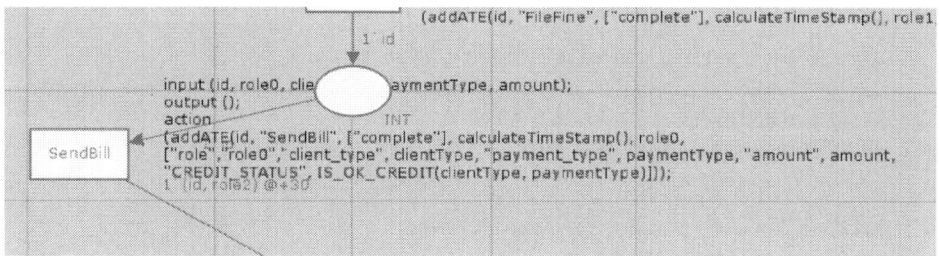

Fig. 7. First extract of the process changed to evaluate the method

- Delivery_released (only for activity "CloseCase"): records the status of product delivery, through values "YES" and "NO";

While the values of the context attributes "Client_type", "Payment_Type" and "Amount" are randomly selected for each application flow, a function does the following to generate the check value of attribute "Credit_Status:

```
fun IS_OK_CREDIT (client_type, payment_type) =
    if (client_type = "Old_Client") then "Approved"
    else  if payment_type = "cash" then "Approved"
          else "Disapproved";
```

The purpose of this formula is forcing that on all executions, only the former clients (client_type = "Old_Client") or new clients who make payment in cash (pay-ment_type = "cash") will have the "Credit_Status" attribute with value "Approved". While the context attributes "Payment_Status" and "Delivery_released" possess its generated values in accordance with following the definitions:

```
fun GET_PAYMENT_STATUS(paymentType, paymentStatus,
            randomStatus) =
    if (payment_type = "money") then "OK";
    else (randomPaymentStatus);

fun IS_DELIVERY_RELEASED(paymentStatus) =
    if paymentStatus = "OK" then "YES"
    else "NO";
```

The first formula makes with that "Payment_Status" always has value "OK" when the "Payment_Type" will be "money" and random value (inside of the attribute scope) when "Payment_type" to possess another value. And the last presented formula, makes with that whenever "Payment_Status" to assume the value "OK", "Deliv-ery_Release" assumes the value "YES", in other cases this attribute assumes the value of "NO".

By forcing the existence of these rules over the executions of the workflow, it be-comes feasible to assess whether it is possible to extract it from the log generated by the application.

A Mxml was generated with more then 10000 event through the simulation result of workflow executions [33] and this log was submitted to the plug-in developed at ProM developed and generates a result containing the rules found by classifier

```
@@@ Start mining of: SendBill                    @@@ Start mining of: CloseCase
@ Label Class attribute: CREDIT_STATUS           @ Label Class attribute: Payment_status
- Correct Instances: 1000.0                      - Correct Instances: 1676.0
- Instances: 1000                                - Instances: 2000
- Tree:                                           - Tree:
payment_type = credit                            payment_type = money: OK (995.0)
|   client_type = New_Client: DISAPPROVED (225.0) payment_type = credit
|   client_type = Old_Client: APPROVED (234.0)   |   delivery_released = NO: Denied (660.0/324.0)
payment_type = money: APPROVED (541.0)           |   delivery_released = YES: OK (345.0)
                  (a)                                             (b)
```

Fig. 8. Mining result for activities "SendBill" (a) and "CloseCase" (b)

attribute used in each activity . For the activity "SendBill," which were added the context attributes and the rules described above, the result generated is shown in the decision tree on Figure 8a. The method could correctly identify the rule while recognizes the value of attribute "Credit_Status", respecting the rule (cited above) that had the existence forced in the model generated in the CPNTools. And in the result of the method application for the activity "CloseCase" was possible to identify the rule presented in the Figure 8b, where was discovered the direct relation between the values of the attributes "Payment_status", "payment_type" and "delivery_released".

5 Conclusions

Business rules have a key role in organization of daily activities both in business and in scientific environments [13], because they determine how the organization should be guided to maintain its structure, to influence all aspects of it and to provide essential information to the business models and technology. The conceptual representation of business rules is important because it provides information source that facilitate the generation and maintenance of technological models, and explicit how the organization works. In particular, condition action assertions rules are essential because they reflect limitations or controls on the rules in the organization; they ultimately restrict the existence of business rules in accordance with the existence of other business rules. But, despite its importance, many organizations do not have their business rules documented. It is therefore important to develop automated mechanisms to discover these rules.

This work proposes a method for a process mining based approach for business rule discovery. The provided examples show the feasibility of our method in automatically discovering condition action assertions and also authorization action assertions. This enables a new and important form of attainment of information on organizations business.

Moreover, the proposed method may also be used to identify conduct deviations or frauds to the defined business rules, through the application of data mining algorithms specific for this purpose [35]. Future work will address this opportunity, as well as other types of business rules.

References

1. van der Aalst, W.M.P., Weijters, A.: Process Mining Process-Aware Information Systems: Bridging People e Software through Process Technology. Wiley & Sons, Chichester (2005)
2. van der Aalst, W.M.P., Günther, C.W.: Finding Structure in Unstructured Processes: The Case for Process Mining. In: ACSD 2007, pp. 3–12 (2007)
3. van der Aalst, W.M.P., De Beer, H.T., Van Dongen, B.F.: Process mining and e verification of properties: An approach based on temporal logic. In: Meersman, R., Tari, Z. (eds.) OTM 2005. LNCS, vol. 3760, pp. 130–147. Springer, Heidelberg (2005)
4. Alberti, M., Sani, F., Gavanelli, M., Lamma, E., Mello, P., Montali, M., Storari, S., Torroni, P.: A Computational Logic-based Approach to Verification of IT Systems. In: Proceedings of the 14th Annual Workshop of HP Software University Association (HP-SUA 2007), Munich, Germany, July 2007, pp. 115–125. Infonomics-Consulting (2007)
5. Amghar, Y., Mezaine, M., Flory, A.: Modeling of business rules for active database application specification. In: Advanced topics in database research, vol. 1, pp. 135–156. IGI Publishing Hershey, PA (2003)
6. BRG (Business Rules Group). Business Rules Group. Business Rules Manifesto. Version 2.0, http://www.businessrulesgroup.org/brmanifesto.htm
7. BRG (Business Rules Group). Defining Business Rules ~ What Are They Really? Rev. 1.3, http://www.businessrulesgroup.org/first_paper/BRG-whatisBR_3ed.pdf
8. Fayyad, U.M., Piatetsky-Shapiro, G., Smith, P., Uthurusamy, R.: Advances in Knowledge Discovery and Data Mining. AAAI/MIT Press (1996)
9. Goedertier, S., Vanthienen: Rule-based business process modeling and execution. In: CTIT Workshop Proceeding Series. International IEEE EDOC Workshop on Vocabularies, Ontologies and Rules for the Enterprise (VORTE 2005), pp. 67–74 (2005)
10. Kovacic, A., Groznik, A.: The business rule-transformation approach. In: 26th International Conference on Information Technology Interfaces, vol. 1, pp. 113–117 (2004)
11. Medeiros, A., Pedrinaci, C., van der Aalst, W.M.P., Domingue, J., Song, M., Rozinat, A., Norton, B., Cabral, L.: An Outlook on Semantic Business Process Mining and Monitoring. In: Workshop: 3rd International IFIP Workshop On Semantic Web & Web Semantics (SWWS 2007) at On The Move Federated Conferences and Workshops (2007)
12. Mirabete, J.F.: Processo Penal. 15 edição, Editora Atlas. 23 (2003) (in Portuguese)
13. Morgado, G.P., Martins, A.E., Alencar, A.J., Seabra, C.M., Silveira, D.S., Schimitz, E.A., Dias, F.G., Lima, P.M.V.: Um Ambiente para Modelagem Organizacional Baseado em Regras de Negócio. In: Simpósio Brasileiro de Sistemas de Informação, Porto Alegre (2004) (in Portuguese)
14. OMG.: Business motivation Model (BMM) Specification, http://www.omg.org/docs/dtc/06-08-03.pdf
15. Prom. The ProM Framework, http://is.tm.tue.nl/~cgunther/dev/prom/
16. Putrycz, E., Kark, A.W.: Recovering Business Rules from Legacy Source Code for System Modernization. In: Paschke, A., Biletskiy, Y. (eds.) RuleML 2007. LNCS, vol. 4824, pp. 107–118. Springer, Heidelberg (2007)
17. Ram, S., Khatri, V.: A comprehensive framework for modeling set-based business rules during conceptual database design. In: Information Systems Archive, pp. 89–118. Elsevier Science Ltd., Amsterdam (2005)
18. Ross, R.G.: Principles of the Business Rule Approach. Addison-Wesley Information Technology Series (2003) ISBN-13: 978-0201788938

19. Ross, R.G.: Expressing Business Rules. In: SIGMOD Conference 2000, pp. 515–516 (2000)
20. Rozinat, A., van der Aalst, W.M.P.: Decision mining in proM. In: Dustdar, S., Fiadeiro, J.L., Sheth, A.P. (eds.) BPM 2006. LNCS, vol. 4102, pp. 420–425. Springer, Heidelberg (2006)
21. Martins, A.: Em direção à captura e representação sistemática das definições dos termos das regras de negócio. Rio de Janeiro. Dissertação de Mestrado. UFRJ/IM/NCE (2006) (in Portuguese)
22. Halle, B.V.: Business Rules Applied: Builing Better Systems Using the Business Rules Approach, 1st edn. John Wiley & Sons, New York (2002)
23. Horrocks, I., Patel-Schneider, P.F., Boley, H., Tabet, S., Grosof, B., Dean, M.: SWRL: A Semantic Web Rule Language Combining OWL and RuleML. W3C Member Submission, http://www.w3.org/Submission/SWRL/
24. OCL. Object Constraint Language. OMG Available Specification. Version 2.0, http://www.omg.org/docs/formal/06-05-01.pdf
25. CPNtools. Computer Tool for Coulored Petri Nets, http://wiki.daimi.au.dk/cpntools/cpntools.wiki
26. Chen, P.P.: The Entity-Relationship Model: Toward a Unified View of Data. ACM Trans. on Database Systems 1(1), 9–36 (1976)
27. ProMimport. Swiss army knife for event logs, http://is.tm.tue.nl/~cgunther/dev/promimport
28. Crerie, R., Baião, F., Santoro, F.M.: Identificação de Regras de Negócio utilizando Mineração de Processos. In: II Workshop de Gestão de Processos de Negócio (WBPM), Vila Velha-ES, Simpósio Brasileiro de Sistemas Multimídia e Web (WEBMEDIA) (2008) (in Portuguese)
29. SBVR, Semantics of Business Vocabulary and Rules, http://www.omg.org/spec/SBVR
30. Kamada, A.: Execução de serviços baseada em regras de negócio. Tese de Doutorado. Universidade Estadual de Campinas, Brazil (2006) (in Portuguese)
31. OMG. Meta Object Facility (MOF) Core. Version 2.0, http://www.omg.org/spec/MOF/
32. OMG. MOF 2.0/XMI Mapping Specification, v2.1, http://www.omg.org/docs/formal/05-09-01.pdf
33. Alves de Medeiros, A.K., Günther, C.W.: Process Mining: Using CPN Tools to Create Test Logs for Mining Algorithms. In: Proceedings of the Sixth Workshop on the Practical Use of Coloured Petri Nets and CPN Tools (CPN 2005), Aarhus, Denmark. DAIMI, vol. 576 (October 2005)
34. Rozinat, A., van der Aalst, W.M.P.: Decision Mining in ProM. In: Dustdar, S., Fiadeiro, J.L., Sheth, A.P. (eds.) BPM 2006. LNCS, vol. 4102, pp. 420–425. Springer, Heidelberg (2006)
35. Bezerra, F., Wainer, J.: Fraud Detection in Process Aware Systems. In: WBPM 2008, Vila Velha. II Workshop de Gestão de Processos de Negócio (2008)
36. Silva, G.Z., Souza, J.M., Miranda, R., Pereira Neto, F.: FalaOCL: Uma ferramenta para Parafrasear OCL. In: XVI Simposio Brasileiro de Engenharia de Software, Rio Grande do Sul. Anais do Simposio Brasileiro de Engenharia de Software, vol. 16, pp. 390–395 (2002) (in Portuguese)
37. OMG. Object Management Group, http://www.omg.org
38. Han, J., Kamber, M.: Data Mining: Concepts and Techniques, 550 pages. Morgan Kaufmann, San Francisco (2000)

39. Alves de Medeiros, A.K., van der Aalst, W.M.P., Pedrinaci, C.: Semantic Process Mining Tools: Core Building Blocks. In: 16th European Conference in Information Systems (ECIS), CD-ROM (2008) ISBN13:978-0-9553159-2-3
40. Alves de Medeiros, A.K.: Genetic Process Mining. Ph. D Thesis, Eindhoven Technical University, Eindhoven, The Netherlands (2006)
41. Weka, http://www.cs.waikato.ac.nz/ml/weka/
42. Arff. Attribute-Relation File Format,
    http://www.cs.waikato.ac.nz/~ml/weka/arff.html

Anomaly Detection Using Process Mining

Fábio Bezerra[1], Jacques Wainer[1], and W.M.P. van der Aalst[2]

[1] Institute of Computing - UNICAMP
Av. Albert Einstein, 1251
Campinas, São Paulo, Brazil
{fbezerra,wainer}@ic.unicamp.br
[2] Dep. of Mathmatics and Computer Science - TU/e
Den Dolech 2, 5600 MB
Eindhoven, The Netherlands
w.m.p.v.d.aalst@tm.tue.nl

Abstract. Recently, several large companies have been involved in financial scandals related to mismanagement, resulting in financial damages for their stockholders. In response, certifications and manuals for best practices of governance were developed, and in some cases, tougher federal laws were implemented (e.g. the Sarboness Oxley Act). Companies adhered to these changes adopting the best practices for corporate governance by deploying Process Aware Information Systems (PAISs) to automate their business processes. However, these companies demand a rapid response to strategic changes, so the adoption of normative PAISs may compromise their competitiveness. On one hand companies need flexible PAISs for competitiveness reasons. On the other hand flexibility may compromise security of system because users can execute tasks that could result into violation of financial loses. In order to re-balance this trade-off, we present in this work how ProM tools can support anomaly detection in logs of PAIS. Besides, we present the results of the application of our approach with a real case.

Keywords: Process mining, anomaly detection, auditing systems.

1 Introduction and Motivation

Management trends in the early 1990's largely motivated the adoption of **P**rocess **A**ware **I**nformation **S**ystems (PAISs) by organizations [1]. The use of PAISs illustrates a shift from data to process-oriented systems, which clearly separates business process logic from application programs, facilitating redesign and extension of process models. Moreover, legal requirements are also motivating companies to adopt PAISs and follow best practices of governance (e.g. COBIT, Control Objectives for Information and related Technology) in order to support the control of their business processes. For example, we can cite the Sarbanes-Oxley Act, which is a United States federal law enacted in response to a number of major corporate and accounting scandals (e.g. Enron and WorldCom).

Despite the automation provided by PAIS, the business process control of competitive companies should not be supported by normative tools like a classical

T. Halpin et al. (Eds.): BPMDS 2009 and EMMSAD 2009, LNBIP 29, pp. 149–161, 2009.

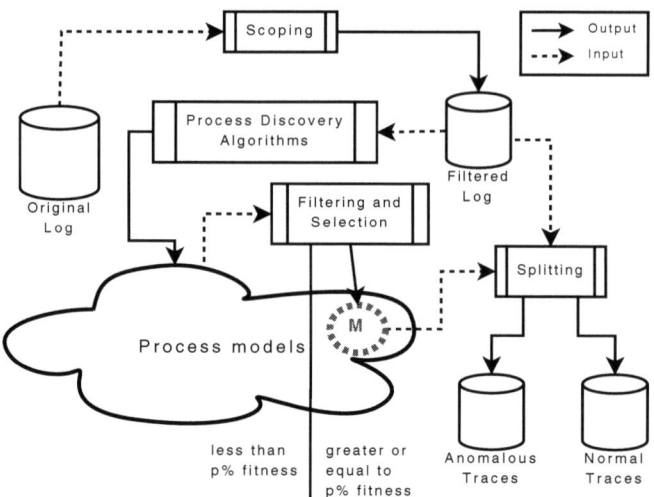

Fig. 1. Overview of our anomaly detection approach

production WMS (Workflow Management System). These companies demand a flexible automation of their business processes, since they need to respond rapidly to new market strategies or new business models. On the other hand, a flexible system may be vulnerable to fraudulent or undesirable executions. These considerations illustrate the trade off between flexibility and security. In other words, the system should provide flexibility for competitiveness reasons, but it also should avoid or *identify* misuse of system.

Therefore, there is clearly a demand for auditing systems, and buzzwords such as BAM (Business Activity Monitoring), BOM (Business Operations Management), and BPI (Business Process Intelligence) illustrate the interest of vendors to support the monitoring and analysis of business activities [2]. Besides, the spectacular growth of log data in the form of audit trails, transaction logs, and data warehouses, and the requirement from a BPM (Business Process Management) perspective, have stimulated and enabled the development of process mining techniques. The process mining is mainly concerned with the discovery of process models from logs generated by information systems [3,4]. Recent developments in the field of process mining have led to a renewed interest in anomaly detection [5,6,7] and security issues [8]. Thus, this paper presents an approach to detect anomalous traces using available process mining tools of ProM framework[1].

Figure 1 provides an overview of our proposed approach which is organized in five steps: (i) scoping, (ii) process discovery, (iii) filtering of fitting models, (iv) model selection, and (v) splitting of log. The *scoping* phase is a domain dependent step by applying some filters where instances and activities that are out-of-scope are removed from the original log. The next two steps deal with

---

[1] http://www.processmining.org

discovering models and *filtering of fitting models*, i.e. the selection of models that satisfy a minimum (p%) fitness criteria - the degree of fitness refers to the ability to reproduce the log. Then, we *select the most appropriate* model among fitting models. An appropriate model is a structuraly simple and behavioraly specific model. Finally, we *classify the instances* of log in anomalous and normal instances using the selected model. In this approach, which focuses on analysis of control-flow perspective, if an execution trace in the log is not an instance of (or does not fit) the appropriate model, it is an anomalous trace.

The remainder of this paper is organized as follow. In Section 2 we present some related work in the area of process mining, conformance checking, trace clustering, and auditing. Albeit it is hard to present a precise definition for anomaly in process-aware context, specially when we consider very dynamic application domains (e.g. health care systems), in Section 3 we present what we believe to be a suitable anomaly definition. In Section 4 we present how ProM framework can be applied to operationalize this definition. Besides, we provide a case study in Section 5 to show how our anomaly detection approach can be applied in a real scenario, and we provide a final discussion and directions for future work in Section 6.

2   Related Work

Process mining techniques allow for various types of analysis based on so-called event logs. For example, using process mining one can reconstruct a process model from a log generated by some information system. In the last ten years researchers around the world have been working on such techniques [3,9,10]. The term was first coined in the context of software processes. Cook and Wolf, in [11], present process discovery as a tool to support the design of software processes because it is a hard, expensive, and a error prone activity, specially for big and complex processes. Also a forerunner work in process mining, the paper of Agrawal et al, in [12], present an algorithm that mine models having three properties in mind: completeness, minimality, and irredundancy.

Among the recent process mining approaches, the most visible one is the $\alpha-$algorithm [10,4]. The effectiveness of that algorithm was formally proved for a class of process models, the WF-Nets (*Workflow Net*), which are Petri nets that require: (i) a single Start place, (ii) a single End place, and (iii) every node must be on some path from Start to End. However, such an algorithm has severe limitations, for example, the inability to deal with short loops.

Noise in the event log is closely related to anomaly detection. Some process mining methods deal with the mining of noisy logs [12,3,13,14,15], yet their approaches are limited to the frequency evaluation of dependency relation between two activities. For example, infrequent dependency relations between two activities may not be modeled in the resulting process model. A more sophisticated and promising approach, called genetic mining, was proposed in [16]. This algorithm is based on genetic algorithms, which search for a solution (an individual) that satisfies a selection criteria, called fitness function. The individuals are generated based on genetic operators such as crossover, mutation, and elitism.

All previously mentioned process mining methods are mainly concerned with the modeling of normal behavior, yet some of them also deal with noisy logs. However, abnormal behavior was not deeply studied by process mining community, although it is a clearly important subject to the development of more accurate auditing systems. Then, in order to fill this gap, recent researches have been addressing the problem of identifying anomalous trace in logs of PAISs [8,17,7,6]. In [8], Aalst and Medeiros present two anomaly detection methods that are supported by α-algorithm. A drawback of this work is that it demands a known "normal" log, but a known "normal" log may not be available in applications domains that demand flexible support. In [17], the authors present a framework to detect fraud and abuse in health insurance systems. In this work clinical pathways are used to construct a detection model, whose features are based on frequent control-flow patterns inferred from two datasets, one with fraudulent instances and other with normal instances. In [6] and [7], Bezerra and Wainer present three different approaches to detect anomalous traces: sampling, threshold, and iterative approaches. Nevertheless, as pointed out by the authors, the methods presented in [6,7] have serious practical limitations, directly resulting from the adopted process mining algorithm, which can not deal with larger logs.

3   Formal Anomaly Definition

There are many meanings associated with the definition of anomaly. An anomaly can be an **exceptional** execution, a **noise** in the log, possibly caused by system failure or error in data input, or even a **fraud** attempt. An exception characterizes an abnormal or unusual execution, but it can be supported by the business. Whereas a fraud attempt and an operational error are unusual executions that lead to undesirable results from a business point of view. However, despite different meanings associated with the term anomaly, there are some common generic definitions such as: (i) a rare or infrequent event; (ii) a deviation from a normal form or rule; (iii) an unexpected result; or (iv) a state outside the usual range of variations.

Nevertheless, a precise definition of normal, norm, or rule is difficult, or even impossible, if one assumes a generic context, e.g. an arbitrary PAIS. Note that, in very dynamic environments, like health care systems, each instance (e.g. patient treatment) may be different from others, so each instance can be viewed as an unexpected occurrence. Next, we present a definition for anomalous traces. We believe that such a definition is a first step towards a more accurate and generic definition. We will make this definition operational using ProM framework, and we point out in Section 4 how ProM can address this definition.

Throughout this paper the term trace will be used to refer to an execution path (or process instance) of a business process model, and it represents the order that the activities of this path were completed. Thus, a trace $[a\ b\ c\ d\ e]$ indicates that activity a finished before activity b, and that activity b finished before activity c, and so on. Using the notion of a trace, we define the concept of an event log.

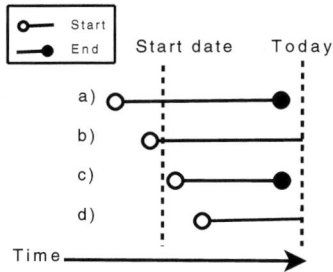

Fig. 2. Problems related with an imported log

Definition 1. *Trace.*
Given that A is a set of activities. Then, a trace t represents a sequence of activities such that t ∈ A*. That is, assuming that A is an alphabet, and A* denotes all possible words over A, then t is a word based on this alphabet.

Definition 2. *Log.*
Given T as the set of all traces defined over A and T' ⊆ T, then a log L is defined as $L \subseteq T'^2$.

In the scoping step of our anomaly detection approach (see Figure 1) the domain analyst will define which activities and traces may be removed from log before anomaly detection. We call the first step scoping because it represents the moment when the domain analyst defines what is important to consider in the analyses. Also, traces that are clearly not fully recorded should be removed. For example, we show in Figure 2 four traces (a, b, c, and d) from a log, and we indicate with dashed lines the period that was used to import the traces for analysis. Thus, it is clear in this figure that: (i) trace a) should be removed because it does not have the expected start activity; (ii) trace b) should be removed because it does not have the expected start and end activities; and (iii) trace d) should be removed because it does not have the expected end activity. The scoping step is formally defined below.

Definition 3. *Scoped Log.*
Given a log L as defined in Definition 2, and a set A^S of scoped activities such that $A^S \subseteq A$. Then, an scoped log L^S is a set of traces t based on scoped activities A^S such that:

$$L^S = \{filter(t, A^S) \mid t \in L \wedge complete(t)\}$$

where filter removes all activities in t that are not in A^S, and complete(t) is a boolean function that evaluates to false if t is not complete or inappropriate.

---

[2] Note that for simplicity we assume that a log is a set of traces. However, in reality a log is a bag (i.e. multiset) of traces since each sequence of activities may appear multiple times in the log. Although we use set in our formal definition, our implementation in ProM takes frequencies of traces into account.

In order to classify the traces of a log as anomalous and normal, we have to use what we call an *appropriate model*, which is a model that has a minimum fitness support (see Definition 5) and maximizes a function called appropriateness (see Definition 6). The minimum fitness support is a parameter used to filter the models that can be discovered from the log, that is, among the models (possibly infinitely many) we are interested in the models that can classify at least $p\%$ of traces as normal, where $p\%$ refers to the minimum fitness support.

Definition 4. *Fitness Instance Test Function.*
$f_M : L \to \mathbb{B}$ *is the fitness instance test function that indicates if a trace from a log L is an instance of a model M. A trace t is instance of a model M if t can be completely parsed by M. It can be defined as follows:*

$$f_M(t) = \begin{cases} true, & if\ t\ can\ be\ replayed\ by\ model\ M \\ false, & otherwise \end{cases}$$

Definition 5. *Fitness Model Test Function.*
It is a function $f : \{(M, L) | M$ is a model $\wedge\ L$ is a log$\} \to [0, 1]$ that indicates the degree of fitness between a model M and a log L, that is, how many traces from log L fit or can be completely parsed in model M. Function f is defined as follows:

$$f(M, L) = \frac{|\{t \in L | f_M(t)\}|}{|L|}$$

Therefore, the *fitness model test function* indicates how much of the observed behavior in the log can be supported by a model. That is, a fitness of 100% means that the model supports the whole log, so it is able to replay each trace from the log correctly. Nevertheless, a model with 100% of fitness does not mean an appropriate model. For example, the generic model depicted in Figure 3 can replay whatever trace defined over the set of activities {A, B, C, D}, so this model will never be able to detect anomalous traces in a log whose traces are based on these activities. On the other hand, a model with low fitness value would classify many traces in log as anomalous. Hence, *appropriateness test function* is important to help us choose which fitting model is more appropriate, that is, given two fitting models which one better describes the log in a simple and specific way. Therefore, we present a formal definition of *appropriateness test function*, which supports the fourth step of our anomaly detection approach, the model selection step. Then, after selecting the *appropriate model*, a trace from the log is anomalous if it is not fitting model (cf. Definition 7).

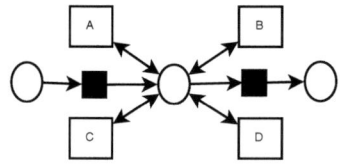

Fig. 3. Example of a generic model (Flowered model)

Definition 6. *Appropriateness Test Function.*
$a : \{(M, L)|M \text{ is a model } \land L \text{ is a log}\} \rightarrow [0, 1]$ *is a function that indicates how appropriate is a model M when compared with log L, where appropriate means that a simple model is preferable than complex one, and that "too much" additional behavior is undesirable. Therefore, such a function represents a balance between structural complexity and extra-behavior support.*

Finally, once we selected an appropriate model, we perform the last step of our anomaly detection approach, the splitting of log in two sets: *anomalous traces* and *normal traces*. Below, we present a formal definition of anomalous trace.

Definition 7. *Anomalous Trace.*
Given log L, $p \in [0, 1]$ the desired minimal degree of fitness between a model and a log, and M^* an appropriate model *such that:*

- $f(M^*, L) \geq p$;
- $\forall M'\ f(M', L) \geq p \Rightarrow a(M', L) \leq a(M^*, L)$.

Then, an anomalous trace $t' \in L$ is defined as follows: $\neg f_{M^*}(t)$, i.e.
$\{t \in L \mid \neg f_{M^*}(t)\}$ is the set of anomalous traces.

Summarizing, among the models that can be discovered from a scoped log L^S, we are interested in the model M^*, which we call *appropriate model* and has a minimum fitness degree p, but whose appropriateness is greater or equal to the appropriateness of all others models with minimum fitness p that can also be discovered from this log L^S. Then, the **anomalous traces** are those traces from log that do not fit the *appropriate model M^**. In the following section we address this formal anomaly definition operational by using ProM.

4   Application Based on ProM

The ProM framework is a pluggable environment for process mining [18]. It is platform independent as it is implemented in Java, and it is open-source. The framework is flexible with respect to the input and output format, and it is also open enough to allow for the easy reuse of code during the implementation of new process mining techniques. ProM supports the analysis of three main perspectives: (i) the process perspective that focuses on the control-flow mining; (ii) the organizational perspective that focuses on the performers of activities; and (iii) the case perspective that focuses on properties, data, and values manipulated by activities. Because our anomaly detection approach is focusing on control-flow deviations, we are specially interested in the plug-ins dealing with process perspective in ProM. In this section, we show how the ProM framework can be used in the identification of anomalous traces based on our formal definition (cf. Definition 7).

4.1   Scoping

The first step of our anomaly detection approach is concerned with the removal
of activities and traces from log that are not interesting for analysis or that may
lead the definition of anomalies that are the result of an incomplete log. ProM
has a lot of log filtering tools that can be applied in this step. For example, in
ProM is possible to indicate what are the start and end activities of traces from
log, so every trace that does not start and end with selected activities will be
removed from log.

ProM also provides inspecting tools that can be used to evaluate the frequency
of activities. Using filtering it is possible to perform an analysis based only on
frequent traces. Besides, ProM provides an analysis plug-in called *LTL Checker*
that can be used to filter traces that satisfy certain properties, for example,
traces with a causal relation between two activities.

4.2   Process Discovery and Filtering

The next two steps of our anomaly detection approach address the discovery and
filtering of models. The process discovery step deals with the automated construction of a process model that describes the log used during discovery, while
the filtering step is related with the selection of models that satisfy a minimum
fitness constraint (the *p value* in Definition 7). In order to address the discovery process step, ProM provides several algorithms, and all available process
discovery algorithms can be used. On the other hand, the fitness instance test
function, as described in Definition 4, is not provided separately by ProM, yet
it can be obtained indirectly through the *conformance checker* plug-in [18]. The
fitness(f) metric of conformance checker plug-in is a more fine-grained metric
that evaluates how much a model fits a log considering both trace and activity
perspectives.

Moreover, the fitness of a model can be evaluated through a metric in ProM
called *PM (Parsing Measure)* that directly supports Definition 5. Such a metric
can be used with *control-flow benchmark* plug-in, but it works only with heuristic models, and because there is not a direct conversion plug-in from Petri nets
to heuristic models, we can not use this metric with process mining algorithms
that output Petri nets models. On the other hand, we can accomplish this limitation using conformance checker plug-in, which provides an interface where it
is possible to select only the fitting traces (100% of fitness), and then we can see
the percentage of traces that fits the model.

4.3   Model Selection

Model selection is the fourth step of our approach, and it is concerned with the
selection of what we call *appropriate model*, that is, a simple and non-generic
model. In order to objectively help us choose such an appropriate model we need
an appropriateness test function that supports Definition 6. Although ProM does
not provide a plug-in that directly selects the most appropriate model, the appropriateness metrics implemented in both *conformance checker* and *control-flow*

benchmark plug-ins can be used in for a suitable definition of an appropriateness test function (cf. Equation (1)). Hence the appropriateness test function may be evaluated in ProM as follows:

- using a metric called *structural appropriateness*, which assesses the complexity of a model, and we represent here as a function $f_S(M)$, where M is a model;
- using a metric called *behavioral appropriateness*, which assesses how specific is a model regarding a log, and we represent here as a function $f_B(M, L)$, where M is a model and L is a log;
- finally, since both functions are defined for the same codomain ($[0, 1]$), we could objectively define appropriateness as a balance value between these structural and behavioral metrics, as follows:

$$a(M, L) = \frac{f_S(M) + f_B(M, L)}{2} \tag{1}$$

4.4   Splitting

Finally, since we have an *appropriate model*, the last step of our anomaly detection approach can be easily achieved through *conformance checker* plug-in of ProM. That is, once we have got a model that supports a minimum fitness threshold (value p of definition), and such a model also has the greatest appropriateness value amongst other models, we can simply select those traces that do not fit the model as follows: (i) selecting fitting traces as normal traces; and then (ii) inverting selection to identify the anomalous traces.

5   Municipal Household Support System

In this section we present a real application of ProM tools for supporting our anomaly detection approach. It refers to a log of the information system of the Dutch municipality. The process is about supporting citizens that need help in the form of a wheelchair, scootmobiel, adaptation of house (elevator), and household help. The log used in this analysis comprises event data from January 2007 to August 2008, and it contains information of 876 process instances that together represent 5497 activities, among 10 different activities available in the log. Besides, the shortest trace from log has 1 activity, while the longest has 12 activities. On average, the traces have 6 activities.

Because many models can be discovered from a log (maybe infinite), and considering the lack of automated tools to generate all possible candidates, we explored the set of possible process models in a semi-automatic fashion, i.e., the appropriate model was discovered through manual parameter selection. In the following we present how we applied our anomaly detection approach.

Table 1. Frequency of start and end activities obtained from ProM

Frequency of start activities		Frequency of end activities	
Activity	Frequency	Activity	Frequency
Request registration	96,12%	Final Phase	94,52%
Reporting & Decision	3,43%	Reporting & Decision	2,06%
Private research	0,34%	Request registration	1,03%
Research	0,11%	Left filing	0,91%
		Keys and decide	0,69%
		Accounting	0,34%
		Waiting recovery	0,23%
		Research	0,11%
		Return	0,11%

5.1   Scoping

During scoping, we first made an analysis based on frequencies of start and end activities. As stated in Section 3, depending of period used to import the log, some traces may start and/or end with an intermediate activity. These incomplete traces were removed. Then we applied the following filters on the original log, which were also supported by users of the system.

  - define "Request registration" as the unique start activity because it is a predominant start activity, as we can notice in Table 1;
  - define "Final Phase" as the unique end activity (see Table 1);

In the end of scoping step we obtained a log with 796 traces that as a whole comprise 5191 activities. Besides, the shortest trace from log has 5 activities, while the longest has 12 activities. On average, the traces have 6 activities.

5.2   Discovering, Filtering, and Selection

Our proposal approach deals with the search of an appropriate model, which satisfies a minimum fitness and maximizes appropriateness. Figure 4 depicts three models that we mined from the scoped log, and their respective properties (**f** for fitness, **s** for structural appropriateness, **b** for behavioral appropriateness, and **a** for appropriateness). We considered 80% as the minimum fitness support in this analisys. We used heuristics mining plug-in for process discovery because it is robust for noise and exceptions since it outputs a model based on frequent patterns.

   Then, we got the Petri net A (after converting from a heuristic net model). Specifically in the case of this log, whose activity frequencies are reported in Table 2, the two most infrequent activities ("Private research" and "Research") add an unnecessary complexity to model A although they are significantly infrequent when compared with other activities. For that reason, we applied heuristic mining over a filtered version of scoped log, which does not consider activities "Private research" and "Research". This way, we got Petri net B, which is a model more appropriate than model A.

   However, although "Return" activity is significantly more frequent than "Private research" and "Research" activities, it is also significantly infrequent when

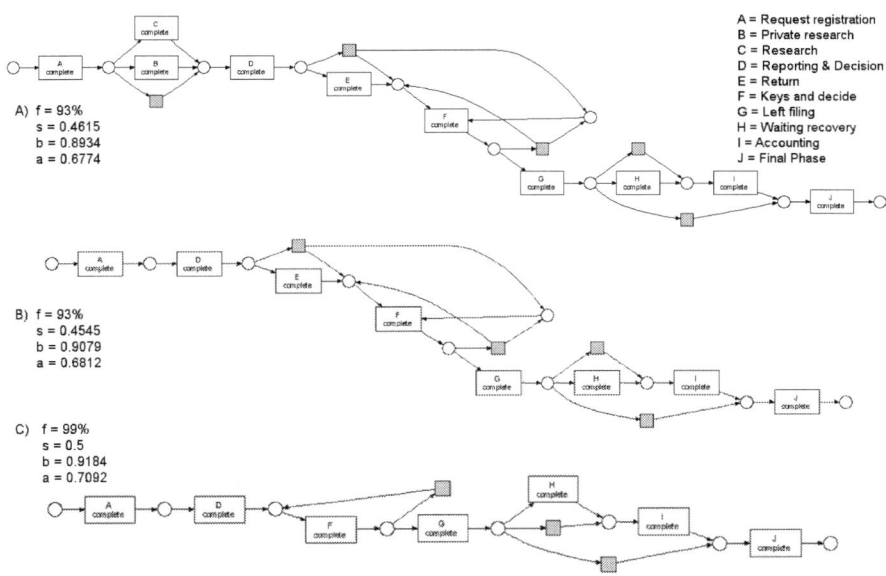

A = Request registration
B = Private research
C = Research
D = Reporting & Decision
E = Return
F = Keys and decide
G = Left filing
H = Waiting recovery
I = Accounting
J = Final Phase

A) f = 93%
    s = 0.4615
    b = 0.8934
    a = 0.6774

B) f = 93%
    s = 0.4545
    b = 0.9079
    a = 0.6812

C) f = 99%
    s = 0.5
    b = 0.9184
    a = 0.7092

Fig. 4. Petri net models based on frequency filtering analysis

Table 2. Activity Frequencies

Model element	Occurrences (relative)
Keys and decide	16,41%
Reporting & Decision	15,43%
Left filing	15,39%
Request registration	15,33%
Final Phase	15,33%
Accounting	11,42%
Waiting recovery	9,59%
Return	1,00%
Private research	0,04%
Research	0,04%

compared with other activities of log (see Table 2). That is, "Return" activity adds an unnecessary complexity to model in Figure 4 A. For that reason, we also mined scoped log, but filtered from "Private research", "Research", and "Return". As a result, we obtained the Petri net C, which is more appropriate than other models, and it also has a better fitness. Therefore, we selected Petri net C as the appropriate model, so it was utilized for splitting step. Note that the selection of this model was not automated and we did not do an exhaustive search. Moreover, manual inspection showed that this is indeed the most appropriate model having a fitness of at least 80%.

5.3   Splitting

Finally, we got the fitting and non-fitting traces using the appropriate model (Petri net C in Figure 4). In this analysis we considered 80% for **p** (minimum fitness support), so we supported to find at most 20% of anomalous traces in the log. However, because we got an appropriate model whose fitness was 99%, we detected only 6 anomalous traces from a total of 796 traces of *scoped log.*

6   Conclusion and Future Work

Recent management trends and the adoption of rigorous best practices of corporate governance stimulated companies to deploy PAIS in order to automate and control their business processes, and also to track misuse of their systems (e.g. financial scandals related to mismanagement). However, the control provided by normative systems may compromise the necessary flexibility to companies in being agile and competitive in the market. This work presents an approach to identify anomalous traces, which may represent a misuse, for deal with this problem. For example, the identification of anomalous traces can lead to an investigation and probable evolution of the business process models. Our approach is based on a formal definition of anomalous trace, which is defined through two parameters: (i) fitness model degree (p%); and (ii) appropriateness of model (a). We described how ProM framework can be utilized for support this formal definition. Then, we carried out an application of approach with a real log from a Dutch municipality.

The presented anomaly detection approach is limited to the control-flow perspective. For example, fraud may follow a normal flow, but producing anomalous data (e.g. very large amount of money) or being executed by unauthorized roles or users (e.g. violation of four eyes principle). Therefore, we believe that data and organizational perspectives should also be considered to provide more accuracy, yet they may require a more complex anomaly detection framework. Because our approach relies on the selection of an *appropriate model*, we believe that a precise appropriateness metric should be defined. Besides, we think that an automated solution might be implemented, for example, through the use of genetic algorithms.

References

1. Dumas, M., van der Aalst, W., ter Hofstede, A.: Process-Aware Information Systems: Bridging People and Software through Process Technology. Wiley, Chichester (2005)
2. Rozinat, A., van der Aalst, W.: Conformance checking of processes based on monitoring real behavior. Information Systems 33(1), 64–95 (2008)
3. van der Aalst, W.M.P., van Dongen, B.F., Herbst, J., Maruster, L., Schimm, G., Weijters, A.J.M.M.: Workflow mining: A survey of issues and approaches. Data & Knowledge Engineering 47(2), 237–267 (2003)
4. van der Aalst, W.M.P., Weijters, A.J.M.M.: Process mining: a research agenda. Computers in Industry 53(3), 231–244 (2004)
5. Bezerra, F., Wainer, J.: Towards detecting fraudulent executions in business process aware systems. In: WfPM 2007 - Workshop on Workflows and Process Management, Timisoara, Romania (September 2007); In conjunction with SYNASC 2007

6. Bezerra, F., Wainer, J.: Anomaly detection algorithms in logs of process aware systems. In: SAC 2008: Proceedings of the 2008 ACM symposium on Applied computing, pp. 951–952. ACM Press, New York (2008)
7. Bezerra, F., Wainer, J.: Anomaly detection algorithms in business process logs. In: ICEIS 2008: Proceedings of the Tenth International Conference on Enterprise Information Systems, Barcelona, Spain, June 2008. AIDSS, pp. 11–18 (2008)
8. van der Aalst, W.M.P., de Medeiros, A.K.A.: Process mining and security: Detecting anomalous process executions and checking process conformance. Electronic Notes in Theoretical Computer Science 121(4), 3–21 (2005)
9. de Medeiros, A.K.A., van der Aalst, W.M.P., Weijters, A.: Workflow mining: Current status and future directions. In: Meersman, R., Tari, Z., Schmidt, D.C. (eds.) CoopIS 2003, DOA 2003, and ODBASE 2003. LNCS, vol. 2888, pp. 389–406. Springer, Heidelberg (2003)
10. van der Aalst, W.M.P., Weijters, T., Maruster, L.: Workflow mining: Discovering process models from event logs. IEEE Transactions on Knowledge and Data Engineering 16(9), 1128–1142 (2004)
11. Cook, J.E., Wolf, A.L.: Discovering models of software processes from event-based data. ACM Trans. Softw. Eng. Methodol. 7(3), 215–249 (1998)
12. Agrawal, R., Gunopulos, D., Leymann, F.: Mining process models from workflow logs. In: Schek, H.-J., Saltor, F., Ramos, I., Alonso, G. (eds.) EDBT 1998. LNCS, vol. 1377, pp. 469–483. Springer, Heidelberg (1998)
13. Cook, J.E., Du, Z., Liu, C., Wolf, A.L.: Discovering models of behavior for concurrent workflows. Computers in Industry 53(3), 297–319 (2004)
14. Pinter, S.S., Golani, M.: Discovering workflow models from activities' lifespans. Computers in Industry 53(3), 283–296 (2004)
15. Herbst, J., Karagiannis, D.: Workflow mining with inwolve. Computers in Industry 53(3), 245–264 (2004)
16. de Medeiros, A.K.A., Weijters, A.J.M.M., van der Aalst, W.M.P.: Genetic process mining: A basic approach and its challenges. In: Bussler, C.J., Haller, A. (eds.) BPM 2005. LNCS, vol. 3812, pp. 203–215. Springer, Heidelberg (2006)
17. Yang, W.S., Hwang, S.Y.: A process-mining framework for the detection of healthcare fraud and abuse. Expert Systems with Applications 31(1), 56–68 (2006)
18. van Dongen, B., de Medeiros, A., Verbeek, H., Weijters, A., van der Aalst, W.: The prom framework: A new era in process mining tool support. In: Ciardo, G., Darondeau, P. (eds.) ICATPN 2005. LNCS, vol. 3536, pp. 444–454. Springer, Heidelberg (2005)

Pattern Mining in System Logs: Opportunities for Process Improvement

Dolev Mezebovsky, Pnina Soffer, and Ilan Shimshoni

University of Haifa, Carmel Mountain 31905, Haifa, Israel
dkmezebov@gmail.com, spnina@is.haifa.ac.il,
ishimshoni@mis.haifa.ac.il

Abstract. Enterprise systems implementations are often accompanied by changes in the business processes of the organizations in which they take place. However, not all the changes are desirable. In "vanilla" implementations it is possible that the newly operational business process requires many additional steps as "workarounds" of the system limitations, and is hence performed in an inefficient manner. Such inefficiencies are reflected in the event log of the system as recurring patterns of log entries. Once identified, they can be resolved over time by modifications to the enterprise system. Addressing this situation, the paper proposes an approach for identifying inefficient workarounds by mining the related patterns in an event log. The paper characterizes such patterns, proposes a mining algorithm, and rules for prioritizing the required process improvements.

Keywords: Process mining, Enterprise systems, Event log.

1 Introduction

Enterprise systems implementations are often accompanied by changes in the business processes of the organizations in which they take place. In fact, the desired change in the business processes is in many cases one of the reasons that motivate the enterprise system implementation. Changes in the business processes can also stem from the need to adapt the enterprise to the enterprise system rather than the other way around [10]. In such cases, some process changes can be considered improvements relatively to the original processes prior to the implementation, but not necessarily all of them.

This is especially true in implementations that take a "vanilla" strategy [15], in which the system is implemented as it is with minimal customizations and adaptations. In such situations, a typical scenario would be that the newly operating business process is still capable of achieving its operational goal, but requires many additional steps as workarounds of the system's limitations. Thus, the achievement of operational goals is at the cost of more effort, resources, and time.

To illustrate the situation, we will consider the following case taken from a university and use it as a running example throughout this paper. In the university, a student registers for a program, and may decide to switch to another program while he studies. Prior to the implementation of an enterprise system, changing the program to

T. Halpin et al. (Eds.): BPMDS 2009 and EMMSAD 2009, LNBIP 29, pp. 162–173, 2009.

which a student was registered was done through a legacy system. When the secretary was reporting a change in a student's program, all the courses the student had already taken were "converted" to the new program. Then the secretary could specifically remove the credits of the courses which were not relevant for the new program. Such activity is not supported by the enterprise system implemented in the university. Hence, when a student wishes to change the program he is registered to, the secretary has to separately detach all the course credits the student already has, and attach them again under the new program. This task is both time consuming and error-prone.

Typically, such situations arise shortly after the system becomes live, and are intended to be addressed later on, as incremental improvements of the already running system. For example, such an improvement could be achieved by adding a function to the university enterprise system. This function would automatically detach all the credits of a student and attach them again under a new program, while all the secretary has to do is to indicate the program change. However, since this may be the case with a large number of processes, they cannot all be immediately addressed. Furthermore, as time passes by, the people who operate the process may get used to the inefficient way of performing their task, and thus they will not require its improvement. As a result, the process will remain in its inefficient form. The problem which is then faced by the organization is first to identify the inefficient processes, and second, to prioritize them so they can gradually be improved. To the best of our knowledge, this problem has not been addressed so far.

This paper proposes an approach for identifying and prioritizing requirements for process improvement. Specifically, we address inefficient processes whose inefficiency stems from workarounds forced by a newly introduced enterprise system. The identification is based on mining event logs of the system, and prioritization is based on the frequency of these workarounds and on their magnitude.

The situation addressed here is when technology (new enterprise system) drives changes in the business processes, albeit in an undesirable way. The approach uses a technological solution (mining event logs) to drive desirable changes in the processes.

The remainder of the paper is organized as follows. Section two demonstrates and characterizes the reflection of workarounds in the event log of a system; Section three provides a basic formalization of a pattern in a log file and an algorithm for pattern mining; Section four addresses the prioritization and utilization of the patterns for process improvement; Section five discusses the proposed approach as compared to related work; conclusions are given in Section six.

2 The Reflection of Workarounds in an Event Log

Our premise is that a series of steps that logically reflect an activity from the business process point of view is reflected in the event log of an enterprise system as a recurring pattern performed by the same user. In this section we illustrate this by an example related to the above mentioned university process.

Although a log file includes actions performed by all the system users, we show in our example (Table 1) only the log entries that relate to one user (YPRESS). Table 1 includes log entries, specifying the process code and name, where "process" is

Table 1. Event Log Example

Row Num	Process Name	Process Name	Date	Time	User Name	Student Name	Course Name	Program Name
1	PR12	Attach Course	15.06.08	13:45:52	YPRESS	Fredrick	Linear Algebra	MIS Major
2	PR12	Attach Course	15.06.08	13:46:26	YPRESS	Fredrick	Algorithms	MIS Major
3	PR12	Attach Course	15.06.08	13:47:44	YPRESS	Fredrick	Data Structures	MIS Major
4	PR11	Detach Course	15.06.08	13:49:18	YPRESS	Fredrick	Linear Algebra	CS Minor
5	PR11	Detach Course	15.06.08	13:49:24	YPRESS	Fredrick	Algorithms	CS Minor
6	PR11	Detach Course	15.06.08	13:49:31	YPRESS	Fredrick	Data Structures	CS Minor
7	PR12	Attach Course	15.06.08	13:54:19	YPRESS	Fredrick	Information Technology	MIS Major
8	PR11	Detach Course	15.06.08	13:55:28	YPRESS	Fredrick	Information Technology	MIS Minor
9	PR12	Attach Course	15.06.08	13:56:40	YPRESS	Fredrick	Business Intelligence	MIS Major
10	PR11	Detach Course	15.06.08	13:58:20	YPRESS	Fredrick	Business Intelligence	MIS Minor
11	PR12	Attach Course	15.06.08	13:59:35	YPRESS	Fredrick	Programming Design	MIS Major
12	PR11	Detach Course	15.06.08	14:01:29	YPRESS	Fredrick	Programming Design	MIS Minor

actually a transaction, the timestamp (date and time), the user name, and the parameters to which the transaction applies (in this case course name, program name, and student name). All entries include two types of processes (transactions): attach course and detach course. They all apply to the same student (Fredrick), three programs (MIS Major, CS Minor, and MIS Minor), and different course names. Finally, all the entries relate to the same date and were performed within about 15 minutes.

The short time frame, within which a series of operations concerning a recurrent set of parameters was performed, may indicate a pattern that stands for one "logical" activity. Our goal is to be able to automatically identify such patterns in an event file, and successfully indicate a larger activity that has been done by the user. Note that the patterns we address do not bear a meaning which is similar in any sense to the workflow patterns [4]. They are not generic. Rather, they capture a recurrent set of related log entries. To get a better understanding about patterns and their structure, we represent the log entries of Table 1 graphically in Fig. 1 and Fig. 2.

Fig. 1 shows two distinct sets of entries along time. The first three entries perform the operation PR12 (attach course) to MIS Major program with three different courses, and the last three entries perform the operation PR11 (detach course) to CS Minor program with the same three courses. All the operations are performed by the same user to the same student. In Fig. 2 no such distinct sets of operations exist over

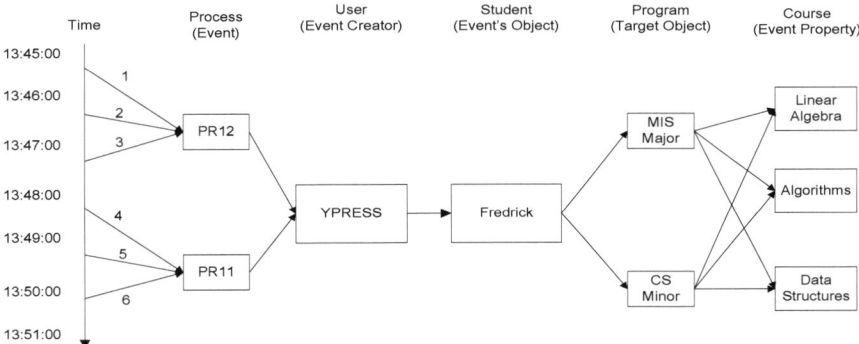

Fig. 1. A graphical representation of rows 1 to 6 of Table 1

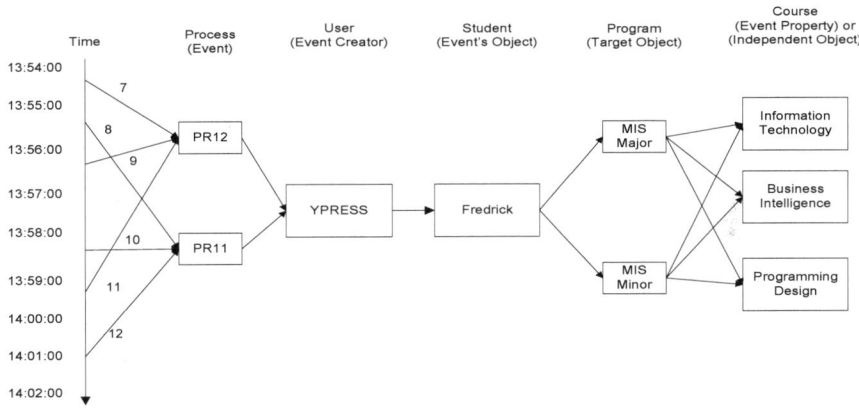

Fig. 2. A graphical representation of rows 7 to 12 of Table 1

the time axis. Rather, the operations PR12 and PR11 alternate. Still, they are per-formed to two programs of the same student and by the same user.

We classify all these entries as belonging to the same pattern, and draw the follow-ing general indications for the existence of a pattern. (a) All the entries are performed by the same user and within a limited time frame. The maximal time frame for pattern identification can be given as a parameter to an automated application which will identify patterns in a system log. (b) The entries have at least one parameter whose value is fixed. We term the fixed parameter(s) the *invariant* set of the pattern. (c) The entries have at least one parameter whose value is different for different entries. We term the parameter(s) whose value changes throughout the entries the *variant* set of the pattern. As to the order of performing the operations in the pattern, we do not con-sider it mandatory for a fixed order (e.g., all PR12 and then all PR11, or alternating operations). Since we assume that for the person who performs these operations they all belong to one logical activity, the specific execution order is not necessarily of importance.

In the following section we formalize the pattern definition and propose an algorithm for pattern detection.

3 Pattern Mining

3.1 Basic Concepts

To formalize the pattern concept, we need to start by providing formal definitions of an entry in a log file and its components.

User – A field in the log entry that indicates who made the commit of the event.

$User \in \{System\ Users\}$.

Timestamp – The time the log entry was committed.

$Timestamp > 0$.

Operation – The type of activity (transaction) that was performed.

$Operation \in \{System\ Operations\ \}$.

Operand – Parameter of a mathematical function. In a log file entry an operand is a pointer to an object or a pointer to a parameter value of the function (transaction).

$Operand \in \{Operands : Operands \notin \emptyset\}$.

ORSO – An ordered set of operands, with at least one operand in the set.

$ORSO = (< Operands > : |Operands| \geq 1)$.

Entry – An event in the log file, which is represented by a tuple. The entry includes user, timestamp, operation and an ordered list of operands.

$Entry = < User, Timestamp, Operation, ORSO >$.

TimeFrame – Delta of timestamps that are used to set pattern start and end entry.

$TimeFrame \geq [(end\ entry).timestamp - (start\ entry).timestamp]$.

For defining a pattern, we rely on the following two assumptions.

1. For every two entries in a log file, if they employ the same operation, then their number of operands, order of operands, and type of operands are the same.
2. Each log file entry has all the needed operands to perform the event transaction. Both these assumptions are logical when considering an event log. First, the operands characterize an operation, hence it makes sense to assume that entries with the same operation have the same set of operands. As well, there is no reason to believe that the order in which the operands are given in the log file varies in different entries. Second, we consider a complete log file without missing information.

Based on the above definitions and assumptions, we may now define a pattern. We consider a pattern as a combination of entries that satisfy certain conditions. For the entries to relate to a single "logical" activity, they need to (a) relate to the same set of operands, and (b) include repetition in the values of some fields and some fields whose values differ. Fields whose value does not change in the pattern are termed *invariant* while the others are termed *variant*.

For a legal pattern the user must be invariant and the timestamp variant with a timeframe smaller than a user defined constant. In addition, the union of operation and operands must have at least one invariant field and one variant field. We represent a pattern as an entry whose components are sets that can be variant or invariant. Note that:

If S is a set such that $S \in \{invariant\}$ then $|S| = 1$

If S is a set such that $S \in \{variant\}$ then $|S| \geq 1$

ORSO includes the same operand types for all entries. Then a pattern is formally defined as:

Pattern $= \ < User, Timestamps, Operations, ORSOs >$:
$\quad\quad User \ \in \{invariant\}, \ Timestamps \in \{variant\}, \ \ ORSO \ \neq \emptyset,$
$\quad\quad (\text{Operations} \cup \text{ORSOs}) \cap \{invariant\} \neq \emptyset$
$\quad\quad (\text{Operations} \cup \text{ORSOs}) \cap \{variant\} \neq \emptyset$

The order of components in the pattern is the same as in the entry. A log file entry is by definition a trivial pattern.

3.2 Pattern Finder Algorithm

For two given patterns (entryA and entryB), we will determine if their composition yields a pattern using the algorithm DIPFinder depicted in Fig. 3.

The algorithm verifies that the entries have the same user and fall within the predetermined timeframe. Then it goes through their operations and list of operands, compares their values, and classifies them as variant or invariant. If there is at least one variant and at least one invariant, the algorithm returns the pattern (specified as a combined entry).

Entries that were recognized as patterns will be considered as a single entry for the next iteration of recurrence. The algorithm uses a variable patternEntry that contains the specific values of the pattern invariants and sets of values for the pattern variants. This variable will be returned by the function in order to be used by the algorithm in the next iteration.

3.3 DIPFinder Example

We demonstrate the algorithm by applying it to data from Table 1 as inputs. Fig. 4 shows the entries that relate to rows 1-6 in Table 1. The rest of the entries can be similarly analyzed.

We select entries (1) and (2) as first inputs to our algorithm. Timeframe for the process is set to 20 minutes. The output is the combined entry (1, 2).

DIPFinder [(1): < YPRESS, '13.45.52', PR12, Fredrick, 'Linear Algebra', 'MIS Major'>,
$\quad\quad\quad$ (2): < YPRESS, '13.46.26', PR12, Fredrick, 'Algorithms', 'MIS Major'>] →
$\quad\quad\quad$ (1, 2) : < YPRESS, ('13.45.52', '13.46.26'), PR12, Fredrick, (L.A., 'Alg.'), 'MIS Major'>

```
∯ DIPFinder  entry  (entryA, entryB, TimeFrame)
    If (entryA ≠ Empty and entryB ≠ Empty)
        Tf = max(entryA.timestamp ∪ entryB.timestamp)- min(entryA.timestamp ∪
entryB.timestamp);
      If  Tf ≠ 0 and entryA.user = entryB.user and  Tf  <  TimeFrame then
          invariantCounter ← 0;
          variantCounter ← 0;
          patternEntry ← Empty;
          patternEntry.user = entryA.user;
          patternEntry.timestamp = entryA.timestamp ∪ entryB.timestamp;
          opSetLength ← entryA.ORSO.length;
          If entryA.oprtSet = entryB.oprtSet or
             entryA.oprtSet ⊂ entryB.oprtSet or
             entryB.oprtSet ⊂ entryA.oprtSet  then
            invariantCounter++;
                patternEntry.operation = entryA.operation ∪ entryB.operation;
          Else
                variantCounter++;
                patternEntry.oprtSet = entryA.oprtSet ∪ entryB.oprtSet;
          End
          For i = 1 → opSetLength do
                      If entryA.ORSO[i].ordSetValues =
entryB.ORSO[i].ordSetValues or
                      entryA.ORSO[i].ordSetValues ⊂
entryB.ORSO[i].ordSetValues or
                      entryB.ORSO[i].ordSetValues ⊂
entryA.ORSO[i].ordSetValues then
                         patternEntry.ORSO[i].ordSetValues ←
                            entryA.ORSO[i].ordSetValues ∪
entryB.ORSO[i].ordSetValues;
                         invariantCounter++;
                      Else                         // we met some new value/s
                         patternEntry.ORSO[i].ordSetValues ←
                            entryB.ORSO[i].ordSetValues ∪
entryA.ORSO[i].ordSetValues
                         variantCounter++;
          End   // end for loop
              If variantCounter = 0 or   invariantCounter = 1 /* no pattern */
                 patternEntry ← Empty;
              End
              return patternEntry
        End
  End
  return Empty
```

Fig. 3. DIPFinder algorithm

(1) : < YPRESS, '13.45.52', PR12, Fredrick, 'Linear Algebra', 'MIS Major'>
(2) : < YPRESS, '13.46.26', PR12, Fredrick, 'Algorithms', 'MIS Major'>
(3) : < YPRESS, '13.47.44', PR12, Fredrick, 'Data Structures', 'MIS Major'>
(4) : < YPRESS, '13.49.18', PR11, Fredrick, 'Linear Algebra', 'CS Minor'>
(5) : < YPRESS, '13.49.24', PR11, Fredrick, 'Algorithms', 'CS Minor'>
(6) : < YPRESS, '13.49.31', PR11, Fredrick, 'Data Structures', 'CS Minor'>

Fig. 4. Log entries for rows 1-6 in Table 1

We will now apply the algorithm again to the combined entry (1, 2) and to entry (3).

DIPFinder [(1, 2), (3)] =
    [(1, 2) : < YPRESS, ('13.45.52', '13.46.26'), PR12, Fredrick, (L.A., 'Alg.'), 'MIS Major'>,
     (3): < YPRESS, '13.47.44', PR12, Fredrick, 'Data Structures', 'MIS Major'>] →

(1, 2, 3): < YPRESS, ('13.45.52', '13.47.44'), PR12, Fredrick, ('L.A.', 'Alg.', 'DS'), 'MIS Major'>

A similar processing of the entries 4, 5, and 6 yields the following output:

(4, 5, 6): < YPRESS, ('13.49.18', '13.49.31'), PR11, Fredrick, ('L.A.', 'Alg.', 'DS'), 'CS Minor'>

Next, we try to process together the pattern entries (1,2,3) and (4,5,6).

DIPFinder [(1, 2, 3), (4, 5, 6)] =

[(1, 2, 3) : < YPRESS, ('13.45.52', '13.47.44'), PR12, Fredrick, ('L.A.', 'Alg.', 'DS'), 'MIS Major'>,
(4, 5, 6) : < YPRESS, ('13.49.18', '13.49.31'), PR11, Fredrick, ('L.A.', 'Alg.', 'DS'), 'CS Minor'>] →
(1, 2, 3, 4, 5, 6): < YPRESS, ('13.45.52', '13.49.31'), (PR12, PR11), Fredrick, ('L.A.', 'Alg.',
'DS'), ('MIS Major', 'CS Minor') >

We have a pattern in which the User is invariant, the start and end times meet the limits of TimeFrame, the operation is variant (PR12, PR11), and there is at least one invariant operand – the student 'Fredrick'. With this recognition of pattern we can draw a conclusion that this is a set of related activities, which may stand for one "logical" activity which is inefficiently performed by the users. To make further conclusions we have to determine what the purpose of this set of activities is, or basically what it does. Section 4 deals with this question.

While the DIPFinder algorithm is capable of incrementally aggregating log entries into a pattern, some higher-level algorithm is still needed for managing the entire log file, and particularly for reducing the complexity of the search. This algorithm, which is currently under development, will be a version of a divide and conquer algorithm. It will recurrently employ DIPFinder for combinations of entries whose size increases gradually until all patterns are identified.

4   Utilizing the Identified Patterns for Process Improvement

Having identified patterns in the log file, it is still not certain that they really stand for a "workaround" of the limitations imposed by the enterprise system. It may be possible that they reflect the normal and expected way the business process should be performed. For example, when a student registers to a number of courses at the beginning of a semester, this will be manifested as a pattern in the log file. Nevertheless, this is a series of operations which should be performed sequentially and do not require process improvement. Hence, patterns that are identified serve as a basis for interviews with the system users, to verify that they stand for inefficiencies in the business processes.

Once patterns that stand for inefficient process execution are identified, the process can be improved by introducing changes to the enterprise system. Such changes can be, considering our example, a designated user interface in which the user indicates the student whose program should be changed as well as the source and target programs. The attaching and detaching of courses is then automatically performed by the system. However, since many such patterns may be identified, some prioritization should be made for performing the required changes. For this purpose, we propose the following prioritization rule.

Assuming the log file relates to a given period of time (e.g., a month), it is possible to calculate the following metrics:

The *count* of a pattern: given a pattern P, its count C_P is the number of times the pattern appears in the log file.

The *average size* of a pattern: given a pattern P, its average size AS_P is the average number of entries it includes. Let P occur C_P times in a log file, so occurrence i includes n_i entries. Then $AS_P = \frac{1}{C_P}\sum_{i=1}^{C_P} n_i$.

The *weighted count* of a pattern (weighted by size): $SC_P = AS_P * C_P$.

Priority for process improvement can be given to patterns whose occurrence is frequent and which entail a relatively large number of entries, namely, patterns whose weighted count is high. Alternatively, it is possible to consider the actual time span of a pattern (average or median) instead of the count. Such a measure does not assume that the entries of different patterns are equally time-consuming.

Note that the patterns and the proposed priority rules are merely an indication of potential improvement. Usually, when metrics are not applied, prioritization can only rely on human considerations. These are influenced by the interaction with the system users who raise their complaints. The proposed rules provide an objective measure which can be used, possibly in addition to other prioritization considerations. Additional considerations are mainly related to specific business and organizational priorities which can only be assigned by humans in the organization.

5 Related Work

The approach presented in this paper relates to the area of process mining, since it analyzes data in a system log in order to get some understanding about a business process. In this section we review process mining literature to establish the unique features of our approach.

Process mining primarily aims at discovering a process model based on the process reflection in an event log of a system. Processes that are actually performed by users have in most cases a flow which is different than the flow that the process designing team has thought of. Process mining is capable of discovering these actual flows and composing an actual process model. The motivation for developing this approach was to find an alternative way of analyzing processes in less time than the traditional way of interviews and observations. Creating a workflow design is a complicated time-consuming process and typically there are discrepancies between the actual workflow processes and the processes as perceived by the management [18]. In addition the analysis made by people is error prone, may lead to inconsistencies between individual views of the same process, and is subject to possible incompleteness of information collected from employees about the process [8].

An early work that relied on event logs for discovering behavioral patterns was reported in [9]. The technique is based on a probability analysis of the event traces. Metrics such as frequency and regularity of the event occurrences behavior were saved by the system. This technique is useful in many tasks of software engineering, including architecture discovery, reengineering, user interaction modeling, and software process improvement.

Relating specifically to business processes, the main challenges involved in extracting a process models include definitions of edge conditions, identifying concurrency of events, and overcoming diversity which leads to complex models that are difficult to interpret. The presence of duplicate activities, hidden activities, and non-free-choice constructs are also challenges when a process mining technique is applied.

Besides the construction of an actual process model, process mining has served for other purposes as well. Delta analysis and conformance testing compares the actual process with some predefined process, and detects differences between the model constructed in the design phase and the actual use that was registered in the log files [1]. Another use of mining techniques was presented in [6]. It focuses on the performer of the event and derives social networks using this information. Another investigated aspect, which is quite close to our focus, is efficiency analysis based on timestamps [3]. Timestamps indicate activities which cause delays in the process. In contrast, we use the timestamps as indication of actions that were performed sequentially and within a short period of time, as representing an inefficient way of performing one "logical" activity.

Pattern discovery is mentioned in several works. Dealing with flexible processes [17], the mining approach is to divide the log file to homogeneous subsets by using a clustering technique, and then to build a process model for each subset. Our pattern discovery approach differs from that since we look for a pattern (subset) performed by a single user, while [17] does not. Pattern discovery is also possible in [7], where the event log is clustered iteratively so each of the resulting clusters relates to a set of cases that can be represented by a process model. This work relies on the frequency of an event for pattern discovery regardless of its type. In contrast, our work identifies a pattern based on event types regardless of their frequency.

Process mining has been used for various domains. In particular, healthcare [13], as an environment of very dynamic behavior, was indicated as a challenging domain, where process mining can significantly contribute. Examples include [12] where process mining techniques discover paths followed by particular groups of patients. Three different perspectives were analyzed using the ProM framework [11]: control flow, organizational, and performance. Another domain where process mining was applied is the public sector [5], where it was used for office work analysis. In the domain of industry and supply chain [14] the discovered process enabled analysis across the supply chain, and could be used as a tool to improve business processes in networked organizations. The application in the software development domain raised several challenges [16]. Since process models and software process models cover different aspects, the work considered the main aspects that can connect between the models such as the control flow aspect, the information aspect which records the data produced by the event, and the organization aspect. This approach is somehow close to our approach, but our goal is different. The use of process mining in the security domain was presented in [2], using process mining techniques to analyze audit trails for security violations. The purpose was to support security levels ranging from low-level intrusion detection to high-level fraud prevention.

Our approach differs from the above reviewed process mining works in two main issues. First, as opposed to the process mining aim of creating a process model, we use the system event log with the aim of discovering a pattern which may reflect a single activity from the user's point of view. Hence, the focus of our approach is narrower than the entire process model aimed at by process mining approaches. Second, the specific use for which these patterns are intended is the identification of process inefficiencies resulting from a lack of system support. This specific use has not been proposed yet.

6 Conclusions

The paper deals with two ways in which technology can drive business processes. First, the introduction of an enterprise system results in changes in the business processes. However, these are not necessarily desirable changes. Second, mining technology can be utilized in such situations as a driver for process improvement.

The problem of inefficient processes as a result of enterprise system adoption is very common in practice (e.g., 10]), and, to the best of our knowledge, has not received a technology-based solution so far. One contribution of the paper is, therefore, making this problem explicit and discussing it. Besides that, the main contribution of the paper is the approach proposed for addressing such situation. This includes (a) a clear definition of the reflection of inefficient workarounds as patterns in an event log of the system, (b) an algorithm for pattern identification, and (c) rules for prioritizing improvement requirements.

The algorithm presented here is still an initial step towards a complete and efficient algorithm, needed for addressing the high volume of data in a real system log file. In future, we intend to complete the development and implementation of the algorithm and to apply it to real data of the university case study, as well as in other domains.

References

1. van der Aalst, W.M.P.: Business alignment: using process mining as a tool for Delta analysis and conformance testing. Requirements Engineering Journal 10(3), 198–211 (2005)
2. van der Aalst, W.M.P., de Medeiros, A.K.A.: Process Mining and Security: Detecting Anomalous Process Executions and Checking Process Conformance. In: Busi, N., Gorrieri, R., Martinelli, F. (eds.) Second International Workshop on Security Issues with Petri Nets and other Computational Models (WISP 2004). STAR, Servizio Tipografico Area della Ricerca, CNR Pisa, Italy, pp. 69–84 (2004)
3. van der Aalst, W.M.P., van Dongen, B.F.: Discovering Workflow Performance Models from Timed Logs. In: Han, Y., Tai, S., Wikarski, D. (eds.) EDCIS 2002. LNCS, vol. 2480, pp. 45–63. Springer, Heidelberg (2002)
4. van der Aalst, W.M.P., ter Hofstede, A.H.M., Kiepuszewski, B., Barros, A.P.: Workflow Patterns. Distributed and Parallel Databases 14(1), 5–51 (2003)
5. van der Aalst, W.M.P., Reijers, H.A., Weijters, A.J.M.M., van Dongen, B.F., Alves de Medeiros, A.K., Song, M., Verbeek, H.M.W.: Business Process Mining: An Industrial Application. Information Systems 32(5), 713–732 (2007)
6. van der Aalst, W.M.P., Reijers, H.A., Song, M.: Discovering Social Networks from Event Logs. Computer Supported Cooperative Work 14(6), 549–593 (2005)
7. Alves de Medeiros, A.K., Guzzo, A., Greco, G., van der Aalst, W.M.P., Weijters, A.J.M.M., van Dongen, B., Saccà, D.: Process Mining Based on Clustering: A Quest for Precision. In: ter Hofstede, A.H.M., Benatallah, B., Paik, H.-Y. (eds.) BPM Workshops 2007. LNCS, vol. 4928, pp. 17–29. Springer, Heidelberg (2008)

8. Bandinelli, S., Fuggetta, A., Lavazza, L., Loi, M., Picco, G.: Modeling and improving an industrial software process. IEEE Trans. Softw. Eng. 21(5), 440–454 (1995)
9. Cook, J.E., Wolf, A.L.: Discovering Models of Software Processes from Event-Based Data. ACM Transactions on Software Engineering and Methodology 7(3), 215–249 (1998)
10. Davenport, T.: Putting the Enterprise into the Enterprise System. Harvard Business Review 76(4), 121–131 (1998)
11. van Dongen, B.F., de Medeiros, A.K.A., Verbeek, H.M.W., Weijters, A.J.M.M., van der Aalst, W.M.P.: The ProM framework: A new era in process mining tool support. In: Ciardo, G., Darondeau, P. (eds.) ICATPN 2005. LNCS, vol. 3536, pp. 444–454. Springer, Heidelberg (2005)
12. Mans, R.S., Schonenberg, M.H., Song, M., van der Aalst, W.M.P., Bakker, P.J.M.: Process Mining in Health Care. In: Azevedo, L., Londral, A.R. (eds.) International Conference on Health Informatics (HEALTHINF 2008), Funchal, Maldeira, Portugal, January 28-31, 2008, pp. 118–125 (2008)
13. Maruster, L., van der Aalst, W.M.P., Weijters, A.J.M.M., van den Bosch, A., Daelemans, W.: Automated Discovery of Workflow Models from Hospital Data. In: Kröse, B., de Rijke, M., Schreiber, G., van Someren, M. (eds.) Proceedings of the 13th Belgium-Netherlands Conference on Artificial Intelligence (BNAIC 2001), pp. 183–190 (2001)
14. Maruster, L., Wortmann, J.C., Weijters, A.J.M.M., van der Aalst, W.M.P.: Discovering Distributed Processes in Supply Chains. In: Proceedings of the International Conference on Advanced Production Management Systems (APMS 2002), pp. 119–128 (2002)
15. Parr, A.N., Shanks, G.: A taxonomy of ERP implementation approaches. In: Proceedings of the 33rd Annual Hawaii International Conference on System Sciences, vol. 1, pp. 1–10. IEEE Press, Los Alamitos (2000)
16. Rubin, V., Günther, C.W., van der Aalst, W.M.P., Kindler, E., van Dongen, B.F., Schäfer, W.: Process Mining Framework for Software Processes. In: Wang, Q., Pfahl, D., Raffo, D.M. (eds.) ICSP 2007. LNCS, vol. 4470, pp. 169–181. Springer, Heidelberg (2007)
17. Song, M., Günther, C.W., van der Aalst, W.M.P.: Trace Clustering in Process Mining. In: 4th Workshop on Business Process Intelligence (BPI 2008) (2008)
18. Weijters, A.J.M.M., van der Aalst, W.M.P.: Process mining: discovering workflow models from event-based data. In: Kröse, B., de Rijke, M., Schreiber, G., van Someren, M. (eds.) Proceedings of the 13th Belgium–Netherlands Conference on Artificial Intelligence (BNAIC 2001), pp. 283–290 (2001)

Regulatory Compliance in Information Systems Research – Literature Analysis and Research Agenda

Anne Cleven and Robert Winter

Institute of Information Management, University of St. Gallen
Mueller-Friedberg-Strasse 8, 9000 St. Gallen, Switzerland
{anne.cleven, robert.winter}@unisg.ch

Abstract. After a period of little regulation, many companies are now facing a growing number and an increasing complexity of new laws, regulations, and standards. This has a huge impact on how organizations conduct their daily business and involves various changes in organizational and governance structures, software systems and data flows as well as corporate culture, organizational power and communication. We argue that the implementation of a holistic compliance cannot be divided into isolated projects, but instead requires a thorough analysis of relevant components as well as an integrated design of the very same. This paper examines the state-of-the-art of compliance research in the field of information systems (IS) by means of a comprehensive literature analysis. For the systemization of our results we apply a holistic framework for enterprise analysis and design. The framework allows us to both point out "focus areas" as well as "less travelled roads" and derive a future research agenda for compliance research.

Keywords: compliance, regulations, information systems research, literature analysis.

1 Introduction

As of shortly, information systems (IS) and the IS discipline were rather marginally affected by compliance concerns. One of the reasons for the comparatively inferior meaning of compliance can be seen in the various deregulation endeavors that have characterized past years. Another reason lies in the fact that – with regard to companies – compliance has long been seen as an unswayable factor that only limits the flexibility of organizational design, but not as an element of design itself like, for example, in the context of electronic government.

In the more recent past, however, – not least because of the current financial crisis – growing legal and regulatory burdens demand for the development of new strategies, processes, and systems that adequately support organizations in a compliant conduct of business. Some approaches like the Control Objectives for Information and Related Technology (COBIT) framework, the Committee of Sponsoring Organizations of the Treadway Commission (COSO) model, or the information security

T. Halpin et al. (Eds.): BPMDS 2009 and EMMSAD 2009, LNBIP 29, pp. 174–186, 2009.

principles of the Code of Practice for Information Security Management ISO/EIC 17799, developed by different non-profit organizations, already provide valuable guidelines.

Nonetheless, organizations are still struggling with a holistic implementation of regulatory and legal requirements. This fact holds true for several reasons which include a lacking sense of urgency [19], indistinct responsibilities [14], and missing insights into the interplay of design elements that are relevant for an integrated compliance management [28]. However, "holistic compliance is an enterprise-wide and long-term approach" [33] that "stands in contrast to simply complying with the rules" [33] and, thus, imperatively requires an integrated design of both relevant elements and the relationships amongst these.

This paper intends to provide an overview of the existing body of knowledge on compliance in the IS discipline. The focus of our literature analysis lies on legal and regulatory compliance and respective contributions from an information systems research (ISR) perspective. Our aim is to identify both areas that have already gained some attention in the discipline and those that have so far rather been neglected. We systematize the results of our search based on a framework for enterprise analysis and design. On this basis, we point out demand for further research.

The remainder of this paper proceeds as follows. In section 2, we introduce a framework as a basis to analyze and systemize our findings. Our literature search strategy as well as the junction of the results is presented in section 3. In section 4, we recapitulate the current state of research on legal and regulatory compliance in the IS discipline, point out those areas that require for the development of further solutions, and present a potential future research agenda.

2 Business Engineering

The enterprise-wide character of regulatory compliance usually influences many, if not all business areas. In every affected business area, it impacts all layers of analysis/design from purely business related aspects (strategy, organization) to purely IT related aspects (software, data, IT infrastructure). Since enterprise architecture (EA) intends to cover all business areas over the entire "business-to-IT" range, suitable frameworks for the analysis and design of regulatory compliance might be identified in the EA field.

According to ANSI/IEEE Standard 1471-2000, architecture is defined as the "fundamental organization of a system, embodied in its components, their relationships to each other and the environment, and the principles governing its design and evolution" [15]. On this basis, EA is understood as the fundamental organization of a government agency or a corporation, either as a whole, or together with partners, suppliers and/or customers ("extended enterprise"), or in part (e.g. a division, a department), as well as the principles governing its design and evolution [21]. According to its primary purpose to support "coherency management", EA covers all relevant artifacts and structures in the "business-to-IT" range in a "wide and flat" manner, i.e. EA focuses on aggregate models and dependencies [1].

The above definition of architecture restricts comprised components to be "fundamental". Due to the broad range of relevant component types, EA may nevertheless comprise a huge number of such artifacts. As a consequence, most EA frameworks distinguish several architecture layers and architecture views in order to reduce the number of artifacts per model type and per model [25]. When several architecture layers and architecture views are differentiated, design and evolution principles have to address consistency and integration issues.

As a basis for consolidating artifact types that are considered as being important for EA, widely used EA frameworks such as The Open Group Architecture Framework (TOGAF), the Federal Enterprise Architecture Framework (FEAF) and the ARIS Framework have been analyzed in [37]. The following set of core EA artifact types has been identified:

- *Business strategy layer:* organizational goals and success factors, products/services, targeted market segments, core competencies and strategic projects
- *Organization/business process layer:* organizational units, business locations, business roles, business functions, business processes including inputs/outputs (internal and external business services including service levels), metrics (performance indicators) and service flows, business information objects and aggregate information flows
- *IT/business alignment layer:* enterprise services, applications and domains
- *IT implementation layer:* software components and data resources, hardware and network architecture

While an EA framework constitutes a suitable foundation to represent EA models and their (static) dependencies, dynamic aspects as well as "soft" factors are not sufficiently covered. "Soft" factors like company culture, leadership style, behavior patterns, incentive/sanctioning systems and communication practices are considered to have a pivotal role for business analysis and successful business engineering [22]. Although such factors are much harder than "hard" artifacts to analyze, represent and include in solution design, there is ongoing research in integrated analysis/design approaches. Regarding the framework, the traditional "hard" EA layers are therefore often complemented by a "soft" layer which, due to the fact that cultural issues, leadership issues and behavioral issues are relevant over the entire "business-to-IT" range, is modeled along all "hard" layers [22].

The system of four "hard" layers and one complementary "soft" layer is limited to static as-is or to-be modeling. In order to capture the dynamics of business innovation, a transformation process view has to be added. Regarding regulatory compliance, (1) an analysis and evaluation process and (2) a transformation process should be differentiated [22]. While the "innovation management style" analysis and evaluation process continuously tracks legislation and current industry developments in order to identify transformation triggers, the transformation process defines and implements discrete transformation projects which apply regulatory measures consistently throughout the organization.

It is important to mention that the holistic, enterprise wide character of regulatory compliance demands an integrated, consistent methodological analysis/design approach. By means of such an approach, the compliance-related knowledge base (terminologies, theories, generic methods and reference models, exemplary successful practices, etc. [36]) is translated into consistent, effective compliance solutions.

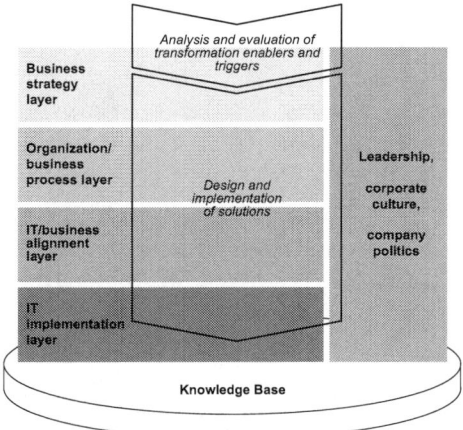

Fig. 1. Business Engineering Framework

Figure 1 illustrates the described architectural framework that includes not only "business-to-IT" as well as "soft" representation layers ("models"), but also the innovation and transformation process view ("methods").

3   Literature Analysis

3.1   Source Selection

Compliance is not a new concept. However, not least due to the current financial crisis it just now experiences an enormous hype in both practice and academia. New laws and regulations are changing IT work, structure, and governance and confront IT managers with a myriad of novel challenges [30]. In order to grasp the meaning of compliance in the context of ISR, "bring coherence and perspective" [9] to this field of research, and identify areas that demand for further solutions from the IS discipline, we conduct a systematic review of existing literature. We base the selection of sources to be included in the review on a capacious catalog of IS outlets provided by the London School of Economics (LSE) [35]. We consider this catalog to be particularly appropriate for our purposes, since it incorporates not only the mainstream IS journals, but covers also those focusing on the social study of IS as well as practitioner journals and the most significant IS conferences [35].

Subsequently, we work out an understanding of compliance that allows us to delineate the body of papers to become part of our analysis. The term compliance is often sloppily used as an umbrella term for the adherence to any piece of rule or directive. Due to the ongoing evolution of the topic, however, it is indeed challenging, if at all feasible to provide a universal definition [31]. Consequently, we decide to limit the scope of our literature analysis to take into consideration only those papers that directly address issues of regulatory and/or legal compliance.

As our aim is to provide a broad overview of recent research on compliance within the IS discipline the time span we cover with our analysis ranges from 2002 – the year the most popular and most cited regulation, the Sarbanes-Oxley Act , was enacted – until present. We identify relevant papers by first conducting a keyword search using the search term 'compliance' and then limiting the results by means of an abstract evaluation. Following this search strategy, 26 IS articles on legal and regulatory compliance are analyzed and systemized in the subsequent section.

No.	Title	Source
1	Regulation as a Barrier to Electronic Commerce in Europe: The Case of the European Fund Management Industry (Fisher, J.; Harindranath, G.)	European Journal of Information Systems
2	How to Build Enterprise Data Models to Achieve Compliance to Standards or Regulatory Requirements (and share data) (Schekkerman, J.)	Journal of the AIS
3	Diffusing Management information for Legal Compliance: The Role of the Is Organization Within the Sarbanes-Oxley Act (Braganza, A.; Hackney, R.)	Journal of Organizational and End User Computing
4	The Role of External and Internal Influences on Information Systems Security – A Neo-Institutional Perspective (Hu, Q.; Hart, P.; Cooke, D.)	Journal of Strategic Information Systems
5	Information Technology and Regulatory Policy: New Directions for Digital Government Research (Coglianese, C.)	Social Science Computer Review
6	Compliance to the Fair Information Practices: How Are the Fortune 500 Handling Online Privacy Disclosures? (Schwaig, K. S.; Kane, G. C.; Storey, V. C.)	Information & Management
7	An Overview of Leading Current Legal Issues Affecting Information Technology Professionals (Matsuura, J. H.)	Information Systems Frontiers
8	Cybercrime: Legal Standards Governing the Collection of Digital Evidence (Schwerha IV, J. J.)	
9	Managing the False Alarms: A Framework for Assurance and Verification of Surveillance Monitoring (Goldschmidt, P.)	
10	Analyzing Regulatory Rules for Privacy and Security Requirements (Breaux, T. D.; Antón, A. I.)	IEEE Transactions on Software Engineering
11	Information Technology Auditing: A Value-Added IT Governance Partnership between IT Management and Audit (Merhout, J. W.; Havelka, D.)	
12	A Framework for Integrating Sarbanes-Oxley Compliance into the Systems Development Process (Mishra, S.; Weistroffer, H. R.)	
13	Implementing Section 404 of the Sarbanes Oxley Act: Recommendations for Information Systems Organizations (Braganza, A.; Desouza, K. C.)	
14	Developments In Practice XXI: IT in the New World of Corporate Governance Reforms (Smith, H. A.; McKeen, J. D.)	Communications of the AIS
15	Spreadsheets and Sarbanes-Oxley: Regulations, Risks, and Control Frameworks (Panko, R. R.)	
16	Framing the Frameworks: A Review of IT Governance Research (Brown, A. E.; Grant, G. G.)	
17	ISO 17799: "Best Practices" in Information Security Management? (Ma, Q.; Pearson, J. M.)	
18	Holistic Compliance with Sarbanes-Oxley (Volonino, L.; Gessner, G. H.; Kermis, G. F.)	
19	The Ethical Commitment to Compliance: Building Value-based Cultures (Tyler, T.; Dienhart, J.; Thomas, T.)	California Management Review
20	SOX, Compliance, and Power Relationships (Braganza, A.; Franken, A.)	
21	The Sarbanes-Oxley Act: Implications for Large-Scale IT-Outsourcing (Hall, J. A.; Liedtka, S. L.; Gupta, P.; Liedtka, J.; Tompkins, S.)	Communications of the ACM
22	Corporate Governance of IT: A Framework for Development (Raghupathi, W. "Rp")	
23	The Unexpected Benefits of Sarbanes-Oxley (Wagner, S.; Dittmar, L.)	Harvard Business Review

Fig. 2. Literature Search Results (part 1)

No.	Title	Source
24	Adopting IT to Manage Compliance and Risks: An Institutional Perspective *(Butler, T.; McGovern, D.)*	European Conference on Information Systems
25	Risk Management and Regulatory Compliance: A Data Mining Framework Based on Neural Network Rule Extraction *(Setiono, R.; Mues, C.; Baesens, B.)*	International Conference on Information Systems
26	Institutionalization of IT Compliance: A Longitudinal Study *(Currie, W.)*	

Fig. 3. Literature Search Results (part 2)

Figure 2 and 3 list the contributions on regulatory compliance that we identified in our literature search.

3.2 Literature Systemization

Systemizing the literature according to the different layers of the proposed BE framework reveals that some research areas have gained a lot of attention whereas others show only a small number of solutions. In the following, we briefly outline which contribution addresses which layers and/or relations of the framework.

Transformation enablers and triggers: Due to the multitude of laws and regulations that has come up for different industry sectors, countries, and application areas it is complicated for organizations to firstly identify relevant regulations and secondly derive adequate measures to actually achieve compliance. With his paper MATSUURA aims at providing an overview of leading current legal issues that affect IT and IT professionals [18]. Structured subject to major application areas, he briefly introduces the most important laws IT professionals are likely to encounter in the course of their daily business. Exemplary fields include information privacy and computer security, trade secrets and proprietary information, intellectual property, and antitrust, competition, and commercial law.

SCHWERHA concentrates on legal standards regulating the collection of digital evidence in the case of cybercrime [27]. Starting from the Fourth Amendment that preserves citizens from unreasonable search and seizure he introduces a variety of statutory provisions that have been issued to supplement the initial law. The author points out that the rapid evolution of new technologies requires a continuous adjustment of the respective laws. He emphasizes that not only officers but also civil litigants have to be familiar with the Fourth Amendment and its complementing laws as they are held to these standards when acquiring digital evidence.

VOLONINO et al. focus on the Sarbanes-Oxley Act and its impact on IT [33]. They discuss the act's mandates as well as the purpose of regulatory agencies and point out the line of accountability from the Security and Exchange Commission via executives through to the IS departments and IS auditors that are ultimately expected to implement compliance requirements. The authors point out why and how a variety of research areas, e.g. information quality assurance, business intelligence, transaction control and integration are affected by Sarbanes-Oxley compliance requirements.

Knowledge Base: Three of the above itemized papers are considered to primarily contribute to the compliance-related knowledge base. FISHER and HARINDRANATH investigate the effect of financial services regulation on electronic commerce in the European Union (EU) [11]. On the basis of an exploratory study the authors reveal that current regulations – tough established to support the electronic distributions of funds – in fact rather act as a barrier and inhibitor. They conclude that due to a missing consistency of present regulations with their theoretical underpinnings the EU is far from realizing a single market in the financial services.

Fair information practices (FIP) represent another example of regulations that especially organizations dealing with the acquisition and use of personal consumer information must adhere to. SCHWAIG et al. investigate the privacy policies of the Fortune 500 in order to assess the degree to which these companies comply with the FIP [26]. Based on their examinations the authors develop a reference-matrix that allows for the evaluation of a company's maturity stage with regard to its privacy policy implementation. Four stages are identified that range from mature privacy policies to policies that merely serve a public relations tool.

Business strategy layer: The intention to implement and establish a holistic compliance management represents a strategic project. Such projects require a sound cost-benefit analysis, a mandate at the top management level, and a thorough project plan. MERHOUT and HAVELKA pick up on the fact that IT auditing is often seen as a "necessary evil" by IT management rather than as a means that may generate value [19]. The authors elaborate an extensive list of explicit benefits of an internal IT function and propose a capacious framework comprising 8 fundamental success factors for quality IT auditing. It is argued that adhering to rules and regulations should be regarded as an opportunity to constitute governance frameworks and establish partnerships between IT management and auditors. This in turn enhances top management's appreciation of the role of IT, leads to better decision making, and frees up resources for other value-added projects.

In their article HALL and LIEDTKA explore how the Sarbanes-Oxley Act affects large-scale IT outsourcing [13]. The authors identify key clauses of the act and derive a capacious list of risks and negative implications for outsourcing thereof. They defer to the need of a tight relation of corporate and IT strategy and appeal to view the act as an opportunity to (re-)integrate IT departments and invest in strategic IT assets.

Four years after the Sarbanes-Oxley Act went into effect, WAGNER and DITTMAR analyze the different ways organizations deal with the new law and discover that only a minor group was able to gain benefits from its implementation [34]. While the majority of companies complained about having to comply with the act, a few used the law as an opportunity to strategically and rigorously redesign their business. The authors portray how benefits like e.g. process standardization and consolidation, were achieved by those companies that successfully implemented the Sarbanes-Oxley Act.

Organization/business process layer: New laws and regulations not only require organizations to provide a more detailed disclosure of their operating results but also imply the need for change in organizational structures and processes. In their contribution 'IT in the New World of Corporate Governance Reforms' of the series 'Development in Practice' SMITH and MCKEEN survey how compliance frameworks and governance reforms affect and change IT work [30]. In collaboration with a focus group of senior IT managers the authors investigate the following five areas: general implications of regulatory acts for IT, the short-term impact, impacts on IT processes as well as impacts on IT structure and governance, and finally the anticipated long-term impacts. The survey reveals that IT managers expect a much more professional, controlled, and bureaucratized IT.

Leadership, corporate culture, and company politics: The successful implementation of a holistic compliance approach not only requires adequate organizational structures and IT. It furthermore necessitates the commitment of a company's workforce and the willingness of every employee to support the whole project. An article written by TYLER ET AL. explores the effect of the 1991 Federal Sentencing Guidelines for Organizations on the way organizations set up culture and policies to assert a compliant behavior of their employees throughout the whole organization. The authors find out that a common behavior of ethics and compliance officers is to promote a "values-and-integrity approach" to the outside but live a "command-and-control approach" at work [32]. The latter approach, however, proves to be the more effective in assuring a compliant behavior. The authors provide a number of cross-organizational benchmarks regarding relevant compliance procedures.

Organization/business process layer & Leadership, corporate culture, and company politics: There are several contributions that examine the combined impact of regulatory and legal compliance on 'hard' organizational and 'soft' cultural aspects and provide solutions for their design. BRAGANZA and HACKNEY, for example, use institutional theory as a lens through which they investigate experiences made by three global organizations with the implementation of Section 404 of the Sarbanes-Oxley Act [4]. Following institutional theory, the authors take a distinct set of implementation tactics as a basis and survey how these are applied to change controls, processes, and behavior. Based on the insights won in their exploratory study they suggest a number of intervention drivers that are considered most appropriate for reducing the potential for financial deficiencies. Another paper by BRAGANZA and DESOUZA addresses the same topic, but directly focuses on providing and discussing six action guidelines for the implementation of Section 404 of the Sarbanes-Oxley Act [2]. BRAGANZA and FRANKEN investigate the relationships between different stakeholders of Sarbanes-Oxley compliance, namely: the chief executive officer (CEO), the chief financial officer (CFO), the chief information officer (CIO), and the auditors [3]. Again, institutional theory and the concept of power relationships are used as the theoretical basis. The authors conclude with a set of compliance implementation tactics that fit best for four given types of power relationships.

In her contribution CURRIE goes into the matter of how societal, organizational and individual pressures change institutionalized processes over time [10]. The author focuses on how the introduction of an investment management system influences the compliance function and its respective processes. For the analysis of data won in a longitudinal study she develops a conceptual framework that borrows from the concepts of institutional theory. With her findings she contributes to the knowledge on implications of technology change.

BUTLER and MCGOVERN likewise apply institutional theory to scrutinize the exogenous factors influencing IT adoption decisions on compliance solutions[7]. The authors complement their findings by additionally using organizational theory to describe endogenous institutional arrangements. On the basis of a case study the authors derive general rules for the adoption of compliance software.

A contribution by HU et al. aims at providing a better understanding of external and internal influences on the success of intentions to establish a corporate IS security [14]. Neo-institutional theory is applied as a framework for analyzing the data gathered in a case study. The authors observe coercive, normative, and mimetic forces that affect an organization's success with the implementation of IS security practices and controls. The investigation shows that regulatory forces, such as the Sarbanes-Oxley Act, are potent drivers for motivating top managers to set off and execute company-wide security initiatives. The contribution points out how regulatory and legal requirements influence an organization's IS security and presents valuable guiding principles for enterprises developing an IS security.

Organizational/business process layer & IT/business alignment layer: Based on the concluding thoughts from two workshops held by Harvard University's Regulatory Policy Program, COGLIANESE discusses how IT affects government in making regulatory decisions [8]. The author points out the necessity of an integrated consideration of both the opportunities associated with new information technologies and the organizational design of regulatory policy making. He provides advice on how to enhance the receptiveness, efficiency, and manageability of decision making in regulatory concerns and outlines objectives for future research on digital government.

Organization/business process layer, IT/business alignment layer, IT implementation layer & Leadership, corporate culture, and company politics: The assurance of an integrated and holistic compliance management calls for approaches that involve all of the layers outlined in the BE framework. However, existing practitioner frameworks often only address specific aspects and neglect the required holism. In his contribution PANKO picks up on the compliance risks that are induced by the widespread use of spreadsheets in financial reporting [23]. Based on the alarming fact that on average 94% of these spreadsheets are faulty the author analyses how general as well as IT-specific control frameworks can be used in order to reduce spreadsheet-related compliance risks. He comes to the conclusion that existing frameworks mainly support error-testing and that "operational procedures, auditing, documentation methods, and secure spreadsheet operations" are still in need of development.

The demand for rigorous and transparent frameworks for corporate governance was significantly increased when the Sarbanes-Oxley Act went into effect. BROWN and GRANT use this as an opportunity to conduct a comprehensive review on existing governance research and literature [6]. They identify two main research streams, one on IT governance forms and the other one on IT governance contingency analysis which conjointly led to the contemporary IT governance research. The author's analysis reveals that especially the fit between IT and organization remains to be of dominant importance and that both practitioners and academicians show a constant effort to further refine instruments and methods to govern corporate IT decisions.

MA and PEARSON conduct a survey of information security professionals in order to validate if the standard ISO 17799 actually represents a best practice approach for information security and if the framework's dimensions address the right aspects [17]. The second objective of their survey consists in the improvement of the standard by generating a parsimonious model. The author's findings indicate that ISO 17799 dimensions and items are highly valid, but should be complemented by a new dimension that additionally addresses the aspect of business partner security.

A lot of regulations and standards require a complete control of the corporate IT. RAGHUPATHI picks up on this fact and discusses how enterprise-wide IT governance

(ITG) can be established [24]. He identifies three different stages in corporate ITG. Starting from the finding that IT needs to generate a high return on investment (ROI) the author analyzes the role of the CIO and the IS organization as well as the way the IS function is regulated by the top management.

IT implementation layer: "Increasingly, regulations are requiring software engineers to specify, design, and implement systems that are accountable to and in compliance with laws and regulations" [5]. The subsequent contributions explicitly focus on technological solutions for the implementation of compliance requirements. KIM et al. propose a concept for model-based proof of compliance [16]. They postulate the use of computational ontologies for the development of enterprise data models in order to both overcome business analysis problems – in particular those related to compliance issues and improve the possibility to inter-organizationally share data models. The paper not only introduces the concept but also provides an exemplary implementation that proves the applicability of the approach.

Another characteristic subject of legal compliance is addressed by GOLDSCHMIDT, who suggests a method to support the assertion of surveillance monitoring alarms by means of the so called compliance verification knowledge management (CV-KM) [12]. Primary monitoring systems (PMS) are systems that ensure internal control and generate exceptions in case of potential anomalies and possible non-compliance events, e.g. fraud or intrusion detection. CV-KM systems represent second-tier monitoring systems that assist the user in analyzing and categorizing the exceptions reported by the PMS and in identifying evidence either verifying or refuting generated alarms. Thus, CV-KM systems act as decision support systems for analysts.

One of the major challenges of automating compliance lies in the fact that regulatory requirements are mostly specified in complex and betimes ambiguous legal language. BREAUX and ANTÓN attend to this defiance and propose a method for extracting rights and obligations from laws and other regulatory texts [5]. Therewith, the authors contribute a design artifact that supports organizations in assuring and systematically demonstrating their compliance with policies and regulations.

The Sarbanes-Oxley Act not only concerns aspects of corporate governance and financial practice but also introduces a set of requirements regulating software development processes. On the basis of the COBIT reference structure MISHRA and WEISSTROFFER develop a conceptual framework that integrates respective requirements into the workflows of software development and, thereby, facilitates the internal control over systems development activities [20].

For the simple reason that an increasing number of regulations require the disclosure of management control SETIONO ET AL. propose a new type of IS designed to support quality decision making [29]. Their novel data mining algorithm is especially designed for verification, validation, and performance monitoring in the Basel II context.

Figure 4 displays how the 26 papers considered in our literature analysis scatter on the BE framework according to the content they address. The papers can be identified based on the numbers they have been assigned in figures 2 and 3.

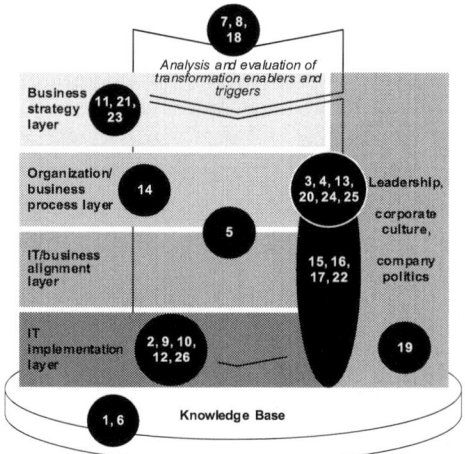

Fig. 4. Systemization of literature

4   Conclusion

The objective we pursued with this paper was to bring light into the darkness of compliance research in the IS discipline. As has been said by a variety of authors, new regulations and laws have huge impacts on how organizations conduct their daily business [30], [33], [34]. Thus, a number of publications address different aspects of implementing regulatory compliance. We conducted a literature analysis and systemized the results according to the BE framework. The systemization reveals that some layers and relations have been considered intensely while others have fairly been neglected. Especially the influences of regulations on organizational and behavioral structures of organizations have thoroughly been investigated, often applying institutional theory as a conceptual basis. Furthermore, a number of contributions propose different software or IT solutions that support the implementation of compliance. Other areas, however, remain clearly under-researched. In particular the relations between different layers have been neglected so far. We could not find any contribution that addresses the topic of how to operationalize strategic compliance objectives. Moreover, methods and approaches for the identification of those regulations that are especially relevant for an organization are missing. The knowledge base alike is still lacking in sound theories, methods and terminologies for the context of regulatory compliance. Moreover, an approach to combine existing methods and adapt these according to specific organizational contexts is not yet available. We thus conclude that – although the implications of regulatory compliance have been thoroughly investigated [20] – the IS discipline is limping behind with the development of suitable concepts and solutions. Compliance represents a challenging new research area in ISR and demands for a unified system of concepts and a pool of methods and models that can be combined for a holistic compliance implementation.

References

1. Aier, S., Kurpjuweit, S., Saat, J., Winter, R.: Business Engineering Navigator – A Business to IT Approach to Enterprise Architecture Management. In: Bernard, S., Doucet, G., Gøtze, J., Saha, P. (eds.) Coherency Management – Architecting the Enterprise for Alignment, Agility, and Assurance Ed. (2009)
2. Braganza, A., Desouza, K.C.: Implementing Section 404 of the Sarbanes Oxley Act: Recommendations for Information Systems Organizations. Communications of the Association for Information Systems 18, 464–487 (2006)
3. Braganza, A., Franken, A.: SOX, Compliance, and Power Relationships. Communications of the ACM 50(9), 97–102 (2007)
4. Braganza, A., Hackney, R.: Diffusing Management Information for Legal Compliance: the Role of the IS Organization within the Sarbanes-Oxley Act. Journal of Organizational and End User Computing 20, 1–24 (2008)
5. Breaux, T.D., Antón, A.I.: Analyzing Regulatory Rules for Privacy and Security Requirements. IEEE Transactions on Software Engineering 34(1), 5–20 (2008)
6. Brown, A.E., Grant, G.G.: Framing the Frameworks: A Review of IT Governance Research. Communications of the Association for Information Systems 15, 696–712 (2005)
7. Butler, T., McGovern, D.: Adoption IT to Manage Compliance and Risks: An Institutional Perspective. In: Proceedings of the 16th European Conference on Information Systems (ECIS), Galway, Ireland, pp. 1034–1045 (2008)
8. Coglianese, C.: Information Technology and Regulatory Policy: New Directions for Digital Government Research. Social Science Computer Review 22(1), 85–91 (2004)
9. Cooper, H.M.: Organizing knowledge syntheses: A taxonomy of literature reviews. Knowledge in Society 1, 104–126 (1988)
10. Currie, W.: Institutionalization of IT Compliance: A Longitudinal Study. In: Proceedings of the 29th International Conference on Information Systems (ICIS), Paris, France (2008)
11. Fisher, J., Harindranath, G.: Regulation as a barrier to electronic commerce in Europe: the case of the European fund management industry. European Journal of Information Systems 13, 260–272 (2004)
12. Goldschmidt, P.: Managing the false alarms: A framework for assurance and verification of surveillance monitoring. Information Systems Frontiers 9(5), 541–556 (2007)
13. Hall, J.A., Liedtka, S.L., Gupta, P., Liedtka, J., Tompkins, S.: The Sarbanes-Oxley Act: Implications for Large-Scale IT-Outsourcing. Communications of the ACM 50(3), 95–100 (2007)
14. Hu, Q., Hart, P., Cooke, D.: The Role of External and Internal Influences on Information Systems Security – A Neo-Institutional Perspective. Journal of Strategic Information Systems 16, 153–172 (2007)
15. IEEE: IEEE Recommended Practice for Architectural Description of Software Intensive Systems (IEEE Std 1471-2000). IEEE Computer Society, New York (2000)
16. Kim, H.M., Fox, M.S., Sengupta, A.: How To Build Enterprise Data Models To Achieve Compliance To Standards Or Regulatory Requirements (and share data). Journal of the Association of Information Systems 8(2), 105–128 (2007)
17. Ma, Q., Pearson, J.M.: ISO 17799: Best Practices in Information Security Management? Communications of the Association for Information Systems 15, 577–591 (2005)
18. Matsuura, J.H.: An Overview of Leading Current Legal Issues Affecting Information Technology Professionals. Information Systems Frontiers 6(2), 153–160 (2004)

19. Merhout, J.W., Havelka, D.: Information Technology Auditing: A Value-Added IT Governance Partnership between IT Management and Audit. Communications of the Association for Information Systems 23, 463–482 (2008)
20. Mishra, S., Weistroffer, H.R.: A Framework for Integrating Sarbanes-Oxley Compliance into the Systems Development Process. Communications of the Association for Information Systems 20, 712–727 (2007)
21. Opengroup: TOGAF Enterprise Edition Version 8.1. The Open Group (2003)
22. Österle, H., Winter, R.: Business Engineering - Auf dem Weg zum Unternehmen des Informationszeitalters. In: Österle, H., Winter, R. (eds.) Business Engineering, 2nd edn., pp. 3–19. Springer, Berlin (2003)
23. Panko, R.R.: Spreadsheets and Sarbanes-Oxley: Regulations, Risks, and Control Frameworks. Communications of the Association for Information Systems 17, 647–676 (2006)
24. Raghupathi, W.R.: Corporate Governance of IT: A Framework for Development. Communications of the ACM 50(8), 94–99 (2007)
25. Schekkerman, J.: How to Survive in the Jungle of Enterprise Architecture Frameworks: Creating or Choosing an Enterprise Architecture Framework. Trafford Publishing, Victoria (2004)
26. Schwaig, K.S., Kane, G.C., Storey, V.C.: Compliance to the Fair Information Practices: How are the Fortune 500 handling Online Privacy Disclosures? Information & Management 43(7), 805–820 (2006)
27. Schwerha IV, J.J.: Cybercrime: Legal Standards Governing the Collection of Digital Evidence. Information Systems Frontiers 6(2), 133–151 (2004)
28. Securities Industry Association, C., Legal, D.: The Role of Compliance. Journal of Investment Compliance 6(3), 4–22 (2005)
29. Setiono, R., Mues, C., Baesens, B.: Risk Management and Regulatory Compliance: A Data Mining Framework Based on Neural Network Rule Extraction. In: Proceedings of the 27th International Conference on Information Systems (ICIS), Paris, France (2006)
30. Smith, H.A., McKeen, J.D.: Developments In Practice XXI: IT in the New World of Corporate Governance Reforms. Communications of the Association for Information Systems 17, 714–727 (2006)
31. Taylor, C.: The Evolution of Compliance. Journal of Investment Compliance 6(4), 54–58 (2005)
32. Tyler, T., Dienhart, J., Thomas, T.: The Ethical Commitment to Compliance: Buildung Value-Based Cultures. California Management Review 50(2), 31–51 (2008)
33. Volonino, L., Gessner, G.H., Kermis, G.F.: Holistic Compliance with Sarbanes-Oxley. Communications of the Association for Information Systems 14, 219–233 (2004)
34. Wagner, S., Dittmar, L.: The Unexpected Benefits of Sarbanes-Oxley. Harvard Business Review 84(4), 133–140 (2006)
35. Willcocks, L., Whitley, E.A., Avgerou, C.: The ranking of top IS journals: a perspective from the London School of Economics. European Journal of Information Systems 17, 163–168 (2008)
36. Winter, R.: Design Science Research in Europe. European Journal of Information Systems 17, 470–475 (2008)
37. Winter, R., Fischer, R.: Essential Layers, Artifacts, and Dependencies of Enterprise Architecture. In: Society, I.C. (ed.) Proceedings of the EDOC Workshop on Trends in Enterprise Architecture Research (TEAR 2006). IEEE Computer Society, Los Alamitos (2006)

Actor-Driven Approach for Business Process. How to Take into Account the Work Environment?

Kahina Bessai[1] and Selmin Nurcan[1,2]

[1] Centre de Recherche en Informatique
Université Paris I - Panthéon Sorbonne
90, rue Tolbiac - 75013 Paris
[2] IAE de Paris, 21 rue Broca - 75005 Paris
{Kahina.Bessai,Selmin.Nurcan}@univ-paris1.fr

Abstract. Over the last decade there was a high interest in business process modeling in organizations. In their majority workflow systems support a role-based allocation of work to actors. This allocation does not consider the additional work which comes from the actors environment and which is not visible to the workflow management system. In fact, the WFMS is not aware of the real workload of human resources in the organization. In this paper we propose an *actor-driven approach* for business processes management which aims at taking into account the additional work generated by the environment (telephone, fax, mail, verbally) and thus the the real workload of actors.

1 Introduction

Business process models are recognized as indispensable artefacts to drive business management and evolution [19], [1],[9]. Even if workflow technology became a standard component of many enterprise information systems, the introduction of this technology set also several problems[12].

Failures have been observed in organization during the operation of workflow applications. Such failures are mainly consequences of the modeling of business processes as flows of activities, without any estimation of the availability of human resources (we will call them shortly resources in the following). Often this led to stack parallel processes on resources, considering that they would be always available. The issue of the concurrent solicitation of multiple processes and process instances for the same resource was never dealt with to our knowledge.

This issue is relatively recent and was grown with the proliferation of new information and communication technologies (email, telephone, fax), which allow to address directly to the resources the work to perform. In service companies, the lack of ability to deal with the dynamic allocation of work to resources by taking into account comprehensively the actors environment leads to non mastered and uncontrolled delays. These observations led us to the conclusion that the real workload of actors is opaque for the workflow management system and also for the supervisors of the involved actors.

T. Halpin et al. (Eds.): BPMDS 2009 and EMMSAD 2009, LNBIP 29, pp. 187–196, 2009.

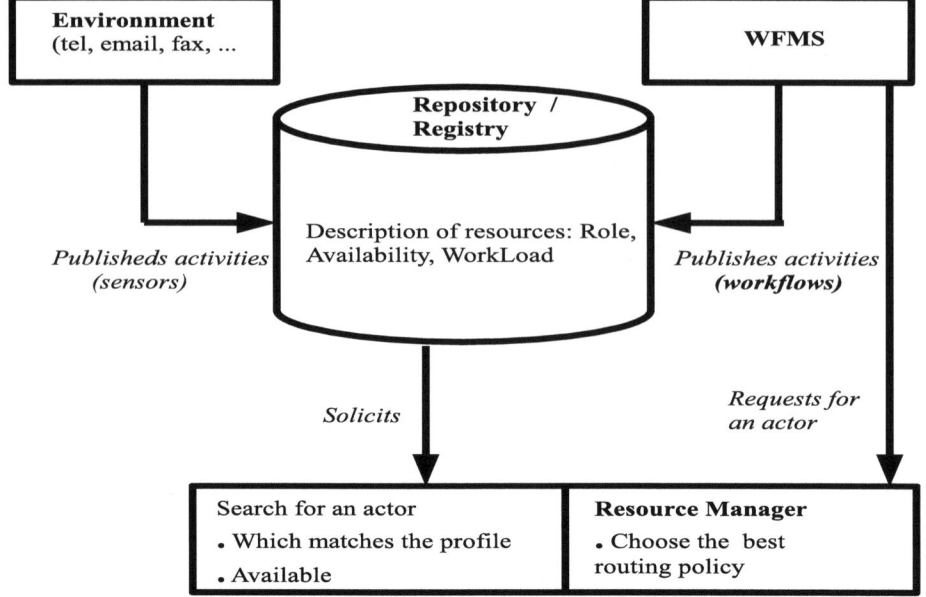

Fig. 1. The approach components

The majority of the workflow management systems(WFMS) are role-based and provide activity-driven modeling capabilities[6]. We focus in this paper on the comprehensive environment of the WFMS users, and more precisely on work allocations taking place outside the WFMS. Figure 1 shows the global picture of our proposition.

We propose an *actor-driven approach* for business processes enactment to deal with the following questions:

– How to capture the work coming from the environment?
– How to integrate the work from the environment in the workloads of resources which are dealt with by the workflow engine and the worklist handler of the WFMS [18]?
– How to take into account the availability of those resources?

This paper is organized as follows. Section 2 presents related works on resource modelling. In section 3, we present our approach for a smooth management of resources taking into account their comprehensive environment. Section 4 concludes the paper.

2   Related Works

In this section we provide a short survey of research on workflow resources. Zur Muhlen [4] presents a meta model which incorporates a technology-driven approach and an organizational-driven approach for resource modeling. In [3] an organizational reference meta model is presented; authors specify users requirements for WFMS, and compare the meta models of two WFMS WorkParty and FlowMark. While the process modeling capabilities of the current WFMS seem to be at a high level, the organizational models provided by these systems are very elementary [4]. In[17] authors characterize a role-based environment focusing on the concepts which need separation of duty. They also define different variations of separation of duty.

In [2] Kumar et *al* propose a systematic approach to create dynamically an equilibrium between quality and performance issues in workflow systems. Russell et *al* [12] describe a series of workflow resource patterns that aim at capturing the various ways resources can be represented and used in workflow technologies. They distinguish a series of specific categories of these patterns. Creation patterns are specific to the built time, and limit the resources that can execute an activity. Push patterns characterize situations where work items which are created are gradually allocated to resources by the WFMS. Pull patterns describe situations where individual resources are informed of a set of work items that must be executed. These resource patterns provided a big advance in the resource modeling for business processes, nevertheless they do not consider the external environment of the WFMS.

In [17], the usage of the concept of role is investigated in the context of flexible business process modelling. In [18], a situational approach for flexible business processes modelling and engineering is suggested in order to deal with the variability problem (which impacts directly human resources) at the meta-model level. Our contribution in this work is the integration of the work items coming from the environment in the workload of resources, and the definition of a resource manager for the orchestration of the dynamic resource allocation.

3   An Actor-Driven Approach for Business Process Enactment

In this section we present an *actor-driven approach* in order to deal with the real workload of human resources. This approach is composed of two main steps. The former aims to capture and identify the work coming from the environment. The later is the dynamic work allocation itself as described below. The principal concepts of the approach are shown in Figure 2:

- Resource: human actors involved in the organization.
- Role: the responsibility that an actor holds when performing an activity.
- Activity: the individual work realized by actors; we distinguish between internal and external activities. *Internal activities* represent work items allocated to the actors by the worklist handler of the WFMS. *External activities* represent the work coming from the environment (telephone, fax, email, verbally). They are closely related to the resource role in the organization and allocated by a manager, collaborator or a business partner. We dont take

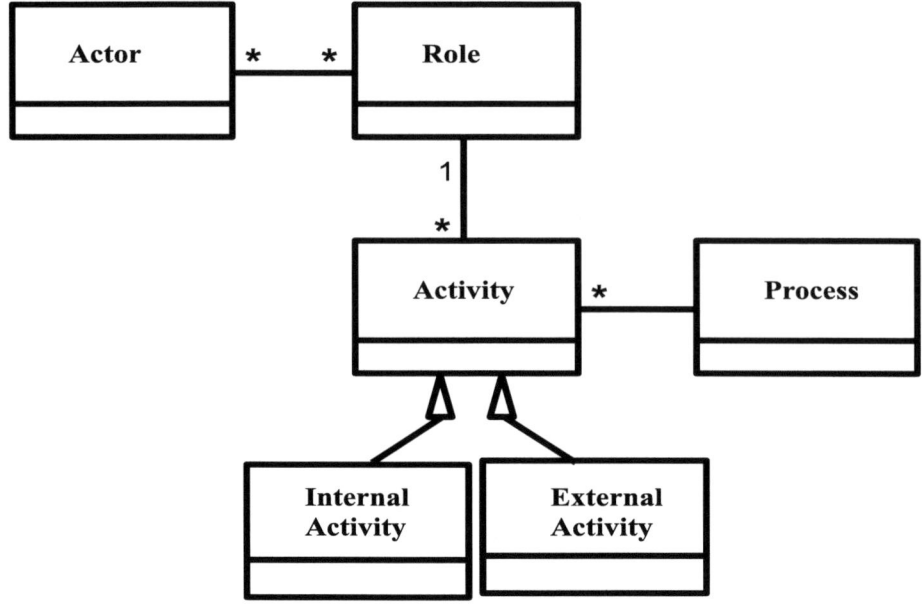

Fig. 2. The approach concepts

into account micro tasks or background tasks like *reading an email, drinking a coffee* and *personal activities.*

– Process: any business process in which the actor is involved.

3.1 Description of the Environment

In our approach, the environment represents all factors that influence either directly or indirectly the WFMS and more particularly the resource manager. Workflow management systems orchestrate resources without having a comprehensive information on their real workload. Numerous interactions between resources and the business environment make this workload opaque for the WFMS. Solicitations from the environment for the performance of a given work can be on different kinds: telephone, fax, email,... These communication channels affect the majority of resources in organizations, although they are not visible by the WFMS. The main purpose of our approach is to define the capability to capture the work items coming from the environment and to perform the resource allocation accordingly. We characterize and describe the environment using a set of factors called contingency factors. These factors will be used to identify the sensors which are necessary to catch the task-flow originated from the environment. Eventually, this will allow us to include those activities in the repository of resources in order to be aware of the real workload of all actors.

Contingency Factors. They are linked to the *external activities* and to *actors*.

- *The contingency factors linked to the environment:* define the communication channels which are used to assign activities to resources and specify some characteristics of these activities.

  - Communication channels: the external activities discussed below can be transported on different channels, such as:

    Email: during the last decade the importance of electronic messages was grown within organizations, for the transmission of information as well as a tool for work assignment to resources.

    Written documents: they correspond to the most often used way to allocate activities to resources. This is also the typical way to delegate a work and can be based on different forms such as fax, memo etc.

    Verbally: this is the less formalized channel, such as telephone communications, nevertheless this is a very usual way to solicit resources for doing "something".

  - The description of external activities: we determined some significant attributes such as: content, priority, impact on other activities, and frequency of occurrence.

- *The contingency factors linked to actors* define in some way the status of the latter. In fact, a resource can be not available for doing something for different raisons like vacancy, illness, vacation etc. This kind of information about availability must be captured and transmitted to the resource manager.

The contingency factors allow thus to formalize the work originated from the environment and to be assigned to resources. They will be used in conjunction with rules for the integration of the external "black box" activities into the resource repository making them "glass box" activities. In that way, the resource manager will have the comprehensive knowledge about the human resource requirements of those external activities without any responsibility for controlling their execution.

Capture and Integration of the Work from the Environment. Sensors will allow us listening/capturing, transforming and integrating *external activities* from the environment to the *repository/registry* of resources. The capture and the integration of *external activities* is mainly dependent on the communication channel and the nature of those activities. This dependence determines the type of sensor to use: automatic, semi- automatic, or manual.

- Automatic capture. As described above emails are frequently used in organizations to assign work to resources. This additional work can be integrated in the *repository of resources* automatically. Emails can be captured automatically if they are formalized in a structured way (key word=value) for instance: (TaskName= write an unexpected report), (Startdate= 14/04/09).

– Semi-automatic capture. Some times emails are not well formalized. In this case, the resource him/her self has to root the email to the resource repository. She can also add additional information, in order to include it more easily into the repository.

– Manual capture. This way will be used when a resource is solicited by telephone, fax or verbally. In these cases, the resource has to complete a form describing the requested work. Once submitted, the repository state is updated.

In most cases, the capture of the external work requires validation before the integration in the *resource repository*. This validation can be performed by a supervisor. The responsibility required for the validation of an activity originated from the environment is determined by the hierarchical position of the resource in the organization. For instance the external activities of a senior manager can be automatically validated, whereas a medium level team member will need the approbation of his/her supervisor for the *external activities* arrived in one of his/her external worklists.. The information about the activity to be included in the resource repository will play an important role in the validation process. Depending on their nature, some activities may be automatically validated like activities of high priority. In some other cases, if information on external activities are missing, the latter will be automatically rejected. A form will be returned to the resource, which is called to perform the activity, to retrieve the missing information. Eventually, the completed information will help the resource who will validate the activity.

The validation of an *external activity* leads to it's integration into the *resource repository*, i.e the update of the workload of the corresponding resource. This makes all *external activities* "glass boxes", and addresses thus the opacity problem presented at the beginning.

The aim of this approach is to balance the load between resources not to monitor their work, therefore it's in the resources' interest to report their external tasks. For this raison we would not carry our interest on background tasks, nevertheless, integration of these tasks in the system would cause privacy issues.

3.2   Work Allocation

In this paper we present an approach for improving the resource allocation in workflow management systems. Our proposition consists of developing a *resource manager* which purpose is to dynamically orchestrate the work allocation. We also suggest assembling necessary information about actors and their real workload into a *resource repository*. In the following sections we will describe this *repository* and the criteria defined for allocating work to the resources.

Resources Repository. Our aim is to construct a *resource repository* which should contain all information about actors and their real workload, the latter being a set of *external and workflow/internal activities*. This *repository* will be the cornerstone of our approach. It will be solicited by workflow management systems, the *resource manager*, resources themselves and the environment through sensors.

– Workflow management systems: the system will update the *repository*, when it will assign an activity to a resource chosen by the *resource manager*. Each time a resource starts or terminates the execution of an activity instance, the WFMS should update the resource repository to modify the *internal/workflow activity* state. The aim is to make the workload of resources as transparent as possible.
– Resource manager: The resource management is based on the information and data available in the repository. The resource manager reacts to the requests of the WFMS by providing the adequate resource for the realization of a given activity instance. Then the WFMS solicits the resource chosen by the resource manager for performing the activity.
– Resources: they integrate their own external activities in the repository and update their state. Otherwise, some other resources, such as supervisors, can integrate be requested for validating the *external activities* of the operational resources which will perform these activities. Thus, the repository has the knowledge about the organizational structure and manages access rights of all resources.
– Sensors: some external activities can be integrated automatically without validation. To realize this, we have to define rules for the repository based on what is listened on these sensors.

The description above sums up the requirements necessary for the implementation of the resource repository, and surveys its functionalities and roles in relation to the other actors (human or software) of the system.

Criteria for Work Allocation. The work allocation in our approach is done by the *resource manager* based on the information stored in the *repository*. This search for the most appropriate actor or the work allocation will be further based on a set of criteria: organizational (roles of resources), real workloads (*external and internal activities*) and the resource availabilities.

4   A Map Illustration of the Way of Working

In this section we use the Map formalism [18] [11] [5] for visualizing the suggested approach. A map as a directed graph from *Start* to *Stop* with intentions as nodes and strategies as edges between them. An *intention* is a goal that can be achieved by the performance of a process. Each map has two special *intentions*, *Start* and *Stop*, to respectively begin and end the process. A strategy is a manner to achieve a goal. The graph is directed because the *strategy* shows the flow from a source to a target *intention*. Each path from *Start* to *Stop* describes a way to reach the result i.e. each of them is a process model.

The map is a navigational structure which supports the dynamic selection of the intention to be achieved next and the appropriate strategy to achieve it whereas guidelines help in the operationalization of the selected intention [18].

We use the map formalism (see Figure 3) to represent the different methodological intentions targeted by our approach and the strategies which can be used for their achievement.

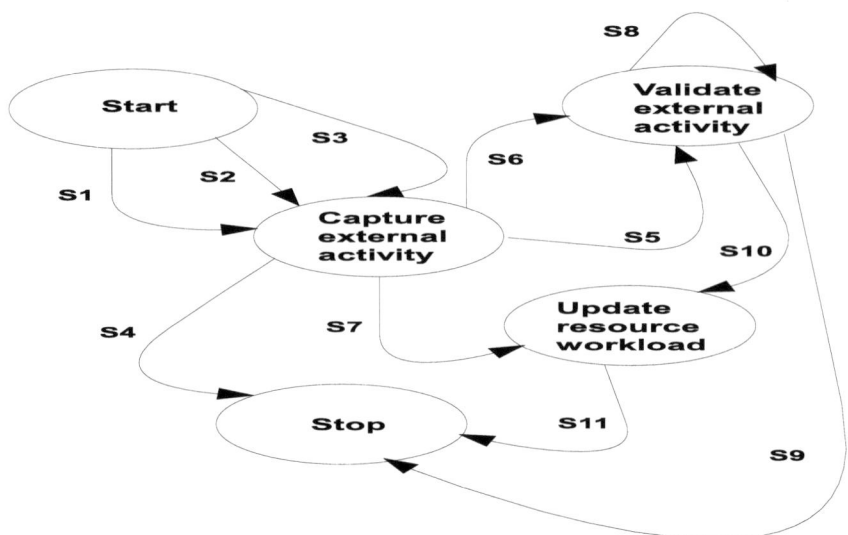

Fig. 3. The map of the actor-driven resource allocation approach

Table 1. Map Strategies Description

N	Strategy Name	Definition
S1	Automatic	This strategy aims to capture formalized mails automatically. Mails contain special keywords for being captured.
S2	Fill a form	An activity is integrated to the resource workload if it's revelant and frequent. The form containing information on requested activity is filled by the resource and validated by his supervisor.
S3	Semi-automatic capture	Not formalized mails which are integrated to the repository by the resource.
S4	Request for an irrelevant sollicitation	If an activity is considered irrelevant or if it requires a tiny execution time.
S5	Manual validation	The activity is manually validated by a supervisor.
S6	Automatic validation	The activity is automatically validated by the system.
S7	Update workload without validation	Some activities do not require validation and are directly added to the resource load work. They are defined as critical activities or the resource has a high rank in the organization.
S8	Missing information	The request for the activity execution is incomplete and it had to be clarified with additional information
S9	Activity is not validated	The activity is rejected by the supervisor or the system. It has no't to be performed by this resource and need to be reassigned.
S10	Workload update	Once validated, the activity is added to the resource workload
S11	By completeness	The system notifies the resource that the activity has been added to his/her workload.

Intentions. The map describing the approach has three intentions other than *Start* and *Stop* : *Capture external activity, validate external activity* and *Update the workload of a resource.*

Strategies. For the realization of these intentions (except Start) we can use the set of strategies, shown in table 1.

5 Conclusion

In this paper we proposed an *actor-driven approach* for the smooth enactment of business processes. This approach aims to make transparent the comprehensive workload of resources and thus smoothing it across time, which is impossible when the work items arrive to the actors from different communication channels including the WFMS itself.

We propose to develop a *repository/registry* which contains *external* and *internal/workflow activities* and all the information about resources (role, availability, workload). This repository up to date by the workflow management system(s) after each work allocation, of a work item to an actor by the workflow engine and worklist handler, and also by the environment through the *sensors* (if complete automation is possible) or by the resources themselves (otherwise). We define a sensor for each *communication channel* (telephone, fax, email). Moreover, we propose a centralized *resource manager* to deal with the comprehensive work allocation, i.e also on behalf of the WFMS, taking into account the availability of resources, the organizational structure and the real workloads of human resources.

At this stage of our research we have not chosen yet the implementation technology for the resource repository, although we envisage some solutions closer to service oriented architectures.

Our future works will also include an extension of the *contingency factors* related to the resources and the definition of additional facets such as the localization of the resource and his/her context of work. We also envisage defining other sensors for the capture of *external activities*, and an allocation mechanism for the *resource manager.*

References

1. Burlton, R.T.: Business Process Management - Profiting from process. SAMS Publishing (2001)
2. Kumar, A., van der Aalst, W.M.P., Verbeek, E.M.W.: Dynamic Work Distribution in Workflow Management Systems: How to balance quality and performance? Journal of Management Information Systems 18(3), 157–193 (2002)
3. Mühlen zur, M.: Evaluation of Workflow Management Systems Using Meta Models. In: Proceedings of the 32nd Hawaii International Conference on System Sciences (1999)
4. Mühlen zur, M.: Resource modeling in workflow applications. In: Proceedings of the 1999 Workflow Management Conference, November 1999, pp. 137–153 (1999)

5. Nurcan, S., Etien, A., Kaabi, R., Zoukar, I., Rolland, C.: A Strategy Driven Business Process Modelling Approach. Special issue of the Business Process Management Journal on Goal-oriented business process modeling, Emerald 11, 6 (2005)
6. Nyanchama, M., Osborn, S.L.: The role graph model and conflict of interest. ACM Transaction on Information and System Security, 3–33 (1999)
7. Regev, G., Wegmann, A.: Regulation-Based View on Business Process and Supporting System Flexibility. In: Proceedings of the CAiSE 2005 Workshop (2005)
8. Rosemann, M., zur Muehlen, M.: Evaluation of workflow Management systems-A Meta Model Approach. Australian Journal of Information Systems (1998)
9. Rolland, C., Prakash, N.: On the Adequate Modeling of Business Process Families. In: 8th Workshop on Business Process Modeling, Development, and Support (BPMDS 2007) in conjunction with CAISE 2007 (2007)
10. Rolland, C., Prakash, N., Benjamen, A.: A Multi-Model View of Process Modelling. Requirements Engineering Journal (REJ), 169–187 (1999)
11. Rolland, C., Loucopoulos, P., Kavakli, V., Nurcan, S.: Intention based modelling of organisational change: an esperience report. In: Proceedings of the fourth CAISE/IFIP 8.1 International Workshop on Evaluation of Modeling Methods in Systems Analysis and Design (EMMSAD 1999), Heidelberg, Germany, June 14-15 (1999)
12. Russell, N., van der Aalst, W.M.P., ter Hofstede, A.H.M., Edmond, D.: Workflow resource patterns: Identification, representation and tool support. In: Pastor, Ó., Falcão e Cunha, J. (eds.) CAiSE 2005. LNCS, vol. 3520, pp. 216–232. Springer, Heidelberg (2005)
13. Russell, N., ter Hofstede, A.H.M., van der Aalst, W.M.P., Mulyar, N.: Workflow Control-Flow Patterns, BPM Center Report BPM-06-22. BPMcenter.org (2006)
14. Russell, N., Hofstede, A., Edmond, D., Van der Aalst, V.M.P.: Workflow Resource Patterns, BETA Working Paper Series, WP 127, Eindhoven University of Technology, Eindhoven (2004)
15. Saidani, O., Nurcan, S.: A role based approach for modeling flexible business processes. In: The 7th Workshop on Business Process Modelling, Development, and Support (BPMDS 2006 (in association with the CAISE 2006 Conference), June 5-6. Springer, Heidelberg (2006)
16. Saidani, O., Nurcan, S.: Towards situational Business Process Modeling. In: 20th International Conference on Advanced Information Systems Engineering (CAISE 2008 Forum), June 16-20 (2008)
17. Simon, R., Zurko, M.E.: Separation of duty in role-based environments. In: Proceedings of the 10th Computer Security Fondations Workshop, pp. 183–194 (1997)
18. WfMC-TC-1011 v3 Workflow Terminology Glossary (February 1999)
19. Van der Aalst, W.M.P., Desel, J., Oberweis, A. (eds.): Business Process Management - Models, techniques and empirical studies. Springer, Heidelberg (2000)

Towards Object-Aware Process Management Systems: Issues, Challenges, Benefits

Vera Künzle and Manfred Reichert

Institute of Databases and Information Systems, Ulm University, Germany
{vera.kuenzle, manfred.reichert}@uni-ulm.de

Abstract. Contemporary workflow management systems (WfMS) offer promising perspectives in respect to comprehensive lifecycle support of business processes. However, there still exist numerous business applications with hard-coded process logic. Respective application software is both complex to design and costly to maintain. One major reason for the absence of workflow technology in these applications is the fact that many processes are data-driven; i.e., progress of process instances depends on value changes of data objects. Thus business processes and business data cannot be treated independently from each other, and business process models have to be compliant with the underlying data structure. This paper presents characteristic properties of data-oriented business software, which we gathered in several case studies, and it elaborates to what degree existing WfMS are able to provide the needed object-awareness. We show that the activity-centered paradigm of existing WfMS is too inflexible in this context, and we discuss major requirements needed to enable object-awareness in processes management systems.

Keywords: Workflow Management, Object-aware Process Management Systems, Data-driven Process Execution.

1 Introduction

Nowadays, specific application software (e.g., ERP, CRM, and SCM systems) exists for almost every business division. Typically, respective software enables access to business data and offers a variety of business functions to its users. In addition, it often provides an integrated view on the business processes. Though such tight integration of process, function and data is needed in many domains, current application software still suffers from one big drawback; i.e., the hard-coding of the process and business logic within the application. Thus, even simple process changes require costly code adaptations and high efforts for testing. Existing application software typically provides simple configuration facilities; i.e., based on some settings one can configure a particular process variant. Problems emerging in this context are the lack of transparency of the configurable processes and the mutual dependencies that exist between the different configuration settings. In addition, like the overall process logic the settings are often (redundantly) scattered over the whole application code, which therefore

T. Halpin et al. (Eds.): BPMDS 2009 and EMMSAD 2009, LNBIP 29, pp. 197–210, 2009.

becomes complex and difficult to maintain over time. This results in long development cycles and high maintenance costs (e.g., when introducing new features).

In principle, *workflow management systems* (WfMS) offer promising perspectives to cope with these challenges. Basically, a WfMS provides generic functions for modeling and executing processes independent from a specific application. Contemporary WfMS, however, are not broadly used for realizing data- and process-oriented application software, particularly if a close integration of the process and the data perspective is needed. In the latter case the processes are typically data-driven; i.e., the progress of single process instances does not directly depend on the execution of activities, but on changes of attribute values of data objects. Thus business processes and data cannot be treated independently from each other, and business process models need to be compliant with the underlying data structure; i.e. with the life cycles of the used data objects.

In this paper we demonstrate why the activity-centered paradigm of existing WfMS is inadequate for supporting data-oriented processes. For this purpose, we elaborate important properties of existing application software and show to what degree they can be covered by existing WfMS. Based on the identified shortcomings, we define major requirements for a generic system component enabling *data-oriented processes* with integrated view on both business processes and business data. To clearly distinguish this approach from existing WfMS we denote it as *Object-aware Process Management System* in the following.

Section 2 summarizes characteristics of contemporary WfMS and introduces an example of a data-oriented process. We use this running example throughout the paper to illustrate different issues relevant for the support of data-oriented processes. In Section 3 we describe five key challenges for realizing an Object-aware Process Management System. We check to what degree contemporary WfMS cover the properties of data-oriented applications. Based on the problems identified in this context we derive the requirements for Object-aware Process Management Systems. Section 4 describes related work. The paper concludes with an outlook on our future research in Section 5.

2   Backgrounds and Illustrating Example

This section describes basic workflow terminology and introduces an illustrating example. Based on this information we discuss the deficiencies of contemporary WfMS in the following sections.

Existing WfMS. In existing WfMS, a process definition consists of a set of activities and their control flow [1]. The latter sets out the order and constraints for executing the activities. It can be defined based on a number of workflow patterns which, for example, allow to express sequential, alternative and parallel routing as well as loop backs [2]. Each activity, in turn, represents a particular task and is linked to a specific function of an application service. To be able to assign human tasks to the respective actors, in addition, actor expressions (e.g., user roles) need to be defined for the corresponding activities. At runtime, for each business case an instance of the corresponding process definition is created and executed according to the defined control flow. A particular activity may be only enabled if all activities preceding in the control flow are completed or cannot be executed anymore (except loop backs). When an interactive activity becomes enabled, corresponding work items are added to the work lists of responsible users. Finally, when a work item is selected by a user, the WfMS launches the associated application service.

Example of a Data-Oriented Process. We consider the (simplified) process of a job application as it can be found in the area of human resource management. Using an online form on the Internet, interested candidates may apply for a vacancy. The overall goal of the process then is to decide which applicant shall get the offered job. A personnel officer may request internal reviews for each job applicant. Corresponding review forms have to be filled out by employees from functional divisions until a certain deadline. Usually, they evaluate the application(s), make a proposal on how to proceed (e.g., whether or not a particular candidate shall be invited for an interview), and submit their recommendation to the personnel officer. Based on the provided reviews the personnel officer makes his decision on the application(s) or he initiates further steps like an interview or another review. In general, different reviews may be requested and submitted respectively at different points in time. In any case, the personnel officer should be able to sign already submitted reviews at any point in time.

3   Findings, Problems, Requirements

In several case studies we have evaluated the properties of data- and process-oriented application software. This section summarizes basic findings from these studies and illustrates them along our running example. We then reveal characteristic problems that occur when using existing workflow technology for implementing the identified properties. This leads us to a number of fundamental requirements to be met by *object-aware process management systems*.

3.1   Challenge 1: Integration of Data

Findings. Usually, application systems manage data in terms of different *object types* represented by a set of *attributes*. At runtime, for each object type several *object instances* exist, which differ in the values of their attributes. Each object type has at least one attribute representing its *object ID*. Using this attribute any object instance can be uniquely identified. Relationships between object types are described using attributes as well. At runtime, object IDs of other object instances are then assigned to these attributes. Generally, an object instance may be referenced by multiple other object instances of a particular object type.

Business Data is represented by a variable number of object instances of different object types which are related to each other.

Fig. 1a depicts the data structure for our running example. For each application multiple reviews can be requested (cf. Fig. 1b). Thereby the precise number of related object instances varies from case to case; i.e., the number of requested reviews may differ from application to application, and it may also change during runtime (e.g., if for an application some reviews are requested or completed later than others).

In data- and process-oriented applications, available information can be accessed by authorized users at any point in time regardless of the process status.

From a user perspective, the instances of a particular object type correspond to rows in a table. Table columns, in turn, relate to selected attributes of the object type or – more precisely – to attribute values of the object instances. Attributes representing object relationships are resolved; i.e., their values are substituted by (meaningful) attribute values of the related object instances. Additional information on object instances (e.g., attributes not displayed by default within the table or detailed information about referenced object instances) can be viewed on-demand. Using this data- or object-centric view, besides working on *mandatory process activities* , authorized users may optionally edit attribute values of single object instances at arbitrary points in time (*optional activities*).

Problems. Existing WfMS are unable to provide such object-centric views. Most of them only cover simple data elements, which store values of selected object attributes, while the object instances themselves are stored in external databases. More precisely, only the data needed for control flow routing and for supplying input parameters of activities are maintained within the WfMS (i.e., so-called workflow relevant data), while other application data is unknown to it. Obviously, this missing link between application data and business process prohibits an integrated access to them; i.e., access to detailed business information is only possible when executing an activity and its related application function respectively. Fig. 1c shows a process activity for perusing a particular review. Which review shall be displayed can be controlled by the WfMS by handing over its objectID to the invoked activity. However, the WfMS cannot control which attributes of the review object or of related objects (e.g., the application) can be accessed. Missing or incomplete context information, however, often leads to inefficient work and erroneous results [3].

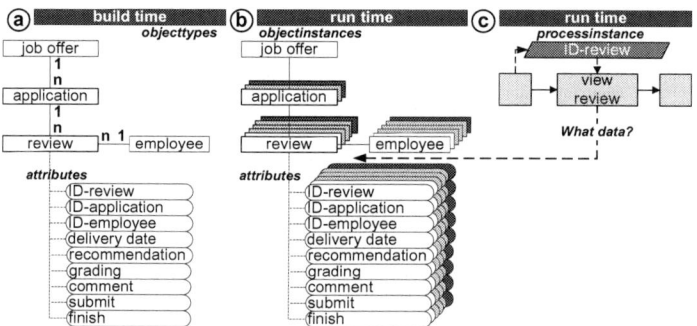

Fig. 1. Data structure and access to context information

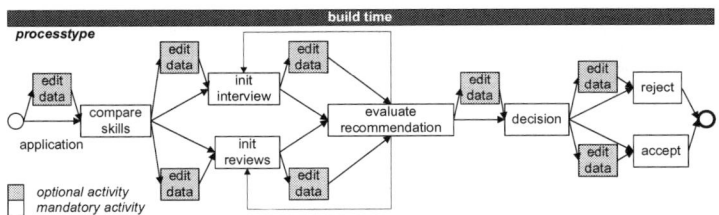

Fig. 2. Mandatory and optional activities in contemporary WfMS

In principle, optional activities, enabling access to application data at arbitrary points in time, could be emulated in WfMS by explicitly modeling them at different positions in the control flow. However, this would lead to spaghetti-like process models with high number of redundant activities, which are difficult to comprehend for users. Besides this, users would not be able to distinguish optional activities from mandatory ones. Fig. 2 illustrates this problem along our running example. Here, optional activity `edit data` is embedded multiple times in the process definition in order to be able to access application data if required. Note that without such an explicit integration of optional activities, needed changes of application data would have to be accomplished directly within the applications system. When bypassing either the WfMS or appl. system, however, inconsistencies with respect to attributes, redundantly maintained in both systems, might occur. Worst case, this can result in runtime errors or faulty process executions.

Requirements. Object-aware process management systems need to be tightly integrated with application data. In particular, these data should be manageable and accessible based on complex objects rather than on atomic data elements. Another challenge is to cope with the varying and dynamic number of object instances to be handled at runtime. Thereby, the different relations between the object instances have to be considered as well. Finally, regardless of process status, it should be possible to access object information at any time.

3.2   Challenge 2: Choosing Granularities for Processes and Activities

Findings. *For different object types separate process definitions exist [4]. The creation of a process instance is directly coupled with the creation of an object instance; i.e., for each object instance exactly one process instance exists.*

Fig. 3 illustrates the mapping between object and process types as well as between object and process instances. The object type of a job application has its own process type. At runtime, there are several instances of a job application object. Correspondingly, for each of them a separate process instance is created.

Regarding the process type associated with a particular object type, each activity refers to one or more attributes of the object type. There is one action per attribute to read or write its value. Each activity consists of at least one action.

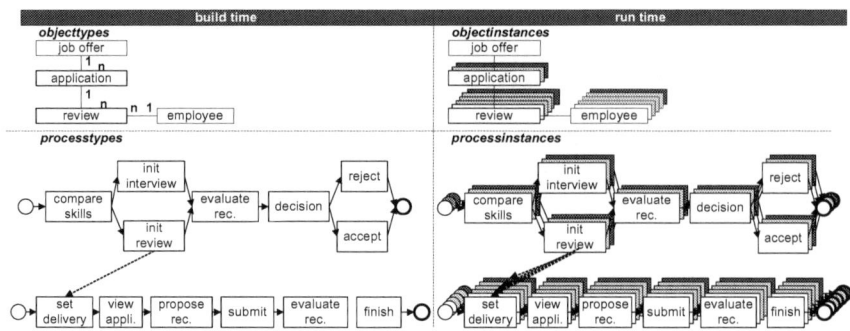

Fig. 3. Analogy between data and process structure

When executing a particular process instance related subordinate processes may be triggered. Results collected during their execution are relevant for the execution of the superordinate process instance as well. In this context the creation of a subordinate process instance is also coupled with the creation of a corresponding object instance. The latter has to refer to the object instance of the superordinate process instance. Consequently, the number of subordinate process instances depends on the number of object instances which reference the object instance associated with the superordinate process instance.

The relations between process types correspond to the relations between object types within the overall data structure [4].

Fig. 3 illustrates the analogy between data structure and process structure. For each job application an arbitrary number of reviews may be requested, and for each review object one process instance is running. The latter constitutes a subordinate process of the process instance related to the job application.

Problems. Granularity issues are not adequately addressed in existing WfMS; i.e., processes, sub-processes and activities may be modeled at arbitrary level of granularity. Neither a uniform methodology nor practical guidelines exist for process modeling [5], often resulting in inconsistent or non-comparable models. Furthermore, when modeling and executing processes in WfMS, there exists no direct support for considering the underlying data structure; i.e., the objects and their relations. In particular, two drawbacks can be observed: First, the creation of (sub) process instances cannot be coupled with the creation of object instances. Second, in many WfMS the number of sub process instances has to be fixed already at build time [6]. Note that WfMS enabling multi-instance patterns constitute an exception in the latter respect [2].

Requirements. The modeling of processes and data constitute two sides of the same coin and therefore should correspond to each other [5]. Thereby, we have to distinguish between object level and (data) structure level: First, a process type should always be modeled with respect to a specific object type; process activities then may directly relate to attributes of this object type. Second,

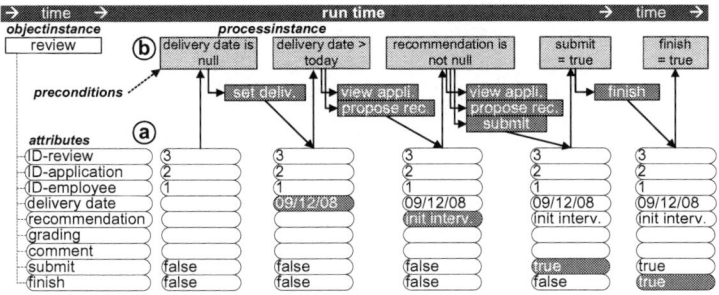

Fig. 4. Progress within data and data-based modeling

at the structure level, process relations should correspond to the ones between the corresponding data objects. Finally, instantiation of processes needs to be coupled with the creation of related object instances.

3.3   Challenge 3: Data-Based Modeling

Findings. *The progress of a process instance correlates with the attribute values of the associated object instance. Corresponding to this, the steps of a process are less defined on basis of black-box activities, but more on explicit data conditions.*

Fig. 4 shows an instance of a review object together with the related process instance. For each process step, pre-conditions on the attribute values of the object instance as well as the attribute values changed within this step are depicted. In particular, the process is defined by setting goals described in terms of conditions on object attribute values. Regarding our example from Fig. 4, these data conditions are related to the attributes of the review object. This way, process state and object state sync at any point in time. Mandatory activities can be identified by analyzing the data conditions. More precisely, they comprise those actions changing object attributes in a way such that the conditions for executing subsequent activities become fulfilled [3]. For each process step at least one mandatory activity exists.

Problems. In existing WfMS, process designers have to explicitly define the activities to be carried out as well as their order constraints. In particular, no support exists for verifying whether or not the (semantic) goals of a process can be achieved [7,8,9]. Some approaches define pre- and post-conditions for certain activities in relation to application data. If the pre-conditions of such an activity cannot be met during runtime, however, process execution is blocked. In this context, it is no longer sufficient to only postulate certain attribute values for executing a particular activity. It then must be also possible, to dynamically react on current attribute values.

Requirements. In object-aware process management systems, the modeling of a process type should not be based on the activities to be carried out. Instead,

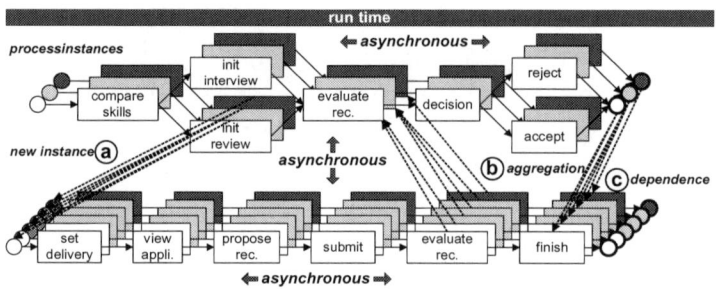

Fig. 5. Synchronizing process instances

process steps should be defined in terms of data conditions. The latter, in turn, should relate to the attributes belonging to the corresponding object type.

3.4 Challenge 4: Synchronizing Process Instances

Findings. A subordinate process is always instantiated during the execution of another process instance [6]. Like for the superordinate process instance, a corresponding object instance is then created. In particular, this object instance references the one related to the superordinate process instance. Finally, the pre-condition of the process step, in which the subordinate process instance is created, corresponds to a data condition on the superordinate object instance.

The creation of a particular object instance depends on the progress of the process instance related to the superordinate object instance.

Fig. 5a illustrates this relationship. A new review object cannot be created before the skills of the applicant have been compared with the job profile.

During the execution of a superordinate process instance, information from its subordinate process instances may be used for decissions within the superordinate process instance.

To accomplish such evaluation, data of multiple subordinate object instances may be required [6]; i.e., we need to aggregate the values of particular attributes of subordinate object instances. Which subordinate object instances shall be taken into account may depend on the execution progress of their corresponding process instances. Fig. 5b illustrates this along our running example. Within the parental process instance handling a particular job application, the requested reviews (i.e., results from different subordinate processes) are jointly evaluated. Thereby, only submitted reviews are considered.

The executions of different process instances may be mutually dependent [4,6]. Respective dependencies may exist between instances of the same process type as well as between instances of different process type.

Considering this, the data conditions for executing process steps are even more complex in existing application software than described above; i.e., these data conditions may be not only based on the attributes of the corresponding object type, but also on the attributes of related object types. For example, a review may only be marked as `completed` after a decision on the job application has been made (cf. Fig. 5c).

Problems. In existing WfMS, process instances are executed in isolation to each other [6]. Neither dependencies between instances of different process types nor dependencies between instances of the same process type can be defined at a reasonable semantical level. Often, the modeling of subordinate processes serves as a workaround. However, in existing WfMS the execution of subordinate process instances is tightly synchronized with their superordinate process instance; i.e., the latter is blocked until the sub process instances are completed. Thus, neither aggregated activities nor more complex synchronization dependencies as described above can be adequately handled in WfMS [6].

Requirements. Generally, it should be possible to execute both instances of the same and instances of different process types in a loosely coupled manner, i.e., asynchronously to each other. However, due to data dependencies at object instance level, we need to be able to synchronize their execution at certain points. Furthermore, to a superordinate process instance several subordinate process instances should be assignable in accordance with the relationships between corresponding object instances as well as their cardinalities.

3.5 Challenge 5: Flexibility

Findings. As described, there are optional as well as mandatory activities. The former are used to gather object information at any point in time regardless from the progress of the corresponding process instance. Opposed to this, the latter are mandatory and comprise actions that change the values of the object attributes used within the data conditions of one or multiple process steps.

The activation of an activity does not directly depend on the completion of other activities; i.e., it may be executed as soon as its data condition is satisfied.

An activity can be also executed repeatedly as long as its data condition is met. Depending on how the data conditions of the different activities look like, a more or less asynchronous execution becomes possible (cf. Fig. 6).

Generally, activities consist of one or more atomic actions for reading or writing the different attributes of an object instance. Which object attributes can be actually modified in a given context depends on the progress of the related process instance. For example, Fig. 7 shows the different actions available within

→ time →		run time		→ time →
delivery date is null	delivery date > today	recommendation is not null	submit = true	finish = true
		view review		
		edit review		
set delivery date		view application		
	propose recommendation			
		submit	finish	

Fig. 6. Asynchronous and overlapping execution of activities

objecttype review	processtype delivery date is null	delivery date > today	recommend. is not null	submit = true	finish = true
attributes					
ID-review	read	read	read	read	read
ID-application	read	read	read	read	read
ID-employee	read	read	read	read	read
delivery date	*write*	read	read	read	read
recommendation		*write*	write	read	read
grading		write	write	read	read
comment		write	write	read	read
submit			*write*	read	read
finish				*write*	read

Fig. 7. Granularity of activities with optional and mandatory actions

the (optional) activity for entering the data of a review object. As can be seen, the concrete set of selectable actions depends on the conditions actually met by the object instance; i.e., (optional) activities dynamically adapt their behavior to the progress of the corresponding process instance (denoted as *horizontal dynamic granularity*). Interestingly, the attribute changes required to fulfill the data condition of a particular process step can be also realized when executing an optional activity. Since this can be done asynchronously at arbitrary point in time, high process flexibility can be achieved. Furthermore, for a particular activity optional and mandatory actions can be differentiated. Fig. 7 shows the mandatory actions for a review. Note that these actions may differ from step to step. As opposed to optional activities, mandatory ones only include those actions necessary for the fulfillment of the data conditions of subsequent steps.

Mandatory activities belonging to different instances of the same process type may be executed together.

Required data is only entered once by the user; i.e., users may group a number of activities for which they want to provide the same input data (denoted as *vertical dynamic granularity*). Fig. 8 illustrates this for activity `finish`.

Problems. Due to the activity-driven execution of process instances in existing WfMS, an activity can usually be activated only once (except loop backs). Furthermore, activity execution must take place in a precisely defined context. However, such rigid behavior is not always adequate. Sometimes an activity needs to be repeated spontaneously; or it has to be executed in advance, or first be stopped and then be caught up at a later point in time [3]. Conventional WfMS

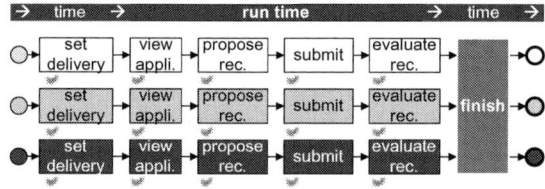

Fig. 8. Grouping of activities

do not allow for this kind of flexibility. Furthermore, users are typically involved in the execution of multiple instances of a particular process type. Thus, their worklist usually contains many activities of same type. However, each of them needs to be processed separately in WfMS, which does not always comply with common work practice. In summary, the isolated execution of process instances in existing WfMS is too inflexible [10].

Requirements. Data-driven process execution is needed; i.e., process execution should be not guided by activities, but rather be based on the state of the processed object instances. Thereby, a much more flexible execution behavior and optional activities can be realized. Furthermore, it should be possible to make the selectable actions within an activity execution dependable on the state of the process instances. Finally, it should be possible to work on several activities with same type, but belonging to different process instances, in one go.

The above discussions have revealed the limitations of current WfMS. Only being able to cope with atomic or stateless data elements is by far not sufficient. Instead, tight process and data integration is needed. This integration can based on objects, object attributes and object relations. Therefore, these three levels need to be reflected in process definitions as well; i.e., activities should be related to object attributes and process modeling should be based on objects. The hierarchical relations between processes and other process interdependencies then depend on object relations; i.e., on references between objects. In summary, we need comprehensive support for the data-based modeling and data-driven execution of business processes.

4 Related Work

The described challenges have been partially addressed by existing work. However, a comprehensive solution for object-aware process management is still missing. Fig. 9 summarizes what challenges have been addressed by which approach.

Challenge 1: Integration of Data. Concepts for better integration of processes and data are suggested in Artifact-Centric Modeling [11], Production-Based Workflow Support [5,12], Data-Driven Process Coordination (Corepro) [4], and Case Handling [3]. [12] establishes relations between atomic data elements, but neither supports complex objects nor varying numbers of data elements. Corepro, in turn, allows to model objects and object relations [4,13]; object definition does not consider attributes and cardinalities of object relations. In [11], so-called *artifacts* have to be identified first. Like objects, artifacts consist of different attributes which can be also used to define relations between them. Unlike objects, they are not defined at type level and therefore cannot be instantiated multiple times. In all approaches, access to data is only possible in the context of an activity execution, i.e. at a certain point during process execution. Only *Case Handling* [3] allows access to data outside the scope of activities, but does not provide explicit support for complex objects and data structures.

		Artifact Centric Modelling (IBM Research USA)	Production Based Support (University of Eindhoven)	Data Driven Coordination (University of Twente / Ulm)	Case Handling (University of Eindhoven, Hasso Plattner Institute Potsdam)	Proclets (University of Eindhoven, Colorado, Carmelina)	Batch activities (University of Queensland)
integration of data	atomic elements / attributes	X	X		X	X	X
	objects	X		X	O		
	relations between data	X	X	X			
	flexible quantity			O			
	access beyond activities				X		
granularity	activity	X	X		X		
	process		O	X	O	X	
databased modelling		O	X	O	X		
synchronisation				X		X	
flexibility	horizontal dynamic granul.			X			
	vertical dynamic granularity						X
	data-driven execution		X	O	X		

Fig. 9. Overview of related work

Challenge 2: Choice of Granularity for Activities and Processes. Objects and object relations constitute guidelines for choosing the granularity for processes, sub-processes and activities. Process definitions are based on objects and activities are used to modify the values of corresponding attributes. Furthermore, a process structure should be in accordance with the data structure. Granularity issues are addressed by the previously mentioned approaches and by Proclets [6]. However, none of them enables complete process definition with references to attributes, objects and object relations. In [11] activities are modeled based on one ore more artifacts, but without deriving the granularity of processes automatically. Proclets [6] are lightweight processes, which communicate with each other via messages. The granularity of a process is not explicitly defined. By considering the quantity of process instances, an implicit analogy between processes and objects can be drawn. Corepro [4] explicitly coordinates individual processes based on the underlying data structure. The granularity of processes and activities can be chosen freely. [5,12] consider both the granularity of activities and the one of processes. Activities always relate to one or more atomic data elements. The structure of the process corresponds to the relationships between the data elements. Sub-processes do not exist. In [3] activities are described in terms of atomic data elements as well. Due to their indirect encapsulation, a process is defined based on an individual "case". However, relationships are not considered.

Challenge 3: Data-Based Modeling. Though [11] does not allow for data-based modeling, activities are defined with references to the identified artifacts. In Corepro, process coordination is realized in accordance with the objects and their relations. Objects are defined in terms of states and transitions between them. Furthermore, processes assigned to different objects can be related to each other based on external transitions. The most advanced approaches in relation to data-based modeling are provided by [3] and [5,12]. Data-based modeling of activities in terms of atomic data elements is possible. However, for each process step still an activity has to be explicitly defined.

Challenge 4: Synchronization. In [6], processes are synchronized based on messages. Thereby, a variable number of process instances is considered. However, their synchronization is not explicitly based on the data structure. The most powerful approach in the given context is provided by the data-driven coordination of processes in Corepro [4]. Process synchronization is in accordance with the related data structure. Thereby, a variable number of instances can be created. The creation of new object instances at runtime is possible, but requires an ad-hoc change of the related data structure [13].

Challenge 5: Flexibility. Case Handling [3] enables *horizontal dynamic granularity*. A data element can be read and written within several activities. These data elements can either be free, mandatory or optional. A data element which is mandatory for an activity can be optional for preceding ones. [10] enables *vertical dynamic granularity* of activities; same activities of different process instances can be grouped and executed together. [3,12] enable the data-driven execution of processes based on current values of the data elements. In Corepro [4] processes themselves are still activity-driven, whereas process synchronization follows a data-driven approach.

5   Outlook

Our overall vision is to develop a framework for object-aware process management; i.e., a generic component for enabling data-driven processes as well as an integrated view on process and data. On the one hand we want to provide similar features as can be found in some hard-coded, data-oriented applications. On the other hand we want to benefit from the advantages known from workflow technology. However, a tight integration of data and process is only one of the challenges to be tackled. Other ones arise from the involvement of users and the handling of access privileges; e.g., depending on object data. In future papers we will provide detailed insights into the different components of an object-aware process management system as well as their complex interdependencies.

References

1. Aalst, W., Hee, K.: Workflow-Management - Models, Methods and Systems. MIT Press, Cambridge (2004)
2. Aalst, W., Hofstede, A., Kiepuszewski, B., Barros, A.: Workflow patterns. Distr. & Parallel Databases 14, 5–51 (2003)
3. Aalst, W., Weske, M., Grünbauer, D.: Case handling: A new paradigm for business process support. DKE 53(2), 129–162 (2005)
4. Müller, D., Reichert, M., Herbst, J.: Data-driven modeling and coordination of large process structures. In: Meersman, R., Tari, Z. (eds.) OTM 2007, Part I. LNCS, vol. 4803, pp. 131–149. Springer, Heidelberg (2007)
5. Reijers, H., Liman, S., Aalst, W.: Product-based workflow design. Management Information Systems 20(1), 229–262 (2003)
6. Aalst, W., Barthelmess, P., Ellis, C., Wainer, J.: Workflow modeling using proclets. In: Scheuermann, P., Etzion, O. (eds.) CoopIS 2000. LNCS, vol. 1901, pp. 198–209. Springer, Heidelberg (2000)
7. Ryndina, K., Küster, J., Gall, H.: Consistency of business process models and object life cycles. In: Kühne, T. (ed.) MoDELS 2006. LNCS, vol. 4364, pp. 80–90. Springer, Heidelberg (2007)

8. Redding, G., Dumas, M., Hofstede, A., Iordachescu, A.: Transforming object-oriented models to process-oriented models. In: ter Hofstede, A.H.M., Benatallah, B., Paik, H.-Y. (eds.) BPM Workshops 2007. LNCS, vol. 4928, pp. 132–143. Springer, Heidelberg (2008)
9. Gerede, C., Su, J.: Specification and verification of artifact behaviors in business process models. In: Krämer, B.J., Lin, K.-J., Narasimhan, P. (eds.) ICSOC 2007. LNCS, vol. 4749, pp. 181–192. Springer, Heidelberg (2007)
10. Sadiq, S., Orlowska, M., Sadiq, W., Schulz, K.: When workflows will not deliver: The case of contradicting work practice. In: Proc. BIS 2005 (2005)
11. Liu, R., Bhattacharya, K., Wu, F.: Modeling business contexture and behavior using business artifacts. In: Krogstie, J., Opdahl, A.L., Sindre, G. (eds.) CAiSE 2007 and WES 2007. LNCS, vol. 4495, pp. 324–339. Springer, Heidelberg (2007)
12. Vanderfeesten, I., Reijers, H., Aalst, W.: Product-based workflow support: Dynamic workflow execution. In: Bellahsène, Z., Léonard, M. (eds.) CAiSE 2008. LNCS, vol. 5074, pp. 571–574. Springer, Heidelberg (2008)
13. Müller, D., Reichert, M., Herbst, J.: A new paradigm for the enactment and dynamic adaptation of data-driven process structures. In: Bellahsène, Z., Léonard, M. (eds.) CAiSE 2008. LNCS, vol. 5074, pp. 48–63. Springer, Heidelberg (2008)

Supporting Ontology-Based Semantic Annotation of Business Processes with Automated Suggestions

Chiara Di Francescomarino and Paolo Tonella

FBK—IRST, Trento, Italy
{dfmchiara,tonella}@fbk.eu

Abstract. Business Process annotation with semantic tags taken from an ontology is becoming a crucial activity for business designers. In fact, semantic annotations help business process comprehension, documentation, analysis and evolution. However, building a domain ontology and annotating a process with semantic concepts is a difficult task.

In this work, we propose an automated technique to support the business designer both in domain ontology creation/extension and in the semantic annotation of process models expressed in BPMN. We use natural language processing of the labels appearing in the process elements to construct a domain ontology skeleton or to extend an existing ontology, if available. Semantic annotations are automatically suggested to the business designer, based on a measure of similarity between ontology concepts and the labels of the process elements to be annotated.

1 Introduction

Available modelling notations for business processes, such as BPMN (Business Process Modelling Notation)[1], lack the ability to specify semantic properties of the processes, including those related to their business domain. The labelling of activity constructs, in fact, is often arbitrarily performed [1], resulting in unclear labels, characterized by mismatching and overlapping terms, and therefore implying a difficult comprehension [2] and loss of domain semantic knowledge. However, semantic information is important for tasks that involve reasoning over the process and for which automated support is desirable [3]. For example, documenting or querying a process [4], enforcing a policy, or verifying constraints on the business logics [5] involve semantic reasoning that cannot be carried out on process models expressed in BPMN or similar languages.

We propose to add semantic annotations to business processes to allow better understanding, documenting, querying and reasoning about properties, constraints and design choices that cannot be expressed in a purely syntactic way. In detail, in order to augment business processes with semantic information from a business domain, we propose to semantically annotate them with concepts taken from a domain ontology by means of standard BPMN textual annotations, with the semantic concept prefixed by an "@". Such annotations allow us to categorize BPMN elements by unifying labels that represent the same concept and abstracting them into meaningful generalizations.

---

[1] http://www.bpmn.org/

T. Halpin et al. (Eds.): BPMDS 2009 and EMMSAD 2009, LNBIP 29, pp. 211–223, 2009.

The idea of adding semantic information to business processes has already been proposed by several authors, for different process description languages and goals. Generalizing, they can be classified into two big groups: semantic annotation approaches for specifying the process dynamic behaviour ([6]) and those aimed at clarifying the meaning of process elements ([7], [8], [9]). In the former category, Koschmider and Oberweis [6] use an ontology to give a precise semantics to the elements and data of a business process (represented as a Petri Net). In the second, Thomas and Fellman [7] present a semantic extension of event-driven process chains (EPC) for solving ambiguities and reasoning over process models; De Nicola et al. [8] introduce BPAL, an ontological framework for the representation of the business process semantics; the SUPER ontology [9] is used for the creation of semantic annotations of both BPMN and EPC process models in order to overcome problems with composition and execution.

Our work falls in the second category: in detail, it is focused on domain-related semantic annotations and deals with the problem of supporting business designers in the difficult task of process semantic annotation. Born et al. [10] proposed a tool for the user-friendly integration of domain ontology information in the process modelling. In order to match process elements and ontology concepts, they exploit: (1) information about domain objects, actions, states and transitions from the ontology; (2) structural knowledge from the process; (3) techniques for string matching (e.g., distance metrics), synonyms and homonyms. Our approach, instead, relies on linguistic analysis (natural language parsing) of the process element labels and of the concept names. Matching is based on a measure of information content similarity. By taking advantage of this similarity measure, we support business designers by providing them with annotation suggestions for the semantic annotation of business process elements with concepts from a domain ontology, and, if necessary, in the domain ontology creation/extension.

After a short overview about concepts and notation that will be used in the remainder of the paper (Section 2), we describe our technique for the semi-automated annotation of process elements (Section 3) and our approach for supporting business analysts in ontology creation and extension (Section 4). A case study is reported in Section 5 and conclusions and future works are finally presented in Section 6.

2 Background

2.1 Linguistic Analysis

Natural language processing is a wide research area, including a number of different tasks and approaches. The analysis of short sentences, like those characterizing labels or ontology concepts, is one such task. Linguistic analyzers, as for example MINIPAR[2] [11], do not only allow to tokenize (short) sentences, reduce words to their stem and classify terms into grammatical categories (e.g. verbs, nouns, adjectives), but they are also able to find dependencies and grammatical relationships between them (e.g. verb-object, article-noun, specifier-specified).

In detail, given a sentence s, MINIPAR is able to tokenize it, thus extracting its word list, $WS(s) = \{w_i \in Dict | s = w_1...w_n\}$, where $Dict$ is a given dictionary of words[3].

---

[2] http://www.cs.ualberta.ca/~lindek/minipar.htm
[3] MINIPAR takes advantage of WordNet.

Term	Grammatical category	Grammatical relationship type	Head
Choose	V (Verb)		
a	Det (Determiner)	det (N det Det)	Group
product	N (Noun)	nn (N nn N)	Group
group	N (Noun)	obj (V obj N)	Choose

Term	Grammatical category	Grammatical relationship type	Head
Select	V (Verb)		
quantity	N (Noun)	obj (V obj N)	Select

Term	Grammatical category	Grammatical relationship type	Head
Store	N (Noun)	nn (N nn N)	method
payment	N (Noun)	nn (N nn N)	method
method	N (Noun)		

Fig. 1. Information extracted by MINIPAR

Moreover, for each word w_i it identifies the grammatical category $GCat(w_i) \in GCS$, as well as the grammatical relationship $gRel(w_i) \in GREL$ and the head word guiding such a relationship ($head(w_i)$), if any. $GCS = \{V, N, V\_BE, A, ...\}$ is the set of the MINIPAR classification of grammatical categories (e.g., V = verb, N = noun, V_BE = "to be" verb, A = adjective or adverb, ...), while $GREL = \{subj, obj, nn, det, ...\}$ is the set of the MINIPAR grammatical relationships (e.g., $subj$ = verb-subject, obj =verb-object, nn = specified-specifier and det = determined-determiner relationship).

Henceforth, we will refer to a verb of a parsed sentence with the character v (i.e., $GCat(v) = V$) and to a noun with the character n (i.e., $GCat(n) = N$). Moreover, we introduce the function $o(v)$ for denoting the object of the verb v (i.e., $gREL(o(v)) = obj$ and $head(o(v)) = v$) and $S(n)$ for representing the set of the specifiers of n (i.e., $gREL(s) = nn$ and $head(s) = n$, where $s \in S(n)$).

For example, by applying MINIPAR to the short sentence "Choose a product group", we obtain the information in Figure 1 (top left); by applying it to the sentence "Select quantity", we get the results shown in Figure 1 (top right).

Unfortunately, short sentences are intrinsically difficult to analyze through linguistic processing, because they carry limited and compact information. Sometimes, it happens that the analysis performed by the parser is wrong or inaccurate. For example, parsing of the label "Store payment method" by means of MINIPAR gives the result in Figure 1 (bottom).

Moreover, parsing a sentence is not enough for determining its semantics. The same term, in fact, can have multiple meanings (*polisemy*), as well as more terms (*synonyms*) can represent the same concept. WordNet [12] is one of the most known resources allowing to categorize terms according to their meaning (sense) and synonym set (synset). A word can have multiple senses and each of them is a key able to disambiguate the word meaning. A synset groups words with the same, specific meaning into a synonym set. According to their semantics, synsets can be classified into five different type categories: verbs, nouns, adjectives, adverbs and satellite adjectives. A pair *(word, wordsense)*, (w, s_i), identifies a unique synset for the sense s_i of the word w; hereafter we will use the function $SynsetRepr(syn) = (w, s_i)$, where syn is a synset, for denoting the synset canonical representative.

2.2 Information Content Similarity Measure

The information content similarity approach is based on the *term information content*: the more frequently a term occurs, the less information it conveys. The information content can be measured as the negative logarithm of the normalized term frequency. Given two concepts, their semantic similarity depends on the amount of information they share. Assuming we can map them onto a hierarchical structure, such as Word-Net, the semantic similarity is given by the information content of the Most Specific Common Abstraction ($MSCA$). The information content of a term can be measured on the basis of the term occurrences in large text corpora (normalized with respect to the hierarchical structure). An approximation of such a measure can be obtained by analyzing the hierarchical structure and counting the number of hyponyms, under the assumption that a term with lots of hyponyms tends to occur quite frequently in large corpora. In this work, we approximate the probability of terms by using hyponyms in WordNet: $p(t) = \frac{hypo(t)+1}{max_{WN}}$, where $hypo(t)$ is the number of hyponyms of the term t and max_{WN} is the total number of WordNet words.

One of the most used ways of computing the information content similarity between two terms t_1 and t_2 is Lin's formula [13]:

$$ics(t_1, t_2) = \frac{2 * \log(p(MCSA(t_1, t_2)))}{\log(p(t_1)) + \log(p(t_2))}$$

Henceforth, when talking about the information content similarity, we refer to Lin's formula.

3   Business Process Semantic Annotation Suggestions

Though the semantic annotation of business processes with concepts taken from a domain ontology provides remarkable advantages, e.g. the possibility of querying and reasoning over processes, it can be a time consuming and error prone task for business designers. Hence, we propose to support them with semantic annotation suggestions semi-automatically generated by exploiting a linguistic resource, such as WordNet, for measuring the information content similarity between process element labels and ontology concepts. Moreover, in order to improve the automatic suggester performance, we propose a semi-automatic domain analysis technique aimed at mapping, when possible, ontology concepts to WordNet synsets.

3.1   Domain Ontology Analysis

In the literature, several WSD (Word Sense Disambiguation) algorithms have been proposed. They determine senses for words appearing in large corpora of texts, written in natural language [14]. Only a few WSD works, in particular in the context of the semantic web [15], deal with the mapping between ontology concepts and WordNet synsets. In order to simplify the semantic annotation of process activities and make it more accurate, we also need to solve the semantic ambiguity of ontology concepts, by mapping them to unique synsets. For this purpose, we exploit the information we can gather from the ontology itself (in particular from its hierarchical structure) and its comparison with the WordNet taxonomy. However, the mapping, as well as the comparison, presents several issues. The first challenge is the structural difference between strings representing ontology concepts and words with a specific sense characterizing a synset.

A concept name can be a single word or a short sentence describing the concept. While in the first case the concept name can be clearly mapped to one of the synonyms in a synset (representing the sense with the highest similarity value), in the second case, the short sentence needs to be linguistically analyzed in order to mine the sentence *head* word, i.e. the word that, representing the dominant meaning of the concept, also determines its ontology relationships (in particular the *is_a* relationship).

Let us consider, for example, the domain ontology concept "record information". By assuming that concept names have been meaningfully assigned, the concept will very likely represent the action of storing information. Therefore, the concept head word is the verb "to record", which probably has an is_a relationship with some "action" or "event" concept in the ontology (see for example SUMO[4] or OntoSem[5]).

The head word in a short sentence can be mined by applying a linguistic analyzer, as for example MINIPAR, to the sentence itself. The head word, in fact, will be the root word in the parsing tree produced by the parser.

Once that the head word has been identified for each concept, it has to be mapped to a WordNet synset. We exploit the hierarchical structure of the ontology for extracting the sense of the head word. In detail, for each concept c we consider its similarity with concepts of the same synset type and belonging to its relative concept set $RC(c) = PC(c) \cup SC(c) \cup CC(c)$, where $PC(c)$ is the set of the superconcepts of c, $SC(c)$ the set of sibling concepts of c and $CC(c)$ the set of subconcepts of c. Given the synset type of the head word $\overline{w}_c$ of the current concept c (it can be inferred from the grammatical category of $\overline{w}_c$), for each sense s_i of such a word and for each relative concept $r_c \in RC(c)$ of the same type, we compute the maximum information content similarity value $maxics((\overline{w}_c, s_i), \overline{r}_c)$ (see Subsection 2.2) between the two head words ($\overline{w}_c$ and $\overline{r}_c$) with respect to all the possible senses of $\overline{r}_c$. The identified synset, characterized by the pair $(\overline{w}_c, s_i)$ chosen for the current concept c, will be the one with the best average of $maxics((\overline{w}_c, s_i), \overline{r}_c)$ computed over all the relative concepts.

Let us consider the word sense disambiguation of the concept "search". Table 1 shows the average information content similarity measure for each sense of the word. The chosen sense for the head word "search" is the one associated with the highest average semantic similarity, i.e. 0.86: sense #1. We do not expect that automated disambiguation of ontology concepts is completely error free, especially because we deal with short sentences, while the available approaches have been proven to work well with long texts in natural language. Hence, we assume the automatically produced disambiguation is revised by the user before moving to the next step of process annotation.

Table 1. Average semantic similarity measures for each sense of the verb "search"

Concept	Sense description	$avgICS(\overline{w}_c, s_i)$
search#1	the activity of looking thoroughly in order to find something or someone	0.86
search#5	boarding and inspecting a ship on the high seas	0.76
search#2	an investigation seeking answers	0.37
search#4	the examination of alternative hypotheses	0.36
search#3	an operation that determines whether one or more of a set of items has a specified property	0.25

---

[4] http://protege.stanford.edu/ontologies/sumoOntology/sumo_ontology.html

[5] http://morpheus.cs.umbc.edu/aks1/ontosem.owl

3.2   Semantic Suggestions

Once the ontology concepts are linked to a single WordNet sense, the business designer can be supported in the semantic annotation, by receiving suggestions for each process activity she intends to annotate. The choice of the suggestions is based on the semantic similarity between pairs of BPMN element labels and ontology concepts: the higher the similarity measure, the closer the candidate ontology concept c is to the BPMN element label l. The semantic similarity of a pair (l, c) can be based on the semantic similarity between pairs of words respectively in l ($W_l = \{w_i \in Dict | l = w_1...w_n\}$) and in c ($W_c = \{w_j \in Dict | c = w_1...w_m\}$). We define the *candidate set of pairs* CSP as $CSP \subseteq W_l \times W_c$ such that: (1) each word $w_i \in W_l$ and $w_j \in W_c$ appears at most once in CSP; and, (2) the total semantic similarity (i.e., the sum of similarity values over each pair in CSP) is maximized by CSP.

We take advantage of the linguistic information available from linguistic analysis (parsing and synset computation) to choose proper candidate pairs (e.g., verbs are never paired with nouns), but also to give weights to the semantic similarity measures (e.g., in the annotation of an activity, the verb has greater importance than the object, in turn more important than the specifier).

Once the semantic similarity measure is known for all pairs, consisting of a BPMN element label and an ontology concept, we determine the subset of such pairs which maximizes the total semantic similarity (maximum cut [16] in the bipartite graph of BPMN element labels and ontology concepts). The result is a suggested semantic annotation for each BPMN element.

The matching $CSP(W_l, W_c)$ between the words in label l and the words in concept c, is built in three steps: (1) maximum similarity pairs of verbs are determined ($CSP(V(l), V(c))$, with $V(l)$ and $V(c)$ respectively the verbs in l and c); (2) the respective objects $(o(v_l), o(v_c))$ of each verb pair $(v_l, v_c) \in (V(l), V(c))$ are added to $CSP(W_l, W_c)$, when both verb objects exist; (3) the CSP of the verb object specifiers, $CSP(S(o(v_l)), S(o(v_c)))$, is also added to $CSP(W_l, W_c)$. So the final matching contains the union of the pairs of maximal similarity verbs, the pairs of respective objects and the pairs of maximal similarity object specifiers.

In practical cases, for short sentences such as those used in process labels and ontology concept names, there is at most one verb, so step (1) produces an initial CSP with at most one pair, containing the two verbs. Step (2) adds the pair of objects for the two verbs, when such objects exist in both short sentences. Finally, maximal similarity object specifiers are added.

Let us consider, for example, the semantic similarity of the label "Choose a product group" and the semantic concept "toSelectProductCategory". In this case, the label and the concept contain a verb, an object and an object specifier, which are easily matched ($CSP = \{(choose, select), (group, category), (product, product)\}$). We weight these three different linguistic components according to the proportions: 4:2:1. So the formula for the semantic similarity becomes: $SemSim(l, c) = (4 * ics_{Lin}(verb_1, verb_2) + 2 * ics_{Lin}(obj_1, obj_2) + ics_{Lin}(objSpec_1, objSpec_2))/7$, where l is the label and c is the ontology concept. In Table 2 we show the result for this pair.

Table 3 shows the five highest values of semantic similarity between the label "Choose a product group" and each of the concepts in a manually built ontology.

Table 2. Semantic similarity measure between a label and an ontology concept

$term_1$	$term_2$	Synset	$p(term_1)$	$p(term_2)$	MCSA	p(MCSA)	ics_{Lin}
choose#1	select#1	{choose#1, take#10, se-lect#1, pick out#1}					1.0
group#1	category#1		0.0399	3.4309E-4	group#1	0.0399	0.5754
product#1	product#1						1.0
$SemSim(l, c)$							0.8787

Table 3. Five ontology concepts most similar to the label "Choose a product group"

Ontology concept	$SemSim(l, c)$
toSelectProductCategory	0.879
toSelectProductQuantity	0.834
toSelectCategory	0.736
toSelectQuantity	0.691
toSelectMethodPayment	0.624

The highest score determines the concept automatically suggested to annotate the task labelled "Choose a product group".

4   Domain Ontology Extension

In many practical cases, available domain ontologies do not perfectly satisfy the requirements of the semantic annotation of business processes. We propose a semi-automatic approach that, suggesting new concepts missing in the available ontology, supports business designers in the domain ontology extension, while avoiding term redundancy.

The starting point for the ontology extension is the introduction of new concepts obtained by combining concepts already in the ontology. In this case, the name of the new concept will be a short sentence, i.e. a compound name created from other concept names so that, in order to determine the superconcept of the concept to add, we apply the following heuristic rules: (1) the new concept is a subconcept of the concept whose name is the head word of the sentence; (2) if the compound name of the new concept combines a verb and an object concept, it will be the subconcept of the verb concept; (3) if the compound name of the new concept combines a specified noun and a specifier noun concept, it will be the subconcept of the specified noun concept; (4) if the verb (the specified noun) in the compound verb-object (specified-specifier) name of the new concept appears in the ontology in the form of the combination of the verb with another object (of the specified noun with another specifier), the verb (the specified noun) is added to the ontology as single word and a new is_a relationship is added between the verb (the specified noun) and both the old and the new concepts with compound names.

Let us consider, for example, the label "Choose a product" and let us imagine that the ontology already contains a "select" concept, whose semantic similarity with the "choose" verb is 1.0 and a concept "good", whose semantic similarity with the word "product" is 0.45. Though no concept exists with an acceptable semantic similarity for the whole label, the two concepts "select" and "good" can be composed, thus generating a new concept "selectGood" (that will be a subconcept of the concept "select"), whose similarity value, with respect to the "Choose a product" label, is 0.92.

Of course, there are also cases in which absolutely new concepts, i.e. made of single words, have to be introduced in the ontology. In order to provide a quite flexible way for managing such a situation we introduce the possibility to specify two thresholds t_w and t_s. The former is referred to single words, i.e. it allows to discard pairs of words whose semantic similarity value is under the threshold. The latter, instead, is a parameter referring to whole sentences, i.e. it allows to determine which pairs (label, ontology concept) have an acceptable global similarity, thus considering these concepts as good candidate annotations for the given process activity label.

Whenever no ontology concept (directly contained in the ontology or composed by other ontology concepts) reaches the t_s threshold, a new concept is added to the domain ontology. In order to discriminate which sentence component, i.e. the verb, the object or the object specifier, to add, we follow the ranking given to the various parts of a sentence (verb: 4; object: 2; specifier: 1). If the label contains the verb and the concept name with the best similarity value does not, we add the verb; otherwise we repeat the same check for the object and, eventually, in case of failure, for the object specifier. If for each of them there exists a concept in the ontology (with a low semantic similarity value), the word pair with the lowest semantic similarity value among those characterizing each sentence component is chosen to be replaced.

The introduction of a new concept in the ontology raises the problem of its relationships with the concepts already in the ontology. To this purpose, we again exploit the properties of Lin's semantic similarity. For each possible position p in the hierarchical structure of the ontology (i.e., for each possible direct superconcept), restricted to the concept type category, we compute $ics(\overline{w}_{ca}, RC(p))$, i.e., the average of the semantic similarity values between the head word of the new concept $\overline{w}_{ca}$ and the head word of each of the relatives, $RC(p)$, that the concept would have if it were in the hypothetical position p. The highest similarity value with respect to all the possible positions, allows to infer the new concept direct superconcept.

Let us consider the ontology in Figure 2 (left), an activity labelled "Choose a product group" and word and sentence thresholds equal to 0.6 and 0.8, respectively. Since none of the possible combinations of concepts already in the ontology (those with the highest values are shown in Table 4) allows to satisfy the two thresholds, the "group" concept needs to be added. Figure 2 (right) reports the semantic similarity values $ics(\overline{w}_{ca}, RC(p))$ for the head word $\overline{w}_{ca}$ = "group". The direct is_a relationship with the "family" concept, corresponding to the best value, is suggested to the designer.

4.1 Ontology Skeleton Creation

In the worst case, no domain ontology is available at all. In these situations business designers can be supported in building an ontology skeleton from scratch. To this purpose we suggest them an automatically generated candidate ontology, based on linguistic analysis of the process element labels. The idea is to build the ontology by combining the output of MINIPAR, applied to process element labels, and some heuristic rules.

The first assumption we make is to base the ontology on two macro concepts, *Action* and *Object*, and their relationships, *hasTargetObject*, having the concept "Action" as domain and "Object" as range, and *hasObjectSpecifier*, having the concept "Object" as domain and range. Starting from this ontology skeleton, we incrementally enrich it by

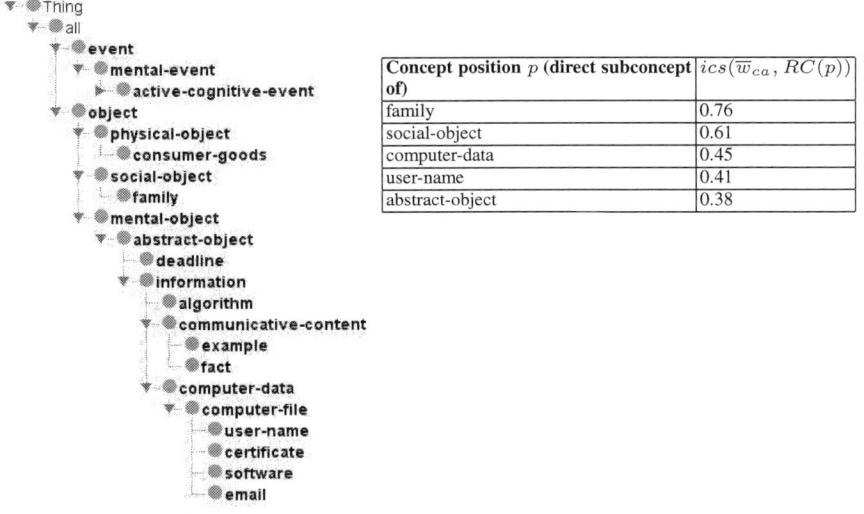

Concept position p (direct subconcept of)	$ics(\overline{w}_{ca}, RC(p))$
family	0.76
social-object	0.61
computer-data	0.45
user-name	0.41
abstract-object	0.38

Fig. 2. Automatically suggested position for concept "group"

Table 4. Three composed concepts most similar to the label "Choose a product group"

Label word w_1	Concept word w_2	$ics_{Lin}(w_1, w_2)$	Activity label	Concept name	$SemSim(l, c)$
Choose#1	select#1	1.0			
group#1	event#1	0.5	Choose a product group	selectGoodEvent	0.823
product#1	good#4	0.76			
Choose#1	select#1	1.0			
group#1	family#2	0.47	Choose a product group	selectGoodFamily	0.815
product#1	good#4	0.76			
Choose#1	determine#1	0.97			
group#1	event#1	0.5	Choose a product group	determineGoodEvent	0.82
product#1	good#4	0.76			

means of some heuristics applied to the output of the linguistic analyses, which include natural language parsing and synonym set identification (based on WordNet synsets).

In detail, we use the following heuristics (summarized in Table 5): ($H1$) words marked as verbs by the parser are subconcepts of the class "Action" (either a new subconcept or an existing one, if a synonym was added previously); ($H2$) words marked as nouns are subconcepts of the class "Object" (either a new subconcept or an existing synonym); ($H3$) pairs of verbs and objects related by a verb-object relationship originate a verb subconcept whose "hasTargetObject" property is restricted to the given object; ($H4$) pairs of nouns related by a specified-specifier relationship originate a specific object subconcept whose "hasObjectSpecifier" property is restricted to the specifier object; ($H5$) subconcepts of verb-object concepts are also added if the object has a specifier (the "hasTargetObject" relationship is restricted to the object with specifier).

Let us consider for example the label "Choose a product group" and let us suppose that this is the first label we are going to analyze (i.e. the skeleton ontology is still empty). By MINIPAR, we obtain the information in Figure 1 (top left). According to the heuristics $H1$, $H2$, the concept "toChoose" is added to the ontology skeleton as an "Action"

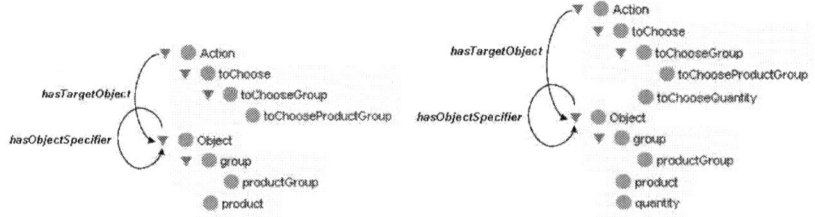

Fig. 3. Candidate ontology skeleton construction

subconcept, and "product" and "group" concepts as "Object" subconcepts. Since the word "group" is the object of the verb "choose", we can apply $H3$ and build the subconcept "toChooseProduct", whose "hasTargetObject" relationship is restricted to the concept "group". Since the word "product" specifies the word "group", "productGroup" is added as "group" subconcept, with "hasObjectSpecifier" object property restricted to the concept "product" (heuristics $H4$). The concept "toChooseProductGroup", whose "hasTargetObject" property is restricted to "productGroup", is added as a subconcept of "toChooseGroup". The resulting ontology fragment is shown in Figure 3 (left).

For the label "Select quantity" MINIPAR suggests (top right in Figure1) that "select" is a verb and "quantity" a noun. Since the ontology already contains the concept "to-Choose", returned by *SynsetRepr* as the canonical representative of the "select" synset, "toSelect" is not added to the ontology. The concept "quantity" is added as an "Object" subconcept and the concept "toChooseQuantity" as a subconcept of the concept "toChoose", with the "hasTargetObject" property restricted to "quantity". The resulting updated ontology structure is shown in Figure 3 (right).

Table 5. Heuristic rules to create a candidate ontology

Id	Linguistic Analysis	Ontology
H1	$v \in WS; GCat(v) = V$	$v' = SynsetRepr(v)$: v' is_a Action
H2	$n \in WS; GCat(n) = N$	$n' = SynsetRepr(n)$: n' is_a Object
H3	$v \in WS; GCat(v) = V$ $o \in WS; GCat(o) = N$ $v\ obj\ o$	$v' = SynsetRepr(v)$: v' is_a Action $o' = SynsetRepr(o)$: o' is_a Object $v'o'$ is_a v', $v'o'$ hasTargetObject o'
H4	$n \in WS; GCat(n) = N$ $s \in WS; GCat(s) = N$ $n\ nn\ s$	$n' = SynsetRepr(n)$: n' is_a Object $s' = SynsetRepr(s)$: s' is_a Object $s'n'$ is_a n', $s'n'$ hasObjectSpecifier s'
H5	$v \in WS; GCat(v) = V$ $o \in WS; GCat(o) = N$ $s \in WS; GCat(s) = N$ $v\ nn\ o$ $o\ nn\ s$	$v' = SynsetRepr(v)$: v' is_a Object $o' = SynsetRepr(o)$: o' is_a Object $s' = SynsetRepr(s)$: s' is_a Object $v'o'$ is_a v', $v'o'$ hasTargetObject o' $s'o'$ is_a o', $s'o'$ hasObjectSpecifier s' $v's'o'$ is_a $v'o'$, $v's'o'$ hasTargetObject $s'o'$

5   Case Study

The approaches proposed for the business process semantic annotation and, if necessary, ontology extension, have been applied to an on-Line Shop process and to an extract of a generic ontology (both available at http://selab.fbk.eu/OnLineShop). The process contains 36 activities to be annotated. The ontology, instead, is an extract of 231 classes out of the 7956 of the OntoSem ontology, whose concepts, we assume, have already been mapped to WordNet synsets.

For this case study we chose as thresholds for word and sentence acceptances $t_w = 0.6$ and $t_s = 0.85$, respectively, based on our previous experience in similar annotation exercises. When considering the first label, "Choose a product group", the business designer is suggested to extend the ontology with the concept "group". In fact, the maximum similarity value of the label with a concept in the ontology, is obtained with the "select" concept and is equal to 0.57, i.e. the weighted average over the semantic similarity values of the sentence components ($\frac{1.0}{4+2+1} = 0.57$), which is below t_s. Moreover, introducing new concepts by composing concept names already in the ontology is also not enough for satisfying the threshold: the best information content similarity value for the object "group" is $0.5 < t_w$; for the sentence it is $0.68 < t_s$. A "group" concept has therefore to be added to the ontology, as well as the composed concepts "selectGroup", "goodGroup" and "selectGoodGroup", since the word "product" is matched with the concept "good" in the maximized information content similarity.

When analyzing the label "Update product quantity" the concept "product" is proposed as a new concept for the ontology, since its best information content similarity value with respect to the ontology concepts is lower than those characterizing the other parts of the sentence. The business designer's acceptance of the suggestion implies not only the possibility of annotating the current activity with a new "modifyProduct" concept, but also an improvement in the annotation of the "Choose a product group" activity: the new annotation will be, in fact, "selectProductGroup" and the new similarity value 1.0. Whenever the ontology is extended, the previous annotation suggestions are automatically revised to identify cases where a better match has become possible.

Going ahead with the annotation of the other activities, the process will finally be annotated and the ontology extended with new concepts. The automatically suggested annotations are shown in the second column in Table 6. The single words added as new concepts to the ontology are marked by an asterisk. On the contrary, since the starting ontology does not contain composite concepts of the form verb-object, specified-specifier, verb-specifier-object, almost all the composite concepts have been automatically added to the ontology during the process analysis.

In order to evaluate the approach, we asked a human to perform the same task, starting from the same domain ontology and giving her the possibility to add new concepts, when necessary, but working without any automated suggestion. The guidelines followed in the execution of this exercise were similar to those implemented in our approach. We compared (Table 6) the manual semantic annotations, i.e. our gold standard, with those obtained with the automated approach. The comparison has been performed separately on the three main label components (i.e., verb, object, and object specifier). We base the evaluation on two assumptions: (1) if a concept for the annotation of a part of a sentence is in the ontology, in order to be correct, it has to be exactly the same in both manual and automated result; (2) if a new concept has to be added to the ontology it will likely have the same name of the sentence part it is required to match.

We define: (1) *reported and correct (R&C)*, the number of the label parts semantically annotated by our technique with exactly the same concepts used in the gold

Table 6. Case study data

Activity label	Automated suggestion	S.sim	Manual annotation	$R\&C$	R	TBR
Choose a product group	selectProduct*Group*	1.0	selectProductGroup	3	3	3
Search for a product		0.0	searchForProduct	0	0	2
Read policies	readDocument	0.9	readPolicy	1	2	2
Choose a product	selectProduct*	1.0	selectProduct	1	2	2
Select quantity	selectNumber	0.93	selectNumber	2	2	2
Add the product to the cart	addProduct*	1.0	addProduct	2	2	2
Update product quantity	modifyProduct*Number	0.86	modifyProductNumber	3	3	3
Remove product from cart	removeProduct*	1.0	removeProduct	2	2	2
Ask for checkout	requestCheckout*	0.97	requestCheckout	2	2	2
Provide personal data	supplyData	1.0	supplyData	2	2	2
Log-in	logIn*	1.0	login	1	1	1
Choose shipment method	selectProduct*Method	0.98	selectShipmentMethod	2	3	3
Choose a payment method	selectMarketingMethod	0.96	selectPaymentMethod	2	3	3
Provide payment information	supplyMarketingData	0.96	supplyPaymentData	2	3	3
Confirm order	confirmOrder	1.0	confirmOrder	2	2	2
Show the home page	showPage*	0.86	showHomePage	2	2	3
Provide summarized product info	supply	1.0	supplyProductData	1	1	3
Search for a product		0.0	searchForProduct	0	0	2
Provide policy information	supplyDocumentData	0.95	supplyPolicyData	2	3	3
Show product data	showProduct*Data	1.0	showProductData	3	3	3
Provide detailed product information	supplyProduct*Data	1.0	supplyProductData	3	3	3
Check product quantity availability	confirmProduct*Availability*	0.96	checkProductAvailability	2	3	3
Create cart	createCart*	1.0	createCart	2	2	2
Warn buyer	warn*Buyer*	1.0	warnBuyer	2	2	2
Compute total	calculateModel	0.86	calculateTotal	1	2	2
Visualize cart	visualize*Cart*	1.0	showCart	1	2	2
Check out	confirm	0.93	check out	0	1	1
Collect personal data	accumulateData	1.0	accumulateData	2	2	2
Check login data		0.0	checkLoginData	0	0	3
Store shipment method		0.0	storeShipmentMethod	0	0	3
Store payment method		0.0	storePaymentMethod	0	0	3
Store payment information		0.0	storePaymentData	0	0	3
Update stocked product data	modifyProduct*	0.92	modifyProductData	3	3	3
				52	61	80

standard; (2) *reported* (R), the number of the label parts for which our technique has been able to provide a suggestion; (3) *to be reported* (TBR), the number of annotation concepts (already in the ontology or added later) in the gold standard. We computed precision and recall for our case study: $precision = R\&C/R = 0.85$ and $recall = R\&C/TBR = 0.65$.

6   Conclusions and Future Work

In this work we addressed the problem of supporting business designers in the semantic annotation of process activities. In detail we propose an approach for: (1) suggesting, given the domain ontology, candidate ontology concepts to be used for the annotation of process activities; (2) whenever a domain ontology does not exist or does not contain concepts sufficient for precise annotation of a process element, creating an ontology skeleton or extending the domain ontology with new concepts.

In our future work we plan to: (1) study more complex short sentences, e.g. also including adverbials of location and time; (2) further analyze the information available in WordNet, domain ontologies and process structure; (3) further investigate heuristics and similarity measures; (4) exploit other resources for measuring word similarity.

References

1. Storey, V.C.: Comparing relationships in conceptual modeling: Mapping to semantic classifications. IEEE Trans. on Knowl. and Data Eng. 17(11), 1478–1489 (2005)
2. Mendling, J., Recker, J.: Towards systematic usage of labels and icons in business process models. In: Proc. of EMMSAD 2008. CEUR WS, vol. 337, pp. 1–13 (2008)
3. Hepp, M., Leymann, F., Domingue, J., Wahler, A., Fensel, D.: Semantic business process management: A vision towards using semantic web services for business process management. In: Proc. of ICEBE 2005 (2005)
4. Di Francescomarino, C., Tonella, P.: Crosscutting concern documentation by visual query of business processes. In: Proc. of BPD 2008 (2008)
5. Di Francescomarino, C., Ghidini, C., Rospocher, M., Serafini, L., Tonella, P.: Reasoning on semantically annotated processes. In: ICSOC, pp. 132–146 (2008)
6. Koschmider, A., Oberweis, A.: Ontology based business process description. In: Proc. of CAiSE 2005. LNCS, pp. 321–333. Springer, Heidelberg (2005)
7. Thomas, O., Fellmann, M.: Semantic epc: Enhancing process modeling using ontology languages. In: Proc. of ESWC 2007. CEUR-WS, vol. 251 (2007)
8. De Nicola, A., Lezoche, M., Missikoff, M.: An ontological approach to business process modeling. In: Proc. of IICAI 2007, December 2007, pp. 1794–1813 (2007)
9. Dimitrov, M., Alex Simov, S.S., Konstantinov, M.: A bpmo based semantic business process modelling environment. In: Proc. of the ESWC 2007. CEUR-WS, vol. 251 (2007)
10. Born, M., Dörr, F., Weber, I.: User-friendly semantic annotation in business process modeling. In: Weske, M., Hacid, M.-S., Godart, C. (eds.) WISE Workshops 2007. LNCS, vol. 4832, pp. 260–271. Springer, Heidelberg (2007)
11. Lin, D.: Dependency based evaluation of minipar. In: Proc. of the Workshop on the Evaluation of Parsing Systems, LREC, Granada, Spain (1998)
12. Miller, G.A.: Nouns in WordNet. In: WordNet: An Electronic Lexical Database (1998)
13. Lin, D.: An information-theoretic definition of similarity. In: ICML 1998, pp. 296–304 (1998)
14. Ide, N., Véronis, J.: Word sense disambiguation: The state of the art. Computational Linguistics 24, 1–40 (1998)
15. Wang, X.: OWSD: A tool for word sense disambiguation in its ontology context. In: International Semantic Web Conference (Posters & Demos) (2008)
16. Cormen, T.H., Leiserson, C.E., Rivest, R.L.: Introduction to Algorithms. MIT Press, Cambridge (1990)

On the Importance of Truly Ontological Distinctions for Ontology Representation Languages: An Industrial Case Study in the Domain of Oil and Gas

Giancarlo Guizzardi[1], Mauro Lopes[2,3], Fernanda Baião[2,3], and Ricardo Falbo[1]

[1] Ontology and Conceptual Modeling Research Group (NEMO), Computer Science Department, Federal University of Espírito Santo, Espírito Santo, Brazil
[2] NP2Tec – Research and Practice Group in Information Technology, Federal University of the State of Rio de Janeiro (UNIRIO), Rio de Janeiro, Brazil
[3] Department of Applied Informatics, Federal University of the State of Rio de Janeiro (UNIRIO), Rio de Janeiro, Brazil
{gguizzardi, falbo}@inf.ufes.br,
{fernanda.baiao, mauro.lopes}@uniriotec.br

Abstract. Ontologies are commonly used in computer science either as a reference model to support semantic interoperability, or as an artifact that should be efficiently represented to support tractable automated reasoning. This duality poses a tradeoff between expressivity and computational tractability that should be addressed in different phases of an ontology engineering process. The inadequate choice of a modeling language, disregarding the goal of each ontology engineering phase, can lead to serious problems in the deployment of the resulting model. This article discusses these issues by making use of an industrial case study in the domain of Oil and Gas. We make explicit the differences between two different representations in this domain, and highlight a number of concepts and ideas that were implicit in an original OWL-DL model and that became explicit by applying the methodological directives underlying an ontologically well-founded modeling language.

Keywords: Ontology, Ontology Languages, Conceptual modelling, Oil and Gas domain.

1 Introduction

Since the word ontology was mentioned in a computer related discipline for the first time [1], ontologies have been applied in a multitude of areas in computer science. The first noticeable growth of interest in the subject in mid 1990's was motivated by the need to create principled representations of domain knowledge in the knowledge sharing and reuse community in Artificial Intelligence (AI). Nonetheless, an explosion of works related to the subject only happened in the past eight years, highly motivated by the growing interest on the Semantic Web, and by the key role played by ontologies in that initiative.

T. Halpin et al. (Eds.): BPMDS 2009 and EMMSAD 2009, LNBIP 29, pp. 224–236, 2009.

There are two common trends in the traditional use of the term ontology in computer science: (i) firstly, ontologies are typically regarded as an explicit representation of a shared conceptualization, i.e., a concrete artifact representing a model of consensus within a community and a universe of discourse. Moreover, in this sense of a reference model, an ontology is primarily aimed at supporting semantic interoperability in its various forms (e.g, model integration, service interoperability, knowledge harmonization, and taxonomy alignment); (ii) secondly, the discussion regarding representation mechanisms for the construction of domain ontologies is, typically, centered on computational issues, not truly ontological ones.

An important aspect to be highlighted is the incongruence between these two trends. In order for an ontology to be able to adequately serve as a reference model, it should be constructed using an approach that explicitly takes foundational concepts into account; this is, however, typically neglected for the sake of computational complexity.

The use of foundational concepts that take truly ontological issues seriously is becoming more and more accepted in the ontological engineering literature, i.e., in order to represent a complex domain, one should rely on engineering tools (e.g., design patterns), modeling languages and methodologies that are based on well-founded ontological theories in the philosophical sense (e.g., [2]; [3]). Especially in a domain with complex concepts, relations and constraints, and with potentially serious risks which could be caused by interoperability problems, a supporting ontology engineering approach should be able to: (a) allow the conceptual modelers and domain experts to be explicit regarding their ontological commitments, which in turn enables them to expose subtle distinctions between models to be integrated and to minimize the chances of running into a *False Agreement Problem* [4]; (b) support the user in justifying their modeling choices and providing a sound design rationale for choosing how the elements in the universe of discourse should be modeled in terms of language elements.

This marks a contrast to practically all languages used in the tradition of knowledge representation and conceptual information modeling, in general, and in the semantic web, in particular (e.g., RDF, OWL, F-Logic, UML, EER). Although these languages provide the modeler with mechanisms for building conceptual structures (e.g., taxonomies or partonomies), they offer no support neither for helping the modeler on choosing a particular structure to model elements of the subject domain nor for justifying the choice of a particular structure over another. Finally, once a particular structure is represented, the ontological commitments which are made remain, in the best case, tacit in the modelers' mind. In the worst case, even the modelers and domain experts remain oblivious to these commitments.

An example of an ontologically well-founded modeling language is the version of UML 2.0 proposed in [5] and, thereafter, dubbed *OntoUML*. This language has its real-world semantics defined in terms of a number of ontological theories, such as theory of parts, of wholes, types and instantiation, identity, dependencies, unity, etc. However, in order to be as explicit as possible regarding all the underlying subtleties of these theories (e.g., modal issues, different modes of predication, higher-order predication), this language strives for having its formal semantics defined in a logical system as expressively as possible. Now, as well understood in the field of knowledge representation, there is a clear tradeoff between logical expressivity and computational efficiency [6]. In particular, any language which attempts at maximizing the explicit characterization of the aforementioned ontological issues risks sacrificing reasoning efficiency and computational tractability. In contrast, common knowledge representation and deductive database languages (e.g., some instances of Description Logics) have been specifically designed to afford efficient automated reasoning and decidability.

In summary, ontology engineering must face the following situation: on one side, we need ontologically well-founded languages supported by expressive logical theories in order to produce sound and clear representations of complex domains; on the other side, we need lightweight ontology languages supported by efficient computational algorithms. How to reconcile these two sets of contradicting requirements? As advocated by [7], actually two classes of languages are required to fulfill these two sets of requirements. Moreover, as any other engineering process, an ontology engineering process lifecycle should comprise phases of conceptual modeling, design, and implementation. In the first phase, a reference ontology is produced aiming at representing the subject domain with truthfulness, clarity and expressivity, regardless of computational requirements. The main goal of these reference models is to help modelers to externalize their tacit knowledge about the domain, to make their ontological commitments explicit in order to support meaning negotiation, and to afford as best as possible the tasks of domain communication, learning and problem solving. The same reference ontology can then give rise to different lightweight ontologies in different languages (e.g., F-Logic, OWL-DL, RDF, Alloy, and KIF) and satisfying different sets of non-functional requirements. Defining the most suitable language for codifying a reference ontology is then a choice to be made at the design phase, by taking both the end-application purpose and the tradeoff between expressivity and computational tractability into account.

In this article, we illustrate the issues at stake in the aforementioned tradeoff by discussing an industrial case study in the domain of Oil and Gas Exploration and Production. However, since we were dealing with a pre-existing OWL-DL codified ontology, we had to reverse the direction of model development. Instead of producing a reference model in OntoUML which would then give rise to an OWL-DL codification, we had to start with the OWL-DL domain ontology and apply a reverse engineering process to it in an attempt to reconstruct the proper underlying reference model in OntoUML. By doing that, we manage to show how much of important domain knowledge had either been lost in the OWL-DL codification or remained tacit in the minds of the domain experts.

The remainder of this article is organized as follows. Section 2 briefly characterizes the domain and industrial setting in which the case study reported in this article took place, namely, the domain of oil and gas exploration and production and in the context of a large Petroleum Organization. Section 3 discusses the reengineering of the original lightweight ontology produced in the settings described in section 2. This reengineering step was conducted by transforming the original ontology to well-founded version represented in OntoUML. Section 4 discusses some final considerations.

2   Characterization of the Case Study Domain and Settings

The oil and gas industry is a potentially rich domain for application of ontologies, since it comprises a large and complex set of inter-related concepts. Ontology-based approaches for data integration and exchange involves the use of ontologies of rich and extensive domains combined with industry patterns and controlled vocabularies, reflecting relevant concepts within this domain [8]. According to this author, the motivating factors for the use of ontologies in the oil and gas industry include:

- The great data quantity generated each day, coming from diverse sources, involving different disciplines. Integrating different disciplines to take advantage of the real value of your information has been a complex and costly task.
- The existence of data in different formats, including structured in databases and semi-structured in documents. To deal with the great quantity of information, as well as heterogeneous formats, a new approach is needed to handle information search and access.
- The necessity of standardization and integration of information along the frontiers of systems, disciplines and organizations, to support the decision-making with the collaborators, to the extent that better quality data will be accessible on the opportune time.

The case study reported in this paper was conducted in a large Petroleum Corporation, by analyzing and redesigning a pre-existing ontology in the domain of Oil and Gas Exploration and Production, henceforth named *E&P-Reservoir Ontology*. Due to the extensiveness and complexity of this domain, only few sub domains were taken into consideration on the initial version of this ontology, namely, the *"Reserve Assessment"* sub domain, and the *"Mechanical pump"* sub domain. The knowledge acquisition process used to create the original *E&P-Reservoir Ontology* ontology was conducted via the representations of business process models following the approach proposed in [9] and extended in [10]. The original E&P-Reserve ontology was codified in OWL-DL comprising 178 classes, which together contained 55 data type properties (OWL datatypeProperties) and 96 object properties (OWL objectProperties).

In a nutshell, a *Reservoir* is composed of *Production Zones* and organized in *Fields* – geographical regions managed by a Business Unit and containing a number of *Wells*. *Reservoirs* are filled with *Reservoir Rock* – a substance composed of quantities of Oil, Gas and Water. *Production* of Oil and Gas from a Reservoir can occur via different lifting methods (e.g., natural lifting, casing's diameter, sand production, among others) involving different Wells. One of these artificial lifting methods is the *Mechanical Pump*. The simultaneous production of oil, gas and water occurs in conjunction with the production impurities. To remove these impurities, facilities are adopted on the fields (both off-shore and on-shore), including the transfer of hydrocarbons via *Ducts* to refineries for proper processing. The notion of *Reserve Assessment* refers to the process of estimating, for each Exploration Project and Reservoir, the profitably recoverable quantity of hydrocarbons (Oil and Gas) for that given reservoir. The *Mechanical Pump* subdomain ontology, in contrast, defines a number of concepts regarding the methods of Fluid lifting, transportation, and other activities that take place in a reservoir during the Production process.

For a more extensive definition of the concepts in this domain, one should refer to, for instance, [11] or *The Energy Standard Resource Center* (www.energistics.org).

3   Reverse Engineering an OntoUML Version of the E&P-Reserve Ontology

In this section, we discuss some of the results of producing an OntoUML version of the original E&P-Reserve Ontology in this domain. In particular we focus at illustrating a number of important concepts in this domain which were absent in the original OWL model and remained tacit in the domain experts' minds, but which became manifest by the application of methodological directives underlying OntoUML. It is important to emphasize that this section does not aim at serving as an introduction to OntoUML neither as a complete report on the newly produced version of the E&P-Reserve Ontology.

3.1   Making the Real-World Semantics of Relationships Explicit

Figure 1 depicts a fragment of the OWL ontology and figure 2 depicts the correspondent fragment transformed to OntoUML.

The OntoUML language, with its underlying methodological directives, makes an explicit distinction between the so-called *material* and *formal relationships*. A formal relationship can be reduced to relationships between intrinsic properties of its relata. For example, a relationship *more-dense-than* between two fluids can be reduced to the relationship between the individual densities of the involved fluids (*more-dense-than(x,y) iff the density of x is higher than of y's*). In contrast, material relationships cannot be reduced to relationships between individual properties of involved relata in this way. In order to have a material relationship established between two concepts C1 and C2, another entity must exist that makes this relationship true. For example, we can say that the Person John works for Company A (and not for company B) if an employment contract exists between John and Company A which makes this relationship true. This entity, which is the truthmaker of material relationships, is termed *relator* in OntoUML and the language determines that (for the case of material relationships) these *relators* must be explicitly represented on the models [12].

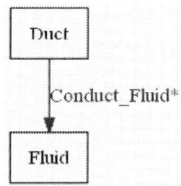

Fig. 1. Representation of *Fluid transportation* (OWL)

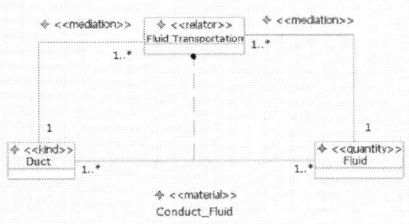

Fig. 2. Alternative Representation of Fluid transportation (OntoUML), an interpretation of Fluid transportation with unique Duct and Fluid

The *Conduct_Fluid* relationship of figure 1 is an example of a material relationship. Therefore, this relationship only takes place (i.e., the *Conduct_Fluid* relationship is only established) between a specific duct x and a specific portion of fluid y, when there is at least a fluid transportation event that involves the participation of x and y.

Besides making explicit the truthmakers of these relations, one of the major advantages of the explicit representation of *relators* is to solve an inherent ambiguity of cardinality constraints that exists in material relationships. Take for example the cardinality constraints of one-to-many represented for the relationship *Conduct_Fluid* in figure 1. There are several possible interpretations for this model which are compatible with these cardinality constraints but which are mutually incompatible among themselves. Two of these interpretations are depicted in figures 2 and 3.

On the model of figure 2, given a fluid transportation event, we have only one duct and only one portion of fluid involved; both fluid and duct can participate in several transportation events. In contrast, on the model of figure 3, given a fluid transportation event, we have possibly several ducts and portions of fluid involved; a duct can be used in several transportation events, but only one fluid can take part on a fluid transportation.

When comparing these two models in OntoUML we can see that the original OWL model collapses these two interpretations (among others) in the same representation, which have substantially different real-world semantics. This semantic overload can be a source of many interoperability problems between applications. In particular, applications that use different models and that attach distinct semantics to relationships such as discussed above can wrongly assume that they agree on the same semantics (an example of the previously mentioned *False Agreement Problem*).

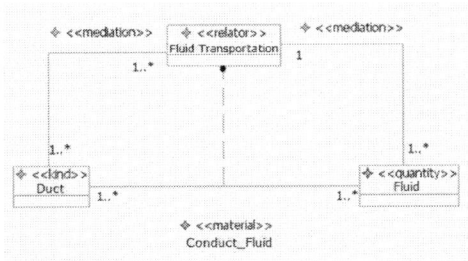

Fig. 3. Interpreting Fluid transportation with multiples Ducts and Fluids

Finally, in the OntoUML models in this section, the dotted line with a filled circle on one of its endings represents the *derivation* relationship between a *relator type* and the *material relationship* derived from it [5]. For example, the derivation relationship *Fluid Transportation* (*relator type*) and *Conduct_Fluid* (*material relationship*) represents that for all x, y we have that: <x,y> is an instance of *Conduct_Fluid* iff there is an instance z of *Fluid Transportation* that mediates x and y. As discussed in depth in [5,12], mediation is a specific type of existential dependence relation (e.g., a particular Fluid Transportation can only exist if that particular Duct and that particular Fluid exist). Moreover, it also demonstrated that the cardinality constraints of a material relationship R derived from a relator type U_R can be automatically derived from the corresponding *mediaton* relationships between U_R and the types related by R. In summary, a relator is an entity which is existentially dependent on a number of other individuals, and via these dependency relationships it connects (mediates) these individuals. Given that a number of individuals are mediated by a relator, a material relationship can be defined between them. As this definition makes clear, relators are ontologically prior to material relationships which are mere logical/linguistic constructions derived from them [5,12]. To put it in a different way, knowing that x and y are related via R tells you very little unless you know what are the conditions (state of affairs) that makes this relationship between this particular tuple true.

3.2 The Ontological Status of Quantities

Figures 4 and 5 represent fragments of the domain ontology that deal with the notion of Fluid.

In general, quantities or amounts of matter (e.g., water, milk, sugar, sand, oil) are entities that are homeomerous, i.e., all of their parts are the same type as the whole. Alternatively, we can say that they are infinitely divisible in subparts of the same type. Homeomerousity and Infinite divisibility causes problems both to determine the referent of expressions referring to quantities and, as a consequence, also problems to specify finite cardinality constraints of relationships involving quantity types [5]. In OntoUML, these problems are avoided by defining a modelling primitive <<quantity>> whose semantics are defined by invoking the ontological notion of *Quantity*. In OntoUML, a type stereotyped as <<quantity>> represents a type whose instances represent portions of amounts of matter which are maximal under the relation of topological self-connectness [5].

In figure 5, the type Fluid is represented as a *quantity* in this ontological sense. As a consequence we have that Fluid: (i) is a rigid type, i.e., all instances of this type are necessarily instances of this type (in a modal sense); (ii) provides an identity principle obeyed by all its instances; (iii) represent a collection of essential properties of all its instances [5,13]. Specializations of a *quantity* are represented with the stereotype *subkind*. In figure 5, these include the specific types of Fluid:Water, Oil and Gas. Subkinds of Fluid have meta-properties (i) and (iii) above by inheriting the principle of identity defined by the quantity kind Fluid that should be obeyed by all its subtypes.

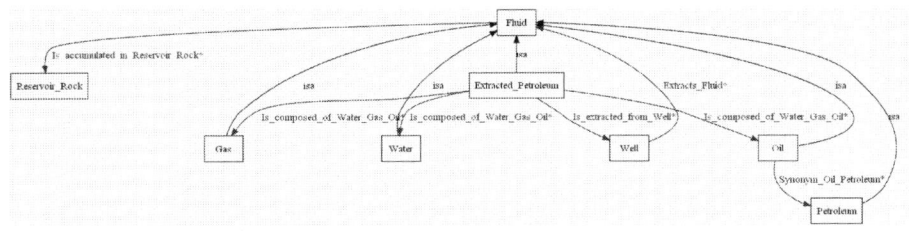

Fig. 4. The representation of *Fluid* and related notions in OWL

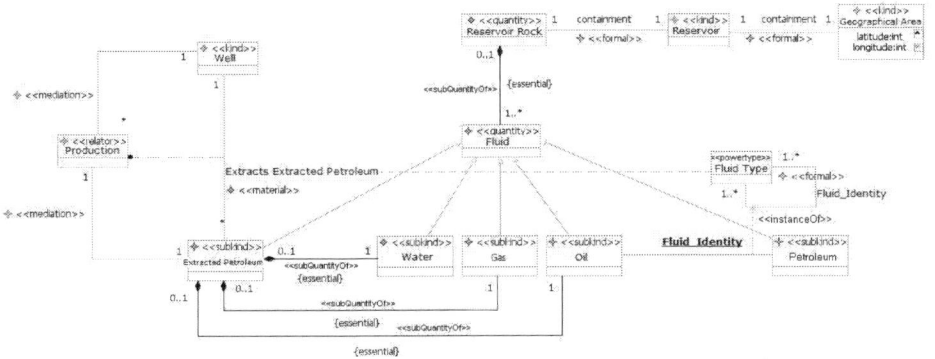

Fig. 5. The Representation of *Fluid* and related notions in OntoUML

On the original ontology in OWL, the equivalence between the Oil and Petroleum concepts is represented by the *Oil_Petroleum_synonym* relationship defined between these concepts. This relationship is declared as being symmetric. On the original ontology, these concepts simply represent the general concepts of Oil or Petroleum and do not represent genuine types that can be instantiated. As consequence in this case, the *Oil_Petroleum_synonym* relationship represents also a relational type that cannot be instantiated and only exists in fact between this pair of concepts. Therefore, it does not make sense to characterize it as a symmetric relationship, since it functions as an instance and not genuinely as a type.

In the semantics adopted on the revised model, Oil and Petroleum are *quantity* types, the instances of which are specific portions of these Fluids. Therefore, in this case, there is no sense in defining an *Is_synonym_of* relationship between Oil and Petroleum. After all, defined this way, since these are genuine types that can be instantiated, this relationship would have as instances ordered pairs formed by specific portions of Oil and Petroleum, which definitely does not correspond to the intended semantics of this relationship. In fact, the relationship *Is_synonym_of* is a relationship between the Oil and Petroleum types and not between its instances. In particular, this relationship has a stronger semantics than simply symmetry, being an equivalence relationship (reflexive, symmetric, transitive).

The problem of the proper representation of an *Is_synonym_of* relationship that could be established between any two types of fluid is solved on the model of figure 5. Firstly, the model makes an explicit distinction between the fluid types instances of which are individual portions of fluid and a type instances of which are the concepts of Oil, Water, Gas and Petroleum themselves. Since OntoUML is an extension of standard UML, this can be represented by the use of notion of *power-type[1]*. In a nutshell, a *powertype* is a type instances of which are other types. On this specific model, the relationship between the *Fluid Type powertype* and *Fluid* defines that the subtypes of the latter (Oil, Water, Gas and Petroleum) are instances of the former. Once this distinction is made, the formal relationship of *Fluid_identity[2]* can be defined among the instances of *Fluid Type*. This relationship can, then, be defined as an equivalence relationship which semantics is characterized by the following rule: two fluid types are identical iff they possess necessarily (i.e., at any given circumstance) the same instances. In the OntoUML language, this rule is defined outside the visual syntax of the language and as part of the axiomatization of the resulting model (ontology).

Finally, as a result of this modeling choice, particular instances of the *Fluid_identity* relationship can be defined. For example, in figure 5, the *link* (instance of a relationship) between Oil and Petroleum (instances of *Fluid Type*) is defined explicitly as an instance of *Fluid_Identity*.

In the revised model of figure 5, in the same manner as Fluid and its subtypes, *Reservoir Rock* is explicitly represented as a *quantity* type. Once more, this type represents a genuine type instances of which are particular portions of *Reservoir Rock*. The *Is_accumulated_in_Reservoir_Rock* relationship in the original model of figure 4 is, hence, replaced by a special type of part-whole relationship (*subQuantityOf*) between Reservoir Rock and Fluid. The SubQuantityOf relationship defined as a primitive in OntoUML contains a formal characterization that implies: (i) a partial order (irreflexivity, asymmetry, transitivity) relation; (ii) An existential dependency relation, i.e., in this particular example a particular portion of Reservoir Rock is defined by the aggregation of the specific particular portions of its constituent Fluids; and (iii) Non-sharing of parts, i.e., each particular portion of fluid is part of at most one portion of Reservoir Rock. It is important to emphasize that the explicit representation of the semantics of this relationship eliminates an implicit ambiguity on the original model.

3.3 The *Containment* Relation to Represent the Spatial Inclusion among Physical Entities: Reservoir, Reservoir Rock and Geographic Area

The model on figure 5 also depicts the Reservoir and Geographic Area concepts and defines the formal relationship of *containment* [14] between Reservoir and Reservoir Rock and between Reservoir and Geographic Area. This relationship contains the semantic of spatial inclusion between two physical entities (with the spatial extension) that is also defined on the ontology's axiomatization, e.g., outside the visual syntax of the model.

On the original model of figure 4, there is only one relationship *Is_composed_of_Water_Gas_Oil* defined between the Extracted Petroleum and the Water, Gas and Oil concepts. On the revised ontology, this relationship is replaced by

---

[1] http://www.omg.org/spec/UML/2.1.2/

[2] The preference for the term *Fluid_identity* instead of *Is_synonym_of* is motivated by the fact that the former refers to an identity relation among types while the latter refers merely to an identity relation among terms.

composition relationships (*subQuantityOf*). As previously discussed, the richer semantics of this relationship type makes important meta-properties of the relationship among these elements explicit in the model. As discussed in [5, 15, 16], the formal characteristics of this relationship, modeled as a partially order, existential dependency relation with non-sharing of parts, have important consequences both to the design and implementation of an information system as to the automated processes of reasoning and model evaluation.

3.4 Making the *Production* Relator Explicit

As already discussed, OntoUML makes an explicit distinction between formal and material relationships. The *Extracts_Fluid* relationship between *Fluid* and *Well* in the original model is an example of the latter. In this way, following the methodological directives of the language, the modeling process seeks to make explicit which is the appropriate relator that would substantiate that relationship. The conclusion would one come to is that the relationship *Extracts_Fluid(x,y)* is true iff there is a *Production* event involving the Well x from where the Fluid y is produced. The semantic investigation of this relationship makes explicit that the resulting fluid of this event in fact only exists after the occurrence of this event. In other words, the portion of the Extracted Petroleum only exists after it is produced from the event of production involving a well. Therefore, a mixture of water, gas and oil is considered *Extracted Petroleum* only when it is produced by an event of this kind. The *Extract_Fluid* relationship between Well and Fluid and the *Is_extracted_from_Well* relationship between Extracted Petroleum and Well on the original ontology are replaced by the material relationship *Extracts_Extracted_Petroleum* between Well and Extracted Petroleum and by the *subQuantityOf* relationships between the Extracted Petroleum portion and its sub portions of Water, Gas and Oil. This representation has the additional benefit of making clear that an event of Production has the goal of generating an Extracted Petroleum portion that is composed of particular portions of these Fluid types and not by directly extracting portions of these other types of fluid. Finally, as previously discussed, the explicit representation of the *Production* relator makes the representation of the cardinality constraints involving instances of Well and Extracted Petroleum precise, eliminating the ambiguity on the representation of the *Extract_Fluid* relationship on the original model.

3.5 Representing the Historical Dependence between *Extracted Petroleum* and *Reservoir Rock*

As previously discussed, the *subquantityOf* relation defined in OntoUML to hold between portions of quantities is a type of existential dependency relation from the whole to the part. In other words, all parts of a quantity are essential parts of it. For instance, in figure 6, we have the type Reservoir Rock stereotyped as <<quantity>>. As a consequence, once we have the case that specific portions of water, gas and oil are extracted from a specific portion of Reservoir Rock x (creating a portion of Extracted Petroleum y) that specific portion x ceases to exists. Indeed, the resulting portion of Extracted Petroleum y and the Reservoir Rock x from which y originates cannot co-exist at the same circumstances. In fact, the same event that creates the

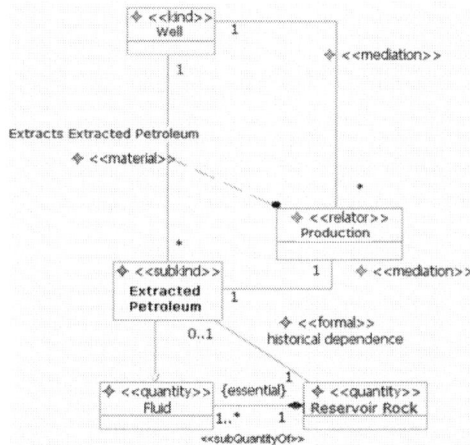

Fig. 6. Extracted Petroleum and its historical dependence to a Reservoir Rock

former is the one that destroys the latter. However, it is important to represent the specific connection between x and y, for instance, because some characteristics from an Extracted Petroleum could result from characteristics of that Reservoir Rock. Here, this relation between x and y is modeled by the formal relation of *historical dependence* [17]: in this case, since y is historically dependent on x it means that y could not exist without x having existed.

4 Final Considerations

An ontology engineering process is composed of phases, among them are conceptual modeling and implementation. During the whole process, the ontology being built must be made explicit by a representation language. The diverse ontology representation languages available in the literature contain different expressivity and different ontological commitments, reflecting on the specific set of available constructs in each one of them. Therefore, different ontology representation languages, with different characteristics, are suitable to be used in different phases of the ontology engineering process so as to address the different set of requirements which characterize each phase. In particular, conceptual ontology modeling languages aim primarily at improving understanding, learning, communication and problem solving among people in a particular domain. Therefore, these languages have being designed to maximize expressivity, clarity and truthfulness to the domain being represented. In contrast, ontology codification languages are focused on aspects such as computational efficiency and tractability and can be used to produce computationally amenable versions of an ontologically-well founded reference conceptual model. The inadequate use of a representation language, disregarding the goal of each ontology engineering phase, can lead to serious problems to database design and integration, to domain and systems requirements analysis within the software development processes, to knowledge representation and automated reasoning, and so on.

This article presents an illustration of these issues by using an industrial case study in the domain of Oil and Gas Exploration and Production. The case study consists in the generation of a Conceptual Ontological Model for this domain from an existing domain ontology in the organization where the case study took place.

The ontology representation language used to produce the redesigned model was OntoUML, a theoretically sound and highly expressive language based on a number of Formal Ontological Theories. The choice of this language highlights a number of explicit concepts and ideas (tacit domain knowledge) that were implicit in the original model coded in OWL-DL. To cite just one example, in the original representation of *Conduct_Fluid* relationship, it is possible to define that a duct can conduct several fluids and a fluid can be conducted by several different ducts. However, the lack of the Fluid Transportation concept (a relator uncovered by the methodological directives of OntoUML) hides important information about the domain. For instance, it is not explicit in this case how many different fluids can be transported at the same time or even if a duct can have more than a fluid transportation at a time. By making these concepts explicit as well as defining a precise real-world semantics for the notions represented, the newly E&P-Reserve ontology produced in OntoUML prevents a number of ambiguity and interoperability problems which would likely be carried out to subsequent activities (e.g., database design) based on this model.

In [18], an extension of OntoUML (OntoUML-R) is presented. This version of the language allows for the visual representation of domain axioms (rules), including integrity and derivation axioms in OntoUML. As future work, we intend to exploit this new language facility to enhance the transformed E&P-Reserve Ontology with visual representations of domain axioms. This enhanced model can then be mapped to a new version of the OWL-DL codified lightweight ontology, now using a combination of OWL-DL and SWRL rules. This enhanced lightweight model, in turn, shall contemplate the domain concepts uncovered by the process described in this article and, due to the combination of OWL-DL and SWRL, afford a number of more sophisticated reasoning tasks.

References

1. Mealy, G.H.: Another Look at Data. In: Proceedings of the Fall Joint Computer Conference, Anaheim, California, November 14–16. AFIPS Conference Proceedings, vol. 31, pp. 525–534. Thompson Books, Academic Press, Washington, London (1967)
2. Burek, P., et al.: A top-level ontology of functions and its application in the Open Biomedical Ontologies. Bioinformatics 22(14), e66–e73 (2006)
3. Fielding, J., et al.: Ontological Theory for Ontology Engineering. In: International Conf. on the Principles of Knowledge Representation and Reasoning (KR 2004), 9th, Whistler, Canada, Proceedings (2004)
4. Guarino, N.: Formal Ontology and Information Systems. In: 1st International Conference on Formal Ontologies in Information Systems, Trento, Italy, June 1998, pp. 3–15 (1998)
5. Guizzardi, G.: Ontological Foundations for Structural Conceptual Models, Telematica Instituut Fundamental Research Series No. 15. Universal Press, The Netherlands (2005)
6. Levesque, H., Brachman, R.: Expressiveness and Tractability in Knowledge Representation and Reasoning. Computational Intelligence 3(1), 78–93 (1987)

7. Guizzardi, G., Halpin, T.: Ontological Foundations for Conceptual Modeling. Applied Ontology 3(1-2), 91–110 (2008)
8. Chum, F.: Use Case: Ontology-Driven Information Integration and Delivery - A Survey of Semantic Web Technology in the Oil and Gas Industry, W3C (April 2007), http://www.w3.org/2001/sw/sweo/public/UseCases/Chevron/ (accessed in Decemeber 2007)
9. Cappelli, C., Baião, F., Santoro, F., Iendrike, H., Lopes, M., Nunes, V.T.: An Approach for Constructing Domain Ontologies from Business Process Models. In: II Workshop on Ontologies and Metamodeling in Software and Data Engineering (WOMSDE) (2007) (in Portuguese)
10. Baião, F., Santoro, F., Iendrike, H., Cappelli, C., Lopes, M., Nunes, V.T., Dumont, A.P.: Towards a Data Integration Approach based on Business Process Models and Domain Ontologies. In: 10th International Conference on Enterprise Information Systems (ICEIS 2008), Barcelona, pp. 338–342 (2008)
11. Thomas, J.E.: Fundamentals of Petroleum Engineering. Rio de Janeiro, Interciência (2001) (in Portuguese)
12. Guizzardi, G., Wagner, G.: What's in a Relationship: An Ontological Analysis. In: Li, Q., Spaccapietra, S., Yu, E., Olivé, A. (eds.) ER 2008. LNCS, vol. 5231. Springer, Heidelberg (2008)
13. Guizzardi, G., Wagner, G., Guarino, N., van Sinderen, M.: An Ontologically Well-Founded Profile for UML Conceptual Models. In: Persson, A., Stirna, J. (eds.) CAiSE 2004. LNCS, vol. 3084, pp. 112–126. Springer, Heidelberg (2004)
14. Smith, B., et al.: Relations in biomedical ontologies. Genome Biology 6(5) (2005)
15. Artale, A., Keet, M.: Essential and Mandatory Part-Whole Relations in Conceptual Data Models. In: 21st International Workshop on Description Logics, Dresden (2008)
16. Keet, M., Artale, A.: Representing and Reasoning over a Taxonomy of Part-Whole Relations. In: Guizzardi, G., Halpin, T. (eds.) Special Issue on Ontological Foundations for Conceptual Modeling, Applied Ontology, vol. 3(1-2), pp. 91–110 (2008) ISSN 1570-5838
17. Thomasson, A.L.: Fiction and Metaphysics. Cambridge University Press, Cambridge (1999)
18. das Graças, A.: Extending a Model-Based Tool for Ontologically Well-Founded Conceptual Modeling with Rule Visualization Support. In: Computer Engineering Monograph, Ontology and Conceptual Modeling Research Group (NEMO), Federal University of Espirito Santo, Brazil (2008)

UML Models Engineering from Static and Dynamic Aspects of Formal Specifications

Akram Idani

Laboratoire d'Informatique de Grenoble
681 Rue de la Passerelle − BP72
F-38402 Saint Martin d'Hères cedex
Akram.Idani@imag.fr

Abstract. While formal methods are focused on some particular parts of software systems, especially secure ones, graphical techniques are the most useful techniques to specify in a comprehensible way large and complex systems. In this paper we deal with the B method which is a formal method used to model systems and prove their correctness by successive refinements. Our goal is to produce graphical UML views from existing formal B specifications in order to ease their readability and then help their external validation. In fact, such views can be useful for various stakeholders in a formal development process: they are intended to support the understanding of the formal specifications by the requirements holders and the certification authorities; they can also be used by the B developers to get an alternate view on their work. In this paper, we propose an MDE framework to support the derivation of UML class and state/transition diagrams from B specifications. Our transformation process is based on a reverse-engineering technique guided by a set of structural and semantic mappings specified on a meta-level.

1 Introduction

The complex requirements of software systems justify the use of the best existing techniques to guarantee the quality of specifications and to preserve this quality during the programming phase of a software life-cycle. Formal methods, such as B, make it possible to reach such a level of quality. Their main characteristics are: (i) they allow to precisely check the correctness of a program against its specification; and (ii) they need a great knowledge of logic.

The first point, which represents the major advantage of these methods, raises from the fact that mathematic models allow to rigorously reason about the coherence of a software system. The second point, which is the primary "brake" to a wide adoption of formal methods, is strongly related to formal languages notations which are often complex. These two characteristics motivated industrial communities to use formal methods uniquely for safety-critical systems. One of the solutions developed by several research teams [5,7,8] is to specify the whole system using a semi-formal language (*e.g.* UML) and then translate the semi-formal model into a formal one. The resulting formal specifications can then be

T. Halpin et al. (Eds.): BPMDS 2009 and EMMSAD 2009, LNBIP 29, pp. 237–250, 2009.

used in order to achieve a rigorous reasoning of the same system. However, these techniques present the following limitations:

- The derived formal specifications are complex and far from what the B developer could have written directly in a formal language. In fact, the systematic translation must take into account semi-formal notions.
- A great effort of comprehension is necessary in order to be able to refine the formal specifications, to correct them and carry out proofs. In case of inconsistency, changing the formal model doesn't induce changes in the semi-formal model.

Our work is intended to contribute to a better comprehension of B specifications[1] in a formal development process by bridging the gap between B and UML. In our approach, UML is not a starting point but a result which aims at documenting the B specifications with graphical notations more intuitive and readable. In order to render formal notations more accessible we proposed theoretical and effective tools [2,4,3] which produce a standardized graphical documentation – in form of UML diagrams – from B specifications. The concerned diagrams are mainly class and state/transition diagrams, which are useful to visualize static as well as dynamic aspects of a B specification. Still, the major drawback which needs inevitably to be considered is that our B-to-UML translation rules are not formally defined. Indeed, as it is difficult to know on what semantic basis the transformation has taken place, then there may be a conceptual gap between the resulting class and state/transition diagrams.

This paper improves our previous works by defining explicitly mappings between B and UML in a reusable MDA-based framework. Such a conceptual base allows to circumvent the shortcomings of our tools and presents an efficient technique to build conjointly coherent static and behavioural views from B models. Indeed, a fundamental idea of Model Driven Engineering is that transformations between heterogeneous models can be described uniformly in terms of meta-model mappings. Based on the fact that meta-models define an abstract syntax from which one can describe model semantics, transformation rules that arise from MDA-based techniques are explicit and precise. This MDA-based framework allowed us to clearly identify translation patterns from B to UML and to automatically produce abstract state predicates.

We also point up in this paper how our approach improves automation of UML diagrams construction.

2   A Simple Example

In order to illustrate our approach we present in Fig. 1 the *AccessControl* specification (inspired by [1]) which deals with access control of peoples to buildings. In this specification the abstract sets *PERSON*, *PASS* and *BUILDING* specify

---

[1] In this paper we consider the classical B approach. Further research are needed in order to cover the B event.

> **MACHINE**
> *AccessControl*
> **SETS**
> *PERSON*; *PASS*; *BUILDING*;
> *STATE* = {*closed*, *open*}
> **VARIABLES**
> *building_state,belong_to,*
> *usable_for,used_for,*
> *VALID*
> **INVARIANT**
> *building_state* ∈ *BUILDING* → *STATE* ∧
> *belong_to* ∈ *PASS* ⤔ *PERSON* ∧
> *usable_for* ∈ *PASS* ↔ *BUILDING* ∧
> *VALID_PASS* ⊆ *PASS* ∧
> *used_for* ∈ *VALID_PASS* ⤔ *BUILDING* ∧
> *used_for* ⊆ *usable_for* ∧
> *building_state*[**ran**(*used_for*)] ≠ {*closed*} ∧
> *VALID_PASS* ⊆ **dom**(*belong_to*) ∧
> *VALID_PASS* ⊆ **dom**(*usable_for*)

Fig. 1. The *AccessControl* machine

respectively persons, access cards and buildings of the studied system. In order to describe states *closed* and *open* of buildings we define the total function *building_state* which associates to each element of set *BUILDING* one of the enumerated elements of set *STATE*. Each pass belongs to at the most one person (variable *belong_to*). Relation *usable_for* lists the buildings for them a pass can be used to go in. In order to be used, a pass must be validated (variable *VALID_PASS*). The partial function *used_for* specifies the set of valid access cards actually used to accede buildings. Buildings couldn't be closed if they are not empty (invariant *building_state*[**ran**(*used_for*)] ≠ {*closed*}). Finally, before be validated a pass must be assigned to a person and must assure access to at least one building.

The dynamic part of the *AccessControl* machine corresponds to the following operations[2]:

- *open_building* and *close_building* which open and close buildings.
- *assign_pass* and *deassign_pass*.
- *validate*: allows the validation of a pass which belongs to a person and which is usable for at least one building. After be validated a pass can be used to enter a building (operation *enter_building*).
- *add_access* and *delete_access*: the first operation adds a building to the list of buildings for which a pass is usable, while the second one deletes all accesses allowed by a pass. In order to activate this last operation, the pass mustn't be actually used.

---

[2] For space reasons we don't give the complete syntax of *AccessControl* operations.

- *enter_building* and *leave_building*: allow to a person to enter or to leave a building. The first action is triggered only if: (*i*) the person is outside the building, (*ii*) the person's pass is valid, (*iii*) the person's pass is usable for the building, and (*iv*) the building is open.

3   Structural Links between B and UML

In order to establish links between the structural aspects of B specifications and UML diagrams, we propose a UML syntax for the B language using a meta-model. Then, we adopt a deep embedding approach in which we explicitly define mappings from the proposed B meta-model to the UML meta-model. The B constructs taken into account in this paper are mainly sets, relations between sets, elements of sets, invariants and operations.

Let $\mathcal{M}_B$ be our B meta-model and $\mathcal{M}_{\mathrm{UML}}$ the UML meta-model[3]. The proposed mappings between these two meta-models, provided by arrows in Fig. 2, are formally defined by the above relation $\mathcal{F}$:

$$\mathcal{F} \in \mathcal{M}_B \leftrightarrow \mathcal{M}_{\mathrm{UML}}$$

For example, the projection established between meta-classes *BSet* and *Class* is defined by: ($BSet \mapsto Class) \in \mathcal{F}$, and means that a B abstract set can be translated into a UML class.

The core concept of the given part of the B meta-model is meta-class *BData*. It specifies data used in operations body and declared in clauses: *SETS*, *VARIABLES* and *CONSTANTS*. B data addressed by our translation schemas are abstract sets and enumerated sets (meta-class *BSet*), functional relations (meta-class *BRelation*) and set elements (meta-class *BSetElem*). A *BSet* is translated into a class, a class attribute or an attribute type.

A *BRelation* can be translated into: a UML association which links classes and two *AssociationEnd*, a class attribute or an associative class. Finally, invariants are translated into constraints over model elements of the resulting UML class diagram. In this paper, we will not discuss translation patterns which produce OCL constraints from B invariants. However, we will look mainly at typing invariants from which we identify five translation patterns.

> **Definition 1.** *Consider abstraction function $\mathcal{A}_{\mathrm{B}}$ (respectively $\mathcal{A}_{\mathrm{UML}}$) which associates to each element issued from a B specification (respectively from a UML class diagram) a meta-concept in $\mathcal{M}_{\mathrm{B}}$ (respectively in $\mathcal{M}_{\mathrm{UML}}$) :*
>
> $$\mathcal{A}_{\mathrm{B}} \in \mathcal{B} \to \mathcal{M}_{\mathrm{B}}$$
> $$\mathcal{A}_{\mathrm{UML}} \in \mathcal{D} \to \mathcal{M}_{\mathrm{UML}}$$
>
> *Where $\mathcal{B}$ denotes the set of concepts of a B machine, and $\mathcal{D}$ the set of model elements of a UML class diagram.*

---

[3] Note that for clarity we present only some fragments of UML and B meta-models.

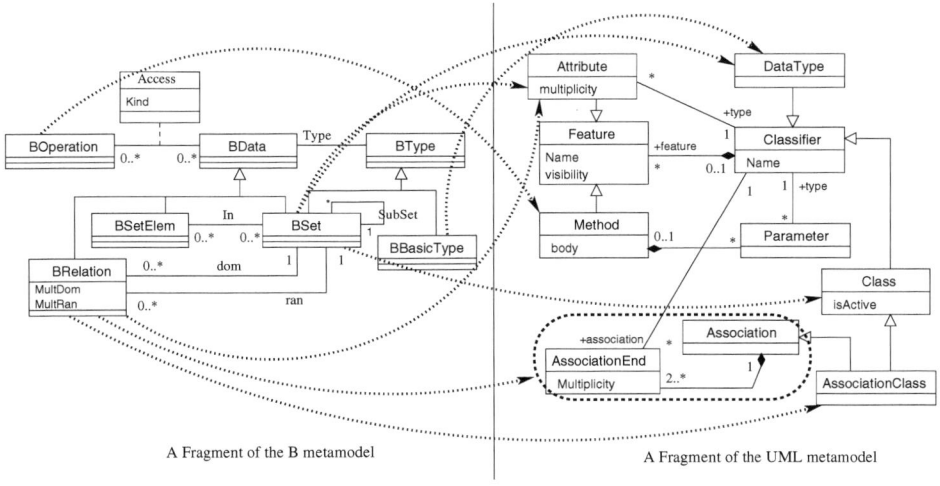

Fig. 2. Mappings between B and UML meta-models

We use the B and UML meta-models, and also relation $\mathcal{F}$ in order to build UML class diagrams from B specifications. Hence, translation of a B data a into a UML model element b must satisfy relation $\mathcal{F}$ between the two meta-concepts $\mathcal{A}_\mathrm{B}(a)$ and $\mathcal{A}_\mathrm{UML}(b)$ associated respectively to a and b.

> **Definition 2.** *Mappings between B and UML concepts are defined by relation Mapping as follows:*
> $$Mapping \in \mathcal{B} \leftrightarrow \mathcal{D} \; ; \; such \; that$$
> $$\forall(a, b) \cdot ((a, b) \in Mapping \Rightarrow (\mathcal{A}_\mathrm{B}(a), \mathcal{A}_\mathrm{UML}(b)) \in \mathcal{F})$$

3.1   B to UML Translation Patterns

Class diagrams generated by our tool (B/UML) [4] from B specifications are formally instances of relation *Mapping*. Providing explicit translation patterns based on this relation allows, on the one hand, automation of the derivation of UML state/transition diagrams (Sect. 4), and on the other hand, to ensure consistency between static and dynamic UML views issued from a same B specification.

Relation "SubSet". Relation "SubSet" in the B meta-model models set inclusion in B. It is translated either into an inheritance between classes or by a Boolean attribute (figure 3).

From a conceptual point of view, the first choice is justified by the fact that the inheritance mechanism in UML means a relationship *"is a"* or *"is a kind of"* between a subclass and a super-class, and allows to encapsulate information and additional operations in the subclass. This mechanism corresponds typically to the set inclusion in B. Indeed, consider sets S and S' such that $S' \subseteq S$, then

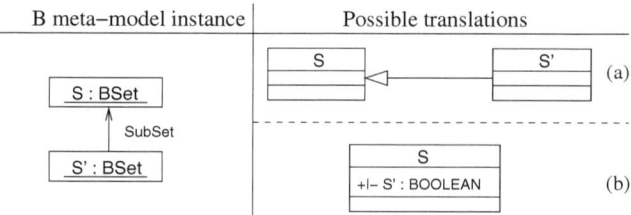

Fig. 3. Translation of relation "SubSet"

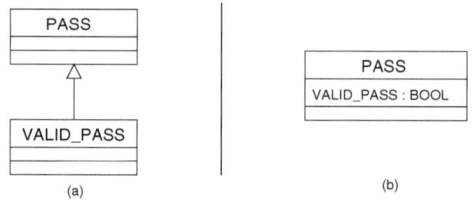

Fig. 4. Translations of $VALID\_PASS \subseteq Pass$

an element x in S' is also an element of S. Furthermore, the B subset indicates the existence of treatments and/or additional information specifically related to the subset. The second choice of translation is justified by the fact that a subset may be defined in the B specification in order to identify a subset of state space from which some operations may be activated. Thus, an element x in S can be seen as an instance of a class S in which the attribute S' is *true*.

For example, invariant VALID_PASS $\subseteq$ PASS of machine *AccessControl* can be translated: (a) into a super-class *PASS* and a sub-class of *PASS* called *VALID_PASS*; or (b) into a class *PASS* having a boolean attribute (private or public) named *VALID_PASS*. These translations are illustrated in figure 4.

Relations "dom" and "ran". Associations "*dom*" and "*ran*" of the B meta-model link meta-classes "*BSet*" and "*BRelation*", and mean respectively the domain and the range of a functional relation between B sets. In this case, the "*BRelation*" can be translated following three possible patterns: (c) an association, (d) an attribute, or (e) an association class (figure 5). Attributes *MultDom* and *MultRan* of meta-class *BRelation* are respectively identified for the domain and the range of the *BRelation*[4]. For example, the partial injection *belong_to* between *PASS* and *PERSON* can be translated into: (i) an association linking classes *PASS* and *PERSON*, (ii) an attribute of type *PERSON* in class *PASS* or an attribute of type *PASS* in class *PERSON*, or finally (iii) an association class linking classes *PASS* and *PERSON*. Values a and b of attributes *MultDom* and *MultRan* in are respectively 0..1 and 0..1 in the case of a partial relation. The

---

[4] For computation details of multiplicities, refer to [3].

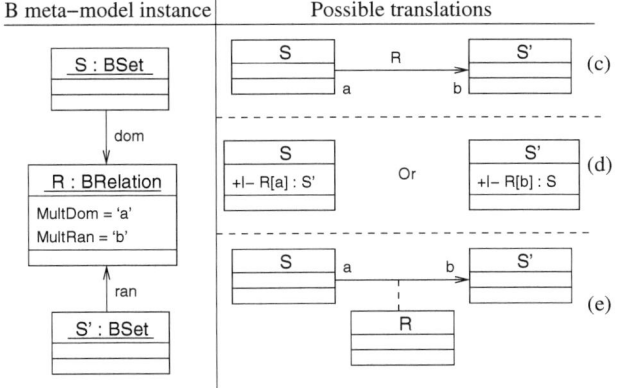

Fig. 5. Translations of *"dom"* and *"ran"*

choice of a particular transformation among others depends on the operations and attributes that the various classes are likely to encapsulate.

Relation "Access". Relation *Access* between a *BOperation* o and a *BData* d means that o uses[5] d in its body. Translation of a B operation into a method of a class $\mathcal{C}$ is based on the fact that the operation uses either the B data translated into $\mathcal{C}$ or one (or more) B data translated into attributes of $\mathcal{C}$. The *Access* relation controls the choice among translation patterns.

For example, consider *BDatas* d and d' of type *BSet* and such that $d' \subseteq d$, if operation o uses d' without using d then it is more pertinent to translate d' into a subclass having method o (*i.e.* application of pattern Fig. 3 (a)) than translating it into a Boolean attribute and encapsulate o and d' in class d (*i.e.* application of pattern Fig. 3 (b)). Thus, several scenarios are possible and vary according to kinds of dependencies between meta-classes *BData* and *BOperation*. Figure 6 shows various translations depending on operation *deassign_pass*. This operation uses three *BData*: set *PERSON*, sub-set *VALID_PASS*, and relation *belong_to*.

3.2   Translation of Machine *AccessControl*

Figure 7 gives a class diagram issued from machine *AccessControl* and which is conform to function $\mathcal{M}apping$. In this diagram, we identify three classes: *PERSON*, *PASS* and *BUILDING*. From a documentation point of view, the boolean attribute of class *PASS* gives the validity of a pass and it is updated by method $+validate()$. Methods $+assign\_pass(pp : PERSON)$ and $+deassign\_pass()$ allow respectively to create and to delete an instance of association *belong_to* between a pass and a person. Methods $+open\_building()$ and $+close\_building()$ of class *BUILDING* allow to open or to close the door of a building by modifying the

---

[5] Attribute *Kind* of *Access* is intended to identify the right kind of access (precondition, writing, etc).

244   A. Idani

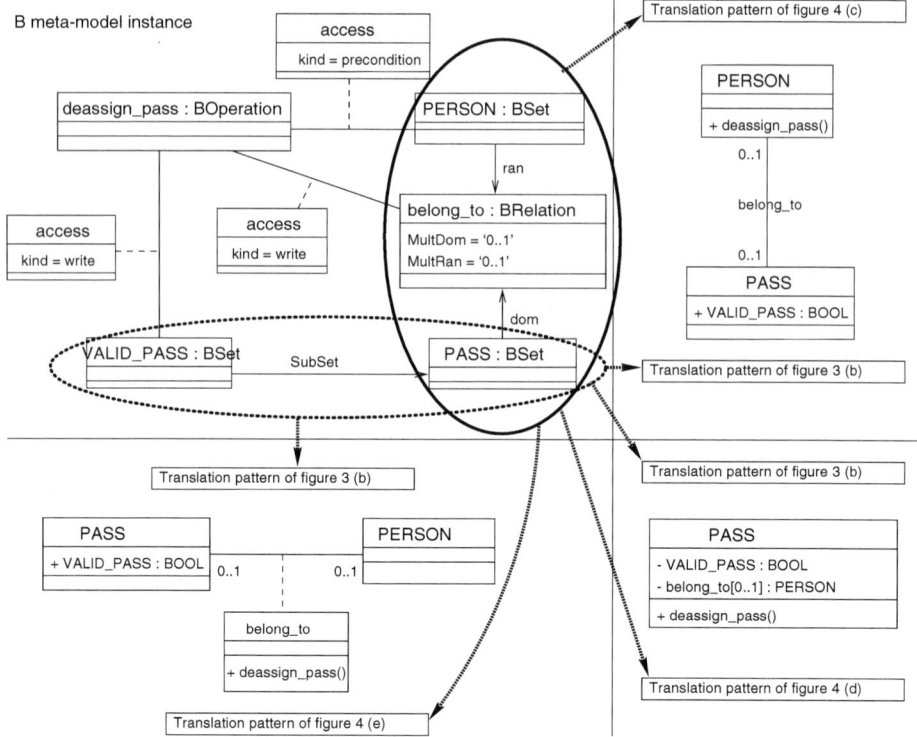

Fig. 6. Translations dependent on the "Access" relation

value of attribute *building_state*. This attribute takes its values from enumerated set $STATE = \{closed, open\}$. Creation and deletion of link *used_for* between an object of type *PASS* and an object of type *BUILDING* are done via methods *enter_building*($cc : PASS$) and *leave_building*($cc : PASS$) of class *BUILDING*.

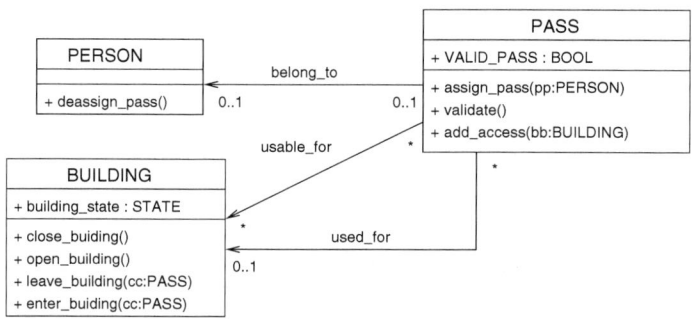

Fig. 7. Produced class diagram

4   Derivation of State/Transition Diagrams

In [2] we proposed a technique that help build graphical state machine representations of the behaviour of a B specification. These diagrams are intended as an accompanying documentation in a process which involves customers or certification authorities not trained in formal methods and who are interested by an alternate view of the dynamic aspects of B models. However, these diagrams don't document the behaviour of model elements of class diagrams which could be derived from the same specification. In this paper, we propose to bridge the gap between structural and behavioural views on the base of the established mappings between B and UML meta-models (relation $\mathcal{Mapping}$) and translation patterns outlined in the previous section. The state/transition diagrams presented in this section will relate to the description of classes behaviour.

In order to produce state machines from B specifications we proposed an abstraction technique based on exhaustive exploration of the B machine behaviour. First, our tool builds exhaustively an accessibility graph using the ProB model-checker [6] and then it applies a proof technique in order to identify concrete states which satisfy some abstract state predicates. The derivation of state machines is then done by running an abstraction algorithm over the accessibility graph. In the following, we will not present our accessibility graph abstraction technique since this approach is detailed in [2]. The major drawback of our previous work is that the choice of abstract state predicates is done manually by the user. In this paper we use the translation patterns of section 3 in order to automatically identify these state predicates, and hence produce state machines related to a derived class diagram. We will also precise the semantics of our state/transition diagrams in terms of events activation and states attainability.

4.1   Abstract State Predicates

A UML state describes the internal state of an object of one particular class. It indicates a particular situation during the life cycle of the object. In our approach, a UML class $\mathcal{C}$ ($\mathcal{A}_{\mathrm{UML}}(\mathcal{C}) = Class$) is uniquely issued from abstract sets ($\mathcal{F}^{-1}[\{Class\}] = \{\mathrm{BSet}\}$) as shown in figure 2. Consequently, a state of class $\mathcal{C}$ can be defined by a predicate expressed over elements of the $BSet$ which corresponds to $\mathcal{Mapping}^{-1}(\mathcal{C})$. In general, an object state is characterized by:

(i) the conjunction of the object attributes values (*e.g.*, an instance of class *BUILDING* is in state *closed* if the value of attribute *building_state* is *closed*),
(ii) the existence of links between the considered object and other objects (*e.g.* an instance of *BUILDING* is in state *empty* if it is not linked to any instance of *PASS* by association *used_for*).

State Predicates Issued from Class Attributes. An attribute t of a class $\mathcal{C}$ is issued either from an abstract set or from a relation. Indeed, $\mathcal{F}^{-1}[\{Attribute\}]$ $= \{\mathrm{BSet}, \mathrm{BRelation}\}$. In the first case, t is a boolean attribute (translation pattern (b) of figure 3). In the second case, t is typed either by the domain or by the range of the $BRelation$ (translation pattern (d) of figure 5).

– If $(\mathcal{A}_\mathrm{B}(\mathcal{M}apping^{-1}(t)) = \mathrm{BSet})$ then two abstract state predicates could be attached to class $\mathcal{C}$ dependent on the logic value of t (e_{true}^t and e_{false}^t). These states are expressed as follows:

$$e_{true}^t(c) \; \widehat{=} \; c \in \mathcal{M}apping^{-1}(t)$$
$$e_{false}^t(c) \; \widehat{=} \; c \notin \mathcal{M}apping^{-1}(t)$$

For example, states $valid$ and $invalid$ attached to class $PASS$ and dependent on values of the boolean attribute $VALID\_PASS$ are:

$$valid(cc) \; \widehat{=} \; cc \in \mathrm{VALID\_PASS}$$
$$invalid(cc) \; \widehat{=} \; cc \notin \mathrm{VALID\_PASS}$$

– If $(\mathcal{A}_\mathrm{B}(\mathcal{M}apping^{-1}(t)) = \mathrm{BRelation})$ and such that t is typed by an enumerated set ($e.g.$ attribute $building\_state$), then abstract state predicates e_i are expressed for each element $elem_i$ ($i.e.$ instance of meta-class $BSetElem$) of the enumerated set. Having $\mathcal{M}apping^{-1}(t)$ is a $BRelation$ then

– If t is typed by the range of $\mathcal{M}apping^{-1}(t)$:
$$e_i^t(c) \; \widehat{=} \; \mathcal{M}apping^{-1}(t)(c) = elem_i$$
– If t is typed by the domain of $\mathcal{M}apping^{-1}(t)$:
$$e_i^t(c) \; \widehat{=} \; (\mathcal{M}apping^{-1}(t))^{-1}(c) = elem_i$$

For example, states $closed$ and $open$ of class $BUILDING$ are defined by possible values of attribute $building\_state$ as:

$$Closed(bb) \; \widehat{=} \; building\_state(bb) = closed$$
$$Open(bb) \; \widehat{=} \; building\_state(bb) = open$$

State Predicates Issued from Associations. Classes derived from a B specification can be linked by an inheritance mechanism (translation pattern (a) of figure 3), an association (translation pattern (c) of figure 5), or by an association class (translation pattern (e) of figure 5). In the case of an inheritance link, the abstract state predicates are produced like a boolean attribute. In the case of an association link or an association class link $\mathcal{R}$ between two classes $\mathcal{C}_1$ and $\mathcal{C}_2$ such that $\mathcal{C}_1$ and $\mathcal{C}_2$ are respectively the source and the target of $\mathcal{R}$, the abstract state predicates depend from the existence of links $\mathcal{R}$ between instances of $\mathcal{C}_1$ and $\mathcal{C}_2$:

For $\mathcal{C}_1$:
$$e_\exists(c) \; \widehat{=} \; c \in dom(\mathcal{M}apping^{-1}(\mathcal{R}))$$
$$e_{\not\exists}(c) \; \widehat{=} \; c \notin dom(\mathcal{M}apping^{-1}(\mathcal{R}))$$
For $\mathcal{C}_2$:
$$e_\exists(c) \; \widehat{=} \; c \in ran(\mathcal{M}apping^{-1}(\mathcal{R}))$$
$$e_{\not\exists}(c) \; \widehat{=} \; c \notin ran(\mathcal{M}apping^{-1}(\mathcal{R}))$$

For example, the existence of a link $used\_for$ between an instance of class $PASS$ and an instance of class $BUILDING$ allows to define states In and Out of class $PASS$:

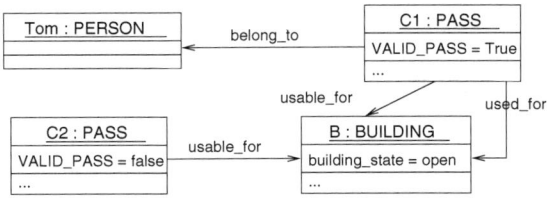

Fig. 8. Object diagram of state "s"

$$In(cc) \ \widehat{=} \ cc \in dom(used\_for)$$
$$Out(cc) \ \widehat{=} \ cc \notin dom(used\_for)$$

These two states express that the person who has pass cc is inside or outside a building.

Concrete States/Abstract States. Concrete states correspond to valuations of a B machine state variables. They are identified by the model-checker ProB tool [6] for finite systems. For example, we consider state s below.

$$s \ \widehat{=} \quad VALID\_PASS = \{C_1\} \ ;$$
$$belong\_to = \{(C_1 \mapsto Tom)\} \ ;$$
$$usable\_for = \{(C_1 \mapsto B), (C_2 \mapsto B)\} \ ;$$
$$used\_for = \{(C_1 \mapsto B)\} \ ;$$
$$building\_state = \{(B \mapsto open)\}$$

This concrete state is a possible state of the abstract state *Open*, defined previously, because it satisfies the abstract state predicate *building_state(bb)* = *open*. We say that state s satisfies state *Open*. Having the function $\mathcal{M}apping$, concrete state e can be translated into an object diagram (figure 8). This diagram describes a state where *Tom*, having a valid pass C_1, acceded to the open building B using his pass. Pass C_2, which allow to enter building B, is not yet validated and it doesn't belong to any person.

4.2   Transitions Properties

The abstraction technique we proposed in [2] builds state/transition diagrams where transitions are operations call. A transition t between two abstract states $\mathcal{S}_1$ and $\mathcal{S}_2$ ($t = \mathcal{S}_1 \xrightarrow{o} \mathcal{S}_2$) indicates the existence of at least one call of operation o allowing the transition between two concrete states s_1 and s_2 such that s_1 satisfies $\mathcal{S}_1$ and s_2 satisfies $\mathcal{S}_2$. This leads to the following properties:

- t is always activable from $\mathcal{S}_1$ if for each concrete state s source of a transition labeled by o then s satisfies the abstract state $\mathcal{S}_1$. Otherwise, t is said possibly activable from $\mathcal{S}_1$ and it will be labeled by o preceded by stereotype ≪*possibly*≫.

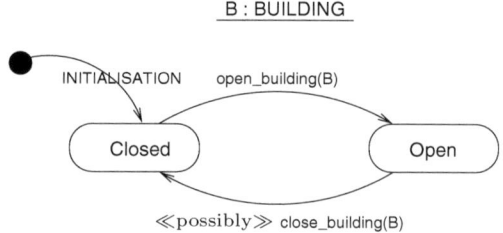

Fig. 9. State/Transition diagram of class BUILDING

- $\mathcal{S}_2$ is always attainable by t from $\mathcal{S}_1$ if all transitions, labeled by o and released from concrete states satisfying $\mathcal{S}_1$, reach at least one concrete state which satisfy $\mathcal{S}_2$. Otherwise, state $\mathcal{S}_2$ is said possibly attainable by t from $\mathcal{S}_1$, and transition t will be labeled by o followed by stereotype ≪possibly≫.
- t is said always feasible if it is always activable from $\mathcal{S}_1$, and state $\mathcal{S}_2$ is always attainable by t from $\mathcal{S}_1$. Otherwise, t is said possibly feasible and it will be represented by a dotted line.

4.3   Application

Simple State/Transition Diagrams. Considering the abstract states *Closed* and *Open* of class *BUILDING*, and an accessibility graph generated for $PERSON = \{\,Tom\}$; $PASS = \{\,C\}$; $BUILDING = \{B\}$, then the state/transition diagram built for class *BUILDING* is that of figure 9. This diagram shows that the instance B of class *BUILDING* is either in state *Closed* or in state *Open*. Transitions between these two states are triggered uniquely by operations *open_building* and *close_building*. Finally, when the system is initialized the building is in state *Closed*. Transition *open_building*(B) is always feasible from state *Closed*, contrary to transition *close_building*(B) which is possibly activable from state *Open*. Indeed, a building can be closed only if it is empty. However, state *Closed* is always attainable by transition *close_building*(B) from state *Open*.

Concurrent State/Transition Diagrams. Concurrent states are combinations of several abstract states. They are obtained by identifying possible relationships between the various state/transition diagrams for a given class.

For example, we identified six abstract states for class *BUILDING*: two states issued from the class attributes (*Open/Closed*), and four states issued from the existence of relations between instances of class *BUILDING* and instances of class *PASS* (*Accessible/Inaccessible* and *Busy/Empty*). Diagram of figure 10 shows that a building is simultaneously *Closed* (or *Open*) and *Accessible* (or *Inaccessible*) and *Busy* (or *Empty*). Considering that each couple of abstract states leads to a simple state/transition diagram, then the concurrent state/transition diagram is obtained by composing simple state/transition diagrams. In this diagram dependencies between concurrent states are given by transitions guards.

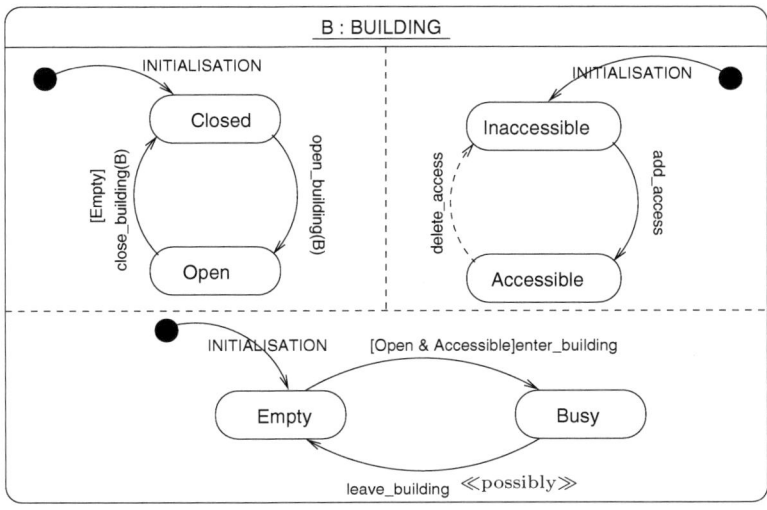

Fig. 10. Concurrent state/transition diagram of class BUILDING

For example, transition *enter_building* is activated only if the building is simultaneously *Empty*, *Open* and *Accessible*.

5   Conclusion

It is well-known that formal methods use specific notations and concepts which are often difficult to understand. This limitation makes difficult their integration in the development and the certification processes. Contrary to these methods, visual specification languages (such as UML) are usually preferred because they allow structuring and intuitive views of the system. In this paper we proposed a useful technique to the research works which aim at graphically documenting formal developments. Indeed, the documentation we provide is expressed by static and dynamic UML diagrams. We are interested by the B method which is a formal method used to model systems and prove their correctness by successive refinements. In order to produce UML class diagrams (*e.g.* figure 7) and associated state/transition diagrams (*e.g.* figures 9 and 10) we proposed a set of projections from a B meta-model to the UML meta-model.

Using our technique, we were able to scale up from small B specifications (several dozens of lines) to medium size ones (several hundreds or thousand lines) such as the secure flight specifications taken from the EDEMOI project[6] (about 300 source lines). Today, the largest B specification (i.e. the METEOR subway) is about 100,000 lines. Scaling up to such sizes may bring interesting new problems to our tool.

---

[6] http://www-lsr.imag.fr/EDEMOI/

The MDA-based CASE tool, issued from our state/transition generator [2] and our class diagram generator [4], is not only intended to provide a useful UML documentation of B developments, but also to circumvent the lack of traceability of existing UML-to-B approaches [5,7,8].

References

1. Abrial, J.-R.: System study: Method and example (1999),
   www-lsr.imag.fr/B/Documents/ClearSy-CaseStudies/
2. Idani, A., Ledru, Y.: Dynamic Graphical UML Views from Formal B Specifications. Journal of Information and Software Technology 48(3), 154–169 (2006)
3. Idani, A., Ledru, Y.: Object Oriented Concepts Identification from Formal B Specifications. Journal of Formal Methods in System Design 30(3), 217–232 (2007)
4. Idani, A., Ledru, Y., Bert, D.: Derivation of UML Class Diagrams as Static Views of Formal B Developments. In: Lau, K.-K., Banach, R. (eds.) ICFEM 2005. LNCS, vol. 3785, pp. 37–51. Springer, Heidelberg (2005)
5. Laleau, R., Mammar, A.: An Overview of a Method and Its Support Tool for Generating B Specifications from UML Notations. In: 15th IEEE Int. Conference on Automated Software Engineering, pp. 269–272. IEEE CS Press, Los Alamitos (2000)
6. Leuschel, M., Butler, M.: ProB: A Model Checker for B. In: Araki, K., Gnesi, S., Mandrioli, D. (eds.) FME 2003. LNCS, vol. 2805, pp. 855–874. Springer, Heidelberg (2003)
7. Sekerinski, E.: Graphical Design of Reactive Systems. In: Bert, D. (ed.) B 1998. LNCS, vol. 1393, pp. 182–197. Springer, Heidelberg (1998)
8. Snook, C., Butler, M.: U2B − A tool for translating UML-B models into B. In: Mermet (ed.) UML-B Specification for Proven Embedded Systems Design (2004)

MDA-Based Reverse Engineering of Object Oriented Code

Liliana Favre[1,2], Liliana Martinez[1], and Claudia Pereira[1]

[1] Universidad Nacional del Centro de la Provincia de Buenos Aires
[2] Comisión de Investigaciones Científicas de la Provincia de Buenos Aires
Tandil, Argentina
lfavre@arnet.com.ar, {lmartine, cpereira}@exa.unicen.edu.ar

Abstract. The Model Driven Architecture (MDA) is an architectural framework for information integration and tool interoperation that could facilitate system modernization. Reverse engineering techniques are crucial to extract high level views of the subject system. This paper describes a reverse engineering approach that fits with MDA. We propose to integrate different techniques that come from compiler theory, metamodeling and formal specification. We describe a process that combines static and dynamic analysis for generating MDA models. We show how MOF (Meta Object Facility) and QVT (Query, View, Transformation) metamodels can be used to drive model recovery processes. Besides, we show how metamodels and transformations can be integrated with formal specifications in an interoperable way. The reverse engineering of class diagram and state diagram at PSM level from Java code is exemplified.

Keywords: Reverse Engineering, Model Driven Architecture (MDA), Metamodeling, Meta-Object Facility (MOF), Formal Specification.

1 Introduction

Reverse engineering is the process of analyzing software systems to extract software artifacts at a higher level of abstraction [21]. A central idea in reverse engineering is exploiting the source code as the most reliable description both of the system behavior and of the organization and its business rules.

Twenty years ago, reverse engineering was focused mainly on recovering high-level architecture or diagrams from procedural code to face up to problems such as comprehending data structures or databases, or the Y2K problem. At that time, many different kinds of static analysis techniques, basically based on compiler theory and abstract interpretation, were developed.

A growing demand of reverse engineering systems appeared on the stage when object oriented languages emerged. The compiler techniques were adapted to perform a propagation of proper data in an essentially dynamic context. During this time, the focus of software analysis moved from static analysis to dynamic one.

When the Unified Modeling Language (UML) emerged, a new problem was how to extract higher level views of the system expressed by different kind of diagrams [24].

T. Halpin et al. (Eds.): BPMDS 2009 and EMMSAD 2009, LNBIP 29, pp. 251–263, 2009.

Nowadays, software and system engineering industry evolves to manage new platform technologies, design techniques and processes. A new architectural framework for information integration and tool interoperation such as the Model Driven Development (MDD) had created the need to develop new analysis tools and specific techniques. MDD refers to a range of development approaches that are based on the use of software models as first class entities, one of them is the Model Driven Architecture (MDA), i.e., MDA is a realization of MDD [15].

The outstanding ideas behind MDA are separating the specification of the system functionality from its implementation on specific platforms, managing the software evolution from abstract models to implementations increasing the degree of automation and achieving interoperability with multiple platforms, programming languages and formal languages. MDA distinguishes at least three main models: platform independent model (PIM), platform specific model (PSM) and implementation specific model (ISM).

One of the main issues behind MDA is that all artifacts generated during software development are represented using metamodels. The essence of MDA is MOF (Meta Object Facility) metamodel that allows different kinds of artifacts from multiple vendors to be used together in a same project [16]. The MOF 2.0 Query, View, Transformation (QVT) metamodel is the standard for expressing transformations [19].

With the emergence of MDA, new approaches should be developed in order to reverse engineering, both platform independent and platform specific models, from object oriented code. Our approach is based on the integration of different techniques that come from compiler theory, metamodeling and formal specification. We describe a process that combines static and dynamic analysis for generating MDA models. We show how MOF metamodels can be used to analyze the consistency of model recovery processes. The reverse engineering of PSM models, including class diagrams and state diagrams, from Java code is exemplified.

This paper is organized as follow. Section 2 describes a three-layer framework for reverse engineering MDA models from object oriented code. Section 3 presents an MDA process based on static and dynamic analysis for reverse engineering MDA models from Java code. Section 4 explains the reverse engineering of PSMs including class diagrams and state diagrams from object oriented code. Section 5 describes reverse engineering process formalization in terms of MOF metamodels. Section 6 summarizes how to integrate this formalization with algebraic specification. Finally, related work and conclusions are presented.

2   An MDA Framework for Reverse Engineering

We propose a framework to reverse engineering MDA models from object oriented code that is based on the integration of compiler techniques, metamodeling and formal specification. It distinguishes three different abstraction levels linked to models, metamodels and formal specifications (Fig. 1).

The model level includes code, PIMs and PSMs. A PIM is a model with a high level of abstraction that is independent of an implementation technology. A PSM is a tailored model to specify a system in terms of specific platform such J2EE or .NET. PIMs and PSMs are expressed in UML and OCL. The subset of UML diagrams that are useful for PSMs includes class diagram, object diagram, state diagram, interaction diagram and package diagram. On the other hand, a PIM can be expressed by means of use case diagrams, activity diagrams, interactions diagrams to model system processes and state diagrams to model lifecycle of the system entities. An ISM is a specification of the system in source code.

At model level, transformations are based on classical compiler construction techniques. They involve processes with different degrees of automation, which can go from totally automatic static analysis to human intervention requiring processes to dynamically analyze the resultant models. All the algorithms that deal with the reverse engineering share an analysis framework. The basic idea is to describe source code or models by an abstract language and perform a propagation analysis in a data-flow graph called in this context object-data flow. This static analysis is complemented with dynamic analysis supported by tracer tools.

The metamodel level includes MOF metamodels that describe the transformations at model level. A metamodel is an explicit model of the constructs and rules needed to construct specific models. MOF metamodel uses an object modeling framework that is essentially a subset of UML 2.1.2 core [25]. The modeling concepts are classes which model MOF metaobjects, associations, which model binary relations between metaobjects, data types which model other data, and packages which modularize the models. At this level MOF metamodels describe families of ISMs, PSMs and PIMs. Every ISM, PSM and PIM conforms to a MOF metamodel. Metamodel transformations are specified as OCL contracts between a source metamodel and a target metamodel. MOF metamodels "control" the consistency of these transformations.

The level of formal specification includes specifications of MOF metamodels and metamodel transformations in the metamodeling language NEREUS that can be used to connect them with different formal and programming languages [9] [10].

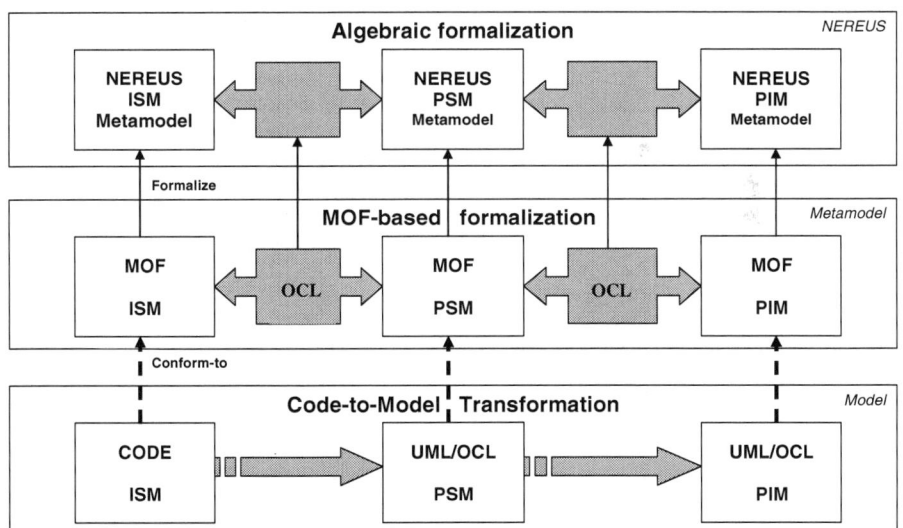

Fig. 1. A framework for MDA-based reverse engineering

NEREUS, like MDA, was designed for improving interoperability and reusability through separation of concerns. It is suited for specifying metamodels such as MOF based on the concepts of entity, associations and systems. Two types of consistency are distinguished: vertical consistency between different levels of refinements and horizontal consistency between models at the same abstraction level. This paper emphasizes the description of transformations at level of models and MOF metamodels.

3   Integrating Static and Dynamic Analysis

At model level, transformations are based on static and dynamic analysis. Static analysis extracts static information that describes the software structure reflected in the software documentation (e.g., the text of the source code) whereas dynamic analysis information describes the structure of the run-behavioral. Static information can be extracted by using techniques and tools based on compiler techniques such as parsing and data flow algorithms. Dynamic information can be extracted by using debuggers, event recorders and general tracer tools.

We suppose that the reverse engineering process starts from an ISM that could reflect, for instance, the migration of legacy code to object oriented code. The first step in the migration towards MDA is the introduction of PSMs. Then, a PIM is abstracted from the PSMs omitting platform specific details.

Next, we describe the process for recovery PSMs from code. Fig. 2 shows the different phases. The source code is parsed to obtain an abstract syntax tree (AST) associated with the source programming language grammar. Then, a metamodel extractor extracts a simplified, abstract version of a language that ignores all instructions that do not affect the data flows, for instance all control flows such as conditional and loops.

The information represented according to this metamodel allows building the data-flow graph for a given source code, as well as conducting all other analysis that do not depend on the graph. The idea is to derive statically information by performing a propagation of data. Different kinds of analysis propagate different kinds of information in the data-flow graph, extracting the different kinds of diagrams that are included in a PSM.

The static analysis is based on classical compiler techniques [2] and abstract interpretation [13]. On the one hand, data-flow graph and the generic flow propagation algorithms are specializations of classical flow analysis techniques [23]. On the other hand, abstract interpretation allows obtaining automatically as much information as possible about program executions without having to run the program on all input data and then ensuring computability or tractability. These ideas were applied to optimizing compilers.

The static and dynamic information could be shown as separated views or merged in a single view. In general, the dynamic behavior could be visualized as an execution scenery which describes interaction between objects. To extract specific information, it is necessary to define particular views of these sceneries. Although, the construction of these views can be automated, their analysis requires some manual processing in most cases.

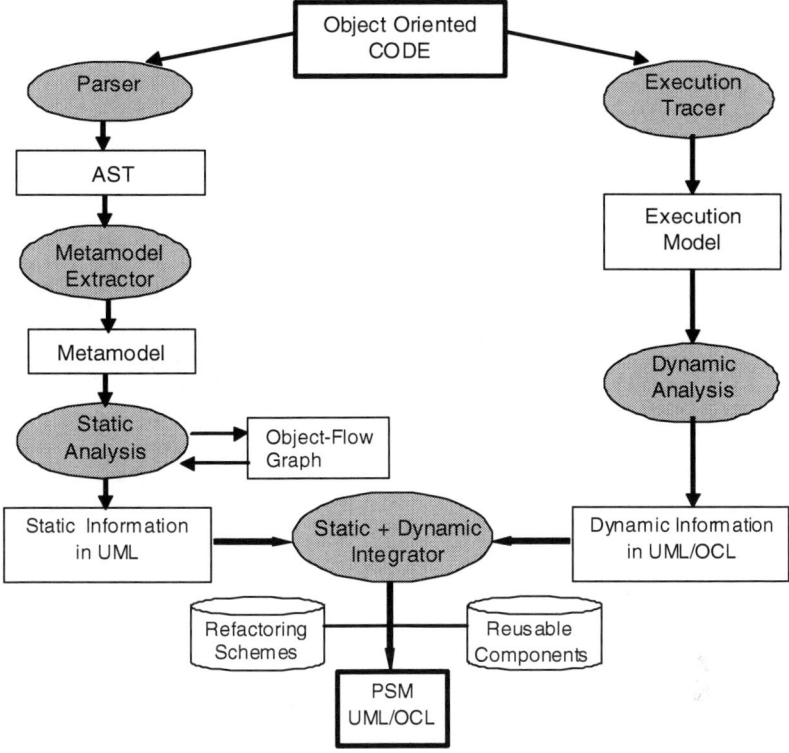

Fig. 2. Reverse engineering at model level: static and dynamic analysis

Dynamic analysis is based on an execution model including the following components: a set of objects, a set of attributes for each object, a location and value of an object type for each object, and a set of messages. Additionally, types such as Integer, String, Real and Boolean are available for describing types of attributes and parameters of methods or constructors.

Fig. 2 also shows that the integration of static and dynamic analysis is supported by refactoring schemes [11] and reusable components [8].

4   Reverse Engineering at Model Level: From Code to PSMs

4.1   The Bases for Recovering Class Diagrams

A class diagram is a representation of the static view that shows a collection of static model elements, such as classes, interfaces, methods, attributes, types as well as their properties (e.g., type and visibility). Besides, the class diagram shows the interrelationships holding among the classes [24] [25].

Reverse engineering of class diagram from code is a difficult task that cannot be automated. The static analysis is based on program models whereas dynamic analysis is based on execution models. For instance, a basic algorithm for the recovery of class diagram can be obtained by a static analysis. By analyzing the syntax of the source code, internal class features such as attributes and methods and their properties (e.g. the parameters of the methods and visibility) can be recovered. From the source code, associations, generalization, realizations and dependencies may be inferred too.

However, to distinguish between aggregation and composition, or to include OCL specifications (e.g. preconditions and postconditions of operations, invariants and association constraints) we need to capture system states through dynamic analysis.

The association between two classes, A and B, could be an aggregation or a composition. An aggregation models the situation where an object is made up of several parts. The whole shows at least an emergent property, i.e. "the whole is more than the sum of its parts". Other properties that characterize the aggregation are: type-antisymmetry, instance-reflexivity and instance anti symmetry. The aggregation from a type A (as whole) to a type B (as part), prevents the existence of other aggregation from B (as a whole) to A (as part).

A composition is a particular aggregation in which the lifetime of the part is controlled by the whole (directly or transitively). Then, we can detect a composition by generating tests and scanning dependency configurations between the birth and the death of a part object according to those of the whole. In the same way, the execution traces of different instances of the same class or method, could guide the construction of invariants or pre- and post-conditions respectively.

4.2   The Bases for Recovering State Diagram

A state transition diagram describes the life cycle of objects that are instances of a class from the time they are created until they are destroyed. Object state is determined by the value of its attributes and possibly by the variables involved in attribute computations. The basic elements of a state diagram are states, identified as equivalence classes of attribute values and, transitions triggered by method invocation.

Our approach to recover state diagrams has similar goals to abstract interpretation that allows obtaining automatically as much information as possible about program executions without having to run it on all input data and then ensuring computability or tractability. These ideas were applied to optimizing compilers, often under the name data-flow analysis [2]. In our context, an abstract interpretation performs method invocation using abstract domains instead of concrete attribute values to deduce information about the object computation on its actual state from the resulting abstract descriptions of its attributes. This implies to abstract equivalence classes that group attribute values corresponding to the different states in which the class can be and the transitions among state equivalence classes.

Then, the first step is to define an appropriate abstract interpretation for attributes (which give the state of the object) and transformer class methods (which give the transitions from state to state to be represented in the state diagram).

The recovery algorithm iterates over the following activities: the construction of a finite automata by executing abstract interpretations of class methods and the minimization of the automata for recovering approximate state equivalence classes.

To ensure tractability, our algorithm proposes an incremental minimization every time a state is candidate to be added to the automaton. When it is detected that two states are equivalents, they are merged in an only state. This could lead to modification

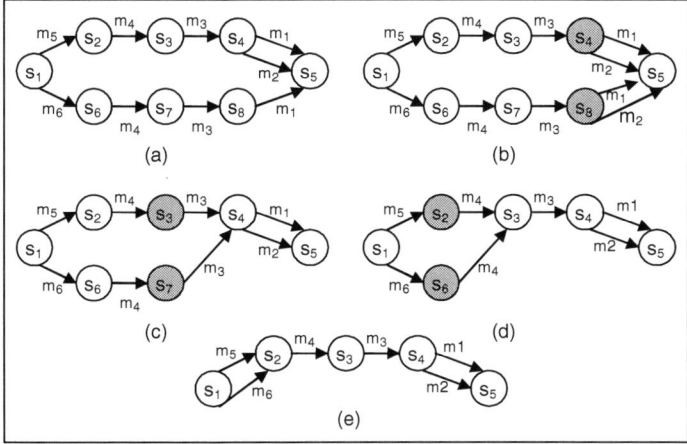

Fig. 3. Recovering minimum State Diagram

of the parts of the automaton that had been previously minimized. To optimize the comparison of pairs of states, these are classified according to their emerging transitions. Let m be a bound of the number of transformer methods of a class, the idea is to generate subsets of the set of transformer methods. The subset of emerging transitions of a new state belongs, in a particular snapshot, to one of them. Two states are candidates to be equivalent if they belong to the same subset. Then, it is sufficient to compare all the pairs composed by the state and one element of the subset. Considerable human interaction to select which abstract interpretations should be executed is required. Then, our approach is so significantly less automatic than traditional abstract interpretation [13].

```
-- initialization of different sets
   set-of-states initialStates = {};
   set-of-states pendingStates ={};
   set-of-states allStates = {};

--defining initial states for the objects
-- of the class
   for each class constructor c
   {-- executing an abstract interpretation
   -- of each class constructor
   state s = abstractInterpretationState (c, {});
   initialStates = initialStates  U {s};
   pendingStatesPending= pendingStates U {s};
   allStates = allStates U {s};     }

-- initializating transition set
   set-of-transitions transitionSet = {};

--generating subsets of transformer methods
   set-of-bins b = classifiedStates (allStates);
   while |pendingStates | > 0
```

```
{ state r = extract (pendingStates);
   pendingState = pendingStates – {r};
   for each class method m
   {– generating transitions of the state r
      s = abstractInterpretationState (m, r);
      if s ∉ allStates
         {pendingStates = pendingStates U {s};
         allStates = allStates U {s};
         transitionSet= transitionSet U
         abstractInterpretationTransition (m,r,s);}
   --updating subsets of transformer methods
      b= modifyBins (s, transitionSet, allStates); }
   for each e ∈ b
   {– defining equivalence of states and
   -- merging equivalent states
      if s ∈ b
         for each q ∈ e and s<> q
         if equivalents (p, q)
         mergeStates(transitionSet, allStates,p,q);}
}
```

Fig. 4. Recovering State Diagrams: algorithm

As an example, Fig. 3 (a) shows a diagram including states (s_1, s_2,.., s_8) and transitions (m_1,m_2,...,m_6). Fig. 3 (b) shows a simplified snapshot of the automaton when a transition to s_5 is added. Then, the shaded states could belong to the same equivalence state class. s_8 belongs to the same subset of s_4 and an equivalence analysis is carried out concluding that s_8 and s_4 can be merged. Fig 3 (c) (d) (e) shows the successive transformations. Fig. 4 shows the pseudo code of the recovery algorithm. A C++ implementation was developed to test the feasibility of this recovering algorithm.

5   Reverse Engineering at MOF Metamodel Level

We specify reverse engineering processes as MOF-defined transformations. It allows capturing all the diversity of modeling standards and interchange constructs that are used in MDA. We call anti-refinement the process of extracting from a more detailed specification (or code) another one, more abstract, that is conformed by the more detailed one.

Fig. 5 shows partially an ISM-Java metamodel that includes constructs for representing classes, fields and operations. It also shows different kind of relationships such as generalization and composition. For example, an instance of JavaClass could be related to another instance of JavaClass that takes the role of superclass or, it could be composed by other instances of JavaClass that take the role of *nestedClass*. Fig. 6 (a) shows partially a PSM-Java metamodel that includes constructs for representing classes, fields, operations and association-end. It also shows different kind of

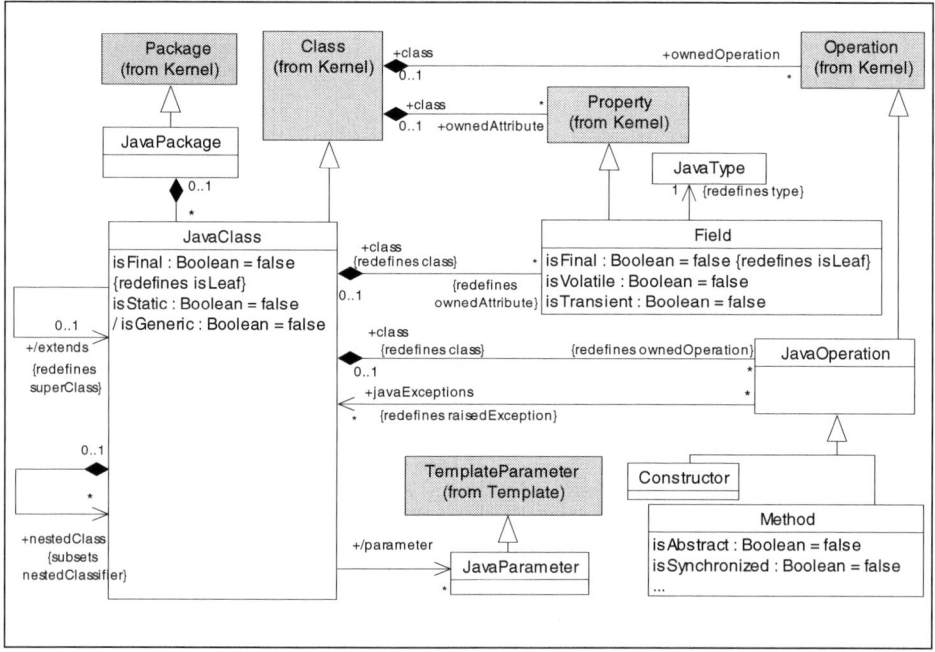

Fig. 5. ISM-Java metamodel

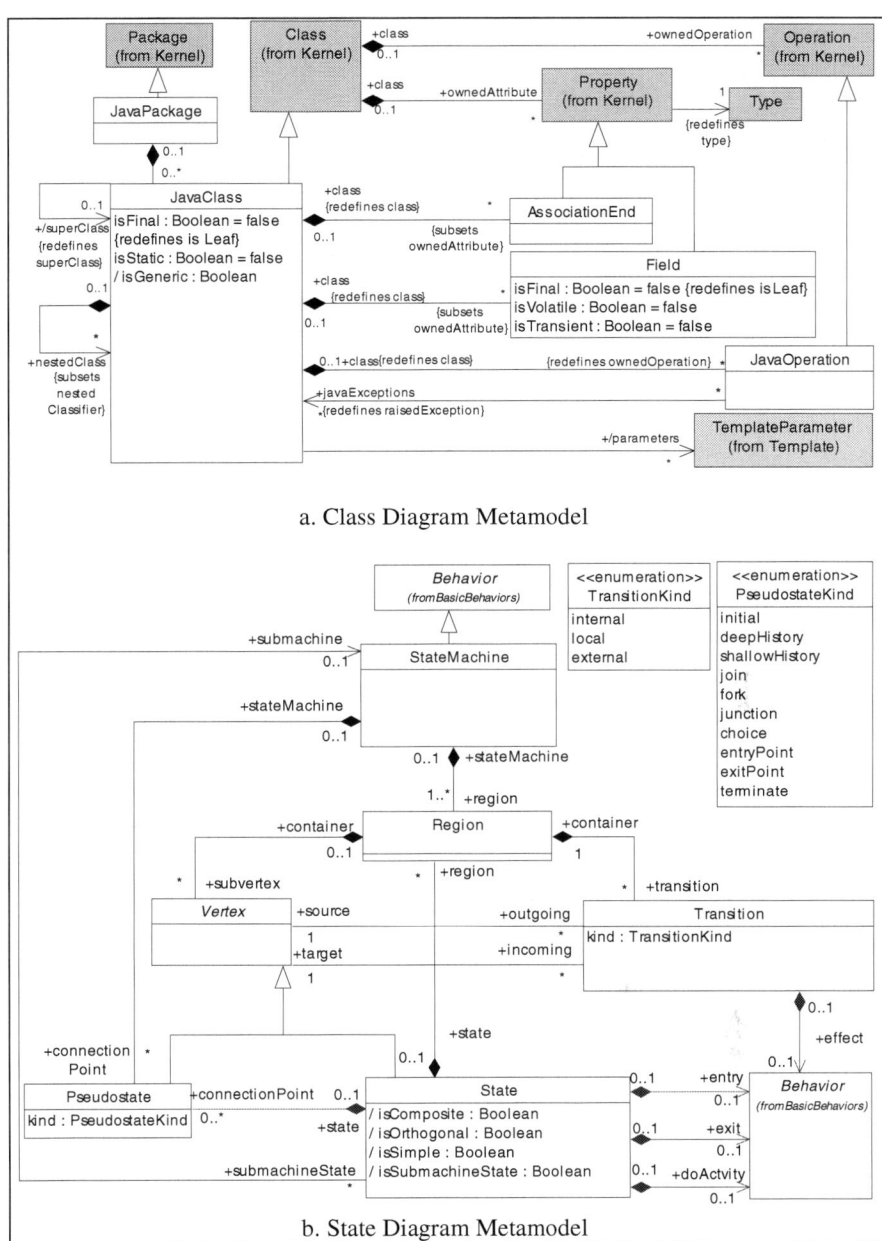

a. Class Diagram Metamodel

b. State Diagram Metamodel

Fig. 6. PSM-Java metamodel

relationships such as composition and generalization. The main difference between an ISM-Java and a PSM-Java is that the latter includes constructs for associations.

The State Diagram metamodel (Fig. 6.b) defines a set of concepts than can be used for modeling discrete behavior through finite state transition systems such as state machines, states and transitions.

Transformation ISM-JAVA to PSM-JAVA {

parameter   sourceModel: ISM-JAVA-Metamodel:: JavaPackage
                     targetModel: PSM-JAVA-Metamodel:: JavaPackage

postconditions

-- For each class 'sourceClass' in the sourceModel
sourceModel.ownedMember->select(oclIsTypeOf(JavaClass))->forAll(sourceClass |

  --there is a class 'targetClass' in the targetModel so that both classes have the same name,
  targetModel.ownedMember-> select(oclIsTypeOf(JavaClass))-> exists (
   targetClass | targetClass.name = sourceClass.name **and**

    -- if 'sourceClass' has an extends relation, targetModel has a superclass so that
    -- both superclasses are equivalent.
   sourceClass.extends->size()=1 **implies** (targetClass.superClass->size()=1 **and**
    targetClass.superClass.**classMatch**(sourceClass.extends))   **and**

    --For each operation of 'sourceClass' there is an operation in targetClass so that
    --both operations are equivalent.
   sourceClass.javaOperation->forAll(sourceOp|targetClass.javaOp->exists(targetOp|
    targetOp.**operationMatch**(sourceOp))) **and**

    --For each field in 'sourceClass' whose type is a primitive type there is a field in
    --'targetClass' so that:
   sourceClass.field-> select(f | f.javaType.oclIsTypeOf(Primitive))->forAll
    (sourceField | targetClass.field -> exists (targetField |

    -- 'targetField' and 'sourceField' have the same name, type,…
   targetField.name=sourceField.name **and** targetField.type=sourceField.javaType…)) **and**

    -- For each field in 'sourceClass' whose type is a user defined type there is an
    --association end in ' targetClass' so that:
   sourceClass.field->select(f|f.javaType.oclIsTypeOf(UserJavaClass))->forAll
    (sourceField | targetClass.associationEnd -> exists (targetAssocEnd |

    -- 'targetAssocEnd' and 'sourceField' have the same name, type,…
   targetAssocEnd.name = sourceField.name **and**
   targetAssocEnd.opposite.type = sourceField.javaType **and ...)) and...**

  --If 'sourceClass' has some significant dynamic behavior, targetModel has
  -- a 'stateMachine' so that:
  sourceClass.**hasSignificantDynamicBehavior() implies**
  targetModel.ownedMember->select(oclIsTypeOf(JavaStateMachine))-> exists (
     targetMachine |

    -- 'targetMachine' and 'sourceClass' have the same name and
   targetMachine.name = sourceClass.name   **and**

    -- For each modifier operation in the 'sourceClass' there is a transition in 'targetClass'
   sourceClass.javaOperation-> select (op| op.**isModifier()**)-> forAll(op|
   targetMachine.region.transition-> exists(t | t.**isCreatedFrom**(op)))
))   **and**
... }

Fig. 7. ISM-JAVA to PSM-JAVA transformation

We specify metamodel-based model transformations as OCL contracts that are described by means of a transformation name, parameters, preconditions, postconditions and additional operations. Transformation semantics is aligned with QVT, in particular with the QVT Core. QVT depends on EssentialOCL [17] and EMOF [16]. EMOF is a subset of MOF that allows simple metamodels to be defined using simple concepts. Essential OCL is a package exposing the minimal OCL required to work with EMOF.

In Fig. 7 we partially exemplify a transformation from an ISM-Java to a PSM-Java. This transformation uses both the specialized UML metamodel of Java code and the UML metamodel of a Java platform as source and target parameters respectively. The postconditions state relations at metamodel level between the elements of the source and target model. The transformation specification guarantees that for each class in Java code there is a class in the PSM-Java, both of them with the same name, the same parent class, equivalent operations and so on. Besides, the PSM-Java has a 'stateMachine' for each class having a significant dynamic behavior.

With respect to reverse engineering processes, two types of consistency can be distinguished, vertical consistency between different levels of refinements and horizontal consistency or interconsistency between models at the same abstraction level. For instance, a vertical consistency analysis detects when a state model is associated to a class that does not exist in the ISM. A horizontal consistency analysis could detect that the sequence of interactions shown in the sequence diagram does not exist as a trace of the state diagram linked to the respective class.

6 Reverse Engineering at Algebraic Level

In [9] and [10], we show results that are strongly related with the process described in this paper. We use the NEREUS language to formalize metamodels and transformations in a way that fits with MDA. NEREUS takes advantage of all the existing theoretical background on formal specifications and can be integrated with property-oriented approaches such as algebraic languages.

NEREUS focuses on interoperability of formal languages in MDD. It would eliminate the need to define formalizations and specific transformations for each different formal language.

We define a bridge between MOF metamodels and NEREUS consisting of a system of transformation rules to convert automatically MOF into NEREUS [9] [10]. Also, we show how to integrate NEREUS with the Common Algebraic Specification Language (CASL) [3].

7 Related Work

[5] provides a survey of existing work in the area of software reverse engineering, discusses success and provides a road map for possible future developments in the area. [22] describes an experimental environment to reverse engineer JAVA software that integrates dynamic and static information. [23] provides a relevant overview of techniques that have been recently investigated and applied in the field of reverse engineering of object oriented code. [12] proposes an study of class diagram constituents with respect to their recovery from object oriented code.

[18] presents an approach to bridging legacy systems to MDA that includes an architecture description language and a reverse engineering process. [14] describes a tool-assisted way of introducing models in the migration towards MDA. [7] shows the first steps towards the definition of a metamodel that unifies a conceptual view on programs with the classical structure-based reverse engineering metamodels. [20] reports on a

project that assessed the feasibility of applying MDD to the evolution of a legacy system. [4] presents MOMENT, a rigorous framework for automatic legacy system migration in MDA. OMG is involved in the definition of standards to successfully modernize existing information systems [1].

In contrast to the research mentioned in this section, our approach has the following advantages. Our work could be considered as an MDA-based formalization of the process described in [23]. Additionally, we propose algorithms for extracting UML diagrams that differs on the ones proposed in [23]. For instance, a different algorithm for extracting State Diagrams is proposed. We also propose to include OCL specifications (preconditions, postconditions and invariants) in Class Diagrams.The functionality proposed in this paper is not supported by existing MDA CASE tools that assist only in the reverse engineering of basic notational features with a direct representation in the code [6].

Other advantages are linked to the automation of the formalization process and interoperability of formal languages. This work is strongly integrated with previous ones that show how to formalize metamodels and metamodel-based transformations in NEREUS [8] [9] [10] [11]. This formalization is the only one that shows how to generate automatically formal specifications from MOF metamodels. With respect to interoperability, NEREUS allows us to connect different source languages (e.g., Domain Specific Languages) with target languages (e.g. different formal languages) without having to define explicit metamodel transformations for each pair of language.

8   Conclusions

In this paper we describe MDA based reverse engineering processes based on the integration of different techniques that come from compiler theory, metamodeling and formal specification. We analyze the relationship between static and dynamic analysis and metamodeling on reverse engineering object oriented software. We emphasize the importance of dynamic analysis in MDA processes. Besides, we propose a specification of MDA based reverse engineering processes as contracts between MOF metamodels.

Although we exemplify our approach in terms of Java reverse engineering, the underlying ideas can be applied in the context of object oriented languages. In this paper we analyze the bases to recover PSMs. To date, we are analyzing the recovery of PIMs from PSMs linked to different platforms.

References

1. ADM Task Force: Architecture Driven Modernization Roadmap. OMG.adm.omg.org (2007)
2. Aho, A., Sethi, R., Ullman, J.: Compilers. Principles, Techniques, and Tools. Addison-Wesley, Reading (1985)
3. Bidoit, M., Mosses, P.: CASL User Manual. LNCS, vol. 2900. Springer, Heidelberg (2004)
4. Boronat, A., Carsi, J., Ramos, I.: Automatic reengineering in MDA using rewriting logic as transformation engine. In: Proc. of the Ninth European Conference on Software Maintenance and Reengineering (CSMR 2005), USA, pp. 228–231. IEEE Computer Society, Los Alamitos (2005)

5. Canfora, G., Di Penta, M.: New Frontiers of Reverse Engineering. In: Future of Software Engineering (FOSE 2007), pp. 326–341. IEEE Press, Los Alamitos (2007)
6. CASE TOOLS (2008), http://www.objectbydesign.com/tools
7. Deissenboeck, F., Ratiu, D.: A Unified Meta Model for Concept-Based Reverse Engineering. In: Proceedings of 3rd International Workshop on Metamodels, Schemes, Grammars, and Ontologies for Reverse Engineering (2006), http://www.planetmde.org
8. Favre, L., Martinez, L.: Formalizing MDA Components. In: Morisio, M. (ed.) ICSR 2006. LNCS, vol. 4039, pp. 326–339. Springer, Heidelberg (2006)
9. Favre, L.: A Rigorous Framework for Model Driven Development. In: Siau, K. (ed.) Advanced Topics in Database Research, ch. I, vol. 5, pp. 1–27. IGP, USA (2006)
10. Favre, L.: Foundations for MDA-based Forward Engineering. Journal of Object Technology (JOT) 4(1), 129–153 (2005)
11. Favre, L., Pereira, C.: Formalizing MDA-based Refactorings. In: 19th Australian Software Engineering Conference (ASWEC 2008), pp. 377–386. IEEE Computer Society, Los Alamitos (2008)
12. Gueheneuc, Y.: A Systematic Study of UML Class Diagram Constituents for their Abstract and Precise Recovery. In: Proc. of 11th Asia-Pacific Software Engineering Conference (APSEC 2004), pp. 265–274. IEEE Computer Society, Los Alamitos (2004)
13. Jones, N., Nielson, F.: Abstract interpretation: A semantic based tool for program analysis. In: Gabbay, D., Abramsky, S., Maibaum, T. (eds.) Handbook of Logic in Computer Science, vol. 4, pp. 527–636. Clarendon Press, Oxford (1995)
14. Mansurov, N., Campara, D.: Managed architecture of existing code as a practical transition towards MDA. In: Jardim Nunes, N., Selic, B., Rodrigues da Silva, A., Toval Alvarez, A. (eds.) UML Satellite Activities 2004. LNCS, vol. 3297, pp. 219–233. Springer, Heidelberg (2005)
15. MDA. The Model Driven Architecture (2005), http://www.omg.org/mda
16. MOF. Meta Object facility (MOF ^{TM}) 2.0. OMG Specification formal/2006-01-01 (2006), http://www.omg.org/mof
17. Object Constraint Language. Version 2.0. OMG: formal/06-05-01 (2006), http://www.omg.org
18. Qiao, B., Yang, H., Chu, W., Xu, B.: Bridging legacy systems to model driven architecture. In: Proc. 27th Annual International Computer Aided Software and Applications Conference, pp. 304–309. IEEE Press, Los Alamitos (2003)
19. Meta Object Facility (MOF) 2.0 Query/View/Transformation. formal/2008-04-03 (2008), http://www.omg.org
20. Reus, T., Geers, H., van Deursen, A.: Harvesting Software System for MDA-based Reengineering. In: Rensink, A., Warmer, J. (eds.) ECMDA-FA 2006. LNCS, vol. 4066, pp. 220–236. Springer, Heidelberg (2006)
21. Sommerville, I.: Software Engineering, 7th edn. Addison-Wesley, Reading (2004)
22. Systa, T.: Static and Dynamic Reverse Engineering Techniques for Java Software Systems. Ph.D Thesis, University of Tampere, Report A-2000-4 (2000)
23. Tonella, P., Potrich, A.: Reverse Enginering of Object Oriented Code. Monographs in Computer Science. Springer, Heidelberg (2005)
24. Unified Modeling Language: Superstructure. Version 2.1.2. OMG Specification: formal/2007-02-05 (2007), http://www.omg.org
25. Unified Modeling Language: Infrastructure. Version 2.1.2. OMG Specification formal/07-02-04 (2007)

Integrated Quality of Models and Quality of Maps

Alexander Nossum and John Krogstie

NTNU, Trondheim, Norway
alexanno@stud.ntnu.no, krogstie@idi.ntnu.no

Abstract. Conceptual modeling traditionally focuses on a high level of abstraction. Even if geographical aspects such as location is included in several enterprise modeling frameworks [26], it is not common to have geographical aspects included in conceptual models. Cartography is the science of visualizing geographical information in maps. Traditionally the field has not included conceptual relationships and the primary focus is on a fairly low abstraction level. Both cartography and conceptual modeling have developed guidelines for obtaining high quality visualizations. SEQUAL is a quality framework developed for understanding quality in conceptual models and modeling languages. In cartography such counterparts are not common to find. An attempt to adapt SEQUAL in the context of cartographic maps has been performed, named MAPQUAL. The paper presents MAPQUAL. Differences between quality of maps and quality of conceptual models are highlighted, pointing to guidelines for combined representations which are the current focus of our work. An example of such combined use is presented indicating the usefulness of a combined framework.

Keywords: Quality of models.

1 Introduction

A *conceptual model* is traditionally defined as a description of the phenomena in a domain at some level of abstraction, which is expressed in a semi-formal or formal visual language. The field has spawn from information systems development and computer science with methodologies like Data Flow Diagram (DFD) [9], Entity Relationship diagrams (ER)[5] and more recently Unified Modeling Language (UML) [8] and Business Process Modeling Notation (BPMN) [29]. The languages used for conceptual modeling largely contain nodes and links between node, and containment relationships. In conceptual modeling and enterprise models a number of perspectives to modeling are distinguished. For instance the Zachman Framework in enterprise modeling [26] describes 6 perspectives or product abstraction; What (material) it is made of, How (process) it works and Where (location) the components are, relative to one another, Who is involved, When is tasks done relative to each other and Why. In conceptual modeling, we often deal with what (data modeling), how (process modeling), who (organizational and actor modeling), when (Behavioral and Temporal modeling), and why (Goal-oriented modeling). On the other hand the location aspect (Where) is seldom dealt with in detail.

T. Halpin et al. (Eds.): BPMDS 2009 and EMMSAD 2009, LNBIP 29, pp. 264–276, 2009.
© Springer-Verlag Berlin Heidelberg 2009

Cartography on the other hand, focuses on aspects of location, through the development of *maps*. In this work we define maps as an abstract representation that preserves the geographical, topological information. Maps can initially seem to be very different from conceptual models. However, many similarities among the disciplines can be found, as also Renolen[22] have recognized. On the other hand, we find current guidelines for quality of maps to be unstructured.

The ultimate goal of the work is to develop an understanding of quality of models when also including geographical constructs. To get to this we have developed a framework for understanding and assessing quality of maps (MAPQUAL), based on the SEQUAL-framework [13] for quality of models and modeling languages. Differences between SEQUAL and MAPQUAL are used to assess how combined geographical and conceptual models should be developed to achieve high quality models.

In section 2, we present background on SEQUAL and cartography. Section 3 provides a brief overview of MAPQUAL by illustrating the differences between SEQUAL and MAPQUAL. The application of a combined framework is illustrated using a case study from the healthcare domain in section 4 before summing up planned work for developing and evaluating an integrated approach.

2   Background and Related Work

This work is based on two areas: conceptual modeling/quality of models and cartography.

2.1   Quality of Models

Since the early nineties, much work has been done relative to analyzing the quality of models. Early proposals for quality goals for conceptual models and requirement specifications as summarized by Davis et al. [7] included many useful aspects, but unfortunately poorly structured. They are also often restricted in the kind of models they regard (e.g. requirements specifications [7]) or the modeling language (e.g. ER-models [16] or process models [11,24]). Another limitation of many approaches to evaluating modeling languages is that they focus almost entirely on the expressiveness of the language (e.g. relative to some ontology, such as Bunge-Wand-Weber [27]). At NTNU one have earlier developed a more comprehensive and generic framework for evaluating modeling approaches, called SEQUAL [12,13]. SEQUAL has the following properties:

- It distinguishes between goals and means by separating what you are trying to achieve from how to achieve it.
- It can be used for evaluation of models and modeling languages in general, but can also be extended for the evaluation of particular types of models.
- It is closely linked to linguistic and semiotic concepts. In particular, the core of the framework including the discussion on syntax, semantics, and pragmatics is parallel to the use of these notions in the semiotic theory of Morris (see e.g. [20] for an introduction).
- It is based on a constructivistic world-view, recognizing that models are usually created as part of a dialogue between the participants involved in modeling, whose knowledge of the modeling domain and potentially the domain itself changes as modeling takes place.

The framework has earlier been used for evaluation of modeling and modeling languages of a large number of perspectives, including data, object, process, enterprise, and goal-oriented modeling. Quality has been defined referring to the correspondence between statements belonging to the following sets:

- *G,* the set of goals of the modeling task.
- *L,* the language extension, i.e., the set of all statements that are possible to make according to the rules of the modeling languages used.
- *D*, the domain, i.e., the set of all statements that can be stated about the situation.
- *M*, the externalized model itself.
- *K*, the explicit knowledge relevant to the domain of the audience.
- *I*, the social actor interpretation, i.e., the set of all statements that the audience interprets that an externalized model consists of.
- *T*, the technical actor interpretation, i.e., the statements in the model as 'interpreted' by modeling tools.

The main quality types are described briefly below:

- Physical quality: The basic quality goal is that the externalized model *M* is available to the relevant social and technical actors.
- Empirical quality deals with predictable error frequencies when a model *M* is read or written by different social actors
- Syntactic quality is the correspondence between the model *M* and the language extension *L*.
- Semantic quality is the correspondence between the model *M* and the domain *D*. This includes validity and completeness.
- Perceived semantic quality is the similar correspondence between the social actor interpretation *I* of a model *M* and his or hers current knowledge *K* of domain *D*.
- Pragmatic quality is the correspondence between the model *M* and the actor interpretation *(I* and *T)* and application of it. One differentiates between social pragmatic quality (to what extent people understand and are able to learn from and use the models) and technical pragmatic quality (to what extent tools can be made that can interpret the models). In addition, one include under pragmatic quality the extent that the participants after interpreting the model learn based on the model (increase *K*) and that the audience are able to change the domain *D* if this is beneficially to achieve the goals of modeling.
- The goal defined for social quality is agreement among social actor's interpretations.
- The organizational quality of the model relates to that all statements in the model *M* contribute to fulfilling the goals of modeling *G*, and that all the goals of modeling *G* are addressed through the model *M*.

Language quality relates the modeling language used to the other sets. Six quality areas for language quality are defined.

- Domain appropriateness. This relates the language and the domain. Ideally, the language must be powerful enough to express anything in the domain, not having what [27] terms construct deficit. On the other hand, you should not be able to express things that are not in the domain, i.e. what is termed construct excess [27]. Domain appropriateness is primarily a mean to achieve semantic quality.

- Participant appropriateness relates the social actors' explicit knowledge to the language. Do the participants have the necessary knowledge of the modeling language to understand the models created in the language? Participant appropriateness is primarily a mean to achieve pragmatic quality.
- Modeler appropriateness: This area relates the language extension to the participant knowledge. The goal is that there are no statements in the explicit knowledge of the modeler that cannot be expressed in the language. Modeler appropriateness is primarily a mean to achieve semantic quality.
- Comprehensibility appropriateness relates the language to the social actor interpretation. The goal is that the participants in the modeling effort using the language understand all the possible statements of the language. Comprehensibility appropriateness is primarily a mean to achieve empirical and pragmatic quality.
- Tool appropriateness relates the language to the technical audience interpretations. For tool interpretation, it is especially important that the language lend itself to automatic reasoning. This requires formality (i.e. both formal syntax and semantics being operational and/or logical), but formality is not necessarily enough, since the reasoning must also be efficient. This is covered by analyzability (to exploit any mathematical semantics) and executability (to exploit any operational semantics). Different aspects of tool appropriateness are means to achieve syntactic, semantic and pragmatic quality (through formal syntax, mathematical semantics, and operational semantics).
- Organizational appropriateness relates the language to standards and other organizational needs within the organizational context of modeling. These are means to support achievement of organizational quality.

2.2 Quality of Maps

Maps have a solid history related to the making, studying and use. The area of cartography focus on this. A map is commonly a reference to a depiction of the world. We have defined maps as an abstract representation that preserves the geographical topological information. The definition thus also includes more unusual maps (e.g. diagrams such as metro-maps) as well as preserving the common understanding of maps. Although the history of map-making is much longer than the history of conceptual modeling, guidelines for quality of maps is less structured than guidelines for quality of models. On the other hand since the main purpose of a map is communication of meaning using signs (just as models), one would expect many of the same issues to be relevant.

In cartography the notion of map communication [14] has been recognized and methods towards understanding this have been developed. Human interpretation relates directly to this notion and one could argue that the communication models developed, including MacEachren's map use cube [14], are enabling methods for increasing the comprehension of the map.

Related to comprehension is the work by Bertin [3] on visual variables. In addition to the visual variables, attention towards classification of symbols has been suggested [23]. The foundation is the notion of the graphic primitives; *point*, *line* and *area*, which is considered to be main elements for constructing a map (the meta-meta model). Emphasizing these primitives can thus affect the empirical quality, such as for instance emphasizing of points to increase attention towards this concept. Another field that has been influential for discussion of empirical quality of maps is Gestalt psychology [28].

3 MAPQUAL

In [19] guidelines for quality of maps following the categories of SEQUAL have been developed. This section aims at investigating the most significant differences between the two frameworks. The results from the investigation will provide a basis for identifying problem areas when combining conceptual models and cartographic maps and thus pose as a basis for developing new guidelines with respect to this kind of combined models which will be exemplified in section 4.

The discussion is structured by each quality facet for both map/model quality and language quality highlighting the differences.

3.1 Language Quality

The differentiation between language and model (map) are not common to find in cartography. There exists no tradition of defining proper languages for making maps, although standardizations towards both symbol sets and rules for applying them exist. MAPQUAL recognize this and aims at investigating how legacy cartographic research can be structured following the SEQUAL structure of language quality. The discussion will first go into some foundational differences on the meta-meta level and then investigate each quality facet and shed light on whether there are differences between the two frameworks or not.

Cartography revolves, generally, around geographical information which is strongly reflected in the visualization used. Generally the visualization method can be said to comprise three graphic primitives, namely; point, line and area and relations between these (Points being within an area, line crossing an area etc). This is inherently different from meta-meta models in conceptual modeling which usually comprise only nodes and links between notes, in addition to containment.

- Domain appropriateness: Due to the lack of discussion and formal separation of domain and language in cartography, MAPQUAL is similar to SEQUAL with respect to domain appropriateness. It is believed that most of the rational in SEQUAL holds true for a cartographic context even when a formal separation and definition of cartographic domain and language occurs.
- Participant appropriateness: As mentioned by Nossum [19], cartography has a tradition of exploiting the "natural" or cognitive knowledge of participants to a large extent. In conceptual modeling the tradition of creating a new language and thus disseminate this knowledge is more common. While of course both approaches consider the fundamental human perception research they approach it slightly differently. Although they have different approaches to participant appropriateness, the understanding and discussion of participant appropriateness of a language is fairly similar in both MAPQUAL and SEQUAL.

- Cartographer (modeler) appropriateness: Similar to participant appropriateness, MAPQUAL and SEQUAL are similar with respect to cartographer appropriateness. Although it should be mentioned that there seems to be less emphasis in cartography towards this quality facet than in conceptual modeling.
- Comprehensibility appropriateness: Comprehensibility is divided into two discussions; conceptual basis and external representation. Conceptual basis comprise the discussion on which concepts that are included in the language. SEQUAL provides several concrete guidelines for the conceptual basis. These guidelines have validity in cartography as well as for conceptual modeling. Thus MAPQUAL and SEQUAL are similar in this respect. External representation focus on how the notation of the language is formed, i.e. the graphical aspects of the language. In this facet there are significant differences between MAPQUAL and SEQUAL. Cartography has a strong tradition of investigating graphic design principles and especially mentioned are so-called visual variables [3]. SEQUAL also draw on the visual variables, however MAPQUAL and cartography are more geared towards extensive use of these properties. Traditionally maps have a heavier focus on the use of colors and the use of texture as a visual technique. SEQUAL takes a free approach to composition of symbols. Such free composition of symbols cannot be a general guideline in cartography as the geographical attributes often are constraining this freedom. Thus one can argue that achieving high aesthetics in cartography is more complex than in conceptual modeling, where graph aesthetics can support the achievement of aesthetics. Concrete guidelines where SEQUAL differs from MAPQUAL are [12];

  - "Composition of symbols in aesthetically pleasing way (i.e. crossing lines, long lines etc)" Generally not applicable in cartography.
  - "A linking line between concepts indicates relationship" Semantics of lines are generally different in cartography.
  - "A line linking closed contours can have different colors or other graphical attributes -indicating an attribute or type of relationship" Semi-valid for cartography, however not in the context of relationship.

- Tool appropriateness: Tool appropriateness is traditionally not considered in cartography. Thus MAPQUAL are similar to SEQUAL on the discussion of tool appropriateness.
- Organizational quality: MAPQUAL is fairly similar to SEQUAL with respect to organizational appropriateness, although MAPQUAL focus more on a cartographic context and the current standardization efforts in this area.

3.2 Map/Model Quality

- Physical quality: MAPQUAL is fairly similar to SEQUAL with respect to physical quality. Cartography is traditionally more geared towards making tangible representation of maps (i.e. printed) -although this is shifting towards more intangible representations for instance in a software environment (i.e. web mapping tools). SEQUAL focus much on guidelines for a model environment and different functionalities that it should provide. It should be noted that these guidelines are adapted to an information systems context, however, the guidelines should hold true for a cartographic environment as well -especially for navigational functionality.

- Empirical quality: MAPQUAL shows significant differences from SEQUAL on the empirical quality of a map. This is mainly due to the differentiation between conceptual modeling and cartography and their inherent differences when it comes to abstraction of the information visualized. Colors are heavily used in cartography to separate different concepts from each other. In conceptual modeling the use of colors has been sparse and avoided to a large degree. [12] suggests to incorporate colors more in conceptual models, but to limit the numbers of different colors used. The inherent geographical attributes of cartographic concepts often restricts the freedom of layout modifications, such as choosing where a concept should be placed on a map. In more "radical" maps (such as a metro map) this freedom exists to some extent. There the freedom of layout is restrained mostly by the geographical topology posed by the concepts which is clearly more similar to conceptual modeling. The restriction of layout freedom induces quite strict possibilities of aesthetic changes to the map. Guidelines for increasing empirical quality of conceptual models base themselves, mostly, on the freedom of layout, supported by graph aesthetics. These guidelines can thus not be directly applied to a cartographic map. In cartography one could see the aesthetics and geographical attributes as orthogonal dimensions. Empirical quality is the facet of map/model quality where MAPQUAL and SEQUAL are most different. In cartography the domain is (mostly) concrete and physical of some sort. The visualization method conforms to this and attempts to preserve most of the concreteness of the information, for instance by restraining visualization by geographical attributes (i.e. location). Conceptual modeling, on the other hand, is much more geared towards information as such, showing relations among different information. An abstract representation of this information is thus preferred as a visualization method, for instance by keeping only core information and relations. Conceptual modeling and cartography shares the background for the guidelines for empirical quality. Shared roots can be found in Gestalt psychology and graphic design principles as well as the general field of aesthetics.
- Syntactical quality: In cartography there is a lack of formal languages in designing maps[19], thus the guidelines for syntactical quality in MAPQUAL are solely based on the syntactical quality presented in SEQUAL.
- Semantic and perceived semantic quality is the relation between the domain, map/model and social actor knowledge and interpretation. Thus, this facet is assumed to be generally applicable for cartography as well as for conceptual modeling. In cartography the quality of the data, in terms of measure errors and similar, is quite common to use as a semantic quality measure. It should be noted that such metrics does not necessarily cover all aspects of semantic quality as semantic and perceived semantic quality concentrates more on the statements made in the map versus the statements in the domain and their human perception and interpretation.
- Pragmatic quality: MAPQUAL has generally the same understanding of pragmatic quality as the understanding in SEQUAL. Human interpretation is probably the most covered aspect of pragmatic quality in cartography. It should be noted that MAPQUAL [19] does not include an extensive investigation in the research of human interpretation of maps (i.e. map communication) in cartography, but recognize that there are significant similarities between this and SEQUAL's

understanding of human interpretation. MAPQUAL and SEQUAL are thus more or less equal with respect to pragmatic quality. It should, however, not be neglected to take this quality facet into account when investigating quality properties of maps and models as pragmatic quality is recognized to be one of the most important quality facets for cartographic maps [19].

- Social quality: MAPQUAL base the discussion of social quality of cartographic maps solely on the discussion of social quality in SEQUAL.
- Organizational quality: Similar to social quality, organization quality in MAPQUAL is similar to organizational quality in SEQUAL. Emphasize is put into the potential benefits that cartography could receive by more applications of the understanding of organizational quality of maps.

An evaluation of MAPQUAL, reported in [19], was performed consisting of using one cartographic expert to evaluate the quality of a set of maps without using the framework. We then evaluated two maps in the same set using MAPQUAL as the guiding framework. Juxtaposing the overall results from these two evaluations provides an overview of differences and similarities. We found that most of the findings from the cartographic expert evaluation are recognized. Additionally the evaluation is more structured and covering all facets of the framework.

4 Quality of Integrated Conceptual and Topological Models

So far we have defined maps to be a kind of models. An underlying assumption has been that cartographic maps represent, primarily, geographic concepts. However, cartographic maps can easily represent also non-geographic concepts. Some research has been put into applying cartographic visualization techniques on general non-geographic information [18,25] and the opposite, applying general information visualization techniques on geographic information. However, little work has looked on the possibilities of combining conceptual models with cartographic maps. When investigating and comparing MAPQUAL and SEQUAL, we found the largest difference being rooted in the difference of the underlying meta-meta model of maps and conceptual models, and how this influences guidelines for language design to achieve comprehensibility appropriateness of the combined language and thus potentially empirical and pragmatic quality of the model. Some important aspects are:

1. Clearly discriminate between geographical oriented lines and conceptual lines (relationships)
2. Clearly differentiate between nodes (concept) which are often depicted by a geometric shape, and geographic areas (by texture or color for instance)
3. Indicate topological information by positioning of conceptual nodes according to the topology where relevant.
4. Position concepts according to their temporal nearness.
5. Conceptualize geographical position when the conceptual structures are the most important (e.g. as a location-concept)

To investigate this further, we are currently experimenting with applications in the medical domain. Work in the medical domain is often highly dependent on the spatial properties of concepts, such as the location of tasks, equipment, staff and patients.

Additionally the conceptual properties are important, such as staffs relation to tasks (e.g. scheduled tasks), doctors responsibilities for specific patients and similar.

One particular complex task in medical work is the self-coordination each staff member needs to undertake. At any given day a doctor has a set of tasks that needs to be performed. These tasks may be scheduled in advance, or they may occur spontaneously (i.e. emergencies). The doctor needs to coordinate himself by deciding what tasks he performs, and when he performs them. This decision can potentially be a complex task, involving elements like;

- Most effective sequence of tasks based on
    o Location of task (e.g. nearness from current position)
    o Importance of tasks
    o Magnitude of task
- When the task is to be performed (i.e. present or future)
    o Involved patients
    o State (health status of patients)
    o Location (if they are at the task location)
- Involved actors (other staff members)
    o Location (if they are at (or near) the task location)
    o State (availability etc.)

Research, mainly from the field of CSCW, suggests that providing awareness of the hospital environment is one mean to lower the complexity of the decision-making. Both a focus towards the spatial dimension (i.e. location), but also the conceptual dimension (i.e. state, relationship etc.) is needed [1,2].

The spatial dimension in indoor environments is commonly visualized either directly in a floor-plan (i.e. a map) [15] or as an attribute in a diagram-like fashion [2]. Both approaches aim at visualizing the spatial dimension as well as the conceptual dimension including relationships, state and similar - which is an instance level conceptual model of the environment in question. However, both approaches focus the visualization towards their respective field (i.e. floor map on spatial dimension, diagram on conceptual dimension) without successfully obtaining a good communication of both dimensions at the same time.

The following will illustrate two distinctly different ways of representing a situation which is directly associated with a typical situation at a hospital. The scenario is based in an operating ward. Several different actors (patients, doctors, surgeons, nurses etc) are working in the environment each having their respective relations to activities (tasks) and other actors. Two activities (surgeries) are included, one which is in progression and one that is scheduled. Additionally a patient (L.S.) is having an emergency. The main user is intended to be the surgeon; ``B.L.''. Combined this provides an illustrative model which can be visualized in different ways. The following two different visualizations illustrate the necessity of developing guidelines for understanding of quality of such mixed representations.

Figure 1 illustrates a floor plan visualization of the model. Concepts are placed absolute in the floor plan and relationships are visualized by traditional arrows. The temporal nearness of the environment is communicated, although not explicitly. Taken into account that the scenario is situated only in one floor minimizes the complexity the visualization has to deal with. When incorporating several floors and buildings (as was the case in e.g. [2] will increase this complexity.

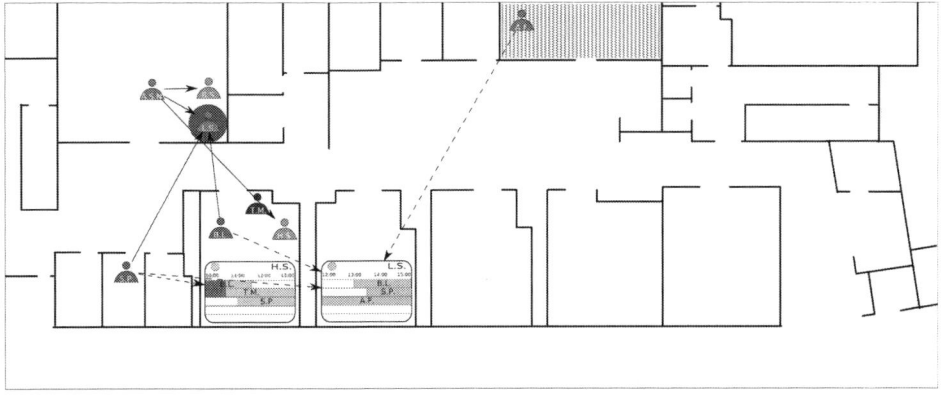

Fig. 1. Floor plan visualization of operating ward

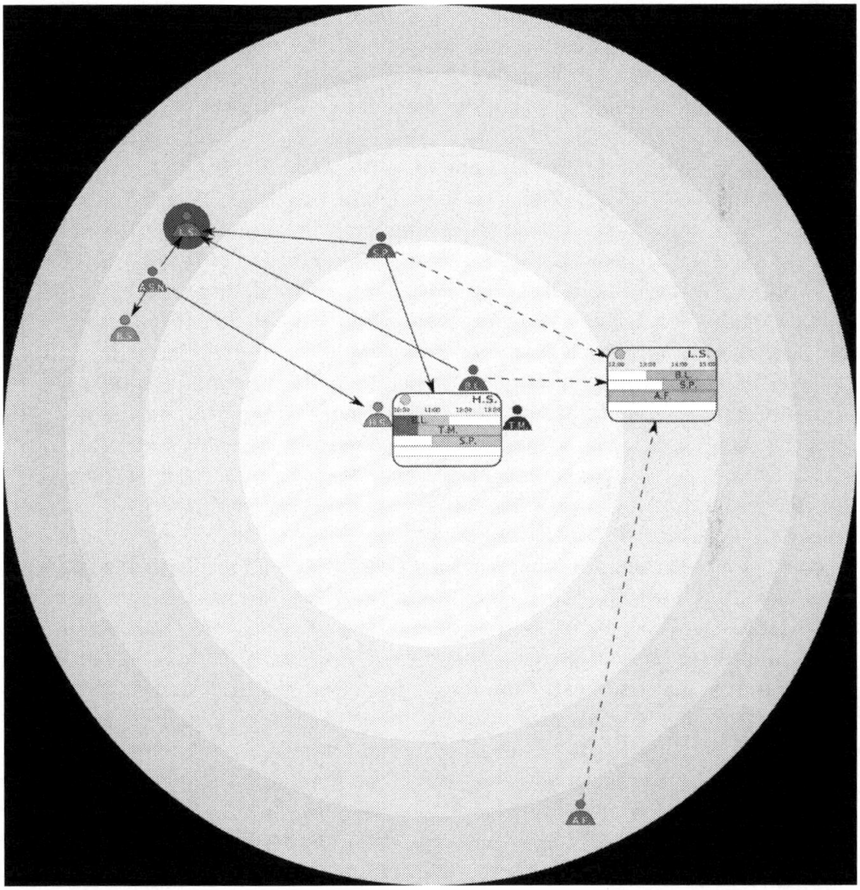

Fig. 2. Visualization of operating ward emphasizing the temporal nearness

Figure 2 positions the concepts according to their relative temporal nearness (i.e. temporal topology). The temporal nearness is communicated using scaled circles [4]. Relative nearness is conveyed by using the same scaled circles approach on the different actors. It is believed this visualization is better suited at visualizing the model when the actors know the spatial environment of the model, which is the case for the scenario, following guideline 3 and 4 above.

5   Conclusion and Future Work

Map quality as structured in MAPQUAL is a new approach to understanding quality in maps. During this work we have primarily adapted the notion of SEQUAL into a cartographic context. We believe all facets of map quality could benefit from a more thorough investigation. Specifically we would suggest that more effort is put into adapting current knowledge of map design into the MAPQUAL map quality facets, thus making it more comprehensive with respect to cartography. The work by MacEachren, especially MacEachren [14] should be further investigated, as well as more recent cartographic research such as mobile and ubiquitous cartography [10]. Including current scientific knowledge on map quality, further efforts in identifying needs from the society/industry is also suggested in an effort to minimize issues with acceptance as discussed by Moody [17].

Cartographic language quality and understanding should be investigated in a similar matter as the research on conceptual modeling languages. We would like to put emphasize on the importance of the meta-language (meta-meta-model) and modeling of this, for instance in a fashion similar to domain-specific languages (DSL) [6]. Much effort is put into this in the field of conceptual modeling, and we strongly believe much of this knowledge is directly applicable in cartography. However, cartographic languages often inherit more complexity than conceptual modeling languages, thus resulting in more complex meta-languages (including point, line and area) - investigation in the complexity of cartographic meta-languages and the possibilities for modeling languages based on them should be performed.

As indicated in the previous section, we are also investigating the issues when removing the separation of conceptual models and cartographic maps by combining them in one single model. It is hypothesized that an integrated visualization focusing on the conceptual information while emphasizing the spatial properties is better suited for communicating the information as a whole and thus, supporting the coordination work of hospital workers. A realization that the location property of concepts implicitly states the temporal topology of concepts is important in the experiments. This allow for variants that emphasize the temporal nearness and abstract away the absolute location from the visualization. To test the hypothesis, several different ways of representing the situation will be developed. The properties of the different representations will exhibit different qualities based on the guidelines of such mixed representations. Experimentation of the comprehensibility of different representations that either breaks of fulfill quality aspects from both SEQUAL, MAPQUAL and a combination where differences are eradicated will be undertaken. Results from this experimentation will provide a sound basis for developing guidelines for models which integrates the conceptual and spatial dimension.

References

1. Bardram, J., Bossen, C.: Mobility Work: The Spatial Dimension of Collaboration at a Hospital. Computer Supported Cooperative Work 14, 131–160 (2005)
2. Bardram, J., Hansen, T.R., Soegaard, M.: AwareMedia – A Shared Interactive Display Supporting Social, Temporal, and Spatial Awareness in Surgery. In: Proceedings of CSCW 2006, Banff, Alberta, Canada, November 4-8 (2006)
3. Bertin, J.: Semiology of Graphics: Diagrams, Networks, Maps. University of Wisconsin Press (1983)
4. Bjørke, J.T.: Kartografisk kommunikasjon (2005),
   http://www.geoforum.no/forskOgUtdan/
   kartografisk-litteratur/kartografisk_kommunikasjon.pdf/
5. Chen, P.: The Entity-Relationship model – Toward a Unified View of Data. ACM Transactions on Database Systems (TODS) 1(1), 9–36 (1976)
6. Cook, S.: Domain-Specific Modeling and Model Driven Architecture. MDA Journal, 2–10 (January 2004)
7. Davis, A., Overmeyer, M., Jordan, S., Caruso, K., Dandashi, J., Dinh, F., Kincaid, A., Ledeboer, G., Reynolds, G., Sitaram, P., Ta, P., Theofanos, M.: Identifying and Measuring Quality in a Software Requirements Specification. In: Proceedings of the First International Software Metrics Symposium, pp. 141–152 (1993)
8. Fowler, M.: UML Distilled: Applying the Standard Object Modeling Language. Addison Wesley, Reading (2003)
9. Gane, C., Sarson, T.: Structured Systems Analysis: Tools and Techniques. Prentice Hall Professional Technical Reference (1979)
10. Gartner, G., Bennett, D., Morita, T.: Towards Ubiquitous Cartography. Cartography and Geographic Information Science 34(4), 247–257 (2007)
11. Hepp, M., Roman, D.: An Ontology Framework for Semantic Business Process Management. In: 8th International Conference Wirtschaftsinformatik, Karlsruhe, Germany, pp. 423–440 (2007)
12. Krogstie, J., Sølvberg, A.: Information Systems Engineering - Conceptual Modeling in a Quality Perspective, Kompendiumforlaget (2003)
13. Lillehagen, F., Krogstie, J.: Active Knowledge Modeling of Enterprises. Springer, New York (2008)
14. MacEachren, A.: How Maps Work. Guilford Press, New York (1995)
15. McCarty, J.F., Meidel, E.S.: ActiveMap: A Visualization Tool for Location Awareness to Support Informal Interactions. In: Gellersen, H.-W. (ed.) HUC 1999. LNCS, vol. 1707, p. 158. Springer, Heidelberg (1999)
16. Moody, D.L., Shanks, G.G.: What Makes a Good Data Model? Evaluating the Quality of Entity Relationship Models. In: Loucopoulos, P. (ed.) ER 1994. LNCS, vol. 881, pp. 94–111. Springer, Heidelberg (1994)
17. Moody, D.: Theoretical and Practical Issues in Evaluating the Quality of Conceptual Models: Current State and Future Directions. Data & Knowledge Engineering 55(3), 243–276 (2005)
18. Moody, D., van Hillergersberg, J.: Evaluating the Visual Syntax of UML: Improving the Cognitive Effectiveness of the UML Family of Diagrams. In: Proceedings of Software Language Engineering (SLE 2008), Toulouse, France, September 29-30 (2008)
19. Nossum, A.: MAPQUAL: Understanding Quality in Cartographic Maps, Technical report, Norwegian Technical University of Science and Technology (2008)
20. Nöth, W.: Handbook of Semiotics. Indiana University Press (1990)

21. Opdahl, A., Henderson-Sellers, B.: Ontological Evaluation of the UML Using the Bunge–Wand–Weber Model. Software and Systems Modeling (2002)
22. Renolen, A.: Concepts and Methods for Modeling Temporal and Spatiotemporal Information, PhD thesis, NTNU (1999)
23. Robinson, A., Sale, R., Morrison, J.: Elements of Cartography. John Wiley & Sons, New York (1995)
24. Sedera, W., Rosemann, M., Doebeli, G.: A Process Modelling Success Model: Insights From A Case Study. In: 11th European Conference on Information Systems, Naples, Italy (2005)
25. Skupin, A., Fabrikant, S.: Spatialisation Methods: A Cartographic Research Agenda for Non-geographic Information Visualization. Cartography and Geographic Information Science 30(2), 99–119 (2003)
26. Zachman, J.A.: A framework for information systems architecture. IBM Systems Journal 26(3), 276–291 (1987)
27. Wand, Y., Weber, R.: On the Ontological Expressiveness of Information Systems Analysis and Design Grammars. Journal of Information Systems 3(4), 217–237 (1993)
28. Ware, C.: Information Visualization: Perception for Design. Morgan Kaufmann, San Francisco (2004)
29. White, S.A.: Introduction to BPMN, IBM Cooperation (2004)

Masev (Multiagent System Software Engineering Evaluation Framework)

Emilia Garcia, Adriana Giret, and Vicente Botti

Departamento de Sistemas Informaticos y Computacion,
Universidad Politecnica de Valencia
{mgarcia,agiret,vbotti}@dsic.upv.es

Abstract. Recently a great number of methods and frameworks to develop multiagent systems have appeared. It makes difficult the selection between one and another. Because of that the evaluation of multiagent system software engineering techniques is an open research topic. This paper presents an evaluation framework for analyzing and comparing methods and tools for developing multiagent systems. Furthermore, four examples of usage are presented and analyzed.

1 Introduction

Nowadays, on the market there are a great number of methods and frameworks to develop multiagent systems (MAS), almost one for each agent-research group. Each proposal has focused on different aspects, offering different functionality with different level of detail [1,2].

This situation makes the selection of one or another multiagent development tool, a very hard task. In the last few years the evaluation of MAS software engineering techniques has gained the research community attention, deriving in standardization efforts. Despite this, there is no complete and systematic way to evaluate MAS development methods and tools.

In this work we try to contribute a framework that deals with some open issues in the field of software engineering MAS evaluation. Masev[1] (MAs Software engineering EValuation framework) is an online application that allows analyzing and comparing methods, techniques and environments for developing MAS. Moreover, Masev allows the evaluation of how these methods and tools support the development of Organizational MAS and Service-oriented MAS.

The evaluation process followed by Masev is based on the standard ISO 14598 and some critical reviews of it [3]. Firstly, the purpose of the evaluation and which types of tools to evaluate were identified based on different studies of the state of the art (Section 2). Secondly, the evaluation framework was defined specifying the evaluation criteria and a metric that allows obtaining quantitative results (Section 3). Thirdly, Masev was implemented (Section 4) and a case study was designed to prove the evaluation framework (Section 4.1). Finally, the case study was executed in order to get some empirical evaluation of the tool.

---

[1] http://masev.gti-ia.dsic.upv.es/

T. Halpin et al. (Eds.): BPMDS 2009 and EMMSAD 2009, LNBIP 29, pp. 277–290, 2009.

2   Background

Following, some of the most relevant studies on the evaluation of MAS engineering techniques are presented.

Some works, like [5,4,2] focus their efforts on the analysis of methodologies, but do not analyze the tools that provide support for these methodologies. Nevertheless, this is a very important feature because a well-defined methodology loses a great part of its functionality if there is no sound and complete tool to apply it easily. Furthermore, these works do not analyze economical aspects (like the availability of documentation and examples of the studied methodologies) and the offered support for MAS issues such as ontologies, organizational MAS and so on.

Eiter and Mascardi [6] analyze environments for developing software agents. They provide a methodology and general guidelines for selecting a MASDK (MAS Development Kit). Bitting and Carter [7] use the criteria established by Eiter and Mascardi to analyze and compare five MASDKs. In order to obtain objective results from the evaluation Bitting and Carter add a quantitative evaluation. This work does not analyze the gap between modeling and platform implementation which is studied by Sudeikat and Braunch in [8].

Works like [9,10] not only provide a list of concepts to analyze but they facilitate the evaluation task providing a questionnaire. The use of questionnaires makes the answers be more concrete and easy to compare. Also it reduces the evaluation time and simplifies the evaluation process.

The main lack of [9,10] is that they only evaluate methodologies and do not take into account the other tools and techniques needed in the MAS development process. Furthermore, they do not take into account the gap between what is proposed by the methods and the final models and implementation code.

Currently, there is no tool that implements and simplifies the evaluation process and the comparison task. The works related with this topic only provide theoretical guidelines and some comparison of a few methods and tools in a specific moment. If any of these methods or tools improves or adds new functionality, the evaluation results will be outdated. Furthermore, there is no comparative repository of the current methods and techniques to develop MAS.

Finally, from these studies we have detected two approaches that are getting more and more importance as powerful paradigms for developing complex systems: Organizational MAS and Service-oriented MAS. Both approaches require new techniques and specific features to be developed. For this reason, studies of the state of the art in these paradigms and about which new requirements arise in their development process have been done. The results of these studies can be consulted in [11,12].

3   Specification of the Evaluation

Because of the different perspectives, the identification of a set of independent, orthogonal features which completely characterize the MAS development process

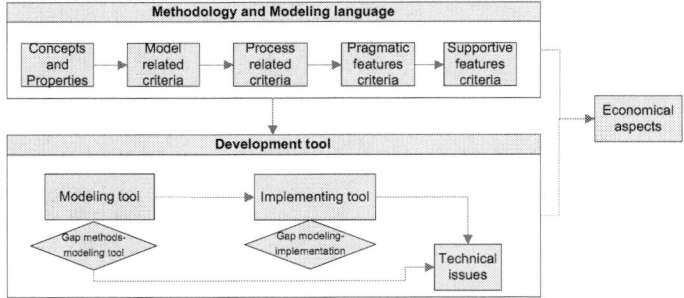

Fig. 1. Criteria classification

is a difficult task. The selected criteria for this evaluation framework are derived from the studies related in Section 2. These criteria takes into account traditional software engineering features and MAS specific characteristics. It tries to cover the whole development process, from the extraction of requirements to the implementation stage.

The use of evaluation questionnaires help in facilitating, standardizing and simplifying the evaluation task. For that reason, the selected criteria are specified as a set of questions and their possible answers.

Due to space limitations, Section 3.1 does not explain in detail each criterion and only a brief overview of each evaluated dimension is presented. For further information see [13].

A quantitative evaluation offers a fast and general evaluation overview which allows to compare and evaluate methods and tools easily. For that reason in Section 3.2 a method to obtain numerical results of the evaluation is presented. This metric is based on previous works like [7,14].

3.1   Criteria

In order to cover all the necessary method characteristics and tools features from the requirements extraction stage to the final implementation code, the evaluation criteria are structured in two main dimensions: (1) Methodology and Modeling language; (2) Development tools that involves the Modeling tool and the Implementation tool (See Figure 1).

The **Methodology and modeling language** dimensions defines a process for evaluating methodologies and modeling languages, comparing their strengths, their weaknesses and identifying ways to improve on a particular methodological feature. These criteria include 71 criteria and analyze methodologies from five different points of view: (1) *Concepts and properties criteria* that evaluate whether or not a methodology adheres to the features of agent and MAS; (2) *Model related criteria* that deal with various aspects of a methodology's models and notational components, including the concepts represented by the models, and their expressiveness and other software engineering issues; (3) *Process related criteria* that analyze the development process and which guidelines offer the methodology for each development stage; (4) *Pragmatic features criteria* that assess software engineering features that evaluate the techniques provided by the methodology for the execution of its process steps and for the development of its models; (5) *Supportive feature criteria* that include high-level and complementary features of MAS and the offered support to the integration with other techniques and technologies. This classification is based on [2].

The methodology provides guidelines to help developers during the development process, but methodologies are only theoretical specifications and **Development tools** are needed to create the models and the final implementation. The analysis of the development tools includes 65 criteria and, as shown in Figure 1, it is divided into five dimensions: (1) the *Modeling tool*; allows the transformation of the abstract concepts and ideas of the methodology into diagrams and models using a specific modeling language. This dimension analyzes the features and the functionality of these tools. (2) The *Gap between methods and the modeling tool dimension* analyzes how the modeling tool covers the specific features of a methodology. (3) The *Implementing tool* allows the transformation between the models and the design of the application into final execution code. This category analyzes which support offers the implementing tool to develop MAS and also, it analyzes traditional software engineering features of this kind of tools. (4) *The gap between modeling and implementation dimension* analyze the gap between what is modeled and what can be finally implemented [8] and which parts of the code are derived automatically from the models. (5) *Technical issues dimension* analyzes traditional software engineering features that are related with the requirements of a tool to be installed, executed and used. These criteria should be applied to evaluate both for the modeling and the implementing tool.

Finally, *Economical aspects* have to be evaluated both for the methodologies and for the development tools. These criteria do not only include the cost of the application, also features like the vendor organization and the documentation offered are analyzed.

Masev also tries to analyze the new requirements for developing MAS in open-systems, with an organizational structure [11] and when MAS are integrated with web services [12].

In order to analyze which support is offered to develop **organizational MAS**, a set of 51 criteria is defined. These criteria are structured using the main classification presented in Figure 1. The methodology and modeling language dimension analyzes how the methodology and its models support the model of organizational MAS and which social guidelines are offered. Moreover, specific organizational concepts are analyzed based on five dimensions [15]: (1) Structural dimension; (2) Dynamic dimension; (3) Functional dimension; (4) Normative dimension; and (5) Environment dimension. The Development tools dimension analyzes how the Modeling tool and Implementing tool support the model and implementation of organizational concepts. These criteria analyzes which facilities are offered and how organizations are materialized in the models and in the final implementation.

In order to analyze which support is offered to develop service-oriented MAS, a set of 44 criteria is defined. These criteria are structured using the main classification presented in Figure 1. The Methodology and modeling language dimension analyzes the way in which the relationship between agents and services is considered. Furthermore, these criteria analyze in which development stages is considered this integration and which guidelines are offered. The Development tools dimension considers the Modeling tool and the Implementing tool. These criteria analyze the facilities offered to model and implement this kind of systems and, their communication and definition standards. Moreover, these criteria analyze how this integration is implemented and which tools are offered to translate between service and agent standards and viceversa.

3.2   Metric

Each established criterion is associated with a weight that represents the importance of this criterion ($\mathbf{W}$).

$\mathbf{max(P)}$ represents the best possible answer for each criterion.

$\mathbf{R}$ represents the evaluator answer for each criterion. Each possible answer is associated with a weight.

$$result = \frac{\sum(W \cdot R)}{\sum(W \cdot max(P))} \cdot 100 \tag{1}$$

When the answer can have multiple values, i.e., when the evaluator checks which features of a list support its approach, the second formula is used.

$$result = \frac{\sum(W \cdot \sum(R))}{\sum(W \cdot max(\sum(P)))} \cdot 100 \tag{2}$$

$\sum(R)$ represents the summation of the checked answers weight.

$max(\sum(P))$ represents the summation of all the answers that could be checked.

Finally, the numerical evaluation is the result of the dot product between the weight vector and the evaluation vector. This formula will be applied to each dimension and a global vision of the development state and the completeness of each method or tool in this category is obtained. These values are useful to compare different approaches rapidly because they give a fast overview that can be completed with the qualitative evaluation.

4   Masev

Masev is an online application that allows analyzing and comparing methods, techniques and environments for developing MAS. The main objective of Masev is to facilitate and simplify the evaluation and comparison task. For that reason, the criteria summarized in Section 3.1, including the special criteria to analyze Organizational MAS and Service-oriented MAS, are presented as a set of questionnaires. The use of questionnaires makes the answers be more concrete and

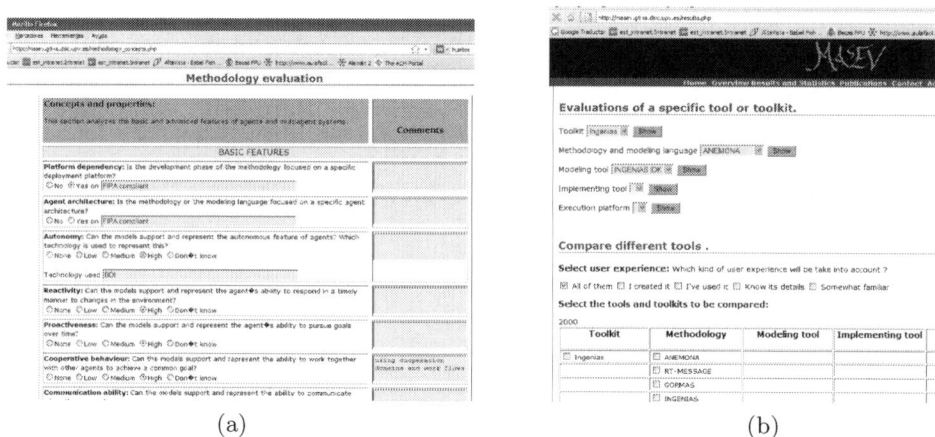

(a)   (b)

Fig. 2. a)Masev questionnaire b)Masev comparison module

easy to compare. Also it reduces the evaluation time and simplifies the evaluation process.

Other objectives of Masev are to achieve the greatest possible number of evaluations and to keep these evaluations constantly updated. For that reason, Masev is implemented as an online application that can be accessed anywhere and anytime. Moreover, the evaluation process has been simplified and the time needed to evaluate a tool has been reduced as much as possible.

The evaluation process consists of completing a sequence of forms about the method or tool to evaluate (Figure 2.a). Masev shows only the questionnaires related to the type of tool to evaluate. Moreover, it only shows the questionnaires related to organizations and services whether the evaluated tool offers some support to them. Furthermore, users can compare different evaluations of a specific method or tool or compare some methods or tools of the same type (Figure 2.b). The results are presented as summarized tables like Figure 3.

Masev also implements the metric proposed in Section 3 and allows obtaining numerical results of the evaluations. The weight of each criteria and the value of each answer has been defined taking into account the study summarized in Section 2 and it can be used as a default value. Despite this, users can define their own vector of weight.

4.1   Case Study

This section summarizes a case study in which four methodologies have been evaluated using Masev. Each methodology has been evaluated by his creator or by an expert. A brief introduction of each one is presented bellow.

RT-MESSAGE [16] is a methodology that covers the analysis, design and implementation of real-time multi-agent systems. In the analysis activity, RT-MESSAGE uses the same set of models set as the MESSAGE methodology. The method adds some real-time extensions in order to specify behaviors with

	RT_Message	Ingenias	Anemona	Gormas
	Concepts			
Platform dependency	Yes on ARTIS	No	Yes on FIPA compliant	No
Autonomy	High	Medium	High	Medium
Reactivity	High	High	High	High
Proactiveness	Medium	Medium	High	High
Cooperative behaviour	Medium	High	High	High
Communication ability	High	High	High	High
Communication language	Speech acts	Speech acts	Speech acts	Speech acts
Non-cooperative agents	Agree	Agree	Agree	Strongly Agree
Mental attitudes	Medium	High	High	Medium
Adaptability	Low	Low	Low	Low
Temporal continuity	High	Medium	High	Medium
Inferential capability	High	Low	Medium	Medium
Meta-management	Medium	Low	Low	Medium

Fig. 3. Results: Concept dimension

temporal restrictions. In the design, RT-MESSAGE proposes the use of SIMBA architecture in order to model real-time multiagent systems.

INGENIAS [17] is a methodology that covers the analysis, design and implementation of MAS, by integrating results from research in the area of agent technology with a well-established software development process, which in this case is the Rational Unified Process. It is also based on MESSAGE and it is supported by an integrated set of tools, the INGENIAS Development Kit (IDK).

ANEMONA [18] is a multi-agent system (MAS) methodology for holonic manufacturing system (HMS) analysis and design, based on HMS requirements. ANEMONA defines a mixed top-down and bottom-up development process, and provides HMS-specific guidelines to help the designer in identifying and implementing holons. In ANEMONA, the specified HMS is divided into concrete aspects that form different "views" of the system.

GORMAS [15] is a methodology for the analysis and design of open MAS, following an organizational point-of-view. It is based on INGENIAS and ANEMONA, extending all meta-models of this last one method. It covers the requirement analysis, the design of the organizational structure of the system and the design of its dynamics, mainly specifying the services offered by the organization, its internal structure and the norms that control its behavior.

Following, the evaluation results offered by Masev are shown. Due to space limitations, only some comments and conclusions of the evaluation are presented.

Figure 3 shows the results of the evaluation of the Concept dimension. From this table, it can be concluded that all the methodologies consider the basic features of agents and MAS. INGENIAS and GORMAS are independent of the execution platform, but ANEMONA is designed for Fipa compliant platforms and RT-MESSAGE for the ARTIS platform. A developer who has to choose between these methodologies should take into account which execution platform is going to use.

	RT_Message	Ingenias	Anemona	Gormas
		Model		
Modeling language representation	Mixed	Mixed	Mixed	Mixed
Metamodels	Yes	Yes	Yes	Yes
Model functionality	Roles, abilities, capabilities: agent, tasks/goals, organization Functionality: tasks/goals Interaction between agents: interaction Interaction with the environment: agent, environment Agent features: agent, organization	Roles, abilities, capabilities:agent model, organization model, task and goal model Functionality: agent model, organization model, task and goal model Interaction between agents: interaction model Interaction with the environment: environment model Agent features: agent model	Roles, abilities, capabilities: Agent model, and organization model Functionality: agent model and task and goal model Interaction between agents: interaction model Interaction with the environment: environment model Agent features: agent model and organization model	Roles, abilities, capabilities: organization, activity Functionality: organization, activity Interaction between agents: activity, interactions Interaction with the environment: environment Agent features: agent
Models dependence	Agree	Agree	Strongly Agree	Agree
Concurrency	Strongly Agree	Agree	Agree	Agree
Complete notation	Agree	Agree	Strongly Agree	Strongly Agree
Clarity	Agree	Agree	Strongly Agree	Agree
Completeness	Agree	Agree	Strongly Agree	Agree
Protocols	Strongly Agree	Agree	Strongly Agree	Strongly Agree
Different levels of abstraction	Neutral	Strongly Disagree	Strongly Agree	Strongly Agree
Human Computer Interaction	Disagree	Disagree	Neutral	Agree
Modularity	Agree	Neutral	Strongly Agree	Neutral
Extensible	Agree	Strongly Agree	Strongly Agree	Agree
Environment	Strongly Agree	Agree	Strongly Agree	Strongly Agree
Dynamic environment	Agree	Agree	Strongly Agree	Agree
Dynamic roles	Neutral	Disagree	Agree	Neutral
Resources	Strongly Agree	Agree	Strongly Agree	Strongly Agree
External systems	Agree	Agree	Strongly Agree	Agree

Fig. 4. Results: Model dimension

As shown in Figure 4, all the methodologies are based on meta-models and they use formal and informal modeling language to model the applications. They use different meta-models, but all of them offer the most important functionalities.

Figure 5 analyzes the development process of each methodology. All of them follow an established development process and cover the analysis and design stages. Despite this, INGENIAS does not support the extraction of requirements stage and GORMAS does not support the implementation stage.

The analysis of the pragmatic dimension shows there are no remarkable differences between them (Figure 6). On the contrary, this figure shows considerable differences respect to the architectures that support each methodology. Mobile agents are only supported by ANEMONA. All the approaches offer some support for developing Organizational MAS and how it is offered, is studied in Figures 7 and 8. Only GORMAS supports the integration between agents and services (Figure 9).

Despite that all the approaches offer some support for organizations, Figure 7 shows that each one offers different functionality. For example, GORMAS offers more facilities to develop several topology structures and it is the

	RT_Message	Ingenias	Anemona	Gormas
Process				
Development lifecycle	Iterative	RUP	Recursive, iterative and incremental	Iterative
Coverage of the lifecycle:				
Extraction of requirements:	Medium	None	Medium	Médium
Analysis:	High	High	High	High
Design:	High	Medium	High	High
Implementation:	High	Medium	Medium	None
Development approach	Top-down approach	Indeterminate	Both	Top-down approach
Approach towards MAS development	OO-based	Knowledge-engineering based	Agent oriented	OO-based
Application domain	Yes	Yes	Yes	No
Model-central element	Agents	Agents	Abstract agent or holon	Organizations
Interaction protocols	Agree	Neutral	Disagree	Agree
Consistency guidelines	Neutral	Agree	Agree	Agree
Estimating guidelines	Agree	Disagree	Disagree	Disagree
Support for decisions	Agree	Agree	Strongly Agree	Agree
Model derivation	Agree	Agree	Strongly Agree	Agree
Support for verification and validation	Disagree	Neutral	Neutral	Disagree
Client communication	Disagree	Disagree	Strongly Agree	Disagree
Models Reuse	Agree	Disagree	Neutral	Agree

Fig. 5. Results: Process dimension

	RT_Message	Ingenias	Anemona	Gormas
Pragmatic				
Unambiguity	Agree	Agree	Strongly Agree	Neutral
Preciseness of models	Agree	Agree	Strongly Agree	Neutral
Expressiveness	Agree	Agree	Strongly Agree	Neutral
Consistency checking	Disagree	Agree	Neutral	Agree
Notation simplicity	Agree	Agree	Strongly Agree	Neutral
Facility to understand	Neutral	Agree	Strongly Agree	Neutral
Facility to learn	Neutral	Agree	Strongly Agree	Neutral
Facility to use	Neutral	Neutral	Strongly Agree	Neutral
Refinement	Agree	Disagree	Strongly Agree	Agree
Documentation	Disagree	Agree	Strongly Agree	Agree
Examples	Neutral	Agree	Strongly Agree	Agree
Supportive				
Open systems	Disagree	Strongly Disagree	Disagree	Agree
Mobile agents	Disagree	Disagree	Neutral	Disagree
Security	Disagree	Strongly Disagree	Neutral	Disagree
Scalability	Small	Large	Large	Large
Support for mobile agents	Disagree	Disagree	Neutral	Disagree
Support for ontology	Agree	Disagree	Agree	Neutral
Support for MAS organizations	Agree	Agree	Neutral	Strongly Agree
Support for the integration with web services	Disagree	Strongly Disagree	Disagree	Agree

Fig. 6. Results: Pragmatic and Supportive dimensions

	RT_Message	Ingenias	Anemona	Gormas
Model central-element	No	No	No	Yes
Coverage of the lifecycle: Extraction of requirements:	High	None	Low	Medium
Analysis:	High	Medium	Medium	High
Design:	Médium	Medium	Medium	High
Implementation:	Low	Low	Low	Low
Social patterns	Neutral	Strongly Disagree	Disagree	Strongly Agree
Structural				
Topologies	Flat-Structure Pyramid Style	Flat-Structure	Holonic	Flat-Structure Pyramid Style Chain of Values matrix Structure-in-Five Co-optation
Topology guidelines	Disagree	Strongly Disagree	Strongly Agree	Agree
Other guidelines	No	No	No	Yes
Composed organization	Disagree	Strongly Disagree	Strongly Agree	Agree
Social relationships	Communication links Authority links	Knowledge links Communication links Authority links	Knowledge links Communication links Authority links	Knowledge links Communication links Authority links
Role dependencies	Communication Coordination Authority	Communication Coordination Authority	Communication Coordination Authority	Heritage Coordination Authority
Topology patterns	No	No	Patterns of role dependencies	Patterns of social relationships
Meta-management based on norms	None	None	None	High
Dynamical models	---	----	The creation and destruction of the organizations How agents change their roles The creation and destruction of new roles	The creation and destruction of the organizations How agents go in/out of the organizations How agents change their roles The creation and destruction of new roles
Dynamic				
Context	Disagree	Strongly Disagree	Disagree	Agree
Heterogeneous agents	Agree	Strongly Disagree	Disagree	Agree
Functional				
Goals	Both	Both	Both	Both
Global goal decomposition	Agree	Agree	Strongly Agree	Strongly Agree
Functionality	Neutral	Agree	Strongly Agree	Agree

Fig. 7. Results: Organizational dimension

only one that offers guidelines to choose the most appropriate topology depending on the application requirements. Moreover, GORMAS is the only one that allows the definition of the internal norms of the agents and the organization, and the norms related to the interaction between them (Figure 8).

The analysis of how the methodologies support the integration of agents with service-oriented architectures shows that only GORMAS offers some support. GORMAS is focused on the analysis and design, and offers some guidelines for this stages. The type of integration proposed by GORMAS is bidirectional, which means that the agents can invoke services, and services can be invoked to agents.

Finally, Figure 10.a analyzes economical aspects and shows that neither methodology has a property license and all of them have been created in an academical environment. ANEMONA and RT-MESSAGE do not have recent updates, but INGENIAS and GORMAS are in constant development.

	RT_Message	Ingenias	Anemona	Gormas
	Normative			
Social norms	Disagree	Strongly Disagree	Disagree	Strongly Agree
Dynamic social norms	Disagree	Strongly Disagree	Disagree	Agree
Kinds of norms:	None	None	Deontic Legislatives Rewards	None
Temporal norms	Agree	Strongly Disagree	Strongly Disagree	Agree
Application level	Internal norms of the agents	None	None	Organization norms
Inconsistent states	Disagree	Strongly Disagree	Disagree	Neutral
Formal representation	No	No	No	Yes
	Environment			
Stakeholders	Agree	Strongly Disagree	Neutral	Strongly Agree
Depends on	Neutral	Strongly Disagree	Neutral	Agree
Resources	Neutral	Strongly Disagree	Strongly Agree	Strongly Agree
Perceptors and effectors	Neutral	Strongly Disagree	Strongly Agree	Strongly Agree
	Modeling language			
Modeling language representation	Informal	Informal	Mixed	Formal
Organizational models	None	there is an organizational model, but it is very simple	None	structural, functional, social, dynamic
Complete notation	Agree	Agree	Strongly Agree	Agree

Fig. 8. Results: Organizational dimension

	Gormas
Integration type	Agents and services can communicate in a bidirectional way.
Integrated methodology	Yes
Coverage of the lifecycle: Extraction of requirements:	Low
Analysis:	Médium
Design:	Médium
Implementation:	Low
Business process	Neutral
Development guidelines	Agree
Agents or services	Neutral
Services and norms	Agree
	Modeling language
Complete modeling language	Agree
Relationship between roles and services	Agree
Modeling language representation	Formal
Unambiguity	Neutral
Service descriptions	Formal
Completeness of service descriptions	Its functionality. Which entities provide it. Which entities are allowed to use it.
Semantics services	Agree
Interaction protocols	Service composition Service and agent composition
Publishing services	Service advertisement Service discovery

Fig. 9. Results: Services dimension

The numerical results presented in Figure 10.b have been obtained using the metric presented in Section 3 and Masev default criteria weights. The numbers in parentheses show the weight of each dimension to calculate the total value.

	RT_Message	Ingenias	Anemona	Gormas
Cost of the application	Free	Free	Free	Free
Cost of its documentation	Free	Free	Free	Free
Vendor organization	Academical vendor: UPV	Academical vendor:GRASIA, UCM	Academical vendor: UPV	Academical vendor: UPV
Updates	Neutral	Strongly Agree	Neutral	Agree
Technical service	Neutral	Agree	Agree	Disagree
Examples of academic use	2-5	More than 10	2-5	One
Examples of industrial use	One	2-5	2-5	Any

(a)

		RT-Message	Ingenias	Anemona	Gormas
Methodology	Concepts (3)	66,66	62,5	78,12	69,79
	Model (3)	78,04	66,46	93,29	80,48
	Process (3)	71,66	45,00	68,33	60,00
	Pragmatic (2)	57,40	69,44	96,30	59,26
	Supportive (1)	39,70	27,94	51,47	55,88
Economical aspects (1)		75	90,63	81,25	70,31
Total		67,59	59,95	80,35	67,35
Organizations		41,38	19,39	46,55	71,98
Services		0,00	0,00	0,00	52,00

(b)

Fig. 10. Results: Economic dimension

These results allow an overview comparison of the methodologies. For example, the results of the Concepts and Model dimension show that there are no significant differences between them in this area. The good results obtained in the Economical dimension show that they are free and offer good documentation. Finally, the results show that all the approaches offer some support for organizations, but GORMAS offers more functionality. Moreover, GORMAS is the only one that offers support for the development of service-oriented MAS.

4.2   Discussion

Masev has been successfully used to analyze and compare four MAS methodologies: RT-MESSAGE, INGENIAS, ANEMONA and GORMAS.

Despite the fact that no evaluator knew Masev, each evaluation process lasted about 15 minutes and facilitated the necessary information to analyze and compare these methodologies. Therefore, one can conclude that Masev simplifies the evaluation process. It produces a large volume of information in a very short time. No evaluator had problems during the evaluation process and the information was easily structured through Masev.

The comparatives provided by Masev have been very useful to analyze the tools and detect their weakness. MASEV structures the information in tabular form so it is very easy to find similarities and differences between the evaluated tools. Finally, the numerical results obtained allow an overview of the evaluated methodologies and a quick comparison of them.

The experiences from the case studies reveal that the informal evaluation makes the results totally dependent on the opinion of the evaluator. This fact introduces too much subjectivity in the process. Thus, Masev was prepared to support multiple evaluations of the same tool or methodology and to calculate the average value at the time of showing the comparative. Furthermore, Masev allows the user to select which types of evaluators will be considered, for example, a user can use only the information provided by the creators of the tool.

5   Conclusions and Future Work

Despite all the conferences and papers related to this topic there is no general and commonly adopted evaluation framework to analyze and compare all the necessary methods and tools for developing MAS. There is a fundamental need to have evaluation frameworks in order to get a measurement of the completeness or correctness of a given MAS development tool.

In this work, Masev has been presented. It is an online evaluation framework that allows analyzing and comparing methods, techniques and environments for developing MAS. Masev analyzes methods and tools through a set of criteria selected by studying the state of the art. These criteria are related to both system engineering dimensions and MAS features. They analyze the MAS development process from the requirement stage to the implementation of the final code taking into account the most important features and tools involved in the process. Furthermore, the support for developing organizational and service-oriented MAS is studied. In order to obtain quantitative results of the evaluation a metric has been added to Masev.

Finally, an analysis and comparison of four methodologies have successfully done using the Masev application. Masev simplifies the evaluation and comparison task. It is implemented as a web application in order to improve its accessibility and facilitate that users and creators of current agent methodologies and development tools evaluate them.

Masev could help developers to select the most appropriate MAS method and tools for developing a specific system. Moreover, developers can define the criteria weights taking into account the requirements of the system to be developed. With this information, Masev shows a ranking of the most appropriate methods and tools.

Furthermore, the Masev questionnaire summarizes the most important issues for developing MAS, organizational MAS and service-oriented MAS, so it could be used for MAS software engineering developers to detect and improve lacks in their methods and tools. Also, developers of new tools can understand this application as a way to publish their tools and demonstrate which is their contribution to the state of the art.

The final objective of Masev is to provide a repository of the most used MAS software engineering methods and tools.For that reason, our current work is to publish Masev in order to obtain the highest possible number of evaluations. Moreover, the evaluation of MAS execution platform will be added. Finally, we plan to study and add some techniques of formal evaluation into Masev.

References

1. Bordini, R.H., Dastani, M., Winikoff, M.: Current issues in multi-agent systems development (invited paper). In: O'Hare, G.M.P., Ricci, A., O'Grady, M.J., Dikenelli, O. (eds.) ESAW 2006. LNCS, vol. 4457, pp. 38–61. Springer, Heidelberg (2007)
2. Lin, C.E., Kavi, K.M., Sheldon, F.T., Daley, K.M., Abercrombie, R.K.: A methodology to evaluate agent oriented software engineering techniques. In: HICSS 2007: Proceedings of the 40th Annual Hawaii International Conference on System Sciences, p. 60. IEEE Computer Society, Los Alamitos (2007)
3. Punter, T., Kusters, R., Trienekens, J., Bemelmans, T., Brombacher, A.: The w-process for software product evaluation: A method for goal-oriented implementation of the iso 14598 standard. Software Quality Control 12(2), 137–158 (2004)

4. Sturm, A., Shehory, O.: A framework for evaluating agent-oriented methodologies. In: Giorgini, P., Henderson-Sellers, B., Winikoff, M. (eds.) AOIS 2003. LNCS, vol. 3030, pp. 94–109. Springer, Heidelberg (2004)
5. Cernuzzi, L., Rossi, G.: On the evaluation of agent oriented modeling methods. In: Proceedings of Agent Oriented Methodology Workshop (2002)
6. Eiter, T., Mascardi, V.: Comparing environments for developing software agents. AI Commun. 15(4), 169–197 (2002)
7. Bitting, E., Carter, J., Ghorbani, A.A.: Multiagent System Development Kits: An Evaluation. In: Proc. of the 1st Annual Conference on Communication Networks and Services Research (CNSR 2003), May 15-16, pp. 80–92 (2003)
8. Sudeikat, J., Braubach, L., Pokahr, A., Lamersdorf, W.: Evaluation of agent-oriented software methodologies examination of the gap between modeling and platform. In: Odell, J.J., Giorgini, P., Müller, J.P. (eds.) AOSE 2004. LNCS, vol. 3382, pp. 126–141. Springer, Heidelberg (2005)
9. Dam, K.H.: Evaluating and Comparing Agent-Oriented Software Engineering Methodologies. Master's thesis, Master of Applied Science in Information Technology - RMIT University, Australia (2003)
10. Tran, Q.N., Low, G.: Comparison of ten agent-oriented methodologies, 341–367 (2005)
11. Garcia, E., Argente, E., Giret, A., Botti, V.: Issues for organizational multiagent systems development. In: Sixth International Workshop From Agent Theory to Agent Implementation (AT2AI-6), pp. 59–65 (2008)
12. Garcia, E., Giret, A., Botti, V.: Software engineering for Service-oriented MAS. In: Klusch, M., Pĕchouček, M., Polleres, A. (eds.) CIA 2008. LNCS(LNAI), vol. 5180, pp. 86–100. Springer, Heidelberg (2008)
13. Garcia, E., Giret, A., Botti, V.: Towards an evaluation framework for MAS software engineering. In: Bui, T.D., Ho, T.V., Ha, Q.T. (eds.) PRIMA 2008. LNCS (LNAI), vol. 5357, pp. 197–205. Springer, Heidelberg (2008)
14. Dubielewicz, I., Hnatkowska, B., Huzar, Z., Tuzinkiewicz, L.: An Approach to Software Quality Specification and Evaluation (SPoQE). IFIP International Federation for Information Processing, vol. 227, pp. 155–166. Springer, Boston (2007)
15. Argente, E., Julian, V., Botti, V.: Mas modelling based on organizations. In: 9th Int. Workshop on Agent Oriented Software Engineering (AOSE2008), pp. 1–12 (2008)
16. Julian, V., Botti, V.: Developing real-time multiagent systems. Integrated Computer-Aided Engineering 11, 135–149 (2004)
17. Pavon, J., Gomez-Sanz, J., Fuentes, R.: The INGENIAS Methodology and Tools, ch. IX, pp. 236–276. Henderson-Sellers (2005)
18. Botti, V., Giret, A.: Anemona. a multi-agent methodology for holonic manufacturing systems. Springer Series in Advanced Manufacturing, vol. XVI, p. 214 (2008)

Transactions in ORM

E.O. de Brock

University of Groningen
Faculty of Economics and Business
P.O. Box 800, 9700 AV Groningen, The Netherlands
e.o.de.brock@rug.nl

Abstract. Languages for specifying information systems should not only contain a data *definition* (sub)language (DDL), i.e., a part for specifying *data structures*, but also a data *retrieval* (sub)language (DRL), i.e., a part for specifying *queries*, and a data *manipulation* (sub)language (DML), i.e., a part for specifying *transactions*.

The language ORM contains a DDL and a DRL (ConQuer), but it does not contain a sufficient DML as yet. We therefore propose an extension of ORM with a DML, for specifying transactions to be easily validated by domain experts.

We introduce the following set of standard classes of specifiable transactions: add an instance, add a query result, remove a subset, and change a subset. We also treat compound transactions in ORM.

In ORM there are usually several ways to specify something. For all transactions we therefore propose syntaxes, verbalizations, and diagrams as well. They allow for type-checking and easy validation by domain experts.

Keywords: ORM, DML, transaction, add, remove, change, syntax, verbalization, diagram, compound transaction.

1 Introduction

Languages for specifying information systems should not only consist of a data *definition* (sub)language (DDL), i.e., a part for specifying *data structures*, but also of a data *retrieval* (sub)language (DRL), i.e., a part for specifying *queries*, and of a data *manipulation* (sub)language (DML), i.e., a part for specifying *transactions*. In the well-known language SQL for example, the DDL typically contain CREATE-, DROP-, and ALTER-statements, the DRL typically SELECT-statements, and the DML typically INSERT-, DELETE- and UPDATE-statements.

The language ORM (Object-Role Modeling), extensively described in [1], started as a DDL. Later on the language was extended with a DRL, called ConQuer [2]. However, the language ORM does not yet contain a good and expressive DML. The operations **add** and **del** in [1] only apply to one fact/instance at a time. And although Balsters et al. do mention transactions in [3] and [4], they concentrate on dynamic rules as such, and do not give a syntax for data manipulation operations. In [3], adding actual operations to the ORM-language that explicitly model transactions is mentioned as future research.

T. Halpin et al. (Eds.): BPMDS 2009 and EMMSAD 2009, LNBIP 29, pp. 291–301, 2009.
© Springer-Verlag Berlin Heidelberg 2009

In this paper we propose an expressive extension of ORM with such a DML part, inspired by the expressiveness of the DML of SQL. We want to introduce a DML that is suitable for end users too (like the rest of ORM), so that transactions can be easily validated by domain experts. The language should also allow for type-checking etc. Our standard classes of specifiable transactions are: add an instance, add a query result, remove a subset, and change a subset. The transactions are used to populate, de-populate and re-populate a type. Together they constitute an expressive collection of transactions. All transactions apply to only one fact type (or one independent entity type) at a time. (Not only fact types but also independent entity types can have populations. However, since independent entity types can be treated similar to (unary) fact types, we will not treat them separately in this paper.)

By a transaction we mean an *attempt* to update the contents of the information system; the attempt fails when any constraint will be violated.

In ORM there are usually several ways to specify something, for instance verbalizations as well as diagrams. For all aforementioned classes of transactions we therefore propose a syntax (textual language), a verbalization, and a diagram (graphical language). The verbalizations of the transactions are "fully communication oriented" and are intended for communication with the domain experts. One of the merits of a separate graphical view of a transaction (one at a time) is that it can alternatively help in the discussion to determine the precise conditions in and effects of a transaction.

In sections 2 – 5 we subsequently treat each of the four aforementioned classes of transactions, i.e. add an instance, add a query result, remove a subset, and change a subset. For each class of transactions we subsequently introduce under (1) its ORM-syntax, under (2) its verbalization, and under (3) its diagram in terms of the ORM-syntax, verbalizations, and diagrams of its constituents respectively. The general structure we give here is more important than the actual syntax, verbalizations, and diagrams we chose. Each section continues with some illustrative examples under (4). In Section 6 we treat compound transactions. We end the paper with some concluding remarks and the future work we will address.

2   Addition of an Instance

We start with a simple class of transactions, the addition of a given instance to a fact type (or to an independent entity type) F. Suppose F is an n-ary fact type and $v_1, \ldots, v_n$ are the respective values for the instance to be added.

(1) We propose the following ORM-syntax: **ADD TO F VALUES** $(v_1; \ldots; v_n)$

(2) We define the verbalization of the transaction in terms of the verbalization of its constituents. We chose the verbalization of each value v to be that value itself.

> Verbalization(**ADD TO F VALUES** $(v_1; \ldots; v_n)$) =
>   ***add to*** Verbalization(F) Verbalization($v_1; \ldots; v_n$)

> where Verbalization(F) = ***fact type F***
> and Verbalization($v_1; \ldots; v_n$) = ***the instance with values*** $v_1, \ldots$ ***and*** v_n
> ***respectively***

In the unary case (i.e. when $n = 1$) the last part reduces to
Verbalization(v_1) = ***the instance with value*** v_1.

(3) We define the diagram for the transaction in terms of the diagrams of its constituents:

Diagram(**ADD TO** F **VALUES** $(v_1; ...; v_n)$) =

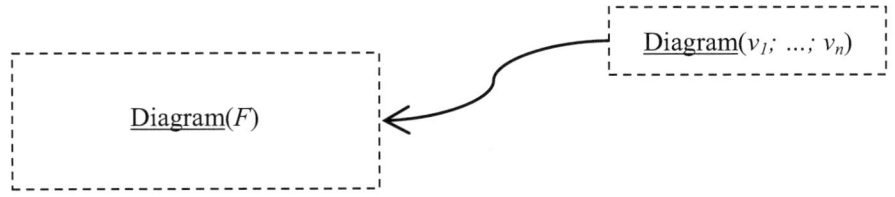

Fig. 1. Diagram for the addition of an instance (schematically)

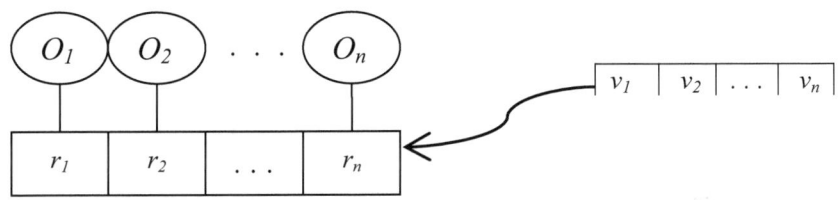

Fig. 2. Diagram for the addition of an instance (more concretely)

We leave out from the diagrams all (constraint) notations, such as those for uniqueness, mandatority, reference modes, (independent) entity/value type distinctions, etc.

(4) **Example.** We give as an example the addition of employee 123 called 'J. Smith' to a (binary) fact type called *Employee has Name*. This fact type has the following diagram:

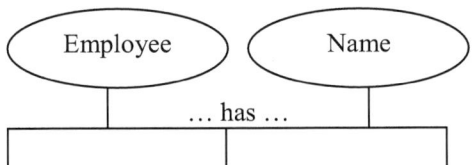

The ORM-syntax given under (1) for this addition will then result in:

ADD TO Employee has Name
VALUES (123, 'J. Smith')

Applying the verbalization rules given under (2) we get:

Verbalization(**ADD TO** Employee has Name **VALUES** (123, 'J. Smith')) =
   add to fact type Employee has Name
   the instance with values 123 ***and*** 'J. Smith' ***respectively***

Applying the diagram rules given under (3) we get the following diagram:

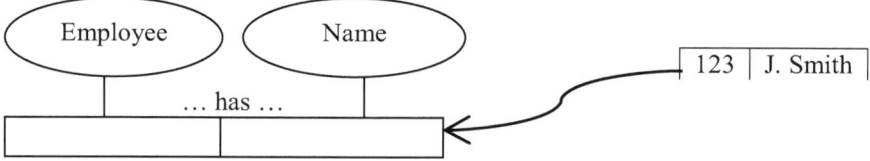

3 Addition of a Query Result

We continue with the addition of the result of a query q (multiple instances) to a fact type F. For the query-part we can make use of the retrieval language ConQuer [2].

(1) We propose the following ORM-syntax: **ADD TO F RESULT q**
   If the role order in q, say $(r_1; ...; r_n)$, is (perhaps) not the same as the role order in F then the expression $(r_1; ...; r_n)$ has to be added:

   ADD TO $F(r_1; ...; r_n)$ RESULT q instead of **ADD TO F RESULT** q.

(2) The verbalization of the transaction is expressed in terms of the verbalization of its constituents:

   Verbalization(**ADD TO F RESULT** q) =
   add to Verbalization(F) **the** Verbalization(q)

   where Verbalization(F) = **fact type F** (see Section 2)
   and Verbalization(q) heavily depends on q itself.

(3) We define the diagram for the transaction in terms of the diagrams of its constituents:

   Diagram(**ADD TO F RESULT** q) =

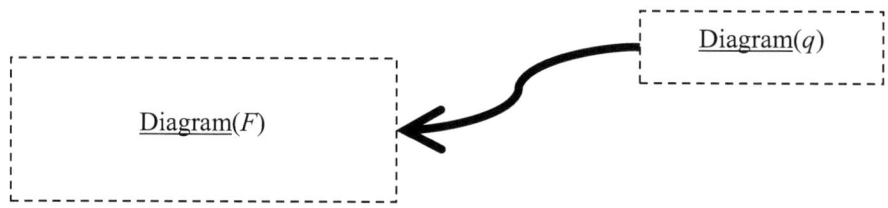

Fig. 3. Diagram for the addition of a query result (schematically)

Here the bold arrow suggests multiple instances, whereas the thin arrow in Figure 1 suggests a single instance.

For the query-part we use the retrieval language ConQuer. We want to represent ConQuer-expressions (such as queries and conditions) by a diagram too. We therefore propose the following graphical representation for a ConQuer-expression:

```
┌─────────────────────────────────┐
│                                 │
│     ConQuer-expression          │
│                                 │
│                              ╱  │
└─────────────────────────────╱───┘
```

Fig. 4. Diagram for a ConQuer-expression

(4) **Example.** We introduce 3 new fact types called *Applicant has Name*, *Applicant obtains Hire Advice*, and *Applicant receives Employee Number*, with the following diagrams:

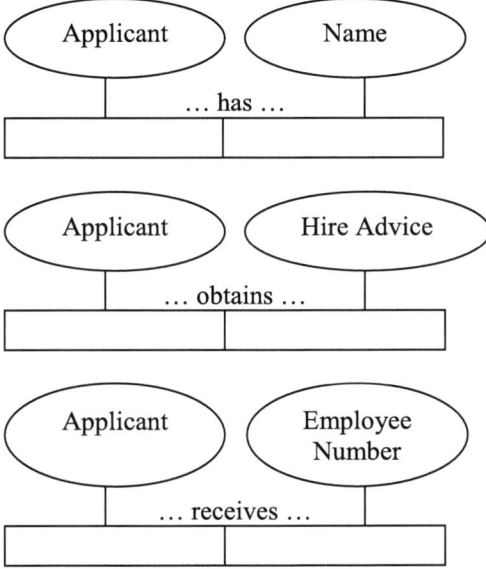

Now we want to add all applicants with the hire advice 'Yes' to the fact type *Employee has Name* introduced in Section 2. Then the underlying query q_0 expressed in ConQuer is

q_0 =Applicant
  └── receives √Employee Number
  └── has √Name
  └── obtains Hire Advice = 'Yes'

The ORM-syntax given under (1) for this addition will then result in:

ADD TO Employee has Name
RESULT Applicant
   └── receives √Employee Number
   └── has √Name
   └── obtains Hire Advice = 'Yes'

The verbalization of the query q_0 will be: Employee Number **and** Name **of each** Applicant **who** obtains Hire Advice **equals** 'Yes'.

Applying the verbalization rules given under (2) we then get:

> Verbalization(**ADD TO** Employee has Name **RESULT** q_0) =
> **add to fact type** Employee has Name **the** Employee Number **and** Name **of each** Applicant **who** obtains Hire Advice **equals** 'Yes'

Applying the diagram rules given under (3) we get the following diagram:

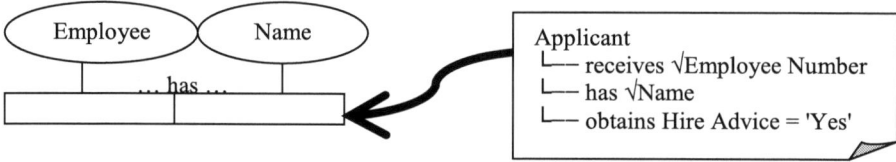

4   Removal of a Subset

We continue with the removal of a subset (multiple instances) from a fact type F. The set to be removed has the form { $t \mid t \in F$ [and C] } for some (optional) condition C on the instances in F; the brackets '[' and ']' denote optionality. The black triangle ▼ in the diagram below represents a 'bottom'-element (or 'sink') and **ALL** represents a new keyword in ORM.

(1)   We propose the following ORM-syntax: **REMOVE FROM** F [**WHEN** C]
      For the condition-part we can again make use of the language ConQuer [2].

(2)   The verbalization of the transaction is expressed in terms of the verbalization of its constituents:

> Verbalization(**REMOVE FROM** F [**WHEN** C]) =
> **remove from** Verbalization(F) **all instances** [**for which** Verbalization(C)]

(3)   We define the diagram for the transaction in terms of the diagrams of its constituents, and distinguish between the cases *with* and *without* a WHEN-condition:

> (a) Diagram *with* a WHEN-condition:

Diagram(**REMOVE FROM** F **WHEN** C) =

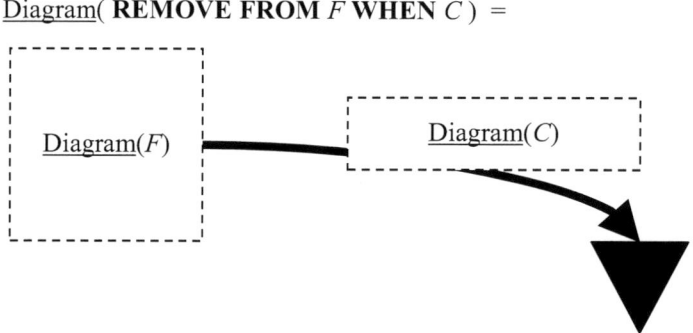

Fig. 5a. Removal of a subset from F

(b) Diagram *without* a WHEN-condition: <u>Diagram</u>(**REMOVE FROM** *F*) =

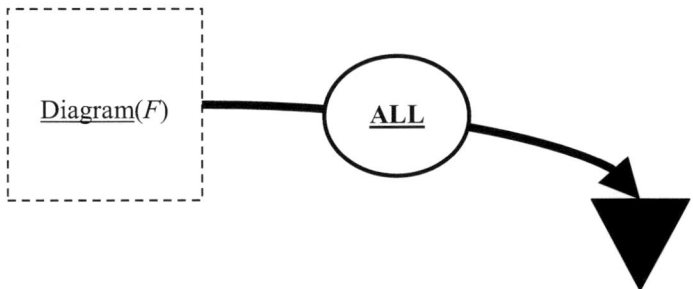

Fig. 5b. Removal of all instances from F

Again, the bold arrows suggest multiple instances, like in Figure 3.

(4) **Example (a).** We continue our running example with the removal of all applicants with the hire advice 'Yes' from the fact type *Applicant obtains Hire Advice*. Hence, the condition C_a is: Hire Advice = 'Yes'. The ORM-syntax will then be:

REMOVE FROM Applicant obtains Hire Advice
WHEN Hire Advice = 'Yes'

Applying the verbalization rules given under (2) we get:

<u>Verbalization</u>(**REMOVE FROM** Applicant obtains Hire Advice
                WHEN Hire Advice = 'Yes')
=   *remove from* <u>Verbalization</u>(Applicant obtains Hire Advice)
    all instances for which <u>Verbalization</u>(C_a)
=   *remove from fact type* Applicant obtains Hire Advice
    all instances for which Hire Advice *equals* 'Yes'

Example (b). Also in the fact type *Applicant has Name* we want to remove all applicants having the hire advice 'Yes'. Therefore we have to look in the fact type *Applicant obtains Hire Advice* for those applicants for which Hire Advice = 'Yes'. This leads to the following ORM-syntax:

REMOVE FROM Applicant has Name
WHEN Applicant
            └── obtains Hire Advice = 'Yes'

Applying the verbalization rules given under (2) will result in the verbalization

remove from fact type Applicant has Name
all instances for which Applicant obtains Hire Advice *equals* 'Yes'

Example (c). To finish our running example, we want to remove from the fact type *Applicant receives Employee Number* all applicants having the hire advice 'Yes'. Again we will look in the fact type *Applicant obtains Hire Advice* for those applicants for which Hire Advice = 'Yes'. This leads to the following ORM-syntax:

REMOVE FROM Applicant receives Employee Number
WHEN Applicant
└── obtains Hire Advice = 'Yes'

Similarly, the verbalization rules given under (2) will result in the verbalization

remove from fact type Applicant receives Employee Number
all instances for which Applicant obtains Hire Advice *equals* 'Yes'

Applying the diagram rules under (3) gives the following diagram for Example (c):

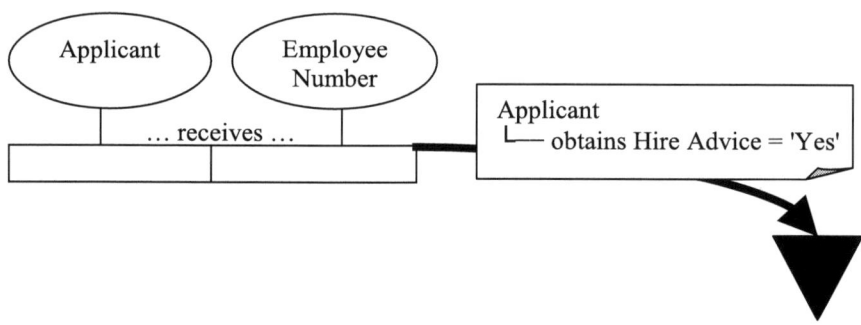

5   Change a Part of a Fact Type

Although a change can be considered as the compound transaction consisting of a delete followed by an addition, we will introduce and treat changes separately. We introduce the change of a part of a fact type F, i.e., replacing the values of some roles $r_1, ..., r_k$ by the (old) values of the expressions $z_1, ..., z_k$ *simultaneously* for *all* instances satisfying a certain (optional) condition C. If the fact type F is elementary then k will be 1, i.e. the values of only one role - the non-key one - will be changed.

(1) We propose the following ORM-syntax:
     CHANGE IN F **SET** $r_1 := z_1, ..., r_k := z_k$ [**WHEN** C]

(2) The verbalization of the transaction is expressed in terms of the verbalization of its constituents:

     Verbalization(**CHANGE IN** F **SET** $r_1 := z_1, ..., r_k := z_k$ [**WHEN** C]) =
          change in Verbalization(F)
          all instances [*for which* Verbalization(C)]
          simultaneously such that
          Verbalization(r_1) *becomes the old value of* Verbalization(z_1),
          ...., and
          Verbalization(r_k) *becomes the old value of* Verbalization(z_k)

(3) We define the diagram for the transaction in terms of the diagrams of its constituents, although Diagram(F) incorporates the expression ":= z_i" within the applicable roles:

Diagram(**CHANGE IN** F **SET** $r_1 := z_1, ..., r_k := z_k$ [**WHEN** C]) =

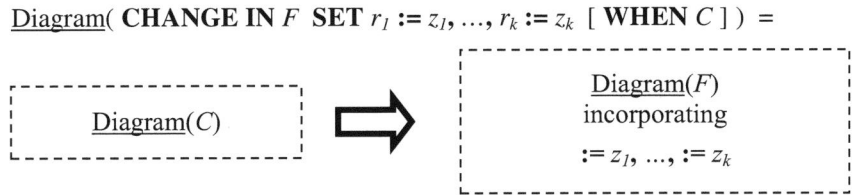

Fig. 6. Change of a part of a fact type (schematically)

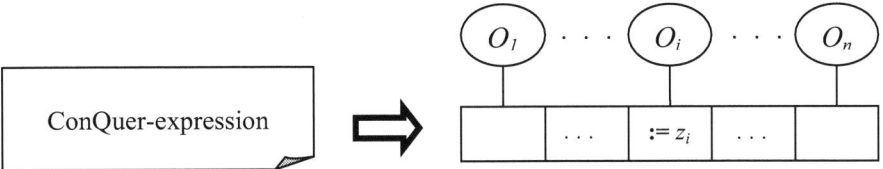

Fig. 7. Change of a part of a fact type (more concretely)

Again, the bold arrow suggests multiple instances, like in Figure 3.

(4) **Example.** We introduce two new fact types called *Employee lives in City* and *Employee earns Salary*, with the following diagrams:

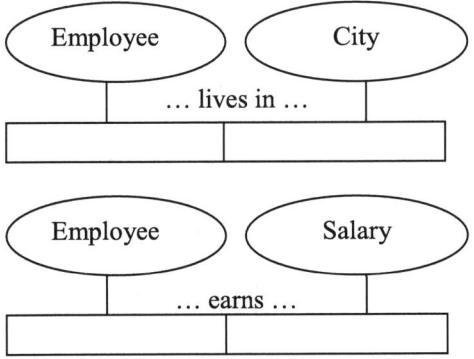

We chose as our change-example an increase of 10% of the salary of all employees living in London with a salary less than 5000 (our new so-called 'London allowance'). So the content of the fact type *Employee earns Salary* has to be changed. And the condition C is:

Employee
  └── lives in City = 'London'
  └── earns Salary < 5000

The ORM-syntax will then be:

CHANGE IN Employee earns Salary
SET   Salary := Salary * 1.10
WHEN   Employee
           └── lives in City = 'London'
           └── earns Salary < 5000

Applying the verbalization rules given under (2) we get:

change in fact type Employee earns Salary
all instances for which Employee lives in City *equals* 'London' *and*
                          Employee earns Salary *less than* 5000
simultaneously such that Salary *becomes the old value of* Salary *times* 1.10

Applying the diagram rules under (3) we get the following diagram:

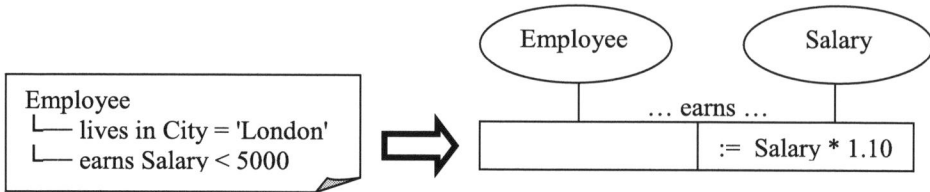

6   Compound Transactions

Sometimes we want several elementary transactions to be considered as one composite update that will be accepted or rejected as a whole. For instance, if the 3 Applicant roles introduced under (4) in Section 3 are all mandatory then the 3 removal transactions under (4) in Section 4 should be treated as one composite update. In line with [1] we indicate the beginning and end of such a compound transaction by means of the keywords **Begin** and **End** as follows:

Begin
    Transaction 1
    Transaction 2
    Transaction 3
End

7   Conclusions

The language ORM did not yet contain a sufficiently expressive data *manipulation* sublanguage (DML), i.e., a part for specifying *transactions*. We proposed an extension of ORM with a DML, for specifying transactions to be easily validated by domain experts. We introduced an expressive set of standard classes of specifiable transactions: add an instance, add a query result, remove a subset, and change a subset. This set was inspired by the expressiveness of the DML of SQL and goes much further than only simple adds and deletes of individual fact instances, which is not sufficient in practice. This extension, which provides ORM with an expressive DML, is the main contribution of this paper. It makes ORM to a certain extent comparable and possibly competitive with SQL. From that perspective this provides an alternative to the almost universally accepted SQL standard language. We also treated compound transactions in ORM. For all transactions we proposed simple syntaxes, verbalizations, and diagrams as well. They allow for type-checking and easy validation by domain experts. In retrospect, we also used or introduced the syntax, verbalizations and diagrams for a fact type, a condition, a query, a role, a value, and an instance here.

8   Future Work

Using the relation mapping procedure Rmap described in e.g. [1], we will work out rules for translation to SQL in a subsequent paper. Although the translation is not exactly one-to-one, the DML-counterparts of our ORM-constructs in SQL are:

ADD VALUES	$\Rightarrow$	INSERT VALUES
ADD RESULT	$\Rightarrow$	INSERT *query*
REMOVE	$\Rightarrow$	DELETE
CHANGE	$\Rightarrow$	UPDATE

We will also provide a formal semantics for these transactions along the lines of [5], formally validating the proposed DML. It will also allow us to study the expressiveness of the DML. Given our space limitations here, we will describe these topics in a separate paper.

Acknowledgments. This paper benefited from discussions with Herman Balsters and from the comments of the EMMSAD-reviewers.

References

1. Halpin, T., Morgan, T.: Information Modeling and Relational Databases. Morgan Kaufmann, San Francisco (2008)
2. Bloesch, A., Halpin, T.: ConQuer: a Conceptual Query Language. In: Thalheim, B. (ed.) ER 1996. LNCS, vol. 1157, pp. 121–133. Springer, Heidelberg (1996)
3. Balsters, H., Carver, A., Halpin, T., Morgan, T.: Modeling Dynamic Rules in ORM. In: Meersman, R., Tari, Z., Herrero, P. (eds.) OTM 2006 Workshops. LNCS, vol. 4278, pp. 1201–1210. Springer, Heidelberg (2006)
4. Balsters, H., Halpin, T.: Formal Semantics of Dynamic Rules in ORM. In: Meersman, R., et al. (eds.) OTM Workshops 2008. LNCS, vol. 5333, pp. 699–708. Springer, Heidelberg (2008)
5. de Brock, E.O.: Foundations of Semantic Databases. Prentice Hall International Series in Computer Science, Hemel Hempstead (1995)

The Orchestration of Fact-Orientation and SBVR

Peter Bollen

Department of Organization and Strategy
Faculty of Economics and Business Administration
University of Maastricht
6200 MD Maastricht, the Netherlands
p.bollen@os.unimaas.nl

Abstract. In this paper we will illustrate how the fact-oriented approach, e.g. ORM, CogNiam can be used in combination with OMG's Semantics of Business Vocabulary and Business Rules' (SBVR) standard. Within the field of modeling methods for information systems analysis and design, this standard can become a dominant force, when it comes to expressing initial domain requirements for an application's ontoloy and business rules, for domain analysis as well for design.

Keywords: Modeling methods, Fact-orientation, ORM, CogNIAM, SBVR.

1 Introduction

In January 2008, OMG has approved an international standard on business rules: Semantics of Business Vocabulary and Business Rules SBVR [1]. SBVR is a standard for expressing 'front-end' models for business requirements in the language that is understandable for the business domain users. Although OMG's SBVR standard is a major breakthrough in the area of business modeling, the standard itself is mainly focused on (potential) 'tool developers' and it is not written with the average domain user or business intelligence consultant in mind. OMG's SBVR standard is defined with the aim that business people can understand models without needing IT skills [2]. Within the field of modeling methods for information systems analysis and design, this standard can become a dominant force, when it comes to expressing initial domain requirements for domain analysis as well for design. In this paper, therefore, we will explore, how existing domain modeling methodologies can capitalize on the SBVR standardization efforts. We will , foremost, focus these capitalizing efforts on fact-oriented methodologies, to which, the specific methodologies: ORM [3], NIAM [4] and CogNIAM [5] belong.

In this article we will link the definitions of a number of SBVR modeling elements to 'familiar' modeling concepts in fact-orientation.

In section 2 we will discus the main concepts of the SBVR [1] and in section 3 we will focus on the different types of business rule statements that exist within SBVR. In section 4 we will see how SBVR vocabulary and rule statements map onto a fact-oriented fact type structure an accompanying application constraints.

T. Halpin et al. (Eds.): BPMDS 2009 and EMMSAD 2009, LNBIP 29, pp. 302–312, 2009.

2   The Main Building Blocks of SBVR Models

In this section we will give an overview of the main elements of the SBVR as they are defined in [1]. The SBVR is applied with the general notion of a model-driven architecture (MDA) in mind and is targeted at business rules and business vocabularies that describe businesses themselves rather than the possible IT system that might support it. In this paper we will focus on those elements in OMG's SBVR standard that refer to meaning or semantics of concepts in an application's ontology and its accompanying business rules. The main building blocks for semantic in the SBVR are the following: *vocabularies and terminology dictionaries*, *noun- and verb concepts*, and *definitional- and operational business rules*. In this paper we will illustrate the definitions in the standard by referencing example applications in the EU-rent case study that is attached to the standard document as Annex E [1].

2.1   Vocabularies and Terminology Dictionaries

One of the new features that has been introduced by the SBVR to the field of conceptual business modeling at large is the explicit definition of (external) vocabularies and namespaces. This allows to qualify signifiers by adding the name of the applicable context vocabulary (e.g., car rental industry standard glossary). In SBVR the applicable context vocabularies are defined as speech communities and vocabularies [1, p.274-275]:

```
' Car Rental Industry Standard Glossary
          Definition: the vocabulary that is defined in English by the Car Rental Industry
          Synonym: CRISG
          Reference Scheme: CRISG terms
CRISG
          Synonym: Car Rental Industry Standard Glossary

Merrian-Webster Unabridged Dictionary
          Definition: the vocabulary that is the 2004 edition,published by Merriam-Webster
          Synonym: MWU
          Reference Scheme: MWU terms.
MWU
          Synonym: Merriam-Webster Unabridged
```

For example in the EU-rental case study, the following vocabulary of concepts can be given (including the references to the defining vocabularies)[1, p.259, p.261]:

```
' rental car
          Source: MWU (1/1d) ["car"], CRISG("rental car")
          Definition: vehicle owned by EU-rent and rented to its customers
          Synonym: car

branch
          Concept type: organization function
          Definition: rental organization unit that has rental responsibility
          Necessity: the concept branch is included in organization units by
                  Function'
```

2.2 Noun- and Verb Concepts

An explicit modeling assumption (or axiom) in the SBVR standard is the reference to *facts* and *terms*, respectively: 'rules are based on facts, and facts are based on terms'[1, p.234]. This 'mantra', implies at least a 'way of working' in which (verbalized) concepts are defined, before fact type (forms) can be phrased. Therefore we need to find (a) the fact type(s) for every business rule that needs to be modeled.

Terms or concepts in SBVR are dived into *noun concepts* and *verb concepts*. Additionally, SBVR uses the concept of *fact type forms*.

2.2.1 Noun Concepts in SBVR

In the SBVR 1.0 specification [1, pp.19-25] a *noun concept* is defined as a 'concept that is the meaning of a noun or noun phrase '. An object type is defined in the SBVR 1.0 standard as follows: 'noun concept that classifies things on the basis of their common properties'. Role is defined as: 'noun concept that corresponds to things based on their playing a part, assuming a function or being used in some situation'. An individual concept is defined in the SBVR specification as follows: ' a (noun) concept that corresponds to only one object [thing]'. In paragraph 1 of clause 8 of the SBVR 1.0 standard document it is clearly explained that the *noun concept* has as subtypes: *individual concept*, *object type* and *fact type role*.

2.2.2 Verb Concepts in SBVR

In the SBVR 1.0 specification a 'verb-concept' is synonym for 'fact type' and is defined as follows: 'a concept that is the meaning of a verb phrase that involves one or more noun concepts and whose instances are all actualities.'[1, p21, p.183].

An example of an expression of a verb-concept or fact type expressed in SBVR-Structured English is the following:

<pre>rental car is stored at branch.</pre>

In SBVR the *verb concept* is synonym to the *fact type*. This means that SBVR does not contain an 'attribute' fact encoding construct as is the case in most non-fact oriented modeling languages like UML and (E)ER and therefore, SBVR prevents the associated modeling anomalies, that can occur when the attribute modeling construct is applied [6]. The SBVR fact type definition is as follows [1, p.21]

'Fact type
      Definition: concept that is the meaning of a verb phrase that involves one or more noun
              concepts and whose instances are all actualities.
      Synonym: verb concept
      Necessity: Each fact type *has* at least one role '

The above definition fragment, clearly demonstrates that the basic fact type definition in the SBVR is a fact-oriented definition that allows for fact types having arity N !. Furthermore, special definitions are provided for unary fact types (or characteristics) and binary fact types.

2.2.3 Fact Type Forms

A designation in SBVR is demonstrated by a *fact type form*. A fact type form contains a fact type reading that includes *place-holders*. This clause implements the *fact type template* and *placeholder* concepts from the fact-oriented approaches.

Table 1. Mapping main SBVR noun and verb concepts on Fact-oriented concepts

SBVR concept	Fact-oriented concept
Object type	Object type
Designation	Individual name
Fact type role	Role
Placeholder	Placeholder
Verb concept/Fact type	Fact type
Fact type form	Fact type reading
Characteristic	Unary fact type
Binary fact type	Fact type having two roles

In table 1 a summary of the mapping between SBVR- and fact-oriented concepts is provided. In the next section we will discuss the types of business rules that are defined in the SBVR 1.0 specification document.

3   Types of Business Rules in SBVR

The most common way of initially expressing business rules in SBVR is by means of a subset of the English Language : SBVR's Structured English [1, annex C] or the RuleSpeak business rule notation [1, Annex F, pp. 343-358]. An example of a rule expression in SBVR Structured English is the following:

> each <u>rental car</u> *is stored at* at most one <u>branch</u>.

In this example we have two designations for an object type: *rental car* and *branch*. Furthermore, we have the quantifiers: *each* and *at most one*. Clause 12 of SBVR v 1.0 [1, pp. 157-177] covers the definition of the types of business statements that can be distinguished in a given business domain. The main types of rule statements are the *operative business rule* statement and the *structural rule* statement. Within each of these groups, SBVR uses two styles of keywords for expressing the business rule statements.

3.1   Definitional (or Structural) Business Rules

In the SBVR 1.0 specification, a structural rule is defined as: a rule that is a claim of necessity[1, pp. 161] . A structural business rule statement can take one of the following forms: *necesssity business rule statement, impossibility business rule statement, restricted possibility rule statement*. A necessity statement is defined : '.. as a structural rule statement that is expressed positively in terms of necessity rather than negatively in terms of impossibility.'[1, pp. 168]. An example of a structural business rule expressed as a necessity business rule statement in pre-fix style is:

> '**It is necessary** that *each* rental has *exactly one* requested car group.'

We note that in the above necessity business rule statement, we have put in italics, the quantification keywords *each* and *exactly one*. An example of a structural business rule expressed in a impossibility business rule statement in pre-fix style is:

'**It is impossible that** the pick-up branch of a one-way rental is the return branch of that rental.'

A structural business rule expressed as a pre-fix restricted possibility statement is the following:

'**It is possible that** a rental is an open rental only if the rental car of the rental has been picked up.'

The structural business rules in SBVR are so-called alethic constraints, that are true by definition and therefore cannot be violated by the business.

Our example fact type and the example business rule are expressed in SBVR using the following SBVR expressions [1, p.316]:

' <u>rental car</u> *is stored* at <u>branch</u>
Necessity: Each <u>rental car</u> *is stored at* most one <u>branch</u> '

3.2 Operative (or Behavioural) Business Rules

In the SBVR 1.0 specification an operative business rule is defined as follows: '..business rule that is a claim of obligation" [1, p. 161]. An operative business rule is expressed in SBVR as an *operative business rule statement*, that can take one of the following forms: *obligation statement, prohibitive statement* and *restricted permissive statement*. An example of an operative business rule expressed in an obligation statement in a mix-fix style is:

'A rental **must** incur a location penalty charge if the drop-off location of the rental is not the EU-Rent site of the return branch of the rental.'

An example of an operative business rule expressed in a prohibitive statement is:

'A rental **must not** be open if a driver of the rental is a barred driver.'

An operative business rule expressed as a restrictive permissive statement is the following:

' **It is permitted that** a rental is open only if an estimated rental charge is provisionally charged to the credit card of the renter of the rental.'

An operative business rule is actionable, but not necessarily automatable, it can therefore be broken by people. The existence of operative business rules or deontic constraints, furthermore, allows the SBVR to document work-instructions and other rules of guidance, that have been traditionally outside the scope of traditional languages for (conceptual) business modeling.

The SBVR standard has been created to help business to model explicit (enforceable at all times) rules as well as tacit rules (in which the action that has to be undertaken depends upon for example the experience of a business user) and the (static) alethic and deontic constraints that exist in the business domain. In sub-clause 10.1.1.4 through 10.1.1.6 of the SBVR 1.0 standard [1, pp. 97- 107]the semantic and logic foundation for the standard are provided, in which the formal equivalence between each of the 3 forms for each of the two statement types is provided. In table 2, the rule templates are provided for each style/rule type combination [1, p.345, 24].

Table 2. Rule templates in SBVR for keyword style/rule type combinations

Modality Type	Prefixed Style	(Mix-fix) Embedded Style
Definitional/Structural		
Necessity	It is necessary that	…always…
Impossibility	It is impossible that	…never…
Restricted possibility	It is possible that	…sometimes…
Operative/behavioural		
Obligation	It is obligatory that	….must…
Prohibation	It is prohibited that	….must not…
Restricted permission	It is permitted that	….may…

4   A Methodology to Define the Complete Set of Uniqueness, Mandatory Role, Set-Comparison and Value Constraints for an Application Subject Area from Structural Rule Necessity Statements

Although the definition of SBVR is complete and based upon first-order logic, it might not always be possible to assess whether all relevant constraints on the states of subjects in the application area have been made explicit. Fact oriented methods provide a modeling procedure that will derive all uniqueness and mandatory role constraints in an application subject area, based upon a dialogue between the business rule modeler and the domain expert in which only concrete examples are shown

The example fact types expressed in SBVR-Structured English:

> rental car *is stored at* branch
> rental car *has* fuel level
> rental car *has as* service odometer reading
> rental car *has as* total mileage odometer reading

and the accompanying constraints or 'business rules' are:

> each rental car *is stored at* at most one branch.
> a rental car *has* at most one fuel level.
> a rental car *has* at most one service odometer reading
> a rental car *has* at most one mileage odometer reading

The first Structured English business rule can be stated as an impossibility structural rule statement in SBVR as follows:

> '**It is impossible** that a rental car is stored at more than one branch'

or as a SBVR business rule expressed as a necessity business rule statement:

> '**It is necessary** that *each* rental car *is stored at* at most one branch.'

or as a SBVR business rule expressed as a restricted possibility rule statement:

> '**It is possible that** a rental car *is stored in* at most one branch'

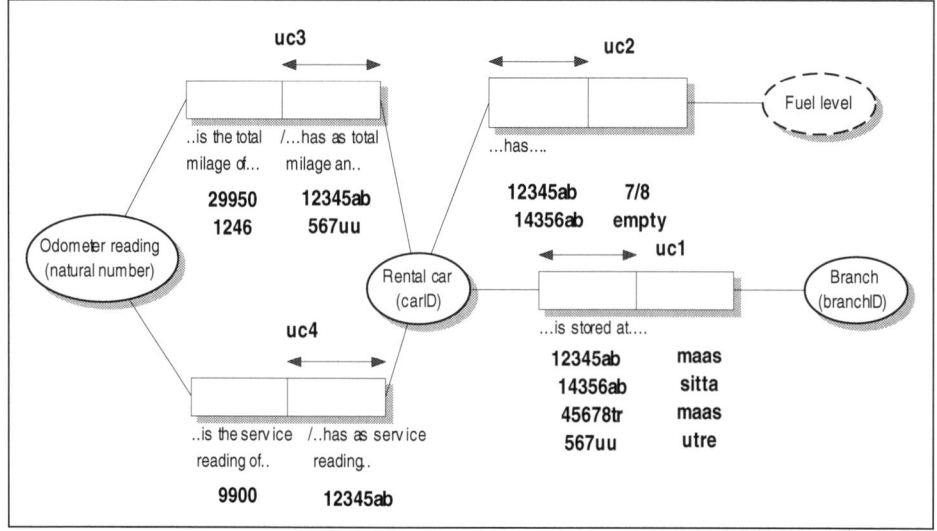

Fig. 1. ORM diagram for example fact types and uniqueness constraints

4.1 Uniqueness Constraints

In fact-orientation a uniqueness constraint is best stated as an obligation claim embedding a logical negation in the form of a prohibitive (rule) statement. In figure 1 we have given an ORM fact diagram of our small EU example, plus an significant population and the uniqueness constraints that is derived in ORM The fact type expressed in SBVR-Structured English:

<code>rental car</code> is stored at <code>branch.</code>

and the accompanying constraint or 'business rule':

each <code>rental car</code> is stored at at most one <code>branch.</code>

If we inspect figure 1 further, we see that the application of the fact-oriented modeling procedure has resulted in the detection of uniqueness constraint *uc2*, which was not listed in the EU rent SBVR model but should have been phrased as the following structural business rule in SBVR:

'**It is impossible** that a rental car has more than one fuel level'

Furthermore we have derived uniqueness constraints uc3 and uc4 who can be phrase as follows in SBVR:

'**It is impossible** that a rental car has more than one total mileage odometer reading'
'**It is impossible** that a rental car has more than one service odometer reading'

4.2 Mandatory Role and Set-Comparison Constraints

After we have found the (intra-fact type) uniqueness constraints that hold in an application subject area, by applying the derivation procedure (e.g. see [7, p.152] on each

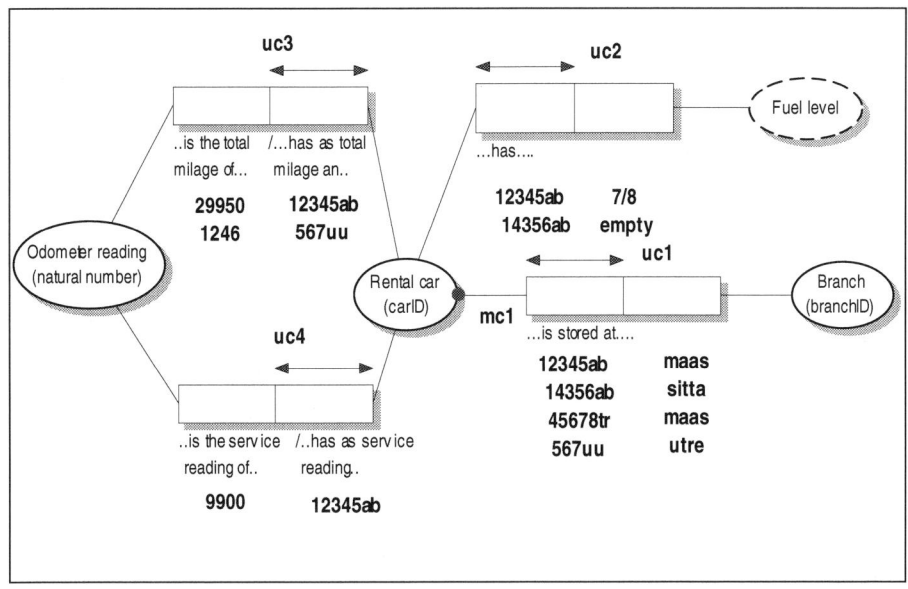

Fig. 2. ORM diagram including uniqueness and mandatory role constraints

fact type in the SBVR fact model we can derive the mandatory role constraints that hold in the universe of discourse (UoD).

In figure 2 we have given the extended fact diagram (based upon parts of the section rental cars in the EU rent-example as given in [8, p. 268-270]) and a significant population and the outcome of the fact-oriented mandatory role constraint derivation procedure: mandatory role constraint *mc1*. This constraint can be stated as a necessity rule statement in SBVR as follows:

'**It is necessary** that *a* <u>rental car</u> *is stored at a* <u>branch.</u>'
OR
'A <u>rental car</u> is **always** stored at a <u>branch</u>
OR
' <u>Each</u> rental car is stored at a <u>branch</u>'

We can now illustrate the phenomenon that a SBVR necessity rule statement coincides with 2 orthogonal fact-oriented constraints:

'Each <u>rental car</u> is stored at exactly one <u>branch</u>'

This necessity statement is the verbalization of fact-oriented constraints *mc1* in combination with uniqueness constraint *uc1* (see figure 3).

The application of the fact-oriented modeling procedure [3, p. 62-63] based on accepting/rejecting combinations of ground facts provided by the analyst to a domain expert leads to set of uniqueness and mandatory role and set comparison constraints that can be mapped onto elementary SBVR rule statements. In figure 3 we have illustrated the detection of subset constraint ssc1, which can be stated as a necessity rule statement in SBVR as follows:

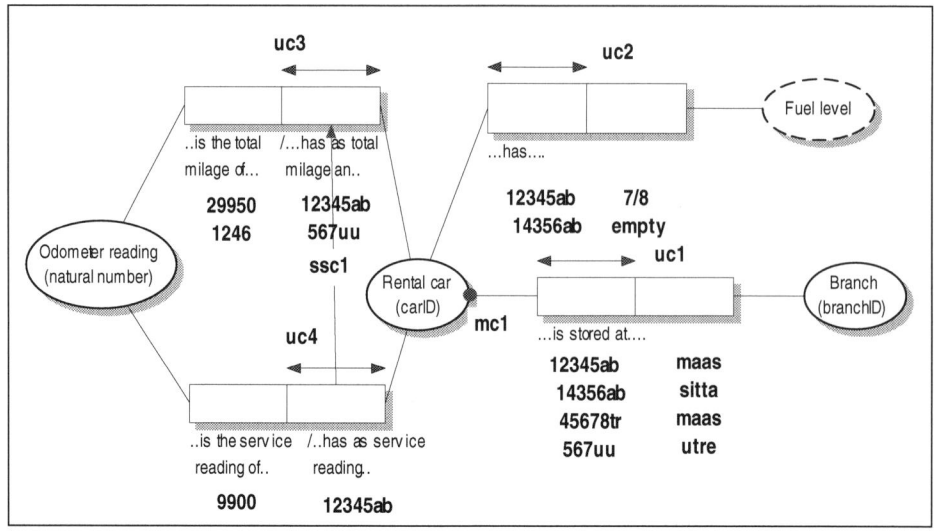

Fig. 3. ORM diagram for uniqueness-, mandatory role and set-comparison constraints

'**It is necessary** that *a* service reading of a rental car is accompanied by a total milage reading of that same car.'

The last groups of pre-defined fact-oriented constraints we will illustrate in this paper is the *value constraint type*. In figure 4 we have illustrated that a value for a fuel level is restricted to the specified values of the value constraint *vc1* (see figure 4). The value constraint that lists the allowed values for an entity type and.or name type can be listed in an SBVR vocabulary as definition [9].

In table 3 we have shown the fact-oriented constraints compare to the phrasing of business rules using and the appropriate SBVR quantifiers [1, p. 195] from the SBVR standard.

In figure 4 we have shown the complete fact-oriented information grammar expressed in the ORM (I) notational convention.

Another way in which fact-orientation can be used is the situation in which analysts have created fact-oriented conceptual models that contain full application domain semantics. In order to share these models with (domain) users that are familiar with SBVR, a mapping can be provided from fact-orientation to SBVR. An example of this 'reversed' transformation, for the case example in this paper is provided in [9].

Table 3. Fact-oriented constraints versus SBVR business rule types and quantifier

Fact-oriented constraints	SBVR business rules	Quantifier
Uniqueness	Structural business rule	at most one
Mandatory role	Structural business rule	each
Set-comparison	Structural business rule	
Value	Vocabulary definition	

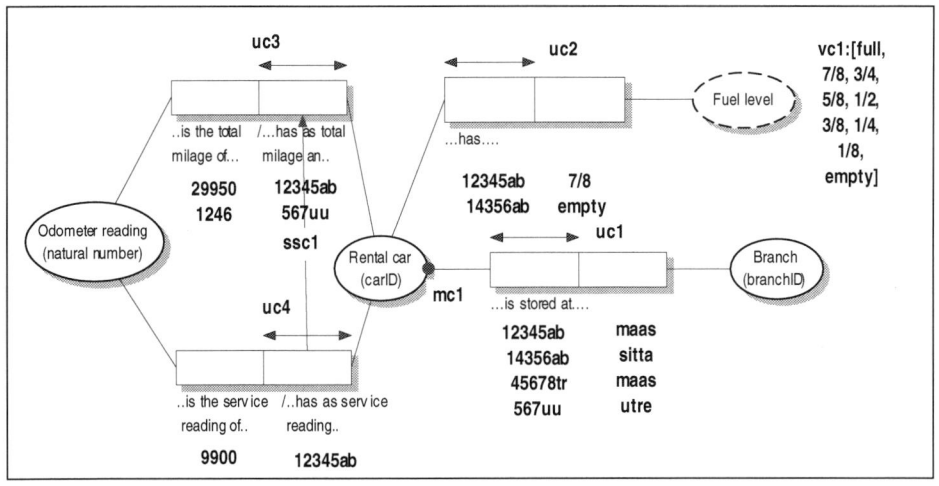

Fig. 4. Complete ORM diagram for example fact types and static constraints

5 Conclusions and Recommendations for Future Research

The SBVR standard gives us the modeling concepts to define most, if not all of the application domain ontology and business rules in the information perpective that can be encountered within organizations. The establishment of an OMG standard for the semantic vocabulary of business rules is a major step forward in the process of making business domain knowledge explicit and transferable in terms of this knowledge itself. However, the SBVR standard for business rules itself does not give guidance on how to arrive at these expressions at all times. We, therefore, strongly advise to use a fact-oriented modeling procedure, e.g. as it is defined in ORM[3] or in CogNIAM [10]. We have illustrated in this chapter that applying such a modeling procedure on the application's fact model, will automatically and completely yield, the uniqueness-, mandatory role-, set-comparison- and value constraints, based on the evaluation of a precise sets of combination of instances from fact types in the application's fact model. With respect to modeling of the process- and event perspectives, we are currently investigating how another OMG standard, the Business Process Modeling (and) Notation (BPMN) can be used for expressing fact-oriented process- and event models. As it stands now, the results show that BPMN has the right set of modeling constructs to model the dynamics aspects of a subject domain. SBVR in combination with BPMN, have provided researchers, practitioners and domain users for the first time in history, a set of tools that allows them to express requirements in the language of the business itself. Once these requirements have been expressed in SBVR (and BPMN), analysts can easily use those results as a semantic rich starting point for further stages towards design and (eventually) implementation.

References

1. OMG, Semantics of Business Vocabulary and Business Rules (SBVR), v1.0 OMG Available Specification (2008)
2. Nijssen, G.: Hooray, SBVR has arrived! Business Rules Journal 9(2) (2008)
3. Halpin, T., Morgan, T.: Information Modeling and Relational Databases; from conceptual analysis to logical design, 2nd edn. Morgan-Kaufman, San-Francisco (2008)
4. Wintraecken, J.: The NIAM Information Analysis Method: Theory and Practice by J.J.V.R. Wintraecken, p. 484. Springer, Heidelberg (1990)
5. Nijssen, G.: SBVR: N-ary fact types and subtypes- understandable and formal. Business Rules Journal 9(4), 12 (2008)
6. Bollen, P.: How to overcome pitfalls of (E)ER and UML in Knowledge Management education. International Journal of Teaching and Case Studies 1(3), 200–223 (2008)
7. Bollen, P.: On the applicability of requirements determination methods. In: Management and Organization, p. 219. University of Groningen, Groningen (2004)
8. OMG, Semantics of Business Vocabulary and Business Rules (SBVR), first interim specification, p. 392 (2006)
9. Bollen, P.: SBVR: a fact oriented OMG standard. In: OTM workshops 2008. Springer, Monterry mexico (2008)
10. Lemmens, I., Nijssen, M., Nijssen, G.: A NIAM 2007 conceptual analysis of the ISO and OMG MOF four layer metadata architectures. In: Meersman, R., Tari, Z., Herrero, P. (eds.) OTM-WS 2007, Part I. LNCS, vol. 4805, pp. 613–623. Springer, Heidelberg (2007)

Goal-Directed Modeling of Self-adaptive Software Architecture

Shan Tang[1], Xin Peng[1], Yijun Yu[2], and Wenyun Zhao[1]

[1] School of Computer Science and Technology, Fudan University, Shanghai, China
{tangshan,pengxin,wyzhao}@fudan.edu.cn
[2] Department of Computing, The Open University, United Kingdom
y.yu@open.ac.uk

Abstract. Today's large-scale computing systems are deployed in open, chang-ing and unpredictable environments. To operate reliably, such systems should be able to adapt to new circumstances on their own to get them running and keep them running. Self-adaptive software system has been proposed as a good solu-tion for this demand. However, very few techniques are available to date for sys-tematically building such kind of system. Aiming at this requirement, this paper presents a sound approach to derive a self-adaptive software architecture model from the requirements goal model in systematic way. At the same time, we illus-trate our approach by applying it to a simplified on-line shopping system.

Keywords: Goal model, Component, Software Architecture, Self-adaptive.

1 Introduction

Nowadays, widespread popularization of internet and emergence of many application patterns such as pervasive computing and grid computing need to operate in open, changing and unpredictable environments. To operate reliably, such systems must have the capabilities of adaptability. Self-adaptive software systems can automatically take the correct actions based on the knowledge of what is happening in the system, guided by objectives and needs of stakeholders [14]. So, self-adaptive software has been proposed as a good solution for this demand. However, there is a troublesome step in the development process of self-adaptive software system which is transform-ing what we want the system to do (requirement analysis model) into a framework for how to do it (software architecture design model). Requirements specifications can be viewed as a contract between the customer and the software developers. Hence, they should be not only easy to understand by the software architects and engineers but also by the end-users (customers) [1]. Traditional requirement analysis approaches, such like those used in structured method and object-oriented method just describe the structure and behavior of the system from developers' view, and do not contain the information that is interest to end-users. Therefore, those approaches are inadequate for transforming the requirement model to software architecture. Among all the kinds of requirements specifications, goal model are more near to the way end-users thinks and are easy to understand by all the stakeholders. So goal model becomes a hot re-search topic in requirement engineering domain [2,3,4].

T. Halpin et al. (Eds.): BPMDS 2009 and EMMSAD 2009, LNBIP 29, pp. 313–325, 2009.

In current goal-based methodologies for developing software systems, requirement-level variability modeling, specifying and analyzing have been well understood and supported. However, their transition to self-adaptive software architecture remains vague, that makes the derivation for this kind of application system hard to achieve on the design level. Aiming at this problem, this paper proposes a promising approach to solve the problem existing approaches met. Specifically, in this work, the requirements model defines the stakeholder objectives in goals and sub goals. The structural view of the software architecture is obtained by converting each goal and subgoal to a corresponding component. The behavioral view of software architecture is defined in terms of FSM. The self-adaptive knowledge base of the component is designed as a part of component to collect the data, analyze it and make decisions according to the high-variability goal model. The approach to derive the self-adaptive software architecture model from the goal requirement specification model is very systematic and can be used for any self-adaptive software development.

The rest of this paper is organized as follows: Section 2 introduces some background knowledge of requirements goal model; Section 3 presents our self-adaptive component model at first, then illustrates the derivation for self-adaptive software architecture model; in Section 4 some related works are discussed; finally, we conclude this paper and point out our future work directions in Section 5.

2   The Goal-Oriented Requirement Model

In our approach, we specify our goal-oriented requirement model under the KAOS modelling framework. The KAOS (Keep All Objectives Satisfied) methodology has been developed by Axel *et al.* [19] for about ten years of research and experience in real projects. And it represents the state-of-the-art specification model for research on the goal-oriented requirement engineering. In this section we first revisit some key concepts and terminologies of the KAOS methodology which will be used later in this paper. Then we present an example of goal modelling. For more details on KAOS, readers can refer to [5,6,7].

KAOS is a goal oriented requirements specification language, and it defines four primary types of concepts: goal, agent, object and operation [7].

Goals are stakeholder objectives that the system should achieve. A goal model generally consists of one or more root goals, and each root goal is AND/OR decomposed repeatedly until every leaf-level goal is realizable by some individual agent assigned to it. If a goal G is AND/OR–refined into subgoals G1,…,Gn, then all/at least one of the subgoals must be satisfied for G to be satisfied. An OR-decomposition of a goal introduces a variation point, which defines alternative ways of fulfilling the goal. It is easy to verify that generally the number of variability represented by a goal model depends exponentially on the number of OR decompositions. The goal refinement process generates a goal refinement tree and the leaves may also be called requisites. The requisites that are assigned to the software system are called requirements, and those assigned to the interacting environment are called assumptions.

Agents are active components such as humans, automated components that play some role assuring the goals satisfaction. Some agents define the software whereas the others define its environment.

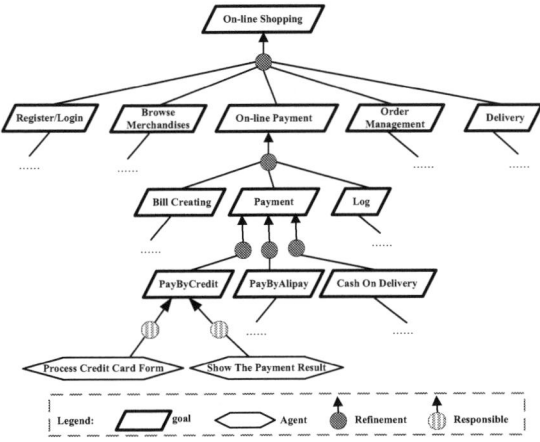

Fig. 1. Segment of the goal model for a simplified On-line Shopping System

Objects can either be entities (passive objects), agents (active objects), events (instantaneous objects), or relationships between objects. The state of the system is defined by aggregation of the states of its objects.

Operations are actions performed by agents to achieve system goal by operationalizing a requirement. In general, an operation is represented by an input-output relation over objects and is used to define state transitions.

Figure 1 shows an example of a goal model describing the requirements for a simplified On-line Shopping System. In this figure, AND-refinements have lines from each subgoal to the same blue circle. OR-refinements have lines from subgoals to different blue circles. For the sake of simplicity, the figure does not depict all the goal elements of this system.

The formal KAOS specification of a goal is described by several fields. The first field *Goal* (*Requirement* or *Operation*) denotes the type of entity and name of the particular instance; the second field is the *Concerns* field, which is used to list the concepts that the entity uses, or is concerned with; the *RefinedTo* field contains the sub-goals and/or requirement into which the goal is refined; the *Refines* field refers to the goal refined by the entity being described; next, the *InformalDef* field describes the informal definition of the entity being described; the optional field *FormalDef* give the formal definition of the entity being described and can be represented in any formal notation, in this paper we adopt the linear temporal logic[12] to formalize this field. Take the "On-line Payment" goal shown in figure 1 for example, its corresponding formal KAOS specification is described as follows:

Goal *Achieve* [On-line Payment]
Concerns OrderNum, TotalCost, CreditCardNum, PayResult...
Refines *Achieve* [On-line Shopping]
RefinedTo *Achieve* [Bill Creating], *Achieve* [Payment], *Achieve* [Log]
InformalDef We require the system to discount before carrying out pay if the customer is a VIP customer.
FormalDef $\Box(\text{VIP} \Rightarrow (\neg \text{Pay} \cup \text{Discount}))$

3   Self-adaptive Software Architecture Model Derivation

In this section, we describe how to derive a self-adaptive software architecture model from goal models. Software architectures provide high-level abstractions for representing the structure, behavior of software systems. Therefore, the software architecture model consists of two design views: the first one is the structural view which is a macro view of a self-adaptive software system, specifying the overall topological structure and considering dynamic changes of the structure in various scenarios; and the second one is the behavior view which is a micro view of self-adaptation.

A fundamental software engineering principle is to modularize a software system into a set of subsystems (i.e. modules, components) that have high cohesion and low coupling [8]. Thus, in this paper we specify a self-adaptive software architecture model in terms of the self-adaptive components. A component is an encapsulation of a computational unit and has interface to specify its provided services and required services. And the self-adaptive component extends the component concept to adapt the structural configuration and dynamic behavior of itself. For elaborating how to derive the self-adaptive software architecture model, we first introduce our self-adaptive component model. Then we explain how to derive the software architecture model from the goal model by mapping the goals in the goal decomposition tree to the components of the software architecture.

3.1   Self-adaptive Component Model Overview

The structural model of a self-adaptive component is presented in figure 2. It is composed of a control center, several internal/external ports and the implementation body. In this paper we extend the component model which was proposed in our previous work [9] by adding an adaptation manager component into the control center.

In this model, a component has a number of ports. Each port defines a logically separable point of interaction with its environment. A component explicitly states its provisions/requirements by its external provide/request ports. Three kinds of ports are

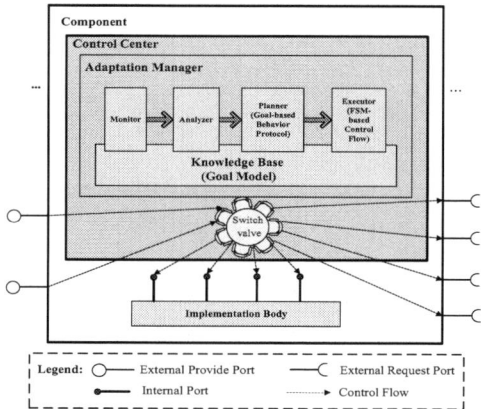

Fig. 2. The structural model of a self-adaptive component

identified [9]: 1) External provide ports. They define how the environment can access the functionalities implemented by the component, and they are also the entries for other components to startup the control flow; 2) External request ports. They define how the component can access the functionalities provided by the environment. At the same time, they are the entries for the control flow to involve external service providers; 3) Internal ports: They are internal functional interfaces provided by the implementation body to fulfill external requests. Usually, after an external request is received, one or more internal ports will be involved in an execution of the control flow to complete the whole service process.

Control center is separated from the component implementation to enforce component-level coordination on its external and internal ports according to the behavioral protocol. At runtime, usually, the control center will be activated by requests of other components on a provide port, then it will perform a series of interactions on internal ports and external request ports on the runtime control flow.

In order to see whether and how well the self-adaptive component achieves its goal, it needs to monitor its managed element, collect the data, analyze it based on its knowledge (in our approach, we use goal model as the knowledge for component's adaptation), plan changes to its behavior if necessary, and execute the plan. The monitor in the adaptation manager senses the environmental components. The analyzer compares event data against patterns in the knowledge base to diagnose symptoms. The planner interprets the symptoms and devises a plan which is a goal-based behavior protocol. And the executor executes the FSM-based control flow which is translated from the goal-based behavior protocol.

The switch valve associates one external request port of one component with two or more alternative external provide ports of other components. Therefore, a switch represents alternative bindings among interaction ports.

The implementation body encapsulates computation logic of the component and exposes some internal ports for the control center.

3.2 Structural Model Derivation

Now, we focus on using goal models to derive self-adaptive software architecture that can accommodate many/all possible functionalities that fulfill stakeholder goals. This is possible because our goals models are extensions of AND/OR graphs, with OR decompositions introducing alternatives into the model. The space of alternatives defined by a goal model can be used as a basis for designing self-adaptive software system (i.e., self-configuring system).

In this paper, the structural model of a software system is defined by components and their bindings through their external provide/request ports. In general, an external request port of a component in the system must be bound to exactly one external provide port of another component. We achieve the alternative bindings of ports by introducing the "switch valve" component. In the most straightforward derivation case, a software component is derived from a goal as follows: for each functional goal, we create a corresponding component to achieve this goal. Specifically, the root goal node corresponds to the whole software system. The leaf-level goal nodes correspond to the actual physical software components. Whereas, the higher-level goal nodes are not directly associated with physical software components, but are used to orchestrate the lower-level nodes. However, these derivation rules are not enough for designing large-scale software systems. To derive the structural model of a software architecture systematically, we adopt a more formal approach in which we take an AND/OR goal decomposition tree and a specification of the inputs and the outputs of each goal as the source model, and return a software architecture model as the target model. Inputs are the data entities that need to be supplied to the agent responsible for the goal in order to fulfill it, and they will become the input parameters of an instances of the external provide ports of the corresponding component. Outputs are data entities that the agent provides to its environment as part of the fulfillments of the goal, and they will become the output parameters of an instance of the external request ports of the corresponding component. Usually, we can derive the external provide port of a component directly from the name of a goal. Whereas, the derivation of the external request ports of the component depend on how the goal is decomposed. Here, we only focus on deriving the external interaction ports of components, and do not prescribe any particular implementation to achieve interoperability in heterogeneous environments.

Next, we use two kinds of goal decomposition patterns to illustrate how to map the goals in the goal model as well as their input and output information to the software components in the software architecture.

■ If a goal **G** is AND-decomposed into N subgoals: **G1,G2,...Gn**, we first derive a software component **C** for the goal **G**, component **C** has an external provide port which is derived directly from the name (or the description) of the goal **G** and N external request ports which are corresponding to the subgoals: **G1,G2,...Gn**. Then N software components **C1,C2,..,Cn** are created for responding **C**'s requests. So each one of them has an external provide port corresponding to one of the external request ports of **C**. meanwhile, we bind the external request ports of component **C** to the external provide ports of **C1,C2,...,Cn**. Finally, we assign the inputs (outputs) of the goals to the corresponding components' external provide (request) ports as their input (output) parameters. The graphical AND decomposition pattern and the corresponding derivation result are illustrated in figure 3. (**I** and **O** denote the set of input parameters and out parameters respectively; the dashed line between an external request port and an external provide port represents the binding relationship.)

For example, goal **"On-line Payment"** is AND-decomposed into three subgoals: **"Bill Creating"**, **"Payment"** and **"Log"**. We can derive a component model (figure 4.b) from the goal "On-line Payment" (figure 4.a).

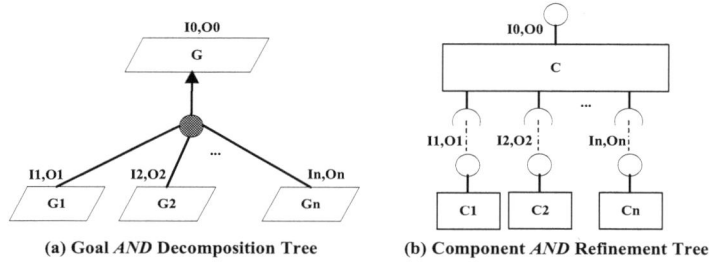

(a) Goal *AND* Decomposition Tree   (b) Component *AND* Refinement Tree

Fig. 3. AND decomposition pattern

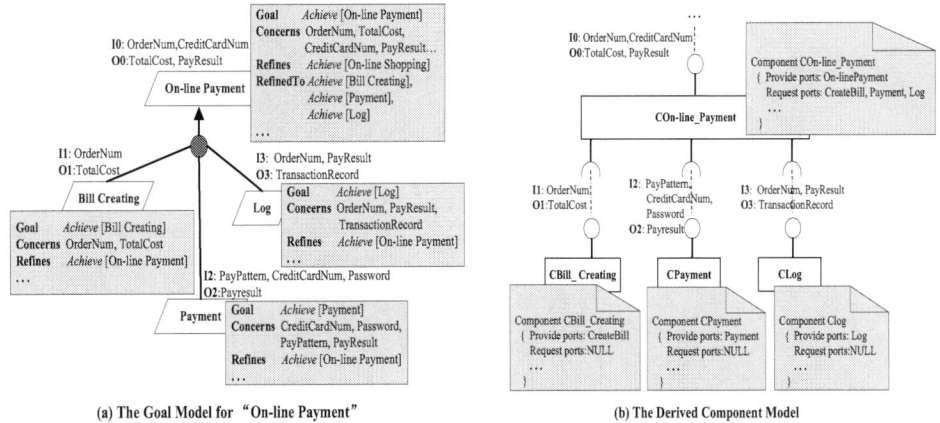

(a) The Goal Model for "On-line Payment"   (b) The Derived Component Model

Fig. 4. The graphical derivation result for goal "On-line Payment"

■ If a goal **G** is OR-decomposed into N subgoals: **G1,G2,...Gn**, at first, a software component **C** and N software component **C1,C2,...,Cn** are created for responding to the goal **G,G1,G2,...,Gn** respectively. Each component has an external provide port. Because all of the goals (**G,G1,G2,...,Gn**) are assigned to perform the identical task, they have the same inputs (**I**) and outputs (**O**). Note that in this decomposition pattern, at this time, each component only has an external provide port, so we cannot bind them directly. We introduce a "**Switcher**" to bind their external provide ports. **Switcher** can distribute the tasks (of the component which is generated for the parent goal **G**) to different components (associated with the subgoals) according to different demand strategies. Then we annotate each binding line (which is located between the individual component's external provide port and the **Switcher**) with the same **I** and **O**. Therefore, an external provide port of the component associated with the parent goal can be binded to any one of its corresponding subgoal's external provide ports. Figure 5 shows the graphical **OR** decomposition pattern and the corresponding derivation result.

Take the goal "**Payment**" for example. It is OR-decomposed into three subgoals: "**PayByCredit**", "**PayByAlipay**" and "**PayByPaypal**". We can derive a component model (figure 6.b) from the goal model (figure 6.a).

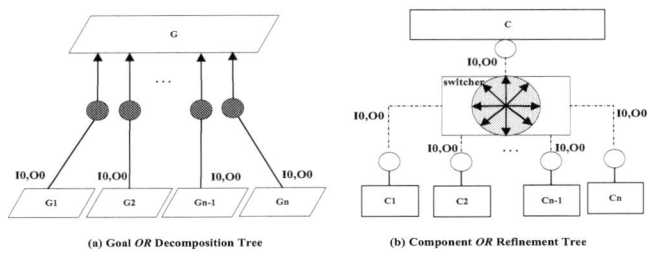

(a) Goal *OR* Decomposition Tree   (b) Component *OR* Refinement Tree

Fig. 5. OR decomposition pattern

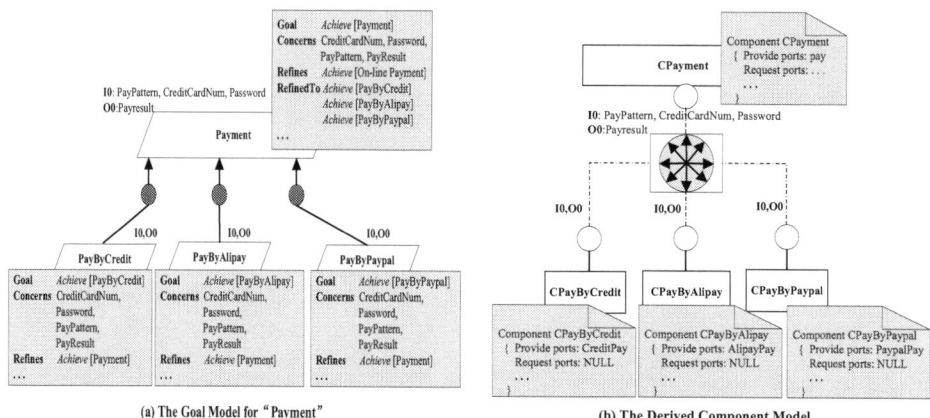

(a) The Goal Model for "Payment"   (b) The Derived Component Model

Fig. 6. The graphical derivation result for goal "Payment"

After the initial components model is generated according to the above derivation patterns. The software architect may choose to merge two or more components into one, if they think their functionalities are too restricted to justify their independent existence. This can be done by introducing compound components and merging individual external ports into ones that contain the union of the original ports. Conversely, the software architect may introduce new ports and components in order to describe functionality in more detail. Thus, the decomposition tree for the goals and the refinement tree for the corresponding software architecture maybe don't have the same shape. It would be a pure coincidence if they did have it.

3.3 Behavioral Model Derivation

Components, as the fundamental building units of software systems, occupy the key position in the component-based software developments. However, the properties of a software system are not a trivial reflection of the simple sum of components. The global system properties emerge from the interactions among components [13]. In this section we expound how to use goal model as a foundation to derive component's behavioral model. In our approach, a component's behavioral model is a separated coordination logic of the component and is described as interacting protocols. We adopt a subset of CSP (Communicating Sequential Processes) notations [10] to describe component's behavior. CSP is a formal method to describe and analyze processes behavior patterns and interactions. Semantically speaking, the architectural components' behaviors model can be modeled as CSP processes. Here, we only introduce a portion of CSP elements we used in this paper due to the space limitation. The major elements are described as follows:

Processes and events: a process is an execution flow of events, standing for the behavior pattern of objects. Processes are described by a series of communication events and other simpler processes. The basic unit of the processes specification is event. An event represents an atomic interaction on external or internal ports. The notation "!" or "?" following each event represents the direction of message sending, in which "!" denotes message sending and "?" denotes message receiving. In this paper, we use the symbol "**SKIP**" to represent the successful termination of a process.

External choice: A process that can behave like *P* or *Q*, where the choice is made by the environment, is denoted *P*□*Q*. ("Environment" refers to the other processes that interact with the process.)

Event transition: A process that engages in event *e* and then becomes process *P* is denoted *e*→*P*.

Parallel composition: Processes can be composed using the " ‖ " operator. Parallel processes may interact by jointly (synchronously) engaging in events that lie within the intersection of their alphabets. Conversely, if an event *e* is in the alphabet of processes *P1* and *P2*, then *P1* can only engage in the event if *P2* can also do so. That is, the process *P1* ‖ *P2* is one whose behavior is permitted by both *P1* and *P2*, and for the events in the intersection of the processes' alphabets, both processes must agree to engage in the event.

Sequential composition: Processes can also be composed using the ";" operator to indicate that the processes are to be performed in sequence from left to right. This operator is useful to model process dependencies.

All of the above conceptual notations and their semantics are summarized as the following Table 1 shows.

A requirements goal model is basically an AND/OR hierarchy, where the AND decomposition of the goals are unordered. These properties require further design-specific annotations on the decompositions in order to generate behavior protocol. i.e., the dependencies are analyzed so as to derive the order that specifies whether the subgoals can be performed in parallel or in sequence. Now we illustrate how to derive the goal-based behavior protocols of a component based on the following three goal decomposition patterns. At the same time, we explain how to transform the protocols into FSM-based control flows.

Table 1. CSP Notations Used in this paper

Behavioral protocol symbol	Semantics
?	message receiving
!	message sending
SKIP	finish successfully
□	external choice
→	event transition
P ‖ Q	parallel composition
P;Q	sequential composition

■ When a goal *G* is AND-decomposed into *N* subgoals *G1,G2,...,Gn sequentially* (;), we first create a process *P* for goal *G* and N subprocesses *P1,P2,...,Pn* for the subgoals, and specify that the subprocesses perform in sequence. At the detailed design stage, the designer may provide solution-specific information to decompose each subprocess into several events. These derived processes characterize the behavior protocol of a component. Then we use the behavior protocol interpreter to translate the behavior protocol into finite state machine (FSM) based control flows. The state

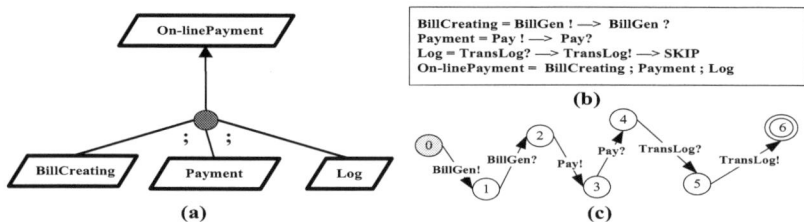

Fig. 7. Example of behavioral model derivation for goal "On-linePayment"

machine consists of a set of states which are also specified at the detailed design stage. Each state represents the status in the process of interaction and has some transitions. A transition corresponds to an event of the behavior protocol. When a transition is fired, state machine changes current state from one state to another. All the states are connected by the transitions as a sequential chain in this case. After translation, state machine information is stored in a container inside the **Executor** component (see figure 2).

For example, the goal "**On-linePayment**" is AND-decomposed into three subgoals sequentially: "**BillCreating**", "**Payment**" and "**Log**" (figure 7a). The corresponding behavior protocol specification and the finite state machine are illustrated in figure 7b and figure 7c respectively. In this example, each subprocess is decomposed into an input event and an output event.

■ When a goal **G** is AND-decomposed into **N** subgoals **G1, G2,...,Gn in parallel** (‖), we first create a process **P** for goal **G** and N subprocesses **P1,P2,...,Pn** for the subgoals, and specify that the subprocesses perform in parallel. The derivation process of the behavior protocol is very similar to the above one. The only difference is the order of execution of the subprocesses. After specifying the behavior protocol, we use the behavior protocol interpreter to translate the behavior protocol into FSM. In this case, we create N pairs of transitions that connect each subprocess state respectively. Take the goal "**Payment Handling**" for example, it is AND-decomposed in parallel (‖) into two subgoals: "**Client-end Handling**" and "**Server-end Handling**" (figure 8a). The corresponding behavior protocol specification and the finite state machine are illustrated in figure 8b and figure 8c respectively.

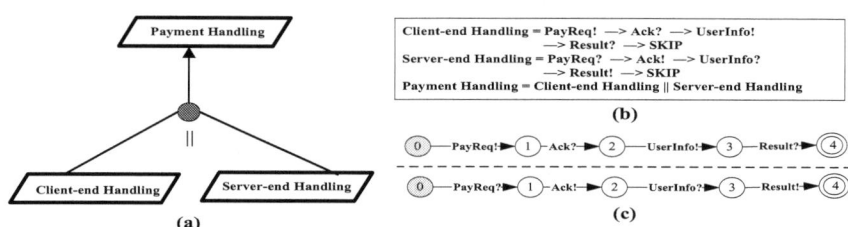

Fig. 8. Example of behavioral model derivation for goal "Payment Handling"

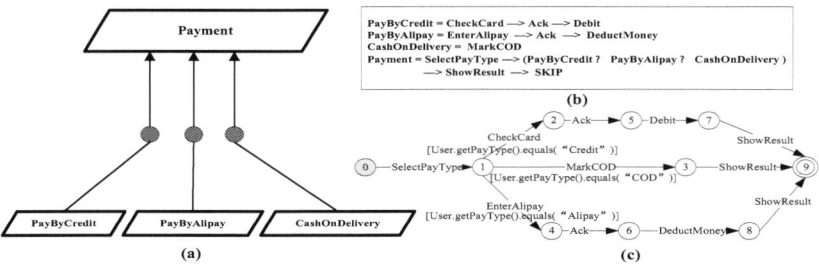

Fig. 9. Example of behavioral model derivation for goal "Payment"

■ When a goal *G* is OR-decomposed into N subgoals: *G1, G2,...,Gn* at first we also create a process *P* for goal *G* and N subprocesses *P1,P2,...,Pn* for the subgoals. These subprocesses are mutually exclusive and each of them can be further decomposed into several events as well. For the derivation of FSM, we create N pairs of transitions that connect each subprocess state with the same initial state and final state respectively. If a state has two or more than two outgoing transitions, each transition from the state should have a guard condition to help event management decide which event would happen. This guard condition is defined by external choice. A triggered event will cause the firing of the transition.

For instance, the goal "**Payment**" is OR-decomposed into three subgoals: "**Pay-ByCredit**", "**PayByAlipay**" and "**CashOnDelivery**" (figure 9a). The corresponding behavior protocol specification and the finite state machine are illustrated in figure 9b and figure 9c respectively. Here, variant events exist as an external choice of candidates in the behavioral protocol and would be decided at runtime by parameters. The external choice may be explicitly decided by control parameter or implicitly decided by data parameter. In this example, the choice of *Payment* could be decided by control parameter *payType*.

4   Related Works

Our approach is related to many other approaches considered by other researchers. For instance, van Lamsweerde *et al.* [6] used the KAOS methodology to elaborate the requirements of a meeting scheduler. Nenad Medvidovic et al. developed a technique to pass from requirements specified in WinWin to an architectural model for the system in [12]. And Brandozzi *et al.* [4] considered that requirements and design are respectively in problem and solution domains. They introduced an architecture prescription language (APL) that specifies the structure of the software system and its components in the language of the application domain. This higher-level architecture specification can be then easily translated, if necessary, in an architecture description, in the solution domain. More recent work by van Lamsweerde *et al.* [7] derived software architectures from the formal specifications of a system goal model using heuristics, that is, by finding design elements such as classes, states and agents directly from the temporal logic formulae representing the goals. However, all these works have not considered the adaptability of the software system that our approach supports. We need a new approach to support the adaptability of the software system.

In [15] Zhang and Cheng proposed a model-driven process to the development of dynamically adaptive programs, and in another work, they integrated the adaptation semantics into the KAOS methodology [16]. Cheng, Garlan *et al.* [17] achieved dynamic adaptation by describing an architectural style for a system and a repair strategy. In [18] Yu *et al.* stated that requirements goal models can be used as a foundation for designing software that supports a space of behaviours, all delivering the same function, and that is able to select at runtime the best behaviour based on the current context, and they used goal models to represent variability in the way high-level stakeholder objectives can be met by the system-to-be. In this regard, there is a close degree of resemblance between our approach and [18].

5   Conclusions and Future Works

This paper has proposed a systematic process for generating a self-adaptive software architecture model from a goal model. Our process generates two design views: the first one is the structural view which is a macro view consisting of self-adaptive software components; and the second one is a micro view specifying the behavioral patterns of the components.

The main contributions of this paper are as follows: First, we expound how to use requirements goal models as a foundation to design a self-adaptive software system that supports a space of behaviors that is able to select at runtime the best behavior based on the current context. Second, keeping the traceability and the consistency in concepts between requirements and designs always are the big games that we pursue. In this work the traceability and consistency between requirements and design is achieved by an explicit transformation from goal models to the design view of software architecture. At the same time, by doing this, we can reuse all the derived artifacts which implement the architectural components to save both developing time and resources. Third, the essential characteristic of self-adaptive computing systems is their ability to reconfigure their topological structure automatically. According to this method, the self-adaptive software architecture model can serve as the basis for developing autonomic computing systems (i.e., self-configuring systems, self-managing systems).

However, the method we propose is far from mature since we only provide a semi-formal representation model for this developing process. Thus, in the future we need a formal representation mechanism to support deriving the software architecture model automatically. On the other hand, we need build supporting tools that take the requirements for a self-adaptive software system and some other parameters and transform them into an architecture prescription for the system.

Acknowledgments. This work is supported by the National Natural Science Foundation of China under Grant No.90818009.

References

1. Brandozzi, M., Perry, D.: From goal-oriented requirements to architectural prescriptions: The preskriptor process. In: Proc. of the 2nd Int'l. Software Requirements to Architectures Workshop, pp. 107–113 (2003)

2. van Lamsweerde, A.: Goal-oriented requirements engineering: From system objectives to UML models to precise software specifications. In: ICSE 2003, pp. 744–745 (2003)
3. Dardenne, A., Fickas, S., van Lamsweerde, A.: Goal-Directed Concept Acquisition in Requirements Elicitation. In: Proc. Sixth Int'l. Workshop Software Specification and Design, pp. 14–21 (1991)
4. Brandozzi, M., Perry, D.E.: Transforming goal oriented requirements specifications into architectural prescriptions. In: STRAW at ICSE 2001 (2001)
5. Dardenne, A., van Lamsweerde, A., Fickas, S.: Goal-directed requirements acquisition. Science of computer Programming 20, 3–50 (1993)
6. Van Lamweerde, A., Darimont, R., Massonet, P.: Goal-Directed Elaboration of Requirements for a Meeting Scheduler: Problems and Lessons Learnt. In: Proc. of the RE 1995 – 2nd IEEE Symposium on Requirements Engineering, York, pp. 194–203 (1995)
7. Van Lamsweerde, A.: From system goals to software architecture. In: Bernardo, M., Inverardi, P. (eds.) SFM 2003. LNCS, vol. 2804, pp. 25–43. Springer, Heidelberg (2003)
8. Parnas, D.: On the criteria to be used in decomposing systems into modules. CACM 15(12), 1053–1058 (1972)
9. Peng, X., Wu, Y., Zhao, W.: A Feature-Oriented Adaptive Component Model for Dynamic Evolution. In: 11th European Conference on Software Maintenance and Reengineering, pp. 49–57 (2007)
10. Hoare, C.: Communicating Sequential Processes. Prentice-Hall International, Englewood Cliffs (1985)
11. Medvidovic, N., Gruenbacher, P., Egyed, A.F., Boehm, B.W.: Bridging Models across the Software Lifecycle. Technical Report USC-CSE-2000-521, University of Southern California (2000)
12. Manna, Z., Pnueli, A.: The Temporal Logic of Reactive and Concurrent Systems. Springer, Heidelberg (1992)
13. Jiao, W., Mei, H.: Dynamic Architectural Connectors in Cooperative Software Systems. In: Proc. of the 10th IEEE International Conference on Engineering of Complex Computer Systems (2005)
14. Ganek, A.G., Corbi, T.A.: The dawning of the autonomic computing era. IBM Systems Journal 42(1), 5–18 (2003)
15. Zhang, J., Cheng, B.H.: Model-based development of dynamically adaptive software. In: Proc. of the 28th International Conference on Software Engineering (2006)
16. Brown, G., Cheng, H.C., Goldsby, H., Zhang, J.: Goal-oriented specification of adaptation requirements engineering in adaptive systems. In: Proc. of the Workshop on Software Engineering for Adaptive and Self-Managing Systems (2006)
17. Cheng, S.W., Garlan, D., Schmerl, B.R., Sousa, J.P., Spitnagel, B., Steenkiste, P.: Using architectural style as a basis for system self-repair. In: WICSA 3: Proceedings of the IFIP 17th World Computer Congress - TC2 Stream / 3rd IEEE/IFIP Conference on Software Architecture, pp. 45–59 (2002)
18. Yu, Y., Lapouchnian, A., Liaskos, S., Mylopoulos, J., Leite, J.C.S.P.: From goals to high-variability software design. In: 17th International Symposium on Methodologies for Intelligent Systems, pp. 1–16 (2008)
19. van Lamsweerde, A., Dardenne, A., Delcourt, B., Dubisy, F.: The KAOS Project: Knowledge Acquisition in Automated Specification of Software. In: Proceedings AAAI Spring Symposium Series, Stanford University, American Association for Artificial Intelligence, pp. 59–62 (1991)

A Goal Modeling Framework for Self-contextualizable Software

Raian Ali, Fabiano Dalpiaz, and Paolo Giorgini

University of Trento - DISI, 38100, Povo, Trento, Italy
{raian.ali,fabiano.dalpiaz,paolo.giorgini}@disi.unitn.it

Abstract. Self-contextualizability refers to the system ability to autonomously adapt its behaviour to context in order to maintain its objectives satisfied. In this paper, we propose a modeling framework to deal with self-contextualizability at the requirements level. We use Tropos goal models to express requirements; we provide constructs to analyse and represent context at each variation point of the goal model; and we exploit the goal and context analysis to define how the system satisfies its requirements in different contexts. Tropos goal analysis provides constructs to hierarchically analyse goals and discover alternative sets of *tasks* the system can *execute* to *satisfy* goals; our framework extends Tropos goal model by considering context at its variation points, and provides constructs to hierarchically analyse context and discover alternative sets of *facts* the system has to *monitor* to *verify* a context. A self-contextualizable promotion information system scenario is used to illustrate our approach.

Keywords: GORE, Context Analysis, Self-Contextualization.

1 Introduction

There is a continuous need for systems that are adaptive and have a degree of autonomy to take decisions by themselves with the minimum intervention of users or designers. As a baseline, we need to identify the parameters that stimulate the need for changing the system behavior, what choices the system has that reflect to each range of parameters, and how to select between choices when more than one are possible. Context, the reification of the environment in which the system is supposed to operate [1], has been considered as a main stimulus for system behavior changes, but still there is a lack of research that involves context with requirements. The relation between context and requirements is tight; context can influence the requirements set, the choices to satisfy a requirement, and the quality of each choice.

Goal analysis (*i** [2], Tropos [3], and KAOS [4]) provides a way to analyse high level goals and to discover and represent alternative sets of tasks that can be adopted to achieve such goals. Goal models – a mainstream technique in requirements engineering – are used to represent the rationale of both humans and software systems, and help for representing software design alternatives. These features are also important for self-contextualizable software that must allow for alternatives and have a rationale to reflect users and software adaptation to context for adopting one useful execution course [5].

T. Halpin et al. (Eds.): BPMDS 2009 and EMMSAD 2009, LNBIP 29, pp. 326–338, 2009.

From a goal-oriented perspective, a self-contextualizable software is assigned a set of goals and has to keep them satisfied in different contexts. Context is out of the control of the system, and we do not expect it to adapt to software; rather, we can build software that adapts to context. Moreover, context may influence not only the software behaviour, but also the behaviour and possible choices of users. Therefore, the software should reflect users adaptation to the variable context to effectively satisfy users expectations. For example, hotel reservation is a common goal for travelers, while reservation procedures can differ from one hotel to another, and the same hotel can have distinct procedures each applying to a specific type of customers.

In our previous work [6,7,8], a modeling and reasoning framework has been presented to tackle some research challenges concerning mobile information systems presented in [9]. The main idea was to associate location (environmental or contextual) properties to the variation points of the goal model, and then to extract a location model from such properties. In that work, location properties are defined without further analysis, i.e. specified in one step as one monolithic block. We believe that a hierarchical analysis and representation of location properties would help for having more understandable, modifiable, and reusable specifications. There is also a need for analysing the domain of discourse[1] of goals and location properties to express explicitly the elements each goal and location property concern. Moreover, modeling the adaptable task execution workflow according to location is still missing.

In this paper, we extend the modeling framework proposed in [6,7,8] trying to overcome its mentioned limitations. We use goal analysis in conjunction with our proposed context analysis to build self-contextualizable goal models[2]. We provide constructs to hierarchically analyse context so to identify the verifiable facts and the monitorable data (i.e., we specify the monitoring requirements). We also identify and illustrate how to create self-contextualizable execution workflow from the resulted goal model, and discuss the utilization of the overall framework.

The rest of this paper is structured as follows. In section 2, we overview Tropos goal modeling. In section 3, we explain our proposed framework, defining the goal model variation points, the context analysis constructs, the self-contextual workflow, and discussing the utilization of the overall framework. We discuss the related work in section 4, and we conclude and discuss our future work in section 5.

2   Tropos Goal Modeling: Overview

Goal analysis represents a paradigmatic shift with respect to object-oriented analysis. While object-oriented analysis fits well to the late stages of requirement analysis, the goal-oriented analysis is more natural for the earlier stages where the organizational goals are analysed to identify and justify software requirements and position them within the organizational system [10]. Tropos goal analysis projects the system as a set of interdependent actors, each having its own strategic interests (*goals*). Goals are

---

[1] Domain (or universe) of discourse refers to the part of the world under discussion.

[2] Although the term *"location"* was used as a synonym of *"context"*, we chose to use *"context"*, because we realized that it has more common and well-accepted definition that also fits to what we meant by *"location"*.

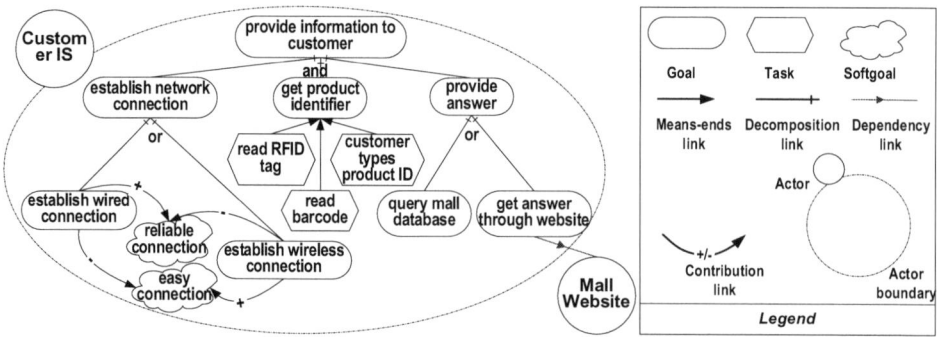

Fig. 1. Tropos goal model example

analysed, iteratively and in a top-down way, to identify the more specific sub-goals needed for satisfying that upper-level goals. Goals can be ultimately satisfied by means of specific executable processes (*tasks*).

In Fig.1, we show a partial Tropos goal model to clarify our goal analysis main concepts. Actors (*Customer IS* and *Mall Website*) have a set of top-level goals (*provide information to customer*), which are iteratively decomposed into subgoals by and-decomposition (all subgoals should be achieved to fulfil the top goal) and or-decomposition (at least one subgoal should be achieved to fulfil the top goal). The goal *provide information to customer* is and-decomposed into *establish network connection*, *get product identifier*, and *provide answer*; the goal *provide answer* is or-decomposed into *query mall database* and *get answer through website*. Goals are finally satisfied by means of executable tasks; the goal *"get product identifier"* can be reached by one of the tasks *"read RFID tag"*, *"read barcode"*, *"let customer type product ID"*.

A dependency indicates that an actor (*depender*) depends on another actor (*dependee*) to attain a goal or to execute a task: the actor *Customer IS* depends on the actor *Mall Website* for achieving the goal *get answer through website*. Soft-goals are qualitative objectives for whose satisfaction there is no clear cut criteria (*easy connection* is a rather vague objective), and they can be contributed either positively or negatively by goals and tasks: *establish wireless connection* contributes positively to *easy connection*, while *establish wired connection* contributes negatively to *easy connection*.

Goal analysis allows for different alternatives to satisfy a goal, but does not specify when each alternative can be adopted. Supporting alternative behaviours without specifying when to follow each of them rises the question *"why does the software support alternative behaviours and not just one?"*. On the other side, the consideration of different contexts the software has to adapt to, without supporting alternative behaviours rises the question *"what can the software do if context changes?"*. Analysing the different alternatives for satisfying a goal, and specifying the relation between each alternative and the corresponding context justify both alternatives and context, and help for having a self-contextualizable software.

3   Self-contextualizable Software Modeling Framework

Fig. 2 represents a goal model for a promotion information system that is intended to interact with customers and sales staff, through their PDAs, in order to promote products in different ways. To make it self-contextualizable, we need to explicitly represent the relation between these alternatives and context. Contexts, labeled by $C1..C12$ in the figure, might be related to the following categories of the goal model variation points:

1. *Or-decomposition*: Or-decomposition is the basic variability construct, we still need to specify in which context each alternative in an Or-decomposition can be adopted. E.g. *"promoting the product by cross-selling"* can be adopted when the product can be used with another product the customer already has $(C2)$, while *"promoting by offering discount"* is adopted when product is discountable and interesting to the customer $(C3)$, and *"promoting by free sample"* can be adopted when product is free sampled and new to the customer $(C4)$. The alternative *"get free sample from a machine"* can be adopted when customer has experience with such machines and can reach the machine and start to use it in a little time $(C5)$.

2. *Actors dependency*: in some contexts, an actor might attain a goal / get a task executed by delegating it to another actor. E.g. the customer information system can satisfy the goal *"deliver a sample of the product to customer by sales staff"* by delegating it to the sales staff information system, when the corresponding sales staff is free, speaks a language common to the customer, has sufficient knowledge about the product, and is close enough to the customer $(C6)$.

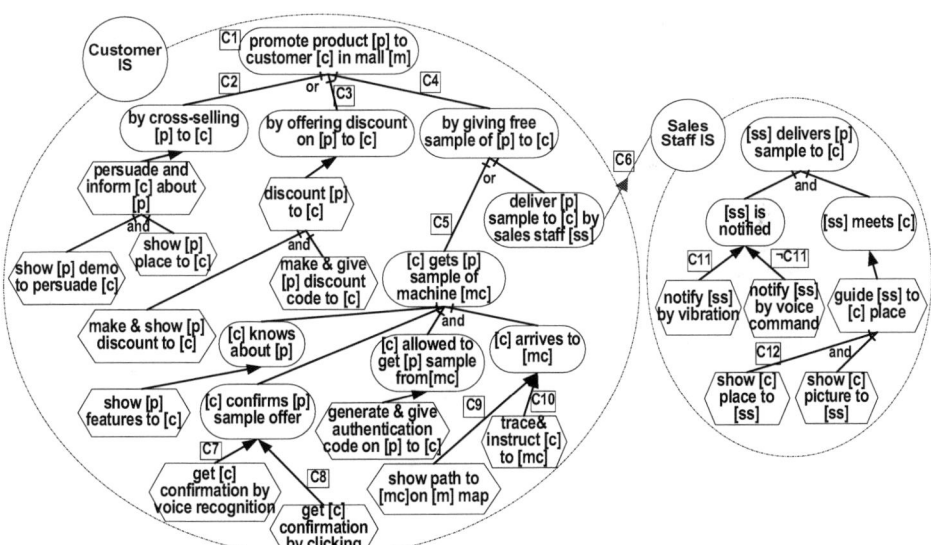

Fig. 2. The parametrized goal model with the variation points annotation

3. *Goal/Task activation*: an actor, and depending on the context, might find necessary or possible triggering (or stopping) the desire of satisfying a goal/ executing a task. E.g. to initiate the goal *"promote product to customer in mall"*, there should be enough time to accomplish the promotion, the customer is not in a hurry or has to work, and the customer did not recently buy the product and does not have it in his/her shopping cart ($C1$).

4. *And-decomposition*: a sub-goal / sub-task might (or might not) be needed in a certain context, that is some sub-goals / sub-tasks are not always mandatory to fulfil the top-level goal / task in And-decomposition. E.g. the sub-task *"show customer current place to sales staff"* is not needed if the customer stays around and can be seen directly by the sales staff ($C12$).

5. *Means-end*: goals can be ultimately satisfied by means of specific executable processes (*tasks*). The adoption of each task might depend on the context. E.g. *"get customer confirmation by voice recognition"* can be adopted when the customer place is not noisy, and the system is trained enough on the customer voice ($C7$), while the alternative *"get customer confirmation by clicking"* can be adopted when the customer has a good level of expertise with regards to using technology and a good control on his fingers, and the used device has a touch screen ($C8$). The task *"show path to sample machine on the mall e-map"* is adopted when customer can arrive easily to that machine ($C9$), while *"trace and instruct customer to sample machine"* task is adopted when the path is complex ($C10$). The task *"notify by vibration"* can be adopted when sales staff is using his PDA for calling ($C11$), while *"notify by headphone voice command"* is adopted in the other case ($\neg C11$).

6. *Contribution to soft-goals*[3]: the contributions to the softgoals can vary from one context to another. We need to specify the relation between the context and the value of the contribution. E.g. the goal *"establish wireless connection"* contributes differently to the softgoal *"reliable connection"* according to the distance between the customer's device and the wireless access point.

We need to analyse context to discover, represent, and agree on how it can be verified. Differently from the other research in context modeling (for a survey see [11]), we do not provide an ontology or a modeling language for representing context, but modeling constructs to hierarchically analyse context. Moreover, and in order to keep the link between the domain of discourse (i.e. the elements of the environment under discussion) between goal and context analysis, we propose parametrizing the goal and context models. Deciding the parameters is not straightforward and we might need several iterations to settle the final set of parameters.

Taking the parametrized goal *"by offering discount on product [p] to customer [c] in mall [m]"*, the analysis of its context ($C3$), and the data conceptual model that the analyst could elicit from the leaf facts are shown in Fig. 3. Each leaf of the context analysis hierarchy represents an atomic fact that is verifiable on a fragment of the data conceptual model that the monitoring system has to instantiate.

---

[3] In the rest of this paper, we do not consider softgoals and contextual contribution.

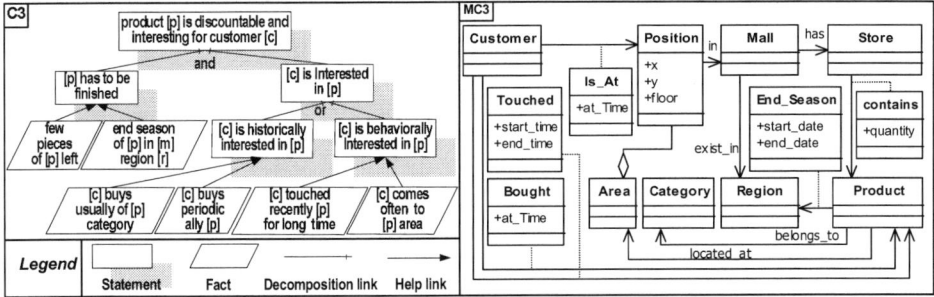

Fig. 3. The statement analysis for $C3$ and the correspondent data conceptual model $MC3$

3.1 Context Analysis Constructs

We provide a set of constructs to analyse high-level contexts and elicit the atomic facts that are verifiable on monitorable data. Context, the reification of the environment surrounding a system, can be monitored but not controlled by the system itself [1]. Under this assumption, systems cannot change the context but should adapt to it for satisfying their objectives.

Definition 1 (Fact). *a boolean predicate specifying a current or a previous context, whose truth value can be computed objectively.*

The objective method to compute a fact truth value requires monitoring some characteristics and history of a set of relevant environment elements. Facts are graphically represented as parallelograms as in Fig.3. Examples of facts are the following:

- *"customer recently bought the product from the mall"*: to compute the truth value of this fact, the system can check the purchase history of the customer since a number x of days ago.
- *"two products are usually sold together"*: the system can check the sales record of all customers and check if the two products $p1$ and $p2$ are often sold together.
- *"product is not in the shopping cart of the customer"*: the system can use an RFID reader in the cart to check if the product (identified by its RFID tag) is in the cart of the customer.

Definition 2 (Statement). *a boolean predicate specifying a current or a previous context, whose truth value cannot be computed objectively.*

Statement verification could not be objectively done because the system is not able to monitor and get all the data needed to compute the truth value of a statement, or because there could be no consensus about the way of knowing the truth value of a statement. Anyhow, to handle such problem we adopt a relaxed confirmation relation between facts, which are objectively computable by definition, and statements, in order to assign truth values to statements. We call this relation *"help"* and define it as following:

Definition 3 (Help). *Let f be a fact, s be a statement.* $help(f, s) \iff f \to s$.

The relation *help* is strongly subjective, since different stakeholders could define differ-ent *help* relations for the same statement, i.e. one stakeholder could say $help(f_1, s) \wedge help(f_2, s)$, whereas another one could say $help(f_2, s) \wedge help(f_3, s)$. Statements are graphically represented as shadowed rectangles, and the relation *help* is graphically represented as a filled-end arrow between a fact and a related statement as in Fig.3. Examples of statements and help relations are the following:

-   *"customer does not have the product"*: is a statement since the system cannot objec-tively compute its truth value. The system can get some evidence of this statement verifying two facts: *"customer did not buy the product from the mall recently"*, and *"the product is not in the cart of the customer"*, but these facts do not ensure that the customer does not have the product (e.g. the system cannot verify if the customer was given the product as a gift).
-   *"customer is interested in the product"*: is a statement that different stakeholders would define differently how we can get an evidence about it. Moreover, to verify it, the stakeholder might state a variety of other conditions which are not necessar-ily computable due to the lack of some necessary data the system cannot monitor. However, we might relax this problem using the *help* relation; a possible solution is to specify several facts that help the verification of the statement like following: *"customer buys the product periodically"*, *"customer buys usually from the prod-uct category"*, *"customer often comes to the product area"*, or *"customer holds recently the product for long time"*.

Definition 4 (And-decomposition). *Let* $\{s, s_1, \ldots, s_n\}$, $n \geq 2$ *be statements (facts).* $and\_decomposed(s, \{s_1, \ldots, s_n\}) \iff s_1 \wedge \ldots \wedge s_n \to s$.

Definition 5 (Or-decomposition). *Let* $\{s, s_1, \ldots, s_n\}$, $n \geq 2$ *be statements (facts).* $or\_decomposed(s, \{s_1, \ldots, s_n\}) \iff \forall i \in \{1, \ldots, n\}, s_i \to s$.

Decomposition is graphically represented as a set of directed arrows from the sub-statements (sub-facts) to the decomposed statement (fact) and annotated by the label *And* or *Or*. Examples of decompositions are the following:

-   *"customer is interested in the product"* is a statement verified if the sub-statements *"customer is historically interested in the product"* **or** *"customer is behaviourally interested in the product"* are verified.
-   *"customer did not get the product from the mall recently"* is a fact that is verified if the sub-fact *"customer does not have the product in his/her cart"* **and** the sub-fact *"the customer did not buy the product from the mall recently"* is true.

As discussed in [1], context is a reification of the environment that is whatever in the world provides a surrounding in which the system is supposed to operate. Each single fact and statement is a context, and our proposed reification hierarchy relates different subcontexts into one more abstract. Moreover, by considering that context is the reifi-cation of the environment, our context analysis is motivated by the need for constructs to analyse context to discover by the end the relevant atomic data that represent that environment, i.e. the data the system has to monitor.

3.2   From Goals to Self-contextualizable Workflow

Specifying the relation between context and goal alternatives is not enough to define how self-contextualizable software will execute tasks to achieve goals depending on the context. In order to handle this issue, two questions should be answered:

1. *How are goals / tasks sequentialized?*. For example, if the achievement of a goal g requires the execution of $t1 \wedge t2$, we have to specify if $t1$ is executed before or after or in parallel with $t2$.
2. *How does the system choose between alternatives when more than one are adoptable?*. For example, if a goal g can be reached through $g1 \vee g2$, we need to specify which one to follow. The intervention of stakeholders is required to prioritize alternatives along the goal hierarchy (for goals and tasks) to face cases where multiple options are possible in some contexts.

A possible self-contextualizable goal achievement workflow is shown in the activity diagram of Fig. 4. We have used activities to represent the tasks of the goal model of Fig. 2. The context of the alternative with the highest priority is evaluated first, and if it is confirmed that alternative is selected and carried out (even if other alternatives are also applicable). In our example, stakeholders stated that the priority for the alternative *"promotion by cross-selling"* is higher than the priority of the alternative *"promotion by free sample"*, whose priority is in turn higher than that of *"promotion by discounting"* alternative. Our depicted workflow reflects such prioritization – and also other prioritization on the other sets of sub-alternatives – by evaluating the contexts associated to the alternative with a higher priority first.

Fig. 4 introduces an additional concern, that is the accumulation of context at each variation point. Looking at Fig 2, we highlight that the confirmation of $C1$ is not sufficient to assure the existence of a workflow for the achievement of the top-level goal. For example, if $C2$-$C3$-$C4$ are all false, no task execution workflow is possible. Thus, finding an alternative for the top-level goal *"promote product [p] to customer [c] in mall [m]"* needs checking $C1^*$, defined as follows:

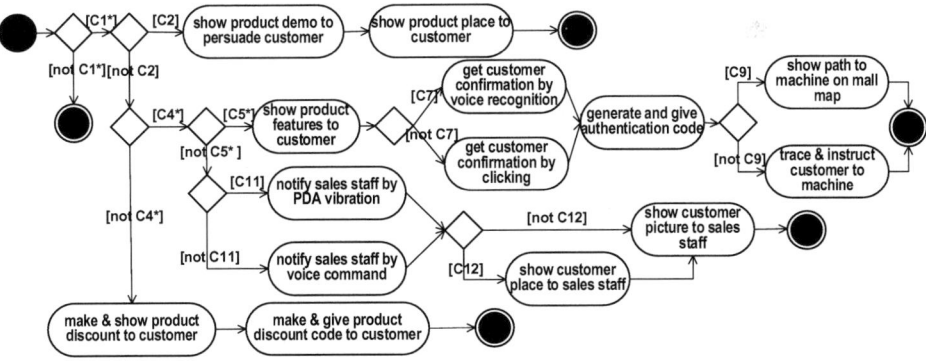

Fig. 4. A possible self-contextualizable goal achievement workflow

$$C1^* = C1 \wedge (C2 \vee C3 \vee C4^*)$$
$$C4^* = C4 \wedge (C5^* \vee C6^*)$$
$$C6^* = C6 \wedge (C11 \vee \neg C11) \wedge (C12 \vee \neg C12) = C6$$
$$C5^* = C5 \wedge (C7 \vee C8) \wedge (C9 \vee C10)$$

In order to evaluate the applicability of the alternative goal *"customer [c] gets product [p] free sample from a dedicated machine [mc]"*, we have to check the accumulated context $C5^*$, evaluating both $C5$ and the contexts that are lower in the goal model hierarchy: ($C7$ or $C8$) and ($C9$ or $C10$). If $C5^*$ is false, this means that no satisfaction alternative for the considered goal can be adopted.

3.3   Framework Utilization

Contextualization: the decomposition of the system into the functional part captured by goal model and the monitoring part that is captured by context analysis, and the association between variation points of goal model and the analysed context allow for a systematic contextualization of the software at the goal level of abstraction. All the functionalities needed by the alternative execution courses to satisfy goals has to be developed and then the contextualization has to be done. Contextualization can be done at two different times:

- *contextualization at deployment time*: when deploying the software to one specific environment, and when we know a priori some contexts that never change in that environment, we can consequently exclude from the deployed software some alternative sets of functionality that are never applied at that environment, as such functionalities will be never used and redundant. E.g. if the software is going to be deployed in a mall where the noise level is always high due to the nature of that mall (for instance, the mall is located in an open area, or the mall sells products of a specific nature), the context $C7$ will never, or rarely, be satisfied, and therefore the deployed software for that mall can exclude the functionality of voice recognition as a way of interaction with customer.
- *contextualization at runtime*: some other contexts are highly variable and should be monitored at runtime to know what behaviour to adopt. Consequently, the software has to monitor context, instantiating the monitoring data conceptual model, validating facts and inferring statements assigned to the variation points, and then adopt the suitable software alternative course of execution. E.g. the distance between customer and the self-service machine is a context which has always different values, and whether the software has to guide the customer to the machine using the alternative functionality *"trace and instruct customer to machine"*, or *"show path to machine on the mall map"* depends on the actual value of this variable distance.

Capturing and justifying monitoring requirements: our framework uses goal analysis in conjunction with context analysis to reduce the gap between the variability of software, at the goal level, and the variability of context, and helps for identifying and justifying both the functional and the monitoring software requirements. While goal analysis helps to elicit and justify each software functionality and to position it within the set of the organizational goals, the context analysis we propose, helps to elicit and justify the data the system has to monitor. The system has to monitor data to validate leaf facts so to confirm top level facts or statements that are used to decide which alternative to adopt for satisfying some organizational goal.

Reusability and scalability: systems change continuously; managing evolution is a hard task that is highly expensive and error-prone. Structuring the software functional requirements using the hierarchy of goal model and the monitoring requirements using the hierarchy of context analysis makes it more feasible to modify, extend, and /or reuse the software for another evolution of the system to operate in a new context or/and for a different group of stakeholders. The same goal model, or parts of it – and hence the same software functionality – can be contextualized differently by different stakeholders. We might need only to change the statements at each variation point, which might influence the data to be monitored.

The hierarchical context analysis has the potential to make a context (i) more understandable for the stakeholders, (ii) easily modifiable as it is not given as one monolithic block, and (iii) more reusable as parts of the statement analysis hierarchy can be also used for other variation points or other stakeholders context specifications. Specifying for each fact the related fragments of the data conceptual model is useful for purpose of tracking. For example, if for some reason, a group of stakeholders decided to drop, to alter, or to reuse one alternative, statement, or fact, we still can track which fragments in the conceptual data model could be influenced.

For example, a certain mall administration could decide that to promote by offering discount, it is not requested that *"few pieces of the product left"*, and it is, instead, requested that the fact *"[p] sales < 60 percent of the [p] historical sales average for the last 15 days"* is true. In this new context specification (*C3'*), one part of *C3* is deleted, one is reused, and another is added as shown in Fig. 5. Removing the fact *"few pieces of product[p] remained"*, leads to remove the corresponding data conceptual model fragments (the class *store*, and the association class *contain*). To verify the new fact, the system needs the sales records that are already represented in the data model fragment *MC3*. Therefore, the new data conceptual model for *C3'* will be like shown in Fig. 5.

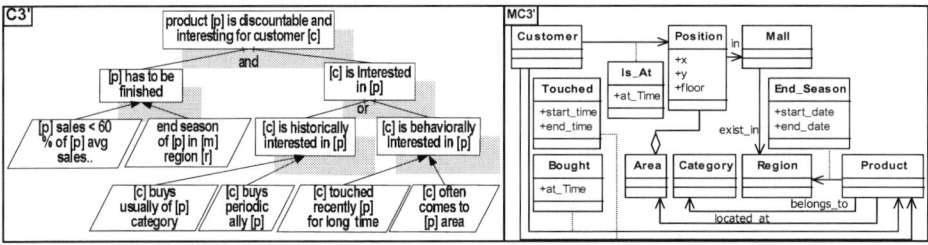

Fig. 5. The modified context *C3'* and the correspondent modified data model *MC3'*

4   Related Work

The research in context modeling, (e.g. [12]), concerns finding modeling constructs to represent software and user context, but there is still a gap between the context model and software behaviour model, i.e. between context and its use. We tried to reduce such gap and to allow for answering questions like: "*how do we decide the relevant context?*", "*why do we need context?*" and "*how does context influence software and user behaviour adaptation?*". Modeling context information should not be done as a standalone activity; context should be defined jointly with the analysis we do for discovering the alternative software behaviours. Salifu et al. [13] investigate the use of problem descriptions to represent and analyse variability in context-aware software; the work recognizes the link between software requirements and context information as a basic step to design context aware systems.

Software variability modeling, mainly feature models [14,15], concerns modeling a variety of possible configurations of the software functionalities to allow for a systematic way of tailoring a product upon stakeholders choices, but there is still a gap between each functionality and the context where this functionality can or has to be adopted, the problem we tried to solve at the goal level. Furthermore, our work is in line, and has the potential to be integrated, with the work in [16] and the FARE method proposed in [17] that show possible ways to integrate features with domain goals and knowledge to help for eliciting and justifying features.

Requirements monitoring is about insertion of a code into a running system to gather information, mainly about the computational performance, and reason if the running system is always meeting its design objectives, and reconcile the system behaviour to them if a deviation occurs [5]. The objective is to have a more robust, maintainable, and self-evolving systems. In [18], a GORE (goal-oriented requirements engineering) framework KAOS [4] was integrated with an event-monitoring system (FLEA [19]) to provide an architecture that enables the runtime automated reconciliation between system goals and system behaviour with respect to a priori anticipated or evolving changes of the system environment. Differently, we propose model-driven framework that concerns an earlier stage, i.e. requirements, with the focus on identifying requirements together with context, and hierarchically analysing and representing context and eliciting the monitoring data.

Customizing goal models to fit to user skills and preferences was studied in [20,21]. The selection between goal satisfaction alternatives is based on one dimension of context, i.e. user skills, related to the executable tasks of the goal hierarchy, and on user preferences which are expressed over softgoals. Lapouchnian et al. [22] propose techniques to design autonomic software based on an extended goal modeling framework, but the relation with the context is not focused on. Liaskos et al [23], study the variability modeling under the requirements engineering perspective and propose a classification of the intentional variability when Or-decomposing a goal. We focused on context variability, i.e. the unintentional variability, which influences the applicability and appropriateness of each goal satisfaction alternative.

5   Conclusions and Future Work

In this paper, we have proposed a goal-oriented framework for self-contextualizable software systems. We have used goal models to elicit alternative sets of executable tasks to satisfy a goal, and we have proposed the association between the alternative software executions and context. In turn, context is defined through statement analysis that elicits alternative sets of facts the system has to verify on monitorable data so to confirm the high level statements. Analysing facts will also lead to identify the data conceptual model the monitoring system has to instantiate to enable facts verification. Facts are verified upon the monitorable data to confirm statements that restrict the space of goal satisfaction alternatives. We have also shown how to construct self-contextualizable goal execution workflows that allow for the construction of an exact execution course of tasks to satisfy goals according to the context. Doing this, we specify the requirements of the monitoring system and the reasoning the system has to do on context to construct, autonomously, a contextualized goal execution course.

As future work, we will define models covering all development phases of self-contextualizable software and a process to facilitate the development of high quality self-contextualizable software. We also want to find a formalization and reasoning mechanisms that fit well to the modeling framework introduced in this paper. We will work on more complex case studies in order to better validate our approach. Similarly to features [24], contexts suffer from interaction problems; for instance, there could be contexts that contradict with others on one goal satisfaction alternative. Therefore, supporting tools and reasoning techniques should be proposed to assist the design and verification of models.

Acknowledgement

This work has been partially funded by EU Commission, through the SERENITY, and COMPAS projects, and by the PRIN program of MIUR under the MEnSA project. We would also like to thank Prof. Jaelson Brelaz de Castro for the valuable discussion we had about this work.

References

1. Finkelstein, A., Savigni, A.: A framework for requirements engineering for context-aware services. In: Proc. 1st Int. Workshop on From Software Requirements to Architectures (STRAW) (2001)
2. Yu, E.: Modelling strategic relationships for process reengineering. Ph.D. Thesis, University of Toronto (1995)
3. Bresciani, P., Perini, A., Giorgini, P., Giunchiglia, F., Mylopoulos, J.: Tropos: An agent-oriented software development methodology. Autonomous Agents and Multi-Agent Systems 8(3), 203–236 (2004)
4. Dardenne, A., Van Lamsweerde, A., Fickas, S.: Goal-directed requirements acquisition. Science of computer programming 20(1-2), 3–50 (1993)
5. Fickas, S., Feather, M.: Requirements monitoring in dynamic environments. In: Proceedings of the Second IEEE International Symposium on Requirements Engineering, p. 140. IEEE Computer Society, Washington (1995)

6. Ali, R., Dalpiaz, F., Giorgini, P.: Location-based variability for mobile information systems. In: Bellahsène, Z., Léonard, M. (eds.) CAiSE 2008. LNCS, vol. 5074, pp. 575–578. Springer, Heidelberg (2008)
7. Ali, R., Dalpiaz, F., Giorgini, P.: Modeling and Analyzing Variability for Mobile Information Systems. In: Gervasi, O., Murgante, B., Laganà, A., Taniar, D., Mun, Y., Gavrilova, M.L. (eds.) ICCSA 2008, Part II. LNCS, vol. 5073, pp. 291–306. Springer, Heidelberg (2008)
8. Ali, R., Dalpiaz, F., Giorgini, P.: Location-based software modeling and analysis: Tropos-based approach. In: Li, Q., Spaccapietra, S., Yu, E., Olivé, A. (eds.) ER 2008. LNCS, vol. 5231, pp. 169–182. Springer, Heidelberg (2008)
9. Krogstie, J., Lyytinen, K., Opdahl, A., Pernici, B., Siau, K., Smolander, K.: Research areas and challenges for mobile information systems. International Journal of Mobile Communications 2, 220–234 (2004)
10. Mylopoulos, J., Chung, L., Yu, E.: From object-oriented to goal-oriented requirements analysis. Commun. ACM 42, 31–37 (1999)
11. Strang, T., Linnhoff-Popien, C.: A context modeling survey. In: Workshop on Advanced Context Modelling, Reasoning and Management as part of UbiComp (2004)
12. Henricksen, K., Indulska, J.: A software engineering framework for context-aware pervasive computing. In: Proc. Second IEEE Intl. Conference on Pervasive Computing and Communications (PerCom 2004), p. 77 (2004)
13. Salifu, M., Yu, Y., Nuseibeh, B.: Specifying Monitoring and Switching Problems in Context. In: Proc. 15th Intl. Conference on Requirements Engineering (RE 2007), pp. 211–220 (2007)
14. Pohl, K., Böckle, G., van der Linden, F.: Software Product Line Engineering: Foundations, Principles, and Techniques. Springer, Heidelberg (2005)
15. Kang, K.C., Kim, S., Lee, J., Kim, K., Shin, E., Huh, M.: Form: A feature-oriented reuse method with domain-specific reference architectures. Ann. Softw. Eng. 5, 143–168 (1998)
16. Yu, Y., do Prado Leite, J.C.S., Lapouchnian, A., Mylopoulos, J.: Configuring features with stakeholder goals. In: SAC 2008: Proceedings of the 2008 ACM symposium on Applied computing, pp. 645–649. ACM, New York (2008)
17. Ramachandran, M., Allen, P.: Commonality and variability analysis in industrial practice for product line improvement. Software Process: Improvement and Practice 10(1), 31–40 (2005)
18. Feather, M.S., Fickas, S., Lamsweerde, A.V., Ponsard, C.: Reconciling System Requirements and Runtime Behavior. In: Proceedings of the 9th international workshop on Software specification and design IWSSD 1998, p. 50. IEEE Computer Society, Los Alamitos (1998)
19. Cohen, D., Feather, M.S., Narayanaswamy, K., Fickas, S.S.: Automatic monitoring of software requirements. In: ICSE 1997: Proceedings of the 19th international conference on Software engineering, pp. 602–603. ACM, New York (1997)
20. Hui, B., Liaskos, S., Mylopoulos, J.: Requirements analysis for customizable software goals-skills- preferences framework. In: RE, pp. 117–126. IEEE Computer Society, Los Alamitos (2003)
21. Liaskos, S., McIlraith, S., Mylopoulos, J.: Representing and reasoning with preference requirements using goals. Technical report, Dept. of Computer Science, University of Toronto (2006), ftp://ftp.cs.toronto.edu/pub/reports/csrg/542
22. Lapouchnian, A., Yu, Y., Liaskos, S., Mylopoulos, J.: Requirements-driven design of autonomic application software. In: Proc. 2006 conference of the Center for Advanced Studies on Collaborative research (CASCON 2006), p. 7. ACM, New York (2006)
23. Liaskos, S., Lapouchnian, A., Yu, Y., Yu, E., Mylopoulos, J.: On goal-based variability acquisition and analysis. In: Proc. 14th IEEE Intl. Requirements Engineering Conference (RE 2006), pp. 76–85 (2006)
24. Cameron, E.J., Griffeth, N., Lin, Y.-J., Nilson, M.E., Schnure, W.K., Velthuijsen, H.: A feature-interaction benchmark for IN and beyond. Communications Magazine, IEEE 31(3), 64–69 (1993)

Security and Consistency of IT and Business Models at Credit Suisse Realized by Graph Constraints, Transformation and Integration Using Algebraic Graph Theory

Christoph Brandt[1], Frank Hermann[2], and Thomas Engel[1]

[1] Université du Luxembourg, SECAN-Lab, Campus Kirchberg,
6, rue Richard Coudenhove-Kalergi, L-1359 Luxembourg-Kirchberg, EU
{christoph.brandt,thomas.engel}@uni.lu
http://wiki.uni.lu/secan-lab
[2] Technische Universität Berlin, Fakultät IV, Theoretische Informatik/Formale
Spezifikation, Sekr. FR 6-1, Franklinstr. 28/29, 10587 Berlin, EU
frank@cs.tu-berlin.de
http://www.tfs.tu-berlin.de

Abstract. This paper shows typical security and consistency challenges regarding the models of the business and the IT universe of the dynamic service-, process- and rule-based environment at Credit Suisse. It presents a theoretical solution for enterprise engineering that is implementable, and fits smoothly with the daily needs and constraints of the people in the scenario. It further enables decentralized modeling based on cognitive and mathematical or logical concepts. Normative aspects of the models are analyzed by graph constraint checks, while consistency is checked and ensured by model integration and transformation. To cope with theoretical and practical necessities, the presented solution is kept sound and usable as well as extensible and scalable. All techniques are based on one theoretical framework: algebraic graph theory. Therefore, the techniques are compatible with each other.

Keywords: enterprise engineering, services, processes, rules, business models, IT models, verification, tests, norms, consistency, algebraic graph theory, model transformation, integration, graph constraints.

1 Introduction

Based on the requirements of Credit Suisse we are presenting how algebraic graph theory can be used as an integration and transformation technique for formal models using their abstract syntax. In our study these models serve as a reference to define the semantics of cognitive models for service landscapes, processes and rules. We claim that the alignment of formal and cognitive models can be realized by model integration using algebraic graph theory. All this is motivated by comparing today's and tomorrows modeling situation at Credit

T. Halpin et al. (Eds.): BPMDS 2009 and EMMSAD 2009, LNBIP 29, pp. 339–352, 2009.
© Springer-Verlag Berlin Heidelberg 2009

Suisse. The contribution encompasses a Mathematica implementation of algebraic graph theory, a new model framework for enterprise engineering, a multi-dimensional approach of model integration, transformation and consistency checks, the use of graph constraints for the purpose of security policy checks, and a sketched propagation of graph constraints beyond model boundaries to evaluate the consistency of security policies of different models. Existing implementations are available for all presented types of formal models. Therefore, model instances can be evaluated automatically.

We claim that one central purpose of a bank's enterprise model is to check for security, risk and compliance. Today, this is done using best practices that focus on interests of certain stakeholders. It is done in an end-of-pipe fashion using checklists and results in partial insights only. The situation is summarized by the following table.

	Today	Tomorrow
Approach	Best Practices	Methods
Focus	Interest	Organization
Control	End-of-pipe	Begin-of-pipe
Judgment	Checklists	Prove, Simulation, Test
Coverage	Partial	Complete

Fig. 1. Security, Risk and Compliance – Today and Tomorrow

Tomorrow's situation, however, should not be built primarily on best-practices. The objective is to use sound methods. In addition to that, today's focus on different stakeholders' interests should be shifted towards organizational qualities, imagining that an organization can be seen as an integrated model of services, processes and rules including their hierarchies. In such a case, where the organization can be represented as an integrated model, controls can be applied in a begin-of-pipe way towards its defining model, making sure that no unwanted definition of an organizational setting comes up later. Because of the methodological basis introduced from the very beginning by the chosen types of models, we claim that prove, simulation and test operations can be automated in an integrated way. Evaluations of formal models enable complete coverage of organizational states.

Business people requested to work with models that are build on cognitive concepts, today's domain models do not use. An example is the use of fuzzy notions. These models can be mapped to mathematical or logical models later on to enable model checking. For practical reasons, services, processes and rules are modeled separately and in a decentralized way. Therefore, model construction, integration and transformation has to be supported. Compliance must be solved. We will show all this in detail based on a small showcase using algebraic graph transformation that has been implemented in Mathematica [17]. Before that, some context information regarding the concrete situation at the bank and the used theory is given.

2   Enterprise Engineering

The first part of this section presents enterprise engineering from a historical point of view. Particular attention is paid to the situation at Credit Suisse. Thereafter, a more methodological understanding is developed based on the bank's needs.

2.1   Today's Situation

Today's enterprise engineering can either be looked at from its perspective of modeling business processes in business departments or from the point of view of running technical services in IT departments. At Credit Suisse, both perspectives exist and both have their own history, document types and people. The current situation is characterized by two views that are not in synch, not integrated, not conflict-free and sometimes over- or under-specified. It can further be characterized as document-oriented, not model-centric. In the documents, different types of models can be found – the following table lists some of them.

	Components	Processes	Requirements
Business Department	–	UML	BO
IT Department	Visio	–	Excel, Word

Fig. 2. Today's Enterprise Modeling at Credit Suisse

The view of Credit Suisse's people is department-oriented and focuses on components, processes and requirements. Landscapes of IT components are often documented using Microsoft Visio, business processes using UML [14] models, and requirements using business object models (BO) [15], or just a natural or standardized business language. The fact that business services and IT processes are not documented shows a mismatch in the involved departments' understanding of the common universe. There is a pressure towards better quality and lower costs.

2.2   Tomorrow's Situation

For the purpose of the requested solution we do not necessarily need UML models here. We like to focus on domain models build on cognitive concepts that have to be aligned with domain models built on mathematical or logical concepts. This assumption helps to clean up the current situation and a new framework for enterprise modeling can be given. Because people at Credit Suisse requested model services, processes and rules using independent, but overlapping models, we focus on model integration and model transformation based on algebraic graph theory. The integration operation is expected to be completely automated.

Therefore, this framework proposes to work with independent models built on cognitive and mathematical or logical concepts. The alignment can be realized by model integration. It does not need to be static over time. Finally, the language space of the business and the IT department should be modeled separately. Here, different ontologies can come into play. That leads to the notion of a business and an IT universe meaning that there is no top-down dependency, but rather a mutual relationship between equals. This assumption enables a round-trip engineering by model transformation that is not feasible in a model-driven architecture approach implying a clear top-down relationship between the business and the IT models. This is something, people at Credit Suisse requested strongly, because they do work in a decentralized organization. As a consequence, business and IT groups need to synchronize their cognitive models driven by model integration from time to time.

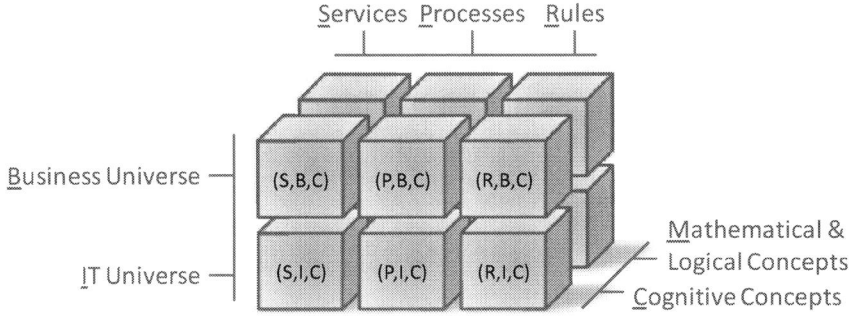

Fig. 3. Model Framework

An advantage of this modeling framework is that the different models themselves can be kept lean, meaning that they only have to deal with a very small fraction of the world. Automatic model integration will generate aggregated views as presented in a first version in the following showcases.

The models based on mathematical and logical concepts used in this context need to be expressive enough, so that models based on cognitive concepts can be fully aligned towards them. By the help of this alignment model checking can be used in an encapsulated way. That is something the people in the field have strongly requested because they do not want to touch formal methods. We propose to use the formal methods listed in the following table. A detailed motivation related to this suggestion is given in [3].

	Service Landscapes	Process Landscapes	Rules and Principles
Business Universe	ABT & Reo	PA & MMC	FOL & LN
IT Universe	ABT & Reo	PA & MMC	FOL & LN

Fig. 4. Tomorrow's Enterprise Engineering at Credit Suisse

Abstract behavior types and Reo connectors (ABT & Reo) [1] can explain the semantics of service landscapes using exogenous coordination. Process algebra in combination with the modal mu-calculus (PA & MMC) [11] can be used to describe the semantics of event-driven process chains and allows checking for process properties. Finally, first-order logic in combination with logical negation (FOL & LN) [12] is expressive enough to grasp the semantics of existing rules and principles related to service landscapes or processes. Because implementations exist for all these formal methods, properties of corresponding models can be checked automatically.

3 Algebraic Graph Transformation

Visual languages and in particular domain specific languages are commonly specified by its abstract together with its related concrete syntax. A diagram of a visual language shows the concrete syntax of a model. Its related abstract syntax is used for model modification as well as model analysis. Meta modeling [13] is one possible technique for defining the abstract syntax of a domain specific language, where models have to conform to a meta model and additionally to all OCL constraints.

An alternative technique is graph transformation [7]. A type graph represents the meta model, and graph transformation rules constructively define how models are build up. Additional graph constraints further restrict models to fulfill certain conditions. This way the technique allows both, specification from the constructive and from the declarative point of view. This section shortly reviews graph transformation, i.e. the rule-based modification of graphs representing the abstract syntax of models for the purpose of this paper. Based on this, main concepts of triple graph transformation used in Section 4 and 5 for fully automated model transformation and integration are presented. An implementation of the theory is presented in [3]. Note that we can also use modeling features like attribution and node type inheritance as presented in [7].

In this context we consider multi graphs, i.e. graphs with possibly parallel edges. A graph $G = (V, E, src, tgt)$ is given by a set of vertices V, a set of edges E and functions $src, tgt : E \rightarrow V$ defining source and target nodes for each edge. Graphs can be related by graph morphisms $m : G_1 \rightarrow G_2$, where $m = (m_V, m_E)$ consists of a mapping m_V for vertices and a mapping m_E for edges, which have to be compatible with the source and target functions of G_1 and G_2.

The core of a graph transformation rule consists of a left-hand side L, an interface K, a right-hand side R, and two injective graph morphisms $L \xleftarrow{l} K$ and $K \xrightarrow{r} R$. Interface K contains the graph objects which are not changed by the rule and hence occur both in L and in R. Applying rule p to a graph G means to find a match m of L in G and to replace this matched part $m(L)$ in G by the corresponding right-hand side R of the rule, thus leading to a graph transformation step $G \xRightarrow{p,m} H$. A graph transformation step is given by a double-pushout (DPO) since both squares in the diagram are pushouts in the category of graphs, where D is the intermediate graph after removing $m(L)$ in G, and in (PO_2) H is constructed as gluing of D and R along K.

$$L \xleftarrow{l} K \xrightarrow{r} R$$
$$m \downarrow (PO_1) \downarrow (PO_2) \downarrow m^*$$
$$G \longleftarrow D \longrightarrow H$$

In this paper, we consider non-deleting rules, which allow model transformation and integration. Therefore, the interface K of a rule is equal to L and we can write a rule p as $p = L \xrightarrow{r} R$. In order to analyze consistency between different models we apply triple graph transformation [18], which is based on triples of graphs instead of single graphs. This allows us to automatically derive model transformation and model integration rules out of a single set of triple rules. Graphs are extended to triple graphs $G = (G_S \xleftarrow{s} G_C \xrightarrow{t} G_T)$, which define a source model by graph G_S, a target model by graph G_T and their correspondences given by graph G_C linked to the source and target models by graph morphisms s and t. A Triple graph morphism $m = (m_S, m_C, m_T) : G_1 \rightarrow G_2$ consists of three graph morphisms - one for each component and it has to be compatible with the inner structure of G_1 and G_2. Given a triple rule $tr : L \rightarrow R$, a triple graph G and an injective triple graph morphism $m = (m_S, m_C, m_T) : L \rightarrow G$, called triple match m, a triple graph transformation step $G \xRightarrow{tr,m} H$ from G to a triple graph H is given by a pushout in the category of triple graphs (see [5]).

Fig. 5 shows triple rule $DepartmentToLAN$, which simultaneously creates two nodes of type "ABT". The rule is part of a set of rules $RULES_{B,I,M}$, which specify how business and IT models in the scenario are co-developed and related with each other. In particular, departments in the business level correspond to LAN-networks in the IT area. Note that we use a compact notation for triple rules. The left hand side L and the right hand side R of a triple rule are combined

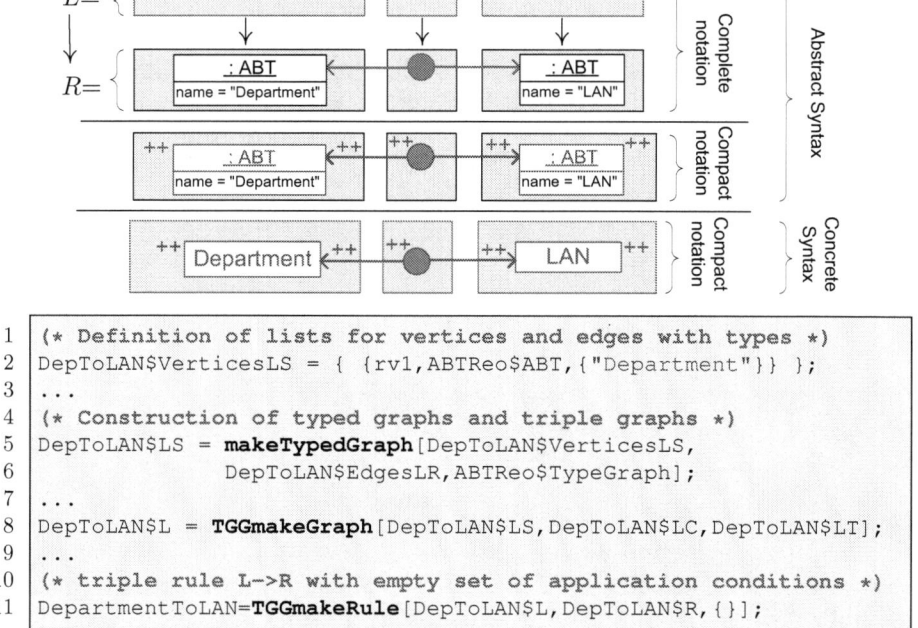

```
1   (* Definition of lists for vertices and edges with types *)
2   DepToLAN$VerticesLS = { {rv1,ABTReo$ABT,{"Department"}} };
3   ...
4   (* Construction of typed graphs and triple graphs *)
5   DepToLAN$LS = makeTypedGraph[DepToLAN$VerticesLS,
6                   DepToLAN$EdgesLR,ABTReo$TypeGraph];
7   ...
8   DepToLAN$L = TGGmakeGraph[DepToLAN$LS,DepToLAN$LC,DepToLAN$LT];
9   ...
10  (* triple rule L->R with empty set of application conditions *)
11  DepartmentToLAN=TGGmakeRule[DepToLAN$L,DepToLAN$R,{}];
```

Fig. 5. Triple Rule $DepartmentToLAN$ and Mathematica Source Code within one triple graph as shown in Fig. 5. The elements, which appear in R only are marked by green line color and labels "++". The bottom line of the figure shows the visualization of the rule, i.e. the concrete syntax. Here, ABT nodes are boxes with a label specifying its name according to the standard notation of abstract behavior types [1]. Further information and full implementation details are given in [3].

4 Case-Study: Consistency of Models

All models in the present scenario are defined as graphs, which specify the abstract syntax of the models. For this reason, consistency of a pair of models can be analyzed and ensured by concepts for graphs and graph transformation. We propose two main techniques for this aim: model transformation and integration based on triple graph transformation [4,6].

Considering the model framework in Fig. 3 we may have the following situations: First of all, we may have that two models are not integrated, thus performing model integration may detect conflicts between them. Furthermore, we may have that some model instances within the model framework are not specified, e.g. business process models and IT service models usually exist while business service models may not be developed. In this case we can apply model transformation on business process models to derive IT process models and check whether they show integration conflicts with respect to the existing IT service models. Therefore, Sec. 4.1 presents model transformation and in Sec. 4.2 we apply model integration to detect conflicts between existing models. All constructions are presented on behalf of an example of a business model $M_{S,B,M}$ and an IT model $M_{S,I,M}$ shown in Fig. 8.

4.1 Model Transformation

As described in Sec. 3 triple rules can be used to specify how two models can be created simultaneously. Thus, triple rules allow the modeler to define patterns of correspondences between elements of two models. Based on these triple rules the operational forward rules are derived and they are used for model transformation from one model of the source language of the transformation into a corresponding model of the target language.

Definition 1 (Derived Forward Rule). *Given a triple rule* $tr = (tr_S, tr_C, tr_T) : L \to R$ *the forward rule* $tr_F = (tr_{F,S}, tr_{F,C}, tr_{F,T})$ *is derived by taking tr and redefining the following components (double subscripts are separated by a comma):* $L_{F,S} = R_S$, $tr_{F,S} = id$, *and* $s_{L,F} = tr_S \circ s_L$.

$$L = (L_S \xleftarrow{s_L} L_C \longrightarrow L_T) \qquad\qquad L_F = (R_S \xleftarrow{tr_S \circ s_L} L_C \longrightarrow L_T)$$
$$tr\downarrow \quad trs\downarrow \qquad\quad \downarrow \qquad\quad \downarrow \qquad\qquad\qquad tr_F\downarrow \quad id\downarrow \qquad\quad \downarrow \qquad\quad \downarrow$$
$$R = (R_S \longleftarrow R_C \longrightarrow R_T) \qquad\qquad R_F = (R_S \longleftarrow R_C \longrightarrow R_T)$$

triple rule tr   forward rule tr_F

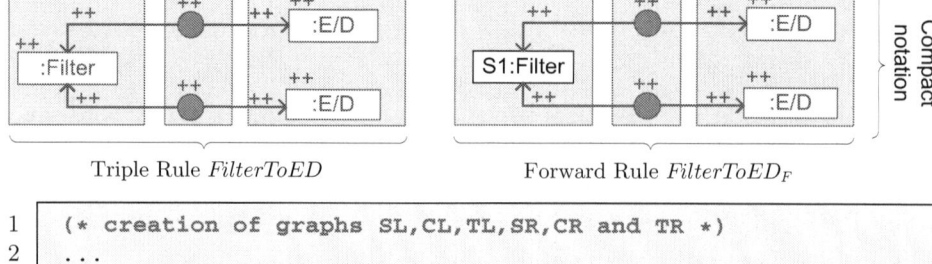

Triple Rule *FilterToED*   Forward Rule *FilterToED$_F$*

```
1    (* creation of graphs SL,CL,TL,SR,CR and TR *)
2    ...
3    FilterToED$L = TGGmakeGraph[SL,CL,TL];
4    FilterToED$R = TGGmakeGraph[SR,CR,TR];
5    (* TGG rule consists of L, R and application conditions *)
6    FilterToED   = TGGmakeRule[FilterToED$L,FilterToED$R,{}];
7    FilterToEDF  = TGGforwardRule[FilterToED];
```

Fig. 6. Triple Rule, Derived Forward Rule and Mathematica Source Code

A model transformation consists of a sequence of applied forward rules, such that the source model is completely translated and conforms to the patterns given by the triple rules. Source consistency [5] is a sufficient condition for this criteria. Intuitively, the source model is parsed using source rules, which are the triple rules restricted to the source component. This leads to a sequence of source transformation steps for building up the source model. The induced forward sequence can then be checked to be completely determined by the source sequence and its corresponding forward rules. An algorithm for checking source consistency is given in [8].

Fig. 6 shows triple rule *"FilterToED"* and its derived forward rule *"FilterToED$_F$"* according to Def. 1. The forward rule is used to transform a filter into two ABT nodes "E/D", which encode and decode communication data. The underlying idea here is that confidential communication in a business universe is filtered out - in an IT universe it is encoded and decoded. Since the left hand side of the forward rule contains already all source elements of the right hand side of the triple rule, the node "S1" appears in both, in the left and in the right hand side. Therefore, the node is named with "S1" to indicate the mapping from L to R. The given operation calls show the specification of the triple rule and the automatic derivation of its forward rule in the AGT Mathematica (AGT_M) implementation.

Rule *"secureConnect"* in Fig. 7 defines that connections with filters at outgoing public connections in a business model correspond to encoded public connections between private communication channels. The security norm here is to forbid that confidential data can be intercepted and used by third parties. The rule can be used for an arbitrary amount of in- and outgoing connections of an ABT node by applying it as often as needed. Fig. 8 shows the source model $M_{S,B,M}$ and the resulting target model $M_{S,I,M}$ using the derived forward rules of the presented triple rules *"DepartmentToLAN"*, *"FilterToED"*,

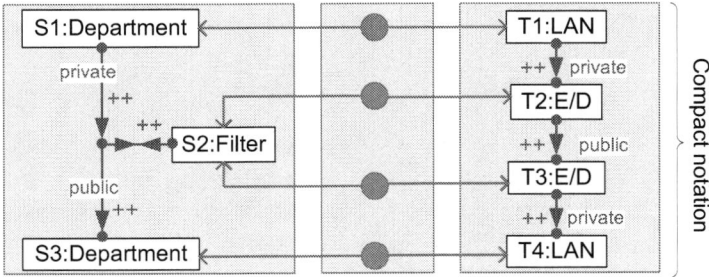

Fig. 7. Triple Rule *secureConnect*

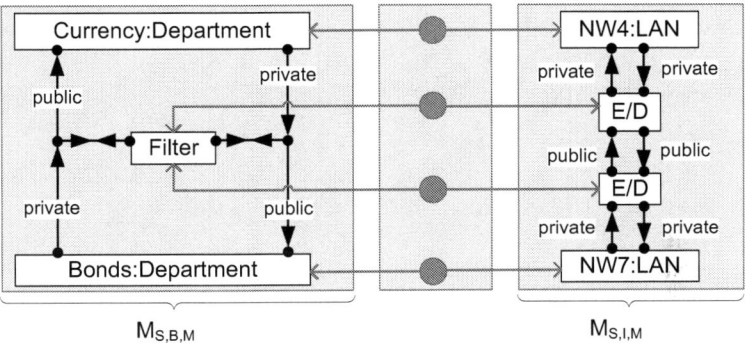

```
1  (* Grammar consists of Forward Triple Rules ABTReo$RulesMT and
2     Integrated Type Graph ABTReo$TypeGraphMT *)
3  ABTReo$GrammarMT={ABTReo$RulesMT, ABTReo$TypeGraphMT};
4  (* Apply Model Transforamation to Model M_SBM *)
5  ModelSIF = TGGmodelTrafo[ModelSBF, ABTReo$GrammarMT];
```

Fig. 8. Integrated Model containing Source Model $M_{S,B,M}$ and Target Model $M_{S,I,M}$

and "*secureConnect*". The model transformation consists of 5 forward transformation steps and is explained in detail in [3].

4.2   Model Integration

Analogously to forward rules, integration rules are derived automatically from the set of triple rules, which describe the patterns of the relations between two models. Integration rules are used to establish or update the correspondences between two models. The scenario shows many possible pairs (see Fig. 3). If two models can be completely integrated they are consistent, otherwise they show conflicts. Consistency between the models is ensured by checking *S-T-consistency* [6], which means that the integration has to conform to a parsing of the existing source and target model.

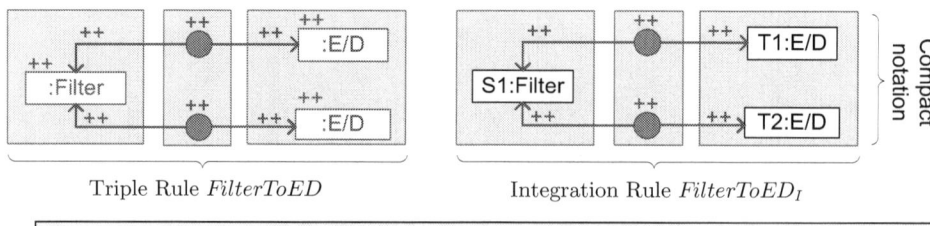

Triple Rule *FilterToED*   Integration Rule *FilterToED$_I$*

```
1  FilterToEDI = TGGintegrationRule[FilterToED];
```

Fig. 9. Derived Integration Rule *FilterToED$_I$* and Mathematica Source Code

Definition 2 (Derived Integration Rule). *Given a triple rule* $tr = (tr_S, tr_C, tr_T) : L \to R$ *the integration rule* $tr_I = (tr_{I,S}, tr_{I,C}, tr_{I,T})$ *is derived by taking* tr *and redefining the following components (double subscripts are separated by a comma):* $L_{I,S} = R_S$, $L_{I,T} = R_T$, $tr_{I,S} = id$, $tr_{I,T} = id$, $s_{L,I} = tr_S \circ s_L$, *and* $t_{L,I} = tr_T \circ t_L$.

$$
\begin{array}{cc}
L = (L_S \xleftarrow{s_L} L_C \xrightarrow{t_L} L_T) & L_I = (R_S \xleftarrow{tr_S \circ s_L} L_C \xrightarrow{tr_T \circ t_L} R_T) \\
tr\downarrow \quad tr_S\downarrow \qquad \downarrow \qquad \downarrow tr_T & tr_I\downarrow \quad id\downarrow \qquad \downarrow \qquad \downarrow id \\
R = (R_S \xleftarrow{} R_C \xrightarrow{} R_T) & R_I = (R_S \xleftarrow{} R_C \xrightarrow{} R_T) \\
\textit{triple rule } tr & \textit{integration rule } tr_I
\end{array}
$$

Fig. 9 shows triple rule "*FilterToED$_I$*" and its derived integration rule according to Def. 2. This corresponds to the derivation of the forward rule in Fig. 6. When applying the integration rule the matching of the left hand side searches for a filter node in the source model and two encoding nodes in the target model. The integration step then relates the nodes by the blue correspondence nodes. There may be several matches which do not lead to a correct integration, but those matches will also lead to sequences that are not *S-T*-consistent and therefore, these sequences will be rejected.

Fig. 8 shows the integration of models $M_{S,B,M}$ and $M_{S,I,M}$ via a correspondence graph containing blue correspondence nodes. The models are integrated by an $S-T$-consistent integration sequence consisting of 5 steps with derived model integration rules. Further details are explained in [3]. Note that correctness is ensured by *S-T*-consistency and if model $M_{S,B,M}$ had only a communication channel from "Currency" to "Bonds" but not in the inverse direction, the inconsistency would be detected. The structures, which are not integrated can be highlighted to support user driven synchronization. Furthermore, a completion can be performed by applying so called backward rules [5], which are also derived from the original triple rules.

5   Case-Study: Compliance

In the domain of enterprise networks, models have to fulfil security norms. In order to automatically analyze and verify the compliance of models to specific

PC: publicIsEncrypted

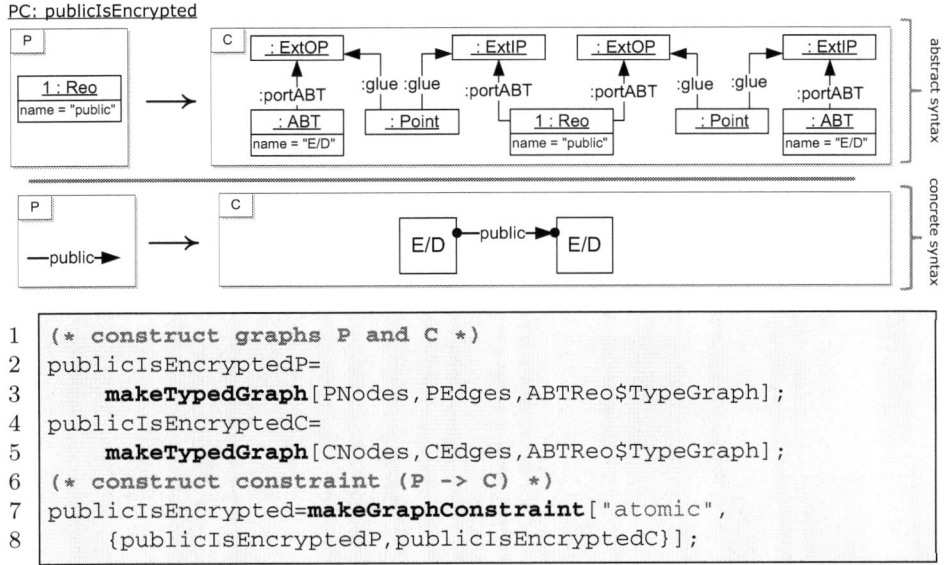

```
1  (* construct graphs P and C *)
2  publicIsEncryptedP=
3      makeTypedGraph[PNodes,PEdges,ABTReo$TypeGraph];
4  publicIsEncryptedC=
5      makeTypedGraph[CNodes,CEdges,ABTReo$TypeGraph];
6  (* construct constraint (P -> C) *)
7  publicIsEncrypted=makeGraphConstraint["atomic",
8      {publicIsEncryptedP,publicIsEncryptedC}];
```

Fig. 10. Constraint for $M_{S,I,M}$ and Mathematica Source Code

norms we propose a formalization by graph constraints. Since the models in the scenario of the paper are graphs we can check the norms by checking the corresponding graph constraints, which offer a compact and intuitive visual notation of the norms.

A graph constraint $c : P \to C$ consists of a premise pattern P together with a conclusion pattern C and a morphism c that relates the elements of the premise with those of the conclusion. A graph G fulfils a graph constraint $c : P \to C$ if for any occurrence of the premise P there is also an occurrence of the conclusion C at the same position of the graph. From the formal point of view we have that G fulfils c if for any injective morphism $p : P \to G$ there is also an injective morphism $q : C \to G$ compatible with p, i.e. $q \circ c = p$. Graph constraints can be used within logic formulae as specified in [7].

Fig. 10 shows a graph constraint for ABT-Reo models [1], which requires that any public Reo element is connected to two ABT nodes for encryption. This ensures the verbal security constraint that confidential communication data cannot be intercepted in plain text by eavesdropping at public channels. Model $M_{S,I,M}$ of Fig. 8 fulfils this constraint, because for each public Reo-element there are ABT-nodes of type "E/D" (encoding/decoding) as required by conclusion C of the constraint.

Fig. 11 shows the operation call in Mathematica for checking the graph constraint "publicIsEncryped" on model $M_{S,I,M}$. Since the model fulfills the constraint the result is "True" as expected.

```
1  In:=    checkGraphConstraint[ModelSIF,publicIsEncrypted]
2  Out:=   True
```

Fig. 11. Source Code for Compliance Check of Graph Constraint "publicIsEncrypted"

6   Related Work

There are two main champs in the area of related work relevant from the point of view of Credit Suise that come up here: one is model driven architecture, another one is software factories.

Model-driven architecture (MDA) [16] is developed by the OMG and introduced as a technique to improve quality and as a way to cut costs in software-development and system-engineering. MDA has shown quite some advantages, however, it still lacks support for round-trip engineering and decentralization. Integration and transformation of models as it was presented in this paper is not inherently supported, MDA set-up costs are high and the final added value is unclear in lots of cases.

Software factories [10] have long been a big hope to address some of the issues related to the work with models. One argument here is that the software industry remains reliant on the craftsmanship of skilled individuals engaged in labor intense manual tasks. Market pressure regarding costs, time and quality created a demand for appropriate models and tools to enable automation. [2] However, even though big investments have been made, they have not been able to deliver solutions being sufficiently suited to cognitive aspects or compatible with requirements of large and decentralized organizations.

Further details regarding ontologies, data graphs and other model integration approaches are given in [3].

7   Conclusion

The concrete situation at Credit Suisse is document-oriented. The presented framework allows a model-centric view. At the same time, the solution supports decentralization by model integration at all levels of abstraction as well as in an incremental way and is able to handle not yet created models by model transformation. Therefore, the problem that models cannot be kept consistent is solvable. A service model in the business universe does not need to be in place right from the beginning. The use of declarative rules is much more flexible and re-use friendly than any generator-driven approach available today. In addition to that, derived rules do not have to be maintained. This leads to lower costs and better quality of results. Because the method of algebraic graph transformation is fully implementable, people can use it and are not bothered by high set-up costs. In contrast to today's fix alignments between conceptual models and their underlying formal models, the alignment between models based on cognitive concepts can be kept flexible towards the models based on mathematical or logical concepts by the help of model integration. This has explicitly been requested and it is not realized by today's solutions. The alignment helps to realize model checking in an encapsulated way as requested by the Credit Suisse management. In contrast to today's situation the implementations of the different pieces of the proposed framework are kept as independent and as orthogonal as possible, so that modules can be reused or exchanged on demand. The current environment at Credit Suisse does not realize that.

In our future work we plan to propagate graph constraints over model boundaries. Details will be presented in the technical report [3]. The objective is to check consistency of security norms related to different but integrated models. Today's solutions do not address this question. From a theoretical point of view, we plan to solve this issue by the help of the notion of a borrowed context [9] that can help to extent graph constraints temporarily to suit the model transformation rules between models.

References

1. Arbab, F.: Abstract Behavior Types: A Foundation Model for Components and Their Composition. Science of Computer Programming 55, 3–52 (2005)
2. Bézivin, J.: On the unification power of models. Software and Systems Modeling 4, 171–188 (2005)
3. Brandt, C., Engel, T., Hermann, F., Adamek, J.: Security and Consistency of IT and Business Models at Credit Suisse realized by Graph Constraints, Transformation and Integration using Algebraic Graph Theory (Long Version). Technical report, Technische Universität Berlin,Fakultät IV (to appear, 2009)
4. Cornelius, F., Hußmann, H., Löwe, M.: The Korso Case Study for Software Engineering with Formal Methods: A Medical Information System. Technical Report 94–5, FB Informatik, TU Berlin (1994)
5. Ehrig, H., Ehrig, K., Ermel, C., Hermann, F., Taentzer, G.: Information Preserving Bidirectional Model Transformations. In: Dwyer, M.B., Lopes, A. (eds.) FASE 2007. LNCS, vol. 4422, pp. 72–86. Springer, Heidelberg (2007)
6. Ehrig, H., Ehrig, K., Hermann, F.: From Model Transformation to Model Integration based on the Algebraic Approach to Triple Graph Grammars. In: Ermel, C., de Lara, J., Heckel, R. (eds.) Proc. Workshop on Graph Transformation and Visual Modeling Techniques (GT-VMT 2008), vol. 10. EC-EASST (2008)
7. Ehrig, H., Ehrig, K., Prange, U., Taentzer, G.: Fundamentals of Algebraic Graph Transformation. EATCS Monographs in Theoretical Computer Science. Springer, Heidelberg (2006)
8. Ehrig, H., Ermel, C., Hermann, F.: On the Relationship of Model Transformations Based on Triple and Plain Graph Grammars (Long Version). Technical Report 2008/05, Technische Universität Berlin, Fakultät IV (2008)
9. Ehrig, H., König, B.: Deriving Bisimulation Congruences in the DPO Approach to Graph Rewriting with Borrowed Contexts. Mathematical Structures in Computer Science 16(6), 1133–1163 (2006)
10. Greenfield, J.: Software Factories: Assembling Applications with Patterns, Models, Frameworks, and Tools. In: Nord, R.L. (ed.) SPLC 2004. LNCS, vol. 3154, p. 304. Springer, Heidelberg (2004)

11. Groote, J.F., Reniers, M.: Modelling and Analysis of Communicating Systems (to appear)
12. Le, T.V., Le, T.U.V., Van, L.T.: Techniques of PROLOG Programming with Implementation of Logical Negation and Quantified Goals. John Wiley & Sons, Chichester (1992)
13. OMG. Meta-Object Facility (MOF), Version 2.0 (2006), http://www.omg.org/
14. OMG. Unified Modeling Language: Superstructure – Version 2.1.2 (2007), http://www.omg.org/.
15. OMG. Catalog of OMG Business Strategy, Business Rules and Business Process Management Specifications (2009), http://www.omg.org/technology/documents/br_pm_spec_catalog.htm
16. OMG. Model driven Architecture (MDA) (2009), http://www.omg.org/mda
17. Pemmaraju, S., Skiena, S.: Computational Discrete Mathematics: Combinatorics and Graph Theory with Mathematica. The University of Iowa and SUNY at Stony Brook. Cambridge University Press, New York (2003)
18. Schürr, A.: Specification of Graph Translators with Triple Graph Grammars. In: Tinhofer, G. (ed.) WG 1994. LNCS, vol. 903, pp. 151–163. Springer, Heidelberg (1995)

Declarative versus Imperative Process Modeling Languages: The Issue of Understandability

Dirk Fahland[1], Daniel Lübke[2], Jan Mendling[1], Hajo Reijers[3], Barbara Weber[4], Matthias Weidlich[5], and Stefan Zugal[4]

[1] Humboldt-Universität zu Berlin, Germany
fahland@informatik.hu-berlin.de, jan.mendling@wiwi.hu-berlin.de
[2] Leibniz Universität Hannover, Germany
daniel.luebke@inf.uni-hannover.de
[3] Eindhoven University of Technology, The Netherlands
h.a.reijers@tue.nl
[4] University of Innsbruck, Austria
barbara.weber@uibk.ac.at, stefan.zugal@uibk.ac.at
[5] Hasso-Plattner-Institute, University of Potsdam, Germany
matthias.weidlich@hpi.uni-potsdam.de

Abstract. Advantages and shortcomings of different process modeling languages are heavily debated, both in academia and industry, but little evidence is presented to support judgements. With this paper we aim to contribute to a more rigorous, theoretical discussion of the topic by drawing a link to well-established research on program comprehension. In particular, we focus on imperative and declarative techniques of modeling a process. Cognitive research has demonstrated that imperative programs deliver sequential information much better while declarative programs offer clear insight into circumstantial information. In this paper we show that in principle this argument can be transferred to respective features of process modeling languages. Our contribution is a pair of propositions that are routed in the cognitive dimensions framework. In future research, we aim to challenge these propositions by an experiment.

Keywords: Process model understanding, declarative versus imperative modeling, cognitive dimensions framework.

1 Introduction

At the present stage, formal properties of process modeling languages are quite well understood [1]. In contrast to these formal aspects, we know rather little about theoretical foundations that might support the superiority of one process modeling language in comparison to another one. There are several reasons why suitable theories are not yet in place for language design, most notably because the discipline is still rather young. Only little research has been conducted empirically in this area so far, e.g. [2,3] relating model understanding to the modeling language and to model complexity.

T. Halpin et al. (Eds.): BPMDS 2009 and EMMSAD 2009, LNBIP 29, pp. 353–366, 2009.
© Springer-Verlag Berlin Heidelberg 2009

The context for process modeling efforts is often that a model builder constructs a process model that aims to facilitate human understanding and communication among various stakeholders. This shows that the matter of understanding is well-suited to serve as a pillar on the quest for theories of process modeling language quality. Furthermore, insights from cognitive research on programming languages point to the fact that 'design is redesign' [4]: a computer program is not written sequentially; a programmer typically works on different chunks of the problem in an opportunistic order which requires a constant reinspection of the current work context. If process builders design their models in a similar fashion, understanding is an important quality factor for the modeler himself.

The lack of theories on modeling language quality with empirical support has contributed both to the continuous invention of new techniques and to the claims on the supposed superiority of such techniques. For instance, Nigam and Caswell introduce the OpS technique in which "the operational model is targeted at a business user and yet retains the formality needed for reasoning and, where applicable, automated implementation" implying that existing languages fall short on these characteristics [5]. In a Popkin white paper, Owen and Raj are less careful and claim a general superiority of BPMN over UML Activity Diagrams because "it offers a process flow modeling technique that is more conducive to the way business analysts model" and "its solid mathematical foundation is expressly designed to map to business execution languages, whereas UML is not" [6]. Smith and Fingar simply state in their book that "BPML is the language of choice for formalizing the expression, and execution, of collaborative interfaces" [7]. We do not want to judge on the correctness of these statements here, but rather emphasize that we currently lack theories to properly assess such claims.

Throughout this paper, we will discuss in how far insights from cognitive research on programming languages could be transferred to the process modeling domain. In particular, it is our aim to investigate the spectrum of imperative versus declarative process modeling languages, as this distinction can be considered as one of the most prominent for today's modeling languages. For example, with respect to the recent development of ConDec (first published as "DecSerFlow"), a declarative process modeling language, the first design criterion that is mentioned is that "the process models developed in the language must be understandable for end-users" [8, p.15]. While it is claimed that imperative (or procedural [1]) languages, in comparison, deliver larger and more complex process models, only anecdotal evidence is presented to support this. Also, in the practitioner community opinions are manifold about the advantages of declarative versus imperative languages to capture business processes, see for example [10,11,12]. These claims and discussions clearly point at the need for an objective, empirically founded validation of the presumed advantages of the different types of process modeling languages.

The contribution of this paper is that it presents a set of theoretically grounded propositions about the differences between imperative and declarative process modeling languages with respect understandability issues. As such, this paper is

---

[1] Computer scientists prefer the term "procedural"; the term "imperative" is popular in other communities [9]. In this paper, we will be using the terms as synonyms.

an essential stepping stone to an empirical evaluation of these languages, which is planned by the authors as future research. To argue and support the hypotheses, this paper is structured as follows. Section 2 summarizes empirical findings and concepts from programming language research. Section 3 characterizes the notational spectrum of process modeling languages. Section 4 derives propositions on when a process modeling language could be superior to another one based on the cognitive dimensions framework. Section 5 concludes the paper and describes the empirical research agenda for validating the propositions.

2   Cognitive Research on Programming Languages

Various authors have noted the similarities between process models and software programs [13,14]. For example, a software program is usually partitioned into modules or functions, which take in a group of inputs and provide some output. Similar to this compositional structure, a business process model consists of activities, each of which may contain smaller steps (operations) that may update the values of data objects. Furthermore, just like the interactions between modules and functions in a software program are precisely specified using various language constructs, the order of activity execution in a process model is defined using logic operators. For software programs and business process models alike, *human agents* are concerned with properly capturing their logic content. This stresses the importance of sense-making for both types of artifacts, both during the construction process and while updating such artifacts at a later stage.

While computer science is a relatively young field in relation to other engineering disciplines or the formal sciences, it has clearly a longer history than business process modeling. Therefore, it is worthwhile to reflect on the insights that are available with respect to the understanding of software code.

In the past, heated debates have taken place about the superiority of one programming language over the other with respect to expressiveness [15] or effectiveness [16], and such debates have extended to the issue of understandability. Edsger Dijkstra's famous letter on the harmfulness of the GOTO statement, for instance, builds on the argument that "our powers to visualize how processes evolving in time are poorly developed" [17]. This made him dismissive of any higher level programming language supporting this construct. Another example is the development of visual programming languages, which have been claimed to be easier to understand than textual languages [18]. Finally, object-oriented programming languages have also been expected to foster understandability in comparison with more traditional languages, see e.g. [19].

During the 1970s and 1980s, alternative views were proposed on how programmers make sense of code as to provide a theoretical explanation of the impact of different programming languages on this process. One view is based on the idea of "cognitive restructuring", in which problem-solving involves the access of information from both the world and memory (short- and long-term), and the restructuring of this information in working memory to provide a solution. Therefore, languages from which information can be easily accessed and transferred to working memory will be easier to understand [20,21].

An alternative view is that every programming language is translated into the same mental representation, and that comprehension performance reflects the extent to which the external program maps to people's internal/cognitive representation primitives. This view is in line with certain theories on natural language processing [22] and forms the theoretical basis for experiments aimed at establishing people's internal representations of computer programs [23,24].

What has proven to be problematic with both these views is that they support the prediction that one programming language is easier or harder to understand than another in an absolute sense – whatever the exact aspect of the program that is studied. In work by Green [25,26], and Gilmore and Green [27], however, it has both been postulated and empirically validated that different tasks that involve sense-making of software code are supported differently by the same programming language. For example, the overall impact of a modification of a single declaration may be difficult to understand in a PASCAL program, but it is relatively easy to develop a mental picture of the control-flow for the same program. The implication of this view is that a programming language may provide superior support with respect to one comprehension task, while it may be outperformed by other languages with respect to a different task.

The latter view was originally the basis for the "mental operations theory" [27], which in essence states that a notation that requires fewer mental operations from a person for any task is the better performing one. In other words, a "matched pair" between the notational characteristics and a task gives the best performance. This view has evolved and matured over the years towards the "cognitive dimensions framework" (CDF) [28,29], which contains many different characteristics to distinguish notations from each other. Several of these dimensions directly matter to process modeling understanding, e.g. whether the model demands *hard mental operations* from the reader, whether there are *hidden dependencies* between notation elements, or whether changes can be applied locally (*viscosity*). The framework has been highly influential in language usability studies and over 50 publications have been devoted to its further development [30]. The CDF extends the main postulate of the mental operations theory towards a broad evaluation tool for a wide variety of notations, e.g. spreadsheets, style sheets, diagrams, etc. While its application to business process models is, to our knowledge, limited to the work in [31], it seems to provide the strongest available theoretical foundation for our aims with this paper.

In particular, an important result that has been established in the development of the CDF relates to the difference between the tasks of looking for sequential and circumstantial information in a program. *Sequential* information explains how input conditions lead to a certain outcome. An example of looking for sequential information is: "In this program, after action X is performed, what might the next action be?". Typically, one can distinguish between sequential information that relates to actions immediately *leading to* or *following from* a certain outcome. On the other hand, given a conclusion or outcome, *circumstantial information* relates to the overall conditions that produced that outcome. An example of looking for *circumstantial* information is: "In this program, what combination of circumstances will cause action X to be performed?". Circumstantial information may either relate to conditions that *have* or *have not* occurred. Empirical evidence is found to support the hypothesis that procedural programming languages display sequential information in a readily-used form, while declarative languages display circumstantial information in a readily-used form [25,27]. The reverse is also true: Just as procedural languages tend to obscure circumstantial information, so do declarative languages tend to obscure sequential information. In other words, one "cannot simple-mindedly claim that procedural languages are easier or harder to read than declarative ones" [28].

The implication for this paper is (a) that we will adopt a similar relativist starting point for the formulation of our hypotheses and (b) that we will refine the distinction between sequential and circumstantial information within the context of process models.

3   The Declarative-Imperative Spectrum

Given the insights from programming language research, this section analyzes in how far an analogy can be established between procedural and declarative programming and respective approaches to process modeling. Section 3.1 elaborates on the difference between imperative and declarative programming; we discuss to which extent the distinction of sequential and circumstantial information is appropriate for process modeling thereafter. Section 3.3 illustrates the declarative-imperative spectrum with examples of process modeling languages.

3.1   Imperative versus Declarative Programming

Assuming that the reader has an intuitive understanding of what an imperative (or procedural) program is, we approach the topic from the declarative angle. According to Lloyd "declarative programming involves stating what is to be computed, but not necessarily how it is to be computed"[32]. Equivalently, in the terminology of Kowalski's equation [33] 'algorithm = logic + control', it involves stating the logic of an algorithm (i.e. the knowledge to be used in problem solving), but not necessarily the control (i.e. the problem-solving strategies). While the logic component determines the meaning of an algorithm, the control component only affects its efficiency [33].

Roy and Haridi [34] suggest to use the concept of a *state* for defining the line between the two approaches more precisely. Declarative programming is often referred to as stateless programming as an evaluation works on partial data structures. In contrast to that, imperative programming is characterized as stateful programming [34]: a component's result not only depends on its arguments, but also on an internal parameter, which is called its "state". A state is a collection of values being intermediate results of a desired computation (at a specific point in time). Roy and Haridi [34] differentiate between implicit (declarative) state and explicit state. Implicit states only exist in the mind of the programmer without requiring any support from the computation model. An explicit state in a procedure, in turn, is a state whose lifetime extends over more than one procedure call without being present in the procedure's arguments. Explicit state is visible in both the program and the computation model.

3.2 Imperative versus Declarative Process Modeling

Process modeling is not concerned with programs, variables, and values, but aims at describing processes. In general, a *process* is a collection of observable actions, events, or changes of a collection of real and virtual objects. A *process modeling language* provides concepts for representing processes. Discussions of declarative versus imperative process modeling are scarce and so are precise distinctions. A description is given in Pesic's PhD thesis [8, p.80]: "[Imperative] models take an 'inside-to-outside' approach: all execution alternatives are explicitly specified in the model and new alternatives must be explicitly added to the model. Declarative models take an 'outside-to-inside' approach: constraints implicitly specify execution alternatives as all alternatives that satisfy the constraints and adding new constraints usually means discarding some execution alternatives." Below, we relate declarative and imperative modeling techniques to the notion of state.

An *imperative* process modeling language focuses on the aspect of *continuous* changes of the process' objects which allows for two principal, dual views. The life of each object in the process can be described in terms of its *state space* by abstractly formulating the object's *locations* in a real or virtual world and its possibilities to get from one location to another, i.e. state changes. The dual view is the *transition space* which abstractly formulates the distinct actions, events, and changes of the process and how these can possibly succeed each other. Based on topological considerations of Petri [35], Holt [36] formally constructs a mathematical framework that relates state space and transition space and embeds it into the theory of *Petri nets* [1]. Holt deducts that Petri net places (or states in general) act as "grains in space" while Petri net transitions (or steps in general) act as "grains in time" providing dedicated concepts for structuring the spatial and the temporal aspect of a process. A directed flow-relation defines pre- and post-places of transitions, and corresponding pre- and post-transitions of places. Thus, in a Petri net model, beginning at any place (state) or transition, the modeler can choose and follow a *continuous* forward trajectory in the process behavior visiting more places (states of objects) and transitions. Likewise, the modeler can follow a continuous backward trajectory to see the process behavior that leads to this place (state) or transition. This interpretation positions Petri nets as a clear imperative process modeling language.

A *declarative* process modeling language focuses on the *logic* that governs the overall interplay of the actions and objects of a process. It provides concepts to describe *key qualities* of objects and actions, and how the key qualities of different objects and actions relate to each other in time and space. This relation can be arbitrary and needs not be continuous; it shall only describe the logic of the process. In this sense, a declarative language only describes *what* the essential characteristics of a process are while it is insensitive to *how* the process works. For instance, a possible key quality of a process can be that a specific action is "just being executed". Formalizing this quality as a predicate ranging over a set of actions, one can use the temporal logic LTL to model how executions of actions relate to each other over time. The logical implication thereby acts as the connective between cause and effect: Each action is executed a specific number of times (e.g. at least once, at most three times); the execution of one action requires a subsequent execution of some other action (at some point); the execution of two given actions is mutually exclusive; etc. Thereby state and step are not explicated in the model, but they are constructed when *interpreting* predicates and formulas. This kind of description relies on an *open-world assumption* leaving room for how the process' changes are continuously linked to each other. Any behavior that satisfies the model is a valid behavior of the process. This approach was formalized for modeling processes in the language ConDec [37].

The probably most notable difference between imperative and declarative modeling is how a given behavior can be classified as satisfying a model or not. In an imperative model, the behavior must be reconstructible from the description by finding a continuous trajectory that looks exactly like the given behavior or corresponds to it in a *smooth* way. For instance, the linear runs of a Petri net are not explicitly visible in the net's structure, but states and steps can be mapped to places and transitions preserving predecessor and successor relations. In a declarative model, all requirements must be satisfied by the given behavior; there is no smooth correspondence required between behavior and model.

The reason for this difference between imperative and declarative modeling is the *degree* to which these paradigms make states and transitions explicit. An imperative process model like a Petri nets explicitly denotes states or transitions or both and their direct predecessor-successor relations. Thus enabled transitions and successor states can be computed locally from a given state or transition; runs can be constructed inductively. In a declarative model like an LTL formula states and transitions are implicitly characterized by the predicates and the temporal constraints over these predicates. Any set of states and transitions that are "sufficiently distinct" and relate to each other "sufficiently correct" are a valid interpretation of the model. This prohibits a construction of runs, but allows for characterizing states and transitions as satisfying or not.

Despite these differences, declarative and imperative models can be precisely related to each other. For instance, any LTL formula can equivalently be translated into a (finite) Büchi automaton [38]. The translation has the price of a technical overhead to express the genuine concepts of one language by the available concepts of another language. While this prohibits a direct transformation of declarative models into well-conceivable imperative models, the resulting imperative model is operational and allows for executing declarative ones [37].

3.3   A Characterization of Process Modeling Languages

As we stated in the previous section, process modeling languages differ with respect to the *degree* in which they make states and transitions explicit. This is in line with Roy and Haridi's [34] suggestion that "declarative" is no absolute property. The following languages lend themselves as evidence for this hypothesis as they position themselves in the imperative-declarative spectrum of process modeling languages. At the imperative end we position Petri nets, and LTL at the declarative end of the spectrum. Because of the large variety of process modeling languages, our list cannot be exhaustive.

Petri nets. We already illustrated the key concepts of imperative process modeling languages by the help of *Petri nets* which make state and transition explicit. A Petri net model of a process provides for each *atomic action* a dedicated transition and for each *atomic state* of a process resource a dedicated place. During modeling, one usually has to augment the model by further transitions and places to implement the desired process logic, e.g. loops, decisions, synchronization, etc. At any stage the modeler may mentally execute the process by placing mental tokens on the given places and mentally firing enabled transitions. These mental operations are supported by the continuous graph-based structure of the model that makes sequential information explicit as explained above. Several techniques like sub-nets transitions or patterns aid in structuring processes and making composite actions explicit.

Colored Petri nets [39] extend Petri nets by offering arbitrary values, objects, and structures to be passed through the net, instead of black tokens; these nets are used for modeling processes with data. Which colored tokens (values) are consumed, and how these are manipulated by firing transitions is specified in arc inscriptions and transition guards being *algebraic terms* with free variables. Thereby, the terms only denote how different colored tokens relate to each other allowing the transition to fire in many different modes. This adds circumstantial information to a transition which is positioned in a sequential context. The modeler has to mentally instantiate the arc inscriptions to get an explicit representation of the behavior. For larger pieces of continuous behavior, inscriptions of several transitions must be instantiated correspondingly.

Flow-based modeling languages like UML Activity Diagrams or BPMN materialize structuring techniques of Petri nets in dedicated concepts. Besides different kinds of actions, these languages know *control-flow nodes* like *AND-split* and *XOR-join* to route control-flow between activities. *Event nodes* explicitly denote process instantiation, communication and termination. These modeling concepts offer a way to represent some of the key corresponding mental concepts of processes requiring fewer mental operations to understand the model.

The **Business Process Execution Language (BPEL)** has a *block-oriented* structure and provides even more specialized concepts for process modeling in a web service context. The block-oriented design allows to read a BPEL model like procedural program. But concepts like *exception handling*, *negative control-flow* and handling of *concurrent events* break the sequential nature of the process. The exact mechanics that coordinate normal process execution and exception handling etc. are not visible in the model, but hidden in the language. The modeler has to reconstruct them mentally to get a consistent image.

Scenario-based languages like Message Sequence Charts (UML Sequence Diagrams) and Life-Sequence Charts provide an explicit notion of behavior in terms of scenarios [40]. A *scenario* denotes a partial execution of the process as a partially ordered set of actions. A model is a set of scenarios sharing some actions. How actions of different scenarios relate to each other is not stated explicitly. Rather, a scenario's structure and annotations describe how it can or cannot be extended by other scenarios. A scenario provides both, sequential and circumstantial information: It describes a continuous piece of behavior. At the same time, when asking "How to execute the last action of this scenario?", it presents the partial answer "Execute all preceding actions of the scenario.".

The **Pockets of Flexibility** approach [41] combines imperative and declarative modeling elements in an integrated manner. Essentially, a *pocket of flexibility* constitutes a placeholder action in a flow-based process model; the pocket is dynamically refined to a flow-based process fragment at run-time. For each pocket declarative modeling constraints can be specified, which have to be obeyed upon refinement. A pocket introduces a region into a process model, where no explicit sequential information is available. The modeler has to link restricting constraints to the surrounding flow, and vice versa, when constructing the model.

TLA. The *Temporal Logic of Actions* (TLA) [42] allows to model process steps in terms of variable values in the current state and in the next state. Together with temporal operators like in LTL, TLA allows to model processes in terms of behavioral invariants as well as in terms of continuous changes.

ConDec. The process modeling language ConDec [37] formalizes key temporal relationships between executions of activities of a process in LTL patterns; e.g. the number of executions of an action or how two (or more) actions must or must not succeed each other. This makes some temporal concepts of process behavior explicit, similar to BPMN compared to Petri nets. The concepts of ConDec are stateless and give only circumstantial information for the (non-) executability of an action. The semantic domain of ConDec is limited to a specific, finite set of activities (out of which the process consists). Thus, the possibilities to relate different circumstances, like "executing action A" and "executing action B", to each other are restricted. This eases a mental construction of continuous behavior that connects them.

LTL. The entire *Linear-Time Temporal Logic (LTL)* neither restricts process models nor the valid interpretations. The model may refer to further key qualities of a process like "availability of resource R". Arbitrary circumstantial information can be constructed with the logical connectives, specifically the implication to relate cause and effect, and the temporal operators *always* (φ holds), *eventually* (φ holds), and *until* (φ holds until ψ holds). The *next* operator allows to express sequential information as it denotes a specific situation holding in the next state.

The languages which we have just presented highlight some points in the imperative-declarative spectrum of process modeling languages. The concepts range from an explicit notion of state and step to an explicit notion of process logic. Our list shows that an explicit notion of step does not exclude an explicit notion of logic as most languages provide concepts for both. An important observation on our examples is that if process logic is explicated, an explicit notion of state is put in relation to that logic, and vice versa. The information that is conveyed by one explicit notion is *relative* to the information conveyed by other explicit notions. The reason for this relativity roots in the following observation.

Every explicit notion conveys some implicit, *hidden information*. Whatever is not explicated is implicit in the model as it can and must be inferred. Whenever step and logic are explicated together in some way, the implied, hidden information of one concept must be consistent with explicit information of the other concept. Picking up the analogy to programs, the process control (states and steps) must enact the process logic, and the process logic must be implemented in the process control. A relative interpretation of the language concepts provides the freedom for a consistent combination of both.

Our illustration of the imperative-declarative spectrum of process modeling languages shows that there are no predetermined points for combining imperative and declarative concepts, but that languages contain both in varying degrees.

4   Propositions

As stated in the introduction, it is our purpose to formulate a set of propositions that can be used as a basis to evaluate the comprehensiveness of process models specified in an imperative or declarative spirit. At this point, we have explored two important elements for this purpose. In the first place, we presented the CDF as the most plausible and dominant theory for sense-making of information artifacts in Section 2. Most notably, it stresses the task-notation relationship, e.g. in the *hard mental operations* and *hidden dependency* dimensions. This has provided us with a relativist viewpoint on the superiority of process modeling techniques – it is the match between the task and the language that will determine the overall effectiveness, not the technique in absolute terms. Also, the important concepts of finding *sequential* and *circumstantial* information give a strong clue to what types of tasks may give a better match with imperative or declarative process models.

Secondly, we reviewed the distinction between declarative and imperative process modeling languages in Section 3. We argued that the more a process modeling language emphasizes *states* and *transitions*, the more imperative it can be regarded. Similarly, the more a process modeling language relies on providing the mere requirements on acceptable behavior, the more declarative it is. Inherent to these views is our acceptance that the distinction between declarative and imperative process modeling languages is not a binary one. By combining the two elements, we arrive at the two following main propositions:

P1. Given two semantically equivalent process models, establishing sequential information will be easier on the basis of the model that is created with the process modeling language that is relatively more imperative in nature.

P2. Given two process models, establishing circumstantial information will be easier on the basis of the model that is created with the process modeling language that is relatively more declarative in nature. Establishing circumstantial information will be easier on the basis of a declarative process model than with an imperative process model.

The reasoning for these propositions can be directly related to the *hard mental operations* and *hidden dependencies* dimensions. Sequence is a hidden dependency from the perspective of a declarative language and requires hard mental operations to construct it. An imperative language, on the other hand, is demanding in terms of circumstantial information because it is hidden and mentally hard to reconstruct. Specifically, we would expect that these propositions hold whether ease of understanding is measured in terms of *accuracy* or *speed*, cf. operationalizations of these notions in [4].

Finally, consistent with the CDF, we would expect these propositions to hold both when subjects have *direct* access to the process model and when they have to establish this information on *recall*, i.e. the memorization of a process model they have seen earlier. Remember that the CDF refutes the idea that people shape a similar problem situation into the same mental model, regardless of the form in which it is presented to them.

5   Conclusion

In this paper, we presented a set of propositions that relate to the understandability of process modeling languages. Specifically, these propositions focus on the distinction between declarative and imperative languages, formulating relative strengths and weaknesses of both paradigms. The most important theoretical foundation for these propositions is the cognitive dimensions framework including the results that are established for programming languages. Also, it is argued that any actual process modeling language finds itself somewhere on the spectrum from a less to a more imperative (declarative) nature. An analysis of existing process modeling languages is provided to support this argument.

This paper is characterized by a number of limitations. First of all, there is a strong reliance on similarities between process modeling languages on the one hand and programming languages on the other. Differences between both ways of abstract expression may render some of our inferences untenable. At this point, however, we do not see a more suitable source of inspiration nor any strong counter arguments. Note that it can be argued that the issue of understandability may be even more important in the domain of process modeling than that of programming. After all, not only designers are reading process models but end users too – which is unusual for computer programs. Furthermore, we have focused exclusively on the issue of understanding but other quality aspects may be equally important. If design is redesign, as argued in this paper, not only understanding but also *ease of change* is important. There are respective cognitive dimensions that need to be discussed for process modeling notations, in particular, *viscosity* (ease of local change) and *premature commitment*.

As follows from the nature of this paper, the next step is to challenge the propositions with an empirical investigation. We intend to develop a set of experiments that will involve human modelers to carry out a set of tasks that involve sense-making of a set of process models. Such tasks will be characterized by establishing both sequential and circumstantial information and including more and less declarative (imperative) languages. The cooperation of various academic partners in this endeavor facilitates extensive testing and replication of such experiments. Ideally, this empirical investigation will lead to an informed voice in the ongoing debate on the superiority of process modeling languages.

References

1. Reisig, W., Rozenberg, G. (eds.): APN 1998. LNCS, vol. 1491. Springer, Heidelberg (1998)
2. Recker, J., Dreiling, A.: Does it matter which process modelling language we teach or use? an experimental study on understanding process modelling languages without formal education. In: Toleman, M., Cater-Steel, A., Roberts, D. (eds.) 18th Australasian Conference on Information Systems, pp. 356–366 (2007)
3. Mendling, J., Reijers, H., Cardoso, J.: What makes process models understandable? In: Alonso, G., Dadam, P., Rosemann, M. (eds.) BPM 2007. LNCS, vol. 4714, pp. 48–63. Springer, Heidelberg (2007)
4. Gilmore, D.J., Green, T.R.G.: Comprehension and recall of miniature programs. International Journal of Man-Machine Studies 21(1), 31–48 (1984)
5. Nigam, A., Caswell, N.: Business artifacts: An approach to operational specification. IBM Systems Journal 42(3), 428–445 (2004)
6. Owen, M., Raj, J.: BPMN and Business Process Management: Introduction to the New Business Process Modeling Standard. Technical report, Popkin (2003), `http://whitepaper.techweb.com/cmptechweb/search/viewabstract/71`
7. Smith, H., Fingar, P.: Business Process Management: The Third Wave (2003)
8. Pesic, M.: Constraint-Based Workflow Management Systems: Shifting Control to Users. PhD thesis, Eindhoven University of Technology (2008)
9. Boley, H.: Declarative and Procedural Paradigms - Do They Really Compete? In: Boley, H., Richter, M.M. (eds.) PDK 1991. LNCS, vol. 567, pp. 383–385. Springer, Heidelberg (1991)
10. Korhonen, J.: Evolution of agile enterprise architecture (April 2006), `http://blog.jannekorhonen.fi/?p=11` (retrieved February 10, 2009)
11. Goldberg, L.: Seven deadly sins of business rules (September 2007), `http://www.bpminstitute.org/articles/article/article/seven-deadly-sins.html` (retrieved February 10, 2009)
12. McGregor, M.: Procedure vs. process (January 2009), `http://www.it-director.com/blogs/Mark_McGregor/2009/1/procedure_vs_process.html` (retrieved February 10, 2009)
13. Vanderfeesten, I., Reijers, H., van der Aalst, W.: Evaluating workflow process designs using cohesion and coupling metrics. Comp. in Ind. 59(5) (2008)
14. Guceglioglu, A., Demirors, O.: Using Software Quality Characteristics to Measure Business Process Quality. In: van der Aalst, W.M.P., Benatallah, B., Casati, F., Curbera, F. (eds.) BPM 2005. LNCS, vol. 3649, pp. 374–379. Springer, Heidelberg (2005)
15. Felleisen, M.: On the Expressive Power of Programming Languages. Science of Computer Programming 17(1-3), 35–75 (1991)

16. Prechelt, L.: An Empirical Comparison of Seven Programming Languages. Computer, 23–29 (2000)
17. Dijkstra, E.: Letters to the editor: go to statement considered harmful. Communications of the ACM 11(3), 147–148 (1968)
18. Glinert, E.: Nontextual programming environments. In: Visual Programming Systems, pp. 144–230. Prentice-Hall, Englewood Cliffs (1990)
19. Wiedenbeck, S., Ramalingam, V., Sarasamma, S., Corritore, C.: A comparison of the comprehension of object-oriented and procedural programs by novice programmers. Interacting with Computers 11(3), 255–282 (1999)
20. Meyer, R.: Comprehension as affected by the structure of the problem representation. Memory & Cognition 4(3), 249–255 (1976)
21. Shneiderman, B., Mayer, R.: Syntactic/semantic interactions in programmer behavior: A model and experimental results. International Journal of Parallel Programming 8(3), 219–238 (1979)
22. Fodor, J., Bever, T., Garrett, M.: The Psychology of Language: An Introduction to Psycholinguistics and Generative Grammar. McGraw-Hill Companies, New York (1974)
23. McKeithen, K., Reitman, J., Rueter, H., Hirtle, S.: Knowledge organization and skill differences in computer programmers. Cogn. Psych. 13(3), 307–325 (1981)
24. Adelson, B.: Problem solving and the development of abstract categories in programming languages. Memory & Cognition 9(4), 422–433 (1981)
25. Green, T.: Conditional program statements and their comprehensibility to professional programmers. Journal of Occupational Psychology 50, 93–109 (1977)
26. Green, T.: Ifs and thens: Is nesting just for the birds? Software Focus 10(5) (1980)
27. Gilmore, D., Green, T.: Comprehension and recall of miniature programs. International Journal of Man-Machine Studies 21(1), 31–48 (1984)
28. Green, T.: Cognitive dimensions of notations. In: Sutcliffe, A., Macaulay, L. (eds.) People and Computers V, Proceedings, pp. 443–460 (1989)
29. Green, T., Petre, M.: Usability Analysis of Visual Programming Environments: A Cognitive Dimensions Framework. J. Vis. Lang. Computing 7(2), 131–174 (1996)
30. Blackwell, A.: Ten years of cognitive dimensions in visual languages and computing. J. Vis. Lang. Computing 17(4), 285–287 (2006)
31. Vanderfeesten, I., Reijers, H., Mendling, J., Aalst, W., Cardoso, J.: On a Quest for Good Process Models: The Cross-Connectivity Metric. In: Bellahsène, Z., Léonard, M. (eds.) CAiSE 2008. LNCS, vol. 5074, pp. 480–494. Springer, Heidelberg (2008)
32. Lloyd, J.: Practical advantages of declarative programming. In: Joint Conference on Declarative Programming, GULP-PRODE 1994 (1994)
33. Kowalski, R.: Algorithm = logic + control. Commun. ACM 22(7), 424–436 (1979)
34. Roy, P.V., Haridi, S.: Concepts, Techniques, and Models of Computer Programming. MIT Press, Cambridge (2004)
35. Petri, C.A.: Concepts of net theory. In: Mathematical Foundations of Computer Science: Proc. of Symposium and Summer School, High Tatras, September 3-8, pp. 137–146. Math. Inst. of the Slovak Acad. of Sciences (1973)
36. Holt, A.W.: A Mathematical Model of Continuous Discrete Behavior. Massachusettes Computer Associates, Inc. (November 1980)
37. van der Aalst, W.M.P., Pesic, M.: DecSerFlow: Towards a truly declarative service flow language. In: Bravetti, M., Núñez, M., Zavattaro, G. (eds.) WS-FM 2006. LNCS, vol. 4184, pp. 1–23. Springer, Heidelberg (2006)
38. Courcoubetis, C., Vardi, M.Y., Wolper, P., Yannakakis, M.: Memory-efficient algorithms for the verification of temporal properties. Formal Methods in System Design 1(2/3), 275–288 (1992)

39. Jensen, K.: Coloured Petri Nets. Springer, Heidelberg (1992)
40. Damm, W., Harel, D.: LSCs: Breathing life into message sequence charts. Form. Methods Syst. Des. 19(1), 45–80 (2001)
41. Sadiq, S., Sadiq, W., Orlowska, M.: A Framework for Constraint Specification and Validation in Flexible Workflows. Information Systems 30(5), 349–378 (2005)
42. Lamport, L.: The temporal logic of actions. ACM Trans. Program. Lang. Syst. 16(3), 872–923 (1994)

The Architecture of the ArchiMate Language

M.M. Lankhorst[1], H.A. Proper[2,3], and H. Jonkers[4]

[1] Telematica Instituut, Enschede, The Netherlands
[2] Radboud University Nijmegen, Nijmegen, The Netherlands
[3] Capgemini, Utrecht, The Netherlands
[4] BiZZdesign, Enschede, The Netherlands

Abstract. In current business practice, an integrated approach to business and IT is indispensable. In many enterprises, however, such an integrated view of the entire enterprise is still far from reality. To deal with these challenges, an integrated view of the enterprise is needed, enabling impact and change analysis covering all relevant aspects. This need sparked the development of the ArchiMate language. This paper is concerned with documenting some of the key design decisions and design principles underlying the ArchiMate language.

1 Introduction

In current business practice, an integrated approach to business and IT is indispensable. In many enterprises, however, such an integrated view of the entire enterprise is still far from reality. This is a major problem, since changes in an enterprise's strategy and business goals have significant consequences within all domains of the enterprise, including organisational structures, business processes, software systems and technical infrastructure [1, 2]. To manage the complexity of any large system, be it an enterprise, an information system or a software system, an architectural approach is needed. To be able to represent the architecture of an enterprise, an architecture description language is needed allowing for the represetation of different core aspects of an enterprise, such as business processes, products, applications and infrastructures, as well as the coherence between these aspects.

As discussed in [2], enterprise architecture is a steering instrument enabling *informed governance*. Important applications of enterprise architecture are therefore the analysis of problems in the current state of an enterprise, determining the desired future state(s), and ensuring that the development projects within transformation programs are indeed on-track with regards to the desired future states. This implies that in enterprise architecture models, coherence and overview are more important than specificity and detail. This also implies the need for more coarse grained modelling concepts than the finer grained concepts which can typically be found in modelling languages used at the level of specific development projects, such as e.g. UML [3] and BPMN [4]. Therefore a new language was needed, leading to the development of the ArchiMate language [1].

The ArchiMate language was developed as part of a collaborative research project, funded partly by the Dutch government and involving several Dutch

T. Halpin et al. (Eds.): BPMDS 2009 and EMMSAD 2009, LNBIP 29, pp. 367–380, 2009.

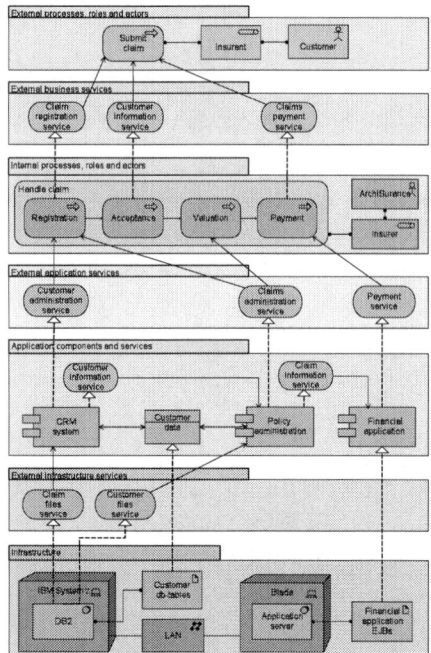

Fig. 1. An example ArchiMate model

research institutes, as well as governmental and financial institutions. The results of the project in general are described in detail in [1] as well as several papers [5, 6, 7, 8]. An illustrative example of an ArchiMate model is provided in Figure 1. Meanwhile, the ArchiMate language has been transferred to the Open Group, where it is slated to become the standard for architectural description accompanying the Open Group's architecture framework TOGAF [9].

The ArchiMate standard consists of six primary components:

A framework – A conceptual framework consisting which allows classification of architectural phenomena.

An abstract syntax – This component contains the formal definition of the language in terms of a meta-model, providing the characteristics of each language construct, and its relationships to other language constructs.

Modelling concepts – A set of modelling concepts allowing for the description of relevant aspects of enterprises at the enterprise level. This set underlies the abstract syntax, focussing on the *concepts* and their meaning, seperate from the language constructs in which they are used.

The language semantics – This component defines the meaning of each language construct and relation type.

A concrete syntax in terms of a visual notation – This syntax defines how the language constructs defined in the meta-model are represented graphically.

A viewpoint mechanism – These mechanisms correspond to the idea of diagram types in UML, though it is much more flexible as there is not a strict partitioning of constructs into views.

The focus of this paper is on documenting some the key design decisions and design principles underlying the language. This also provides a novel perspective on the design, and in particular the evolution, of a modelling language. The ability to evolve the language is of prime importance for languages which are designed as open standards. Languages used as a standard run the risk of becoming a hotchpotch of sorts. Using a clear architecture enables language evolution while still maintaining conceptual integrity of the language.

In the remainder of this paper, we start by discussing in more detail the challenges facing the design of an architecture description language, while consequently discussing the way in which the design of the ArchiMate aims to tackle these. We then continue with a discussion of the modelling concepts needed to domain models in general, which we then first refine to the modelling of dynamic systems, and finally to the modelling of enterprise architectures.

2 Challenges on an Architecture Modelling Language

The design of the ArchiMate language was based on an extensive requirements study. In this study, both practical requirements from the client organisations[1] involved in the ArchiMate project, as well as general requirements on the soundness and other qualities [10] were taken into account [11].

From a modelling perspective, the essential requirements were the following:

Concept coverage – Several domains for grouping concepts have been identified, such as product, process, organisation, information, application and technology. The concepts in the language must at least cover the concepts in these domains.

Enterprise level concepts – At an enterprise level, it is important to be able to represent the core elements from the different domains such as product, process, et cetera, as well as the coherence between these aspects.

Concept mapping – Organisations and/or individual architects must be able to keep using their own concepts and descriptions in development projects. This requires a mapping from the coarse grained concepts in ArchiMate to the fine-grained concepts used in languages at project level.

Unambiguous definitions of concepts – The meaning and definition of the modelling concepts offered by the language must be unambiguous. Every concept must be described taking into account: informal description, specialisation, notation, properties, structuring, rules and restrictions and guidelines for use.

---

[1] ABN AMRO, ABP Pension Fund, and the Dutch Tax and Customs Administration.

Structuring mechanisms – Composition/decomposition, generalisation/specialisation, and aggregation of concepts must be supported.

Abstraction – It must be possible to model relations at different abstraction levels. For example, relations can be formulated between concepts, groups of concepts or different architectural domains.

The ability to perform various kinds of analyses was also recognised as an important benefit of using architecture models. These benefits also contribute towards the *return on modelling effort* (RoME) with regards to the creation of architectural models. The demands following demands were therefore also taken into account in designing the modelling language:

Analysis of architectural properties – It must be possible to perform qualitative and quantitative analysis of properties of architectures.

Impact of change analysis – Impact of change analysis must be supported. In general, such an analysis describes or identifies effects that a certain change has on the architecture or on characteristics of the architecture.

3   Meeting the Challenges

In this section we start with a discussion of the key design principles used in the construction of the ArchiMate language, together with their motivations as well as their actual impact on the design of the language.

Concepts should have a clear contribution – The more concepts are offered by a modelling language, the more ways in which a specific situation can be modelled. When it is clear for each of the concepts what its contribution is, the language becomes easier to use and easier to learn [12].

Underlying set of concepts should be defined incrementally – The language should be based on an incrementally defined set of modelling concepts, level by level refining and specialising the set of underlying concepts. When defining the language in this way, it becomes easier to position and discuss possible extensions of the language in relation to higher level core concepts and/or the specialisations of these at the lower levels.

The language should be as compact as possible – The most important design restriction on the language was that it was explicitly designed to be as compact as possible, while still being usable for most enterprise architecture related modelling tasks. Many other languages, such as UML, try to accommodate as much as possible all needs of all possible users. In the interest of simplicity of learning and use, ArchiMate has been limited to the concepts that suffice for modelling the proverbial 80% of practical cases.

Core concepts shouldn't dependent on specific frameworks – Many architecture frameworks are in existence. Therefore, it is not desirable for a general purpose architecture description language to be too dependent on a specific architecture framework. Doing so will also make the language more extendible in the sense that it can easily be adopted to other frameworks.

Easy mapping from/to concepts used at project level – To enable tracability from the enterprise level to the project level, a strong relationship should exist between the modelling concepts used at project level and those used in the enterprise architecture. Therefore, the ArchiMate language needed to be set up in such a way that project level modelling concepts be expressed easily in terms of the more general concepts defined in the language (e.g., by specialisation or composition of general concepts).

Transitivity of relations – Relations between concepts should be transitive. This will not be further explained in this paper, for more details we refer to [7].

The key challenge in the development of the language meta-model was actually to strike a balance between the specific concepts used by project-level modelling languages on one extreme, and the very general modelling concepts suggested by general systems theory. The triangle in Figure 2 illustrates how concepts can be described at different levels of specialisation. The design of the ArchiMate language started from a set of relatively generic concepts (higher up in the triangle) focussing on domain modelling in general. These were then specialised towards the modelling of dynamic systems (at a course grained level), and consequently to enterprise architecture concepts. At the base of the triangle, we find the meta-models of the modelling concepts used by project-level modelling languages such as UML, BPMN, et cetera. The ArchiMate meta-model defines the concepts somewhere between these two extremes.

In the remainder of the paper, we discuss the stack of meta-models taking us from the top of the triangle to the level of the ArchiMate meta-model. At each level, we will present a meta-model of the additional modelling concepts provided by this level. Each level also inherits the concepts from the previous level, while also providing specialisations of the existing concepts. As an example meta-model stack, involving two levels, consider Figure 3. In this paper we have

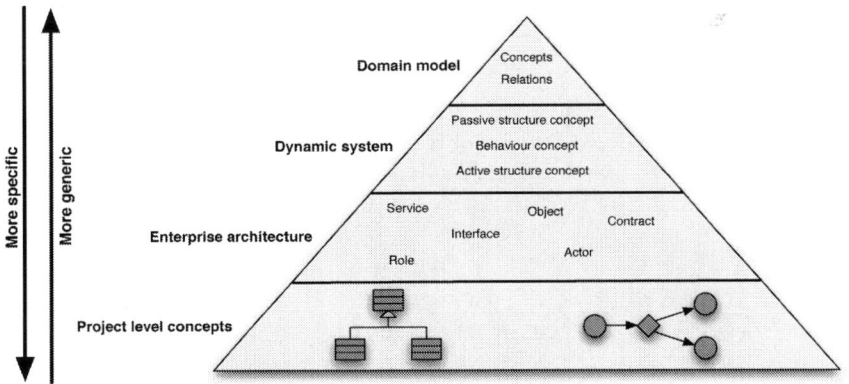

Fig. 2. Concept hierarchy

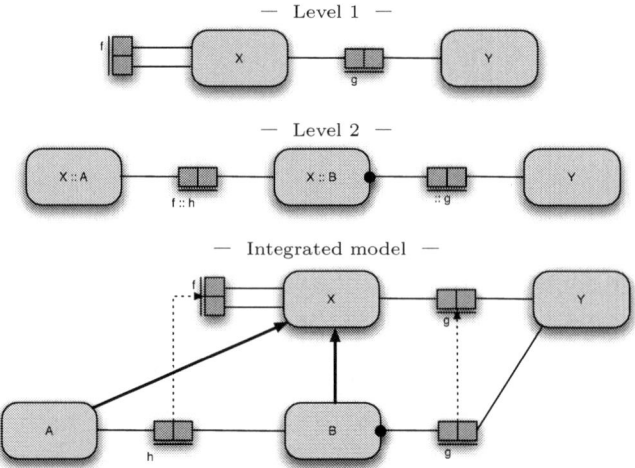

Fig. 3. Example meta-model stack

chosen to use Object-Role Modelling [13] (ORM) as a meta-modelling language, since it allows for precise modelling and elaborate verbalisations, making it well suited for the representation of meta-models. The mappings between modelling concepts at different levels are represented as: $a :: b$. What is also illustrated in Figure 3 is the fact that if a, b are both object types b is subtype of a, while if both are fact-types b is a subset of a. More specifically, in Figure 3 A and B are a sub-type of X, while fact-type h is a sub-set of fact-type f.

Sometimes we will want to repeat fact-types which already exist between two super-types for sub-types of these super-types. In this case we will write $:: a$ as a shorthand for $a :: a$. In the example shown in Figure 3 we see how g is repeated at level 2, while the the mandatory role (the filled circle on object-type B) requires the instances of sub-type B to all play a role in fact-type g.

4   Domain Modelling

In this section we are concerned with the establishment of a meta-model covering a set of modelling concepts that would allow us to model domains in general. We do so by defining three levels as depicted in Figure 4.

The first level in Figure 4 shows a meta-model comprising a single modelling concept: Element. This allows us to discern several elements within a modelled domain (end its environment). On its own, this is of course still highly impractical. We need the ability to at least identify relations between these elements. This, therefore, leads to the refinement suggested by level two. At this level, we identify two kinds of elements: Concepts and Relations. Concepts are the source of Relations as well as the destination of Relations. In other words, Concepts can be related by way of a Relation. This is abbreviated by the derived (as marked by the

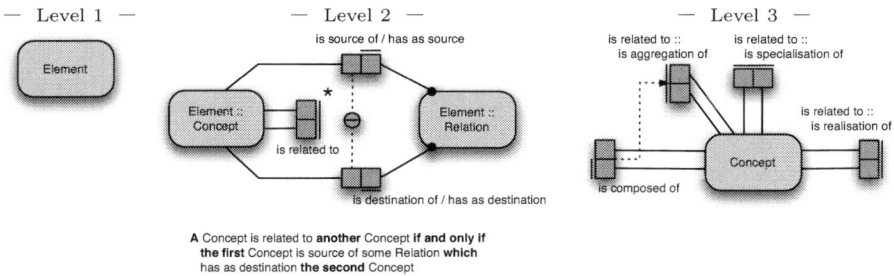

Fig. 4. Basic layers

asterisk) fact-type is related to. The definition of this derived fact-type is provided in the style of SBVR [14].

The domains we are interested in tend to be large and complex. To harness this complexity we need special relationships between Concepts which provide us with abstraction, aggregation and specialisation mechanisms. This leads to three specialisations of the is related to fact-type: is realisation of, is specialisation of, and is aggregation of. A special class of aggregations are compositions, as signified by the is composition of fact-type.

5 Modelling Dynamic Systems

Based on the foundation established in the previous section, we now describe general concepts for the modelling of dynamic systems. A dynamic system is any (discrete-event) system in which one or more subjects (actors or agents) display certain behaviour, using one or more objects. Examples of dynamic systems are business systems, information systems, application systems, and technical systems. In this section, we gradually extend the set of concepts, using three more or less orthogonal aspects or 'dimensions'. We distinguish: the aspects *active structure*, *behaviour* and *passive structure*, an *internal* and an *external* view, and an *individual* and a *collective* view.

5.1 Active Structure, Behaviour and Passive Structure

First, we distinguish *active structure concepts*, *behavioural concepts* and *passive structure concepts*. These three classes have been inspired by structures from natural language. When formulating sentences concerning the behaviour of a dynamic system, concepts will play different roles in the sentences produced. In addition to the role of a *proposition* dealing with some activity in the dynamic system (selling, reporting, weighing, et cetera), two other important roles are the role of *agens* and the role of *patiens*. The *agens* role (the active structure) refers to the concept which is regarded as executing the activity, while the *patiens* role (the passive structure) refers to the concept regarded as undergoing/experiencing the activity.

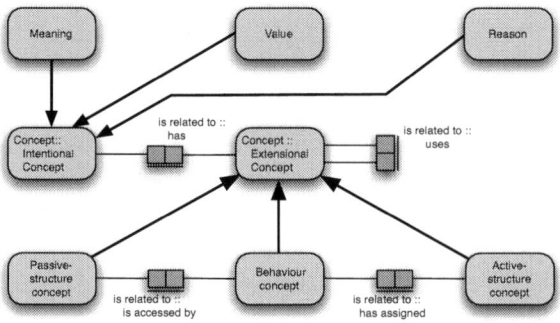

Fig. 5. Level 4

Active structure concepts are concepts concerned with the execution of behaviour; e.g., (human) actors, software applications or devices that display actual behaviour. The *behavioural concepts* represent the actual behaviour, i.e., the
processes and activities that are performed. The active structure concepts can
be *assigned to* behavioural concepts, to show who (or what) performs the behaviour. The *passive structure concepts* are the concepts upon which behaviour
is performed. In the domain that we consider, these are usually information
or data objects, but they may also be used to represent physical objects. This
extension leads to the refined meta-model as shown in Figure 5.

The active structure, behaviour and passive structure concepts provide an *ex-
tensional* perspective on behaviour. In addition, one can discern an *intentional*
perspective in relation to stakeholders observing the behaviour. Mirroring the
passive structure, we identify the *meaning* concept to express the meaning attached to the passive structures. For the *behaviour* aspect, the *value* concept
expresses the value exchange/addition that may be associated to the performance of the behaviour. The *active structure* is mirrored by the *reason* concept,
expressing the rationale underlying the role of the *active structure* concepts.

5.2   Internal versus External

A further distinction is made between an *external* view and an *internal* view
on a system. When looking at the behavioural aspect, these views reflect the
principles of service orientation. The *service* concept represents a unit of essential functionality that a system exposes to its environment. This leads to the
extension as depicted in Figure 6.

A service is accessible through an *interface*, which constitutes the external
view on the active structural concept. An interface is a (physical or logical)
location where the functionality of a service is exposed to the environment.
When a service has assigned an interface, then this assignment must be mirrored
by the assignment of relevant internal active structure concepts to the internal
behaviour concepts involved in the realisation of the service (the dotted arrow
between the two **has assigned** fact-types).

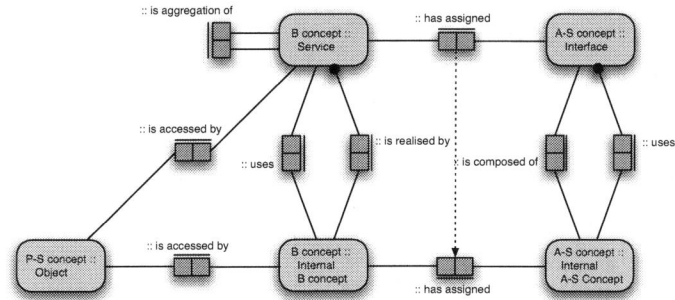

Fig. 6. Level 5

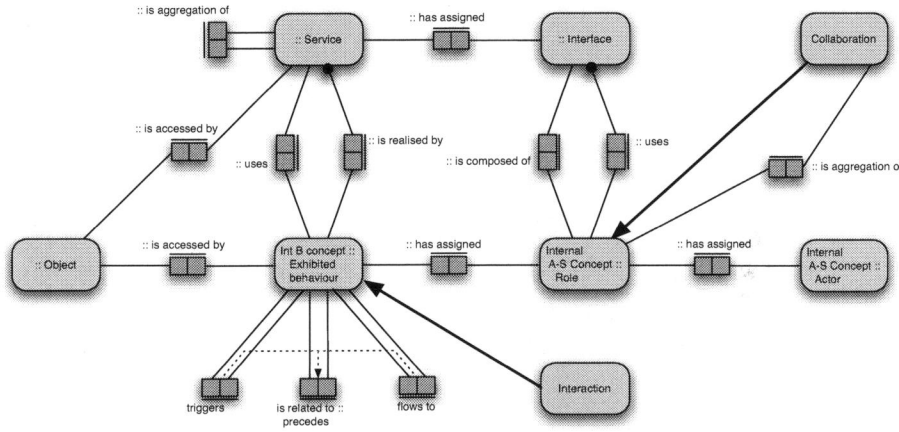

Fig. 7. Level 6

5.3 Individual versus Collective Behaviour

Going one level deeper in the structure of the language, we distinguish between the *individual* behaviour, performed by a single active structure concept, and the *collective* behaviour performed by multiple active structure concepts in a collaboration. This leads to the refinements shown in Figure 7.

In describing individual and/or collective behaviour in more detail, the internal behaviour concept needs refinement in terms of temporal ordering of the exhibited behaviour. This leads to the precedes fact-type and its sub-sets: triggers (for activities) and flows to (for information processing). A further refinement needed is the distinction between *roles* and *actors* as *active structure* concepts. *Actors* represent the essential identities that can ultimately be regarded as executing the behaviour, e.g. an insurance company, a mainframe, a person, et cetera. The actual execution is taken to occur in the context of a *role* played by an *actor*.

A collective of co-operating *roles* is modelled by the *collaboration* concept: a (possibly temporary) aggregation of two or more active structure concepts, working together to perform some collective behaviour. A collaboration is defined as a specialisation of a *role*. The collective behaviour itself is modelled by the *interaction* concept, where interaction is defined as a specialisation of the *exhibited behaviour* concept.

6   Modelling Enterprise Architectures

In this section we further extend the meta-model stack to arrive at the actual ArchiMate language. Two steps remain. The first step involves the introduction of an architecture framework allowing us to consider enterprises as a layered set of systems. The final step is to refine the meta-models to the specific needs of each of these layers.

As a common denominator of the architecture frameworks in use by participating client organisations, as well as a number of standard frameworks used in the industry, a framework was created involving three layers:

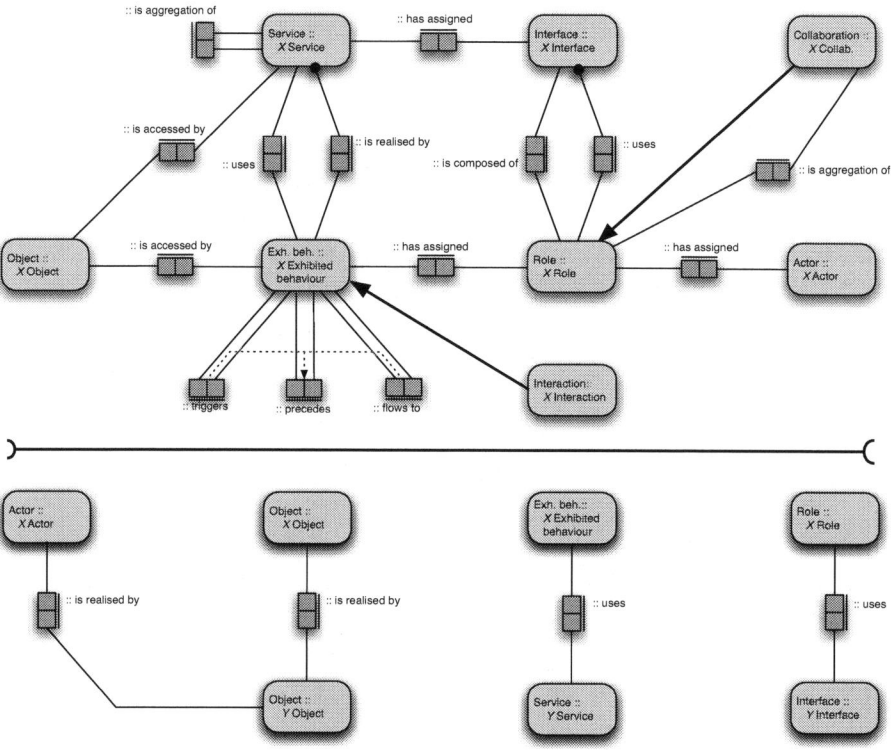

Fig. 8. Level 7 – Fragments

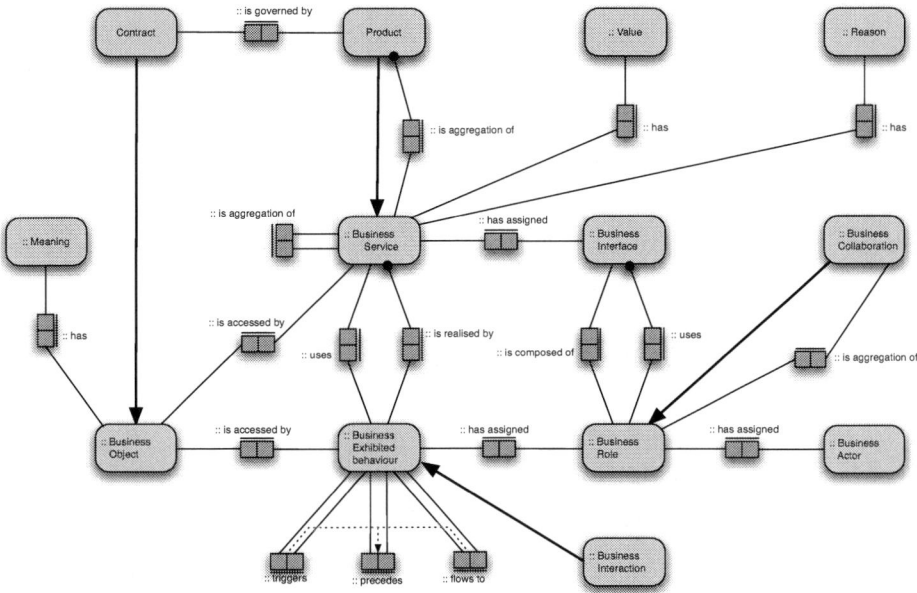

Fig. 9. Level 8 – Business layer

Business layer – Products and services offered to external customers, as well as the realisation of these within the organisation by means of business processes performed by business actors and roles.

Application layer – This layer supports the business layer with application services which are realized by (software) application components.

Technology layer – This layer offers infrastructural services (e.g., processing, storage and communication services) needed to run applications, realised by computer and communication hardware and system software.

Since each of these layers involves a dynamic system, the meta-model at level 7 comprises three copies of the fragment depicted at the top of Figure 8 for Business, Application and Technology respectively. These fragments, however, need to be connected as well, therefore for each of the two combinations: Business, Application and Application, Technology the fragment shown at the bottom of Figure 8 should be added.

Given the focus of each of the layers, further refinements were needed to better cater for the specific needs of the respective layers. For the business layer, as shown in Figure 9, the concepts of *contract* and *product* have been introduced. At the business level, services may be grouped to form *products*, which are treated as (complex) services. A business service offers a certain value (economic or otherwise) to its (prospective) users, which provides the motivation for the service's existence. For the external users, only this external functionality and value, together with non-functional aspects such as the quality of service, costs, et cetera,

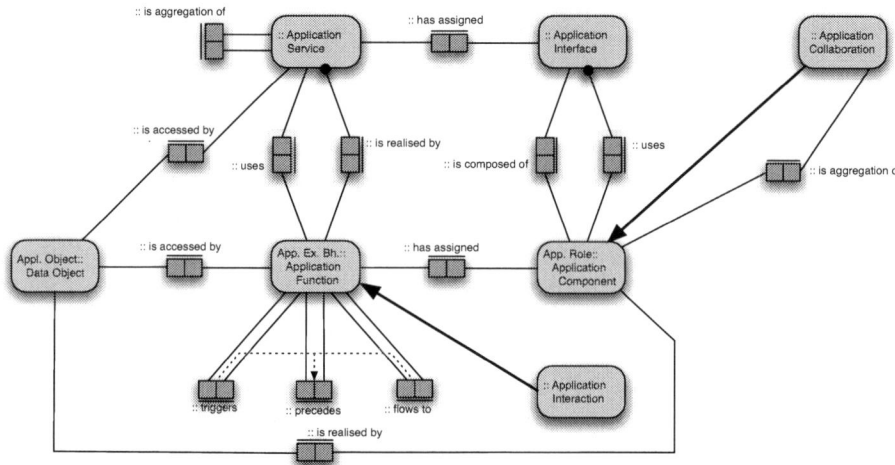

Fig. 10. Level 8 – Application layer

are of relevance. These can be specified in a contract. This leads to the situation as depicted in Figure 9. The concepts of *meaning* and *value* have been repeated to stress the fact that they specifically play a role in the business layer.

The application layer, shown in Figure 10, does not lead to the introduction of additional concepts, and only involves the re-naming of some of the existing concepts. The renamings resulted in new names for existing concepts, which

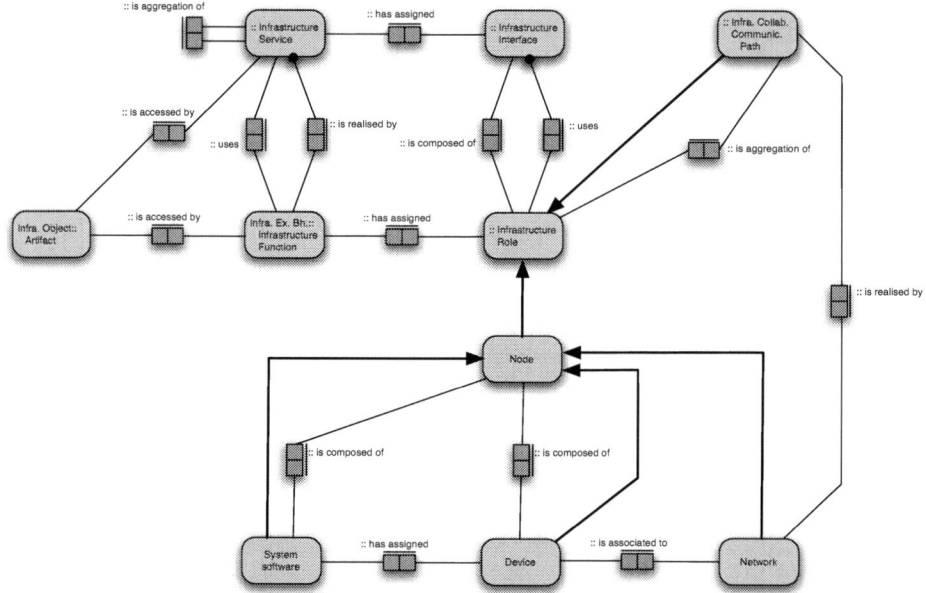

Fig. 11. Level 8 – Technology layer

corresponded better to the names already used by the partners participating in the ArchiMate project, as well as existing standards such as the UML.

The technology layer also involves some renaming of existing concepts. In addition, some further refinements of existing concepts were needed as well, as depicted in Figure 11. The newly introduced concepts deal with the different kinds of elements that may be part of a technology infrastructure: *nodes*, *software systems*, *devices* and *networks*.

7   Conclusion

In this paper we discussed some of the key design decisions and design principles underlying the ArchiMate language. We have reviewed the challenges confronting an architecture description language for enterprise architecture, as well as the design principles aiming to meet these challenges. This also offered a new perspective on the design and evolution of modelling languages, which is of prime importance for languages designed as open standards. We then discussed the modelling concepts needed in the ArchiMate language, where we made a distinction between concepts needed to model domains in general, the modelling of dynamic systems, and the modelling of enterprise architectures.

Recently, the ArchiMate language has been transferred to the Open Group. It is expected that the language will evolve further to better accompany future versions of the Open Group's architecture framework (TOGAF). This can easily be accommodated by taking the meta-model at level 6 as a common denominator. At level 7 a choice has to be made for a specific architecture framework; in the case of TOGAF this corresponds to a *business architecture*, an *information systems architecture* and a *technology architecture*.

References

1. Lankhorst, M., et al.: Enterprise Architecture at Work: Modelling, Communication and Analysis. Springer, Berlin (2005)
2. Op 't Land, M., Proper, H., Waage, M., Cloo, J., Steghuis, C.: Enterprise Architecture – Creating Value by Informed Governance. Springer, Berlin (2008)
3. OMG: UML 2.0 Superstructure Specification – Final Adopted Specification. Technical Report ptc/03–08–02, OMG (2003)
4. Object Management Group: Business process modeling notation, v1.1. OMG Available Specification OMG Document Number: formal/2008-01-17, Object Management Group (2008)
5. Steen, M., Doest, H.t., Lankhorst, M., Akehurst, D.: Supporting Viewpoint–Oriented Enterprise Architecture. In: Proceedings of the 8th IEEE International Enterprise Distributed Object Computing Conference (EDOC 2004), pp. 20–24 (2004)
6. Jonkers, H., Lankhorst, M., Buuren, R.v., Hoppenbrouwers, S., Bonsangue, M., Torre, L.v.d.: Concepts for Modeling Enterprise Architectures. International Journal of Cooperative Information Systems 13, 257–288 (2004)

7. van Buuren, R., Jonkers, H., Iacob, M.-E., Strating, P.: Composition of relations in enterprise architecture models. In: Ehrig, H., Engels, G., Parisi-Presicce, F., Rozenberg, G. (eds.) ICGT 2004. LNCS, vol. 3256, pp. 39–53. Springer, Heidelberg (2004)
8. Arbab, F., Boer, F.d., Bonsangue, M., Lankhorst, M., Proper, H., Torre, L.v.d.: Integrating Architectural Models. Enterprise Modelling and Information Systems Architectures 2, 40–57 (2007)
9. The Open Group: The Open Group Architecture Framework (TOGAF) Version 8.1.1, Enterprise Edition (2007)
10. Lindland, O., Sindre, G., Sølvberg, A.: Understanding quality in conceptual modeling. IEEE Software 11, 42–49 (1994)
11. Bosma, H., Doest, H.t., Vos, M.: Requirements. Technical Report ArchiMate Deliverabe D4.1, TI/RS/2002/112, Telematica Instituut (2002)
12. Proper, H., Verrijn–Stuart, A., Hoppenbrouwers, S.: Towards Utility–based Selection of Architecture–Modelling Concepts. In: Hartmann, S., Stumptner, M. (eds.) Proceedings of the Second Asia–Pacific Conference on Conceptual Modelling (APCCM 2005), Sydney, New South Wales, Australia. Conferences in Research and Practice in Information Technology Series, vol. 42, pp. 25–36. Australian Computer Society (2005)
13. Halpin, T., Morgan, T.: Information Modeling and Relational Databases, 2nd edn. Morgan Kaufmann, San Francisco (2008)
14. SBVR Team: Semantics of Business Vocabulary and Rules (SBVR). Technical Report dtc/06–03–02, Object Management Group, Needham, Massachusetts (2006)

Enterprise Meta Modeling Methods – Combining a Stakeholder-Oriented and a Causality-Based Approach

Robert Lagerström[1], Jan Saat[2], Ulrik Franke[1], Stephan Aier[2], and Mathias Ekstedt[1]

[1] Industrial Information and Control Systems, the Royal Institute of Technology,
Osquldas väg 12, 10044 Stockholm, Sweden
{robertl,ulrikf,mathiase}@ics.kth.se
[2] Institute of Information Management, University of St Gallen,
Mueller-Friedberg-Strasse 8, 9000 St Gallen, Switzerland
{jan.saat,stephan.aier}@unisg.ch

Abstract. Meta models are the core of enterprise architecture, but still few methods are available for the creation of meta models tailored for specific purposes. This paper presents two approaches, one focusing on the stakeholders' information demand of enterprise architecture and the other driven by causal analysis of enterprise system properties. The two approaches are compared and a combined best-of-breed method is proposed. The combined method has merged the strengths of both approaches, thus combining the stakeholder concerns with causality-driven analysis. Practitioners will, when employing the proposed method, achieve a relevant meta model with strong, and goal-adapted, analytic capabilities.

Keywords: Meta modeling, Enterprise Architecture, stakeholder concerns, causal modeling.

1 Introduction

Meta models are at the core of enterprise architecture (EA) concepts. They describe the fundamental artifacts of business and IT as well as their interrelationships in a single aggregate organizational model [42]. Such high level models provide a common language and a clear view on the structure of and dependencies between relevant parts of the organization. Meta models serve three main purposes [23]:

1. Documentation of the enterprise architecture
2. Analysis of the enterprise architecture
3. Planning and design of the enterprise architecture.

These three purposes are in turn crucial to the success of management tasks such as product planning, business development, or business process consolidation [24].

However, devising a good meta model is not trivial. Obviously, it is important that the meta model is relevant in relation to the management tasks it should support. At the same time it is also of outmost importance that the meta model employed is kept minimal so that it can be used in practice where time and resources available to spend on enterprise architecture are limited. Occam's razor – the famous principle that

T. Halpin et al. (Eds.): BPMDS 2009 and EMMSAD 2009, LNBIP 29, pp. 381–393, 2009.

entities must not be multiplied beyond necessity – is a rule of thumb very much valid in the context of meta modeling.

This paper presents two different meta modeling approaches, both based on the idea that minimal meta models are best obtained by maintaining a strict focus on goals when in the phase of meta model creation. However, the two methods differ in important respects, and a combined, best-of-breed, method is therefore proposed.

The first, stakeholder-oriented, approach to meta modeling starts with stakeholder concern elicitation and is strongly driven by practitioners. The resulting meta model seeks to satisfy the stakeholders information demands, each connected to distinct application scenarios. The second, causality-based, approach is based on causal modeling of goals sought. Starting from these goals, the resulting meta model provides a range of elements and attributes linked together by causality. The meta model thus supports the analysis necessary to achieve defined goals [16]. Compared to the stakeholder-oriented approach, focus is set on attributes with causal relations rather than on elements.

According to method engineering literature [4, 5], a method consists of design activities, design results, information models, techniques and roles. The proposed combined method focuses on the design activities, by introducing a meta modeling procedure. The method combines the strengths of its two constituent parts, addressing stakeholder concerns through causality driven analysis.

The remainder of this paper is structured as follows. Section 2 discusses related works, putting the present contribution in context. Section 3 describes the two parent methods in greater detail, and includes an analysis of their strengths and weaknesses. Section 4 outlines the combined method, including a concrete example of a possible application scenario. Section 5 discusses the result and concludes the paper.

2 Related Work

A number of EA initiatives have been proposed, e.g. The Open Group Architecture Framework (TOGAF) [39], the Zachman Framework [45], Enterprise Architecture Planning (EAP) [38], and the General Enterprise Reference Architecture and Methodology (GERAM) [14]. There are also numerous meta models proposed for EA modeling, e.g. the ones presented by O'Rourke [33], Lankhorst [27], Frank [8], and Niemann [31]. These works tend to focus on the differentiation of meta models in viewpoints, often referred to as architecture layers, as well as proposing notations (syntaxes) to display the model content of the different viewpoints. Neither the larger frameworks nor the meta model oriented initiatives typically contain methods for meta model design or adaptation to suit specific stakeholder concerns (except on a very general level). Only a few meta models detail whether and how they support decision making and goal oriented modeling. Even fewer specify how the meta models can support analysis of different scenario designs.

In contrast to the general and enterprise-wide modeling languages found within the discipline of EA, there exist a large number of languages that serve more specific purposes. Software and system architecture description languages, for instance, focus on internal structure and design of software systems. In addition to capturing the overall structure of systems, analysis capabilities are often available, such as deadlock and interoperability analyses in Wright [3], and availability, security, and timeliness analyses in the Architecture Analysis and Design Language (AADL) [35]. Other examples of modeling languages with very specific purposes are found, for instance, in software security engineering, where languages such as UMLsec [18], secure UML [29] and misuse cases [36] have been tailored specifically for security analysis (rather than depicting overall architectural design). These languages provide good support for detailed modeling of concerns. However, they lack holistic scope, which means that a subject such as security is only covered from a limited (typically technical) point of view. Furthermore, they also miss a large class of concerns such as business/IT alignment, system maintainability and flexibility that are highly relevant when considering an enterprise as a whole.

There is also a discussion of business architecture as a complementary concept to IT architecture. Although there are a few contributions dealing with the definition and implementation of business architecture as well as the corresponding models in general [21, 40] or in specific industries [12] there is no discussion of methods for meta model design we are aware of.

Looking even broader we quickly turn to adjacent areas. There is much written on the subject of knowledge elicitation [10], i.e. how to capture existing knowledge about phenomena in a systematic way. This field of research is associated with artificial intelligence [28], requirements elicitation [32], ontological engineering [6], and Bayesian networks [19, 20]. Most of the methods within these research fields focus on conducting experiments or interviews. Most of the methods are customized for a specific purpose, and since none of the methods mentioned deal with meta modeling it is difficult to employ them as meta model design methods off-the-shelf.

More specifically, there are some initiatives focusing on meta model integration [22, 37]. However, these methods do neither detail how to create a meta model or a meta model fragment nor what specific purpose they serve.

Recently it has been reported on how the i* framework [13, 43] could support goal oriented analysis and modeling into EA. In [44] it is demonstrated how business and IT related goals could be explicitly modeled using i* when constructing an EA. i* promotes a meta model including among other things goals (and so called soft goals) and their dependencies. Presently, is i* however not a method for developing meta models, it is rather a meta model for expressing goals. Consequently, it does not help the EA modeler with delimiting the meta models, instead it is an (important) extension of it.

To conclude, frameworks and formal notations for EA are available, most of them evolved from software engineering or business modeling to the EA context. However, general, notation independent, methods for meta modeling, that take business-oriented (and non functional) requirements and potential application scenarios into account are rare. None of the methods, frameworks, and notations examined results in meta models, covers the entire EA domain, and is purpose oriented in the sense that there should be an explicit relation to the purpose of the resulting meta model and support for describing the purpose. Furthermore, there is little support of causality formalization or attributes in the available methods for enterprise meta model creation.

3 Meta Modeling Approaches

3.1 Stakeholder-Oriented Approach

Stakeholder-oriented meta model engineering was first introduced by [23]. The scope of the approach covers the architectural layers strategy, organization, alignment, software and data, and infrastructure as proposed in [2, 42]. Starting point for the meta model creation are the stakeholders and their information needs (concerns). A stakeholder in this case can be understood as a role within an organization that may benefit from the information provided by the enterprise architecture, and therefore by the entities of the meta model. A stakeholder has certain concerns that may be supported by application scenarios of the enterprise architecture. Application scenarios, such as *compliance management*, *product planning*, *business continuity planning* or *technology risk management* can be supported by architectural analysis, such as dependency analysis or coverage analysis. An extensive list of application scenarios and analysis types can be found in [31, 41]. In order to address multiple stakeholders concerns and to support a variety of application scenarios the meta model must include all relevant entities and relations. Therefore the method proposes stakeholder interviews to gather information about concerns and application scenarios. In a next step, meta model fragments to cover the collected concerns are created.

Table 1. Engineering of Meta Model Fragments for Example Scenarios [23]

Scenario	IT Consolidation	Business IT Alignment	Compliance (IT-Ownership)
Object Purpose Concern **Stakeholder Design Strategies**	Processes, Applications Analysis Cost of application operations and maintenance Application architect Consolidation of applications that are in use for a similar purposes	Processes, Applications Analysis Providing adequate IT for business processes Process owner Providing IT functionalities for each process step / Reduction of media breaks	IT-related artifacts Documentation Correct implementation of ownership policies IT audit Assigning explicit owners to applications and other IT-related artifacts
Questions	Which applications are used in the individual processes (sorted by organizational unit, product, and distribution channel)? Which system software of the same type is currently in use?	Which process activities are not IT supported? Which processes include media breaks? Which activities are supported by multiple applications?	Are there applications for which no owners have been defined? Are there applications that have not been audited for more than two years?
Meta Model Fragment	Product — Distribution Channel; Process ⋯ Org. Unit; Application — System Software	specialization / part of — Process; Application	Org. Unit; Application — Person

These fragments are set into relation in order to achieve consistency and to eliminate redundancies. Finally the model fragments are integrated to create one holistic
meta model to cover all entities and relationships needed (Table 1).

The method presented has been used in several industry projects, which led to continuous improvements [24]. Since most organizations do not start enterprise architecture
projects in green field environments, occasionally company specific meta models or
parts of it already exist and need to be integrated in the process sketched above. In this
case modeling of the meta model fragments does not start from scratch but existing
parts are modified according to the results of stakeholder interviews. In other cases,
companies opt for the adoption of reference models for parts of the meta model. To
support this situation, a common level of abstraction has to be found in order to integrate self modeled fragments and reference model fragments. Therefore domains are
used to group semantically related architectural entities and create comparability. Furthermore a quantitative indicator to determine the usefulness of a reference model fragment for a specific model is introduced. This indicator determines the modification
efforts of a reference model necessary to fit the specific meta model of the organization.

Consequently, the method supports

1. the development of meta models starting from scratch with stakeholders'
   concerns,
2. meta modeling using legacy and reference models, and
3. the integration of fragments from steps 1 and 2.

3.2 Causality-Based Approach

The main focus of the causality-based approach is on creating a meta model tailored
to suit specific goals. These goals can be business oriented and "high-level", such as
reduce IT costs or *improve customer satisfaction* as well as more technical and concrete, such as *increase system availability* or *improve system documentation*. In order
to achieve the goal, the approach stipulates that the goal is decomposed into more
tangible and clearly operationalized sub goals. The goal decomposition and operationalization is made by considering the causal dependencies of the goals upon components of enterprises, such as systems, processes, services, information, etc. as well
as their inherent properties such as *process cycle time* or *system cost*. The method thus
focuses heavily on causal relations between attributes of entities in enterprise meta
models. Thus, a meta model will contain entities and entity relations as well as attributes and causal relations between these attributes [25].

The first step is the identification of enterprise goals. The second step is the detection of those enterprise constructs that influence these goals. The effort aims to understand which attributes causally influence the selected goals. In subsequent iterations,
attributes causally affecting the attributes found in the second step are identified. This
iterative process continues until all paths of attributes, and causal relations between
them, have been broken down into attributes that are directly controllable for the
decision maker (Fig. 1). For instance, it might be identified that the goal *improve customer satisfaction* is affected by *customer support process efficiency* and *customer
web portal usability*. In the next iteration the *customer web portal usability* might be
affected by the, for the IT decision maker, directly controllable attributes *web
interface standardization* and *ERP system interoperability*.

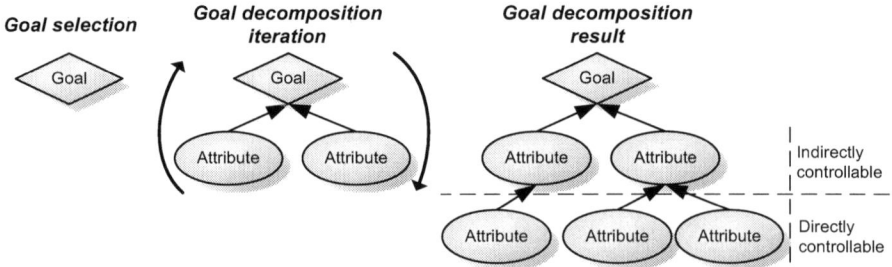

Fig. 1. Goal decomposition method

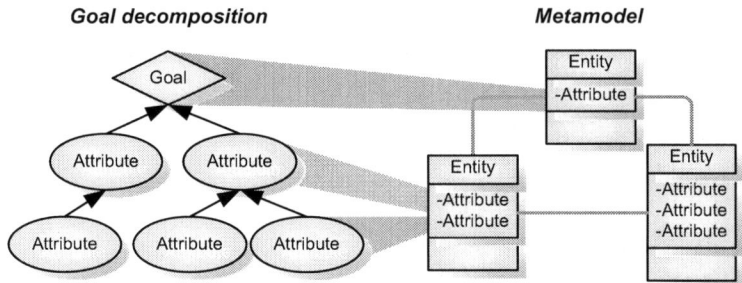

Fig. 2. Goal decomposition result and corresponding meta model

Once a complete set of attributes has been identified, it is time to decide upon enterprise constructs, i.e. meta model entities and relations (Fig. 2). These can either be physical artifacts, such as "computer" and "person", or more conceptual such as "data flow" and "process," depending on the goal decomposition. The previously introduced example uses the entity *web interface* with the attribute *standardization* as well as *ERP system* and *interoperability*. For more information see [11, 16, 26].

The goal decompositions can be visualized and formalized using various languages. By the criteria listed in [17], Extended Influence Diagrams (EIDs), an extension of Bayesian networks, is the preferred language. Employing the notation and mathematical foundation of EIDs provides the user with a language based on causality between a set of discrete variables. Using conditional probabilities and Bayes' rule, it is thus possible to infer the values of the variables in the goal decomposition under different architecture scenarios [15]. By using the EID formalism, the architecture analyses take the potential uncertainties of the knowledge of attribute values as well as the causalities as such.

3.3 Comparison, Strengths and Weaknesses

Both presented approaches propose processes to create meta models for organizations. Also, both approaches are independent of modeling notations. Yet there are differences in process, scope, focus and goals (Table 2).

Table 2. Comparison of Stakeholder-Oriented and Causality-Based Approach

Approach	Stakeholder-Oriented Approach	Causality-Based Approach
Goal	Support concrete application scenarios, such as e.g. IT consolidation, product planning, and post merger integration in organizations based on stakeholders concerns	Support quality goals, such as e.g. business value, IT governance maturity, and system quality (e.g. maintainability, interoperability, security, availability, performance) by decomposing the goals into more controllable metrics
Focus	Entities and relations • What does exist? • What entities are connected?	Causal relations between attributes • How are entities connected? • What is the impact of a changing entity/attribute on the entire architecture?
Scope	• Entities • Entity relations	• Entities • Entity relations with multiplicity • Attributes • Causal relationships between attributes

Meta Modeling Process	1. Define application scenario
	2. Identify stakeholders
	3. Elicit concerns and information demand
	4. Create meta model fragments according to concerns
	5. Integrate fragments
	  5.1. to create a new model
	  5.2. to combine existing fragments or reference models with new fragments, or modify existing models
		1. Define enterprise goals
		2. Decompose in more tangible sub goals
		3. Identify attributes of entities with impact on sub goals
		4. Identify attributes that influence attributes from step 3 until all attributes are broken down to a directly controllable level
		5. Model entities, attributes, and relations between entities

Modeling goals can be diverse and complex, especially if main drivers such as different goals of an organization (causality-based approach) or different stakeholder concerns (stakeholder-oriented approach) cause conflicting modeling decisions. According to the main purposes of enterprise architecture, the meta model has to support documentation, analysis and planning. Both approaches focus on goal orientation and are generally suitable for these purposes. For that matter, the causality-based approach delivers measurable interconnections of entity attributes, which is especially important for analysis and planning capabilities. Stakeholder involvement ensures that there are specific roles with dedicated interest in their special application scenarios, which support the data gathering for the modeling process and also subsequent governance and maintenance aspects.

The focus and scope of the modeling approaches differ. The stakeholder-oriented approach focuses on entities and relations necessary to provide the groundwork for documentation, analysis and planning (What does exist? How are entities connected?). The causality-based approach takes a further step by not only including entities and relations, but focusing on attributes related to the entities and the causal relations between the attributes. This enhances the model, e.g. by using metrics and key performance indicators to evaluate and compare as-is situations and planning scenarios (How are entities connected? What are impacts of changes to one entity on the entire architecture?). Challenging prerequisite is however the existence of accurate data, as well as useful probabilities of occurrence for a certain situation. Not as a matter of meta modeling, but as an issue of operating the enterprise architecture, the cost of gathering and maintaining model information needs to be justified by benefits generated by it. Therefore the desired level of detail for entities and attribute information should be considered according to specific use cases and business needs [9, 30].

The modeling process of the causality-based approach is based on the idea to make strategic aspects measurable and controllable and create a meta model to consider these measures by the use of attributes. The method assumes that the meta model is built from scratch. The stakeholder-oriented approach is based on the information demand of interest groups and considers the scenario where organizations make use of legacy models and/or reference models in combination with new model fragments as well as creating the meta model on the green field.

4 Method Construction

4.1 Goal, Scope, and Focus

In order to create a best-of-breed method strengths of both approaches need to be combined. The resulting method needs a process oriented perspective to support concrete application scenarios and satisfy stakeholder needs as proposed by the stakeholder-oriented approach. At the same time, the metric oriented perspective from the causality-based approach is necessary to ensure sophisticated analysis of the meta model. This enhances the method with important capabilities, e.g. different versions of future scenarios can be compared to each other and evaluated based on the analysis and the impact local changes might cause in the entire enterprise architecture become visible. Thereby the scope of the meta modeling process involves entities, relationships, and attributes. The desired level of granularity results from the usefulness of the depth of information. This might be assessed by difference of the benefits generated from analysis information and the efforts of gathering and maintaining the data. Stakeholder involvement thereby ensures that there are concerns connected to model and analysis information, which is important for acceptance and maintenance matters.

4.2 Method Description

Combining the strengths of the two presented meta modeling methods a novel modeling process is proposed. Table 3 gives an overview on the eight-step procedure.

The method combines the stakeholder orientation with the causality-based approach. The following example illustrates the method using a sample application scenario.

4.3 Example Scenario: IT Consolidation

So far, the presented methods have only been evaluated in industry projects separately [1, 11, 26, 34]. In this first joint proposal, we therefore use an example scenario to illustrate the method. The characteristics of this scenario will be outlined as we proceed through the process steps.

Table 3. Meta Modeling Method Description

Step No.	Step	Description
1*	Define application scenario	Identification of concrete business situations, that enterprise architecture shall support.
2*	Identify stakeholders	Identification of roles and persons that hold responsibility for identified application scenarios.
3*	Elicit concerns and information demand	Investigation of what information stakeholders need in order to fulfill their roles
4 ****	Formalize information demand into metrics	Transform information demand and open questions into high level goals and measures
5 **	Decompose in more tangible sub goals	Break down high level measures in measurable goals
6 **	Identify attributes of entities with impact on sub goals	Identification of model attributes that influence measurable goals
7 ***	Create meta model fragments	Meta modeling including entities, relations and attributes according to concerns and respective analysis metrics. Identification of reusable fragments of existing meta models.
8 *	Integrate fragments	Merge different model fragments to create one meta model addressing all application scenarios selected.
Legend	*based on stakeholder-oriented approach, **based on causality-based approach, ***based on both approaches, ****new step	

In the example case, the company is concerned with a lot of different processes, each supported by its very own IT systems. While the organization is still large, it has gone through considerable downsizing in recent years, and cost reduction is a priority throughout the whole enterprise. The CIO is faced with a decreasing budget, and has to cut costs while maintaining acceptable IT support to the core business.

1. **Define application scenario.** Faced with these circumstances, the CIO decides to make application consolidation a top priority. The CIO believes that there are numerous IT systems currently maintained that provide identical or similar functionality, which causes inefficiencies and high costs.
2. **Identify stakeholders.** To perform an application consolidation, the CIO needs to involve the system owners. These are top executives, each responsible for a certain business area, who also own the IT systems supporting their respective business. While the CIO has a responsibility to co-ordinate these systems, it is the business executives that formally own the systems and the personnel using them.
3. **Elicit concerns and information demand.** To make an informed decision on whether to phase out or keep any given system, the CIO needs to collect information on the characteristics of the system. This means that he must (i) get the consent of his peer executives, so that they will have the actual users collect the data, and (ii) decide on which criteria he is to use for the decisions.
4. **Formalize information demand into quality goals.** To structure his decision, the CIO seeks to make a cost-benefit analysis, with cost and benefits broken down as illustrated in Fig. 3. The need for the system in the organization is combined with the functional and non-functional qualities to define the benefits. The costs to keep the system, on one hand, and the costs to phase out the system, on the other hand, are combined to define the costs.

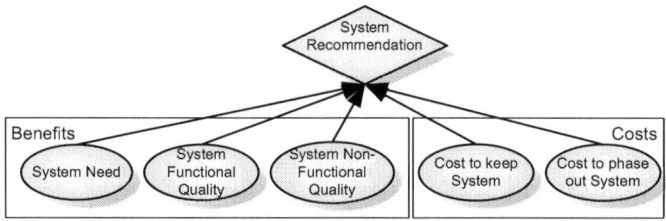

Fig. 3. Formalization of information demand

5. **Decompose in more tangible sub goals.** Clearly, the goals defined above need to be decomposed further. The need for the system can be measured by considering the criticality of the business processes supported by the system combined with an investigation of the redundancy, i.e. whether the processes are supported with the same functionality by several systems. Functional and non-functional qualities (availability, performance, interoperability, etc.) can be indicated by taking the ratio of the quality of service offered over quality that is required. The costs to keep the system can be estimated from current financial records, and those to phase it out depend on the modifiability and the level of coupling of the system at hand with other systems.

6. **Identify attributes of entities with impact on sub goals.** Following the decomposition above, some sample entities are *System*, *Process*, and *Service*. The system entity should have the attribute *Recommendation*, i.e. the top node illustrated above, but also functional and non-functional quality attributes such as *Intrinsical availability* (on an absolute scale) and *Availability ratio* (as compared to the requirements). These requirements, in turn, are attributes of the service offering support to the business process, and the process itself is attributed with, for instance, its *Criticality*. Needless to say, this is only a limited subset of all the attributes actually needed. Fig. 4. below gives a few more causal relationships in this limited example.

7. **Create meta model fragments including entities, relations and attributes according to concerns and quality goals.** The final meta model fragment in this example is illustrated below. The criticality of processes determines the criticality of the services supporting those processes. This is one input into the recommendation of whether to keep or phase out a system. Another input is the availability ratio of the system, as compared to the level of availability needed by the service.

8. **Integrate fragments.** The last step integrates the newly modeled meta model fragments with each other, respectively with already existing meta model fragments.

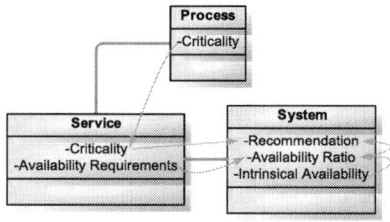

Fig. 4. Meta model fragment

5   Discussion and Conclusion

In this paper we have analyzed existing approaches to EA meta model engineering. Based on this analysis we have proposed an integrated method to define situational EA meta models on a meta model element level as well as on a level of element attributes. Our basic assumption is, that EA models are no ends in themselves but have to provide a business value by supporting informed and well-founded decisions on how to continually transform the EA to fit an organization's goals.

Enterprise architecture data that does not contribute to such decisions should not be maintained in EA models since it often increases the EA maintenance efforts and thus reduces the acceptance of EA in an organization. Therefore our approach strictly derives relevant EA information from relevant application scenarios and stakeholder's concerns down to an attribute level.

Since this paper presents a first proposal of our enhanced method, the method has not yet been evaluated in a real case study. However, the partial evaluation of its components as well as the example given in section 4.3 may indicate the applicability of the method as well as the progressivity of the method compared with existing approaches.

Therefore our next steps will include the evaluation of the method in industry projects as well as the improvement of exiting EA maintenance approaches [e.g. 7] concerning the updates of EA element attributes. We will further investigate into the lifetime of accurate EA model information in order to further enhance EA application and maintenance processes.

References

1. Aier, S., Kurpjuweit, S., Schmitz, O., Schulz, J., Thomas, A., Winter, R.: An Engineering Approach to Enterprise Architecture Design and its Application at a Financial Service Provider. In: Proceedings of Modellierung betrieblicher Informationssysteme (MobIS 2008), Saarbrücken, GI/Köllen, pp. 115–130 (2008)
2. Aier, S., Winter, R.: Virtual Decoupling for IT/Business Alignment - Conceptual Foundations, Architecture Design and Implementation Example. Business & Information Systems Engineering 51(2) (2009)
3. Allen, R.: A Formal Approach to Software Architecture Ph.D. Thesis, Carnegie Mellon University (1997)
4. Brinkkemper, S.: Method Engineering: Engineering of Information Systems Development Methods and Tools. Information and Software Technology 38(4), 275–280 (1996)
5. Brinkkemper, S.: Method-Engineering with Web-Enabled Methods. In: Brinkkemper, S., Lindencrona, E., Solvberg, A. (eds.) Informations Systems Engineering - State of the Art and Research Themes, pp. 123–133. Springer, London (2000)
6. Corcho, O., Gómez-Pérez, A., Fernández-López, M.: Ontological Engineering. Springer, London (2004)
7. Fischer, R., Aier, S., Winter, R.: A Federated Approach to Enterprise Architecture Model Maintenance. Enterprise Modelling and Information Systems Architectures 2(2), 14–22 (2007)
8. Frank, U.: Perspective Enterprise Modeling (MEMO) – Conceptual Framework and Modeling Languages. In: Proceedings of 35th Hawaii International Conference on System Sciences (2002)

9. Franke, U., Johnson, P., Robert, L., Ullberg, J., David, H., Ekstedt, M., Johan, K.: A Method for Choosing Software Assessment Masures using Bayesian Networks and Diagnosis. In: Proceedings of 13th European Conference on Software Maintenance and Reengineering (2009)
10. Gaines, B., Shaw, M.: Using Knowledge Acquisition and Representation Tools to Support Scientific Communities. In: Proceedings of AAAI 1994, pp. 707–7141 (1994)
11. Gustafsson, P., Franke, U., Höök, D., Johnson, P.: Quantifying IT impacts on organizational structure and business value with Extended Influence Diagrams. In: Proceedings of First IFIP WG 8.1 Working Conference: The Practice of Enterprise Modeling (PoEM 2008), Stockholm, Sweden. LNBIP, vol. 15, pp. 138–152. Springer, Heidelberg (2008)
12. Huschens, J., Rumpold-Preining, M.: IBM Insurance Application Architecture (IAA) - An overview of the Insurance Business Architecture. In: Mertins Bernus, K., Schmidt, G. (eds.) Handbook on Architectures of Information Systems, vol. 2, pp. 669–692. Springer, Berlin (2006)
13. i*wiki: I-Star-Wiki (2009), http://istar.rwth-aachen.de (last access: 17.02.2009)
14. Ifip–Ifac: GERAM: Generalised Enterprise Reference Architecture and Methodology, Version 1.6.2, IFIP–IFAC Task Force (1998) (last access: 12.01.2005)
15. Jensen, F.: Bayesian Networks and Decision Graphs. Springer, Heidelberg (2001)
16. Johnson, P., Ekstedt, M.: Enterprise Architecture - Models and Analyses for Information Systems Decision Making. Studentlitteratur, Pozkal (2007)
17. Johnson, P., Lagerström, R., Närman, P., Simonsson, M.: Enterprise Architecture Analysis with Extended Influence Diagrams. Information Systems Frontiers 9(2) (2007)
18. Jürjens, J.: Secure Systems Development with UML. Springer, Heidelberg (2005)
19. Kadane, J., Wolfson, L.: Experiences in Elicitation. The Statistician 47(1) (1998)
20. Keeney, R., von Winterfeldt, D.: Eliciting Probabilities from Experts in Complex Technical Problems. IEEE Transactions on Engineering Management 38(3) (1991)
21. Kilov, H.: Business Models - A Guide for Business and IT. Prentice Hall PTR, Upper Saddle River (2002)
22. Kühn, H., Bayer, F., Jungringer, S., Karagiannis, D.: Enterprise Model Integration. In: Bauknecht, K., Tjoa, A.M., Quirchmayr, G. (eds.) EC-Web 2003. LNCS, vol. 2738, pp. 379–392. Springer, Heidelberg (2003)
23. Kurpjuweit, S., Winter, R.: Viewpoint-based Meta Model Engineering. In: Proceedings of Enterprise Modelling and Information Systems Architectures (EMISA 2007), Bonn, Gesellschaft für Informatik, Köllen, pp. 143–161 (2007)
24. Kurpjuweit, S., Winter, R.: Concern-oriented Business Architecture Engineering. In: Proceedings of 24th Annual ACM Symposium on Applied Computing (SAC), Honolulu, Hawaii (2009)
25. Lagerström, R.: Analyzing System Maintainability using Enterprise Architecture Models. Journal of Enterprise Architecture 3(4), 33–42 (2007)
26. Lagerström, R., Johnson, P.: Using Architectural Models to Predict the Maintainability of Enterprise Systems. In: Proceedings of 12th European Conference on Software Maintenance and Reengineering (CSMR 2008), Athens, Greece, pp. 248–252 (2008)
27. Lankhorst, M.: Enterprise Architecture at Work: Modelling, Communication and Analysis. Springer, Berlin (2005)
28. Liou, Y.: Knowledge acquisition: issues, techniques, and methodology. In: Proceedings of ACM SIGBDP Conference on Trends and Directions in Expert Systems (SIGBDP 1990), pp. 212–236. ACM Press, New York (1990)

29. Lodderstedt, T., Basin, D., Doser, J.: SecureUML: A UML-Based Modeling Language for Model-Driven Security. In: Jézéquel, J.-M., Hussmann, H., Cook, S. (eds.) UML 2002. LNCS, vol. 2460, pp. 426–441. Springer, Heidelberg (2002)
30. Närman, P., Johnson, P., Robert, L., Franke, U., Ekstedt, M.: Data Collection Prioritization for Software Quality Analysis. In: Proceedings of Electronic Notes in Theoretical Computer Science (2008)
31. Niemann, K.D.: From Enterprise Architecture to IT Governance. Elements of Effective IT Management. Vieweg, Wiesbaden (2006)
32. Nuseibeh, B., Kramer, J., Finkelstein, A.: Expressing the relationship between multiple view in requirements specification. In: 15th Int. Conf. on Software Engineering (1993)
33. O'Rourke, C., Fishman, N., Selkow, W.: Enterprise Architecture – Using the Zachman Framework. Thomson Learning, Boston (2003)
34. Raderius, J., Per, N., Ekstedt, M.: Assessing System Availability Using an Enterprise Architecture Analysis Approach. In: Proceedings of 3rd Workshop on Trends in Enterprise Architecture Research (TEAR 2008), Sydney, Australia (2009)
35. SAE: Society of Automotive Engineers: Architecture Analysis and Design Language (AADL) standard, Carnegie Mellon University (2009)
36. Sindre, G., Opdahl, A.L.: Eliciting Security Requirements by Misuse Cases. In: Proceedings of TOOLS Pacific 2000, pp. 120–131. IEEE Press, Los Alamitos (2000)
37. Song, X.: A framework for understanding the integration of design methodologies. ACM SIGSOFT Software Engineering 20(1), 46–54 (1995)
38. Spewak, S.H., Hill, S.C.: Enterprise Architecture Planning - Developing a Blueprint for Data, Applications and Technology. John Wiley & Sons, New York (1993)
39. The Open Group: The Open Group Architecture Framework TOGAF - 2007 Edition (Incorporating 8.1.1). Van Haren, Zaltbommel (2007)
40. Versteeg, G., Bouwman, H.: Business architecture: A new paradigm to relate business strategy to ICT. Information Systems Frontiers 8(2), 91–102 (2006)
41. Winter, R., Bucher, T., Fischer, R., Kurpjuweit, S.: Analysis and Application Scenarios of Enterprise Architecture - An Exploratory Study. Journal of Enterprise Architecture 3(3), 33–43 (2007)
42. Winter, R., Fischer, R.: Essential Layers, Artifacts, and Dependencies of Enterprise Architecture. Journal of Enterprise Architecture 3(2), 7–18 (2007)
43. Yu, E.: Modelling Strategic Relationships for Process Engineering, Dissertation, University of Toronto. Dept. of Computer Science (1995)
44. Yu, E., Strohmaier, M., Deng, X.: Exploring Intentional Modeling and Analysis for Enterprise Architecture. In: Proceedings of Workshop on Trends in Enterprise Architecture Research (TEAR 2006), Hong Kong (2006)
45. Zachman, J.A.: A Framework for Information Systems Architecture. IBM Systems Journal 26(3), 276–292 (1987)

Organizational Patterns for B2B Environments – Validation and Comparison

Moses Niwe and Janis Stirna

Department of Computer and Systems Sciences, Stockholm University and Royal Institute of Technology, Forum 100, SE-16440, Kista, Sweden
{niwe,js}@dsv.su.se

Abstract. This research captures best practices in the business-to-business (B2B) domain as a means of competitive advantage and innovation for organizations striving to adopt B2B environments. We present a case of developing and validating a set of patterns for B2B adoption and then discuss the case in the context of a number of other cases where organizational patterns have been used to capture, document and share competitive organizational knowledge.

Keywords: Organizational patterns, pattern validation, business-to-business (B2B).

1 Introduction

Organizational success depends on capturing and using its knowledge, which may come in many different forms such as employee competence, skills, work experiences, and work procedures. Best practices and collective expertise are particularly important to capture and share in the most efficient ways, because they are the most valuable assets for sustainable competitive advantage, innovation, and success of many IT undertakings. One such area is establishing and running business to business (B2B) environments.

Organizations having B2B environments encounter many knowledge-related problems, for instance, the operation and communication aspects of the B2B environment, problems with accessibility and execution of transactions, lack proper documentation. Furthermore, employees' tasks are shifted frequently and new staff are added or replaced often without knowledge capturing and sharing. As the body of knowledge has grown considerably, it has become very difficult to fast track new employees and to externalize and share valuable knowledge quickly. Since most of this knowledge is problem-solution based, an effective and practicable way of addressing this challenge is to capture the knowledge in the form of patterns.

The objective of this paper is to present a case of developing and validating a set of patterns for B2B adoption and then to discuss it in comparison with a number of other cases where organizational patterns have been used to capture, document, and share competitive organizational knowledge. More specifically, we discuss pattern validation results in terms of the usefulness of the knowledge embedded in the patterns and the usefulness and appropriateness of the pattern format to knowledge capture.

T. Halpin et al. (Eds.): BPMDS 2009 and EMMSAD 2009, LNBIP 29, pp. 394–406, 2009.

The rest of the paper is structured as follows. Section 2 presents the background of organizational patterns and introduces the pattern validation process. This is followed by the pattern language of B2B adoption in section 3. In section 4 we present the pattern validation results and discussion. This is divided into three subsections addressing the usefulness of the knowledge embedded in the patterns, the usefulness of the pattern format followed by a comparison with similar pattern development and application cases. Future work and concluding remarks are presented in sections 5.

2   Background to Organizational Patterns

A pattern is used to: *"describe a problem that occurs over and over again in our environment, and then describes the core of the solution to that problem in such a way that you can use this solution a million times over, without ever doing it the same way twice"* [1]. This principle of describing a reusable solution to a recurrent problem in a context has been adopted in various domains such as software engineering, information system analysis and design (e.g. [2]) and organizational design. Organizational patterns have proven to be a useful way for the purpose of documenting, representing, and sharing best practices (c.f. [3] & [4]). Patterns offer an alternative and flexible approach that bridges between theory, empirical evidence and experience, and help resolve practical problems of organizations. Knowledge sharing and the generic nature of patterns, provides an efficient instrument for capturing various knowledge chunks such as best practices, work processes, organizational solutions, experiences, etc. [5].

Organizational patterns show when and how to solve something [6]. To do this the pattern will have different elements as shown in figure 1. The elements of the pattern allow the potential pattern user to make a judgment as to the pattern's usefulness, appropriateness, and applicability in different contexts. In the B2B adoption case reported in this paper we have used the following fields – (1) pattern name as the general area of application, (2) business problem as the summary of the issue that the pattern intends to solve, (3) proposed solution to the business problem, and (4) motivation explaining the reason for the pattern, emphasizing the practical significance and implications of the pattern. When appropriate the solution is illustrated by a model fragment or referenced to business process descriptions. It is also worth pointing out that in some cases the knowledge embedded in the patterns serves only as a suggestion or inspiration for designing processes in organizations – the proposed solution would have to be

Name of field	Description
Name	Each pattern should have a name that reflects the problem/solution that it addresses. Names of patterns are also used for indexing purposes.
Problem	Describes the issues that the pattern wishes to address within the given context and forces.
Solution	Describes how to solve the problem and to achieve the desired result. Solution describes the work needed. It can be expressed in natural language, drawings, multimedia sequences, etc. Solution can be backed up with references to other knowledge sources and other patterns.
Motivation	Argument and example of applicable areas. In some cases this field also includes citations of expert interviews from the pattern discovery and development stages.

Fig. 1. The pattern template used in the B2B adoption case

Sources of knowledge for eliciting candidate patterns included business documentations (manuals, repositories and intranet), policies, rules, archival sources like project reports, as well as face to face and phone interviews with experts. Examples of the companies that contributed to this process are:

- a firm that solves complex systems integration issues behind state-of-the-art technology partnering with software vendors such as Sterling Commerce, and Business Objects.
- a data exchange company that enables B2B document exchange. It provides a B2B platform with a large number of suppliers, with which, buyers do business often exchanging hundreds or thousands of documents monthly.
- a large multi-service provider (Internet, data, multimedia, and voice),
- and a large wireless service provider.

2.1 Pattern Validation

Part of the process of developing patterns is validating patterns. I.e. the patterns development team needs to assess the reuse potential of the proposed patterns outside the organizational context in which they were developed. The validation process should be performed after a fairly complete and coherent set of patterns has been developed and it shows the external consistency of the knowledge embedded in developing the patterns. Patterns can be evaluated separately and in groups.

The ELEKTRA project developed a pattern evaluation approach [7, 8] that has been tailored and used in a number of subsequent projects. The approach puts forward a number of hypotheses and then validates them with a set of criteria addressed by questionnaires. The questionnaires should be answered by experts who have substantial competence in the respective knowledge domain and who could be seen as the potential pattern users. The ELEKTRA approach to evaluating the usefulness of the knowledge embedded in patterns used the following criteria:

- *Usefulness*: The degree to which the usage of the pattern would provide a substantial contribution in the context of a real problem-solving application.
- *Relevance*: The degree to which a pattern addresses a significant problem in the target industry sector or knowledge domain.
- *Usability*: The degree to which the pattern can be used in the context of a real application.
- *Adaptability*: The degree to which the solution advocated by the pattern can be modified to reflect a particular situation.
- *Adoptability*: The degree of acceptance of the pattern to be used by domain experts for resolving a particular problem of interest.
- *Completeness*: The degree to which a pattern offers a comprehensive and complete view of the problem under consideration and of the proposed solution.
- *Coherence*: The degree to which the pattern constitutes a coherent unit including correct relationships with other patterns.
- *Consistency*: The degree to which the pattern conforms to existing knowledge and vocabulary used in the target industry sector or knowledge domain.

- *Prescriptiveness*: The degree to which the pattern offers a concrete and tangible proposal for solving a problem, in particular with respect to the steps necessary for its implementation as described in the guideline.
- *Granularity*: The level of detail at which the pattern addresses a problem.

3   Pattern Language of B2B Adoption

The overall problem that the pattern language for B2B adoption addresses on the macro level is the lack of standards and structure in the operation and communication of the B2B environment, for example, issues in accessibility and execution of B2B transactions. Table 1 shows the different problems and corresponding patterns.

The goal of constructing a pattern language is to understand the dependencies among patterns and how they contribute to the overall problem of the pattern language. This required us to analyze the B2B environment and business operations. The current set of 25 patterns act as guidelines for B2B transactions. The patterns represent a set of problems that are involved in B2B systems transactions and each pattern's solution and its effect are supported by trading partner experience. The pattern as best practice action provides a means for what organizations need to do in order to compete effectively in a changing and competitive business climate.

Table 1. Problems and corresponding patterns and relationships

Business Problem	No.	Pattern Name	Relationship to patterns
X1:-The problem is dealing with different releases	P16	Versioning and compatibility	P1,P5,P22
X2:-Lack of intervention on errors raises issues	P1	Error handling/management	P10,P12,P24
X3:-Lack of agreed conventions	P3	Single platform	P4,P7
X4:-Set up issues with trading partners	P15	Connectivity	P17,P22
X5:-Multiple entry points	P9	Duplication	P2,P23
X6:-Visibility and monitoring in transaction systems	P8	Visibility and monitoring	P10,P12,P14
X7:-Non-relational tracking mechanism for issues	P24	Tracking and trending	P1,P8,P10
X8:-Documents fail to load because of process	P20	System, process/task failure	P10,P11,P21
X9:-No dialogue across the B2B modules	P5	Architecture/integration	P3,P4
X10:-No automated mechanism for various subtasks	P19	Auto task assignments	P2,P5
X11:-Data problems in disparate locations	P4	Centralized data repository	P3,P7
X12:-Transaction document accuracy	P17	Transaction integrity	P3,P4,P18
X13:-Lack of clear legal environment,	P11	Contractual issues	P3,P7,P12
X14:-Timely receipt and sequence of all files	P14	Timing and sequence	P1,P2,P16
X15:-Frequency and format of archived information	P25	Archiving and/or maintenance	P22,P23
X16:-Change process to support B2B initiatives	P2	Change management	P14,P18
X17:-Complicated B2B tools	P6	Usability/end-user enhancements	P2,P20
X18:- Collectivity in creating networks	P7	Inter-organizational factors	P3,P4,P5
X19:-Processing problematic transactions	P10	Resolution and reconciliation	P1,P24
X20:-Reporting mechanism for transaction activity	P12	Reporting capabilities	P1,P8,P19
X21:-File resends and corresponding enhancements	P13	File resends / re-load option	P1,P17,P23
X22:-Template related issues	P18	Transaction template construction	P1,P9,P23
X23:-Hardware standard thresholds	P21	Hardware scalability	P8,P20
X24:-Controls for communication	P22	Controls and security	P3,P17,P25
X25:-Data ownership is often political	P23	Data and file processing	P9,P25

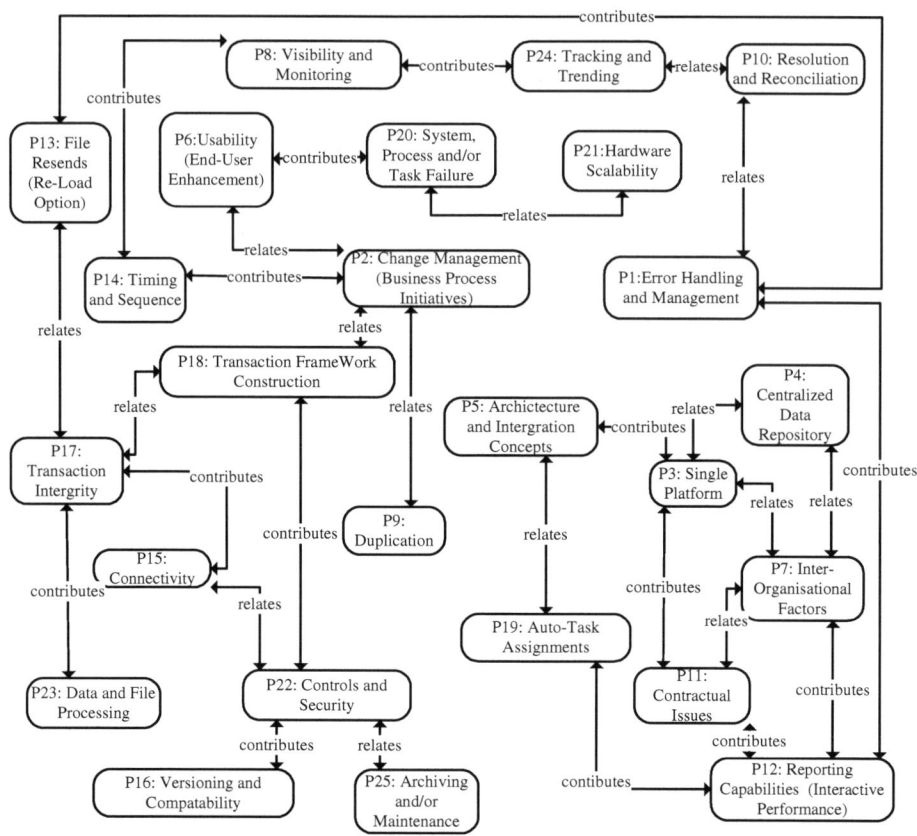

Fig. 2. The pattern language of B2B adoption

The overall structure of the pattern language is shown in figure 2.

The pattern language for B2B adoption shows the structure of the pattern relationships E.g. in table 2 we extrapolate an example of one such pattern. P2:-*change management and business process initiatives* involves following through process to identify deficient, broken and non-existent processes so as to reengineer changes or upgrades to take advantage of P14:- *timing and sequence* (according to process). Company sets up a change initiation process that begins with using a pre-defined template to clarify business need. Company will then assess architectural fit for P18:- *transaction framework construction* to consider component reuse, advancement opportunities, coupling, and technology use when creating scope, vision, and delivery plan for change. P6 *usability and end user enhancements* are related to a successful change process in P2:-*change management and business process initiatives* as users have a direct role in system transition. P9:-*duplication* includes considerations such as: when converting from paper to electronic what business rules should be established for duplicate business documents found? Specifically, which document, paper

Table 2. Example Pattern and Model in the B2B adoption domain

Name	P2-Change Management and Business Process Initiatives
Business Problem	Companies face difficulties in the change process to support B2B initiatives. They try to patch new systems onto the existing system because they are caught up in balancing between needs of tactical survival and strategic viability.
Solution	There is a need for organizations to discuss the best mechanism for initiating changes while evaluating and evolving existing processes to successfully utilize B2B solutions. The overall suggestion is to pick one thing and do it consistently (a key change management concept) then add another-continuous improvement to a standard format while understanding the stages of B2B transaction growth and reengineer business processes (such as order fulfillment and delivery) concurrently with B2B implementation. In addition change management helps companies to implement B2B in a way that addresses "people" issues that may arise while moving from the current state to the desired state. The business context should address the processes, organization, people and technology. Following is a structural layout that could be followed: The first step is to identify the current process. The company implementation manager partners with the trading partner to identify all components of the current process, including: ■ Process Steps – Points within the process when an action, or set of actions, are performed on the business document. For each step, trading partner should specify: • Entrance criteria • Actions that must be performed; actions that may be performed • Exit criteria • The next possible step or steps, and what determining factors should be used when there are multiple possible steps: ■ Work Assignment – For each processing step, identify how the work is assigned. For each step, Trading partner should specify: • To which users or groups the work is assigned • Secondary/default user assignments • The criteria used to identify to whom the work is assigned ■ Processing Controls – Points within the process where work is controlled, either through an approval step or second-level review. Processing controls should include: • Who is performing the approval or second-level review • What occurs when the reviewer accepts or rejects the reviewed work In all this organizations need to build business decision-making capabilities in the B2B processes explaining the underlying principles and approach all aimed at adding trading partner value. E.g. work with the appropriate trading partners to determine the impact of the scope change.
Motivation	Business process reengineering initiatives will help in achieving cost reduction, improved quality, trading partner satisfaction, and time reduction involved in the execution of each of the business process.

or electronic, should be discarded? Under what circumstances (e.g. order in which they were received, level of detail entered/loaded, etc.)? This is related to P2:-*change management and business process initiatives.*

4 Pattern Validation Results and Discussion

This section presents our findings from evaluating the B2B pattern language. The features examined in the evaluation process of the B2B pattern language where: (1) usefulness of the knowledge embedded in the patterns and (2) the usefulness of the pattern format to knowledge capture. This was done after 25 patterns were developed and presented in the pattern language c.f. figure 2. 20 evaluators from 12 organizations in total answered questionnaires addressing the criteria shown below.

The evaluation process starts out by identifying hypotheses that are presented as statements and/or possible theories. Evaluations using these hypotheses tests feature (1)-the usefulness of the knowledge embed in the patterns for the B2B environment. This was in line with the evaluation criterion developed for the ELEKTRA approach as follows:

- *Hypothesis 1 Usefulness*: The knowledge embedded in the pattern would provide a substantial contribution for a transaction oriented trading partner to resolve an existing problem.
- *Hypothesis 2 Relevance*: The pattern addresses a problem that is significant for B2B transaction oriented companies.
- *Hypothesis 3 Usability*: The knowledge embedded in the pattern can be used by a trading partner to resolve an existing problem.
- *Hypothesis 4 Adaptability*: The pattern can be tailored and modified with a reasonable amount of effort in order to produce a template for a specific trading partner.
- *Hypothesis 5 Adoptability*: The pattern is likely to be used in a real situation by domain experts in order to respond to a need in a trading partner.
- *Hypothesis 6 Completeness*: The description of the pattern is complete.
- *Hypothesis 7 Coherence*: The description of the pattern is coherent.
- *Hypothesis 8 Consistency*: The pattern fully conforms to the existing knowledge and vocabulary of the B2B transaction sector.
- *Hypothesis 9 Prescriptiveness*: The pattern clearly describes the solution to the problem addressed and lays out the individual elements of the solution and the steps for their implementation.
- *Hypothesis 10 Granularity*: The pattern provides a solution with a level of detail reflecting the level of abstraction of the problem addressed.

Evaluation feature (2) addresses the usefulness of the pattern format to knowledge capture also used evaluation criterion developed for the ELEKTRA approach as follows:

- *Hypothesis 11 Usefulness*: The language captures and conveys the relevant knowledge for describing patterns.
- *Hypothesis 12 Comprehensiveness*: The different elements of the pattern (e.g. problem, solution, and motivation.) are adequate for understanding its purpose.
- *Hypothesis 13 Richness*: The language is able to describe the different aspects of a pattern one is expecting in such a description.
- *Hypothesis 14 Relevance*: The conceptual primitives chosen are appropriate for expressing the respective parts of pattern knowledge.

The measuring scale was done for 2 options, a "yes" or "no" option such as adoptable and not adoptable.

4.1 Findings Concerning the Usefulness of the Knowledge Embedded in Patterns

This section presents the usefulness of the knowledge embedded in patterns. Due to space limitations we present the overall analysis concerning the whole pattern language. The complete evaluation results will be published later this year. Percentages are used to present a clearer perspective of the evaluators that were for or against a specific pattern. We also present the reasoning behind those for and against. However in some cases the disagreement was not commented on thus warranting a further investigation and analysis.

Hypothesis 1 *Usefulness*: Evaluating the overall usefulness of the pattern language, most evaluators (71%) have regarded them as useful. Most of the comments were in agreement with the usage in terms of the general theme of the pattern language. However for (29%) of the evaluators that disagree, comments are related to some of the patterns being too general and covering a wide scope. In some instances suggestions were made for improvement such as the introduction of specific advice on certain patterns.

Hypothesis 2 *Relevance*: Most of the evaluators (71%) regard the content of the pattern repository as relevant to the B2B domain. It is noted that the same evaluators who considered the pattern language useful also considered the problem described in the pattern as relevant to the problem domain, probably because they viewed them as useful and relevant.

Hypothesis 3 *Usability*: (70%) of evaluators agree to the usability of the repository. However (30%) of evaluators do not agree that the patterns aim at being usable to solve an existing problem in the context of a real application. The argument for this is that in some instances the patterns are too general for the unique needs that surround B2B players.

Hypothesis 4 *Adaptability*: On a slightly lower scale compared to the first three hypotheses, (67%) of the evaluators consider that the solution advocated by the pattern can be tailored and modified in order to produce a model for a specific organization reflecting a particular situation. Some evaluators were skeptical because they argue that this process would involve interpretation of knowledge and, adaptations of this knowledge to fit the situation being addressed. According to them this is not possible to achieve for trading partners in a B2B environment.

Hypothesis 5 *Adoptability*: An equal percentage of evaluators think that the solutions of the patterns are adaptable as adoptable. For (67%) the pattern shall be applied in a real situation by domain experts for resolving a particular problem of interest in order to respond to a need in a specific organization. For the (33%) that disagree comments provided suggest that evaluators were looking for more concrete and detailed solutions.

Hypothesis 6 *Completeness*: Most of the evaluators (70%) consider the pattern offers a complete description of the problem and solution under consideration. Those that regarded the solutions as being incomplete expressed their desire for more elaborated solutions.

Hypothesis 7 *Coherence*: The evaluation results regarding the coherence of the problem description is fairly good (73%). We conclude that most of the evaluators regarded the problems addressed and solutions proposed as related. Furthermore some additional pattern relationships were suggested.

Hypothesis 8 *Consistency*: At (75%) of the evaluators, the results of this evaluation strongly are in favor of Consistency. The evaluators regarded the patterns as being consistent with the knowledge and vocabulary used in the B2B domain. In some instances evaluators advocated for inclusion of more standardized platform solutions.

Hypothesis 9 *Prescriptiveness*: Most of the evaluators (79%) consider that the pattern clearly describes the solution to the problem addressed and lays out the individual elements of the solution and the steps for their implementation. For (21%) the level of abstraction is too high. Evaluators suggested refinement of concepts and presentation in a stepwise format.

Hypothesis 10, *Granularity*: 71% of the evaluators regard that the patterns propose a solution at the appropriate level of detail. However, (29%) of the evaluators are consistent with the previous comments about the patterns being too general and the need for more examples. The main criticism concerned the level of detail and thoroughness of the proposed solutions.

In presenting an overview of evaluator's comments, the idea was that outside the patterns discussed above there are more issues that would fit as business problems. E.g. lack of adequate e-commerce expertise in the firm resulting from little or no time to develop new skills for B2B efforts, limitations posed by existing infrastructure in companies, improper business planning and poor investment decisions coupled with lack of strategic vision for B2B e-commerce which presents problems in measuring benefits of B2B e-commerce efforts.

Evaluators also point out that for B2B initiatives to succeed there is need for time, energy and investment from senior executives. Given that managers are enthusiastic about IT, this can be used to rally top management support for B2B e-commerce efforts. This provides strong and charismatic leadership to craft a marketable and compelling B2B vision.

Furthermore domain expertise and well-defined processes are a prerequisite for effective B2B systems success. Organizations that fail to realize this continually struggle with a myriad of problems.

Finally, organizations need to comply with standards by allowing their organizational processes to get redefined. Identifying clear cut responsibilities and dividing them according to team efforts is crucial to the success of the B2B systems.

4.2 Findings Concerning the Usefulness of the Pattern Format

This section presents the usefulness of the pattern format. There are four hypotheses used for evaluation as follows:

Hypothesis 11, *Usefulness*: The evaluation is more optimistic with regard to the pattern format being able to capture and convey the relevant knowledge for describing patterns. Evaluators that supported the approach recommended the structure of the pattern language, especially the problem-solution guideline. However some evaluators recommended inclusion of more items such as diagrammatic representation in the pattern format. This could include audio and even video where applicable.

Hypothesis 12, *Comprehensiveness*: Most of the evaluators consider the different elements of the pattern (e.g. problem, solution, motivation.) are adequate for understanding its purpose. For the evaluators that disagree suggestions included adding pictures to the pattern format to make explanation much easier.

Hypothesis 13, *Richness*: An equal percentage of evaluators think that the language is able to describe the different aspects of a pattern one is expecting in such a description as in hypothesis 2 above. Comments given here were almost identical to the ones in comprehensiveness. Apart from one evaluator who was of the view that the B2B process can be a very complex network and was skeptic about using the pattern approach to fully describe this in detail. This could be that she did not fully appreciate the pattern approach to knowledge capture.

Hypothesis 14 *Relevance*: For most of the evaluators the conceptual primitives chosen are appropriate for expressing the respective parts of pattern knowledge.

On the basis of the evaluation the following improvements have been proposed: The pattern should be further subdivided, more pictures should be included and example cases for pattern applicability should be included in detail. The argument is that the example cases can work as models for organizations that would be interested in adopting the pattern language.

4.3 Comparison with Other Pattern Application Cases

In this section we review a few example cases of application of organizational patterns. Organizational patterns have been created and applied in practice for considerable time. They have been used for various domains (e.g. electricity supply industry (ESI), public administrations, healthcare) and for various problems (e.g. company restructuring, change management, collaborative engineering (CE), treatment practices). Summary of five such cases and the case reported in chapter 3 is given in table 3.

The early cases of pattern development started the development process in a more top down fashion, i.e. identifying the overall problem and then decomposing it into a number or more manageable sub-problems. The resulting pattern languages of the ELEKTRA project and the cases at Riga City Council and Verbundplan were similar to goal hierarchies. In the later cases the patterns were developed in a more explorative way, i.e. the process started by investigating the initial problems, knowledge needs and requirements. E.g. at Skaraborgs hospital a knowledge map was used to identify the knowledge needs and structure patterns. The MAPPER project performed more than 10 modeling workshops with the domain experts. In the B2B adoption case a series of explorative interviews were carried out with a number or experts in the B2B domain. The evaluation results seem to suggest that this way of working contributes to the overall usefulness of the resulting pattern language. In summary, the explorative way of working allows the pattern developers to identify and address more problems with practical significance.

Concerning the appropriateness of using the pattern format, the results of the six cases show that the domain experts appreciate the problem-solution view on their competitive knowledge and expertise. The pattern template has been tailored in all these cases to improve the comprehensiveness and richness of patterns.

Furthermore it seems that the way the pattern development process engages the domain experts also influences the potential impact of the patterns. In this context additional challenge is to transfer the pattern development knowledge to the domain

Table 3. Summary of different pattern application cases

	ELEKTRA project, [8]	Riga City Council, [9]	Verbundplan GmbH,[3]	Skaraborg Hospital, [5]	MAPPER project, [10]	B2B Adoption
Period of time	1996-1999	2001-2003	2001-2003	2004-2007	2006-2008	2006-2009
Domain	ESI	Public administration	Consulting for the ESI	Healthcare	CE in the automotive sector	B2B
Problems addressed	Best practices of human resources management & electricity distribution	6 pilot cases in areas such as outreach work, police, transport department, and schools	Repairing of serious damages in hydro power plants and project risk management.	Management of treatment best practices. Focusing on treatment of leg ulcers.	Product development, and collaboration [11]	Lack of standards and structure in the operation and communication of the B2B environment.
Repository	~40 patterns	~100 patterns, linked to some multimedia content	~80 patterns, links to documents, definitions and multimedia	~100 patterns, documents and multimedia content	~30 patterns, some linked to executable services	~25 patterns
Use of models to document the solution	In almost all patterns contained fragments of enterprise models.	Some contained enterprise models, other kinds of models were also used	Some contained enterprise models, other kinds of models were also used	Very few models and diagrams were used to convey the solution	Patterns were part of Active Knowledge Modeling (AKM) [12]	Some patterns documented as models using tabular formats
IT support	HTML pages	Content management tool and web export	Content management tool and web export	Web based content management system integrated with the hospital's webpage	METIS tool and the AKM platform.	Document, proposal for HTML pages
Pattern developers	Researchers, developers of approach	Domain experts with heavy involvement of outside experts and consultants	Domain experts with heavy involvement of outside experts and consultants	Domain experts assisted by researchers	Outside experts, consultants researchers and domain experts in a collaboration	Researchers assisted by domain experts
Evaluation	Questionnaire, formal, after the project	Questionnaire, formal, after the project	Questionnaire, formal, after the project	Informal, discussions and workshops, feedback during the project	Scorecard based, iterative, several times during the project.	Informal discussions, and feedback during project
Usefulness of the knowledge content	Low	Low	Medium	High	Medium	Medium
Appropriateness of the pattern format	Medium	Medium	Medium	High	High	High
Potential impact	Low	Low	Medium	High	Medium to high	Medium- more investigation needed

experts and to make the pattern based approach to knowledge sharing an accepted way of working in the organization. From the five cases reported in this section, this has been achieved only at Skaraborg Hospital (for more detailed analysis see [5]). For the MAPPER project it is too early to conclude whether the pattern approach will survive at the target organizations in the long term. Concerning the B2B adoption case, the dissemination process is not yet complete.

5 Concluding Remarks and Future Work

We have presented a validated pattern language of B2B adoption practices. These patterns can be seen as generic and abstract organizational design proposals that can be easily adapted and reused. While the validation process has shown that the quality of the patterns is high, continuous improvement of the patterns can be done through application feedback, reviews and corresponding adjustments.

More specifically, concerning the usefulness of the patterns we conclude the patterns are useful. Concerning the appropriateness of the pattern format we conclude that the format is useful. However depending on the domain, additions to the pattern elements such as pictures should be emphasized. Further more process models can be included to present a high level overview of the system in discussion.

We have also compared the findings from the validation of this case with five other cases which leads to conclude that patterns are valuable means for capturing and sharing various kinds of knowledge in different domains (e.g. engineering, IT, management, and healthcare). On the other hand, considering the varying degree of long term impact of the pattern use in organizations, we would like stress that more research should be devoted to supporting the process of adopting pattern-based ways of working in and knowledge sharing.

Patterns have also showed potential for acting as means for configuring enterprise information systems. Despite initial promising experiences [10] more research should be devoted to connecting patterns to services thus making the solutions proposed by patterns executable. This would make patterns a central part of enterprise architecture.

References

1. Alexander, C.: A pattern language. Oxford University Press, New York (1977)
2. Gamma, E., Helm, R., Johnson, R., Vlissides, J.: Design Patterns: Elements of Reusable Object-Oriented Software Architecture. Addison Wesley, Reading (1995)
3. Persson, A., Stirna, J., Dulle, H., Hatzenbichler, G., Strutz, G.: Introducing a Pattern Based Knowledge Management Approach - the Verbundplan Case. In: The 4th International Workshop on Theory and Applications of Knowledge Management (TAKMA 2003), Proceedings of 14th International Workshop on Database and Expert Systems Applications (DEXA 2003). IEEE, Los Alamitos (2003)
4. Stirna, J., Persson, A., Aggestam, L.: Building Knowledge Repositories with Enterprise Templateling and Patterns-from Theory to Practice. In: Proceedings of the 14th European Conference on Information Systems, Gothenburg, Sweden (2006)
5. Persson, A., Stirna, J., Aggestam, L.: How to Disseminate Professional Knowledge in Healthcare. The Case of Skaraborg Hospital 3, 42–64 (2008); Journal of Cases on Information Technology 10, (2008) ISSN: 1548-7717

6. Bubenko Jr., J.A., Persson, A., Stirna, J.: User guide of the knowledge management approach using enterprise knowledge patterns, deliverable D3, IST project Hypermedia and Pattern Based Knowledge Management for Smart Organisations. Royal Institute of Technology, Sweden (2001)
7. ELEKTRA Consortium, Newton: Validated ESI Knowledge Base, ELEKTRA Project Deliverable Document, ESPRIT Project No. 22927 (1999)
8. Rolland, C., Stirna, J., Prekas, N., Loucopoulos, P., Grosz, G., Persson, A.: Evaluating a Pattern Approach as an Aid for the Development of Organisational Knowledge: An Empirical Study. In: Wangler, B., Bergman, L.D. (eds.) CAiSE 2000. LNCS, vol. 1789, pp. 176–540. Springer, Heidelberg (2000)
9. Mikelsons, J., Stirna, J., Kalnins, J.R., Kapenieks, A., Kazakovs, M., Vanaga, I., Sinka, A., Persson, A., Kaindl, H.: Trial Application in the Riga City Council, deliverable D6, IST Programme project Hypermedia and Pattern Based Knowledge Management for Smart Organisations, project no. IST-2000-28401, Riga City Council, Riga, Latvia (2002)
10. Sandkuhl, K., Stirna, J.: Evaluation of Task Pattern Use in Web-based Collaborative Engineering. In: Proc. of the 34th EUROMICRO Conference on Software Engineering and Advanced Applications (SEAA), EUROMICRO. IEEE, Los Alamitos (2008)
11. Carstensen, A., Högberg, P., Holmberg, L., Johnsen, S., Karlsen, D., Lillehagen, F., Lundqvist, M., Ohren, O., Sandkuhl, K., Wallin, A.: Kongsberg Automotive Requirements Model, deliverable D6, MAPPER, IST proj. no 016527 (2006)
12. Lillehagen, F., Krogstie, J.: Active Knowledge Models and Enterprise Knowledge Management. In: Proceedings of the IFIP TC5/WG5.12 International Conference on Enterprise Integration and Modeling Technique: Enterprise Inter- and Intra-Organizational Integration: Building International Consensus, IFIP Conference Proceedings, vol. 236. Kluwer, Dordrecht (2002)

Anti-patterns as a Means of Focusing on Critical Quality Aspects in Enterprise Modeling

Janis Stirna[1] and Anne Persson[2]

[1] Department of Computer and Systems Sciences, Royal Institute of Technology, Forum 100,
SE-16440, Kista, Sweden
js@dsv.su.se
[2] University of Skövde, P.O. Box 408, SE-541 28 Skövde, Sweden
anne.persson@his.se

Abstract. Enterprise Modeling (EM) is used for a wide range of purposes such as developing business strategies, business process restructuring, business process orientation and standardization, eliciting information system requirements, capturing best practices, etc. A common challenge impeding the value and impact of EM is insufficient model quality. Despite substantial attention from both researchers and commercial vendors of methods the current situation in practice with respect to the quality of models produced is not satisfactory. Many modeling projects produce bad models that are essentially useless. The objective of this paper is to introduce a format, anti-patterns, for documenting critical don'ts in EM and to demonstrate the potential of the format by using it to report a set of common and reoccurring pitfalls of real life EM projects. We use the format of anti-pattern for capturing the bad solutions to reoccurring problems and then explain what led to choosing the bad solution. The anti-patterns in this paper address three main aspects of EM – the modeling product, the modeling process, and the modeling tool support.

Keywords: Enterprise modeling, model quality, anti-patterns.

1 Introduction

Enterprise Modeling (EM) is an activity where an integrated and commonly shared model describing different aspects of an enterprise is created. An Enterprise Model comprises a number of related "sub-models", each focusing on a particular aspect of the problem domain, e.g. processes, business rules, concepts/information/data, vision/goals, and actors. EM is often used for a wide range of purposes such as developing business strategies, restructuring business processes, business process orientation and standardization, eliciting information system requirements, capturing best practices, etc. (cf. i.e. [1]). In these application contexts EM is commonly accepted as a valuable and practicable instrument. Yet, a number of challenges for EM use in practice do exist. One such challenge is enterprise and conceptual model quality. Despite substantial attention from both researchers and practitioners (c.f., for instance, [2, 3, 4, 5, 6, 7, 8]) the current situation with respect to quality of models produced in real life is not satisfactory – many modeling projects produce really bad models thus making them essentially useless. This is best illustrated by the following interview quote: "I

T. Halpin et al. (Eds.): BPMDS 2009 and EMMSAD 2009, LNBIP 29, pp. 407–418, 2009.

claim that only 30 % of what is produced today is at all acceptable as a platform to stand on [for further development work]… Most of what is done today, especially with regard to business processes, is garbage" ([9], p. 197). According to our experience the situation in practice has not improved since this quote was made.

Perhaps one of the reasons for this situation is that many EM projects do not really know what kind of model quality they should strive towards. This then leads to either insufficient model quality, which undermines the usefulness of the model, or "too high" (unnecessary) quality for the project, i.e. in a particular project certain quality criteria e.g. level of detail, could be relaxed. Another problem that causes bad models is that modelers and managers of EM projects are either too uninformed or ignorant when it comes to model quality and means to improve it.

An Enterprise Model, and in essence any type of conceptual model, is produced by a modeler or a team of modelers by combining a modeling language with a modeling process. In that process the knowledge and creativity of the stakeholders are essential driving forces. In addition, how EM is carried out is highly situation dependent. A large number of situational factors need to be taken into account (c.f. [9 and 10]).

Learning how to become a skilled modeler who is able to both manage the modeling language and the modeling process to produce high-quality models is a complicated process that takes substantial time and effort. Learning through practice is essential, but in order to avoid making unnecessary mistakes, there is also a need for some form of documented guidelines and advice for carrying out EM. However, the high degree of situation dependence and the complicated nature of EM make it difficult to produce comprehensive guidelines that specify what to do in all situations.

In this paper we take a complementary approach to guiding modelers. We focus on giving advice with respect to what a modeler should *not* do, making the assumption that the set of don'ts are substantially less than the possible dos. By taking this approach we can focus on avoiding the most common costly mistakes in EM. For this purpose we have chosen the format of anti-pattern because it effectively captures the knowledge about an *appealing but bad* solution to a reoccurring problem and then explains what led to choosing the bad solution and what the consequences of the bad solution are. The focus of anti-patterns is to capture common pitfalls and traps that for some reason appear attractive, but lead to undesired consequences.

The objectives of this paper are twofold: 1) to introduce a format, anti-patterns, for documenting critical don'ts in EM and 2) to demonstrate the potential of the format by using it to report a set of common and reoccurring pitfalls of real life EM projects.

The research approach is conceptual and argumentative based on a number of case studies that were carried out in public and private organizations [11, 12, 13, 14, 15] and interview studies with practitioners experienced in applying EM in practice [9, 10, 16, 17].

The remainder of the paper is organized as follows. In section 2 we provide a brief background to EM methods and ways of working. Section 3 discusses a number of issues of model quality as well as some of the existing work on model quality. The concepts of a pattern and anti-pattern are introduced in section 4. Section 5 comprises a number of anti-patterns for conducting EM using the proposed approach. In section 6 we discuss the proposal and make some concluding remarks.

2 Background to Enterprise Modeling

A great variety of EM approaches and methods have been developed and successfully used in practice (c.f., for instance, [18, 19, 20, 21, 22, 23, 24, 25, 26]). [1] show that EM can be used for two main types of objectives – (1) developing the business, e.g. developing business vision, strategies, redesigning the way the business operates, developing the supporting information systems (IS), or (2) ensuring the quality of the business, e.g. sharing the knowledge about the business, its vision, the way it operates, or ensuring the acceptance of business decisions through committing the stake-holders to the decisions made.

In the reminder of this section we will describe an example EM method, namely, Enterprise Knowledge Development (EKD) [19]. The anti-patterns presented in the paper are mostly based on projects that used EKD or similar approaches. However, adhering to the criteria that patterns (and anti-patterns) should be generic, we have described them independent from the modeling approach used.

EKD is a representative of the Scandinavian strand of EM methods. It defines the modeling process as a set of guidelines for participative way of working and the modeling product in terms of six sub-models each focusing on a specific aspect of an organization (see table 1).

The ability to trace decisions, components and other aspects throughout the enterprise is dependent on the use and understanding of the relationships between the different sub-models addressing the issues in table 1.

When developing a full enterprise model, these relationships between components of the different sub-models play an essential role. E.g. statements in GM allow different concepts to be defined more clearly in the CM. A link is then specified between the corresponding GM component and concepts in CM. In the same way, goals in the GM motivate the existence of processes in the BPM. Links between models make the model traceable. They show, for instance, why certain rules, processes and information system requirements have been introduced.

In order to achieve results of high quality, the modeling process is equally important as the modeling language used. There are two aspects of the process, namely the approach to participation and the process to develop the model.

Table 1. Overview of the sub-models of the EKD method

	Goals Model (GM)	Business Rules Model (BRM)	Concepts Model (CM)	Business Process Model (BPM)	Actors and Resources Model (ARM)	Technical Component & Requirements Model(TCRM)
Focus	Vision and strategy	Policies and rules	Business ontology	Business operations	Organizational structure	IS needs
Issues	What does the organization want to achieve or to avoid and why?	What are the business rules, how do they support organization's goals?	What are the things and "phenomena" addressed in other sub-models?	What are the business processes? How do they handle information and material?	Who are responsible for goals and process? How are the actors interrelated?	What are the business requirements to the IS? How are they related to other models?
Components	Goal, problem, external constraint, opportunity	Business rule	Concept, attribute	Process, external proc., information set, material set	Actor, role, organizational unit, individual	IS goal, IS problem, IS requirement, IS component

When it comes to gathering domain knowledge to be included in Enterprise Models, there are different approaches. Some of the more common ones are interviews with domain experts, analysis of existing documentation, observation of existing work practices, and facilitated group modeling.

EM practitioners and EKD method developers have advocated a participatory way of working using facilitated group modeling (see e.g. [9, 19, 27, 28]). In facilitated group modeling, participation is *consensus-driven* in the sense that it is the domain stakeholders who "own" the model and govern its contents. In contrast, *consultative* participation means that analysts create models and domain stakeholders are then consulted in order to validate the models. In the participatory approach to modeling, stakeholders meet in modeling sessions, led by a facilitator, to create models collaboratively.

3 Enterprise Modeling Quality

The EM process produces two results that are potentially useful:

– the produced models, which are used as input to further development or implementation activities, and
– the changed thinking and the improved knowledge of the participants.

[9] states that the main criteria for successful application of EKD are that (1) the quality of the produced models is high, (2) the result is useful and actually used after the modeling activity is completed, and (3) the involved stakeholders are satisfied with the process and the result.

High quality of models means that they make sense as a whole and that it is possible to implement them as a solution to some problem. Successful EM is when the result of modeling, e.g., a new strategy or a new process, is effectively implemented in the organization. The required quality level of models is usually determined by the project goals and the specific goals that apply to each modeling session. E.g. some modeling sessions might be geared towards creatively gathering ideas in which case model quality (e.g. in terms of the level of detail and completeness) is of lesser importance. In other cases when models are intended to be used as part of, for instance, a requirements specification, the models have to adhere to considerably higher quality requirements (e.g. in terms of completeness, integration, and understandability).

[7] present an overall framework of process model quality and discuss general quality aspects of active knowledge models. [6], [29], and [30] have elaborated quality metrics of process models. These contributions are highly useful for EM when dealing with business process models. In an EM context these factors and metrics should be coupled with specific modeling and analysis guidelines for improving business process models.

[4] presents a set of factors for assessing and improving the quality of data models. [16] provide an initial investigation of whether the model quality criteria of [4] are applicable to Enterprise Models and concludes that the following factors: completeness, correctness, flexibility, integration, simplicity, understandability, and usability

are applicable. This work should be further extended towards specific modeling guidelines for conducting EM and for documenting the modeling result. An example of one such guideline addressing understandability and applicability is to strive towards SMART goals in the Goal Model, meaning that every goal should be specific (S), measurable (M), accepted (A), realistic(R), and time framed (T). This guideline would contribute to increasing the understandability and usability of the model. A guideline for improving simplicity would be to improve the graphical presentation of large and interconnected models, i.e. "spaghetti models", rearranging them into sub-models and by eliminating unnecessary relationships. In order for this guideline to be efficient, tool support that automates some of the activities, by, example, wizards for reviewing and querying relationships would be required.

In summary, what is needed to improve the quality of Enterprise Models in practice is guidance for dealing with the modeling product, the modeling process, as well as the tool support for identifying the quality issues and then resolving them.

4 Patterns and Anti-patterns for Capturing Reusable Knowledge

Alexander et al. [31] define a pattern as describing *"a problem which occurs over and over again in our environment and then describes the core of the solution to that problem, in such a way that you can use this solution a million times over, without ever doing it the same way twice"*. On the basis of this initial definition, the pattern concept has been successfully adopted in software programming, system analysis, software design, and data modeling (c.f. for instance, [32, 33, 34]). The notion of pattern from these areas share two main ideas – (1) a pattern relates a recurring problem to its solution, and (2) each problem has its unique characteristics that distinguish it from other problems. The common objective of applying patterns is to capture, store and share reusable content, such as fragments of design (e.g. Class Diagrams) and software code. Patterns have also been useful in organizational settings for knowledge sharing purposes (c.f., for instance, [15, 35]).

An anti-pattern (see e.g. [26]) is a *bad solution* to a common problem. Besides just presenting a bad solution, a good anti-pattern also explains why this solution looks attractive in the first place and why it backfires and turns out to be bad when applied. We use a template for anti-patterns adopted from [37] which has also been used for representing anti-patterns of adopting Knowledge Management approaches in organizations [38]. The anti-pattern template is shown in figure 1.

Name	The name of the anti-pattern
Problem	EM oriented motivation or problem it tries to solve
Anti-solution	What solution was chosen and how it was applied
Actual results and unintended consequences	What happened after the solution was applied
Primary fallacies	What were the likely causes for failure, e.g. false assumptions.

Fig. 1. The anti-pattern template

5 Examples of Anti-patterns in Enterprise Modeling

In this section we present a number of anti-patterns that demonstrate the proposed approach to capture reusable knowledge about the don'ts of EM. They should be seen as examples, but, in fact, they do contain some of the don'ts that have been collected by the authors of this paper during more than 10 years of applying the EKD EM method in various settings. More about these applications and related experiences can be found in [17 and 38].

In this work we have followed the pattern development guidelines given in [19] and the overall principles outlined in the Pattern Language for Pattern Writing [39].

5.1 Addressing the Modeling Product

Elaborate each model type separately and in detail	
Problem	Your modeling language has a number of model types, all of which are to be elaborated in the modeling effort
Anti-solution	Each model type, e.g. process model, concepts model, goal model, is elaborated separately and in detail until its developers feel that the model is complete.
Actual results and unintended consequences	In a set of model types, each type explains some aspect of the other model types. E.g. The information sets in a process model can be defined in a concepts model. Going into detail with the process model, without defining the information sets, will most likely cause the process model to be of low quality, since it will be based on superficial knowledge and assumptions about the content of the information sets. Wrongful assumptions will cause problems later on in the modeling effort and cause costly re-work of previous models. In the worst case, if all model types are developed in the same manner the modeling result will not be coherent and ultimately cause development efforts based on the models to fail.
Primary fallacies	Assuming that we have to complete one model type before we start with the next.

Relate everything that seems related	
Problem	Analyzing the model you discover that there are a number of relationships between model components that have not been documented.
Anti-solution	Document all possible relationships that you can find between components in the model. Relate components "for good measure" because they "seem somehow related".
Actual results and unintended consequences	The model will become muddled and difficult to read. It will contain many relationships and its interconnectedness could be close to a total graph. Such models are sometimes regarded as "spaghetti models". A more serious problem is that the model will become un-focused and not function well as a basis for different types of development.
Primary fallacies	Assuming that all possible relationships need to be documented.

5.2 Addressing the Modeling Process

Everybody is a facilitator	
Problem	You do not have a modeling facilitator at a modeling seminar. This can be caused by either not realizing the need for a facilitator or not being able to afford the services of an external facilitator. A special case of this problem is when the facilitator is unexpectedly unable to attend due to force majeure.
Anti-solution	The group members attempt to "facilitate each other" in various ways according to the best of their knowledge of what facilitation really is. In doing this the group members might even engage in a pseudo competition about who will facilitate more or louder. It is also not uncommon that the highest ranking manager assumes the role of facilitator.
Actual results and unintended consequences	The discussion in the modeling room might appear creative and inspired at the outset, but usually it is quite chaotic. It runs the risk of discussing only themes and topics that are very commonly discussed in the organization. The resulting model usually contains a large number of various modeling components dealing with an abundance of issues, most of which are not relevant to the problem at hand. The modeling language is not followed and the model may also include "drawings" of various kinds.
Primary fallacies	The assumptions that participative modeling can be done without a dedicated and skillful facilitator, that anyone can facilitate, and that more facilitation leads to better results.

The facilitator acts as domain expert	
Problem	The facilitator has previous knowledge about the domain to be modeled. It is difficult to activate the domain experts in the modeling session and to get them to contribute their knowledge to the model. Modeling progresses slowly and time is running out.
Anti-solution	The facilitator has some knowledge about the domain to be modeled and takes tries to make progress by introducing his/her own knowledge in the model.
Actual results and unintended consequences	The domain experts become even more passive and even less motivated to contribute. The model ends up by being the facilitator's own solution to the problem at hand and, hence, the domain experts will not feel that they are responsible for the model and for its implementation. In the worst case, should the model be incorrect in some way or later cause problems, the credibility of the facilitator will be seriously damaged. This could eventually jeopardize the whole modeling effort.
Primary fallacies	Assuming that it is better to get a model that reflects the views of a select few than no model at all.

Concept dump	
Problem	Your modeling participants are knowledgeable about the domain and reasonably skillful modelers. They produce an abundance of modeling concepts without much discussion. The facilitator might be reasonably inexperienced.
Anti-solution	The facilitator tries to place them all in the model and somehow relate them to each other.
Actual results and unintended consequences	The resulting model contains a lot of concepts and may look really complex and appear advanced. Many of these concepts will be trivial and issues addressed will be peripheral to the problem at hand. Hard problems are not addressed in the model.
Primary fallacies	The assumption that all issues brought up and pieces of paper written need to be placed in the model. Following blindly the guideline that stakeholder wishes must be recorded. Replacing quality with quantity – good models need critical discussion and decisions going into the model need to be weighted.

Please the participants	
Problem	The organization and its participants commit to using participative EM but at the same time they impose very strict conditions about the schedule, cost, location, and who should participate in the modeling seminars.
Anti-solution	To accept the situation as is and to try to do the best possible effort within the frame conditions.
Actual results and unintended consequences	The result usually does not meet the expectations because the recourses have not been allocated adequately. The people allocated to the project have not been able to present the complete picture when it comes to the issues involved. The resulting models and the decisions are not implementable and are not followed in the organization. At best they are seen as an input to the problem solving process.
Primary fallacies	Assuming that participative EM can be done with very little effort and in any setting. The amount of effort required for preparing and conducting modeling seminars is given in [38]. Assuming that it does not matter who the stakeholders are and, hence, using stakeholder representatives or mediators, rather than stakeholders themselves, e.g. involving a secretary or a favorite employee of a manager, rather the manager him/herself.

5.3 Addressing EM Tool Support

Models keep "alive" themselves	
Problem	The company has created a set of enterprise models that are intended to be used in the future for (1) reference purposes such as, for instance, business process standardization, or for (2) reusing them in a new organizational design.

Anti-solution	Store models in the tool repository and/or reports in the hope that people will look at them when they need them.
Actual results and unintended consequences	Once the models are created and stored in the repository they are quickly forgotten. Nobody remembers the details in the models and their purpose and as a result the new modeling activities often "reinvent the wheel".
Primary fallacies	Assuming that the models do not need updating or that when updates are needed people will voluntarily do it. Not allocating responsibilities and resources for model updating. Assuming that models and reusable model parts can be easily identifiable. Not identifying reuse artifacts, i.e. patterns, in Enterprise Models. Assuming that people are well acquainted with the contents of the model repository.

Professionals use only computerized tools	
Problem	You use a modeling tool in a setting where you need to capture knowledge which requires collective thinking or consolidating several opinions.
Anti-solution	The facilitator uses a modeling tool and a beamer. Everyone sits at a round table and tells what they think should be modeled and what part of the model they would like to be shown on the screen.
Actual results and unintended consequences	The process has interruptions because the facilitator has to shift his/her attention between discussing issues with the group and operating the tool. As a result the model looks visually unappealing; it has many broken links, misspelled words, awkward placement of modeling concepts. The progress is slow and not all stakeholders are able to contribute. Several of them are disengaged. The resulting model reflects knowledge of a select few in the room.
Primary fallacies	Assuming that working with paper stickers on a plastic wall is perceived unprofessional. Wanting to immediately come up with the right or the finished model. Not wanting to spend time to document and refine the model.

Everyone embraces a new tool	
Problem	The stakeholders need to review the models produced, you need to communicate with models within the project.
Anti-solution	Purchase many licenses of a tool, train all stakeholders in tool usage, and send them models via email. Ask them to enter comments directly in the tool.
Actual results and unintended consequences	The communication in the project is hampered. Models are not discussed as the stakeholders spend considerable time discussing how to use the new tool.
Primary fallacies	Assuming that the stakeholders have the motivation and sufficient knowledge to use a tool on their own. Failing to focus on well established tools and packages, e.g. the Office software.

6 Concluding Remarks

In this paper we have proposed the format of anti-patterns as the means of capturing reusable knowledge about how EM should *not* be conducted. The underlying assumption is that it is complicated and cumbersome to instruct modelers about everything that they can and should do, e.g. because EM is so highly situation dependant. We have experienced this problem ourselves, having been involved in writing the user guide for the EKD EM approach. Alternatively it should be possible to focus on what modelers should *not* do. In our case we have chosen the form of anti-pattern to achieve this.

We have applied the approach to the knowledge that we have gained through more than 10 years of applying the EKD EM approach in a variety of domains by developing a number of anti-patterns included in this paper. One reflection from developing these patterns is that this format has forced us to focus on the essential aspects of the knowledge: what should you not do, what are the consequences if you still do it, and why do people do what they should not do.

The anti-pattern format is completely generic and could be applicable to capturing knowledge about all or most EM methods and for other methods such as process modeling and concepts modeling methods focusing on issues related to organizational and information systems design or change. The anti-patterns presented in this paper should be seen only as examples and a starting point; many more exist and wait to be captured and shared by the EM community. Furthermore, concerning the anti-pattern approach, more work needs to be devoted to elaborating guidance for their capturing, sharing and adoption.

References

1. Persson, A., Stirna, J.: An explorative study into the influence of business goals on the practical use of Enterprise Modelling methods and tools. In: Proceedings of the 10th International Conference on Information Systems Development (ISD 2001). Kluwer, London (2001)
2. Lindland, O.I., Sindre, G., Sølvberg, A.: Understanding Quality in Conceptual Modeling. IEEE Software 11(2), 42–49 (1994)
3. Davies, I., Green, P., Rosemann, M., Gallo, S.: Conceptual Modelling - What and Why in Current Practice. In: Atzeni, P., Chu, W., Lu, H., Zhou, S., Ling, T.-W. (eds.) ER 2004. LNCS, vol. 3288, pp. 30–42. Springer, Heidelberg (2004)
4. Moody, D.L., Shanks, G.: Improving the quality of data models: empirical validation of a quality management framework. Information Systems (IS) 28(6), 619–650 (2003)
5. Maes, A., Poels, G.: Evaluating Quality of Conceptual Models Based on User Perceptions. In: Embley, D.W., Olivé, A., Ram, S. (eds.) ER 2006. LNCS, vol. 4215, pp. 54–67. Springer, Heidelberg (2006)
6. Mendling, J., Reijers, H.A., Cardoso, J.: What Makes Process Models Understandable? In: Alonso, G., Dadam, P., Rosemann, M. (eds.) BPM 2007. LNCS, vol. 4714, pp. 48–63. Springer, Heidelberg (2007)
7. Krogstie, J., Sindre, G., Jørgensen, H.: Process models representing knowledge for action: a revised quality framework. European Journal of Information Systems 15, 91–102 (2006)

8. Rosemann, M.: Potential Pitfalls of Process Modeling: Part A. Business Process Management Journal 12(2), 249–254 (2006)
9. Persson, A.: Enterprise Modelling in Practice: Situational Factors and their Influence on Adopting a Participative Approach, PhD thesis, Dept. of Computer and Systems Sciences, Stockholm University, No 01-020 (2001) ISSN 1101-8526
10. Stirna, J.: The Influence of Intentional and Situational Factors on EM Tool Acquisition in Organisations, Ph.D. Thesis, Royal Institute of Technology, Sweden (2001)
11. Carstensen, A., Högberg, P., Holmberg, L., Johnsen, S., Karlsen, D., Lillehagen, F., Lundqvist, M., Ohren, O., Sandkuhl, K., Wallin, A.: Kongsberg Automotive Requirements Model, deliverable D6, MAPPER, IST proj. no 016527 (2006)
12. Carstensen, A., Holmberg, L., Högberg, P., Johnsen, S.G., Karlsen, D., Lillehagen, F., Sandkuhl1, K., Stirna, J.: Integrating Requirement and Solution Modelling: Approach and Experiences. In: The 12th Workshop on Exploring Modelling Methods for Information Systems Analysis and Design (EMMSAD), Trondheim, Norway (2007) ISBN 978-82-519-2245-6
13. Carstensen, A., Holmberg, L., Högberg, P., Johnsen, S.G., Karlsen, D., Lillehagen, F., Sandkuhl, K., Stirna, J.: Generalised Active Knowledge Models for Automotive Distributed Product Design, deliverable D16, MAPPER - Model-based Adaptive Product and Process Engineering, IST project no 016527, Kongsberg Automotive, Sweden (2008)
14. Mikelsons, J., Stirna, J., Kalnins, J.R., Kapenieks, A., Kazakovs, M., Vanaga, I., Sinka, A., Persson, A., Kaindl, H.: Trial Application in the Riga City Council, deliverable D6, IST Programme project Hypermedia and Pattern Based Knowledge Management for Smart Organisations, project no. IST-2000-28401. Riga, Latvia (2002)
15. Stirna, J., Persson, A., Aggestam, L.: Building Knowledge Repositories with Enterprise Modelling and Patterns - from Theory to Practice. In: Proceedings of the 14th European Conference on Information Systems (ECIS), Gothenburg, Sweden (June 2006)
16. Larsson, L., Segerberg, R.: An Approach for Quality Assurance in Enterprise Modelling, MSc thesis, Deptment of Computer and Systems Sciences, Stockholm University, no 04-22 (2004)
17. Stirna, J., Persson, A.: An Enterprise Modeling Approach to Support Creativity and Quality in Information Systems and Business Development. In: Halpin, T., Krogstie, J., Proper, E. (eds.) Innovations in Information Systems Modeling: Methods and Best Practices. IGI Global (2008) ISBN 978-1-60566-278-7
18. Bajec, M., Krisper, M.: A methodology and tool support for managing business rules in organisations. Information Systems 30(6), 423–443 (2005)
19. Bubenko, J.A.j., Persson, A., Stirna, J.: User Guide of the Knowledge Management Approach Using Enterprise Knowledge Patterns, IST Programme project Hypermedia and Pattern Based Knowledge Management for Smart Organisations, no. IST-2000-28401, KTH, Sweden (2001), http://www.dsv.su.se/~js/ekd_user_guide.html
20. Castro, J., Kolp, M., Mylopoulos, J.: A Requirements-Driven Software Development Methodology. In: Dittrich, K.R., Geppert, A., Norrie, M.C. (eds.) CAiSE 2001. LNCS, vol. 2068, pp. 108–123. Springer, Heidelberg (2001)
21. Dobson, J., Blyth, J., Strens, R.: Organisational Requirements Definition for Information Technology. In: Proceedings of the International Conference on Requirements Engineering 1994, Denver/CO (1994)
22. Fox, M.S., Chionglo, J.F., Fadel, F.G.: A common-sense model of the enterprise. In: Proceedings of the 2nd Industrial Engineering Research Conference, Institute for Industrial Engineers, Norcross/GA (1993)

23. van Lamsweerde, A., Letier, E.: Handling Obstacles in Goal-Oriented Requirements Engineering. IEEE Trans. Software Eng. 26(10), 978–1005 (2000)
24. Loucopoulos, P., Kavakli, V., Prekas, N., Rolland, C., Grosz, G., Nurcan, S.: Using the EKD Approach: The Modelling Component, UMIST, Manchester, UK (1997)
25. Krogstie, J., Jørgensen, H.D.: Interactive Models for Supporting Networked Organizations. In: Persson, A., Stirna, J. (eds.) CAiSE 2004. LNCS, vol. 3084, pp. 550–563. Springer, Heidelberg (2004)
26. Willars, H.: Handbok i ABC-metoden. Plandata Strategi (1988)
27. Yu, E.S.K., Mylopoulos, J.: From E-R to A-R- Modelling Strategic Actor Relationships for Business Process Reengineering. In: Proceedings of the 13th International Conference on the Entity-Relationship Approach, Manchester, England (1994)
28. F3-Consortium, F3 Reference Manual, ESPRIT III Project 6612, SISU, Sweden (1994)
29. Nilsson, A.G., Tolis, C., Nellborn, C. (eds.): Perspectives on Business Modelling: Understanding and Changing Organisations. Springer, Heidelberg (1999)
30. Cardoso, J.: Process control-flow complexity metric: An empirical validation. In: IEEE International Conference on Services Computing (SCC 2006), pp. 167–173 (2006)
31. Mendling, J., Neumann, G., van der Aalst, W.M.P.: Understanding the Occurrence of Errors in Process Models based on Metrics. In: Meersman, R., Tari, Z. (eds.) OTM 2007, Part I. LNCS, vol. 4803, pp. 113–130. Springer, Heidelberg (2007)
32. Alexander, C., Ishikawa, S., Silverstein, M., Jacobson, M., Fiksdahl-King, I., Angel, S.: A Pattern Language. Oxford University Press, New York (1977)
33. Coplien, J., Schmidt, D. (eds.): Pattern Languages of Program Design. Addison Wesley, Reading (1995)
34. Fowler, M.: Analysis Patterns: Reusable Object Models. Addison-Wesley, Reading (1997)
35. Gamma, E., Helm, R., Johnson, R., Vlissides, J.: Design Patterns: Elements of Reusable Object-Oriented Software. Addison Wesley, Reading (1995)
36. Rolland, C., Stirna, J., Prekas, N., Loucopoulos, P., Persson, A., Grosz, G.: Evaluating a Pattern Approach as an Aid for the Development of Organisational Knowledge: An Empirical Study. In: Wangler, B., Bergman, L.D. (eds.) CAiSE 2000. LNCS, vol. 1789, pp. 176–191. Springer, Heidelberg (2000)
37. Brown, W.J., Malveau, R.C., McCormick III, R.C., Mowbray, T.J.: AntiPatterns: Refactoring Software, Architectures, and Projects in Crisis. John Wiley & Sons, Chichester (1998)
38. Long, J.: Software Reuse Antipatterns. Software Engineering Notes, ACM SIGSOFT 26(4) (2001)
39. Stirna, J., Persson, A., Sandkuhl, K.: Participative Enterprise Modelling: Experiences and Recommendations. In: Krogstie, J., Opdahl, A.L., Sindre, G. (eds.) CAiSE 2007 and WES 2007. LNCS, vol. 4495, pp. 546–560. Springer, Heidelberg (2007)
40. Persson, A., Stirna, J.: How to transfer a KM approach to an organization – a set of patterns and anti-patterns. In: Reimer, U., Karagiannis, D. (eds.) PAKM 2006. LNCS, vol. 4333, pp. 243–252. Springer, Heidelberg (2006)
41. Meszaros, G.: A Pattern Language for Pattern Writing, Object Systems Group (1997), http://www.hillside.net/patterns/writing/patternwritingpaper.htm

Author Index